Mrs. Bateman's Cooking Lite for Life™

by Kristine Bateman

- 13 chapters of recipes with a forward on how to use **Mrs. Bateman's Products** in each chapter.
- You can substitute sugar and fat in any percent in my recipes.
- **ButterLike** fat substitutes fit FDA coronary heart claims.
- Recipes made with **SugarLike** and **ButterLike** lower calories for weight loss.
- Each recipe has been nutritionally broken down to show the fat and cholesterol grams including the Fat Quotient (% of calories from fat).
- Each recipe has been nutritionally broken down to show all carbohydrate information including, total carbohydrates, dietary fiber, sugars, and other carbohydrates.
- Each recipe includes a nutritional comparison when using the Bateman Products or the traditional high fat, high sugar ingredients.
- Each recipe shows the % less fat, % less sugar, and the % less calories compared to the high fat and high sugar recipes
- Tips on how to lower fat, calories, and sugar in your own recipes.
- Important formulas to figure new nutritional information for your recipes using **Mrs. Bateman's Products**.
- Mrs. Bateman's easy substitution formula for changing your difficult high fat ingredients to low fat substitutes.
- The Exchange Per Serving is figured for each recipe for the Exchange Diet.
- The Carbohydrates that a diabetic person would need to count is figured.
- Toll free Bateman Product Info Hotline 1-800-574-6822. Monday through Friday (MST).
- E-mail bateman @bakingbutter.com

Table of Contents

Acknowledgements

Because of the extensive nutritional information we needed for each recipe it became necessary to put the recipe into the computer many times and in different ways. Shilo Nelson did this often for each recipe. She is brilliant.

Shelly Fonnesbeck tested each of the recipes and gave us great tasting opportunities during work. She is such a wonderful cook and I appreciate her work. Thank you!

I would like to thank Evan Bateman for his support. We are a good team and I could not have come this far without him. I'm the dreamer with my head in the clouds and he is the stable one with his feet on the ground.

Brett, Danen, and Anbrea Bateman poured over recipes catching errors for this cookbook. Thank you for your help and support. Brooke and Brian Bateman couldn't catch the errors but they worked hard making our business work. Thank you. I had to include our new family picture. It has been four years since the last family picture was taken and included in the first cookbook. I would be lost without our children.

Nathan Bridges for his dedicated work in our behalf. Our business would not be growing if it weren't for his focused attention to detail. Thank you.

Thank you Lori McNamara, Kris Burnham Shelley Gardner, and Heide Weatherby for their help with the layout, design, and typesetting of this cookbook.

Forward by Dr. David C. Robbins M.D.

Director of Research, Medlantic Research Institute
Professor of Medicine, George Washington University Medical School

Nearly fifty years ago, Dr. Anselm Keys observed that the lowest rates of heart disease occurred among people eating the least amount of fat. Where fat was a larger part of the diet, cholesterol levels and rates of heart disease were higher. These observations led to a public health campaign asking us to eat less fat. Who can pass a city bus without seeing the familiar placard on its side commanding us to "know your cholesterol level."

The response to this has been a good-news, bad-news situation. The fat consumed by Americans is now a smaller part of the diet. Twenty years ago, the average American ate more than 40% of their calories as fat, and much of it was saturated fat, the worst type. Government-sponsored studies estimate that the average American now gets only 34% of their calories from fat. The average cholesterol level dropped, and the rate of heart disease is generally lower. Yet the bad news is that Americans are eating more calories and exercising less. As a nation we are getting fatter and less active. During the past ten years, the percentage of Americans significantly overweight increased at an alarming rate. Now, more than 35% of us are obese. The most apparent consequence of all this obesity is a striking increase in the number of people affected with diabetes. Nearly l0% of American adults now have some form of glucose intolerance, and the rates of diabetes are reaching epidemic proportions among minorities such as Hispanics and American Indians. Diabetes is theoretically one of the most treatable public health conditions, if we could only avoid obesity and exercise more.

Health professionals view these trends with fear. Whatever gains made by eating less fat are lost as we eat too much, becoming a victim to this pattern is easy. Look what's on the grocery store shelves. See how many foods they label as "low fat" or "fat free." Take a careful look at the nutrition summary on the back panel of these foods. They are often dense in calories and have nearly as many calories as the regular brands. They substitute the evils of fat with the dangers of too many calories. These "low fat" claims invite us to eat as much as we please, and the consequences are all too evident. Obesity costs this country more than $58 billion per year in health care costs and we spend nearly $30 billion per year in just trying to lose weight.

The healthy or prudent diet recommended by American Diabetes association, The Cancer Society, the American Heart Association, and the National Academy of Sciences is nearly the same. With uncharacteristic accord, scientists and physicians from a variety of backgrounds agreed upon a common, healthy diet. The same diet that seems to lower the cholesterol level, reduces the sugar in the blood, and minimizes the chances of breast, colon and prostate cancer. They recommend an appropriate number of calories, less fat, more carbohydrates, and greater amounts of fiber. The prudent diet emphasizes several daily portions of fruits and vegetables that are important sources of fiber, vitamins, and minerals. Meat should be used more as a condiment, sprinkled on top of the food. Good sources of carbohydrates like grains, beans, and pasta should assume a more central role in the meal. Less than 30% of the calories should come from fats, and these should include both mono- and polyunsaturated oils such a canola, olive and corn oil. We should reduce simple sugars since they are calorically dense and produce large changes in the blood sugar. This is especially important to people with diabetes who must try to reduce the blood sugar.

How then do we eat well, eat healthy, and enjoy what we eat?

This book is a guide to eating wisely while eating well. Bateman's SugarLike and ButterLike are tools that can painlessly reduce the amount of fat and simple sugar in the diet. The recipes are familiar favorites with all the expected taste and nutrition. However, the Bateman kitchen makes meals with fewer calories and all of the flavor. This cookbook is a guide to fine eating without the guilt. Combine it with a healthy lifestyle. Exercise a little more, take time off from stress, and enjoy our meal. Forgive me for saying so, but here is your chance to have your cake and eat it too. Bon Appetit.

ButterLike, SugarLike, and EggLike are a dream come true. Kristine Bateman's wonderful products will change the way you think about foods. At last, we can all truly enjoy the "unthinkables" - rich desserts, creamy sauces and soups, succulent main dishes, delicious breads, buttery tasting corn and potatoes without a drop of guilt and with just a fraction of the fat and calories. SugarLike products help you control your diabetic diet by not raising blood glucose levels as much as sugar. These products will change the way we eat and prepare our favorite foods.

Use SugarLike wherever you would use sugar. You simply won't be able to tell the difference. The only sacrifice you're making is giving up half the calories.

ButterLike opens a whole new world of cooking for those of us who want to control the amount of fat, cholesterol and calories in our diets. (I guess that's just about everybody these days.) It bakes and cooks just like butter, but with 93% less fat and cholesterol and 65% fewer calories.

Enjoy this cookbook and the great recipes it contains. But don't be afraid to experiment on your own with new creations or family favorites. ButterLIke, SugarLike, and EggLike are used on a one-to-one replacement basis anywhere your recipe calls for sugar or butter. It's just that easy.

Like me, I am sure you will be eternally grateful to Kristine, founder and developer of the wonderful Bateman Products...I only wish she had done so sooner! I hope you will join me in recommending them to others. They have been lovingly crafted for good health and great taste.

I am proud to give them my full endorsement.

Eat healthy and well.

Sybil Ferguson
Diet Center Founder
Rexburg, Idaho

Introduction

I have to credit much of my interest in nutrition to my paternal grandmother. She was ahead of her time in the field of nutrition and felt that nutrition was the key to feeling better, staying healthy, and enjoying life. She must have been right....she lived to be 91 years old. I can remember one time my parents becoming worried about her because she drank so much carrot juice her skin was turning orange. She was juicing before juicing was popular. I've probably tasted every kind of juice conceivable. She also believed that "wheat was for man." Wheat germ was a natural ingredient included in everything she ate. My Aunt Mary's meatloaf, which includes wheat germ, is the most delicious meatloaf I've ever tasted. I add it to my own meatloaf today.

My mother was another role model and inspiration to me. Her interest in low fat cooking and experiences in trying to lose weight left me determined to find better ways of cooking and dieting.

Since my graduation from the University of Utah with a B.S. Degree in Food Science and Nutrition in 1977, and especially since my grandmother's time, there has been an avalanche of information published on nutrition and dieting. Not only can all this information be overwhelming, but it can change - one day recommending one thing, and the next day something else. The consumer can become confused, left wondering what to believe. What foods are healthy? What are safe ways to lose weight? Are there any foods left that are good for me? I personally feel that some things have not changed since my grandmother's time; healthy eating is not about the latest fad diets, but about having choices and eating a well-balanced diet filled with a variety of foods. Part of the legacy I want to leave to my children is the knowledge and the tools necessary to eat healthy — free from the problems of obesity, heart disease, high blood pressure, diabetes, and cancer. I hope my products - **ButterLike Baking Butter**, **ButterLike Saute Butters**, and the **SugarLike** line will help you too feel good about the way you eat.

In the following pages I have compiled some information (from the avalanche of information) that I hope will simplify making healthy choices. Included are the U.S.F.D.A Dietary Food Guides and Food Guide Pyramid, tips for making your own recipes low fat, substitution tables, comparison tables, and **ButterLike** and **SugarLike** product information. There is also a special section just for Diabetics. If you have any questions regarding low fat cooking or the Bateman Products, please write me, call the toll free hot line **(1-800-574-6822)** or send an e-mail. Healthy cooking!

Kristine, sharing new nutritional information on low fat cooking with customers at Barnes and Noble, Idaho Falls, Idaho.

Diabetes Study and SugarLike™

We recently tested the new sweetener **SugarLike**™ for use by people with type 2 diabetes. Type 2 diabetes, the most common form of diabetes, is the type that occurs later in life and often runs in families. People with type 2 diabetes are usually overweight and physically inactive. The study was designed to determine the effects of **SugarLike** on the blood sugar of people with type 2 diabetes in a "double blinded" design. "Double blinded" means that the participants and the doctor in the study did not know which of the meals was made with **SugarLike** or table sugar.

The people in our study ate a breakfast containing **SugarLike** used in a muffin, some fruit, and tea or coffee. Then we took blood samples every 15 minutes for 2.5 hours to measure glucose, insulin, and triglycerides. We found that blood glucose did not increase as much when they ate the breakfast containing **SugarLike**. While blood glucose always goes up after a meal, the rise was not as high with **SugarLike** as with table sugar (see the graph). The average increase in blood glucose was on the average 12% lower with **SugarLike**.

Each of these factors indicates that **SugarLike** is a better choice for people with diabetes than table sugar. Thus, we showed that **SugarLike** can be used more safely than table sugar (sucrose) by people with type 2 diabetes. Current dietary recommendations for people with diabetes encourage reduced amounts of sugar and a diet designed to keep levels of sugars and triglycerides at safe levels.

The importance of this study is that **SugarLike**, unlike Nutrasweet™, can be used for baking. **SugarLike** can withstand baking temperatures to produce sweetened baked produces with a good texture. Therefore, **SugarLike** adds more options for those people with type 2 diabetes. In addition to the beneficial effects on blood glucose, triglycerides, and insulin, **SugarLike** cup-for-cup has fewer calories than table sugar and therefore, it can also help people reduce their calorie intake. Taking in fewer calories, reducing portion sizes and increasing exercise will result in weight loss. Losing weight is often the best thing a person with diabetes can do to improve their health.

In summary, using **SugarLike**, as well as the fat substitute **ButterLike**™ to produce low calorie snacks, can add variety to an otherwise low calorie, healthy diet. These products and this cookbook should make eating a healthy diet and losing weight more pleasant for all of us.

David C. Robbins, MD
Director of Research
Medlantic Research Institute

Judy S. Hannah, PhD
Research Scientist
Penn Medical Lab

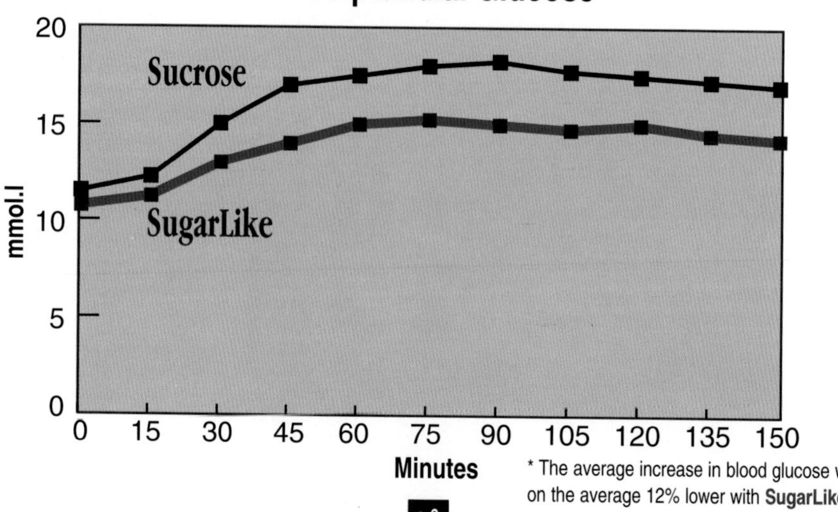

* The average increase in blood glucose was on the average 12% lower with **SugarLike**.

U.S.F.D.A Dietary Food Guides

1. Eat a variety of foods.
2. Balance the food you eat with physical activity; maintain or improve your weight.
3. Choose your diet with plenty of grain products, vegetables and fruit.
4. Choose a diet low in fat, saturated fat, and cholesterol.
5. Choose a diet low in sugars.
6. Choose a diet that's moderate in salt and sodium.
7. If you drink alcoholic beverages, do so in moderation.

I'd like to add two recommendations to the list:

8. Eat smaller meals, eat snacks, and eat more often. Our bodies need to maintain our blood sugar level. As we do this, we are less hungry as our metabolism increases.

   If we go longer periods of time without eating, our bodies go into a starvation mode. As a result, our metabolism slows down. (We get fat by eating less.)
9. Drink at least 8 glasses of water a day.

U.S.F.D.A. Food Pyramid

The pyramid is bigger at the bottom with the foods and food servings that we should eat the most of. It gets smaller at the top with foods we should eat sparingly. Fats, oils, and sweets have not been given serving amounts because we should eat these foods sparingly. Mrs. Bateman's Products give you the ingredients you need to keep the fat and sugar in balance.

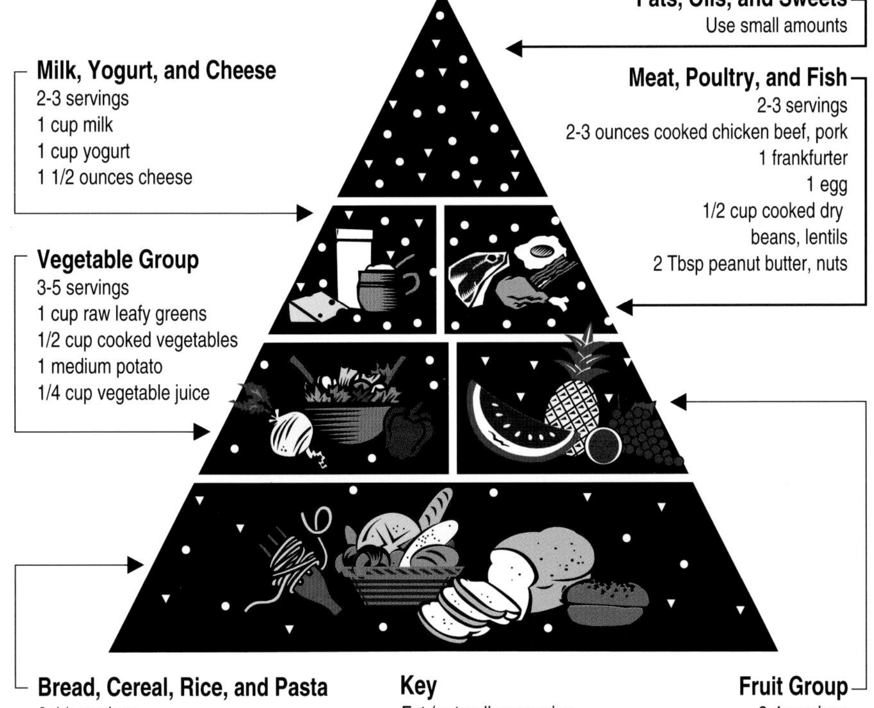

Bread, Cereal, Rice, and Pasta
6-11 servings
1 slice bread
1/2 bagel
1 tortilla
1/2 cup cooked rice, pasta, grits
3/4 cup ready-to-eat cereal

Key
● Fat (naturally occurring and added)
Sugars (added)
▼ These symbols show fat and added sugars in foods.

Fruit Group
2-4 servings
1 medium apple, orange
1/2 cup grapes, berries
1/4 cantaloupe
3/4 cup fruit juice
1/4 cup raisins

Why Use Mrs. Bateman's Products?

Fat and sugar are necessary parts of our diets, and, in certain quantities, are necessary to our health. They give our food wonderful flavor and texture and are a required ingredient in most of our everyday foods. My search for healthy, low fat, low calorie alternatives to fat and sugar began when customers of our family bakery began telling me that while they loved our food, they were getting fat from eating it. My customers, as well as myself, were finding out the repercussions of eating too much fat and sugar - weight gain. Along with weight gain, high fat intake is linked with other health problems such as heart disease, diabetes, hypertension, and cancer.

The first step in my search for healthy alternatives was to try products that were already on the market. There weren't very many choices to begin with, and **all** of them failed to meet one or more of my basic requirements which are:

- It must taste great
- It must be a one-for-one replacement (no complicated measurements)
- It must work in all types of cooking (main dishes, baking, sauteing, canning, etc)
- It must be as natural as possible.

Through experimentation, I developed a formula for **ButterLike Baking Butter** and **ButterLike Sauté Butter**, both now patented, and **SugarLike**, patent pending. They meet all of my requirements and give you, the consumer, the tools you need to eat food that you like and that is healthy at the same time.

ButterLike™ Family Line

What is It?

ButterLike substitutes are the first one-to-one fat substitutes that can be used to bake, cook, and sauté with. **ButterLike** is the family name for the unique maltodextrin based fat replacements made with a small amount of real butter. There is **ButterLike Baking Butter** - an emulsion, **ButterLike Saute Butters** - a liquid, and **ButterLike Powdered Baking Butter** - a powder. The **ButterLike** products are used to replace all fats, not just butter. Not only are the fat substitutes low fat but are also very low calorie - only 2.57 to 2.86 per gram. The **ButterLike** fat substitutes are formulated in a unique way to utilize natural ingredients and to retain the best nutrition as possible. All the ingredients are natural, except for the two preservatives used to keep the shelf life.

How Do I Use ButterLike Products?

To Bake — ButterLike Baking Butter can be used to replace every cup of butter, margarine, oil, shortening or other fat in any recipe. **ButterLike** was developed because there was not a fat substitute that worked in replacing the fat, straight across, in all types of food products such as cinnamon rolls, cookies, cakes, frostings, etc. **ButterLike** has different properties than fat and mixes differently so I have included some mixing instructions, storage instructions, and some helpful hints about using **ButterLike**. The products made with **ButterLike** turn out very similar to the high fat counterpart food products in taste, appearance, texture, and ease of preparation.

Eating healthy is about having choices and eating a well balanced diet filled with a variety of foods.

To Saute — **ButterLike Sauté Butter** was developed specifically as a sauté and has the rich flavor of butter and olive oil sometimes needed in main dish cooking. **ButterLike Sauté Butter** also works as a wonderful buttery seasoning for corn on the cob, baked potatoes, steamed fresh vegetables or anywhere a butter spread is wanted to enhance your foods.

Baking Butter may be used as a sauté medium or in main dish cooking as well, but has a milder flavor and a thicker consistency than **Sauté Butter**.

ButterLike Sauté Butter has real butter and real olive oil as its ingredients so it is a superior additive to any food where more butter flavor is needed. Examples of this would be bread stuffing, candied yams, pasta dishes, cream sauces etc.

Sauté Butter is available in 4 natural flavors: **Butter and Olive Oil Flavor, Toasted Onion Flavor, Toasted Garlic Flavor, and Italian Herb Flavor.**

Nutritional Information

ButterLike Baking Butter Comparison to Butter

Baking Butter (1 cup)	**Butter** (1 cup)	**Healthy Savings** (1 cup)
13 grams fat	184 grams fat	93% less fat
569 Calories	1626 Calories	65% less calories
35 mg cholesterol	497 mg cholesterol	93% less cholesterol
971 mg sodium	1847 mg sodium	47% less sodium

ButterLike Baking Butter

Nutritional Facts

Serving Size	1 Tbsp (14 g)	
Calories		36
Calories from fat		10
		% Daily Value*
Total Fat	1 g	1.5%
Saturated Fat	.5 g	2.5%
Cholesterol	<5 mg	1%
Sodium	60 mg	2%
Total Carbohydrate	8 g	3%
Dietary Fiber	0 g	0%
Sugar	0 g	0%
Other **	1 g	.4%
Protein	0 g	0%

Vit A 10% Vit C 0% Calcium 0% Iron 0%

*Percent Daily Values (DV) are based on 2000 calorie diet

Baking Butter Ingredients: Maltodextrin (made from corn, rice or potatoes), Water, Inulin (natural extract of chicory root), Modified food starch, Butter, Dehydrated butter, Liquid soybean oil, Salt, Whey, Citric acid, Calcium propionate & Sodium Benzoate (preservatives), Natural flavor, Beta-carotene, Vitamin A palmitate added.

* 'Other' Carbohydrates are carbohydrates that do not significantly raise the blood glucose or insulin levels. They have less than 4 calories per gram found in regular carbohydrates. Diabetics do not have to count these carbohydrates.

Powdered Baking Butter Ingredients: Powdered Baking Butter retains the same nutritional statement when hydrated as Baking Butter.

ButterLike Sauté Butter:

- 85% less fat than Olive Oil
- 83% less fat than Butter
- 67% less calories than Olive Oil
- 61% less calories than Butter
- 94% less cholesterol than butter

Sauté Butter Ingredients: Water, Maltodextrin (made from corn, rice & potatoes), Butter, Olive oil, Soybean oil, Modified food Starch, Citric acid, Whey, Xanthum gum, Calcium propionate and Sodium benzoate (preservatives), Natural flavor, Beta-carotene, Vitamin A palmitate added.

ButterLike Saute Butter

Nutritional Facts

Serving Size	1 Tbsp (14 g)	
Calories		40
Calories from fat		10
		% Daily Value*
Total Fat	2 g	3%
Saturated Fat	.5 g	.5%
Cholesterol	<5 mg	1%
Sodium	60 mg	2%
Total Carbohydrate	4 g	1%
Dietary Fiber	0 g	0%
Sugar	0 g	0%
Other **	0 g	0%
Protein	0 g	0%

Vit A 10% Vit C 0% Calcium 0% Iron 0%

*Percent Daily Values (DV) are based on 2000 calorie diet

ButterLike Saute Butters

SugarLike™ Family Line

What is It?

The **SugarLike** Sugar Substitutes are a family of patent pending low calorie, one-to-one, sugar substitutes used in baking, cooking, table top, and in any way real sugar is used or processed. There is **Granulated SugarLike, Brown SugarLike, Powdered SugarLike,** and **Liquid SugarLike**.

SugarLike was developed from direct requests from diabetics using and loving **Baking Butter**, but also needing help to replace the sugar in their recipes. Unlike other substitutes on the market, **SugarLike** is heat stable and retains its sweetness when processed under all types of cooking conditions, and has no aftertaste.

These sugar substitutes contain less than 1/2 the calories of real sugar, no aspartame, no saccharin, and can be listed as sugar free. They are made up of several different ingredients, all of which are tooth friendly, low calorie, and most important of all, diabetic friendly (will not significantly raise the blood glucose and insulin levels.) **SugarLike** is also high in fiber with Bifidobacteria promotion benefits.

SugarLike Family Line

SugarLike Comparison to Sugar

	SugarLike	Sugar
Calories per cup	384 Calories	768 Calories
Suitable for Diabetics?	Yes!	No
Tooth friendly?	Yes!	No

Comparison to Saccharin and Aspartame

	SugarLike	Saccharin	Aspartame
One-to-one substitute?	Yes!	No	No
Retains sweetness?	Yes!	No	No
Solves bulk problem?	Yes!	No	No
Promotes Bifidobacteria?	Yes!	No	No
Lowers cholesterol?	Yes!	No	No
No aftertaste?	Yes!	No	No
Contains fiber?	Yes!	No	No
Some browning?	Yes!	No	No
Non carcinogenic?	Yes!	No	No
Can be used in any recipe without adjustments?	Yes!*	No	No

(Except those leavened with yeast, which requires two Tbsp of sugar to react with one Tbsp of dry yeast).

Nutritional Information

Granulated SugarLike—A granulated sugar substitute used to replace granulated sugar in a one-to-one replacement in any recipe or in any way sugar would be used. From candies, meringue, cakes, cookies, to a sweetener for soft drinks.

Granulated SugarLike Ingredients: Maltitol, Inulin (Natural Extract of Chicory Root), Lactitol, Erythritol, Polydextrose, Acesulfame K, Gum Arabic, Natural Flavor.

Granulated SugarLike

Nutritional Facts

Serving Size	1 tsp (4 g)	
Calories		7
Calories from fat		0
		% Daily Value*
Total Fat	0 g	0%
Saturated Fat	0 g	0%
Cholesterol	0 mg	0%
Sodium	0 mg	0%
Total Carbohydrate	4 g	1%
Dietary Fiber	1 g	4%
Sugar	0 g	0%
Other **	3 g	1%
Protein	0 g	0%
Vit A 0% Vit C 0% Calcium 0% Iron 0%		

*Percent Daily Values (DV) are based on 2000 calorie diet

Brown SugarLike—A brown sugar substitute used to replace brown sugar as a one-to-one replacement in any recipe or in any way brown sugar would be used.

Brown SugarLike Ingredients: Maltitol, Inulin (Natural Extract of Chicory Root), Lactitol, Erythritol, Polydextrose, Caramel Color, Acesulfame K, Natural Flavor.

Brown SugarLike

Nutritional Facts

Serving Size	1 tsp (4 g)	
Calories		7
Calories from fat		0
		% Daily Value*
Total Fat	0 g	0%
Saturated Fat	0 g	0%
Cholesterol	0 mg	0%
Sodium	0 mg	0%
Total Carbohydrate	4 g	1%
Dietary Fiber	1 g	4%
Sugar	0 g	0%
Other **	3 g	1%
Protein	0 g	0%
Vit A 0% Vit C 0% Calcium 0% Iron 0%		

*Percent Daily Values (DV) are based on 2000 calorie diet

Powdered SugarLike—A powdered sugar substitute used to replace powdered sugar as a one-to-one replacement in recipes. Now sugar free cake frostings can be made to top sugar free cakes

Powdered Sugar Ingredients: Maltitol, Inulin (Natural Extract of Chicory Root), Lactitol, Erythritol, Polydextrose, Silicon Dioxide, Acesulfame K, Natural Flavor.

Powdered SugarLike

Nutritional Facts

Serving Size	1/4 cup (30 g)	
Calories		60
Calories from fat		0
		% Daily Value*
Total Fat	0 g	0%
Saturated Fat	0 g	0%
Cholesterol	0 mg	0%
Sodium	0 mg	0%
Total Carbohydrate	30 g	10%
Dietary Fiber	0 g	0%
Sugar	<1 g	.3%
Other **	22 g	7%
Protein	0 g	0%
Vit A 0% Vit C 0% Calcium 0% Iron 0%		

*Percent Daily Values (DV) are based on 2000 calorie diet

Liquid SugarLike—This is used to replace corn syrup, fructose syrup, etc., as a one-to-one replacement in recipes. The need for this SugarLike product became apparent when trying to make candy, when more than half the recipes called for corn syrup. If candy is to be sugar free and diabetic safe, then you need a corn syrup substitute.

Liquid SugarLike Ingredients: Maltitol, Water, Inulin (Natural Extract of Chicory Root), Lactitol, Erythritol, Polydextrose, Acesulfame K, Natural Flavor.

Liquid SugarLike

Nutritional Facts

Serving Size	1/4 cup (60 ml)	
Calories		120
Calories from fat		0
		% Daily Value*
Total Fat	0 g	0%
Saturated Fat	0 g	0%
Cholesterol	0 mg	0%
Sodium	0 mg	0%
Total Carbohydrate	59 g	20%
Dietary Fiber	14 g	56%
Sugar	1 g	.3%
Other **	43 g	14%
Protein	0 g	0%
Vit A 0% Vit C 0% Calcium 0% Iron 0%		

*Percent Daily Values (DV) are based on 2000 calorie diet

EggLike™

What is It?

EggLike is a new natural, dried whole egg substitute used in baking and cooking. This new formulation was made to help increase the volume of cakes and other baked low fat products. In the past I used plain egg whites or egg substitutes to keep the fat down but I found they caused more structural change to the finished product than the **ButterLike** or **SugarLike**. **EggLike** helps to correct these structural changes and helps to make a better finished baked product. I am pleased to present this newest member of the Bateman's Products to help you to truly cook delicious, great tasting, low fat, low cholesterol, low calorie, and low sugar recipes for you and your families.

This cookbook was basically finished by the time **EggLike** was ready to market. However, for your convenience, I have added the nutritional information for **EggLike** here. **EggLike** can be substituted according to the following directions. Each egg or 1/4 cup egg white or egg substitute called for in this cookbook can be replaced with 1/4 cup of the mixed **EggLike.**

EggLike, a natural, dried, whole egg substitute:

- 26% less calories than whole eggs
- 77% less fat
- Cholesterol free
- Contains fiber
- No saturated fats
- Low sodium
- Increases volume in cakes
- Equal mixing
- Fortified with calcium, iron, Vitamin D, Vitamin A

Directions:

Mrs. Bateman's **EggLike** is an easy to mix dried egg substitute made to replace whole eggs, egg substitute, and egg whites in baking and cooking. Mix equal amounts of **EggLike** and water according to the easy mixing chart below, stir well. Store **EggLike** in your cupboard. Store mixed **EggLike** no more than 3 days in the refrigerator.

Easy Mixing Chart

Amount of eggs to be replaced	Equal amounts of Egglike and water
1 or 1/4 cup	1 scoop or 2 Tbsp plus 2 tsp
2 or 1/2 cup	2 scoops or 1/3 cup
3 or 3/4 cup	3 scoops or 1/2 cup
4 or 1 cup	4 scoops or 2/3 cup

Nutritional Information

Comparison to Eggs

	Egg	**EggLike** (mixed with water)
Weight	50 g	50 g
Calories	74.5	55
Total Fat	5 g	1 g
Saturated Fat	1.5 g	0 g
Cholesterol	212 mg	0 mg
Sodium	63 mg	130 mg
Total Carbohydrates	.61 g	3.65 g
Dietary Fiber	0 g	1 g
Sugars	0 g	0 g
Protein	6 g	7 g
Calcium	24.5 mg	24.5 mg
Iron	.72 mg	.72 mg

Ingredients Statement: Dried Egg Whites, Lecithin, Maltodextrin (made from rice, corn or potatoes). Modified Food Starch, Butter, Dehydrated Butter, Liquid Soybean Oil, Salt, Whey, Natural Flavorings, Maltitol, Lactitol, Erythritol, Polydextrose, Xanthum Gum, Beta Carotene, fortified with Vitamin A Palmitate, Calcium, Vitamin K, Iron, Zinc, Thiamin B-1, Pantothenic Acid, Vitamin D.

EggLike

Nutritional Facts

Serving Size 2 Tbsp + 2 tsp (15 g)

Calories		55
Calories from fat		10
		% Daily Value*
Total Fat	1 g	2%
Saturated Fat	0 g	0%
Cholesterol	0 mg	0%
Sodium	130 mg	5%
Total Carbohydrate	4 g	1%
Dietary Fiber	1 g	4%
Sugar	0 g	0%
Other **	0 g	0%
Protein	7 g	

Vit A 10% Vit C 0% Calcium 2% Iron 4%

*Percent Daily Values (DV) are based on 2000 calorie diet

What is Inulin?

One of the main ingredients of SugarLike is Chicory Extract (Inulin). The part of the Inulin used in SugarLike is obtained by hot water extraction. The end product is a medium sized indigestible chain of the natural sugar fructose. Based upon a major industry report, aside from being low in calories Inulin has many health benefits.

Inulin's (prebiotic) bifidogenic effects

- Consumed regularly at about 10 g/day promotes Bifudus as predominant bacterial genus in color
- Bifido Bacteria reduces colonic pH - via VFA production
- Bifido Bacteria produces B-complex vitamins
- Immunododulation (attacks malignant cells and absorbs procarcinogenes)
- Restores normal microflora during antibiotic therapy
- By eating SugarLike you increase the number of good bacteria and decrease the number of bad bacteria.

Inulin: A Dietary Fiber

- Meets physiological definition of dietary fiber
- Inulin functions as a fiber and is used as a dietary fiber in eight European countries and Canada
- Actually been shown to improve glucose tolerance and insulin sensitivity.
- Increases fecal mass and increases triglycerides levels
- Decreases fecal transit time and the risk of some types of colon cancer.

Reduces Fat Absorption

- Increases triglyceride levels in fecal material
- The consumption of Inulin significantly improved the HDL to LDL cholesterol in rats
- Reduces hepatic cholesterol and triglyceride levels.

Inulin is not absorbed as a carbohydrate so it does not significantly raise blood glucose levels.

How to figure SugarLike Nutritional Information in your own recipes.

The following charts and instructions will give you all the information you need to figure calories, total carbohydrates, sugar grams, and fiber grams in your own recipes after substituting SugarLike for sugar.

To figure out the new nutritional information for a recipe you must first know its nutritional information when made the original way using sugar. Most recipes include this information.

To figure the new calories per serving using SugarLike:

1. If you have 1/2 cup of sugar in your recipe, substitute 1/2 cup of SugarLike in the recipe.
2. **Multiply** the number of servings per recipe by the number of calories per serving to get the total calories in the recipe.

Example: 6 servings X 200 calories = 1200 calories per recipe.

3. **Subtract** the sugar calories from the total calories (use the sugar chart on the following page to get the correct amount of calories in 1/2 cup of sugar).

Example: 1200 calories per recipe - 388 sugar calories = 812 remaining calories

4. Looking at the SugarLike chart, now add the SugarLike calories for 1/2 cup to the remaining calories.

Example: 812 remaining calories + 192 (1/2 cup) SugarLike Calories = 996 calories for the whole recipe

5. To figure the total calories per serving, divide the last figure by the number of servings.

Example: 996 calories divided by 6 servings = 166 calories per serving

Sugar Chart

	1 Tbsp	1/8 cup	1/4 cup	1/3 cup	1/2 cup	2/3 cup	3/4 cup	1 cup	2 cup	3 cup
Calories	48	96	192	264	384	528	576	768	1536	2304
Total Carbohydrate g	12.5	25	50	67	100	134	150	200	400	600
Dietary Fiber g	0	0	0	0	0	0	0	0	0	0
Sugars g	12	24	49	65	97	129	146	194	388	582
Other g	0	0	0	0	0	0	0	0	0	0

SugarLike Chart

	1 Tbsp	1/8 cup	1/4 cup	1/3 cup	1/2 cup	2/3 cup	3/4 cup	1 cup	2 cup	3 cup
Calories	24	48	96	132	192	264	288	384	768	1152
Total Carbohydrate g	12	25	49	66	99	132	148	197	394	591
Dietary Fiber g	3	6	12	16	24	32	36	48	96	144
Sugars g	0	.57	1	1.5	2.3	3	3.46	4.6	9.2	13.8
Other g	9	18	36	48	72	96	108	144	288	432

To figure the new Other* grams

Follow the same formula but instead of calories you will be using the Other* grams.

1. If you have 1/2 cup of sugar in your recipe, substitute 1/2 cup of **SugarLike** in the recipe.
2. Since there are no Other* carbohydrates in the recipe made with sugar, all you need to do is to divide the number of Other* Carbohydrates grams by the number of servings found in 1/2 cup **SugarLike**.

Example: 72 grams Other* divided by 6 servings = 12 grams Other* per serving

To figure the new Fiber grams

Follow the same formula, but instead of calories you will be using the fiber grams.

1. If you have 1/2 cup of sugar in your recipe, substitute 1/2 cup of **SugarLike** in the recipe.
2. Since there are no fiber grams in the recipe made with sugar all you need to do is divide the number of fiber grams by the number of servings found in 1/2 cup **SugarLike**.

Example: 24 grams of fiber divided by 6 servings = 4 grams of fiber per serving.

3. If your original recipe contains fiber, make sure you add those fiber grams onto the fiber from the previous step.

Example: Lets say that the original recipe had 1 gram of fiber per serving. Changing 1/2 cup sugar with **SugarLike** added 4 grams of fiber per serving. Just add the original 1 gram of fiber per serving + to the 4 grams of fiber per serving from the **SugarLike** and it = 5 grams of fiber total.

To figure the sugar Grams per serving

Use the following formula:

1. If you have 1/2 cup of sugar in your recipe, substitute 1/2 cup of **SugarLike** in the recipe.
2. Multiply the total of number of sugar grams found per serving in the regular high sugar recipe by the number of servings.

Example: Lets say the recipe had 18 grams of sugar per serving X 6 servings = 108 grams total sugar.

1/2 cup of sugar (look at sugar chart) has 97 grams sugar Subtract 96 grams of sugar - 108 grams total sugar = 11 grams of remaining sugar.

3. Looking at the **SugarLike** chart, add the SugarLike grams of sugar for 1/2 cup to the remaining sugar.

Example: 2.4 grams of sugar + 11 grams of remaining sugar = 13.4 grams of total sugar in the whole recipe.

13.4 grams of total sugar divided by 6 servings = 2.3 grams of sugar per serving. That is a reduction in 2.4 grams of sugar divided by 108 grams of sugar = (0.022 subtracted from 1) 98% less sugar.

* Other carbohydrates in **SugarLike** are digested in a manner that does not significantly affect blood glucose and insulin levels. Diabetics do not need to count these Other carbohydrates as starches or sugars. These Other carbohydrates have less than half the calories than sugar. If you are on a restricted diet you will need to count the calories per gram, which is 2.

Baked goods such as Chocolate Peanut Butter Bars, page 86; Ginger Bread, page 52; and Angel Sugar Crisps, page 84; no longer have to be "bad for you" when you bake them using ButterLike and SugarLike.

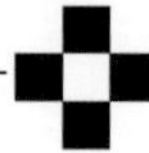

Substitution Formula

The **ButterLike Products** and **SugarLike Products** are very simple to substitute.
Use the same amounts of my products that the recipe calls for.
1 cup sugar = 1 cup SugarLike. 1 cup Corn Syrup = 1 cup Liquid SugarLike

1 Tablespoon of ButterLike for every 11 grams of fat you take out of your recipe.

Use **ButterLike Baking Butter** especially if your recipe is a baked recipe.
Use **ButterLike Sauté Butter** if you need more butter flavor

Heavy cream or whipping cream (1 cup) 89 fat grams	=	**1 cup skim milk plus 1/2 cup ButterLike** 7 fat grams
Half and Half (1 cup) 8 fat grams	=	**1 cup skim milk plus 2 5/8 Tbsp ButterLike** 2.1 fat grams
2% milk (1 cup) 4.7 fat grams	=	**1 cup skim milk plus 1/2 Tbsp ButterLike** 0.4 fat grams
Whole milk (1 cup) 8 fat grams	=	**1 cup skim milk plus 3/4 Tbsp ButterLike** 0.6 fat grams
Evaporated milk (1 cup) 19 fat grams	=	**1 cup evaporated skim milk plus 1 3/4 Tbsp ButterLike** 1.4 fat grams
Buttermilk (1 cup) 2.2 fat grams	=	**I use buttermilk because it is so low in fat**
Yogurt (1 cup) 7.4 fat grams	=	**1 cup skim yogurt plus 5/8 Tbsp ButterLike** .48 fat grams
1 large whole egg 5.6 fat grams	=	**Equal amounts of EggLike and water (2 Tbsp + 2 tsp)** 1 fat gram
Sour cream (1 cup) 20 fat grams	=	**1 cup non fat sour cream plus 2Tbsp ButterLike** 1.6 fat grams
Cream cheese (1 cup) 76 fat grams	=	**1 cup non fat cream cheese plus 7 Tbsp ButterLike** 5.87 fat grams

Altitude Adjustment

Most of these recipes will work at low altitude but have been tested for 5,000 feet above sea level. Altitude and humidity can affect the finished product and adjustments may be made in accordance with where you live

The following chart will help you make the changes necessary.

Recipe adjustments for high altitude

	3000 ft.	*5000 ft.	7000 ft.
Baking Powder For each tsp. decrease	1/8 tsp.	1/8-1/4 tsp.	1/4 tsp.
Sugar For each cup decrease	0-1 Tbsp	0-2 Tbsp	1-3 Tbsp
Liquid For each cup add	1-2 Tbsp	2-4 Tbsp	3-4 Tbsp

(egg works well for the increase in liquid because it helps the cell structure of your cake.

**5000 feet - the recipes in this book were developed at 5000 feet.*

Recipe adjustments for sea level

	Sea Level
Baking Powder, For each tsp. increase	1/8-1/4 tsp
Sugar, For each cup increase	2 Tbsp
Liquid*, For each cup decrease	2-4 Tbsp

**Pie crusts at our altitude (5000 feet) need slightly more liquid.*
You may find in high humidity at sea level that adding water to the eggs to equal 1/4 cup is unnecessary. If you have a problem getting your recipes done, it might be that you have too much liquid.

Abbreviations

Ounce	oz
Pound	lb
Gram	g
Milliliter	ml
Liter	l
Tablespoon	Tbsp
Teaspoon	tsp
Cup	C
Each	ea
Package	pkg

Baking Pan Conversions Chart

Inches (“)	Centimeters
1 inch	2.54 cm
9”X13”	22.86X33 cm
8”X8”	20.32X20.32 cm
9”X9”	22.86X22.86 cm
9” Pie Pan	22.86 cm
8” Pie Pan	20.32 cm
15”X10”X1”	38X25.4X2.54 cm

Oven Conversions Chart

To convert Fahrenheit into Centigrade, subtract 32, multiply by 5, and divide by 9. To convert Centigrade to Fahrenheit reverse the process. Multiply by 9, divide by 5 and add 32.

425° F - 220°C	400°F - 200°C
375°F - 190°C	350°F - 180°C
325°F - 160°C	300°F - 150°C

These recipes were tested in regular, conventional gas or electric ovens. The baking times were tested in those ovens at 5000 feet above sea level. Always set your timer for five minutes before the end of the cooking time given in this cookbook. This way you can see how your oven works in comparison to my baking times. It is easier to reset your time than cry over burnt food. There are a few things that affect the baking time of your product, such as the actual temperature of your oven, the altitude you live at, etc.

If you have a convection, fan or other type of oven please read the directions for baking temperatures and times that came with your particular oven.

Mrs. Bateman's Tips on cooking low fat, low calorie, low cholesterol and sugar free Main Dishes

Cooking low fat, low calorie, low cholesterol and sugar free is more than just using **ButterLike** and **SugarLike** products. It is a new way of cooking using every possible means available to reduce the fat, sugar, calories and cholesterol in your recipes. The result will be delicious foods that you love and that are healthy for you.

General Tips

1. Substitute any fat in your recipe one-to-one with **ButterLike Saute Butter** or with the **Flavored Saute Butters**.
2. Substitute any sugar into your recipes on a one-to-one replacement with the **SugarLike** products.
3. Always use the leanest cuts of meat with the fat trimmed off.
5. Substitute boneless skinless chicken breasts for meats that are higher in fat.
6. Meats are usually the highest source of fat found in recipes. Slightly cut the serving size of the meats for a healthier diet.
7. Rinse and drain lean ground beef in a colander after browning . (I use this technique often. I brown the meat well, rinse and drain it, and then add the sauteed vegetables and seasoning. I cannot tell a difference in the finished dish and neither can my family.)
8. Remove the skin from chicken before serving if it was cooked with the skin on. Recent studies conducted have found that eating chicken without the skin reduce the fat, regardless if it was cooked with the skin or without. I usually use boneless skinless chicken because of ease.
9. Here are some techniques to degrease your sauce or gravies.
   a. Deglaze your pan using a small amount of cold liquid. (At least 1/4 cup of drippings are necessary for the degreaser cup to work.) Pour drippings into a degreaser cup. Pour off the fat free drippings after the fat has raised to the top. Quit pouring as soon as the fat starts to go into the spout of the cup.
   b. Use a plastic baggy to degrease your drippings if you don't have a degreasing cup. Pour drippings into a plastic baggy. Cut or poke a hole in the bottom corner of the baggy. Let the fat free drippings pour into a pan until the fat or grease gets down to the hole. Pinch the hole together and drop the baggy into the garbage. Easy!
   c. Pour drippings into a small container and set in the refrigerator until chilled and grease has solidified at the top of the drippings. Spoon off all the solid grease and discard.
   d. Add 3 or 4 ice cubes to hot drippings and stir until grease solidifies on the ice. Spoon out with a slotted spoon.
10. Use the Substitution Table on page a-15 to substitute other ingredients that are typically high in fat but are not a one-to-one replacement for butter or fat. An example of this is sour cream, cream cheese or cream. I find that I have great success if I use skim milk for the cream, fat free sour cream for the real sour cream, and fat free cream cheese for the cream cheese. The real key to having the end product turn out is to add a small amount of **Baking Butter** or **Saute Butter** to the fat free substitute.
11. I went into cheese substitutions in the first cookbook a little more extensively than I will here. If I mix a small amount of a stronger flavored cheese with a low fat or fat free cheese I have greater success in my end recipe. When a recipe calls for sprinkling cheese on top of recipes I always use fat free cheese topping in in place of parmesan cheese.
12. Sometimes eggs can be replaced in main dish cooking entirely with egg substitutes. Other dishes such as souffle's need some mix of whole eggs, egg whites or egg substitutes. I recommend you use both egg whites and whole eggs for the most successful recipe.

    Our new **EggLike**™ is a natural, dried, whole egg substitute used in baking and cooking. Can be used to substitute any whole egg, 1/4 cup egg whites or egg substitutes in any recipe. See page A-12. **EggLike** is compatible with the recipes in this cookbook. **EggLike** increases volume in cakes and baked products over egg substitutes and egg whites.

Mrs. Bateman's Tips on using ButterLIke Saute Butter, ButterLike Baking Butter and SugarLike

- Use quality, non-stick bakeware and cookware to prevent sticking and promote even cooking.
- Vegetable spray all pans, even non-stick bakeware.
- **Saute Butter** heats up quite well, but it does not have the capacity to be heated to the high temperatures necessary for deep fat frying.
- Plain **Saute Butter** and the **Seasoned Saute Butter's** are interchangeable. **ButterLike Baking Butter** may also be substituted in recipes calling for **Saute Butter**.
  - **Saute Butter** has slightly more fat and a richer flavor than **ButterLike Baking Butter**.
  - When you need a product with a spreading consistency, use **Saute Butter**. **Baking Butter** can be thinned with a small amount of water if you do not have **Saute Butter** available.
- Seasoning cooked vegetables such as baked potatoes and corn on the cob has become a breeze. Just squirt a bit of one of the **Saute Butter** onto the prepared food and serve.

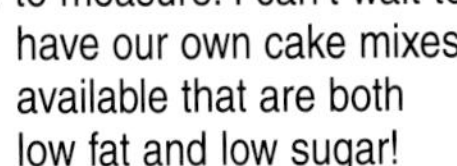

- Use **Saute Butter** in prepackaged side dishes such as macaroni and cheese, stuffing mix or noodles romanoff. Just replace the fat called for in the instructions with **Saute Butter**.
- **Saute Butter** works great in cake mixes. It is easy to use and easy to measure. I can't wait to have our own cake mixes available that are both low fat and low sugar!

- Sauteing with **ButterLike Saute Butter**.
  - Add **Saute Butter** to a non-stick pan **before** heating to saute vegetables or meats.
  - Add enough **Saute Butter** to slightly cover the vegetables and meat. Adjust the size of the pan to fit the amount of the items to be cooked.
  - If the **Saute Butter** sticks to the pan, cover it for a few minutes.
  - If items need to be browned, some sticking may occur. Sprinkling a small amount of water into the pan and stirring may assist in browning.

- Keep your **ButterLike Products** refrigerated. **Baking Butter**, although being shelf stable, will retain flavors better if refrigerated. Unless you are using large quantities of **Baking Butter**, keep it refrigerated even before opening.
- Soften pre-measured **ButterLike** in a microwave for 10-30 seconds before using or let sit out until it reaches room temperature.
- **Baking Butter** can be frozen. We don't recommend freezing **Saute Butter** because of the water content.
- Recipes using the **Bateman Products** can be frozen before or after baking, just like cooking with regular fat or sugar.
- **Do not over mix.** Because **ButterLike** contains only 7% fat, it does not incorporate air when beaten, so mix only until ingredients are combined and lump free
- Once **SugarLike** is mixed with other ingredients, use immediately. Lumps may form if mixture is allowed to sit.
- Because **ButterLike Baking Butter** has very little fat and does not melt like real fat, it should be whisked into other recipe ingredients rather than melted first.

Using Mrs. Bateman's Products in your own recipes

- Read "Tips on using **ButterLIke Saute Butter**, **ButterLike Baking Butter**, and **SugarLike**" on this page and the tips to successful cooking in each category
- **ButterLike** and **SugarLike** products were made to replace the fat and sugar completely in substitution. The nice thing about these products is that they can also be used to replace part of the sugar or fat. Try using 1/2 real fat and 1/2 **Baking Butter**. Any way you choose will give you excellent results.

- **SugarLike** works in every application with the exception of yeast products, which need sugar to feed it. Use two tablespoons of sugar for every tablespoon of dry yeast; mix together with 1/4 cup of warm water and wait until bubbles start forming. The rest of the sugar the recipe calls for can then be replaced with **SugarLike**.
- Baked products using **ButterLike Products** must contain some leavening. Leavening is either baking powder, baking soda, or yeast. Recipes that do not typically contain leavening such as pie crust need a small amount added. For every cup of flour in your recipe, add 1/4 tsp baking soda or baking powder. Some recipes such as shortbread have to have leavening added, but the recipe would then be a raised product instead of shortbread consistency. I recommend that if the shortbread texture is important to you, don't make shortbread using **Baking Butter**.
- **Important:** Each egg called for in a recipe needs to equal 1/4 cup. The recipe may call for whole eggs, egg whites, egg substitutes or dried eggs. But when you measure them, each "egg" must equal 1/4 cup. If your egg is short, add enough water to equal 1/4 cup. Using egg whites can cause some textural changes in your baked goods.

  Our new **EggLike**™ is a natural, dried, whole egg substitute used in baking and cooking. Can be used to substitute any whole egg, 1/4 cup egg whites or egg substitutes in any recipe. See page a-15. **EggLike** is compatible with the recipes in this cookbook. **EggLike** increases volume in cakes and baked products over egg substitutes and egg whites.
- Use the conversion charts, substitution table, and altitude charts on the preceding pages to help make your recipe conversions.
- Cooking times are sometimes slightly longer than when using real fat and sugar. Test with a toothpick or knife to check for doneness.
- Do not overcook. Cook until done, not until as brown as normal.
- Store foods in an airtight container.
- Call our Hotline, 1-800-574-6822, or E-Mail us at bakingbutter@lgcy.com to receive answers to your questions.

Mrs. Bateman's Products are tools for you to use in whatever way you choose, and will help you achieve the goals of low fat, low calorie, low cholesterol, and low sugar foods. Happy cooking!

Roasted Garlic

The Fat Quotient using **ButterLike** is **12%** instead of **35%**
70% less fat **0% less sugar**
16% less Calories

U.S.	Ingredients	Metric
8 tsp	**ButterLike Saute Butter**	37.00 g
1-4 bulbs	Garlic	12.00 g
1 loaf	French bread	310.00 g

Directions

Heat oven to 350°. Peel paperlike skin from around each bulb of garlic, leaving just enough to hold cloves together. Cut 1/4 to 1/2 inches from top of each bulb, place cut side up on 12-inch square of aluminum foil. Drizzle each bulb with 2 tsp of **ButterLike**. Sprinkle with salt and pepper. Wrap with foil and place in shallow baking pan. Bake 45 to 50 minutes or until tender. Cool slightly. To serve, gently squeeze garlic out of cloves and spread on bread. Top with crumbled feta cheese if desired.

Nutrition Facts				
Serving Size	45 g			
Servings Per Recipe	8			
Amount per serving			High Fat/Sugar Comparison	
Calories	109		130	
Calories from fat	10		45	
	% Daily Value*		% Daily Value*	
Total Fat	1.5 g	**2%**	5 g	**8%**
Saturated Fat	0 g	**0%**	0.5 g	**3%**
Cholesterol	0 mg	**0%**	0 mg	**0%**
Sodium	230 mg	**10%**	230 mg	**10%**
Total Carbohydrate	19 g	**6%**	18 g	**6%**
Dietary Fiber	0 g	**0%**	0 g	**0%**
Sugars	0 g		0 g	
Other	0 g		0 g	
Protein	4 g		4 g	

*Percent of Daily Values on Page a-22

Exchanges and 19 g Carbohydrates Per Serving

Breads	1.4	Vegetables	0.1	Fruits	0.0
Meats	0.0	Milk	0.0	Fats	0.5

How to Read a Recipe

A. Fat Quotient: % of calories from fat. Preparing food using **ButterLike** and **SugarLike** products cause the fat grams and calories to be lowered dramatically. When we figure the Fat Quotient using reduced fat grams and reduced calories the Fat Quotient looks higher than if made using the **ButterLike** products alone.

B. % Less Fat: This recipe's fat grams divided by high fat/high sugar recipe's fat grams subtracted from 1.

C. % Less Sugar: This recipe's sugar grams divided by high fat/high sugar recipe's sugar grams subtracted from 1.

% More Sugar: Sometimes our low fat/low sugar recipes contain more sugar than the original recipe. This usually occurs when other fat free substitutes used, such as fat free ham, have slightly more sugar than full fat ham. The recipe's **sugar grams** never go up higher than the original recipe because of adding **SugarLike**.

D. % Less Calories: This recipe's calories divided by high fat/high sugar recipe's calories subtracted from 1.

E. Saute symbol: This recipe uses the technique of sauteing.

F. U.S. measurements of ingredients

G. Ingredients: List of ingredients needed to make this recipe. What if you only want to use the **ButterLIke** products and not the **SugarLike** products? What do you do? Simply replace the **SugarLike** ingredients with the same amount of granulated, brown, powdered or corn syrup called for in the recipe. You may even replace a portion of the **ButterLIke** and **SugarLike** with fat and sugar if you so desire.

H. Metric measurements of ingredients

I. Directions: These directions explain how to use **Mrs. Bateman's Products** in this recipe.

J. Nutrition Facts Box: This box list this recipes nutrition information compared to the same recipe made high fat/high sugar.

Serving Size: Weight in grams

Serving Per Recipe: How many servings this recipe makes

Calories Per Serving

Calories From Fat: The amount of calories that are fat calories

Total Fat Per Serving

Saturated Fat Per Serving

Cholesterol Per Serving

Sodium Per Serving

Total Carbohydrates Per Serving

Dietary Fiber Per Serving

Sugars Per Serving

Other Per Serving: These Other Carbohydrates do not raise the blood glucose or insulin levels. They have less than 4 calories per gram. If you are diabetic you do not need to count the Other grams as Carbohydrates, only the calories.

Protein Per Serving

***Percent of Daily Values on Page a-22:** This recipes nutritional information has a % Daily Value that was figured based on comparison to a 2000 calorie diet.

K. **Exchanges & Carbohydrates Per Serving Box:** This box contains the two most prominent types of diets used by diabetics and weight loss.

The Exchange Per Serving is a list of six food groups that are grouped together by similarity in nutritional information. The Exchange box gives this particular recipes Exchange information so that you can count this food serving as part of an Exchange Diet.

The Carbohydrate figure given in this box is the total amount of carbohydrates you would need to count if you were diabetic. This Carbohydrate Total was figured by subtracting the Fiber grams and the Other grams from the Total Carbohydrates in this recipe. We figured this Carbohydrate figure for you for convenience in reading this recipe. The Other grams and Fiber grams in this recipe do not raise the insulin or glucose level in the blood like starch and sugar. Using **ButterLike** and **SugarLike** Products help you lower the amount of Carbohydrates you need to count if you are diabetic.A.

Appetizers & Snacks

Mexican Eight-Layer Dip, page 9

Appetizers and Snacks

This section includes recipes that show you how to make healthy snacks and treats without sacrificing taste. There are even some typically high fat sweetened nuts to show you how easy and tasty it is to use the **SugarLike**. Normally this section is one of the highest fat and sugar sections in a cookbook; however, the **ButterLike** and **SugarLike** products have changed that. This was a fun section to put together to show how much we can reduce the fat and sugar in regular appetizer recipes. I look forward to expanding this area in the next cookbook.

Tips for making low fat, low calorie, low cholesterol and sugar free appetizers and snacks

- For savory appetizers please read "Tips on cooking low fat, low calorie, low cholesterol and sugar free main dishes" page 127; and "Sauteing with **ButterLIke Saute Butter**", page 128.
- For sweet appetizers please read "Tips for successful desserts using the **Bateman Products**", page 90.
- Most appetizers and snacks can be made using the **ButterLike** and **SugarLike** Products.
- This typical high fat and high sugar section is an excellent way to start eating healthy.

Fruit Salsa, page 7

Roasted Garlic

The Fat Quotient using **ButterLike** is **12%** instead of **35%**
70% less fat **0% less sugar**
16% less Calories

U.S.	Ingredients	Metric
8 tsp	**ButterLike Saute Butter**	37.00 g
1-4 bulbs	Garlic	12.00 g
1 loaf	French bread	310.00 g

Directions

Heat oven to 350°. Peel paperlike skin from around each bulb of garlic, leaving just enough to hold cloves together. Cut 1/4 to 1/2 inches from top of each bulb, place cut side up on 12-inch square of aluminum foil. Drizzle each bulb with 2 tsp of **ButterLike**. Sprinkle with salt and pepper. Wrap with foil and place in shallow baking pan. Bake 45-50 minutes or until tender. Cool slightly. To serve, gently squeeze garlic out of cloves and spread on bread. Top with crumbled feta cheese if desired.

Nutrition Facts				
Serving Size	45 g			
Servings Per Recipe	8			
Amount per serving			High Fat/Sugar Comparison	
Calories	109		130	
Calories from fat	10		45	
	% Daily Value*		% Daily Value*	
Total Fat	1.5 g	**2%**	5 g	**8%**
Saturated Fat	0 g	**0%**	0.5 g	**3%**
Cholesterol	0 mg	**0%**	0 mg	**0%**
Sodium	230 mg	**10%**	230 mg	**10%**
Total Carbohydrate	19 g	**6%**	18 g	**6%**
Dietary Fiber	0 g	**0%**	0 g	**0%**
Sugars	0 g		0 g	
Other	0 g		0 g	
Protein	4 g		4 g	

*Percent of Daily Values on page a-22

Exchanges and 19 g Carbohydrates Per Serving					
Breads	1.4	Vegetables	0.1	Fruits	0.0
Meats	0.0	Milk	0.0	Fats	0.5

Buffalo Chicken Wings

The Fat Quotient **ButterLike** using is **12%** instead of **45%**
83% less fat **0% less sugar**
38% less Calories

U.S.	Ingredients	Metric
12	Chicken wings, skin removed	1134.00 g
2 Tbsp	**ButterLike Saute Butter**	28.00 g
2 Tbsp to 1/4 cup	Bottled hot pepper sauce	31.20 g

Directions

Cut off and discard wing tips and skin from wings. Cut each wing into two sections at its joints. Rinse and pat dry. Arrange pieces in a foil-lined 15x10x1-inch baking pan. Bake in a 375° oven for 20 minutes. Meanwhile, heat **ButterLike** and hot pepper sauce in a small saucepan. Drain fat from wings. Brush wings with **ButterLike**-pepper sauce mixture. Bake 10 minutes more. Turn wings over; brush with mixture again. Bake 5-10 minutes more or until tender and no longer pink. If desired, serve wings with low fat or fat free blue cheese dressing and celery sticks.

Nutrition Facts				
Serving Size	99 g			
Servings Per Recipe	12			
Amount per serving			High Fat/Sugar Comparison	
Calories	111		180	
Calories from fat	15		80	
	% Daily Value*		% Daily Value*	
Total Fat	1.5 g	**2%**	9 g	**14%**
Saturated Fat	0 g	**0%**	3 g	**15%**
Cholesterol	55 mg	**18%**	75 mg	**25%**
Sodium	160 mg	**7%**	190 mg	**8%**
Total Carbohydrate	1 g	**0%**	0 g	**0%**
Dietary Fiber	0 g	**0%**	0 g	**0%**
Sugars	0 g		0 g	
Other	0 g		0 g	
Protein	22 g		26 g	

*Percent of Daily Values on page a-29

Exchanges and 1 g Carbohydrates Per Serving					
Breads	0.1	Vegetables	0.0	Fruits	0.0
Meats	1.9	Milk	0.0	Fats	0.1

Potato Skins

The Fat Quotient using **ButterLike** is **6%** instead of **33%**
86% less fat **0% less sugar**
25% less Calories

U.S.	**Ingredients**	Metric
6 large	Baking potatoes	1212.00 g
2 tsp	**ButterLike Saute Butter**	9.33 g
1 1/2 tsp	Chili powder	4.00 g
Drops	Bottled hot pepper sauce	5.20 g
8 slices	Lean bacon, crisp-cooked	48.00 g
2/3 cup	Tomato, finely chopped	161.00 g
2 Tbsp	Green onion, finely chopped	6.00 g
1/4 cup	Sharp cheddar	28.00 g
3/4 cup	Non fat cheddar cheese, shredded	85.00 g
1/2 cup	Fat free sour cream	128.00 g

Directions

Scrub potatoes and prick with a fork. Bake in a 425° oven for 40-45 minutes or until tender; cool. Cut each potato lengthwise into 4 wedges. Scoop out the inside of each potato wedge, leaving skin 1/4 inch thick. Cover and chill the leftover fluffy white part of potatoes for another use. In the small bowl combine the **ButterLike**, chili powder, and hot pepper sauce. Using a pastry brush, brush the insides of the potato wedges with the **ButterLike** mixture. Place the potato wedges in a single layer on a large baking sheet. Sprinkle wedges with bacon, tomato, and green onion; top with cheese. Bake 10 minutes more or until cheese melts and potatoes are heated through. Serve with sour cream.

Nutrition Facts				
Serving Size	211 g			
Servings Per Recipe	8			
Amount per serving			High Fat/Sugar Comparison	
Calories	226		300	
Calories from fat	10		100	
	% Daily Value*		% Daily Value*	
Total Fat	1.5 g	**2%**	11 g	**17%**
Saturated Fat	.5 g	**3%**	6 g	**30%**
Cholesterol	5 mg	**2%**	30 mg	**10%**
Sodium	270 mg	**11%**	330 mg	**14%**
Total Carbohydrate	43 g	**14%**	40 g	**13%**
Dietary Fiber	4 g	**16%**	4 g	**16%**
Sugars	3 g		3 g	
Other	0 g		0 g	
Protein	11 g		10 g	

*Percent of Daily Values on page a-22

Exchanges and 39 g Carbohydrates Per Serving					
Breads	2.3	Vegetables	0.1	Fruits	0.0
Meats	0.4	Milk	0.2	Fats	0.3

Cheesy Potato Skins

The Fat Quotient using **ButterLike** is **15%** instead of **58%**
82% less fat **0% less sugar**
31% less Calories

U.S.	Ingredients	Metric
2 Tbsp	**ButterLike Saute Butter**	28.00 g
4 large	Potatoes	907.00 g
1 cup	Low fat colby-monterey jack cheese	113.00 g
1/2 cup	Fat free sour cream	128.00 g
1/2 cup	Green onions, sliced (5 medium)	30.00 g

Directions

Pierce potatoes to allow steam to escape. Bake potatoes in a 425° oven for about 45 minutes until tender. Let stand until cool enough to handle. Cut potatoes lengthwise into fourths; carefully scoop out the fluffy white part, leaving 1/4-inch shells. Save potato pulp for other use. Set oven to broil. Place potato shells, skin sides down, on rack in broiler pan. Brush with **ButterLike**. Broil with tops 4-5 inches from heat 8-10 minutes or until crisp and brown. Sprinkle cheese over potato shells. Broil about 30 seconds or until cheese is melted. Serve hot with sour cream and green onions.

Nutrition Facts				
Serving Size	151 g			
Servings Per Recipe	8			
Amount per serving			High Fat/Sugar Comparison	
Calories	118		170	
Calories from fat	20		100	
	% Daily Value*		% Daily Value*	
Total Fat	2 g	**3%**	11 g	**17%**
Saturated Fat	1 g	**5%**	7 g	**35%**
Cholesterol	5 mg	**2%**	25 mg	**8%**
Sodium	280 mg	**12%**	370 mg	**15%**
Total Carbohydrate	18 g	**6%**	14 g	**5%**
Dietary Fiber	1 g	**4%**	1 g	**4%**
Sugars	1 g		1 g	
Other	0 g		0 g	
Protein	7 g		4 g	

*Percent of Daily Values on page a-22

Exchanges and 17 g Carbohydrates Per Serving

Breads	1.0	Vegetables	0.1	Fruits	0.0
Meats	0.7	Milk	0.2	Fats	0.1

Cheesy Potato Skins

Crunchy Party Mix

The Fat quotient using ButterLike is 18% instead of 51%
81% less fat 0% less sugar
45% less Calories

U.S.	Ingredients	Metric
1 cup	**ButterLike Saute Butter**	224.00 g
3 Tbsp	Worcestershire sauce	45.00 g
1/2 tsp	Garlic powder	1.40 g
Drops	Bottled hot pepper sauce	5.00 g
5 cups	Tiny fat free pretzels	255.00 g
4 cups	Round toasted oat cereal	165.00 g
4 cups	Bite-size wheat or bran cereal	220.00 g
4 cups	Bite-size rice or shredded wheat	186.00 g
1/2 cup	Mixed nuts	56.00 g

Directions

Heat **ButterLike**, worcestershire sauce, garlic powder, and hot pepper sauce. In a large roasting pan combine pretzels, cereals, and nuts. Drizzle **ButterLike** mixture; toss to coat. Bake in a 300° oven for 45 minutes, stirring every 15 minutes. Spread on foil; cool. Store in an airtight container.

Nutrition Facts				
Serving Size	45 g			
Servings Per Recipe	26			
Amount per serving			High Fat/Sugar Comparison	
Calories	154		280	
Calories from fat	25		140	
	% Daily Value*		% Daily Value*	
Total Fat	3 g	5%	16 g	25%
Saturated Fat	.5 g	3%	6 g	30%
Cholesterol	0 mg	0%	20 mg	7%
Sodium	230 mg	10%	330 mg	14%
Total Carbohydrate	30 g	10%	28 g	9%
Dietary Fiber	3 g	12%	3 g	12%
Sugars	4 g		4 g	
Other	0 g		0 g	
Protein	4 g		6 g	

*Percent of Daily Values on page a-22

Exchanges and 27 g Carbohydrates Per Serving

Breads	1.7	Vegetables	0.0	Fruits	0.1
Meats	0.1	Milk	0.0	Fats	0.5

Cinnamon-Sugared Nuts

The Fat quotient using ButterLike is 82% instead of 74%
0% less fat 75% less sugar
10% less Calories

U.S.	Ingredients	Metric
1/4 cup	**Granulated SugarLike**	50.00 g
1 Tbsp	Egg whites, slightly beaten	6.30 g
2 cups	Pecan or walnut halves	216.0 g
2 tsp	Cinnamon	4.60 g
1/4 tsp	Nutmeg	.55 g
1/4 tsp	Cloves	.53 g

Directions

Heat oven to 300°. Mix egg whites and nut halves in medium bowl until pecans are coated and sticky. Mix remaining ingredients, sprinkle over nuts, stir until they are completely coated. Spread in single layer in ungreased pan. Bake about 30 minutes or until toasted. Cool completely or serve warm.

Nutrition Facts				
Serving Size	17 g			
Servings Per Recipe	16			
Amount per serving			High Fat/Sugar Comparison	
Calories	99		110	
Calories from fat	80		80	
	% Daily Value*		% Daily Value*	
Total Fat	9 g	14%	9 g	14%
Saturated Fat	.5 g	3%	.5 g	3%
Cholesterol	0 mg	0%	0 mg	0%
Sodium	5 mg	0%	5 mg	0%
Total Carbohydrate	6 g	2%	6 g	2%
Dietary Fiber	2 g	8%	1 g	4%
Sugars	1 g		4 g	
Other	2 g		0 g	
Protein	1 g		1 g	

*Percent of Daily Values on page a-22

Exchanges and 2 g Carbohydrates Per Serving

Breads	0.0	Vegetables	0.0	Fruits	0.0
Meats	0.0	Milk	0.0	Fats	1.8

Cinnamon Tortilla Crisps

The Fat Quotient using **ButterLike** is **0%** instead of **30%**
100% less fat **100% less sugar**
50% less Calories

U.S.	Ingredients	Metric
1/2 cup	**Granulated SugarLike**	100.00 g
1/4 cup	**ButterLike Saute Butter**	56.00 g
1 tsp	Ground cinnamon	2.30 g
12	Fat free flour tortillas (7-inch)	444.00 g

Directions

Combine **SugarLike** and cinnamon. Brush **ButterLike** over tortillas; sprinkle with cinnamon-**SugarLike** mixture. Cut each tortilla into wedges. Spread one-third of the wedges in a 15x10x1-inch baking pan. Bake in a 350° oven 5-10 minutes or until dry and crisp. Repeat with remaining wedges; cool. Store in an airtight container at room temperature up to 3 weeks or in the freezer up to 2 months.

Nutrition Facts				
Serving Size	25 g			
Servings Per Recipe	24			
Amount per serving			High Fat/Sugar Comparison	
Calories	45		90	
Calories from fat	0		30	
	% Daily Value*		% Daily Value*	
Total Fat	0 g	**0%**	3 g	**5%**
Saturated Fat	0 g	**0%**	1.5 g	**8%**
Cholesterol	0 mg	**0%**	5 mg	**2%**
Sodium	90 mg	**4%**	105 mg	**4%**
Total Carbohydrate	11 g	**4%**	14 g	**5%**
Dietary Fiber	4 g	**12%**	1 g	**4%**
Sugars	0 g		4 g	
Other	3 g		0 g	
Protein	1 g		2 g	

*Percent of Daily Values on page a-22

Exchanges and 4 g Carbohydrates Per Serving

Breads	0.5	Vegetables	0.0	Fruits	0.0
Meats	0.0	Milk	0.0	Fats	0.1

Fruit Salsa

The Fat quotient using **ButterLike** is **0%** instead of **0%**
0% less fat **33% less sugar**
20% less Calories

U.S.	Ingredients	Metric
2 Tbsp	**Granulated SugarLike**	25.00 g
1 cup	Strawberries, finely chopped	149.00 g
1 medium	Orange, peeled, finely chopped	86.00 g
2 large	Kiwifruit, peeled, finely chopped	152.00 g
1/2 cup	Pineapple, finely chopped	78.00 g
1/4 cup	Green onions, thinly sliced	12.00 g
1/4 cup	Green or yellow pepper, chopped	57.00 g
1 Tbsp	Lime or lemon juice	15.00 g
1	Fresh Jalapeno pepper, seeded and chopped	19.00 g

Directions

In a mixing bowl stir together **SugarLike**, strawberries, orange, kiwifruit, pineapple, green onions, sweet pepper, lime or lemon juice, and, if desired jalapeno pepper. Cover and chill for 6-24 hours. Serve with **Cinnamon Tortilla Crisps**.

Nutrition Facts				
Serving Size	25 g			
Servings Per Recipe	24			
Amount per serving			High Fat/Sugar Comparison	
Calories	12		15	
Calories from fat	0		0	
	% Daily Value*		% Daily Value*	
Total Fat	0 g	**0%**	0 g	**0%**
Saturated Fat	0 g	**0%**	0 g	**0%**
Cholesterol	0 mg	**0%**	0 mg	**0%**
Sodium	15 mg	**1%**	15 mg	**1%**
Total Carbohydrate	4 g	**1%**	4 g	**1%**
Dietary Fiber	1 g	**4%**	1 g	**4%**
Sugars	2 g		3 g	
Other	1 g		0 g	
Protein	0 g		0 g	

*Percent of Daily Values on page a-22

Exchanges and 2 g Carbohydrates Per Serving

Breads	0.0	Vegetables	0.0	Fruits	0.1
Meats	0.0	Milk	0.0	Fats	0.0

Great Salsa

The fat quotient using **ButterLike** is **0%** instead of **0%**
0% less fat **0% less sugar**
11% less Calories

U.S.	Ingredients	Metric
1/2 tsp	**Granulated SugarLike**	2.00 g
1 quart	Whole tomatoes	824.00 g
2 Tbsp	Bottled jalapeno peppers	33.00 g
1/4 tsp	Coarse pepper	.50 g
1	Red onion, finely chopped	120.00 g
3 Tbsp	Fresh cilantro, finely chopped	36.00 g
	Salt to taste	3.00 g

Directions

Reserve liquid from 1 quart of whole tomatoes. Pour liquid into blender or food processor. Add **SugarLike** and jalapeno peppers; adjust the amount of peppers to your taste. Blend until smooth. Stop blender; add whole tomatoes and pepper. Pulse until there are still chunks of tomatoes left. Stir in chopped onion and cilantro. Add salt to taste. Serve with **Baked Tortilla Chips**.

Nutrition Facts				
Serving Size	32 g			
Servings Per Recipe	32			
Amount per serving			High Fat/Sugar Comparison	
Calories	8		9	
Calories from fat	0		0	
	% Daily Value*		% Daily Value*	
Total Fat	0 g	**0%**	0 g	**0%**
Saturated Fat	0 g	**0%**	0 g	**0%**
Cholesterol	0 mg	**0%**	0 mg	**0%**
Sodium	105 mg	**4%**	105 mg	**4%**
Total Carbohydrate	1 g	**0%**	1 g	**0%**
Dietary Fiber	0 g	**0%**	0 g	**0%**
Sugars	1 g		1 g	
Other	0 g		0 g	
Protein	0 g		0 g	

*Percent of Daily Values on page a-22

Exchanges and 1 g Carbohydrates Per Serving

Breads	0.0	Vegetables	0.3	Fruits	0.0
Meats	0.0	Milk	0.0	Fats	0.0

Baked Tortilla Chips

The fat quotient using **ButterLike** is **23%** instead of **58%**
78% less fat **0% less sugar**
43% less Calories

U.S.	Ingredients	Metric
1 cup	**ButterLike Saute Butter**	56.00 g
6	Corn or flour tortillas (8-inch)	150.00 g

Directions

Heat oven to 375°. Brush tortillas lightly with **ButterLike**. Sprinkle with chili powder (if desired). Cut each into 12 wedges. Place in single layer on 2 cookie sheets. Bake uncovered 6-8 minutes or until light brown and crisp. Cool slightly (chips will continue to crisp as they cool). Store in tightly covered container for up to 3 weeks at room temperature.

Nutrition Facts				
Serving Size	17 g			
Servings Per Recipe	12			
Amount per serving			High Fat/Sugar Comparison	
Calories	40		70	
Calories from fat	10		40	
	% Daily Value*		% Daily Value*	
Total Fat	1 g	**2%**	4.5 g	**7%**
Saturated Fat	0 g	**0%**	2.5 g	**13%**
Cholesterol	0 mg	**0%**	10 mg	**3%**
Sodium	20 mg	**1%**	65 mg	**3%**
Total Carbohydrate	7 g	**2%**	6 g	**2%**
Dietary Fiber	1 g	**4%**	1 g	**4%**
Sugars	0 g		0 g	
Other	0 g		0 g	
Protein	1 g		1 g	

*Percent of Daily Values on page a-22

Exchanges and 6 g Carbohydrates Per Serving

Breads	0.5	Vegetables	0.3	Fruits	0.0
Meats	0.0	Milk	0.0	Fats	0.2

Mexican Eight-Layer Dip

The Fat Quotient using ButterLike is 35% instead of 65%
70% less fat **0% less sugar**
41% less Calories

U.S.	Ingredients	Metric
2-3 cups	Lettuce, shredded	110.00 g
1 can	Fat free bean dip (9 oz)	255.00 g
1/4 cup	Picante or taco sauce	62.00 g
1 carton	Fat free sour cream (8 oz)	227.00 g
1 Container	Frozen avocado dip, thawed (6 oz)	170.00 g
3/4 cup	Sharp cheddar cheese, shredded	28.00 g
1/4 cup	Green onions, sliced	12.00 g
2 Tbsp	Pitted ripe olives, chopped	16.88 g
2/3 cup	Tomato, seeded and chopped	161.00 g

Directions

On a platter arrange lettuce, leaving a 2-inch open rim at edge of platter. Combine bean dip and picante sauce or **Great Salsa** on page 8. Spread bean mixture over lettuce, making a layer 1/4-inch thick. Next layer sour cream and avocado dip. Top with cheese, onion, and olives. Cover and chill 4-24 hours. Before serving, sprinkle with chopped tomato. Arrange **Baked Tortilla Chips**, page 8, on the platter around spread.

Nutrition Facts				
Serving Size	70 g			
Servings Per Recipe	16			
Amount per serving			High Fat/Sugar Comparison	
Calories		65	110	
Calories from fat		25	70	
	% Daily Value*		% Daily Value*	
Total Fat	2.5 g	**4%**	8 g	**12%**
Saturated Fat	0.5 g	**3%**	3.5 g	**18%**
Cholesterol	0 mg	**0%**	15 mg	**5%**
Sodium	220 mg	**9%**	310 mg	**13%**
Total Carbohydrate	7 g	**2%**	5 g	**2%**
Dietary Fiber	2 g	**8%**	2 g	**8%**
Sugars	1 g		1 g	
Other	0 g		0 g	
Protein	4 g		4 g	

*Percent of Daily Values on page a-22

Exchanges and 5 g Carbohydrates Per Serving					
Breads	0.4	Vegetables	0.1	Fruits	0.0
Meats	0.2	Milk	0.1	Fats	0.4

Cinnamon Raisin Oatmeal

The Fat Quotient using ButterLike is 5% instead of 19%
83% less fat **33% less sugar**
32% less Calories

U.S.	Ingredients	Metric
1/4 cup	**Brown SugarLike**	50.00 g
1 1/2 cup	Quick-cooking rolled oats	351.00 g
1 cup	Raisins or mixed dried fruit bits	145.00 g
1/2 tsp	Ground cinnamon	1.20 g
1/4 tsp	Salt	1.50 g
1/4 tsp	Ground nutmeg	.60 g

Directions

Stir together **Brown SugarLike**, oats, raisins or dried fruit bits, cinnamon, salt, and nutmeg. Cover tightly and store at room temperature.

Breakfast Servings: In a medium saucepan bring 3 cups water to a boil. Slowly add oat mix to boiling water, stirring constantly. Cover; remove from heat. Let stand 1-3 minutes or until desired consistency is reached. If desired, serve with skim milk.

Nutrition Facts				
Serving Size	137 g			
Servings Per Recipe	4			
Amount per serving			High Fat/Sugar Comparison	
Calories		189	280	
Calories from fat		10	50	
	% Daily Value*		% Daily Value*	
Total Fat	1 g	**2%**	6 g	**9%**
Saturated Fat	0 g	**0%**	0.5 g	**3%**
Cholesterol	0 mg	**0%**	0 mg	**0%**
Sodium	150 mg	**6%**	160 mg	**7%**
Total Carbohydrate	51 g	**17%**	53 g	**18%**
Dietary Fiber	6 g	**24%**	3 g	**12%**
Sugars	24 g		36 g	
Other	9 g		g	
Protein	4 g		5 g	

*Percent of Daily Values on page a-22

Exchanges and 36 g Carbohydrates Per Serving					
Breads	0.6	Vegetables	0.0	Fruits	1.9
Meats	0.0	Milk	0.0	Fats	0.2

Sugar-Spiced Nuts and Dried Fruit

The Fat quotient using **ButterLike** is **68%** instead of **62%**
18% less fat **86% less sugar**
26% less Calories

U.S.	Ingredients	Metric
1 cup	**Granulated SugarLike**	200.00 g
1/8 cup	Egg whites	28.00 g
1 tsp	Water	5.00 g
1 Tbsp	Pumpkin pie spice	5.00 g
2 cans	Mixed nuts (12 oz each)	680.00 g
2 cups	Dried fruit (apples, peaches, etc.)	510.00 g

Directions

Vegetable spray a non-stick 15x10x1-inch baking pan; set aside. In a large mixing bowl beat egg whites and water until frothy. Add the nuts and toss to coat. Combine **SugarLike** and pumpkin pie spice. Sprinkle over nuts; toss to coat. Spread nuts in a single layer in the prepared baking pan. Bake at 325° for 20 minutes. Cool slightly in pan. Transfer to waxed paper to cool. Break into clusters. Add dried fruit and mix. Store tightly covered up to 1 week.

Nutrition Facts				
Serving Size	36 g			
Servings Per Recipe	40			
Amount per serving			High Fat/Sugar Comparison	
Calories	119		160	
Calories from fat	80		100	
	% Daily Value*		% Daily Value*	
Total Fat	9 g	**14%**	11 g	**17%**
Saturated Fat	1 g	**5%**	1.5 g	**8%**
Cholesterol	0 mg	**0%**	0 mg	**0%**
Sodium	5 mg	**0%**	0 mg	**0%**
Total Carbohydrate	11 g	**4%**	12 g	**4%**
Dietary Fiber	3 g	**12%**	2 g	**8%**
Sugars	1 g		7 g	
Other	4 g		0 g	
Protein	3 g		4 g	

*Percent of Daily Values on page a-22

Exchanges and 4 g Carbohydrates Per Serving					
Breads	0.0	Vegetables	0.0	Fruits	0.1
Meats	0.4	Milk	0.0	Fats	1.8

Note: Fruit can be left out but the fat jumps to 10.96 grams per serving.

Sugar-Spiced Nuts and Dried Fruit

Beverages

Non-Alcoholic Daiquiri Punch, page 18

Now you can make powdered drink mixes, lemonade, hot chocolate or any other beverage you choose sugar free. No more aftertaste! No more aspartame! **Liquid SugarLike** is ideal to sweeten your beverages. **Granulated SugarLike** can be used by the teaspoon to sweeten your drinks.

Fresh Lemonade/Limeade Base, page 19

Fruity Yogurt Sipper

The Fat Quotient using **ButterLike** is **0%** instead of **23%**
100% less fat **14% less sugar**
27% less Calories

U.S.	Ingredients	Metric
2 Tbsp	**Powdered SugarLike**	13.00 g
1 large	Banana or two medium peaches	114.00 g
1 1/2 cup	Skim milk	368.00 g
1 carton	Non fat vanilla yogurt (8-oz)*	227.00 g
1/2 cup	Ice cubes	113.00 g

Directions

Cut fruit into chunks. In a blender container combine the **SugarLike**, fruit, milk, and yogurt. Cover; blend until smooth. With blender running, add ice cubes, one at a time, through lid opening. Blend until smooth.

***Note:** Sugar free, low fat yogurt would be a good substitute here but I could not find any in my store.

Nutrition Facts				
Serving Size	209 g			
Servings Per Recipe	4			
Amount per serving			High Fat/Sugar Comparison	
Calories	117		160	
Calories from fat	0		35	
	% Daily Value*		% Daily Value*	
Total Fat	0 g	**0%**	4 g	**6%**
Saturated Fat	0 g	**0%**	2.5 g	**13%**
Cholesterol	0 mg	**0%**	15 mg	**5%**
Sodium	90 mg	**4%**	95 mg	**4%**
Total Carbohydrate	25 g	**8%**	24 g	**8%**
Dietary Fiber	2 g	**8%**	1 g	**4%**
Sugars	18 g		21 g	
Other	3 g		0 g	
Protein	6 g		6 g	

*Percent of Daily Values on page a-22

Exchanges and 20 g Carbohydrates Per Serving					
Breads	0.0	Vegetables	0.0	Fruits	0.8
Meats	0.0	Milk	0.7	Fats	0.0

Raspberry Apple Punch

The Fat Quotient using **ButterLike** is **0%** instead of **0%**
0% less fat **71% less sugar**
43% less Calories

U.S.	Ingredients	Metric
	Raspberry Sauce, page 231	438.00 g
1/3 cup	Frozen apple juice concentrate	84.00 g
3 Tbsp	Frozen grape juice concentrate	54.00 g
1 small	Apple, thinly sliced	85.00 g
1 quart	Raspberry sparkling water, sugar free	474.00 g

Directions

Follow directions for **Raspberry Sauce** on page 231.

Mix Raspberry Sauce, thawed juice concentrate, and sparkling water in pitcher. Cover and refrigerate 2 hours. Serve with ice cubes and apple slices.

Nutrition Facts				
Serving Size	189 g			
Servings Per Recipe	6			
Amount per serving			High Fat/Sugar Comparison	
Calories	85		160	
Calories from fat	0		0	
	% Daily Value*		% Daily Value*	
Total Fat	0 g	**0%**	0 g	**0%**
Saturated Fat	0 g	**0%**	0 g	**0%**
Cholesterol	0 mg	**0%**	0 mg	**0%**
Sodium	5 mg	**0%**	10 mg	**0%**
Total Carbohydrate	26 g	**9%**	38 g	**13%**
Dietary Fiber	7 g	**28%**	4 g	**16%**
Sugars	9 g		31 g	
Other	8 g		g	
Protein	1 g		1 g	

*Percent of Daily Values on page a-22

Exchanges and 11 g Carbohydrates Per Serving					
Breads	0.0	Vegetables	0.0	Fruits	1.0
Meats	0.0	Milk	0.0	Fats	0.0

Eggnog

The Fat Quotient using **ButterLike** is **23%** instead of **65%**	
81% less fat	**60% less sugar**
46% less Calories	

U.S.	**Ingredients**	Metric
1/3 cup	**Granulated SugarLike**	67.00 g
2 cups	Skim milk	490.00 g
1 tsp	Vanilla	5.00 g
2	Egg yolks	33.00 g
3 Tbsp	Sugar free instant vanilla pudding	57.00 g
1 tsp	Rum flavor (optional)	4.60 g
1/4 tsp	Ground nutmeg	.55 g
2 cups	Lite whipped topping	128.00 g

Directions

In a large heavy saucepan mix the eggs, milk, pudding, and the **SugarLike**. Cook and stir over medium heat until mixture just coats a metal spoon. Remove from heat. Place the pan in a sink or bowl of ice water and stir for 2 minutes. Stir in vanilla. Cover and chill for 4-24 hours. Just before serving, beat whipped topping until smooth. Transfer chilled egg mixture to a punch bowl. Add the whipped topping. Serve at once. Sprinkle each serving with nutmeg.

Note to Diabetics: 1 cup lite whipping cream and 1/4 cup **Granulated SugarLike** may be substituted for 2 cups lite whipped topping. The drink will be sugar free, but fat will increase to 8.5 grams per serving.

Nutrition Facts				
Serving Size	78 g			
Servings Per Recipe	10			
Amount per serving			High Fat/Sugar Comparison	
Calories	97		180	
Calories from fat	25		120	
	% Daily Value*		% Daily Value*	
Total Fat	2.5 g	**4%**	13 g	**20%**
Saturated Fat	2 g	**10%**	7 g	**35%**
Cholesterol	45 mg	**15%**	165 mg	**65%**
Sodium	150 mg	**6%**	40 mg	**2%**
Total Carbohydrate	17 g	**6%**	11 g	**4%**
Dietary Fiber	2 g	**8%**	0 g	**0%**
Sugars	4 g		10 g	
Other	5 g		g	
Protein	2 g		4 g	

*Percent of Daily Values on page a-22

Exchanges and 10 g Carbohydrates Per Serving					
Breads	0.4	Vegetables	0.0	Fruits	0.0
Meats	0.1	Milk	0.2	Fats	0.5

Eggnog

Water Punch

The Fat Quotient using ButterLike is 0% instead of 0%
0% less fat 94% less sugar
47% less Calories

U.S.	Ingredients	Metric
3 cups	**Granulated SugarLike**	600.00 g
5 qt.	Water	4740.00 g
1 Tbsp	Citric acid	14.00 g
1 Tbsp	Lemon extract	15.00 g
2 each	Oranges, thinly sliced	262.00 g
2 each	Lemons, thinly sliced	122.00 g

Directions

Mix all the ingredients together. Add ice and serve cold. This is an excellent punch that isn't too sweet.

Exchanges and 4 g Carbohydrates Per Serving					
Breads	0.0	Vegetables	0.0	Fruits	0.2
Meats	0.0	Milk	0.0	Fats	0.0

Nutrition Facts				
Serving Size	443 g			
Servings Per Recipe	13			
Amount per serving			High Fat/Sugar Comparison	
Calories		106	200	
Calories from fat		0	0	
	% Daily Value*		% Daily Value*	
Total Fat	0 g	**0%**	0 g	**0%**
Saturated Fat	0 g	**0%**	0 g	**0%**
Cholesterol	0 mg	**0%**	0 mg	**0%**
Sodium	10 mg	**0%**	10 mg	**0%**
Total Carbohydrate	49 g	**16%**	49 g	**16%**
Dietary Fiber	12 g	**48%**	1 g	**4%**
Sugars	3 g		47 g	
Other	33 g		0 g	
Protein	1 g		0 g	

*Percent of Daily Values on page a-22

Peach Berry Shake

The Fat Quotient using ButterLike is 0% instead of 26%
100% less fat 16% less sugar
20% less calories

U.S.	Ingredients	Metric
2 Tbsp	**Granulated SugarLike**	25.00 g
1 pkg	Frozen peaches, unsweetened, sliced (16 oz)	454.00 g
2/3 cup	Whole strawberries, unsweetened	99.00 g
1 1/2 cup	Skim milk	368.00 g
1 cup	Non fat, plain yogurt, extra creamy*	227.00 g
1 tsp	Vanilla	5.00 g
1/8 tsp	Ground cinnamon	.29 g

Directions

Place all ingredients in a blender. Cover and blend, stopping blender occasionally to stir mixture, until thickened and smooth. Serve.

* **Note:** Sugar free low fat yogurt would be a good substitute here but I could not find any in my store.

Nutrition Facts				
Serving Size	236 g			
Servings Per Recipe	5			
Amount per serving			High Fat/Sugar Comparison	
Calories		113	140	
Calories from fat		0	35	
	% Daily Value*		% Daily Value*	
Total Fat	0 g	**0%**	4 g	**6%**
Saturated Fat	0 g	**0%**	2.5 g	**13%**
Cholesterol	0 mg	**0%**	15 mg	**5%**
Sodium	75 mg	**3%**	55 mg	**2%**
Total Carbohydrate	25 g	**8%**	22 g	**7%**
Dietary Fiber	3 g	**12%**	2 g	**8%**
Sugars	16 g		19 g	
Other	4 g		0 g	
Protein	6 g		5 g	

*Percent of Daily Values on page a-22

Exchanges and 18 g Carbohydrates Per Serving					
Breads	0.0	Vegetables	0.0	Fruits	0.8
Meats	0.0	Milk	0.6	Fats	0.0

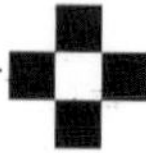

Slushy Punch

The Fat quotient using **ButterLike** is **0%** instead of **0%**
0% less fat **53% less sugar**
20% less Calories

U.S.	Ingredients	Metric
1 cup	**Granulated SugarLike**	200.00 g
2 3/4 cup	Water	652.00 g
2 medium	Ripe bananas, cut up	228.00 g
3 cups	Pineapple juice, unsweetened	750.00 g
1 can	Frozen orange juice concentrate (6 oz)	170.00 g
2 Tbsp	Lemon juice	31.00 g
1-liter	Carbonated water or lemon-lime diet soda	1030.00 g

Slushy Punch

Nutrition Facts				
Serving Size	133 g			
Servings Per Recipe	23			
Amount per serving			High Fat/Sugar Comparison	
Calories	72		90	
Calories from fat	0		0	
	% Daily Value*		% Daily Value*	
Total Fat	0 g	**0%**	0 g	**0%**
Saturated Fat	0 g	**0%**	0 g	**0%**
Cholesterol	0 mg	**0%**	0 mg	**0%**
Sodium	0 mg	**0%**	0 mg	**0%**
Total Carbohydrate	22 g	**7%**	22 g	**7%**
Dietary Fiber	3 g	**12%**	0 g	**0%**
Sugars	8 g		17 g	
Other	6 g		0 g	
Protein	0 g		0 g	

*Percent of Daily Values on page a-22

Exchanges and 13 g Carbohydrates Per Serving					
Breads	0.0	Vegetables	0.0	Fruits	0.6
Meats	0.0	Milk	0.0	Fats	0.0

Directions

Combine water and **SugarLike** until it dissolves. In a blender combine bananas, half of the pineapple juice, and the orange juice concentrate. Cover; blend until smooth. Add to **SugarLike** mixture. Stir in remaining juices. Transfer to a 13x9x2-inch baking pan. Freeze for 4-24 hours. To serve, let mixture stand at room temperature 20-30 minutes. To form slush, scrape a large spoon across frozen mixture; spoon into punch bowl. Slowly pour carbonated water down side of bowl; stir.

Orange Breakfast Nog

The Fat Quotient using **ButterLike** is **8%** instead of **16%**
63% less fat **11% less sugar**
24% less Calories

U.S.	Ingredients	Metric
2 Tbsp	**Brown SugarLike**	25.00 g
1 1/2 cup	Low fat buttermilk	368.00 g
3 oz	Frozen orange juice	85.00 g
1 tsp	Vanilla	5.00 g
2-3 large	Ice cubes	75.00 g

Orange Breakfast Nog

Nutrition Facts				
Serving Size	279 g			
Servings Per Recipe	2			
Amount per serving			High Fat/Sugar Comparison	
Calories	174		230	
Calories from fat	15		35	
	% Daily Value*		% Daily Value*	
Total Fat	1.5 g	**2%**	4 g	**6%**
Saturated Fat	1 g	**5%**	2.5 g	**13%**
Cholesterol	5 mg	**2%**	15 mg	**5%**
Sodium	200 mg	**8%**	170 mg	**7%**
Total Carbohydrate	38 g	**13%**	40 g	**13%**
Dietary Fiber	3 g	**12%**	0 g	**0%**
Sugars	24 g		27 g	
Other	9 g		0 g	
Protein	7 g		9 g	

*Percent of Daily Values on page a-22

Exchanges and 26 g Carbohydrates Per Serving

Breads	0.0	Vegetables	0.0	Fruits	1.1
Meats	0.0	Milk	0.7	Fats	0.4

Directions

In a blender container combine **Brown SugarLike**, buttermilk, orange juice concentrate, and vanilla. Cover and blend until smooth. With blender running, add ice cubes, one at a time, through opening in lid. Blend until smooth and frothy.

Non-Alcoholic Daiquiri Punch

The Fat Quotient using **ButterLike** is **0%** instead of **0%**
0% less fat **74% less sugar**
17% less Calories

U.S.	Ingredients	Metric
1 cup	**Granulated SugarLike**	200.00 g
6 cups	Fresh or frozen strawberries	894.00 g
1/2 cup	Lime juice	123.00 g
3/4 cup	Pineapple juice, unsweetened	178.00 g
16 oz	Diet lemon lime soda	454.00 g

Directions

In a blender or food processor bowl place half the strawberries at a time. Cover; blend or process until smooth. Transfer blended berries to a large pitcher. Stir in lime juice and **SugarLike**. If desired this mixture can be placed in a covered container and chilled for up to 24 hours. Just before serving stir in carbonated beverage and ice.

Nutrition Facts				
Serving Size	231 g			
Servings Per Recipe	8			
Amount per serving			High Fat/Sugar Comparison	
Calories		150	180	
Calories from fat		0	0	
	% Daily Value*		% Daily Value*	
Total Fat	0 g	**0%**	0 g	**0%**
Saturated Fat	0 g	**0%**	0 g	**0%**
Cholesterol	0 mg	**0%**	0 mg	**0%**
Sodium	10 mg	**0%**	10 mg	**0%**
Total Carbohydrate	37 g	**12%**	43 g	**14%**
Dietary Fiber	9 g	**36%**	3 g	**12%**
Sugars	10 g		39 g	
Other	18 g		0 g	
Protein	1 g		1 g	

*Percent of Daily Values on page a-22

Exchanges and 10 g Carbohydrates Per Serving

Breads	0.0	Vegetables	0.0	Fruits	0.8
Meats	0.0	Milk	0.0	Fats	0.0

Non-Alcoholic Daiquiri Punch

Fresh Lemonade/Limeade Base

The Fat Quotient using **ButterLike** is **0%** instead of **0%**
0% less fat **94% less sugar**
50% less Calories

U.S.	Ingredients	Metric
1 1/4 cup	**Granulated SugarLike**	250.00 g
2 1/2 cup	Water	593.00 g
1/2 tsp	Lemon peel, finely shredded	1.00 g
1 1/4 cup	Lemon or lime juice	305.00 g

Directions

For a lemonade or limeade base, in a sauce pan heat and stir **SugarLike** and water over medium heat until it is dissolved. Remove from heat; cool 20 minutes. Add peel and juice to **SugarLike** mixture. Pour into a jar, cover, and refrigerate for up to 3 days. For each glass of lemonade or limeade, combine equal parts base and water in ice-filled glasses; stir.

Note: 3/4 cup (6-oz) of this base equals one 6-oz can frozen lemonade or limeade concentrate.

Nutrition Facts				
Serving Size	144 g			
Servings Per Recipe	8			
Amount per serving			High Fat/Sugar Comparison	
Calories	70		140	
Calories from fat	0		0	
	% Daily Value*		% Daily Value*	
Total Fat	0 g	**0%**	0 g	**0%**
Saturated Fat	0 g	**0%**	0 g	**0%**
Cholesterol	0 mg	**0%**	0 mg	**0%**
Sodium	10 mg	**0%**	10 mg	**0%**
Total Carbohydrate	33 g	**11%**	34 g	**11%**
Dietary Fiber	8 g	**32%**	0 g	**0%**
Sugars	2 g		31 g	
Other	23 g		0 g	
Protein	0 g		0 g	

*Percent of Daily Values on page a-22

Exchanges and 2 g Carbohydrates Per Serving					
Breads	00	Vegetables	00	Fruits	0.2
Meats	00	Milk	00	Fats	00

Fresh Lemonade/Limeade Base

Southwestern Fiesta Hot Chocolate

The Fat Quotient using **ButterLike** is **3%** instead of **26%**
94% less fat **59% less sugar**
42% less Calories

U.S.	Ingredients	Metric
1/3 cup	**Brown SugarLike**	67.00 g
2 Tbsp	**Powdered SugarLike**	13.00 g
1/2 cup	Cocoa	119.00 g
1 Tbsp	Flour	7.00 g
4 cups	Skim milk	980.00 g
3	Whole cloves	9.00 g
1	Cinnamon stick, broken	2.30 g
1 1/2 tsp	Vanilla	7.40 g
4	Cinnamon sticks	9.20 g

Directions

Mix cocoa and flour in 2-quart saucepan. Stir in **Brown SugarLike**, milk, cloves, and one stick cinnamon. Heat to just a boil over medium heat, stirring constantly; reduce heat. Simmer uncovered for 5 minutes; do not boil. Remove from heat; remove cloves and cinnamon. Stir in **Powdered SugarLike** and vanilla. Beat with wire whisk or hand mixer until foamy. Pour into 4 cups or mugs. Serve with whipped topping and cinnamon sticks.

Nutrition Facts				
Serving Size	304 g			
Servings Per Recipe	4			
Amount per serving			High Fat/Sugar Comparison	
Calories	163		280	
Calories from fat	5		80	
	% Daily Value*		% Daily Value*	
Total Fat	0.5 g	**1%**	8 g	**12%**
Saturated Fat	0 g	**0%**	5 g	**25%**
Cholesterol	5 mg	**2%**	35 mg	**12%**
Sodium	150 mg	**6%**	150 mg	**6%**
Total Carbohydrate	39 g	**13%**	41 g	**14%**
Dietary Fiber	7 g	**28%**	2 g	**8%**
Sugars	14 g		34 g	
Other	15 g		0 g	
Protein	10 g		9 g	

*Percent of Daily Values on page a-22

Exchanges and 17 g Carbohydrates Per Serving

Breads	0.1	Vegetables	0.2	Fruits	0.0
Meats	0.0	Milk	1.0	Fats	0.0

Hot Cocoa Mix

The Fat quotient using **ButterLike** is **0%** instead of **10%**
100% less fat **92% less sugar**
13% less Calories

U.S.	Ingredients	Metric
2 cups	**Powdered SugarLike**	210.00 g
3 1/2 cup	Non fat dry milk powder	238.00 g
1 cup	Non fat powdered nondairy creamer	96.00 g
1/2 cup	Unsweetened cocoa powder, sifted	119.00 g

Directions

In a mixing bowl combine **Powdered SugarLike**, dry milk powder, nondairy creamer, and cocoa powder. Store in an airtight container. For each serving, place 1/3 cup of the mix in a mug and add 3/4 cup boiling water. Makes 5 1/2 cups mix.

Nutrition Facts				
Serving Size	41 g			
Servings Per Recipe	16			
Amount per serving			High Fat/Sugar Comparison	
Calories	113		130	
Calories from fat	0		15	
	% Daily Value*		% Daily Value*	
Total Fat	0 g	**0%**	1.5 g	**2%**
Saturated Fat	0 g	**0%**	1.5 g	**8%**
Cholesterol	5 mg	**2%**	5 mg	**2%**
Sodium	85 mg	**4%**	85 mg	**4%**
Total Carbohydrate	27 g	**9%**	24 g	**8%**
Dietary Fiber	4 g	**16%**	0 g	**0%**
Sugars	1 g		12 g	
Other	11 g		0 g	
Protein	5 g		6 g	

*Percent of Daily Values on page a-22

Exchanges and 12 g Carbohydrates Per Serving

Breads	0.3	Vegetables	0.0	Fruits	0.0
Meats	0.0	Milk	0.7	Fats	0.0

Breads

Lemon Granola Muffins, page 30; and Blueberry Muffins, page 31

Notes

This section includes a few recipes for quick breads, yeast breads, and sweet yeast doughs. The first cookbook has more of my traditional yeast breads that I made daily at our bakery. I have not put in the same recipes twice. I have also given an excellent recipe for a sourdough start in this section - use it or one of your own and enjoy great sourdough foods!

Tips for successful bread baking using the Bateman Products

- Yeast needs real sugar to feed it. **SugarLike** will not feed the yeast since it is sugar free. When using **SugarLike** in your doughs, you need to start with 2 tablespoons of real granulated sugar to one package, or 2 1/2 teaspoons, of dry yeast. Mix this with 1/2 cup warm water and set aside until bubbly. The remaining amounts of sugar or honey can be substituted with **SugarLike**. The real sugar that is used in the recipe just feeds the yeast. Very little, if any, sugar is left in your dough by the time it is baked. The additional sweetness required for taste can be substituted with **SugarLike** to make your breads turn out great. After your yeast and sugar start to bubble, continue to follow the recipe according to directions.
- Soften cold **Baking Butter** for 10-30 seconds in the microwave or set out until room temperature before mixing. This is very important if you are using a bread machine. Adding cold **Baking Butter** can result in inconsistency in your dough.
- Cut back on flour if your bread turns out dry. If your bread turns out too soft just add a little bit of flour. Many factors affect how your bread turns out, so experimenting with your bread machine may be necessary. You will be able to enjoy fresh, warm, and delicious bread daily after you have a feel for your machine.

Mixing

Mixing bread using **Mrs. Bateman's Baking Butter** requires no changes in your normal recipes or procedures.

Kneading

Mixer: 5-10 minutes. In the bakery we knead all our breads 10 minutes. It develops the gluten, makes the bread elastic and helps it to have a nice volume.

Food processor: 1 minute. Do not knead longer. If your food processor is labored, take half of dough out and knead in two pieces.

Croissants, page 38

By hand: 15 minutes. Get into it. Get those muscles going. Knead — push down, roll under, push down, turn, repeat.

The process of kneading is done when dough springs slowly back after making an indentation with your finger.

Rising

The dough needs to rise to double in size before rolling and shaping into loaves or rolls.

Regular rise method: Cover kneaded dough with a cloth and let it rise on it's own. A warm, humid spot works best.

Quick rise method:

1. Place a cup of water in the corner of your microwave.
2. Place kneaded dough in a microwave safe bowl.
3. Cover dough with a damp towel or plastic wrap.
4. Put covered dough in the microwave on the very lowest setting (approximately 10% power). If your microwave does not go that low, you might not be able to use the quick rise method.
5. Microwave for 3 minutes. Let dough rest for 3 minutes. Microwave for 3 minutes. Let it rest in microwave. As soon as it is double, you can remove it and continue to the next step of shaping your dough.

Note: Microwave ovens vary. If the dough is too hot, it could kill the yeast. Try microwaving for 2 minutes instead of 3 minutes. You may need to add more yeast and try again. If the dough is too cold, increase the microwave time from 3 minutes to 4.

Delicious Cinnamon Danish Rolls, page 40

Shaping

Shape the dough after it has risen double in size.

Loaves — Flatten ball of dough out to a large rectangle shape. Roll up the dough (like making cinnamon rolls), tucking in the ends. Using the pressure of your hands shape the dough so it is lower on the ends and higher in the middle.

Rolls — One standard recipe of bread can be cut into 12 pieces. Roll the pieces into round balls. Place on a vegetable-sprayed cookie sheet. Brush with egg whites. Let rise until double in size.

Pan rolls — Place close in vegetable-sprayed pie pan - 8 rolls per pan. Brush with egg whites.

Pull apart rolls — White bread or bun dough works great. Take 1/2 cup Mrs. Bateman's Baking Butter thinned with 1/4 cup warm water. Dip each rounded roll into **Mrs. Bateman's Baking Butter** then drop into 1 cup sugar mixed with 3 Tbsp cinnamon. Drop into a vegetable sprayed bundt or angel food cake pan. Let rise until double. Bake at 350° for 35 minutes. Dump out while still warm.

Hamburger buns – Divide your dough into 6 pieces and form into round rolls. Place the rolls on a large cookie sheet that has been sprayed with a vegetable spray; cover with waxed paper and place a cookie sheet on top of the waxed paper. Press down on the top sheet or stand on it to flatten the buns. Take off cookie sheet and wax paper. Brush buns with egg white and sprinkle with sesame seeds if desired. Let rise at least double before you bake.

Hoagie buns – Divide your dough into 8 pieces. Flatten your piece into a rectangle about 6 inches by 4 inches. Roll up like a loaf of bread, tucking in the ends. Brush with egg white and sprinkle with sesame seeds or poppy seeds. Rise at least double.

You can use the quick rise method for the final rise after shaping if your dough is in a glass baking dish.

Baking

- I bake most of my breads in a 350° oven. Wheat breads do well at 325°. Always preheat.
- Bread bakes between 35-40 minutes and is done if it is golden brown on the bottom or sounds hollow when thumped.
- Rolls and buns bake for 20-25 minutes and are done if they are pulling away from each other and are golden brown on bottom.

Flatbread Wafers

The Fat Quotient using ButterLike is 0% instead of 39%
100% less fat **0% less sugar**
21% less Calories

U.S.	Ingredients	Metric
1/4 cup	**ButterLike Baking Butter**, softened	57.00 g
1 3/4 cup	All-purpose flour	201.00 g
1/2 cup	Yellow cornmeal	120.00 g
1/2 tsp	Salt	3.00 g
1/2 tsp	Baking soda	2.30 g
2/3 cup	Warm water	158.00 g

Directions

In a medium bowl, mix flour, cornmeal, salt, and baking soda. Stir in **ButterLike** and warm water. Cover and refrigerate until cold. Shape chilled dough into balls the size of large marbles. On a lightly floured board, roll out each ball of dough to a paper-thin round about 4 inches in diameter. Place rounds slightly apart on a vegetable sprayed baking sheet. Bake in a 375° oven for 5 minutes. Transfer to racks and let cool completely. If made ahead, wrap airtight and store at room temperature. Makes 90 wafers.

Nutrition Facts				
Serving Size	36 g			
Servings Per Recipe	15			
Amount per serving			High Fat/Sugar Comparison	
Calories	63		80	
Calories from fat	0		30	
	% Daily Value*		% Daily Value*	
Total Fat	0 g	**0%**	3.5 g	**5%**
Saturated Fat	0 g	**0%**	2 g	**10%**
Cholesterol	0 mg	**0%**	10 mg	**3%**
Sodium	135 mg	**6%**	150 mg	**6%**
Total Carbohydrate	13 g	**4%**	11 g	**4%**
Dietary Fiber	0 g	**0%**	0 g	**0%**
Sugars	0 g		0 g	
Other	0 g		0 g	
Protein	2 g		2 g	

*Percent of Daily Values on page a-22

Exchanges and 13 g Carbohydrates Per Serving					
Breads	0.9	Vegetables	0.0	Fruits	0.0
Meats	0.0	Milk	0.0	Fats	0.1

German Pancakes

The Fat Quotient using ButterLike is 34% instead of 68%
67% less fat **0% less sugar**
34% less Calories

U.S.	Ingredients	Metric
1/2 cup	**ButterLike Saute Butter**	112.00 g
1 cup	Egg substitute	251.00 g
4 large	Whole eggs	200.00 g
1 cup	All-purpose flour	125.00 g
1/2 tsp	Salt	3.00 g

Directions

Blend eggs, salt, and flour; scrape and blend again. Pour into a preheated 9x13-inch vegetable sprayed baking pan that has been put in a 450° oven for 5 minutes. Pour the **ButterLike** into the pan and tilt to spread around. Pour egg mixture into pan and place in oven. Bake at 450° for 20-25 minutes or until the batter has doubled and is starting to brown on top. Cut into twelve pieces. Puffiness will decrease when cut. Serve with jam, jelly or syrup.

Nutrition Facts				
Serving Size	58 g			
Servings Per Recipe	12			
Amount per serving			High Fat/Sugar Comparison	
Calories	106		160	
Calories from fat	35		100	
	% Daily Value*		% Daily Value*	
Total Fat	4 g	**6%**	12 g	**18%**
Saturated Fat	1 g	**5%**	6 g	**30%**
Cholesterol	75 mg	**25%**	165 mg	**55%**
Sodium	160 mg	**7%**	220 mg	**9%**
Total Carbohydrate	11 g	**4%**	8 g	**3%**
Dietary Fiber	0 g	**0%**	0 g	**0%**
Sugars	0 g		0 g	
Other	0 g		0 g	
Protein	6 g		5 g	

*Percent of Daily Values on page a-22

Exchanges and 11 g Carbohydrates Per Serving					
Breads	0.7	Vegetables	0.0	Fruits	0.0
Meats	0.6	Milk	0.0	Fats	0.5

Homemade Tortillas

The Fat Quotient using ButterLike is 7% instead of 34%
83% less fat **0% less sugar**
18% less Calories

U.S.	Ingredients	Metric
1/3 cup	**ButterLike Saute Butter**	75.00 g
3-4 cups	All-purpose flour	375.00 g
1 tsp	Salt	6.00 g
1 cup	Warm water	237.00 g

Directions

In a medium-size bowl, mix the **ButterLike** and flour until it crumbles. Dissolve salt in warm water and pour it over flour mixture, then use your fingers to combine the dough. Knead the dough on an unfloured surface until elastic, about 4 minutes. Let dough rest in a bowl, covered with damp cloth, for at least 1 hour. Divide into 12 balls and roll each one into vegetable sprayed skillet over medium-high heat and cook each side for 1-3 minutes.

Nutrition Facts				
Serving Size	58 g			
Servings Per Recipe	12			
Amount per serving			High Fat/Sugar Comparison	
Calories	131		160	
Calories from fat	10		50	
	% Daily Value*		% Daily Value*	
Total Fat	1 g	**2%**	6 g	**9%**
Saturated Fat	0 g	**0%**	3.5 g	**18%**
Cholesterol	0 mg	**0%**	15 mg	**5%**
Sodium	190 mg	**8%**	250 mg	**10%**
Total Carbohydrate	26 g	**9%**	24 g	**8%**
Dietary Fiber	1 g	**4%**	1 g	**4%**
Sugars	0 g		0 g	
Other	0 g		0 g	
Protein	4 g		3 g	

*Percent of Daily Values on page a-22

Exchanges and 25 g Carbohydrates Per Serving					
Breads	1.7	Vegetables	0.0	Fruits	0.0
Meats	0.0	Milk	0.0	Fats	0.2

Quick Lemon Bread

The Fat Quotient using ButterLike is 6% instead of 37%
92% less fat **93% less sugar**
46% less Calories

U.S.	Ingredients	Metric
1 cup	**Granulated SugarLike**	200.00 g
1/2 cup	**ButterLike Baking Butter**, softened	114.00 g
1 1/2 cup	All-purpose flour	173.00 g
1 tsp	Baking powder	4.00 g
1/2 tsp	Salt	3.00 g
1/2 cup	Egg whites, lightly beaten	114.00 g
1/2 cup	Skim milk	123.00 g
1 1/2 tsp	Lemon peel, grated	3.00 g
Lemon Glaze:		
1/3 cup	**Granulated SugarLike**	67.00 g
4 1/2 Tbsp	Lemon juice	69.00 g

Nutrition Facts				
Serving Size	87 g			
Servings Per Recipe	10			
Amount per serving			High Fat/Sugar Comparison	
Calories	157		290	
Calories from fat	10		110	
	% Daily Value*		% Daily Value*	
Total Fat	1 g	**2%**	12 g	**18%**
Saturated Fat	0 g	**0%**	2 g	**10%**
Cholesterol	0 mg	**0%**	45 mg	**15%**
Sodium	230 mg	**10%**	180 mg	**8%**
Total Carbohydrate	47 g	**16%**	41 g	**14%**
Dietary Fiber	7 g	**28%**	1 g	**4%**
Sugars	2 g		27 g	
Other	20 g		0 g	
Protein	4 g		3 g	

*Percent of Daily Values on page a-22

Directions

In a large bowl, mix **ButterLike**, **SugarLike**, and egg whites until smooth. Add remaining muffin ingredients and mix until flour is incorporated into batter. Pour batter into a vegetable sprayed and floured 5x9-inch loaf pan. Bake in a 350° oven 45-50 minutes or until a toothpick inserted in center comes out clean. As soon as bread is done, prepare glaze. Leaving loaf in pan, use a long, slender skewer to poke numerous holes all the way to bottom of loaf.

Lemon Glaze: In a small pan, combine **SugarLike** and lemon juice. Cook over medium heat, stirring constantly, until **SugarLike** is dissolved. Remove from heat. Slowly drizzle over top of loaf so that glaze soaks into bread. Let bread cool in pan on rack for 15 minutes; then turn out onto rack to cool completely.

Exchanges and 20 g Carbohydrates Per Serving					
Breads	1.3	Vegetables	0.0	Fruits	0.0
Meats	0.2	Milk	0.0	Fats	0.2

Banana Bread

The Fat Quotient using ButterLike is **9%** instead of **37%**
86 % less fat **83% less sugar**
43% less Calories

U.S.	Ingredients	Metric
1/2 cup	**ButterLike Baking Butter**, softened	114.00 g
1 cup	**Granulated SugarLike**	200.00 g
1/2 cup	Egg whites	114.00 g
1 tsp	Vanilla	5.00 g
2 cups	All-purpose flour	230.00 g
3/4 tsp	Baking soda	3.50 g
1/2 tsp	Salt	3.00 g
1/4 cup	Non fat buttermilk	61.00 g
1 cup	Bananas, mashed	235.00 g
1/8 cup	Nuts, chopped	16.00 g

Directions

Mix **SugarLike**, **ButterLike**, and egg whites until smooth. Add remaining ingredients and mix until combined. Pour into vegetable sprayed bread pans. Bake in a 350° oven for 1 hour or until toothpick comes out clean. Let rest 5 minutes. Take bread out of pan.

Nutrition Facts				
Serving Size	49 g			
Servings Per Recipe	20			
Amount per serving			High Fat/Sugar Comparison	
Calories		98	170	
Calories from fat		10	70	
	% Daily Value*		% Daily Value*	
Total Fat	1 g	**2%**	7 g	**11%**
Saturated Fat	0 g	**0%**	1.5 g	**8%**
Cholesterol	0 mg	**0%**	20 mg	**7%**
Sodium	140 mg	**6%**	115 mg	**5%**
Total Carbohydrate	25 g	**8%**	22 g	**7%**
Dietary Fiber	3 g	**12%**	1 g	**4%**
Sugars	2 g		12 g	
Other	7 g		0 g	
Protein	2 g		3 g	

*Percent of Daily Values on page a-22

Exchanges and 15 g Carbohydrates Per Serving					
Breads	0.8	Vegetables	0.0	Fruits	0.2
Meats	0.1	Milk	0.0	Fats	0.2

Pizza Crust

The Fat Quotient using ButterLike is 0% instead of 15%
100% less fat 0% less sugar
9% less Calories

U.S.	Ingredients	Metric
2 Tbsp	**ButterLike Saute Butter**	28.00 g
1 pkg	Active yeast, regular or quick	7.00 g
1 cup	Warm water	237.00 g
1 tsp	Sugar	4.00 g
2 1/2 cup	All-purpose flour	313.00 g
1/2 cup	Salt	3.00 g
	Cornmeal	17.00 g

Directions

My brother Walter makes wonderful pizza and I would like to share his most famous **Marinated Chicken Pizza** and **Basil Proscuito Pizza**. His crust makes the pizza. Here is how to make the good crust. Dissolve yeast and sugar in warm water in a mixing bowl. Let it just start to bubble. Mix in the flour and salt. If using a mixer, knead for 15 minutes on medium; by hand knead 20 minutes; by food processor divide dough into two pieces and mix for 1 minute each. Dough should not be too stiff. If it feels too stiff sprinkle with water and mix until smooth. Take out of bowl and form two balls. Roll the dough in cornmeal lightly to keep from sticking. Cover and place in a warm spot until raised just over double. Dough should be very pliable at this point. Sprinkle corn meal over a clean working surface. Press dough into a circle; press from the middle out. When your circle is started, lift up the dough and start stretching out the sides, being careful not to let the center get too thin. If you are brave you could toss it a few times. The edges should be thicker than the middle. Again set the pizza dough onto the cornmeal surface. Then set on a seasoned pizza wire. This is what the pizza house uses to cook their pizzas. Top your pizza according to your likes. Place pizza onto a rack in the center of a pre-heated 450° oven. Bake for 13 minutes. Most homemade pizzas are over cooked. Make sure bottom crust is browned and top crust is also browned along the edges. Another light layer of cheese added at this time makes the pizza just delicious. Serve immediately. If cooking two pizzas at a time you will have to switch the positions of the pizzas to make sure they bake evenly half way through cooking.

Nutrition Facts				
Serving Size	38 g			
Servings Per Recipe	16			
Amount per serving			High Fat/Sugar Comparison	
Calories	82		90	
Calories from fat	0		15	
	% Daily Value*		% Daily Value*	
Total Fat	0 g	**0%**	1.5 g	**2%**
Saturated Fat	0 g	**0%**	1 g	**5%**
Cholesterol	0 mg	**0%**	5 mg	**2%**
Sodium	75 mg	**3%**	90 mg	**4%**
Total Carbohydrate	17 g	**6%**	16 g	**5%**
Dietary Fiber	1 g	**4%**	1 g	**4%**
Sugars	0 g		0 g	
Other	0 g		0 g	
Protein	2 g		2 g	

*Percent of Daily Values on page a-22

Exchanges and 16 g Carbohydrates Per Serving					
Breads	1.1	Vegetables	0.0	Fruits	0.0
Meats	0.0	Milk	0.0	Fats	0.1

Pizza Stones: Pizza stones are wonderful but they need to be used correctly. After preparing the pizza wire carefully slip the pizza off onto a hot pizza stone that has heated up the correct amount of time in the center of your oven. If you do not have a pizza wire you will have a very difficult time slipping off the uncooked pizza onto the pizza stone. After cooking slip a large pizza paddle under pizza and remove from oven.

Refrigerated Bran Muffins

The Fat Quotient using ButterLike is 7% instead of 27%
83% less fat **47% less sugar**
34% less Calories

U.S.	Ingredients	Metric
1 cup	**Granulated SugarLike**	200.00 g
1/2 cup	**ButterLike Saute Butter**	112.00 g
2 1/2 cup	All-purpose flour	288.00 g
2 1/2 tsp	Baking soda	12.00 g
1/2 tsp	Salt	3.00 g
3 cups	Whole bran cereal (not flakes)	261.00 g
1 cup	Boiling water	237.00 g
1/2 cup	Egg whites, lightly beaten	114.00 g
2 cups	Non fat buttermilk	490.00 g
1 cup	Raisins, currants, dates, or prunes	145.00 g

Directions

In a medium bowl, mix **SugarLike,** flour, baking soda, and salt; set aside. In a large bowl, mix cereal and boiling water until evenly moistened; let cool. Add **ButterLike**, egg whites, buttermilk, and raisins; stir until combined. Add flour mixture; stir until blended. (This batter can be refrigerated for up to two weeks; stir before baking.) Spoon batter into vegetable sprayed 2 1/2-inch muffin cups, filling cups 2/3 full. Bake in a 425° oven about 20 minutes until tops of muffins spring back when lightly touched.

Nutrition Facts				
Serving Size	78 g			
Servings Per Recipe	24			
Amount per serving			High Fat/Sugar Comparison	
Calories	132		200	
Calories from fat	10		50	
	% Daily Value*		% Daily Value*	
Total Fat	1 g	**2%**	6 g	**9%**
Saturated Fat	0 g	**0%**	1 g	**5%**
Cholesterol	0 mg	**0%**	20 mg	**7%**
Sodium	260 mg	**11%**	250 mg	**10%**
Total Carbohydrate	33 g	**11%**	32 g	**11%**
Dietary Fiber	6 g	**24%**	4 g	**16%**
Sugars	8 g		15 g	
Other	6 g		0 g	
Protein	4 g		4 g	

*Percent of Daily Values on page a-22

Exchanges and 11 g Carbohydrates Per Serving					
Breads	1.3	Vegetables	0.0	Fruits	0.3
Meats	0.1	Milk	0.1	Fats	0.2

Lemon Granola Muffins

The Fat Quotient using ButterLike is **6%** instead of **41%**
92% less fat **87% less sugar**
44% less Calories

U.S.	**Ingredients**	Metric
1/2 cup	**ButterLike Baking Butter**, softened	114.00 g
3/4 cup	**Granulated SugarLike**	150.00 g
3/4 cup	All-purpose flour	86.30 g
3/4 cup	Whole wheat flour	90.00 g
1 Tbsp	Baking powder	12.00 g
1/2 tsp	Salt	3.00 g
1 tsp	Lemon peel, grated	2.00 g
1/2 cup	Egg whites	114.00 g
1/2 cup	Lemon juice	122.00 g
1 cup	Fat free granola-type cereal	83.00 g
1/2 cup	Currants, dried	72.00 g

Directions

In a large bowl, combine flours, baking powder, and salt; set aside. In another bowl, combine **ButterLike** and **SugarLike**. Add lemon peel and egg whites; mix until smooth. Then stir in lemon juice. Gradually add flour mixture, granola, and currants, stirring until blended. Spoon batter equally into 12 vegetable sprayed 2 1/2-inch muffin tins. Bake in a 350° oven 25-30 minutes until the tops of muffins are well browned and spring back when touched.

Nutrition Facts
Serving Size 71 g
Servings Per Recipe 12

Amount per serving			High Fat/Sugar Comparison	
Calories	148		260	
Calories from fat	5		110	
	% Daily Value*		% Daily Value*	
Total Fat	1 g	**2%**	12 g	**18%**
Saturated Fat	0 g	**0%**	6 g	**30%**
Cholesterol	0 mg	**0%**	55 mg	**18%**
Sodium	260 mg	**11%**	290 mg	**12%**
Total Carbohydrate	40 g	**13%**	34 g	**11%**
Dietary Fiber	5 g	**20%**	3 g	**12%**
Sugars	2 g		15 g	
Other	9 g		0 g	
Protein	4 g		4 g	

*Percent of Daily Values on page a-22

Exchanges and 26 g Carbohydrates Per Serving

Breads	1.4	Vegetables	0.0	Fruits	0.3
Meats	0.1	Milk	0.0	Fats	0.1

Lemon Granola Muffins

Blueberry Muffins

The Fat Quotient using **ButterLike** is **5%** instead of **20%**
83% less fat **81% less sugar**
31% less Calories

U.S.	Ingredients	Metric
1 cup + 2 Tbsp	**Brown SugarLike**	225.00 g
1/4 cup	**ButterLike Baking Butter**, softened	57.00 g
1 1/2 cup	All-purpose flour	173.00 g
1 1/2 cup	Whole wheat flour	180.00 g
4 tsp	Baking powder	16.00 g
1 Tbsp	Ground cinnamon	7.00 g
2 tsp	Baking soda	9.20 g
1/4 tsp	Salt	1.50 g
1/2 cup	Egg whites	114.00 g
1 1/2 cup	Non fat buttermilk	386.00 g
2 cups	Fresh or frozen blueberries, unsweetened	310.00 g

Directions

Mix 1 cup **SugarLike**, flours, baking powder, cinnamon, baking soda, and salt. In another bowl, blend **ButterLike**, egg whites, and buttermilk; add to flour mixture and stir just until moistened. Add blueberries and stir until evenly distributed. Spoon batter into 12 vegetable sprayed muffin cups; do not use paper liners. Sprinkle remaining **SugarLike** evenly over batter in cups. Bake in a 375° oven about 35 minutes until tops of muffins are browned and spring back when lightly touched.

Nutrition Facts
Serving Size 122 g
Servings Per Recipe 12

Amount per serving			High Fat/Sugar Comparison	
Calories	185		270	
Calories from fat	10		60	
	% Daily Value*		% Daily Value*	
Total Fat	1 g	**2%**	6 g	**9%**
Saturated Fat	0 g	**0%**	1 g	**5%**
Cholesterol	0 mg	**0%**	20 mg	**7%**
Sodium	460 mg	**19%**	430 mg	**18%**
Total Carbohydrate	48 g	**16%**	47 g	**16%**
Dietary Fiber	8 g	**32%**	3 g	**12%**
Sugars	4 g		21 g	
Other	14 g		0 g	
Protein	6 g		5 g	

*Percent of Daily Values on page a-22

Exchanges and 26 g Carbohydrates Per Serving

Breads	1.6	Vegetables	0.0	Fruits	0.2
Meats	0.1	Milk	0.1	Fats	0.1

Blueberry Muffins

Sourdough Starter

The Fat Quotient using ButterLike is 2% instead of 17%
86% less fat — 6% less sugar
11% less Calories

U.S.	Ingredients	Metric
1 cup	Lukewarm skim milk	245.00 g
2 Tbsp	Non fat plain yogurt	28.00 g
1 cup	All-purpose flour	115.00 g

Directions

Combine milk and yogurt in a dry, heated container. Cover tightly and let stand in a warm place 18-24 hours until a curd forms and mixture doesn't flow readily when container is slightly tilted. If clear liquid rises to top, stir it back in. But if liquid turns light pink, discard starter and begin again. Gradually stir in flour until well blended; cover tightly and let stand in a warm place until mixture is full of bubbles and has a good sour smell. If clear liquid forms, stir in. If liquid is pink, spoon out and discard all but 1/4 cup of starter, then stir in a mixture of 1 cup lukewarm milk and 1 cup flour. Cover tightly and let stand again in a warm place until bubbly and sour smelling. Use at once; or cover and refrigerate.

Each time starter is used, replenish it with equal amounts of flour and milk. (If you use 1/2 cup starter, replenish with 1/2 cup milk and 1/2 cup flour. Let stand, covered, until bubbly. then refrigerate, covered, until next use. Before using starter, let it warm at room temperature.) If you bake regularly, starter should stay active; if not, discard half of starter and replenish with milk and flour every two weeks. Starter can be frozen, if unused for a long period of time.

Nutrition Facts				
Serving Size	388 g			
Servings Per Recipe	1			
Amount per serving			High Fat/Sugar Comparison	
Calories		132	200	
Calories from fat		10	50	
	% Daily Value*		% Daily Value*	
Total Fat	1.5 g	**2%**	11 g	**17%**
Saturated Fat	0 g	**0%**	6 g	**30%**
Cholesterol	5 mg	**2%**	40 mg	**13%**
Sodium	150 mg	**6%**	140 mg	**6%**
Total Carbohydrate	102 g	**34%**	102 g	**34%**
Dietary Fiber	3 g	**12%**	3 g	**12%**
Sugars	15 g		16 g	
Other	0 g		0 g	
Protein	22 g		21 g	

*Percent of Daily Values on page a-22

Exchanges and 99 g Carbohydrates Per Serving					
Breads	5.9	Vegetables	0.0	Fruits	0.0
Meats	0.0	Milk	1.1	Fats	0.2

Cottage Cheese Sourdough Rolls

The Fat Quotient using ButterLike is 0% instead of 17%
100% less fat — 0% less sugar
11% less Calories

U.S.	Ingredients	Metric
1 cup	**Sourdough Starter**, room temperature, page 32	259.00 g
2 Tbsp	**ButterLike Baking Butter**, softened	28.00 g
1 pkg	Active dry yeast	7.00 g
1/4 cup	Warm water	59.00 g
1 cup	Fat free cottage cheese	226.00 g
1/4 cup	Egg whites	57.00 g
1 Tbsp	Sugar	12.50 g
2 tsp	Baking powder	8.00 g
1 tsp	Salt	6.00 g
1/4 tsp	Baking soda	1.20 g
4 1/2 cups	All-purpose flour	518.00 g

Nutrition Facts				
Serving Size	66 g			
Servings Per Recipe	18			
Amount per serving			High Fat/Sugar Comparison	
Calories		142	160	
Calories from fat		0	25	
	% Daily Value*		% Daily Value*	
Total Fat	0 g	**0%**	3 g	**5%**
Saturated Fat	0 g	**0%**	1.5 g	**8%**
Cholesterol	0 mg	**0%**	20 mg	**7%**
Sodium	260 mg	**11%**	260 mg	**11%**
Total Carbohydrate	28 g	**9%**	27 g	**9%**
Dietary Fiber	1 g	**4%**	1 g	**4%**
Sugars	2 g		2 g	
Other	0 g		0 g	
Protein	6 g		6 g	

*Percent of Daily Values on page a-22

Directions

Follow directions for **Sourdough Starter** on page 32; set aside.

Combine yeast and warm water; let stand 5 minutes until yeast is softened. Blend **Sourdough Starter,** cottage cheese, and egg whites until smooth. In a large bowl, mix sugar, baking powder, salt, baking soda, and 4 cups flour. Cut in **ButterLike** until mixture resembles coarse crumbs. Stir in cottage cheese mixture and yeast mixture. Turn dough out onto a floured board and knead until smooth; add more flour as needed to prevent sticking. Place dough in a vegetable sprayed bowl; turn over to coat top. Cover and let rise in a warm place until doubled. Punch dough down. Shape into 18 balls. Arrange 9 balls in each of 2 vegetable sprayed 8-inch round baking pans. Let rise, covered, 25-30 minutes until puffy. Bake in a 350° oven 30-35 minutes until golden. Turn rolls out onto racks to cool. Makes 1 1/2 dozen.

Exchanges and 27 g Carbohydrates Per Serving

Breads	1.8	Vegetables	0.0	Fruits	0.0
Meats	0.3	Milk	0.0	Fats	0.1

Sourdough French Bread

The Fat Quotient using ButterLike is 0% instead of 5%
100% less fat **50% less sugar**
19% less Calories

U.S.	Ingredients	Metric
1 cup	**Sourdough Starter**, page 32	259.00 g
1 pkg	Active dry yeast	7.00 g
1 1/2 cup	Warm water	356.00 g
6 cups	All-purpose flour, divided	690.00 g
2 tsp	Salt	12.00 g
2 tsp	Sugar	8.30 g
1/2 cup	Cornmeal, divided	61.00 g
1/2 tsp	Cornstarch	1.30 g
1/2 cup	Cold water	119.00 g

Nutrition Facts

Nutrition Facts			High Fat/Sugar Comparison	
Serving Size	63 g			
Servings Per Recipe	24			
Amount per serving				
Calories	131		160	
Calories from fat	0		5	
	% Daily Value*		% Daily Value*	
Total Fat	0 g	**0%**	1 g	**2%**
Saturated Fat	0 g	**0%**	0 g	**0%**
Cholesterol	0 mg	**0%**	0 mg	**0%**
Sodium	200 mg	**8%**	240 mg	**10%**
Total Carbohydrate	27 g	**9%**	33 g	**11%**
Dietary Fiber	1 g	**4%**	1 g	**4%**
Sugars	1 g		2 g	
Other	0 g		0 g	
Protein	4 g		5 g	

*Percent of Daily Values on page a-22

Exchanges and 26 g Carbohydrates Per Serving

Breads	1.8	Vegetables	0.0	Fruits	0.0
Meats	0.0	Milk	0.0	Fats	0.1

Directions

Follow directions for **Sourdough Starter**, set aside.

In a large bowl, combine yeast and warm water; let stand about 5 minutes until yeast is softened. Add **Sourdough Starter**, 4 cups flour, salt, and sugar; beat until smooth and well blended. Cover; let rise about 1 1/2 hours in a warm place until doubled. Stir in enough remaining flour to make a stiff dough. Knead dough on a lightly floured board until smooth and satiny. Add more flour as needed to prevent sticking. Divide dough in half. Place on half in a vegetable sprayed bowl; let stand, covered, at room temperature until first loaf is shaped and placed in oven. For an oblong loaf, roll dough into a 14-inch log. Set each loaf on a piece of stiff cardboard sprinkled with 1/4 cup cornmeal. Let rise, covered lightly, in a warm place about 1 hour until almost doubled. Set oven racks in the 2 lowest positions; place 12x15-inch baking sheet on lower rack and pour in boiling water to a depth of about 1/4 inch. In a small pan, blend cornstarch and cold water; bring to a boil, stirring constantly. Remove from heat and let cool slightly. Evenly brush cornstarch mixture over entire surface of loaf. Cut 1/2-inch-deep slashes on top of loaf. Slip loaf off cardboard onto top baking sheet in oven. Bake in a 400° oven for 10 minutes; brush with cornstarch mixture again. Continue to bake 20-25 minutes until loaves are golden and sound hollow when tapped. Let cool on racks. Makes two 14-inch loaves.

Giant Cheese Rolls

The Fat Quotient using **ButterLike** is **6%** instead of **37%**
88% less fat **57% less sugar**
30% less Calories

U.S.	Ingredients	Metric
1/8 cup	**ButterLike Baking Butter**, softened	28.00 g
1/4 cup	**Granulated SugarLike**	50.00 g
1 pkg	Yeast, not instant	7.00 g
1/3 cup	Warm water	79.00 g
4 cups	All-purpose flour	460.00 g
1 Tbsp	Baking powder	12.00 g
1/2 tsp	Salt	3.00 g
3/4 cup	Egg whites	170.00 g
1/2 cup	Evaporated skim milk	128.00 g
1/3 cup	Sharp cheddar cheese, shredded	38.00 g
2 cups	Fat free cheddar cheese, shredded	227.00 g
2 Tbsp	Sugar	25.00 g

Directions

Dissolve yeast in water. Sift flour, baking powder, and salt together twice. Stir sugar and 1/2 cup flour mixture into the yeast mixture. Cover and let rise in warm place for 20 minutes, until doubled in size. Combine **ButterLike**, **SugarLike**, and egg whites; mix until smooth. Beat in remaining flour mixture, alternating with evaporated milk. Stir in the yeast mixture and beat until smooth. Turn the dough onto a lightly floured surface and divide into 12 parts. Roll each part into an 8-inch circle. Combine cheeses. Sprinkle 2 Tbsp cheese onto each circle.

Nutrition Facts				
Serving Size	102 g			
Servings Per Recipe	12			
Amount per serving			High Fat/Sugar Comparison	
Calories	219		310	
Calories from fat	15		120	
	% Daily Value*		% Daily Value*	
Total Fat	1.5 g	**2%**	13 g	**20%**
Saturated Fat	1 g	**5%**	7 g	**35%**
Cholesterol	5 mg	**2%**	140 mg	**47%**
Sodium	370 mg	**15%**	370 mg	**15%**
Total Carbohydrate	39 g	**13%**	37 g	**12%**
Dietary Fiber	3 g	**12%**	1 g	**4%**
Sugars	3 g		7 g	
Other	3 g		0 g	
Protein	13 g		12 g	

*Percent of Daily Values on page a-22

Exchanges and 33 g Carbohydrates Per Serving

Breads	2.2	Vegetables	0.0	Fruits	0.0
Meats	0.8	Milk	0.1	Fats	0.2

Roll circles like jelly roll and coil into crescent shape. Place on ungreased baking sheets. Cover and let rise in a warm place 1 1/2 hours until doubled in size. Preheat oven to 400° and bake rolls for 15-20 minutes or until golden brown. Remove from oven and immediately brush with some **ButterLike**; sprinkle with **SugarLike** and remaining cheese. Serve while warm.

Wheat Germ and Honey Bread

The Fat Quotient using **ButterLike** is **0%** instead of **11%**
100% less fat **0% less sugar**
2% less Calories

U.S.	Ingredients	Metric
1 Tbsp	**ButterLike Baking Butter**, softened	14.00 g
2 Tbsp	Sugar	25.00 g
1 pkg	Yeast	7.00 g
1/3 cup	Water	79.00 g
1 cup	Whole wheat flour	120.00 g
2 cups	Bread flour	274.00 g
1 Tbsp	Wheat germ	6.50 g
1/2 tsp	Salt	3.00 g

Directions

Mix together sugar, yeast, and warm water. Set aside until bubbles start. Add remaining ingredients gradually. Knead. Let the dough rise double and shape into desired shapes. Let rise at least 2 1/2 times.

Exchanges and 15 g Carbohydrates Per Serving					
Breads	1.0	Vegetables	0.0	Fruits	0.0
Meats	0.0	Milk	0.0	Fats	0.0

Nutrition Facts				
Serving Size	26 g			
Servings Per Recipe	20			
Amount per serving			High Fat/Sugar Comparison	
Calories	79		80	
Calories from fat	0		10	
	% Daily Value*		% Daily Value*	
Total Fat	0 g	**0%**	1 g	**2%**
Saturated Fat	0 g	**0%**	0 g	**0%**
Cholesterol	0 mg	**0%**	0 mg	**0%**
Sodium	60 mg	**3%**	65 mg	**3%**
Total Carbohydrate	16 g	**5%**	16 g	**5%**
Dietary Fiber	1 g	**4%**	1 g	**4%**
Sugars	1 g		1 g	
Other	0 g		0 g	
Protein	3 g		3 g	

*Percent of Daily Values on page a-22

Whole Wheat Bread

The Fat Quotient using **ButterLike** is **4%** instead of **19%**
83% less fat **0% less sugar**
22% less Calories

U.S.	Ingredients	Metric
1/3 cup	**ButterLike Baking Butter**	76.00 g
1/3 cup	**Granulated SugarLike**	67.00 g
2 1/2 cup	Hot water	593.00 g
2 Tbsp	Sugar	25.00 g
1 Tbsp	Salt	18.00 g
1 Tbsp	Yeast	11.00 g
1/2 cup	Powdered skim milk	34.00 g
3 cups	Whole wheat flour	360.00 g
3 1/2 cup	White flour	403.00 g

Directions

Combine softened **ButterLike**, **SugarLike**, water sugar, salt, and yeast. Let stand 10 minutes until yeast activates and **ButterLike** melts. Add powdered milk and flours. Knead and let raise until it doubles. Punch down and knead again. Divide into two loaves. Place in vegetable sprayed baking pans and let raise a few more. Bake at 350° for 45 minutes or until browned. Makes two 1 1/2 lb loaves.

If using a bread mixer, mix 15 minutes. Divide into two loaves. Then do as instructions indicate.

Nutrition Facts				
Serving Size	53 g			
Servings Per Recipe	30			
Amount per serving			High Fat/Sugar Comparison	
Calories	109		140	
Calories from fat	5		25	
	% Daily Value*		% Daily Value*	
Total Fat	0.5 g	**1%**	3 g	**5%**
Saturated Fat	0 g	**0%**	1 g	**5%**
Cholesterol	0 mg	**0%**	0 mg	**0%**
Sodium	250 mg	**10%**	260 mg	**11%**
Total Carbohydrate	24 g	**8%**	24 g	**8%**
Dietary Fiber	2 g	**8%**	2 g	**8%**
Sugars	1 g		1 g	
Other	2 g		0 g	
Protein	4 g		4 g	

*Percent of Daily Values on page a-22

Exchanges and 22 g Carbohydrates Per Serving					
Breads	1.4	Vegetables	0.0	Fruits	0.0
Meats	0.0	Milk	0.1	Fats	0.1

Buttermilk Cheese Bread

The Fat Quotient using ButterLike is 9% instead of 24%
66% less fat **0% less sugar**
12% less Calories

U.S.	Ingredients	Metric
1 Tbsp	**ButterLike Baking Butter**	14.00 g
1 Tbsp	Sugar	12.50 g
1 pkg	Yeast	7.00 g
1/3 cup	Warm water	79.00 g
3 cups	Bread flour	411.00 g
1 tsp	Double-acting baking powder	4.60 g
1 cup	Low fat buttermilk	245.00 g
3/4 cup	Fat free cheddar cheese, shredded	84.00 g
1/4 cup	Sharp cheddar cheese, shredded	28.00 g

Directions

Mix together sugar, yeast, and warm water. Set aside until bubbles start. Add remaining ingredients gradually. Knead. Let the dough rise double and shape into desired shapes. Let rise at least 2 1/2 times. Bake for 40 minutes at 350°.

Note: 1/4 cup oats or 1/4 cup cornmeal may be substituted for 1/2 cup flour, if preferred.

Nutrition Facts				
Serving Size	44 g			
Servings Per Recipe	20			
Amount per serving			High Fat/Sugar Comparison	
Calories	97		110	
Calories from fat	10		30	
	% Daily Value*		% Daily Value*	
Total Fat	1 g	**2%**	3 g	**5%**
Saturated Fat	0 g	**0%**	1.5 g	**8%**
Cholesterol	0 mg	**0%**	5 mg	**2%**
Sodium	80 mg	**3%**	70 mg	**3%**
Total Carbohydrate	17 g	**6%**	16 g	**5%**
Dietary Fiber	1 g	**4%**	1 g	**4%**
Sugars	1 g		1 g	
Other	0 g		0 g	
Protein	5 g		4 g	

*Percent of Daily Values on page a-22

Exchanges and 16 g Carbohydrates Per Serving

Breads	1.0	Vegetables	0.0	Fruits	0.0
Meats	0.2	Milk	0.0	Fats	0.1

Basic Bun Dough

The Fat Quotient using ButterLike is 5% instead of 22%
86% less fat **100% less sugar**
16% less Calories

U.S.	Ingredients	Metric
1/2 cup	**ButterLike Baking Butter**, softened	114.00 g
1/2 cup	**Granulated SugarLike**	100.00 g
2 Tbsp	Sugar	25.00 g
2 cups	Warm water	474.00 g
1 1/2 Tbsp	Dry yeast	16.00 g
1 tsp	Salt	6.00 g
7 cups	Bread flour	959.00 g
1/4 cup	Egg white	57.00 g

Directions

Mix together sugar, yeast and warm water; let sit until bubbly. Combine all ingredients except half of bread flour. Add the remaining bread flour gradually until dough pulls away from the bowl. Knead. Set aside and let dough raise until doubled in size.

See pages 23-24 for further instructions on mixing, kneading, rising, shaping, and baking.

Nutrition Facts				
Serving Size	48 g			
Servings Per Recipe	36			
Amount per serving			High Fat/Sugar Comparison	
Calories	113		130	
Calories from fat	5		30	
	% Daily Value*		% Daily Value*	
Total Fat	0.5 g	**1%**	3.5 g	**5%**
Saturated Fat	0 g	**0%**	2 g	**10%**
Cholesterol	0 mg	**0%**	15 mg	**5%**
Sodium	80mg	**3%**	95 mg	**4%**
Total Carbohydrate	24 g	**8%**	22 g	**7%**
Dietary Fiber	1 g	**4%**	1 g	**4%**
Sugars	0 g		3 g	
Other	3 g		0 g	
Protein	4 g		4 g	

*Percent of Daily Values on page a-22

Exchanges and 20 g Carbohydrates Per Serving

Breads	1.4	Vegetables	0.0	Fruits	0.0
Meats	0.0	Milk	0.0	Fats	0.0

Basil-Parmesan Bread

The Fat Quotient using ButterLike is 11% instead of 32%
71% less fat **0% less sugar**
81% less Calories

U.S.	Ingredients	Metric
1/4 cup	**ButterLike Saute Butter**	56.00 g
2 Tbsp	Non fat grated parmesan	15.00 g
1 Tbsp	Fresh basil or 1 tsp dried basil	2.70 g
1/8 tsp	Garlic powder or 1 garlic clove	3.00 g
1/8 tsp	Pepper	.26 g
1 loaf	French bread, unsliced (16 oz)	454.00 g

Directions

Spread: In a small mixing bowl combine **ButterLike**, Parmesan cheese, basil, garlic, and pepper.

Cut bread into 1-inch thick slices, cutting to, but not through, the bottom crust. Spread cut surfaces with the spread. Tear off a 48x18-inch piece of heavy foil. Fold in half to make a double thickness of foil that measures 24x18 inches. Place bread in the center of the foil. Bring up two opposite edges of foil and seal with a double fold. Fold remaining ends to completely enclose the bread, yet leaving space for the steam to build. Grill bread on the rack of an uncovered grill directly over medium coals for 15-20 minutes or until the bread is heated through, turning once halfway through. Makes 16 side-dish servings.

Nutrition Facts				
Serving Size	33 g			
Servings Per Recipe	16			
Amount per serving			High Fat/Sugar Comparison	
Calories	81		100	
Calories from fat	10		35	
	% Daily Value*		% Daily Value*	
Total Fat	1 g	**2%**	3.5 g	**5%**
Saturated Fat	0 g	**0%**	2 g	**10%**
Cholesterol	0 mg	**0%**	10 mg	**3%**
Sodium	180 mg	**8%**	210 mg	**9%**
Total Carbohydrate	14 g	**5%**	13 g	**4%**
Dietary Fiber	0 g	**4%**	0 g	**0%**
Sugars	0 g		0 g	
Other	0 g		0 g	
Protein	3 g		3 g	

*Percent of Daily Values on page a-22

Exchanges and 14 g Carbohydrates Per Serving					
Breads	1.0	Vegetables	0.0	Fruits	0.0
Meats	0.3	Milk	0.0	Fats	0.3

Basil-Parmesan Bread

Croissants

The Fat Quotient using ButterLike is 8% instead of 26%
72% less fat **67% less sugar**
15% less Calories

U.S.	Ingredients	Metric
2 1/4 lbs	**ButterLike Baking Butter**	1020.00 g
3/5 lb	Butter	272.00 g
1/2 lb	Compressed yeast	227.00g
4 oz	Granulated Sugar	113.00 g
8 oz	**Granulated SugarLike**	227.00 g
4 oz	Salt	113.00 g
16 oz	Powdered skim milk	454.00 g
9 lbs	Bleached flour	4082.00 f
9 lbs	Unbleached flour	4082.00 g
5 1/2 qts	Water	5214.00 g

Directions

Mix together the softened **ButterLike** and butter until smooth. Cool. Mix yeast, lukewarm water, and sugar until yeast dissolves. Set aside for 10 minutes or until bubbles form. Add remaining ingredients except **ButterLike** mixture. Mix on low until combined. Dough should form loose ball. Add more flour if needed. Knead in mixer on second speed for 10 minutes. Roll out dough on a flour table to a 1/2-inch thick large rectangle. Spread 1/2 of **ButterLike** mixture onto the middle third of the dough. Fold one side over **ButterLike** mixture. Spread remaining **ButterLike** on top of folded dough. Fold remaining third of dough over newly applied **ButterLike** mixture. Place dough on a vegetable sprayed cookie sheet and cover with a large plastic bag. Leave in refrigerator until chilled. Remove from refrigerator and roll out until size of first rectangle. If running through a sheeter, spread a small amount of flour on top and bottom. Fold the same as before (1/3 over 1/3, then other 1/3 on top). Chill again. Repeat rolling and chilling step two more times. When rolled out for the last time cut and shape as desired. Each croissant should be 4 1/4 ounces. Place on vegetable sprayed cookie sheets. Raise more than double in size. Bake in a 350° oven for 20-25 minutes.

Cover and freeze the leftover rolled out croissant, raise and bake at a later date.

Nutrition Facts				
Serving Size	116 g			
Servings Per Recipe	136			
Amount per serving			High Fat/Sugar Comparison	
Calories		264	310	
Calories from fat		25	80	
	% Daily Value*		% Daily Value*	
Total Fat	2.5 g	**4%**	9 g	**14%**
Saturated Fat	1 g	**5%**	5 g	**25%**
Cholesterol	5 mg	**2%**	20 mg	**7%**
Sodium	390 mg	**16%**	430 mg	**18%**
Total Carbohydrate	53 g	**18%**	49 g	**16%**
Dietary Fiber	1 g	**4%**	0 g	**0%**
Sugars	1 g		3 g	
Other	1 g		0 g	
Protein	9 g		9 g	

*Percent of Daily Values on page a-22

Exchanges and 51 g Carbohydrates Per Serving					
Breads	3.1	Vegetables	0.0	Fruits	0.0
Meats	0.0	Milk	0.1	Fats	0.5

Raspberry-Filled Croissants

Raspberry-Filled Croissants

The Fat Quotient using ButterLike is 8% instead of 19%
71% less fat **73% less sugar**
32% less Calories

U.S.	Ingredients	Metric
Raspberry Filling:		
1 cup	**Granulated SugarLike**	200.00 g
5 cups	Fresh or frozen raspberries, thawed	615.00 g
2 Tbsp	Cornstarch	16.00 g
Croissants:		
1/2 cup + 1 Tbsp	**ButterLike Baking Butter**	127.00 g
2 1/4 Tbsp	Butter	34.00 g
1 oz	Compressed yeast	28.00 g
3 1/2 tsp	Granulated sugar	15.00 g
2 3/4 Tbsp	**Granulated SugarLike**	34.40 g
2 1/4 tsp	Salt	13.50 g
1 cup + 1/4 Tbsp	Powdered skim milk	56.00 g
3 3/4 cup	Bleached flour	514.00 g
3 3/4 cup	Unbleached flour	514.00 g
2 3/4 cup	Lukewarm water	652.00 g
Glaze:		
1/2 cup	**Powdered SugarLike**	53.00 g
1 Tbsp	Skim milk	15.00 g
1/4 tsp	Vanilla	1.20 g

Nutrition Facts				
Serving Size	120 g			
Servings Per Recipe	24			
Amount per serving			High Fat/Sugar Comparison	
Calories	225		330	
Calories from fat	20		70	
	% Daily Value*		% Daily Value*	
Total Fat	2 g	**3%**	7 g	**11%**
Saturated Fat	1 g	**5%**	4 g	**20%**
Cholesterol	5 mg	**2%**	20 mg	**7%**
Sodium	270 mg	**11%**	350 mg	**15%**
Total Carbohydrate	52 g	**17%**	59 g	**20%**
Dietary Fiber	5 g	**20%**	2 g	**8%**
Sugars	4 g		15 g	
Other	9 g		0 g	
Protein	7 g		7 g	

*Percent of Daily Values on page a-22

Exchanges and 38 g Carbohydrates Per Serving

Breads	2.3	Vegetables	0.0	Fruits	0.2
Meats	0.0	Milk	0.1	Fats	0.3

Directions

Filling: Combine **SugarLike**, raspberries, and cornstarch; set aside.

Croissants: Mix **ButterLike** and butter until smooth; cool. Mix yeast, water, and sugar until yeast dissolves. Set aside for 10 minutes or until bubbles form. Add remaining ingredients except **ButterLike** mixture. Mix on low until combined. Should form a loose ball. Add more flour if needed. Knead in mixer on second speed for 10 minutes. Roll out dough on a flour table until you have a large rectangle, 1/2-inch thick. Spread 1/2 of **ButterLike** mixture onto the middle third of the dough. Fold on side over **ButterLike** mixture. Spread remaining **ButterLike** on top of folded over dough. Fold remaining third of dough over newly applied **ButterLike** mixture. Place the dough on a vegetable sprayed cookie sheet and cover with a large plastic bag. Chill in refrigerator. After refrigerated, roll until dough is size of first rectangle. If running through a sheeter, spread a small amount of flour on top and bottom. Fold the same as before, 1/3 over 1/3 and then fold the other 1/3 on top. Refrigerate until chilled as before. Repeat rolling and chilling step two more times. When rolled out the last time, cut and shape as desired. Spread a small amount of **Raspberry Filling** within 1-inch of edges. Roll up and bend tips in. Each croissant should be about 4 1/4 ounces. Place on vegetable sprayed cookie sheets. Raise more than double in size. Bake in 350° oven for 20-25 minutes.

Cover and freeze leftover rolled out croissant; raise and bake at a later date.

Glaze: Combine **Powdered SugarLike**, skim milk, and vanilla; mix until smooth. Drizzle glaze over cooled croissants.

Delicious Cinnamon Danish Rolls

The Fat Quotient using ButterLike is 4% instead of 29%
88% less fat 80% less sugar
21% less Calories

U.S.	Ingredients	Metric
Dough:		
3/8 cup	**ButterLike Baking Butter**	85.00 g
1/2 cup	**Granulated SugarLike**	100.00 g
3/8 cup	Sugar	75.00 g
1 1/2 cups	Water	356.00 g
4 Tbsp	Yeast	44.00 g
5 1/2 cups	Bread flour	754.00 g
7/8 cup	Cake flour	95.00 g
3/8 cup	Non fat dry milk	26.00 g
2 1/8 tsp	Salt	13.00 g
1/2 cup	Egg whites	114.00 g
Glaze:		
1/8 cup	**ButterLike Baking Butter**	28.00 g
1 1/8 cup	**Powdered SugarLike**	118.00 g
1/8 cup	Skim milk	31.00 g
7/8 tsp	Vanilla	4.00 g
Cinnamon Mixture:		
1/3 cup	**ButterLike Baking Butter**	76.00 g
1/3 cup	**Granulated SugarLike**	67.00 g
2 3/8 tsp	Cinnamon	5.50 g

Nutrition Facts				
Serving Size	133 g			
Servings Per Recipe	15			
Amount per serving			High Fat/Sugar Comparison	
Calories		317	400	
Calories from fat		15	120	
	% Daily Value*		% Daily Value*	
Total Fat	1.5 g	**2%**	13 g	**20%**
Saturated Fat	0.5 g	**3%**	8 g	**40%**
Cholesterol	0 mg	**0%**	60 mg	**20%**
Sodium	410 mg	**17%**	470 mg	**20%**
Total Carbohydrate	74 g	**25%**	64 g	**21%**
Dietary Fiber	7 g	**28%**	2 g	**8%**
Sugars	5 g		25 g	
Other	15 g		0 g	
Protein	9 g		8 g	

*Percent of Daily Values on page a-22

Exchanges and 52 g Carbohydrates Per Serving

Breads	3.4	Vegetables	0.0	Fruits	0.0
Meats	0.1	Milk	0.1	Fats	0.1

Directions

Dough: Mix together sugar, 1 cup warm water, and dry yeast. Let sit until bubbly. Add the rest of the dough ingredients to the yeast mixture and mix together on low. (Thin **ButterLike Baking Butter** with 2 Tbsp water). Scrape down sides and knead for 10 minutes to develop gluten. Place dough on a vegetable sprayed sheet pan. Cover with plastic and place in the refrigerator. When cool, place on floured surface and roll out into a rectangle about 3/4-inch thick.

Cinnamon Danish Rolls: Spread dough with cinnamon mixture and roll into a log. Cut rolls into 1 inch slices approximately 4 1/2 ounces each. Place in a vegetable sprayed baking dish, proof until at least double in size, and bake in a pre heated 350° oven for 12-15 minutes or until lightly browned. Cover with Glaze.

Glaze: Combine **ButterLike Baking Butter**, **Powdered SugarLike**, skim milk, and vanilla; mix until smooth. Drizzle glaze over cooled Cinnamon Danish Rolls.

Variation

Danish rolled in Baking Butter: Thickly spread dough with 5/8 cup **Baking Butter** mixed with 1/8 cup water or 3/4 cup **ButterLike Saute Butter**. Fold into a three part book as shown. Cover with plastic and chill again in refrigerator. Roll out again about 3/4-inch thick. Spread on the same consistency of **Baking Butter** and form into desired shape. Proof, bake in a pre heated 350° oven until lightly brown. Cover with Glaze.

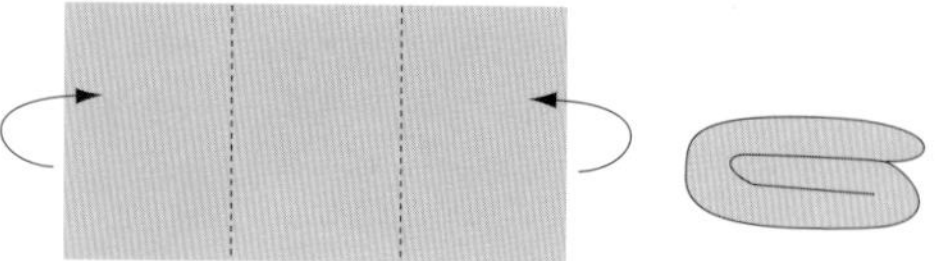

Cakes & Frostings

Holiday Pound Cake, page 48

Powdered SugarLike has had a big impact in making our cake frostings sugar free and delicious. It was easy making a great cake using **Granulated SugarLike**, and now your frostings are a breeze as well. I have enjoyed putting this section together and hope you enjoy the recipes as much as I have!

Tips on successful cakes and frostings using the Bateman Products

Frostings:

- Gradually add **SugarLike Products** to your recipe, mixing well between each addition.
- Foods using **Granulated SugarLike** and **Powdered SugarLike** don't require as much liquid as foods using regular sugar, so start out with the minimum liquid listed, then add as needed for your frosting consistency preference.
- It is important to have your cake cooled and ready to frost. Frostings get a glossy surface and stiffen up if allowed to set.

Cakes:

- Use quality, non-stick bakeware and cookware to prevent sticking and promote even cooking.
- Vegetable spray all pans, even non-stick bakeware.
- **Important:** Each egg called for in a recipe needs to equal 1/4 cup. The recipe may call for whole eggs, egg whites, egg substitutes or dried eggs, but when you measure them, each "egg" must equal 1/4 cup. If your egg is short, add enough water to equal 1/4 cup. Using egg whites can cause some textural changes in your baked goods.

Our new **EggLike™** is a natural, dried, whole egg substitute used in baking and cooking. Can be used to substitute any whole egg, 1/4 cup egg whites or egg substitutes in any recipe. See page a-12. **EggLike** is compatible with the recipes in this cookbook. **EggLike** increases volume in cakes and baked products over egg substitutes and egg whites.

- Check the low altitude cooking chart on page a-17 for altitudes other than 5000 feet.
- **Mixing steps:**
  - Soften premeasured **Baking Butter** in the microwave for 10-30 seconds. If you do not have a microwave or are mixing large quantities, place the cold **Baking Butter** in a mixing bowl and mix until lump free and smooth.
  - Beat eggs for a couple of minutes first to incorporate more air into the cake. This helps the cake to be light and fluffy.
  - Add softened **Baking Butter** or **Saute Butter** to the sugar or **SugarLike** mix, then add the beaten eggs, mixing until smooth.
  - Add the rest of the ingredients and mix until lump free. Because **ButterLike** contains only 7% fat, it does not incorporate air when beaten, so mix only until ingredients are combined and lump free
- Once **SugarLike** is mixed with other ingredients, use immediately. Lumps may form if mixture is allowed to sit.
- Cooking times are sometimes slightly longer than when using real fat and sugar. Test with a toothpick or knife to check for doneness.
- Do not overcook. Cook until done, not until as brown as normal.
- Store foods in an airtight container.

Banana Praline Spice Layer Cake, page 47

Grandma's Applesauce Cake

The Fat Quotient using ButterLike is 8% instead of 24%
80% less fat **79% less sugar**
42% less Calories

U.S.	Ingredients	Metric
1/2 cup	**ButterLike Baking Butter**	114.00 g
2 cups	**Granulated SugarLike**	400.00 g
3/4 cup	Raisins	109.00 g
1 cup	Hot water	237.00 g
1/4 cup	Egg whites	57.00 g
1 1/2 cup	Applesauce	383.00 g
2 3/4 cup	All-purpose flour	344.00 g
1/4 cup	Chopped walnuts	31.00 g
1/2 tsp	Salt	3.00 g
1/2 tsp	Ground cinnamon	1.00 g
1/2 tsp	Ground cloves	1.00 g
1/2 tsp	Ground nutmeg	1.00 g
2 tsp	Baking soda	9.00 g
1/3 cup	Boiling water	79.00

Directions

Place raisins and hot water in a small bowl; set aside. In a large mixing bowl, combine remaining ingredients except soda and water. Dissolve baking soda in boiling water; add to batter. Mix well. Scrape bowl. Drain raisins and fold into batter. Pour into baking pan. Bake at 300° for 40 minutes.

Nutrition Facts				
Serving Size	118 g			
Servings Per Recipe	15			
Amount per serving			High Fat/Sugar Comparison	
Calories	214		370	
Calories from fat	20		90	
	% Daily Value*		% Daily Value*	
Total Fat	2g	**3%**	10 g	**15%**
Saturated Fat	0 g	**0%**	4.5 g	23%
Cholesterol	0 mg	**0%**	30 mg	**10%**
Sodium	290 mg	**12%**	320 mg	**13%**
Total Carbohydrate	59 g	**20%**	68 g	**23%**
Dietary Fiber	8 g	**32%**	1 g	**4%**
Sugars	10 g		48g	
Other	19 g		0 g	
Protein	4 g		4 g	

*Percent of Daily Values on page a-22

Exchanges and 32 g Carbohydrates Per Serving

Breads	1.4	Vegetables	0.0	Fruits	0.7
Meats	0.1	Milk	0.0	Fats	0.3

If desired, dust top with **Powdered SugarLike.** Serve warm or cold. Store in an airtight container.

Blackberry Jam Cake

The Fat Quotient using ButterLike is 12% instead of 47%
86% less fat **52% less sugar**
42% less Calories

U.S.	Ingredients	Metric
1 cup	**ButterLike Baking Butter**	227.00 g
1 cup	**Granulated SugarLike**	200.00 g
1 can	Crushed pineapple with unsweetened juice (8 oz)	227.00 g
1 cup	Raisins	145.00 g
1 cup	Egg whites	227.00 g
2/3 cup	Non fat buttermilk	163.00 g
2 1/2 cup	All-purpose flour	313.00 g
1/3 cup	Unsweetened cocoa	79.00 g
1 tsp	Baking soda	4.60 g
1 tsp	Ground cinnamon	2.30 g
1 tsp	Ground nutmeg	2.20 g
1/2 tsp	Ground cloves	1.00 g
1/4 cup	Chopped pecans	27.00 g
1 1/2 cup	Fresh or frozen blackberries	216.00 g

Nutrition Facts				
Serving Size	131 g			
Servings Per Recipe	14			
Amount per serving			High Fat/Sugar Comparison	
Calories		231	400	
Calories from fat		25	190	
	% Daily Value*		% Daily Value*	
Total Fat	3 g	**5%**	21 g	**32%**
Saturated Fat	0.5 g	**3%**	10 g	**50%**
Cholesterol	5 mg	**2%**	100 mg	**33%**
Sodium	200 mg	**8%**	270 mg	**11%**
Total Carbohydrate	55 g	**18%**	47 g	**18%**
Dietary Fiber	6 g	**24%**	3 g	**12%**
Sugars	12 g		25 g	
Other	11 g		0 g	
Protein	6 g		6 g	

*Percent of Daily Values on page a-22

Exchanges and 38 g Carbohydrates Per Serving					
Breads	1.7	Vegetables	0.0	Fruits	0.8
Meats	0.2	Milk	0.1	Fats	0.5

Directions

Soak the raisins in the crushed pineapple and juice for several hours or overnight. (This can be sped up by placing in microwave for 2 minutes on high and setting aside for 15 minutes.) You can use 1 cup of store bought jam, but it is not sugar free. Mix together the blackberries and 1/2 cup **SugarLike** in a small saucepan to make your own jam. Heat and stir until boiling. Set aside and cool. In a large mixing bowl, mix the softened **ButterLike**, 1 cup **Granulated SugarLike**, and egg whites until smooth. Add the jam, buttermilk, flour, cocoa, soda, cinnamon, nutmeg, and cloves. Mix until combined and lump free. Stir in the pecans, raisins, and pineapple. Pour into two, vegetable sprayed 9-inch cake pans. Bake at 350° for 50 minutes or until cakes test done. Cool in pans 10 minutes and remove from pans.

Blackberry Jam Cake

Chocolate Nougat Cake

The Fat Quotient using **ButterLike** is **11%** instead of **29%**
74% less fat **94% less sugar**
45% less Calories

U.S.	Ingredients	Metric
1/3 cup	**ButterLike Baking Butter**	75.00 g
1 1/4 cup	**Granulated SugarLike**	276.00 g
2 Tbsp	**ButterLike Saute Butter**	28.00 g
1/2 cup	Egg whites, divided	114.00 g
6 Tbsp	Cocoa	89.00 g
1 1/3 cup	All-purpose flour	166.00 g
1 1/4 tsp	Baking powder	5.00 g
1/2 tsp	Salt	3.00 g
3/4 cup + 2 Tbsp	Skim milk	216.00 g
1/4 cup	Nuts, finely chopped	33.00 g
Frosting:		
1 1/2 cup	**Granulated SugarLike**	300.00 g
1/3 cup	Cold water	78.00 g
1/4 cup	Egg whites	57.00 g
1/4 tsp	Cream of tarter	.75 g
1 tsp	Vanilla	4.70 g

Nutrition Facts				
Serving Size	120 g			
Servings Per Recipe	12			
Amount per serving			High Fat/Sugar Comparison	
Calories	203		370	
Calories from fat	20		110	
	% Daily Value*		% Daily Value*	
Total Fat	2.5 g	**4%**	12 g	**18%**
Saturated Fat	0 g	**0%**	6 g	**30%**
Cholesterol	0 mg	**0%**	35 mg	**12%**
Sodium	200 mg	**8%**	210 mg	**9%**
Total Carbohydrate	64 g	**21%**	62 g	**21%**
Dietary Fiber	12 g	**48%**	2 g	**8%**
Sugars	3 g		48 g	
Other	35 g		0 g	
Protein	5 g		4 g	

*Percent of Daily Values on page a-22

Exchanges and 17 g Carbohydrates Per Serving					
Breads	1.0	Vegetables	0.0	Fruits	0.0
Meats	0.2	Milk	0.1	Fats	0.4

Directions

In a large mixing bowl, mix softened **ButterLike Baking Butter**, 3/4 cup plus 2 Tbsp **SugarLike**, and 1/4 cup egg whites until smooth. Add cocoa and **Saute Butter**; mix. Sift together flour, baking powder, and salt; add alternately with milk to mixture. Stir in nuts. Beat remaining egg whites with remaining **SugarLike** until stiff peaks form; fold gently into batter. Pour into two vegetable sprayed and floured 8-inch baking pans. Bake at 350° for 30-35 minutes. Cool in pans on a rack for 10 minutes before removing from pans. Cool completely.

Frosting: Combine all ingredients except vanilla in the top of a double boiler. Beat on low for 30 seconds. Cook over boiling water for 7 minutes, beating constantly on high until stiff peaks form. Remove from heat and add vanilla. Beat 2-3 minutes or until frosting has a spreading consistency. Frost cake.

Chocolate Nougat Cake and Seven-Minute Frosting, page 58

Gingerbread

The Fat Quotient using ButterLike is 5% instead of 40%
91% less fat **31% less sugar**
34% less Calories

U.S.	Ingredients	Metric
1/2 cup	**ButterLike Baking Butter**, softened	114.00 g
1/4 cup	**Brown SugarLike**	50.00 g
1 1/2 cup	All-purpose flour	173.00 g
3/4 tsp	Cinnamon	1.70 g
3/4 tsp	Ginger	1.40 g
1/2 tsp	Baking powder	2.00 g
1/2 tsp	Baking soda	2.30 g
1/4 cup	Egg whites	57.00 g
1/2 cup	Light molasses	160.00 g
1/2 cup	Water	

Directions

In a bowl combine flour, cinnamon, ginger, baking powder, and baking soda; set aside. In another mixing bowl beat **ButterLike**, **SugarLike**, egg whites, and molasses until smooth. Add dry mixture and water alternately to beaten mixture, beating on low after each addition. Pour batter into a vegetable sprayed 9x1 1/2-inch round baking pan. Bake at 350° for 35-40 minutes. Cool for 30 minutes on wire rack. Serve warm.

Nutrition Facts				
Serving Size	75 g			
Servings Per Recipe	9			
Amount per serving			High Fat/Sugar Comparison	
Calories	166		250	
Calories from fat	10		100	
	% Daily Value*		% Daily Value*	
Total Fat	1 g	**2%**	11 g	**17%**
Saturated Fat	0 g	**0%**	3 g	**15%**
Cholesterol	0 mg	**0%**	25 mg	**8%**
Sodium	160 mg	**7%**	110 mg	**5%**
Total Carbohydrate	40 g	**13%**	33 g	**11%**
Dietary Fiber	2 g	**8%**	1 g	**4%**
Sugars	11 g		16 g	
Other	5 g		0 g	
Protein	3 g		3 g	

*Percent of Daily Values on page a-22

Exchanges and 33 g Carbohydrates Per Serving					
Breads	1.4	Vegetables	0.0	Fruits	0.0
Meats	0.1	Milk	0.0	Fats	0.2

Gingerbread

Banana Praline Spice Layer Cake

The Fat Quotient using ButterLike is 10% instead of 56%
91% less fat **75% less sugar**
55% less Calories

U.S.	Ingredients	Metric
3/4 cup	**Granulated SugarLike**	150.00 g
3/4 cup	**Brown SugarLike**	150.00 g
3/4 cup	**ButterLike Baking Butter**, softened	170.00 g
3/4 cup	Egg whites	170.00 g
2 1/4 cup	All-purpose flour	259.00 g
2 1/2 tsp	Baking powder	10.00 g
1 1/2 tsp	Nutmeg	3.30 g
1/2 tsp	Baking soda	2.30 g
1/2 tsp	Cinnamon	1.20 g
1/4 tsp	Salt	1.50 g
1 cup	Fat free sour cream	256.00 g
1 1/2 tsp	Vanilla extract	7.40 g
Topping:		
2/3 cup	**Brown SugarLike**	133.00 g
6 Tbsp	**ButterLike Saute Butter**	84.00 g
1/2 tsp	Nutmeg	1.10 g
1/4 tsp	Cinnamon	.58 g
1 1/2 tsp	Vanilla extract	7.40 g
1/4 cup	Pecans, chopped	28.00 g
1 Tbsp	Water	15.00 g
2 tsp	Lemon juice	10.00 g
3 medium	Firm, ripe bananas, sliced thin	573.00 g
Frosting:		
3 Tbsp	**Brown SugarLike**	38.00 g
2 cups	Fat free whipped topping	144.00 g
1 tsp	Nutmeg	2.20 g
1/2 tsp	Cinnamon	1.20 g

Nutrition Facts				
Serving Size	185 g			
Servings Per Recipe	12			
Amount per serving			High Fat/Sugar Comparison	
Calories	329		720	
Calories from fat	35		400	
		% Daily Value*		% Daily Value*
Total Fat	4 g	**6%**	45 g	**69%**
Saturated Fat	1 g	**5%**	24 g	**120%**
Cholesterol	5 mg	**2%**	160 mg	**53%**
Sodium	290 mg	**12%**	420 mg	**18%**
Total Carbohydrate	84 g	**28%**	72 g	**24%**
Dietary Fiber	12 g	**48%**	3 g	**12%**
Sugars	12 g		48 g	
Other	29 g		0 g	
Protein	7 g		7 g	

*Percent of Daily Values on page a-22

Exchanges and 43 g Carbohydrates Per Serving

Breads	1.9	Vegetables	0.0	Fruits	0.6
Meats	0.2	Milk	0.2	Fats	0.7

Directions

In a large bowl blend **SugarLikes**, **ButterLike**, and egg whites until smooth. Add remaining cake ingredients; beat until smooth. Pour into 2 vegetable sprayed and floured 9-inch round cake pans. Bake at 350° for 25-30 minutes or until cakes spring back when touched lightly in the center.

Topping: In a small bowl blend **Brown SugarLike**, **ButterLike**, nutmeg, cinnamon, and vanilla. In another small bowl coat pecans with 3 Tbsp **Brown SugarLike** mixture. Set aside. Stir water and lemon juice into remaining **Brown SugarLike** mixture. Arrange bananas over cake layers. Pour and spread **Brown SugarLike** mixture evenly over bananas. Place 1 cake at a time on vegetable sprayed cookie sheet. Broil 4-6 inches from heat for 30-90 seconds or until topping is bubbly. Cool cakes 16 minutes. Remove from pans. Cool, banana side up, on wire cooling racks. Place **SugarLike** coated pecans in a single layer on a vegetable sprayed cookie sheet. Bake at 350° for 5-10 minutes or until pecans are slightly toasted and **SugarLike** coating begins to harden. Cool completely.

Frosting: Combine all ingredients. Stir until **SugarLike** dissolves. Assemble cake by placing 1 layer, banana side up, on serving plate; top with half of the frosting. Sprinkle with half of the coated pecans. Top with remaining cake layer, banana side up. Spoon remaining frosting over bananas. Garnish with remaining coated pecans. Store in refrigerator.

Note to Diabetics: Reduce sugar by substituting whipped topping with 1 cup light whipping cream and 1/4 cup **Granulated SugarLike**. Whip cream until soft peaks form. Add **SugarLike**. The fat grams will increase to 10.3 grams per serving.

Hawaiian Tropical Cake with Frosting

The Fat Quotient using **ButterLike** is **8%** instead of **16%**
70% less fat **93% less sugar**
38% less Calories

U.S.	Ingredients	Metric
2 cups	**Granulated SugarLike**	400.00 g
2 cups	All-purpose flour	250.00 g
1/2 cup	Egg whites	114.00 g
2 cups	Crushed pineapple, unsweetened	492.00 g
1/4 cup	Walnuts, chopped	31.00 g
1 tsp	Baking soda	4.60 g
Frosting:		
2 cups	**Powdered SugarLike**	210.00 g
2 Tbsp	**ButterLike Baking Butter**, softened	28.00 g
2 Tbsp	Skim milk	31.00 g
1/2 tsp	Vanilla extract	2.50 g

Directions

Mix the **SugarLike** and egg whites until smooth. Add the remaining ingredients and mix until combined. Pour into a vegetable sprayed 9x13-inch cake pan and bake at 350° for 45 minutes.

Nutrition Facts				
Serving Size	104 g			
Servings Per Recipe	15			
Amount per serving			High Fat/Sugar Comparison	
Calories	174		280	
Calories from fat	15		45	
	% Daily Value*		% Daily Value*	
Total Fat	1.5 g	**2%**	5 g	**8%**
Saturated Fat	0 g	**0%**	1.5 g	**8%**
Cholesterol	0 mg	**0%**	35 mg	**12%**
Sodium	105 mg	**4%**	110 mg	**5%**
Total Carbohydrate	57 g	**19%**	56 g	**19%**
Dietary Fiber	11 g	**44%**	1 g	**4%**
Sugars	3 g		41 g	
Other	31 g		0 g	
Protein	3 g		4 g	

*Percent of Daily Values on page a-22

Exchanges and 15 g Carbohydrates Per Serving

Breads	0.9	Vegetables	0.0	Fruits	0.2
Meats	0.1	Milk	0.0	Fats	0.3

Frosting: Combine ingredients and frost on completely cooled cake.

Holiday Pound Cake

The Fat quotient using **ButterLike** is **11%** instead of **51%**
89% less fat **86% less sugar**
50% less Calories

U.S.	Ingredients	Metric
1 cup	**ButterLike Baking Butter**	227.00 g
1 1/2 cup	**Granulated SugarLike**	300.00 g
1 pkg	Fat free cream cheese (8 oz)	227.00 g
1 cup	Egg whites	227.00 g
1 1/2 tsp	Vanilla extract	7.00 g
1 1/2 tsp	Baking powder	6.00 g
2 1/4 cup	All-purpose flour	259.00 g
1/2 tsp	Salt	3.00 g
3/4 cup	Maraschino cherries, well drained	113.00 g
1/3 cup	Chopped pecans	36.00 g
Glaze:		
1 1/2	**Powdered SugarLike**	158.00 g
2 tsp	Skim milk	31.00 g
1 Tbsp	Pecans	7.00 g
1 Tbsp	Maraschino cherries	28.00 g

Nutrition Facts				
Serving Size	136 g			
Servings Per Recipe	12			
Amount per serving			High Fat/Sugar Comparison	
Calories	274		550	
Calories from fat	35		280	
	% Daily Value*		% Daily Value*	
Total Fat	4 g	**5%**	31 g	**48%**
Saturated Fat	1 g	**5%**	16 g	**80%**
Cholesterol	3 mg	**2%**	135 mg	**45%**
Sodium	370 mg	**15%**	400 mg	**17%**
Total Carbohydrate	73 g	**23%**	61 g	**20%**
Dietary Fiber	10 g	**40%**	1 g	**4%**
Sugars	6 g		42 g	
Other	30 g		0 g	
Protein	8 g		7 g	

*Percent of Daily Values on page a-22

Directions

Mix softened **ButterLike**, **SugarLike**, and egg whites until smooth. Add vanilla. Sift dry ingredients; stir into creamed mixture. Fold in cherries and 1/4 cup nuts. Sprinkle remaining nuts into a vegetable sprayed 10-inch fluted tube pan. Spoon batter into pan. Bake at 325° for about 70 minutes or until cake tests done. Cool cake in pan 5 minutes on wire rack before removing from pan.

Exchanges and 33 g Carbohydrates Per Serving					
Breads	1.8	Vegetables	0.0	Fruits	0.3
Meats	0.3	Milk	0.1	Fats	0.7

Glaze: Combine **SugarLike** and milk; drizzle over cake. Garnish with cherries and pecans.

Moist Chocolate Cake with Frosting

The Fat Quotient using **ButterLike** is **7%** instead of **52%**
93% less fat **92% less sugar**
51% less Calories

U.S.	Ingredients	Metric
1 cup	**ButterLike Baking Butter**	227.00 g
2 cups	**Granulated SugarLike**	400.00 g
2 cups	All-purpose flour	250.00 g
1 tsp	Salt	6.00 g
1 tsp	Baking powder	4.00 g
2 tsp	Baking soda	9.20 g
3/4 cup	Unsweetened cocoa	179.00 g
1 cup	Hot water	237.00 g
1 cup	Skim milk, sour	245.00 g
1/2 cup	Egg whites	114.00 g
1 tsp	Vanilla extract	5.00 g
Frosting:		
1 cup	**ButterLike Baking Butter**	227.00 g
1 cup	**Granulated SugarLike**	200.00 g
1 cup	Skim milk	245.00 g
5 Tbsp	All-purpose flour	39.00 g
1 tsp	Vanilla extract	5.00 g

Directions

Mix softened **Baking Butter**, **SugarLike**, egg whites, and vanilla until smooth. Add remaining ingredients to the mixture. Mix at medium speed until smooth. Pour into two vegetable sprayed and floured 9-inch cake pans (or two 8-inch cake pans and six muffin cups). Bake at 325° for 25-30 minutes.

Nutrition Facts				
Serving Size	199 g			
Servings Per Recipe	12			
Amount per serving			High Fat/Sugar Comparison	
Calories	316		640	
Calories from fat	25		330	
	% Daily Value*		% Daily Value*	
Total Fat	2.5 g	**4%**	37 g	**57%**
Saturated Fat	1 g	**5%**	9 g	**45%**
Cholesterol	5 mg	**2%**	65 mg	**22%**
Sodium	640 mg	**27%**	560 mg	**23%**
Total Carbohydrate	92 g	**31%**	72 g	**24%**
Dietary Fiber	13 g	**52%**	1 g	4%
Sugars	4 g		52 g	
Other	37 g		0 g	
Protein	6 g		6 g	

*Percent of Daily Values on page a-22

Exchanges and 42 g Carbohydrates Per Serving					
Breads	2.5	Vegetables	0.0	Fruits	0.0
Meats	0.1	Milk	0.2	Fats	0.4

Frosting: Combine milk and flour in a saucepan; cook until thick. Cover and refrigerate. In another bowl, beat softened **ButterLike**, **SugarLike**, and vanilla until creamy. Add chilled mixture; beat for 10 minutes. Frost cooled cake.

Variation: For Moist Chocolate Mocha Cake, substitute 1 cup hot coffee for 1 cup hot water.

Angel Food Cake

The Fat Quotient using ButterLike is 0% instead of 0%
0% less fat **96% less sugar**
33% less Calories

U.S.	Ingredients	Metric
1 1/2 cup	**Powdered SugarLike**	158.00 g
1 cup	**Granulated SugarLike**	200.00 g
1 1/2 cup	Egg whites	341.00 g
1 cup	All-purpose flour	115.00 g
1 1/2 tsp	Cream of tartar	4.50 g
1 tsp	Vanilla extract	5.00 g

Nutrition Facts				
Serving Size	69 g			
Servings Per Recipe	12			
Amount per serving			High Fat/Sugar Comparison	
Calories	114		170	
Calories from fat	0		0	
	% Daily Value*		% Daily Value*	
Total Fat	0 g	**0%**	0 g	**0%**
Saturated Fat	0 g	**0%**	0 g	**0%**
Cholesterol	0 mg	**0%**	0 mg	**0%**
Sodium	45 mg	**2%**	45 mg	**2%**
Total Carbohydrate	39 g	**12%**	37 g	**12%**
Dietary Fiber	8 g	**32%**	0 g	**0%**
Sugars	1 g		28 g	
Other	23 g		0 g	
Protein	4 g		4 g	

*Percent of Daily Values on page a-22

Exchanges and 8 g Carbohydrates Per Serving					
Breads	0.5	Vegetables	0.0	Fruits	0.5
Meats	0.4	Milk	0.0	Fats	0.1

Directions

In large mixing bowl, allow egg whites to stand at room temperature for 30 minutes. Meanwhile, sift **Powdered SugarLike** and flour together 3 times; set aside. Add cream of tartar and vanilla to egg whites. Beat with an electric mixer on medium speed until soft peaks form. Gradually add **Granulated SugarLike**, about 2 tablespoons at a time, beating until stiff speaks form. Sift 1/4 of the dry mixture over beaten egg whites, fold in gently. Repeat, folding in remaining dry mixture by fourths. Pour into an ungreased 10-inch tube pan. Gently cut through batter to remove any large air pockets. Bake on the lowest rack in a 350° oven for 40-45 minutes or until top springs back when lightly touched. Immediately invert cake (leave in pan); cool thoroughly. Loosen sides of cake from pan; remove cake.

Maple Nut Angel Food Cake

The Fat quotient using ButterLike is 10% instead of 20%
70% less fat **97% less sugar**
43% less Calories

U.S.	Ingredients	Metric
3/4 cup	**Brown SugarLike**	150 .00 g
1 1/4 cup	Cake flour	136.00 g
1 1/2 cup	Egg whites	341.00 g
1/4 tsp	Salt	2.00 g
1 tsp	Vanilla extract	5.00 g
1/4 tsp	Maple extract	2.00 g
1 1/2 tsp	Cream of tartar	6.00 g
1 cup	**Granulated SugarLike**	200.00 g
1/4 cup	Walnuts, chopped	30.00 g

Nutrition Facts				
Serving Size	73 g			
Servings Per Recipe	12			
Amount per serving			High Fat/Sugar Comparison	
Calories	131		230	
Calories from fat	15		45	
	% Daily Value*		% Daily Value*	
Total Fat	1.5 g	**2%**	5 g	**8%**
Saturated Fat	0 g	**0%**	0 g	**0%**
Cholesterol	0 mg	**0%**	0 mg	**0%**
Sodium	150 mg	**6%**	135 mg	**6%**
Total Carbohydrate	39 g	**313%**	41 g	**14%**
Dietary Fiber	7 g	**28%**	0 g	**0%**
Sugars	1 g		29 g	
Other	21 g		0 g	
Protein	4 g		5 g	

*Percent of Daily Values on page a-22

Directions

Combine flour and **Brown SugarLike**; set aside. In a large mixing bowl beat egg whites, salt, and cream of tartar until soft peaks form. Add vanilla and maple flavoring. Add **Granulated SugarLike** a little at a time, beating until stiff. Gradually flour mixture, about 1/4 at a time. Spoon half the batter into an ungreased angel food cake pan; sprinkle with nuts. Cut through batter with knife; spoon in remaining batter. Bake at 375° for about 35 minutes. Cool inverted on a wire rack.

Exchanges and 11 g Carbohydrates Per Serving					
Breads	0.6	Vegetables	0.0	Fruits	0.0
Meats	0.4	Milk	0.0	Fats	0.3

Prune Cake

The Fat quotient using **ButterLike** is **12%** instead of **53%**
89% less fat **90% less sugar**
53% less Calories

U.S.	Ingredients	Metric
1 cup	**ButterLike Baking Butter**	227.00 g
1 1/2 cup	**Granulated SugarLike**	300.00 g
3/4 cup	Egg whites	170.00 g
2 cups	All-purpose flour	250.00 g
1 tsp	Baking soda	5.00 g
1 tsp	Ground nutmeg	2.00 g
1 tsp	Ground cinnamon	2.00 g
1 tsp	Salt	6.00 g
1/2 cup	Fat free buttermilk	123.00 g
1 tsp	Vanilla extract	5.00 g
1 cup	Prunes, cut up and cooked	227.00 g
1/4 cup	Walnuts, chopped	31.00 g
Topping:		
1/2 cup	**ButterLike Baking Butter**	114.00 g
3/4 cup	**Granulated SugarLike**	150.00 g
1/3 cup	Fat free buttermilk	82.00 g
1 tsp	Vanilla extract	5.00 g
1/2 tsp	Baking soda	2.00 g

Nutrition Facts				
Serving Size	113 g			
Servings Per Recipe	15			
Amount per serving			High Fat/Sugar Comparison	
Calories	218		460	
Calories from fat	25		250	
	% Daily Value*		% Daily Value*	
Total Fat	3 g	**5%**	27 g	**42%**
Saturated Fat	1 g	**5%**	7 g	**35%**
Cholesterol	5 mg	**2%**	60 mg	**20%**
Sodium	410 mg	**17%**	370 mg	**15%**
Total Carbohydrate	59 g	**20%**	48 g	**15%**
Dietary Fiber	8 g	**32%**	1 g	**4%**
Sugars	3 g		31 g	
Other	22 g		0 g	
Protein	4 g		6 g	

*Percent of Daily Values on page a-22

Exchanges and 29 g Carbohydrates Per Serving					
Breads	1.6	Vegetables	0.0	Fruits	0.2
Meats	0.2	Milk	0.0	Fats	0.5

Directions

Mix the softened **ButterLike**, **SugarLike**, and egg whites until smooth. Add the remaining cake ingredients. Mix until combined. Pour into a vegetable sprayed 13x9-inch pan and bake at 350° for 45-50 minutes.

Topping: Combine all ingredients in a saucepan and bring to boil. Boil 2 minutes and pour over hot cake.

Prize-Winning Cranberry Coffee Cake

The Fat Quotient using ButterLike is 4% instead of 24%
90% less fat **96% less sugar**
41% less Calories

U.S.	Ingredients	Metric
Cranberry Sauce:		
1/3 cup	**Granulated SugarLike**	67.00 g
1 cup	Cranberries, fresh or frozen	110.00 g
Cake:		
1/2 cup	**ButterLike Baking Butter**	114.00 g
1 1/2 cup	**Granulated SugarLike**	300.00 g
1/2 cup	Egg whites	114.00 g
1 tsp	Almond extract	14.00 g
1 cup	Non fat yogurt	227.00 g
2 cups	All-purpose flour	250.00 g
1 1/4 tsp	Baking powder	5.00 g
1/2 tsp	Baking soda	2.30 g
Glaze:		
1 cup	**Powdered SugarLike**	200.00 g
1/2 tsp	Almond extract	8.50 g
1 Tbsp	Skim milk	15.00 g

Nutrition Facts				
Serving Size	119 g			
Servings Per Recipe	12			
Amount per serving			High Fat/Sugar Comparison	
Calories	221		370	
Calories from fat	10		90	
	% Daily Value*		% Daily Value*	
Total Fat	1 g	2%	10 g	18%
Saturated Fat	0 g	0%	6 g	30%
Cholesterol	0 mg	0%	60 mg	20%
Sodium	170 mg	7%	190 mg	8%
Total Carbohydrate	71 g	24%	67 g	22%
Dietary Fiber	12 g	48%	1 g	4%
Sugars	2 g		48 g	
Other	34 g		0 g	
Protein	5 g		4 g	

*Percent of Daily Values on page a-22

Exchanges and 24 g Carbohydrates Per Serving

Breads	1.4	Vegetables	0.0	Fruits	0.1
Meats	0.1	Milk	0.1	Fats	0.1

Directions

Cranberry Sauce: Grind cranberries, then mix with **SugarLike**. Heat in microwave for 2 minutes. Set aside, let cool.

Cake: Stir softened **ButterLike**, **SugarLike**, egg whites, and almond extract together with a spoon until smooth. Add remaining ingredients. Mix until combined. Pour half of the mixture into a vegetable sprayed bundt pan. Spread cranberry sauce on top of mixture. Spread remaining cake dough on top of sauce. Bake at 350° for 55-60 minutes. Let cool in pan for 10 minutes.

Glaze: Combine **Powdered SugarLike**, almond extract, and milk. Drizzle over cooled cake.

Hot-Milk Sponge Cake

The Fat Quotient using ButterLike is 4% instead of 23%
89% less fat **95% less sugar**
39% less Calories

U.S.	Ingredients	Metric
1 cup	**Granulated SugarLike**	200.00 g
2 Tbsp	**ButterLike Saute Butter**	28.00 g
1 cup	All-purpose flour	115.00 g
1 tsp	Baking powder	4.00 g
1/2 cup	Egg whites	114.00 g
1/2 cup	Skim milk	123.00 g

Directions

Stir together flour and baking powder; set aside. In another bowl, blend egg whites until frothy. Add **SugarLike**, beating on medium 4-5 minutes until light and fluffy. Add dry mixture; beat on low-medium just until combined. In a small saucepan heat and stir **ButterLike** and milk; add to batter, beating until combined. Pour batter into a vegetable sprayed 9x9x2-inch baking pan. Bake in a 350° oven for 20-25 minutes or until toothpick comes out clean. Cool cake in pan on wire rack. Dust with **Powdered SugarLike** or frost.

Exchanges and 11 g Carbohydrates Per Serving					
Breads	0.7	Vegetables	0.0	Fruits	0.0
Meats	0.2	Milk	0.1	Fats	0.1

Nutrition Facts				
Serving Size	65 g			
Servings Per Recipe	9			
Amount per serving			High Fat/Sugar Comparison	
Calories		110	180	
Calories from fat		5	40	
	% Daily Value*		% Daily Value*	
Total Fat	0.5 g	**1%**	4.5 g	**7%**
Saturated Fat	0 g	**0%**	2.5 g	**13%**
Cholesterol	0 mg	**0%**	55 mg	**18%**
Sodium	75 mg	**3%**	90 mg	**4%**
Total Carbohydrate	33 g	**11%**	33 g	**11%**
Dietary Fiber	6 g	**24%**	0 g	**0%**
Sugars	1 g		22 g	
Other	16 g		g	
Protein	3 g		3 g	

*Percent of Daily Values on page a-22

Cream Cheese Pound Cake

The Fat quotient using **ButterLike** is **8%** instead of **48%**
91% less fat **96% less sugar**
49% less Calories

U.S.	Ingredients	Metric
1 1/2 cup	**ButterLike Baking Butter**	341.00 g
3 cups	**SugarLike Granulated Sugar**	600.00 g
1 pkg	Non fat cream cheese (8 oz)	227.00 g
1 cup	Egg whites	227.00 g
2 large	Eggs	100.00 g
3 cups	All-purpose flour	345.00 g
1 1/2 tsp	Baking powder	6.00 g

Directions

In a large mixing bowl mix the egg whites until frothy. Stir in the softened **ButterLike**, **SugarLike**, room temperature cream cheese, and eggs; mix until smooth. Add flour and baking powder and mix until combined. Pour into a vegetable sprayed 10-inch tube pan. Bake at 325° for 1 hour and 20 minutes or until cake tests done. Cool in pan 10 minutes before removing. Cake ages and freezes well. Keep in air tight container. Great served warm with ice cream.

Nutrition Facts				
Serving Size	154 g			
Servings Per Recipe	4			
Amount per serving			High Fat/Sugar Comparison	
Calories		318	620	
Calories from fat		25	300	
	% Daily Value*		% Daily Value*	
Total Fat	3 g	**5%**	33 g	**51%**
Saturated Fat	1 g	**5%**	20 g	**100%**
Cholesterol	40 mg	**13%**	190 mg	**63%**
Sodium	325 mg	**14%**	360 mg	**15%**
Total Carbohydrate	88 g	**29%**	73 g	**24%**
Dietary Fiber	13 g	**52%**	1 g	**4%**
Sugars	2 g		49 g	
Other	37 g		0 g	
Protein	10 g		8 g	

*Percent of Daily Values on page a-22

Exchanges and 51 g Carbohydrates Per Serving					
Breads	2.5	Vegetables	0.0	Fruits	0.0
Meats	0.4	Milk	0.1	Fats	0.5

Red Velvet Cake

The Fat Quotient using ButterLike is 6% instead of 42%
92% less fat **88% less sugar**
48% less Calories

U.S.	Ingredients	Metric
1/2 cup	**ButterLike Baking Butter**	114.00 g
1 1/4 cup	**Granulated SugarLike**	250.00 g
1/2 cup	Egg whites	114.00 g
1/4 cup	Red food coloring	113.00 g
3 Tbsp	Unsweetened cocoa	45.00 g
2 1/4 cup	All-purpose flour	281.00 g
1 tsp	Baking soda	4.60 g
1/2 tsp	Salt	3.00 g
1 cup	Non fat buttermilk	245.00 g
1 Tbsp	Vanilla extract	15.00 g
1 Tbsp	Vinegar	15.00 g
Frosting:		
3/4 cup	**ButterLike Baking Butter**	170.00 g
1 1/2 cup	**Granulated SugarLike**	300.00 g
1 cup	Skim milk	245.00 g
5 Tbsp	All-purpose flour	39.00 g
2 tsp	Vanilla extract	10.00 g

Nutrition Facts				
Serving Size	164 g			
Servings Per Recipe	12			
Amount per serving			High Fat/Sugar Comparison	
Calories	290		560	
Calories from fat	15		240	
	% Daily Value*		% Daily Value*	
Total Fat	2 g	**3%**	26 g	**40%**
Saturated Fat	1 g	**5%**	12 g	**60%**
Cholesterol	5 mg	**2%**	75 mg	**25%**
Sodium	380 mg	**16%**	400 mg	**17%**
Total Carbohydrate	84 g	**28%**	76 g	**25%**
Dietary Fiber	12 g	**48%**	1 g	**4%**
Sugars	6 g		52 g	
Other	34 g		0 g	
Protein	6 g		6 g	

*Percent of Daily Values on page a-22

Exchanges and 38 g Carbohydrates Per Serving

Breads	2.2	Vegetables	0.0	Fruits	0.0
Meats	0.1	Milk	0.2	Fats	0.3

Directions

In a large mixing bowl, mIx softened **ButterLike SugarLike**, and egg whites until smooth. Combine food coloring and cocoa; add to mixture. Combine flour, baking soda, and salt; add alternately with buttermilk to mixture. Stir in vanilla and vinegar. Pour into two 9-inch round vegetable sprayed cake pans. Bake at 350° for 35 minutes or until toothpick inserted near center comes out clean.

Frosting: Whisk together milk and flour in a saucepan. Cook, stirring constantly, until thick, about 5 minutes. Cool. Place in a mixing bowl with remaining ingredients. Beat on high speed until consistency of whipped cream. Frost one cake layer; top with second layer and frost entire cake.

Red Velvet Cake

Walnut Pound Cake

The Fat quotient using **ButterLike** is **9%** instead of **46%**
91% less fat **96% less sugar**
51% less Calories

U.S.	Ingredients	Metric
1 1/2 cup	**ButterLike Baking Butter**	341.00 g
3 cups	**Granulated SugarLike**	600.00 g
1 1/4 cup	Egg whites	284.00 g
3 cups	All-purpose flour	375.00 g
1 1/2 tsp	Baking powder	6.00 g
1 cup	Skim milk	245.00 g
1 tsp	Vanilla extract	5.00 g
1 tsp	Almond extract	9.00 g
1/4 cup	Black walnuts, chopped	31.00 g
Frosting:		
1/4 cup	**ButterLike Baking Butter**	57.00 g
3 cups	**Powdered SugarLike**	315.00 g
1 pkg	Non fat cream cheese (8 oz)	227.00 g
1 tsp	Vanilla extract	5.00 g

Directions

In a large mixing bowl mix egg whites until frothy. Add softened **ButterLike** and **SugarLike** to eggs and mix until smooth. Add remaining ingredients. Mix until combined. Pour into a vegetable sprayed and floured 10-inch tube pan and bake at 325° for 1 hour and 20-25 minutes or until cake tests done. Cool ten minutes and then remove from pan. Cool thoroughly.

Nutrition Facts				
Serving Size	208 g			
Servings Per Recipe	12			
Amount per serving			High Fat/Sugar Comparison	
Calories	417		850	
Calories from fat	35		390	
	% Daily Value*		% Daily Value*	
Total Fat	4 g	**6%**	44 g	**68%**
Saturated Fat	1 g	**5%**	24 g	**120%**
Cholesterol	5 mg	**2%**	185 mg	**62%**
Sodium	350 mg	**15%**	440 mg	**18%**
Total Carbohydrate	124 g	**39%**	103 g	**34%**
Dietary Fiber	20 g	**80%**	1 g	**4%**
Sugars	3 g		73 g	
Other	59 g		0 g	
Protein	11 g		11 g	

*Percent of Daily Values on page a-22

Exchanges and 45 g Carbohydrates Per Serving

Breads	2.7	Vegetables	0.0	Fruits	0.0
Meats	0.4	Milk	0.2	Fats	0.7

Frosting: Beat the softened **ButterLike** and room temperature cream cheese until smooth. Add the **Powdered SugarLike** and mix well. Add vanilla. Spread on cooled cake.

Walnut Pound Cake

Lemon Coffee Cake

The Fat quotient using ButterLike is 7% instead of 37%
90% less fat **90% less sugar**
42% less Calories

U.S.	Ingredients	Metric
Streusel:		
3 Tbsp	**ButterLike Baking Butter**	43.00 g
1/3 cup	**Granulated SugarLike**	67.00 g
1/2 cup	All-purpose flour	63.00 g
1/4 cup	Coconut, flaked	30.00 g
Coffee Cake:		
3/4 cup	**ButterLike Baking Butter**	170.00 g
1 cup	**Granulated SugarLike**	200.00 g
2 1/4 cup	All-purpose flour	281.00 g
1/2 tsp	Baking powder	2.00 g
1/2 tsp	Baking soda	2.00 g
1/2 tsp	Salt	3.00 g
2/3 cup	Vanilla yogurt	151.00 g
2 tsp	Grated lemon peel	4.00 g
1 Tbsp	Lemon juice	15.00 g
1/3 cup	Egg whites	75.00 g
1 pkg	Lemon pudding and pie filling mix (2.9 oz)	85.00 g
1/2 cup	**Granulated SugarLike**	100 g
2 cups	Water	474.00 g
2 tsp	Lemon juice	10.00 g
Glaze:		
1/2 cup	**Powdered SugarLike**	53.00 g
1 tsp	Lemon juice	5.00 g
1 tsp	Water	5.00 g

Nutrition Facts				
Serving Size	153 g			
Servings Per Recipe	12			
Amount per serving			High Fat/Sugar Comparison	
Calories	276		480	
Calories from fat	20		180	
	% Daily Value*		% Daily Value*	
Total Fat	2 g	**3%**	20 g	**31%**
Saturated Fat	1 g	**5%**	12 g	**60%**
Cholesterol	5 mg	**2%**	100 mg	**33%**
Sodium	310 mg	**13%**	400 mg	**17%**
Total Carbohydrate	77 g	**25%**	71 g	**44%**
Dietary Fiber	10 g	**40%**	1 g	**4%**
Sugars	4 g		41 g	
Other	26 g		0 g	
Protein	5 g		5 g	

*Percent of Daily Values on page a-22

Exchanges and 41 g Carbohydrates Per Serving					
Breads	2.5	Vegetables	0.0	Fruits	0.2
Meats	0.1	Milk	0.1	Fats	0.4

Directions

Streusel: Mix the softened **ButterLike**, **SugarLike**, and flour with a fork until coarse crumbs form. Stir in coconut.

Coffee Cake: In a large bowl, combine flour, **SugarLike**, baking powder, baking soda, and salt. Add softened **ButterLike**, yogurt, lemon peel, 1 Tbsp lemon juice, and egg whites. Stir until mixture is well blended. Prepare the lemon pudding mix in a small sauce pan with 2 cups water, 1/2 cup **SugarLike**, and 2 tsp lemon juice. Bring to a full boil while stirring. Remove from heat and let cool slightly. Spread 2 cups of the batter in vegetable sprayed 9- or 10-inch springform pan. Sprinkle with 1/2 cup of the streusel. Drop 3/4 cup of the lemon pudding by 1/2 teaspoonful to within 1/2 inch of edge. Spoon remaining batter over lemon pudding; sprinkle with remaining streusel. Bake at 350° for 50 minutes. Cool 10 minutes. Remove from pan.

Lemon Coffee Cake

Glaze: In a small bowl combine **Powdered SugarLike**, lemon juice, and water. Drizzle over warm coffee cake.

Lemon Custard Pudding Cake

The Fat Quotient using **ButterLike** is **4%** instead of **32%**
94% less fat **93% less sugar**
51% less Calories

U.S.	Ingredients	Metric
6 Tbsp	**ButterLike Baking Butter**	85.00 g
2 cups	**Granulated SugarLike**, divided	400.00 g
1 cup	Egg whites, divided	227.00 g
6 Tbsp	All-purpose flour	43.00 g
1 1/2 cup	Skim milk	368.00 g
	Grated peel of 1 lemon	100.00 g
2 Tbsp	Fresh lemon juice	31.00 g

Directions

In a large bowl, combine softened **ButterLike**, 1 1/2 cups **SugarLike,** and 1/2 cup egg whites. Mix until smooth. Add flour, milk, and lemon peel. Mix well. Add lemon juice. In another bowl, beat 1/2 cup egg whites until stiff, slowly adding remaining 1/2 cup **SugarLike** while beating. Fold into batter. Pour into a vegetable sprayed 2-quart baking dish or individual dishes. Place in shallow pan of hot water and bake at 350° for 55-60 minutes or until lightly brown.

Serve with **Powdered SugarLike** dusted on top .

Nutrition Facts				
Serving Size	209 g			
Servings Per Recipe	6			
Amount per serving			High Fat/Sugar Comparison	
Calories	245		500	
Calories from fat	10		160	
	% Daily Value*		% Daily Value*	
Total Fat	1 g	**2%**	18 g	**28%**
Saturated Fat	0.5 g	**3%**	10 g	**50%**
Cholesterol	5 mg	**2%**	180 mg	**60%**
Sodium	160 mg	**7%**	200 mg	**8%**
Total Carbohydrate	84 g	**28%**	77 g	**26%**
Dietary Fiber	17 g	**68%**	1 g	**4%**
Sugars	5 g		68 g	
Other	49 g		0 g	
Protein	8 g		7 g	

*Percent of Daily Values on page a-22

Exchanges and 18 g Carbohydrates Per Serving

Breads	0.9	Vegetables	0.0	Fruits	0.0
Meats	0.6	Milk	0.2	Fats	0.2

Fudge Frosting

The Fat Quotient using **ButterLike** is **0%** instead of **38%**
100% less fat **0% less sugar**
43% less Calories

U.S.	Ingredients	Metric
1/4 cup	**ButterLike Baking Butter**	57.00 g
1 1/2 cup	**Powdered SugarLike**	180.00 g
1 Tbsp	**Liquid SugarLike**	20.00 g
1/3 cup	Cocoa	79.00 g
2 tsp	Vanilla	10.00 g
2 Tbsp	Skim milk	31.00 g

Directions

Combine all of the ingredients. Mix until smooth. Frost on cooled cake or brownies. For cooked frosting, mix **ButterLike**, cocoa, and skim milk in a microwave safe bowl. Microwave for two minutes. Stir in remaining ingredients and spread over brownies.

Nutrition Facts				
Serving Size	21 g			
Servings Per Recipe	18			
Amount per serving			High Fat/Sugar Comparison	
Calories	34		60	
Calories from fat	0		25	
	% Daily Value*		% Daily Value*	
Total Fat	0 g	**0%**	2.5 g	**4%**
Saturated Fat	0 g	**0%**	1.5 g	**8%**
Cholesterol	0 mg	**0%**	5 mg	**2%**
Sodium	15 mg	**1%**	30 mg	**1%**
Total Carbohydrate	13 g	**4%**	10 g	**3%**
Dietary Fiber	3 g	**12%**	0 g	**0%**
Sugars	16 g		9 g	
Other	8 g		0 g	
Protein	0 g		0 g	

*Percent of Daily Values on page a-22

Exchanges and 2 g Carbohydrates Per Serving

Breads	0.1	Vegetables	0.0	Fruits	0.0
Meats	0.0	Milk	0.0	Fats	0.0

Seven-Minute Frosting

The Fat Quotient using ButterLike is 0% instead of 0%
0% less fat **96% less sugar**
51% less Calories

U.S.	Ingredients	Metric
1 1/2 cup	**Granulated SugarLike**	300.00 g
1/3 cup	Cold water	79.00 g
2	Egg whites	67.00 g
1/4 tsp	Cream of tartar	.75 g
1 tsp	Vanilla	5.00 g

Directions

In the top of a double boiler, combine **SugarLike**, water, egg whites, and cream of tartar. Beat with an electric mixer on low for 30 seconds. Place over boiling water (upper pan should not touch water). Cook, beating constantly with the electric mixer on high, until frosting forms stiff peaks. Remove from the heat; add vanilla. Beat 2-3 minutes more or until it reaches spreading consistency. This frosts the tops and sides of two 8- or 9-inch cake layers or one 10-inch tube cake.

Nutrition Facts				
Serving Size	38 g			
Servings Per Recipe	12			
Amount per serving			High Fat/Sugar Comparison	
Calories	54		110	
Calories from fat	0		0	
	% Daily Value*		% Daily Value*	
Total Fat	0 g	**0%**	0 g	**0%**
Saturated Fat	0 g	**0%**	0 g	**0%**
Cholesterol	0 mg	**0%**	20 mg	**7%**
Sodium	10 mg	**0%**	5 mg	**0%**
Total Carbohydrate	25 g	**8%**	25 g	**8%**
Dietary Fiber	6 g	**24%**	0 g	**0%**
Sugars	1 g		24 g	
Other	18 g		0 g	
Protein	1 g		1 g	

*Percent of Daily Values on page a-22

Exchanges and 1 g Carbohydrates Per Serving					
Breads	0.0	Vegetables	0.0	Fruits	0.0
Meats	0.1	Milk	0.0	Fats	0.0

Caramel Frosting

The Fat Quotient using ButterLike is 12% instead of 34%
83% less fat **96% less sugar**
53% less Calories

U.S.	Ingredients	Metric
1/2 cup	**ButterLike Saute Butter**	112.00 g
1 cup	**Brown SugarLike**	200.00 g
2 cups	**Powdered SugarLike**	240.00 g
1/4 cup	Skim milk	61.00 g

Directions

Place **ButterLike** in 2-quart saucepan over medium heat. Slowly stir in **Brown SugarLike** and heat to boiling, stirring constantly. Reduce heat to low, boil, and stir 2 minutes. Stir in milk and heat to boiling, then remove from heat. Gradually stir in **Powdered SugarLike**. Place saucepan of frosting in bowl of cold water and beat until smooth and spreadable. Spread immediately.

Nutrition Facts				
Serving Size	38 g			
Servings Per Recipe	16			
Amount per serving			High Fat/Sugar Comparison	
Calories	75		160	
Calories from fat	10		60	
	% Daily Value*		% Daily Value*	
Total Fat	1 g	**2%**	6 g	**9%**
Saturated Fat	0 g	**0%**	4 g	**20%**
Cholesterol	0 mg	**0%**	15 mg	**5%**
Sodium	0 mg	**0%**	70 mg	**3%**
Total Carbohydrate	30 g	**10%**	26 g	**9%**
Dietary Fiber	7 g	**28%**	0 g	**0%**
Sugars	1 g		24 g	
Other	20 g		0 g	
Protein	1 g		0 g	

*Percent of Daily Values on page a-22

Exchanges and 3 g Carbohydrates Per Serving					
Breads	0.2	Vegetables	0.0	Fruits	0.0
Meats	0.0	Milk	0.0	Fats	0.2

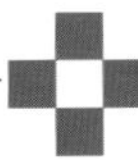

Canning

Pickled Beets, page 67

Canning

SugarLike is the first sugar substitute that keeps its sweetness and withstands the high cooking temperatures of fruit canning, jam making, and pickle making. Testing these canning recipes has been enjoyable and these recipes are my personal favorites. It is nice to know that these products can help make my favorite canning and jam recipes diabetic friendly, sugar free, low calorie, and low fat.

Tips for successful canning using the Bateman Products

- Always add the **SugarLike** gradually and mix well between additions. Follow the directions on each individual recipe. **Mrs. Bateman's Products** work well in all of these recipes.

Notes

Strawberry Jam

The Fat Quotient using ButterLike is 0% instead of 0%
0% less fat **91% less sugar**
51% less Calories

U.S.	**Ingredients**	Metric
1/2 tsp	**ButterLike Saute Butter**	2.33 g
7 cups	**Granulated SugarLike**	1400.00 g
2 qts	Fresh strawberries, hulled	1192.00 g
1 pkg	Powdered pectin (1 3/4 oz)	50.00 g

Directions

Crush 1 cup berries in an 8-quart pot. Continue adding and crushing berries until you have 5 cups crushed berries. Stir in **ButterLike** and pectin. Heat on high, stirring constantly, until mixture comes to a full rolling boil. Add **SugarLike** all at once. Return to boiling; boil 1 minute, stirring constantly. Remove from heat; skim off foam. Ladle at once into hot, sterilized half-pint canning jars, leaving a 1/4-inch headspace. Wipe jar rims; adjust lids. Process in a boiling-water canner 5 minutes. Remove jars; cool. Makes 8 half-pints.

Nutrition Facts				
Serving Size	41 g			
Servings Per Recipe	64			
Amount per serving			High Fat/Sugar Comparison	
Calories	49		100	
Calories from fat	0		0	
	% Daily Value*		% Daily Value*	
Total Fat	0 g	**0%**	0 g	**0%**
Saturated Fat	0 g	**0%**	0 g	**0%**
Cholesterol	0 mg	**0%**	0 mg	**0%**
Sodium	0 mg	**0%**	0 mg	**0%**
Total Carbohydrate	23 g	**8%**	23 g	**8%**
Dietary Fiber	6 g	**24%**	0 g	**0%**
Sugars	2 g		22 g	
Other	16 g		g	
Protein	1 g		1 g	

*Percent of Daily Values on page a-22

Exchanges and 1 g Carbohydrates Per Serving

Breads	0.0	Vegetables	0.0	Fruits	0.1
Meats	0.0	Milk	0.0	Fats	0.0

Berry Freezer Jam

The Fat Quotient using ButterLike is 0% instead of 0%
0% less fat **82% less sugar**
42% less Calories

U.S.	Ingredients	Metric
4 cups	**Granulated SugarLike**	800.00 g
4 cups	Blackberries, raspberries, or hulled strawberries	596.00 g
1/4 tsp	Lemon peel, finely shredded	.50 g
1/2 of a 6 oz pkg	Liquid fruit pectin	85.00 g
2 Tbsp	Lemon juice	31.00 g

Directions

Crush berries until you have 2 cups blackberries or raspberries or 1 3/4 cup strawberries. Mix berries, **SugarLike**, and peel. Let stand for 10 minutes. Combine pectin and lemon juice. Add to berry mixture; stir for 3 minutes. Ladle into half-pint freezer container, leaving 1/2-inch headspace. Seal and label. Let stand at room temperature 24 hours or until set. Store 3 weeks in refrigerator or 1 year in freezer. Makes 4 half-pints.

Nutrition Facts				
Serving Size	47 g			
Servings Per Recipe	32			
Amount per serving			High Fat/Sugar Comparison	
Calories		70	120	
Calories from fat		0	0	
	% Daily Value*		% Daily Value*	
Total Fat	0 g	**0%**	0 g	**0%**
Saturated Fat	0 g	**0%**	0 g	**0%**
Cholesterol	0 mg	**0%**	0 mg	**0%**
Sodium	0 mg	**0%**	0 mg	**0%**
Total Carbohydrate	29 g	**10%**	29 g	**10%**
Dietary Fiber	6 g	**24%**	0 g	**0%**
Sugars	5 g		28 g	
Other	18 g		0 g	
Protein	0 g		0 g	

*Percent of Daily Values on page a-22

Exchanges and 5 g Carbohydrates Per Serving

Breads	0.0	Vegetables	0.0	Fruits	0.4
Meats	0.0	Milk	0.0	Fats	0.0

Pepper Jelly

The Fat Quotient using ButterLike is 0% instead of 0%
0% less fat **86% less sugar**
43% less Calories

U.S.	Ingredients	Metric
5 cups	**Granulated SugarLike**	1000.00 g
2-4	Jalapeno peppers, halved and seeded	38.00 g
1 1/2 cup	Cranberry juice cocktail	378.00 g
1/2 of a 6 oz pkg	Liquid fruit pectin	85.00 g
5	Tiny hot red peppers	57.00 g

Nutrition Facts				
Serving Size	45 g			
Servings Per Recipe	40			
Amount per serving			High Fat/Sugar Comparison	
Calories		68	120	
Calories from fat		0	0	
	% Daily Value*		% Daily Value*	
Total Fat	0 g	**0%**	0 g	**0%**
Saturated Fat	0 g	**0%**	0 g	**0%**
Cholesterol	0 mg	**0%**	0 mg	**0%**
Sodium	40 mg	**2%**	40 mg	**2%**
Total Carbohydrate	29 g	**10%**	29 g	**10%**
Dietary Fiber	6 g	**24%**	0 g	**0%**
Sugars	4 g		28 g	
Other	18 g		g	
Protein	0 g		0 g	

*Percent of Daily Values on page a-22

Directions

Combine jalapeno peppers, cranberry juice, and vinegar. Bring to boil; reduce heat. Simmer, covered, for 10 minutes. Strain mixture through a sieve; press with back of a spoon to remove all liquid. Discard pulp. Combine **SugarLike** and 2 cups liquid in a 4-quart pot. Bring to a full boil over high heat, stirring constantly. Stir in pectin and tiny peppers. Return to rolling boil; boil 1 minute, stirring constantly. Remove from heat. Skim foam off with a metal spoon. Ladle immediately into hot, sterilized half-pint jars, leaving 1/4-inch headspace and making sure each jar contains one tiny red pepper. Wipe jar rims; adjust lids. Process in a boiling-water canner for 5 minutes (start timing when water begins to boil). Remove jars and cool on a wire rack until set. Makes 5 half-pints.

Exchanges and 5 g Carbohydrates Per Serving					
Breads	0.0	Vegetables	0.0	Fruits	0.3
Meats	0.0	Milk	0.0	Fats	0.0

Fruit Juice Jelly

The Fat Quotient using **ButterLike** is **0%** instead of **0%**

0% less fat **90% less sugar**

49% less Calories

U.S.	Ingredients	Metric
4 1/2 cup	**Granulated SugarLike**	900.00 g
4 cups	Orange, apple, or grape juice unsweetened	988.00 g
1/4 cup	Lemon juice	61.00 g
1 pkg	Powdered fruit pectin (1 3/4 oz)	50.00 g

Directions

Pour juices into an 8- or 10-quart pot. Sprinkle with pectin. Let stand 1-2 minutes; stir to dissolve. Bring to a full rolling boil over medium-high heat, stirring frequently. Stir in **SugarLike**. Return to a full rolling boil; stir often. Boil 1 minute, stirring constantly. Remove from heat; quickly skim off foam with a metal spoon. Ladle at once into hot, sterilized half-pint jars, leaving a 1/4-inch headspace. Wipe jar rims and adjust lids. Process in a boiling-water canner 5 minutes. Remove jars; cool on a rack until set. Makes 6 half-pints.

Nutrition Facts				
Serving Size	42 g			
Servings Per Recipe	48			
Amount per serving			High Fat/Sugar Comparison	
Calories	46		90	
Calories from fat	0		0	
	% Daily Value*		% Daily Value*	
Total Fat	0 g	**0%**	0 g	**0%**
Saturated Fat	0 g	**0%**	0 g	**0%**
Cholesterol	0 mg	**0%**	0 mg	**0%**
Sodium	0 mg	**0%**	0 mg	**0%**
Total Carbohydrate	21 g	**7%**	22 g	**7%**
Dietary Fiber	5 g	**20%**	0 g	**0%**
Sugars	2 g		21 g	
Other	14 g		0 g	
Protein	0 g		0 g	

*Percent of Daily Values on page a-22

Exchanges and 3 g Carbohydrates Per Serving					
Breads	0.0	Vegetables	0.0	Fruits	0.1
Meats	0.0	Milk	0.0	Fats	0.0

Quick Refrigerator Cucumber Pickles

The Fat Quotient using ButterLike is 0% instead of 0%
0% less fat — 80% less sugar
36% less Calories

U.S.	Ingredients	Metric
3/4 cup	**Granulated SugarLike**	150.00 g
3 large	Cucumbers	903.00 g
1 large	Red bell pepper	170.00 g
1 medium	Onion, sliced thin	160.00 g
1 Tbsp	Salt	18.00 g
2 tsp	Dill seeds	4.20 g
1/2 cup	White vinegar	120.00 g

Directions

Cut unpeeled cucumbers into 1/16-inch thick slices. Seed bell pepper and cut lengthwise into 1/2-inch wide strips. In a bowl, combine cucumbers, bell pepper, and onion. Stir in salt and dill seeds. Let stand, uncovered 1-2 hours, stirring occasionally. In a small bowl, combine **SugarLike** and vinegar; stir until **SugarLike** is dissolved. Pour over vegetables and mix gently. Spoon into a 2-quart container or into several small containers. Refrigerate, covered, for at least 24 hours or up to 3 weeks. Makes 2 quarts.

Nutrition Facts				
Serving Size	48 g			
Servings Per Recipe	32			
Amount per serving			High Fat/Sugar Comparison	
Calories	16		25	
Calories from fat	0		0	
	% Daily Value*		% Daily Value*	
Total Fat	0 g	**0%**	0 g	**0%**
Saturated Fat	0 g	**0%**	0 g	**0%**
Cholesterol	0 mg	**0%**	0 mg	**0%**
Sodium	220 mg	**9%**	220 mg	**9%**
Total Carbohydrate	6 g	**2%**	6 g	**2%**
Dietary Fiber	2 g	**8%**	0 g	**0%**
Sugars	1 g		5 g	
Other	4 g		0 g	
Protein	0 g		0 g	

*Percent of Daily Values on page a-22

Exchanges and 0 g Carbohydrates Per Serving

Breads	0.0	Vegetables	0.3	Fruits	0.0
Meats	0.0	Milk	0.0	Fats	0.0

Bread and Butter Pickles

The Fat Quotient using ButterLike is 0% instead of 0%
0% less fat — 92% less sugar
43% less Calories

U.S.	Ingredients	Metric
4 cups	**Granulated SugarLike**	800.00 g
4 quarts	Medium cucumbers, sliced	1664.00 g
8 medium	White onions, sliced	960.00 g
1/3 cup	Pickling salt	77.00 g
3 cloves	Garlic, halved	9.00 g
	Cracked ice	226.00 g
3 cups	Cider vinegar	720.00 g
2 Tbsp	Mustard seed	19.00 g
1 1/2 tsp	Turmeric	3.60 g
1 1/2 tsp	Celery seed	2.40 g

Directions

Combine cucumbers, onions, pickling salt, and garlic. Add 2 inches of cracked ice. Refrigerate for 3 hours; drain well. Remove garlic. In a large kettle combine **SugarLike**, vinegar, mustard seed, turmeric, and celery seed. Heat to boiling. Add cucumber mixture. Return to boiling. Pack cucumber mixture and liquid into hot, sterilized pint jars, leaving a 1/2-inch headspace. Wipe jar rims; adjust lids. Process in a boiling-water canner 10 minutes, after water begins to boil.

Exchanges and 3 g Carbohydrates Per Serving					
Breads	0.0	Vegetables	0.3	Fruits	0.0
Meats	0.0	Milk	0.0	Fats	0.0

Nutrition Facts				
Serving Size	64 g			
Servings Per Recipe	70			
Amount per serving			High Fat/Sugar Comparison	
Calories		34	60	
Calories from fat		0	0	
	% Daily Value*		% Daily Value*	
Total Fat	0 g	0%	0 g	0%
Saturated Fat	0 g	0%	0 g	0%
Cholesterol	0 mg	0%	0 mg	0%
Sodium	350 mg	15%	350 mg	15%
Total Carbohydrate	14 g	5%	14 g	5%
Dietary Fiber	3 g	12%	0 g	0%
Sugars	1 g		12 g	
Other	8 g		0 g	
Protein	0 g		0 g	

*Percent of Daily Values on page a-22

Red Bell Pepper Relish

The Fat Quotient using **ButterLike** is 0% instead of 0%
0% less fat **77% less sugar**
40% less Calories

U.S.	Ingredients	Metric
3 cups	**Granulated SugarLike**	600.00 g
3 lbs	Onions, cut into 1-inch chunks	1360.00 g
6 lbs	Red bell peppers, seeded, cut into 1-inch chunks	2721.00 g
4 cups	Distilled white vinegar	960.00 g
2 Tbsp	Salt	36.00 g
1 Tbsp	Mustard seeds	9.60 g

Directions

Pour chopped vegetables into an 8- to10-quart pan. Stir in remaining ingredients. Bring to a boil over medium heat, stirring occasionally. Reduce heat to medium-low and boil gently about 50 minutes, stirring often, until relish is thick, but juicy. Ladle hot relish into hot, sterilized 1-pint canning jars, leaving 1/2-inch headspace. Gently run a narrow non metallic spatula between relish and jar sides to release air bubbles. Wipe rims and threads of jars clean; top with scalded lids, then firmly screw on bands. Place jars, slightly apart, on a rack in a boiling water canner or other deep pan half-full of hot water. Add more water to cover jars by 1-2 inches. Let water simmer for 15 minutes. Lift out jars and let cool on a towel away from drafts. Test seal of each jar by pressing lid; if it pops when pressed, there's no seal. Store unsealed relish in the refrigerator and use within 1 month. Makes 7 pints.

Nutrition Facts				
Serving Size	102 g			
Servings Per Recipe	56			
Amount per serving			High Fat/Sugar Comparison	
Calories		42	70	
Calories from fat		0	0	
	% Daily Value*		% Daily Value*	
Total Fat	0 g	0%	0 g	0%
Saturated Fat	0 g	0%	0 g	0%
Cholesterol	0 mg	0%	0 mg	0%
Sodium	250 mg	10%	250 mg	10%
Total Carbohydrate	15 g	5%	15 g	5%
Dietary Fiber	4 g	16%	1 g	4%
Sugars	3 g		13 g	
Other	8 g		0 g	
Protein	1 g		1 g	

*Percent of Daily Values on page a-22

Exchanges and 3 g Carbohydrates Per Serving					
Breads	0.0	Vegetables	0.9	Fruits	0.0
Meats	0.0	Milk	0.0	Fats	0.0

Cucumber Relish

The Fat Quotient using ButterLike is 0% instead of 0%
0% less fat 90% less sugar
42% less Calories

U.S.	Ingredients	Metric
5 cups	**Granulated SugarLike**	1000.00 g
12	Cucumbers	780.00 g
2	Green peppers	340.00 g
2	Red peppers	340.00 g
3 large	Onions	480.00 g
1 can	Red pimentos (2 oz)	57.00 g
1 Tbsp	Mustard seed	9.60 g
1/3 tsp	Cloves	.70 g
1 tsp	Turmeric	2.50 g
1 tsp	Celery seed	2.00 g
3 cups	Vinegar	720.00 g
1 cup	Water	237.00 g

Directions

Chop vegetables and soak in a large kettle of salt water for 30 minutes. Drain. Add remaining ingredients. Salt to taste. Cook slow for about 1 hour. Bottle in quart jars.

Nutrition Facts				
Serving Size	40 g			
Servings Per Recipe	100			
Amount per serving			High Fat/Sugar Comparison	
Calories		26	45	
Calories from fat		0	0	
	% Daily Value*		% Daily Value*	
Total Fat	0 g	**0%**	0 g	**0%**
Saturated Fat	0 g	**0%**	0 g	**0%**
Cholesterol	0 mg	**0%**	0 mg	**0%**
Sodium	105 mg	**4%**	105 mg	**4%**
Total Carbohydrate	11 g	**4%**	11 g	**4%**
Dietary Fiber	3 g	**12%**	0 g	**0%**
Sugars	1 g		10 g	
Other	7 g		0 g	
Protein	0 g		0 g	

*Percent of Daily Values on page a-22

Exchanges and 1 g Carbohydrates Per Serving

Breads	0.0	Vegetables	0.1	Fruits	0.0
Meats	0.0	Milk	0.0	Fats	0.0

Spaghetti Sauce

The Fat Quotient using ButterLike is 0% instead of 40%
100% less fat 50% less sugar
38% less Calories

U.S.	Ingredients	Metric
1 1/2 cup	**Granulated SugarLike**	300.00 g
12 quarts	Tomato juice	2844.00 g
4 large	Onions, blended	640.00 g
8 cans	Tomato paste (6 oz each)	1360.00 g
2 tsp	Garlic powder	5.60 g
2 Tbsp	Ground oregano	9.00 g
1 Tbsp	Ground basil	4.20 g
1/2 cup	Salt	142.00 g
1 cup	**ButterLike Saute Butter**	224.00 g
5 Tbsp	Chili powder	39.00 g

Directions

Combine all ingredients in a kettle; simmer for 1/2 hour. Bottle in clean pint or quart jars, seal, and process in a boiling-water bath for 20 minutes.

Nutrition Facts				
Serving Size	46 g			
Servings Per Recipe	120			
Amount per serving			High Fat/Sugar Comparison	
Calories		35	45	
Calories from fat		0	15	
	% Daily Value*		% Daily Value*	
Total Fat	0 g	**0%**	2 g	**3%**
Saturated Fat	0 g	**0%**	0 g	**0%**
Cholesterol	0 mg	**0%**	0 mg	**0%**
Sodium	550 mg	**23%**	550 mg	**23%**
Total Carbohydrate	7 g	**2%**	6 g	**2%**
Dietary Fiber	1 g	**4%**	1 g	**4%**
Sugars	2 g		4 g	
Other	2 g		0 g	
Protein	1 g		1 g	

*Percent of Daily Values on page a-22

Exchanges and 4 g Carbohydrates Per Serving

Breads	0.0	Vegetables	0.7	Fruits	0.0
Meats	0.0	Milk	0.0	Fats	0.1

Pickled Beets

The Fat Quotient using ButterLike is 0% instead of 0%
0% less fat 67% less sugar
29% less Calories

U.S.	Ingredients	Metric
1/4 cup	**Granulated SugarLike**	50.00 g
1/3 cup	Vinegar	80.00 g
1/4 cup	Water	59.00 g
1/2 tsp	Cinnamon	1.15 g
1/4 tsp	Salt	1.50 g
1/4 tsp	Ground cloves	.50 g
1 can	Sliced beets, drained (16 oz)	454.00 g

Directions

In a medium saucepan, combine **SugarLike**, vinegar, water, cinnamon, salt, and cloves. Bring to a boil, stirring occasionally. Stir in drained beets. Return to boil; reduce heat. Cover and simmer for 5 minutes. Cool for 30 minutes. Chill beets in liquid at least 8 hours before serving. Cover and store in liquid in the refrigerator up to 1 month. Drain before serving.

Nutrition Facts				
Serving Size	81 g			
Servings Per Recipe	8			
Amount per serving			High Fat/Sugar Comparison	
Calories	32		45	
Calories from fat	0		0	
	% Daily Value*		% Daily Value*	
Total Fat	0 g	**0%**	0 g	**0%**
Saturated Fat	0 g	**0%**	0 g	**0%**
Cholesterol	0 mg	**0%**	0 mg	**0%**
Sodium	230 mg	**10%**	230 mg	**10%**
Total Carbohydrate	11 g	**4%**	11 g	**4%**
Dietary Fiber	3 g	**15%**	1 g	**4%**
Sugars	3 g		9 g	
Other	5 g		0 g	
Protein	1 g		1 g	

*Percent of Daily Values on page a-22

Exchanges and 3 g Carbohydrates Per Serving

Breads	0.0	Vegetables	0.7	Fruits	0.0
Meats	0.0	Milk	0.0	Fats	0.0

Frozen Corn

The Fat Quotient using ButterLike is 16% instead of 48%
0% less fat 90% less sugar
15% less Calories

U.S.	Ingredients	Metric
1/2 lb	**ButterLike Saute Butter**	227.00 g
4 tsp	**Granulated SugarLike**	17.00 g
16 cups	Corn	4000.00 g
3 tsp	Salt	18.00 g

Directions

In a large kettle combine ingredients. Add enough water to not quite cover corn. Boil corn for about 5 minutes or until warm throughout. Pack juice with corn in 1-quart freezer bag.

Nutrition Facts				
Serving Size	133 g			
Servings Per Recipe	32			
Amount per serving			High Fat/Sugar Comparison	
Calories	110		130	
Calories from fat	20		60	
	% Daily Value*		% Daily Value*	
Total Fat	2 g	**3%**	7 g	**11%**
Saturated Fat	0 g	**0%**	3.5 g	**18%**
Cholesterol	0 mg	**0%**	15 mg	**5%**
Sodium	550 mg	**23%**	610 mg	**25%**
Total Carbohydrate	17 g	**6%**	15 g	**5%**
Dietary Fiber	2 g	**8%**	2 g	**8%**
Sugars	5 g		5 g	
Other	0 g		0 g	
Protein	2 g		2 g	

*Percent of Daily Values on page a-22

Exchanges and 15 g Carbohydrates Per Serving

Breads	1.3	Vegetables	0.0	Fruits	0.0
Meats	0.0	Milk	0.0	Fats	0.2

Apple Pie Filling

The Fat Quotient using ButterLike is 3% instead of 3%
0% less fat 95% less sugar
28% less Calories

U.S.	Ingredients	Metric
6 cups	**Granulated SugarLike**	1200.00 g
12 quarts	Apples, peeled, cored, and sliced	8208.00 g
4 cups	Water	948.00 g
1 cup	Cornstarch	128.00 g
2 tsp	Cinnamon	4.60 g
1/4 tsp	Nutmeg	.55 g
1 tsp	Salt	6.00 g

Directions

In a large kettle, cook apples and water about 10 minutes until apples shrink. Drain apples in a colander and pour juice back into kettle. Mix **SugarLike**, cornstarch, cinnamon, nutmeg, and salt thoroughly. Cook until mixture thickens. Stir in lemon juice. Add apples to juice and stir together. Fill quart bottles to 1inch from top; seal and process in a boiling-water bath for 20 minutes. Makes about 7 quarts.

Nutrition Facts
Serving Size 188 g
Servings Per Recipe 56

Amount per serving			High Fat/Sugar Comparison	
Calories	129		180	
Calories from fat	5		5	
	% Daily Value*		% Daily Value*	
Total Fat	0.5 g	**1%**	0.5 g	**1%**
Saturated Fat	0 g	**0%**	0 g	**0%**
Cholesterol	0 mg	**0%**	0 mg	**0%**
Sodium	45 mg	**2%**	45 mg	**2%**
Total Carbohydrate	43 g	**14%**	44 g	**15%**
Dietary Fiber	7 g	**28%**	1 g	**4%**
Sugars	1 g		21 g	
Other	15 g		0 g	
Protein	1 g		0 g	

*Percent of Daily Values on page a-22

Exchanges and 11 g Carbohydrates Per Serving

Breads	0.1	Vegetables	0.0	Fruits	1.3
Meats	0.0	Milk	0.0	Fats	0.0

Cherry Pie Filling

The Fat Quotient using ButterLike is 0% instead of 0%
0% less fat 74% less sugar
35% less Calories

U.S.	Ingredients	Metric
2 1/2 cup	**Granulated SugarLike**	500.00 g
2 1/2 cup	Water	593.00 g
3 Tbsp	Lemon Juice	46.00 g
2 quarts	Sour pie cherries, pitted	1952.00 g
6 Tbsp	Cornstarch	48.00 g
1/4 tsp	Salt	1.50 g

Directions

Combine 2 cups **SugarLike**, 2 cups water, and cherries. Boil gently; no stirring for 5 minutes or until foam ceases. Remove from heat. Combine remaining **SugarLike**, remaining water, cornstarch, and salt. Mix until cornstarch is dispersed. Add cornstarch mixture to cooked cherries. Bring to a gentle boil for 1 minute. While boiling, pour into hot jars. Leave 1-inch head space. Put on lids; screw band tightly. Immediately place in boiling water. Process 30 minutes. Do not double recipe. Makes 3 quarts.

Nutrition Facts
Serving Size 129 g
Servings Per Recipe 24

Amount per serving			High Fat/Sugar Comparison	
Calories	78		120	
Calories from fat	0		0	
	% Daily Value*		% Daily Value*	
Total Fat	0 g	**0%**	0 g	**0%**
Saturated Fat	0 g	**0%**	0 g	**0%**
Cholesterol	0 mg	**0%**	0 mg	**0%**
Sodium	30 mg	**1%**	30 mg	**1%**
Total Carbohydrate	30 g	**10%**	30 g	**10%**
Dietary Fiber	6 g	**24%**	1 g	**4%**
Sugars	7 g		27 g	
Other	15 g		0 g	
Protein	1 g		1 g	

*Percent of Daily Values on page a-22

Exchanges and 9 g Carbohydrates Per Serving

Breads	0.1	Vegetables	0.0	Fruits	0.5
Meats	0.0	Milk	0.0	Fats	0.0

Cookies & Candy

Pumpkin Bars, page 81

Cookies

Cookies are such a big part of my family's diet. They love hot, soft cookies right out of the oven. Cookies are easy to make, and are low in fat and low in sugar when you use **Mrs. Bateman's Products**. Mrs. Bateman's cookie dough can be frozen or refrigerated and baked when you want them.

Tips for successful cookie baking using the Bateman Products

- Please read "Tips for successful desserts using the Bateman Products", page 90.
- Use vegetable spray on all pans before baking and storing cookies.
- Spray your palms with vegetable spray before shaping cookie balls.
- The cookie dough may seem sticky, but resist adding more flour or the cookies will turn out dry. Sprinkle the cookie dough with water and gently mix if the dough becomes too dry.
- It is important to remember to scrape the bowl after mixing the eggs, **SugarLike**, and **ButterLike** together.
- Do not to overbake your cookies. Cookies continue to cook for a few minutes after being removed from the oven. Therefore, cookies should be pulled from the oven when slightly brown on the outside and soft in the middle.
- Leave cookies on the pan for 5-7 minutes to cool before removing with a spatula, which will allow the cookies to keep their shape.
- Store cookies in an airtight container. Separate layers with plastic wrap if needed.
- Cookies freeze well if stored in an airtight container.
- You can use **Mrs. Bateman's Products** in any substitution level you desire. Try using half and half, or even 3 parts **Baking Butter** to 1 part margarine to reduce the fat, yet retain traditional flavor and texture.

Candy

What a joy this has been to make candy that cooks for a long period of time under extremely high heat and still comes out sweet and delicious, but without a high fat or high sugar content. You can't use the intense sweeteners on the market because they either don't handle cooking under heat without losing their sweetness or they don't have the bulk needed to make the candy turn out right.

Liquid SugarLike is a great addition to the candy making section. It will enable you to cook candies that still meet the individual needs of diabetics.

Some of the candies in this section have a slightly different texture or look than their traditional versions. Fudge made with **SugarLike** cooks like fudge, cools like fudge, but when I beat it the fudge never seems to noticeably thicken as much as fudge and it never loses its glossy texture. But it tastes great and is sugar free. Taffy and divinity have the original taste, but set up softer and chewier than their high fat counterparts.

You don't need to completely replace the fat and sugar in these recipes with **Bateman Products**. As they are written, the recipes replace up to 90% of the fat over their high fat version Even if you use some percentage of real fat and sugar in them they can still be a healthier alternative to the originals.

Tips for successful candy making using the Bateman Products

- Please read "Tips for successful desserts using the Bateman Products", page 90.
- Use vegetable spray on all pans before cooking and storing candies.
- Air dry candies for a few hours before trying to embellish or decorate.
- Items can be frozen if stored in an airtight container.
- Cook candies according to directions and following the guides to using a candy thermometer.
- Place candies in a freezer for a short time to make cutting easier.

Coconut Macaroons

The Fat Quotient using ButterLike is 36% instead of 26%
0% less fat **83% less sugar**
29% less Calories

U.S.	Ingredients	Metric
2/3 cup	**Granulated SugarLike**	133.00 g
1/4 cup	Egg whites	57.00 g
1/2 tsp	Vanilla	2.50 g
1 1/3 cup	Coconut	103.00 g

Directions

Vegetable spray a cookie sheet; set aside. In a medium mixing bowl beat egg whites and vanilla with an electric mixer on high until soft peaks form. Gradually add **SugarLike**, about 1 Tbsp at a time, beating until stiff peaks form. Fold in coconut. Drop mixture by rounded teaspoons, 2 inches apart, on a cookie sheet. Bake at 325° for 20 minutes or until edges are lightly browned. Transfer cookies to a wire rack and let cool.

Lemon Macaroons: Prepare as above, except substitute 1 Tbsp lemon juice for the vanilla and add 1 tsp finely shredded lemon peel.

Nutrition Facts				
Serving Size	10 g			
Servings Per Recipe	30			
Amount per serving			High Fat/Sugar Comparison	
Calories	25		35	
Calories from fat	10		10	
	% Daily Value*		% Daily Value*	
Total Fat	1 g	**2%**	1g	**2%**
Saturated Fat	1 g	**5%**	1 g	**5%**
Cholesterol	0 mg	**0%**	0 mg	**0%**
Sodium	0 mg	**0%**	0 mg	**0%**
Total Carbohydrate	6 g	**2%**	6 g	**2%**
Dietary Fiber	1 g	**4%**	0 g	**0%**
Sugars	1 g		6 g	
Other	3 g		0 g	
Protein	0 g		0 g	

*Percent of Daily Values on page a-22

Exchanges and 2 g Carbohydrates Per Serving

Breads	0.0	Vegetables	0.0	Fruits	0.0
Meats	0.0	Milk	0.0	Fats	0.2

Coconut Macaroons

Fudge Oatmeal No Bake Cookies

The Fat Quotient using **ButterLike** is **13%** instead of **36%**
75% less fat **94% less sugar**
32% less Calories

U.S.	Ingredients	Metric
3 cups	**SugarLike Granulated Sugar**	600.00 g
1/2 cup	**ButterLike Baking Butter**	114.00 g
3 Tbsp	Cocoa	45.00 g
1/2 tsp	Salt	3.00 g
3/4 cup	Skim milk	184.00 g
5 cups	Quick oats	405.00 g
1 tsp	Vanilla extract	5.00 g
1/4 cup	Coconut flakes	30.00 g
2 Tbsp	Nuts	17.00 g

Directions

Stir together **SugarLike**, **ButterLike**, cocoa, salt, and milk. Heat in a large saucepan until it comes to a boil. Boil for 5 minutes. Stir in oats, vanilla, coconut, and nuts. Mix until combined. Drop onto vegetable sprayed wax paper or plastic wrap by teaspoonful. Cool. Store in an airtight plastic container.

Nutrition Facts				
Serving Size	56 g			
Servings Per Recipe	25			
Amount per serving			High Fat/Sugar Comparison	
Calories	135		200	
Calories from fat	20		70	
	% Daily Value*		% Daily Value*	
Total Fat	2 g	**3%**	8 g	**12%**
Saturated Fat	0.5 g	**3%**	3.5 g	**18%**
Cholesterol	0 mg	**0%**	10 mg	**3%**
Sodium	75 mg	**3%**	80 mg	**3%**
Total Carbohydrate	38 g	**13%**	28 g	**9%**
Dietary Fiber	8 g	**32%**	2 g	**8%**
Sugars	1 g		18 g	
Other	17 g		0 g	
Protein	3 g		3 g	

*Percent of Daily Values on page a-22

Exchanges and 13 g Carbohydrates Per Serving					
Breads	0.9	Vegetables	0.0	Fruits	0.0
Meats	0.0	Milk	0.0	Fats	0.4

Chocolate Revel Bars

The Fat Quotient using **ButterLike** is **16%** instead of **36%**
75% less fat **66% less sugar**
44% less Calories

U.S.	Ingredients	Metric
Crust:		
1 cup	**ButterLike Baking Butter**, softened	227.00 g
2 cups	**Brown SugarLike**	400.00 g
1 tsp	Baking soda	4.60 g
1/2 cup	Egg whites	114.00 g
2 tsp	Vanilla	10.00 g
2 1/2 cup	All-purpose flour	288.00 g
3 cups	Quick-cooking rolled oats	702.00 g

U.S.	Ingredients	Metric
Filling:		
14 oz	Non fat **Sweetened Condensed Milk**, page 91	397.00 g
1 1/2 cup	Reduced fat semisweet chocolate pieces	360.00 g
1/8 cup	Pecans, chopped	16.00 g
2 tsp	Vanilla	10.00 g

Directions

Crust: Set aside 2 Tbsp of **ButterLike**. In a large mixing bowl beat the remaining **ButterLike** with an electric mixer on medium-high for 30 seconds. Add the **SugarLike**, eggs, vanilla, and baking soda. Beat until combined, scraping sides of bowl occasionally. Beat in as much of the flour as you can with the mixer. Then stir in remaining flour and the rolled oats.

Filling: Follow directions for **Sweetened Condensed Milk**. In a medium saucepan combine the reserved 2 Tbsp **ButterLike**, chocolate pieces, and Sweetened Condensed Milk. Cook over low heat until chocolate melts, stirring occasionally. Remove from heat. Stir in pecans and 2 tsp vanilla.

Press 2/3 of the rolled oats mixture into the bottom of a vegetable sprayed 15x10x1-inch baking pan. Spread filling evenly over the oat mixture. Dot remaining rolled oats mixture on filling. Bake at 350° for about 25 minutes or until top is lightly browned (chocolate filling will still look moist). Cool on a wire rack and let set for one hour. Cut into bars.

Nutrition Facts				
Serving Size	42 g			
Servings Per Recipe	60			
Amount per serving			High Fat/Sugar Comparison	
Calories	84		150	
Calories from fat	10		60	
	% Daily Value*		% Daily Value*	
Total Fat	1.5 g	**2%**	6 g	**9%**
Saturated Fat	1 g	**5%**	3.5 g	**18%**
Cholesterol	0 mg	**0%**	20 mg	**7%**
Sodium	45 mg	**3%**	75 mg	**3%**
Total Carbohydrate	21 g	**7%**	20 g	**7%**
Dietary Fiber	2 g	**8%**	1 g	**4%**
Sugars	4 g		10 g	
Other	7 g		0 g	
Protein	2 g		2 g	

*Percent of Daily Values on page a-22

Exchanges and 12 g Carbohydrates Per Serving					
Breads	0.7	Vegetables	0.0	Fruits	0.0
Meats	0.0	Milk	0.0	Fats	0.4

Chocolate Revel Bars

Basic Non Fat Cookie Dough

The Fat Quotient using **ButterLike** is **0%** instead of **45%**
100% less fat **100% less sugar**
40% less Calories

U.S.	Ingredients	Metric
3/4 cup	**ButterLike Baking Butter**	170.00 g
3/4 cup	**Granulated SugarLike**	150.00 g
1/4 cup	**Liquid SugarLike**	85.00 g
1/4 cup	Egg whites	57.00 g
2 1/2 cup	All-purpose flour	285.00 g
1 tsp	Baking powder	4.00 g
1 tsp	Baking soda	5.00 g
1/2 tsp	Salt	3.00 g

Directions

Mix room temperature **ButterLike**, **SugarLike**, and egg whites until smooth. Add remaining ingredients; mix until combined. Watch mixing time; does not require excessive mixing. Bake at 350° for 7-9 minutes. Bake until lightly browned on bottom.

Ginger Cookies: Replace **Liquid SugarLike** with molasses. Replace white sugar with **Brown SugarLike**. Add 1 tsp cinnamon and 1/2 tsp ginger.

Nutrition Facts				
Serving Size	21 g			
Servings Per Recipe	36			
			High Fat/Sugar Comparison	
Amount per serving				
Calories	54		90	
Calories from fat	0		40	
	% Daily Value*		% Daily Value*	
Total Fat	0 g	**0%**	4.5 g	**7%**
Saturated Fat	0 g	**0%**	2.5 g	**13%**
Cholesterol	0 mg	**0%**	15 mg	**5%**
Sodium	100 mg	**4%**	125 mg	**5%**
Total Carbohydrate	14 g	**5%**	12 g	**4%**
Dietary Fiber	2 g	**8%**	0 g	**0%**
Sugars	0 g		5 g	
Other	4 g		0 g	
Protein	1 g		1 g	

*Percent of Daily Values on page a-22

Exchanges and 8 g Carbohydrates Per Serving

Breads	0.6	Vegetables	0.0	Fruits	0.0
Meats	0.0	Milk	0.0	Fats	0.1

Cinnamon Raisin Cookies: Add 1 tsp cinnamon, raisins, and nuts.

Snickerdoodles

The Fat Quotient using **ButterLike** is **0%** instead of **39%**
100% less fat **100% less sugar**
47% less Calories

U.S.	Ingredients	Metric
1/2 cup	**ButterLike Baking Butter**, softened	114.00 g
1 cup + 2 Tbsp	**Granulated SugarLike**, divided	225.00 g
1/4 tsp	Baking soda	1.20 g
1/4 tsp	Cream of tarter	.75 g
1/4 cup	Egg whites	57.00 g
1/2 tsp	Vanilla	2.50 g
1 1/4 cup	All-purpose flour	144.00 g
1 tsp	Ground cinnamon	2.30 g

Directions

In a medium mixing bowl beat softened **ButterLike**, 1 cup **SugarLike**, baking soda, cream of tarter, egg whites, and vanilla until smooth. Beat in as much of the flour as you can with the mixer. Stir in remaining flour. Cover and chill 1 hour. Combine the 2 Tbsp **SugarLike** and cinnamon. Shape dough into 1-inch balls. Roll balls in **SugarLike**-cinnamon mixture to coat. Place 2 inches apart, pressing down slightly, on a vegetable sprayed cookie sheet. Bake at 375° for 10-11 minutes or until edges are golden. Transfer cookies to a wire rack and let cool.

Exchanges and 4 g Carbohydrates Per Serving					
Breads	0.3	Vegetables	0.0	Fruits	0.0
Meats	0.0	Milk	0.0	Fats	0.0

Nutrition Facts				
Serving Size	15 g			
Servings Per Recipe	36			
Amount per serving			High Fat/Sugar Comparison	
Calories	37		70	
Calories from fat	0		25	
	% Daily Value*		% Daily Value*	
Total Fat	0 g	**0%**	3 g	**5%**
Saturated Fat	0 g	**0%**	1.5 g	**8%**
Cholesterol	0 mg	**0%**	15 mg	**5%**
Sodium	25 mg	**1%**	40 mg	**2%**
Total Carbohydrate	11 g	**4%**	9 g	**3%**
Dietary Fiber	2 g	**8%**	0 g	**0%**
Sugars	0 g		6 g	
Other	5 g		0 g	
Protein	1 g		1 g	

*Percent of Daily Values on page a-22

Biscotti

The Fat Quotient using **ButterLike** is **11%** instead of **40%**
85% less fat **94% less sugar**
44% less Calories

U.S.	Ingredients	Metric
2/3 cup	**ButterLike Saute Butter**	149.00 g
1 1/2 cup	**Granulated SugarLike**	300.00 g
4 cups	Flour	460.00 g
1/2 tsp	Salt	3.00 g
2 tsp	Baking powder	8.00 g
1 cup	Egg whites	227.00 g
1 tsp	Vanilla extract	5.00 g
1 tsp	Almond extract	5.00 g
1 Tbsp	Anise seed	6.30 g
1/8 cup	Almonds, ground	17.00 g

Nutrition Facts				
Serving Size	66 g			
Servings Per Recipe	18			
Amount per serving			High Fat/Sugar Comparison	
Calories	163		290	
Calories from fat	20		120	
	% Daily Value*		% Daily Value*	
Total Fat	2 g	**3%**	13 g	**20%**
Saturated Fat	0.5 g	**3%**	4.5 g	**23%**
Cholesterol	0 mg	**0%**	60 mg	**20%**
Sodium	130 mg	**5%**	160 mg	**7%**
Total Carbohydrate	39 g	**13%**	38 g	**13%**
Dietary Fiber	5 g	**20%**	2 g	**8%**
Sugars	1 g		17g	
Other	12 g		0 g	
Protein	5 g		6 g	

*Percent of Daily Values on page a-22

Exchanges and 22 g Carbohydrates Per Serving					
Breads	1.5	Vegetables	0.0	Fruits	0.0
Meats	0.2	Milk	0.0	Fats	0.4

Directions

Sift together **SugarLike**, flour, salt, and baking powder. Beat softened **ButterLike**, egg whites, and extracts until smooth. Quickly smooth **ButterLike** mixture, anise seed, and almonds into dry ingredients. Turn out on a floured board and knead until dough is no longer sticky. Divide dough into 6-8 pieces. Roll with hands into long rolls. Place rolls on greased baking pans and flatten slightly with hands. Bake at 325° for 25-30 minutes.

Slice each roll diagonally into 3/4-inch pieces. Return to baking pan, cut side up, and bake at 375° for 5 minutes. Turn over and bake 5 minutes more.

Angel Sugar Crisps

The Fat Quotient using **ButterLike** is **0%** instead of **51%**
100% less fat **100% less sugar**
30% less Calories

U.S.	Ingredients	Metric
1 cup	**ButterLike Baking Butter**	227.00 g
1/2 cup	**Granulated SugarLike**	100.00 g
1/2 cup	**Brown SugarLike**	100.00 g
1/4 cup	Egg whites	57.00 g
1 tsp	Vanilla extract	5.00 g
3 cups	All-purpose flour	345.00 g
1 tsp	Baking soda	4.60 g
1 tsp	Cream of tarter	3.00 g
1/2 tsp	Salt	3.00 g

Directions

In a mixing bowl, cream softened **ButterLike**, **SugarLikes**, egg whites, and vanilla until smooth. Sift together flour, soda, cream of tarter, and salt. Add to mixture; mix until blended. Shape into large marble-size balls. Dip half of ball into water, then in **SugarLike**. Place, sugared side up, on vegetable sprayed cookie sheets. Bake at 400° for 6 minutes or until done. Cool.

Nutrition Facts				
Serving Size	18 g			
Servings Per Recipe	48			
Amount per serving			High Fat/Sugar Comparison	
Calories	49		70	
Calories from fat	0		40	
	% Daily Value*		% Daily Value*	
Total Fat	0 g	**0%**	4 g	**6%**
Saturated Fat	0 g	**0%**	2 g	**10%**
Cholesterol	0 mg	**0%**	10 mg	**3%**
Sodium	75 mg	**3%**	75 mg	**3%**
Total Carbohydrate	13 g	**4%**	8 g	**3%**
Dietary Fiber	1 g	**4%**	0 g	**0%**
Sugars	0 g		4 g	
Other	3 g		0 g	
Protein	1 g		1 g	

*Percent of Daily Values on page a-22

Exchanges and 9 g Carbohydrates Per Serving					
Breads	0.5	Vegetables	0.0	Fruits	0.0
Meats	0.0	Milk	0.0	Fats	0.0

Angel Sugar Crisps

Peanut Butter Cookies

The Fat Quotient using ButterLike is 26% instead of 54%
66% less fat **86% less sugar**
32% less Calories

U.S.	Ingredients	Metric
1/2 cup	**ButterLike Baking Butter**	114.00 g
1/2 cup	**Brown SugarLike**	100.00 g
1/2 cup	**Granulated SugarLike**	100.00 g
1/4 cup	Egg whites	57.00 g
1/2 cup	Reduced fat peanut butter	144.00 g
1 1/4 cup	All-purpose flour	144.00 g
3/4 tsp	Baking soda	3.00 g
1/2 tsp	Baking powder	2.00 g
1/4 tsp	Salt	1.50 g

Directions

Mix **ButterLike**, **SugarLikes**, and egg whites until smooth. Add the remaining ingredients; mix until combined. Watch mixing time; does not require excessive mixing. Bake until light brown; middle should be soft.

Nutrition Facts				
Serving Size	22 g			
Servings Per Recipe	30			
Amount per serving			High Fat/Sugar Comparison	
Calories	68		100	
Calories from fat	15		50	
	% Daily Value*		% Daily Value*	
Total Fat	2 g	**3%**	6 g	**9%**
Saturated Fat	0 g	**0%**	2.5 g	**13%**
Cholesterol	0 mg	**0%**	15 mg	**5%**
Sodium	105 mg	**4%**	115 mg	**5%**
Total Carbohydrate	14 g	**5%**	11 g	**4%**
Dietary Fiber	0 g	**0%**	0 g	**0%**
Sugars	2 g		7 g	
Other	5 g		0 g	
Protein	2 g		2 g	

*Percent of Daily Values on page a-22

Exchanges and 7 g Carbohydrates Per Serving

Breads	0.5	Vegetables	0.0	Fruits	0.0
Meats	0.2	Milk	0.0	Fats	0.4

Peanut Butter Marshmallow Treats

The Fat Quotient using ButterLike is 13% instead of 34%
66% less fat **0% less sugar**
15% less Calories

U.S.	Ingredients	Metric
1/4 cup	**ButterLike Saute Butter**	56.00 g
32 large	Marshmallows	230.00 g
1/2 tsp	Vanilla	2.50 g
5 cup	Peanut butter, chocolate puff cereal	180.00 g

Directions

Microwave **ButterLike** and marshmallows in 3-quart microwave safe bowl for 2 minutes; stir. Microwave 1 more minute; stir until mixture is smooth. Add vanilla. Stir in half of the cereal at a time until evenly coated. Press out treats evenly, with vegetable sprayed sandwich bags, into vegetable sprayed pan; cool to harden.

Nutrition Facts				
Serving Size	20 g			
Servings Per Recipe	24			
Amount per serving			High Fat/Sugar Comparison	
Calories	68		80	
Calories from fat	10		25	
	% Daily Value*		% Daily Value*	
Total Fat	1 g	**2%**	3 g	**5%**
Saturated Fat	0 g	**0%**	1.5 g	**8%**
Cholesterol	0 mg	**0%**	5 mg	**2%**
Sodium	65 mg	**3%**	85 mg	**4%**
Total Carbohydrate	15 g	**5%**	14 g	**5%**
Dietary Fiber	0 g	**0%**	0 g	**0%**
Sugars	4 g		4 g	
Other	0 g		0 g	
Protein	1 g		1 g	

*Percent of Daily Values on page a-22

Exchanges and 15 g Carbohydrates Per Serving

Breads	0.4	Vegetables	0.0	Fruits	0.0
Meats	0.0	Milk	0.0	Fats	0.2

Chocolate Peanut Butter Bars

The Fat Quotient using **ButterLike** is **24%** instead of **43%**
66% less fat **46% less sugar**
41% less Calories

U.S.	Ingredients	Metric
Crumb Mixture:		
1 3/4 cup	**Brown SugarLike**	350.00 g
1 cup	**ButterLike Baking Butter**, softened	227.00 g
2 cups	Quick-cooking rolled oats	468.00 g
1 cup	All-purpose flour	115.00 g
1/2 cup	Whole wheat flour	60.00 g
1 tsp	Baking powder	4.00 g
1/2 tsp	Baking soda	2.30 g
1/4 cup	Peanuts, chopped	36.50 g
Topping:		
2 cups	Reduced fat chocolate pieces	480.00 g
Crust:		
1/4 cup	Beaten egg whites	57.00 g
Filling:		
14 oz	Non fat **Sweetened Condensed Milk**, page-91	397.00 g
1/3 cup	Peanut butter	96.00 g

Nutrition Facts				
Serving Size	48 g			
Servings Per Recipe	48			
Amount per serving			High Fat/Sugar Comparison	
Calories	112		190	
Calories from fat	25		90	
	% Daily Value*		% Daily Value*	
Total Fat	3 g	**5%**	9 g	**14%**
Saturated Fat	1.5 g	**8%**	5 g	**25%**
Cholesterol	0 mg	**0%**	20 mg	**7%**
Sodium	65 mg	**3%**	95 mg	**4%**
Total Carbohydrate	25 g	**8%**	23 g	**8%**
Dietary Fiber	2 g	**8%**	1 g	**4%**
Sugars	7 g		13g	
Other	8 g		0 g	
Protein	2 g		3 g	

*Percent of Daily Values on page a-22

Exchanges and 15 g Carbohydrates Per Serving					
Breads	1.0	Vegetables	0.0	Fruits	0.0
Meats	0.1	Milk	0.0	Fats	0.7

Directions

Crumb Mixture: In a large mixing bowl combine **Brown SugarLike**, rolled oats, all-purpose flour, whole wheat flour, baking powder, and baking soda. Using a pastry blender, cut in the **ButterLike** until mixture resembles fine crumbs. Stir in peanuts.

Topping: Combine 1 3/4 cups of the crumb mixture and the chocolate pieces; set aside.

Crust: Stir egg whites into the remaining crumb mixture. Press into bottom of a vegetable sprayed 15x10x1-inch baking pan. Bake at 350° for 15 minutes.

Filling: Follow directions for **Sweetened Condensed Milk** . Stir together Sweetened Condensed Milk and peanut butter until well combined. Pour filling evenly over crust. Bake for 12-15 minutes more or until lightly browned around the edges. Cool on a wire rack. Cut into bars.

Chocolate Peanut Butter Bars

Raisin Sheet Cookies

The Fat Quotient using ButterLike is 10% instead of 45%
88% less fat **73% less sugar**
45% less Calories

U.S.	Ingredients	Metric
1 cup	**ButterLike Baking Butter**	227.00 g
1 1/2 cup	**Granulated SugarLike**	300.00 g
1 cup	Raisins	145.00 g
1 1/4 cup	Water	296.00 g
1/2 cup	Egg whites	114.00 g
1 tsp	Baking soda	4.60 g
3 cups	All-purpose flour	345.00 g
1/4 tsp	Ground nutmeg	.60 g
1/4 tsp	Ground cinnamon	.60 g
1/2 tsp	Salt	3.00 g
1/4 cup	Walnuts, chopped	31.00 g

Directions

In a small saucepan, combine raisins and water; bring to a boil. Drain; reserve 1 cup liquid and set aside. In a mixing bowl, combine **SugarLike**, softened **ButterLike**, and egg whites until smooth. Add baking soda to raisin liquid. Sift together flour, nutmeg, cinnamon, and salt; add alternately with raisin liquid to wet mixture. Stir in raisins and nuts. Spread in a vegetable sprayed 15x10-inch baking pan. Bake at 350° for 25-30 minutes. If desired, glaze with **Powdered SugarLike** icing while hot. Cut while warm.

Nutrition Facts				
Serving Size	41 g			
Servings Per Recipe	36			
Amount per serving			High Fat/Sugar Comparison	
Calories	88		160	
Calories from fat	10		70	
	% Daily Value*		% Daily Value*	
Total Fat	1 g	**2%**	8 g	**12%**
Saturated Fat	0 g	**0%**	1.5 g	**8%**
Cholesterol	0 mg	**0%**	10 mg	**3%**
Sodium	100 mg	**4%**	90 mg	**4%**
Total Carbohydrate	22 g	**7%**	19 g	**6%**
Dietary Fiber	2 g	**8%**	1 g	**4%**
Sugars	3 g		11g	
Other	6 g		0 g	
Protein	2 g		2 g	

*Percent of Daily Values on page a-22

Exchanges and 14 g Carbohydrates Per Serving					
Breads	0.7	Vegetables	0.0	Fruits	0.2
Meats	0.0	Milk	0.0	Fats	0.2

Caramel Oatmeal Chews

The Fat Quotient using **ButterLike** is **23%** instead of **45%**
90% less fat **88% less sugar**
81% less Calories

U.S.	Ingredients	Metric
1 cup	**Caramel Sauce**, page 233	319.00 g
3/4 cup	**ButterLike Saute Butter**	168.00 g
3/4 cup	**Brown SugarLike**	150.00 g
1 1/4 cup	Oatmeal	293.00 g
1 1/2 cup	Flour	173.00 g
1 tsp	Baking soda	4.60 g
1/4 tsp	Salt	1.50 g
1/2 cup	Flour	58.00 g
1/4 cup	Chopped nuts	31.00 g
1 pkg	Reduced fat chocolate chips (12 oz)	340.00 g

Directions

Follow directions for **Caramel Sauce**; set aside.

Combine **SugarLike**, oatmeal, flour, baking soda, and salt. Mix **ButterLike** with dry ingredients. In a separate mixing bowl, mix 1 cup Caramel Sauce and 1/2 cup flour. Press 1/2 of the oatmeal mixture into a 9x13-inch vegetable sprayed pan. Spread caramel and flour mixture over oatmeal mixture. Sprinkle with nuts and chocolate chips. Drop the remaining oatmeal mixture by small teaspoonful over chocolate chips. Bake at 350° for 30 minutes.

Nutrition Facts				
Serving Size	48 g			
Servings Per Recipe	32			
Amount per serving			High Fat/Sugar Comparison	
Calories	117		610	
Calories from fat	25		280	
	% Daily Value*		% Daily Value*	
Total Fat	3 g	**5%**	31 g	**48%**
Saturated Fat	2 g	**10%**	19 g	**95%**
Cholesterol	0 mg	**0%**	30 mg	**10%**
Sodium	60 mg	**3%**	210 mg	**9%**
Total Carbohydrate	25 g	**8%**	73 g	**24%**
Dietary Fiber	2 g	**8%**	3 g	**12%**
Sugars	7 g		60 g	
Other	7 g		0 g	
Protein	2 g		7 g	

*Percent of Daily Values on page a-22

Exchanges and 14 g Carbohydrates Per Serving					
Breads	1.1	Vegetables	0.0	Fruits	0.0
Meats	0.0	Milk	0.0	Fats	0.8

Pecan Puffs

The Fat Quotient using **ButterLike** is **39%** instead of **36%**
50% less fat **100% less sugar**
54% less Calories

U.S.	Ingredients	Metric
1 cup	**Brown SugarLike**	200.00 g
3	Egg whites	85.00 g
1/8 tsp	Salt	.75 g
1/2 tsp	Vanilla extract	2.50 g
1/2 cup	Pecans, chopped	55.00 g

Directions

In a mixing bowl, beat egg whites and salt until soft peaks form. Gradually add **Brown SugarLike**, beating until stiff peaks form, about 5-8 minutes. Fold in vanilla and pecans. Drop by well-rounded teaspoonful onto vegetable sprayed cookie sheets. Bake at 200° for 50-55 minutes or until firm to the touch. Store in airtight container.

Nutrition Facts				
Serving Size	10 g			
Servings Per Recipe	36			
Amount per serving			High Fat/Sugar Comparison	
Calories	23		50	
Calories from fat	10		20	
	% Daily Value*		% Daily Value*	
Total Fat	1 g	2%	2 g	3%
Saturated Fat	0 g	0%	0 g	0%
Cholesterol	0 mg	0%	0 mg	0%
Sodium	15 mg	1%	15 mg	1%
Total Carbohydrate	6 g	2%	7 g	2%
Dietary Fiber	1 g	4%	0 g	0%
Sugars	0 g		6 g	
Other	4 g		0 g	
Protein	0 g		0 g	

*Percent of Daily Values on page a-22

Exchanges and 1 g Carbohydrates Per Serving					
Breads	0.0	Vegetables	0.0	Fruits	0.0
Meats	0.1	Milk	0.0	Fats	0.2

Pumpkin Bars

The Fat Quotient using **ButterLike** is **0%** instead of **30%**
100% less fat **75% less sugar**
40% less Calories

U.S.	Ingredients	Metric
2/3 cup	**ButterLike Baking Butter**	151.00 g
2 cups	**Granulated SugarLike**	400.00 g
1 cup	Egg whites	227.00 g
16 oz	Pumpkin	454.00 g
2 cups	All-purpose flour	230.00 g
1/2 tsp	Nutmeg	1.00 g
2 tsp	Baking powder	8.00 g
1 tsp	Cinnamon	2.30 g
1/2 tsp	Salt	3.00 g
1/2 tsp	Baking soda	2.30 g
1 cup	Raisins (optional)	145.00 g

Directions

In a large mixing bowl, mix **ButterLike**, **SugarLike**, and egg whites until smooth. Add the rest of your ingredients and mix until combined. Spread batter into a vegetable sprayed 9x13-inch pan. Bake at 350° for 30-40 minutes.

Nutrition Facts				
Serving Size	65 g			
Servings Per Recipe	25			
Amount per serving			High Fat/Sugar Comparison	
Calories	108		180	
Calories from fat	0		60	
	% Daily Value*		% Daily Value*	
Total Fat	0 g	0%	6 g	9%
Saturated Fat	0 g	0%	3.5 g	18%
Cholesterol	0 mg	0%	50 mg	17%
Sodium	150 mg	6%	170 mg	7%
Total Carbohydrate	32 g	11%	29 g	10%
Dietary Fiber	4 g	16%	1 g	4%
Sugars	5 g		20g	
Other	12 g		0 g	
Protein	2 g		2 g	

*Percent of Daily Values on page a-22

Exchanges and 16 g Carbohydrates Per Serving					
Breads	0.7	Vegetables	0.0	Fruits	0.3
Meats	0.1	Milk	0.0	Fats	0.1

Chocolate Chip Cookies

The Fat Quotient using **ButterLike** is **11%** instead of **36%**
81% less fat **74% less sugar**
38% less Calories

U.S.	Ingredients	Metric
1 1/2 cup	**ButterLike Baking Butter**	341.00 g
1 5/8 cup	**Granulated SugarLike**	326.00 g
2 1/8 cup	**Brown SugarLike**	425.00 g
1 1/2 tsp	Salt	9.00 g
7/8 tsp	Baking soda	4.00 g
1 5/8 Tbsp	Vanilla	24.00 g
5/8 cup	Egg whites	142.00 g
1/2 cup	Skim milk	123.00 g
5 cups	Cake flour	545.00 g
1 5/8 cup	Reduced fat chocolate chips	391.00 g

Directions

Mix softened **ButterLike**, **Granulated SugarLike**, and egg whites until smooth. Add the rest of the ingredients and mix until combined. Do not over mix. Drop by teaspoonful onto a vegetable sprayed cookie sheet. Bake at 350° for 9-10 minutes. Bake until lightly browned.

Cookies should still be soft in middle. Cookies continue to cook on hot tray. Remove from tray after about 5 minutes.

Nutrition Facts				
Serving Size	47 g			
Servings Per Recipe	50			
Amount per serving			High Fat/Sugar Comparison	
Calories	123		200	
Calories from fat	15		80	
	% Daily Value*		% Daily Value*	
Total Fat	1.5 g	**2%**	8 g	**12%**
Saturated Fat	1.5 g	**8%**	3 g	**15%**
Cholesterol	0 mg	**0%**	10 mg	**3%**
Sodium	130 mg	**5%**	110 mg	**5%**
Total Carbohydrate	33 g	**11%**	29 g	**10%**
Dietary Fiber	4 g	**16%**	0 g	**0%**
Sugars	5 g		19 g	
Other	11 g		0 g	
Protein	2 g		2 g	

*Percent of Daily Values on page a-22

Exchanges and 18 g Carbohydrates Per Serving					
Breads	1.2	Vegetables	0.0	Fruits	0.0
Meats	0.0	Milk	0.0	Fats	0.4

Chocolate Chip Cookies

Cream Cheese Mints

The Fat Quotient using **ButterLike** is **0%** instead of **32%**
100% less fat **96% less sugar**
36% less Calories

U.S.	Ingredients	Metric
1 Tbsp	**ButterLike Baking Butter**, softened	14.00 g
4 cups	**Powdered SugarLike**	480.00 g
1 pkg	Fat free cream cheese (3 oz)	85.00 g
1/2 tsp	Peppermint extract	2.50 g

Directions

Stir together softened **ButterLike**, softened cream cheese, and peppermint extract. Gradually add **Powdered SugarLike**, stirring until smooth. (Knead in the last of the **Powdered SugarLike** by hand.) Add food coloring; knead until evenly distributed. Form cream cheese mixture into 3/4-inch balls. Roll each ball in **Granulated SugarLike**; place on waxed paper. Flatten each ball with the bottom of a juice glass or with the tines of a fork. (Or, sprinkle small candy molds lightly with **Granulated SugarLike**. Press about 3/4-1 tsp cream cheese mixture into each mold. Remove from molds.) Cover mints with paper towels; let dry overnight. Store in an airtight container in the refrigerator or freezer up to 1 month.

Nutrition Facts				
Serving Size	48 g			
Servings Per Recipe	12			
Amount per serving			High Fat/Sugar Comparison	
Calories	90		140	
Calories from fat	0		30	
	% Daily Value*		% Daily Value*	
Total Fat	0 g	**0%**	3.5 g	**5%**
Saturated Fat	0 g	**0%**	2 g	**10%**
Cholesterol	0 mg	**0%**	10 mg	**3%**
Sodium	45 mg	**2%**	30 mg	**1%**
Total Carbohydrate	40 g	**13%**	25 g	**8%**
Dietary Fiber	10 g	**40%**	0 g	**0%**
Sugars	1 g		24 g	
Other	29 g		0 g	
Protein	1 g		1 g	

*Percent of Daily Values on page a-22

Exchanges and 11 g Carbohydrates Per Serving					
Breads	0.0	Vegetables	0.0	Fruits	0.0
Meats	0.0	Milk	0.0	Fats	0.0

Candied Nuts

The Fat quotient using **ButterLike** is **59%** instead of **56%**
20% less fat **89% less sugar**
24% less Calories

U.S.	**Ingredients**	Metric
1/2 cup	**Granulated SugarLike**	100.00 g
2 Tbsp	**ButterLike Saute Butter**	28.00 g
1 1/2 cup	Raw or roasted nuts	206.00 g
1/2 tsp	Vanilla	2.50 g

Directions

Line a baking sheet with foil. Vegetable spray the foil; set aside. In a heavy 10-inch skillet combine nuts, **SugarLike**, **ButterLike**, and vanilla. Cook over medium-high heat, shaking skillet occasionally, until **SugarLike** begins to melt. Do not stir. Reduce heat to low; cooking until **SugarLike** is golden brown, stirring occasionally. Remove from heat. Pour onto prepared baking sheet. Cool completely. Break into clusters. Store tightly covered.

Note: These are great to add to a trail mix, and if you add lower fat fillers the total fat is reduced.

Fat quotient is higher in this recipe even though we have lowered the fat. Since we lowered the calories our fat quotient goes up.

Nutrition Facts				
Serving Size	28 g			
Servings Per Recipe	12			
Amount per serving			High Fat/Sugar Comparison	
Calories	122		160	
Calories from fat	80		90	
	% Daily Value*		% Daily Value*	
Total Fat	8 g	**12%**	10 g	**15%**
Saturated Fat	1.5 g	**8%**	3 g	**15%**
Cholesterol	0 mg	**0%**	5 mg	**2%**
Sodium	0 mg	**0%**	25 mg	**1%**
Total Carbohydrate	15 g	**5%**	14 g	**5%**
Dietary Fiber	3 g	**12%**	1 g	**4%**
Sugars	1 g		9 g	
Other	6 g		0 g	
Protein	3 g		3 g	

*Percent of Daily Values on page a-22

Exchanges and 6 g Carbohydrates Per Serving

Breads	0.1	Vegetables	0.0	Fruits	0.0
Meats	0.0	Milk	0.0	Fats	1.6

Old-Fashioned Popcorn Balls

The Fat Quotient using **ButterLike** is **0%** instead of **0%**
0% less fat **96% less sugar**
36% less Calories

U.S.	**Ingredients**	Metric
2 cups	**Granulated SugarLike**	400.00 g
1/2 cup	**Liquid SugarLike**	170.00 g
18 cups	Popcorn, popped	187.00 g
1 cup	Water	237.00 g
1 tsp	Vinegar	5.00 g
1/2 tsp	Salt	3.00 g
1 Tbsp	Vanilla	15.00 g

Nutrition Facts				
Serving Size	51 g			
Servings Per Recipe	20			
Amount per serving			High Fat/Sugar Comparison	
Calories	89		140	
Calories from fat	0		0	
	% Daily Value*		% Daily Value*	
Total Fat	0 g	**0%**	0 g	**0%**
Saturated Fat	0 g	**0%**	0 g	**0%**
Cholesterol	0 mg	**0%**	0 mg	**0%**
Sodium	60 mg	**3%**	70 mg	**3%**
Total Carbohydrate	33 g	**11%**	33 g	**11%**
Dietary Fiber	7 g	**28%**	1 g	**4%**
Sugars	1 g		23 g	
Other	18 g		0 g	
Protein	1 g		1 g	

*Percent of Daily Values on page a-22

Directions

Remove all unpopped kernels from popped popcorn. Put popcorn in a vegetable sprayed 17x12x2-inch baking or roasting pan. Keep popcorn warm in a 300° oven while making syrup. For syrup mixture, vegetable spray the sides of a 2-quart saucepan. In saucepan combine **SugarLikes**, water, vinegar, and salt. Cook and stir over medium-high heat until mixture boils, stirring to dissolve **Granulated SugarLike**. Clip a candy thermometer to side of pan. Reduce heat to medium; continue boiling at a moderate, steady rate, stirring occasionally, for 20 minutes or until thermometer registers 250°, hard-ball stage. Remove from heat; remove thermometer. Stir in vanilla. Pour syrup mixture over the hot popcorn and stir gently to coat. Cool until the popcorn mixture can be handled easily. With vegetable sprayed hands, quickly shape the mixture into 2 1/2-inch diameter balls. Wrap each popcorn ball in plastic wrap.

Exchanges and 6 g Carbohydrates Per Serving					
Breads	0.5	Vegetables	0.0	Fruits	0.0
Meats	0.0	Milk	0.0	Fats	0.1

Hard Candy

The Fat Quotient using **ButterLike** is **0%** instead of **0%**

0% less fat **100% less sugar**

48% less Calories

U.S.	Ingredients	Metric
2 cups	**Granulated SugarLike**	400.00 g
1 cup	**Liquid SugarLike**	340.00 g
1/2 cup	Water	119.00 g
1/4 tsp	Food coloring of choice	1.40 g
Few drops	Peppermint or cinnamon extract	7.00 g

Directions

Line a 8x8x2-inch baking pan with foil, extending foil over edges of pan. Vegetable spray foil; set aside. Vegetable spray sides of a heavy 2-quart saucepan. In saucepan combine **SugarLikes** and water. Cook and stir over medium-high heat until mixture boils, stirring to dissolve **Granulated SugarLike** for about 5 minutes. Clip the candy thermometer to side of pan. Reduce heat to medium; continue boiling at a moderate, steady rate, stirring occasionally, until thermometer registers 290°, soft-crack stage, 20-25 minutes. Remove from heat; remove thermometer. Quickly stir in food coloring and flavor. Immediately pour mixture into the prepared pan. Let stand for 5-10 minutes or until a film forms over the surface of candy. Using a broad spatula or pancake turner, begin marking candy by pressing a line across surface 1/2 inch from edge of pan. Do not break film on surface. Repeat along other three sides of pan, intersecting lines at corners to form squares. (If lines do not remain in candy, it is not cool enough to mark. Let candy stand a few more minutes and start again.) Continue marking lines along all sides, 1/2 inch apart, until you reach the center. Retrace previous lines, pressing spatula deeper, but still not breaking the film on surface. Repeat until the spatula can be pressed to bottom of pan along all lines. Cool completely. Use foil to lift candy out of pan; break candy into squares. Store tightly covered. Makes 216 pieces.

Nutrition Facts				
Serving Size	16 g			
Servings Per Recipe	54			
Amount per serving			High Fat/Sugar Comparison	
Calories	24		50	
Calories from fat	0		0	
	% Daily Value*		% Daily Value*	
Total Fat	0 g	**0%**	0 g	**0%**
Saturated Fat	0 g	**0%**	0 g	**0%**
Cholesterol	0 mg	**0%**	0 mg	**0%**
Sodium	0 mg	**0%**	5 mg	**0%**
Total Carbohydrate	11 g	**4%**	12 g	**4%**
Dietary Fiber	3 g	**12%**	0 g	**0%**
Sugars	0 g		10 g	
Other	8 g		0 g	
Protein	0 g		0 g	

*Percent of Daily Values on page a-22

Exchanges and 0 g Carbohydrates Per Serving					
Breads	0.0	Vegetables	0.0	Fruits	0.0
Meats	0.0	Milk	0.0	Fats	0.0

Penuche

The Fat Quotient using ButterLike is 28% instead of 25%
40% less fat **93% less sugar**
43% less Calories

U.S.	Ingredients	Metric
1 1/2 cup	**Granulated SugarLike**	300.00 g
1 cup	**Brown SugarLike**	200.00 g
2 Tbsp	**ButterLike Saute Butter**	28.00 g
1/3 cup	Light cream substitute	80.00 g
1/3 cup	Skim milk	82.00 g
1 tsp	Vanilla	4.70 g
1/2 cup	Pecans or walnuts, chopped	63.00 g

Nutrition Facts				
Serving Size	24 g			
Servings Per Recipe	32			
Amount per serving			High Fat/Sugar Comparison	
Calories		48	90	
Calories from fat		32	32	
	% Daily Value*		% Daily Value*	
Total Fat	1.5 g	**2%**	2.5 g	**4%**
Saturated Fat	0 g	**0%**	1 g	**5%**
Cholesterol	0 mg	**0%**	5 mg	**2%**
Sodium	0 mg	**0%**	10 mg	**0%**
Total Carbohydrate	17 g	**6%**	16 g	**5%**
Dietary Fiber	4 g	**16%**	0 g	**0%**
Sugars	1 g		15 g	
Other	11 g		0 g	
Protein	1 g		1 g	

*Percent of Daily Values on page a-22

Exchanges and 2 g Carbohydrates Per Serving					
Breads	0.0	Vegetables	0.0	Fruits	0.0
Meats	0.0	Milk	0.0	Fats	0.2

Directions

With foil, line an 8x4x2 or 9x5x3-inch loaf pan; extend foil over edges. Vegetable spray foil; set aside. In 2-quart vegetable sprayed saucepan, combine **SugarLikes**, cream, and milk. Bring to a boil over medium-high heat while stirring. Attach a candy thermometer to side of pan. Reduce heat to medium-low. Continue boiling at a steady rate, stirring frequently, until thermometer registers 236°, soft-ball stage. Remove from heat; add **ButterLike** and vanilla; don't stir. Cool to 110°. Remove thermometer from saucepan. Beat mixture with wooden spoon until it begins to thicken. Add nuts. Continue beating until mixture becomes very thick and begins to lose its gloss. Immediately, spread into foil lined pan. Score into squares while warm. When Penuche is firm, lift out of pan on foil. Cut into squares. Store tightly covered. Makes 1 1/4 pounds.

Saltwater Taffy

The Fat Quotient using ButterLike is 0% instead of 0%
0% less fat **100% less sugar**
57% less Calories

U.S.	Ingredients	Metric
2 cups	**Granulated SugarLike**	400.00 g
1 cup	**Liquid SugarLike**	320.00 g
2 Tbsp	**ButterLike Saute Butter**	28.00 g
1 cup	Water	237.00 g
1 1/2 tsp	Salt	9.00 g
1/4 tsp	Peppermint, rum, or cinnamon extract	1.20 g
	Few drops food coloring (optional)	3.00 g

Nutrition Facts				
Serving Size	10 g			
Servings Per Recipe	100			
Amount per serving			High Fat/Sugar Comparison	
Calories		13	30	
Calories from fat		0	0	
	% Daily Value*		% Daily Value*	
Total Fat	0 g	**0%**	0 g	**0%**
Saturated Fat	0 g	**0%**	0 g	**0%**
Cholesterol	0 mg	**0%**	0 mg	**0%**
Sodium	35 mg	**1%**	40 mg	**2%**
Total Carbohydrate	6 g	**2%**	6 g	**2%**
Dietary Fiber	2 g	**8%**	0 g	**0%**
Sugars	0 g		6 g	
Other	5 g		0 g	
Protein	0 g		0 g	

*Percent of Daily Values on page a-22

Directions

In a vegetable sprayed 2-quart saucepan, combine **SugarLikes**, water, and salt. Cook, stirring, over medium-high heat until mixture boils. Attach candy thermometer to side of pan. Reduce heat to medium. Continue boiling at a steady rate 40 minutes or until thermometer registers 265°, hard-ball stage. Remove saucepan from heat and remove thermometer. Stir in **ButterLike**, extract, and food coloring, if desired. Pour into a vegetable sprayed 15x10x1-inch baking pan. Cool for 15-20 minutes or until taffy mixture is easy to handle. Butter hands and twist and pull candy about 10-15 minutes until it turns stiff and difficult to pull and has a creamy color. Candy shows doneness by cracking when tapped on counter. Divide into 4 pieces; twist and pull into long 1/2-inch thick strands. With vegetable sprayed scissors, snip strands into bite-size pieces. Wrap pieces in plastic. Makes 1 1/2 pounds.

Exchanges and 0 g Carbohydrates Per Serving

Breads	0.0	Vegetables	0.0	Fruits	0.0
Meats	0.0	Milk	0.0	Fats	0.0

Pralines

The Fat Quotient using **ButterLike** is **50%** instead of **45%**
36% less fat **94% less sugar**
42% less Calories

U.S.	Ingredients	Metric
3 Tbsp	**ButterLike Saute Butter**	42.00 g
1 1/2 cup	**Granulated SugarLike**	300.00 g
1 1/2 cup	**Brown SugarLike**	300.00 g
1 cup	Light cream substitute	240.00 g
2 cups	Pecan halves	216.00 g

Directions

In a 2 quart vegetable sprayed saucepan, combine **SugarLikes** and cream. Cook and stir over medium-high heat until mixture boils. Attach a candy thermometer to side of pan. Reduce heat to medium-low. Continue boiling at a steady rate, stirring frequently, 16-18 minutes, until thermometer registers 234°, soft-ball stage. Remove from heat; add **ButterLike**; don't stir. Cool 30 minutes or until 150°. Remove thermometer from saucepan. Stir in pecans. Beat mixture with wooden spoon until it begins to thicken, but remains glossy. Immediately drop candy by spoonfuls onto waxed paper. When firm, store tightly covered.

Nutrition Facts			High Fat/Sugar Comparison	
Serving Size	31 g			
Servings Per Recipe	36			
Amount per serving				
Calories	81		140	
Calories from fat	40		60	
	% Daily Value*		% Daily Value*	
Total Fat	4.5 g	**7%**	7 g	**11%**
Saturated Fat	0 g	**0%**	2 g	**10%**
Cholesterol	0mg	**0%**	10 mg	**3%**
Sodium	0 mg	**0%**	15 mg	**1%**
Total Carbohydrate	19 g	**6%**	18 g	**6%**
Dietary Fiber	5 g	**20%**	0 g	**0%**
Sugars	1 g		17 g	
Other	12 g		0 g	
Protein	1 g		1 g	

*Percent of Daily Values on page a-22

Exchanges and 2 g Carbohydrates Per Serving

Breads	0.0	Vegetables	0.0	Fruits	0.0
Meats	0.0	Milk	0.0	Fats	0.8

Divinity

The Fat Quotient using ButterLike is 23% instead of 13%
0% less fat **100% less sugar**
47% less Calories

U.S.	Ingredients	Metric
2 2/3 cup	**Granulated SugarLike**	533.00 g
2/3 cup	**Liquid SugarLike**	213.00 g
1/2 cup	Water	119.00 g
2 large	Egg whites	67.00 g
1 tsp	Vanilla	5.00 g
2/3 cup	Nuts, coarsely chopped	83.00 g

Directions

Over low-heat, cook **SugarLikes** and water, stirring until **SugarLike** is dissolved. Cook, without stirring, to 260° on a candy thermometer or until mixture reaches hard-ball stage. Beat egg whites on high until stiff peaks form. Beat on medium while pouring hot syrup into egg whites. Add vanilla. Beat until mixture holds shape. Fold in nuts. Drop mixture from vegetable sprayed spoon onto waxed paper. Let stand uncovered at room temperature at least 12 hours, turning candies over once, until candies feel firm. Store tightly covered.

Nutrition Facts				
Serving Size	21 g			
Servings Per Recipe	48			
Amount per serving			High Fat/Sugar Comparison	
Calories	40		70	
Calories from fat	10		10	
	% Daily Value*		% Daily Value*	
Total Fat	1 g	**2%**	1 g	**2%**
Saturated Fat	0 g	**0%**	0 g	**0%**
Cholesterol	0 mg	**0%**	0 mg	**0%**
Sodium	00 mg	**0%**	10 mg	**0%**
Total Carbohydrate	14 g	**5%**	15 g	**5%**
Dietary Fiber	3 g	**12%**	0 g	**0%**
Sugars	0 g		13 g	
Other	10 g		0 g	
Protein	1 g		1 g	

*Percent of Daily Values on page a-22

Exchanges and 8 g Carbohydrates Per Serving

Breads	0.0	Vegetables	0.0	Fruits	0.0
Meats	0.0	Milk	0.0	Fats	0.2

Desserts

Old-Fashioned Ice Cream Roll, page 115

Desserts

Wow! We can now make luscious, decadent, and heavenly desserts and still have them low fat, low calorie, low cholesterol, and sugar free. In fact it seems the more ingredients and the richer the original recipe was intended to be the better the dessert turns out. We have loaded this dessert section with recipes that have all been tried and tested and turned out great. We included some old family favorites such as cheesecakes, as well as some new tortes. We even have a few great ice cream and sorbet recipes. Enjoy!

Tips for successful desserts using the Bateman Products

- Use quality, non-stick bakeware and cookware to prevent sticking and promote even cooking.
- Vegetable spray all pans, even non-stick bakeware.
- Your recipe can be frozen before or after baking, just like cooking with regular fat or sugar.
- **Important:** Each egg called for in a recipe needs to equal 1/4 cup. The recipe may call for whole eggs, egg whites, egg substitutes or dried eggs, but when you measure them, each "egg" must equal 1/4 cup. If your egg is short, add enough water to equal 1/4 cup. Using egg whites can cause some textural changes in your baked goods.

  Our new **EggLike™** is a natural, dried, whole egg substitute used in baking and cooking. Can be used to substitute any whole egg, 1/4 cup egg whites or egg substitutes in any recipe. See page a-12. **EggLike** is compatible with the recipes in this cookbook. **EggLike** increases volume in cakes and baked products over egg substitutes and egg whites.
- Check the low altitude cooking chart on page a-17 for altitudes other than 5000 feet.
- **Mixing steps**
  - Soften premeasured **Baking Butter** in the microwave for 10-30 seconds. If you do not have a microwave or are mixing large quantities, place the cold **Baking Butter** in a mixing bowl and mix until lump free and smooth. Then add the sugar and eggs and mix until combined.
  - Mix softened **ButterLike** with sugar or **SugarLike** and eggs until combined and smooth. Stop. Because **ButterLike Baking Butter** contains only 7% fat, it does not incorporate air when beaten, so further mixing or creaming is unnecessary.
  - Once **SugarLike** is mixed with other ingredients, use immediately. Lumps may form if mixture is allowed to sit.
  - Gradually add remaining ingredients for easier mixing.
- Cooking times are sometimes slightly longer than when using real fat and sugar. Test with a toothpick or knife to check for doneness.
- Do not overcook cookies and other baked goods. Foods that do not require a long cooking time sometimes do not brown as much as the high fat counterpart. Cook until done, not until as brown as normal.
- Store foods in an airtight container.

Sweetened Condensed Milk

The Fat Quotient using ButterLike is 0% instead of 10%
100% less fat **98% less sugar**
37% less Calories

U.S.	Ingredients	Metric
2/3 cup	**Granulated SugarLike**	132.00 g
1 cup	Evaporated skim milk	227.00 g

Directions

In a medium saucepan, combine milk and **SugarLike**. Heat until **SugarLike** is dissolved. Bring to a boil; remove from heat. Store in an airtight container.

Nutrition Facts				
Serving Size	359 g			
Servings Per Recipe	1			
Amount per serving			High Fat/Sugar Comparison	
Calories	438		690	
Calories from fat	0		70	
	% Daily Value*		% Daily Value*	
Total Fat	0 g	**0%**	8 g	**12%**
Saturated Fat	0 g	**0%**	5 g	**25%**
Cholesterol	10 mg	**3%**	35 mg	**12%**
Sodium	260 mg	**11%**	120 mg	**5%**
Total Carbohydrate	156 g	**52%**	145 g	**48%**
Dietary Fiber	32 g	**128%**	0 g	**0%**
Sugars	3 g		141 g	
Other	95 g		0 g	
Protein	18 g		8 g	

*Percent of Daily Values on page a-22

Exchanges and 29 g Carbohydrates Per Serving

Breads	0.0	Vegetables	0.0	Fruits	0.0
Meats	0.0	Milk	2.1	Fats	0.0

Blueberry Slump

The Fat Quotient using ButterLike is 5% instead of 12%
67% less fat 74% less sugar
25% less Calories

U.S.	Ingredients	Metric
Sauce:		
1/2 cup	**Granulated SugarLike**	100.00 g
3 cups	Fresh Blueberries	435.00 g
1 1/4 cup	Water	296.00 g
1 tsp	Lemon peel, finely grated	2.00 g
1 Tbsp	Lemon juice	15.00 g
Dumplings:		
2 Tbsp	**ButterLike Baking Butter**	28.00 g
2 Tbsp	**Granulated SugarLike**	25.00 g
1 cup	All-purpose flour	115.00 g
2 tsp	Baking powder	8.00 g
1/2 tsp	Salt	3.00 g
1/2 cup	Skim milk	123.00 g

Nutrition Facts				
Serving Size	192 g			
Servings Per Recipe	6			
Amount per serving			High Fat/Sugar Comparison	
Calories	172		230	
Calories from fat	5		30	
	% Daily Value*		% Daily Value*	
Total Fat	1 g	**2%**	3 g	**5%**
Saturated Fat	0 g	**0%**	1.5 g	**8%**
Cholesterol	0 mg	**0%**	10 mg	**3%**
Sodium	360 mg	**15%**	360 mg	**15%**
Total Carbohydrate	49 g	**16%**	47 g	**16%**
Dietary Fiber	8 g	**32%**	3 g	**12%**
Sugars	7 g		27 g	
Other	15 g		0 g	
Protein	3 g		3 g	

*Percent of Daily Values on page a-22

Exchanges and 26 g Carbohydrates Per Serving

Breads	1.2	Vegetables	0.0	Fruits	0.7
Meats	0.0	Milk	0.1	Fats	0.1

Directions

Sauce: In a large saucepan, combine ingredients; bring to a boil. Reduce heat and simmer, uncovered, for 5 minutes.

Dumplings: Combine flour, **SugarLike**, baking powder, and salt; cut in softened **ButterLike** until mixture resembles coarse meal. Add milk quickly, mixing until dry ingredients are moistened. Drop dough by spoonfuls into simmering berries; makes 6 dumplings. Cook, covered, over low heat for 10 minutes. Do not lift lid. Serve warm with sauce and fat free whipped topping, if desired.

Individual Caramel Flans

The Fat Quotient using ButterLike is 29% instead of 25%
43% less fat 30% less sugar
26% less Calories

U.S.	Ingredients	Metric
2/3 cup	**Granulated SugarLike,** divided	133.00 g
3 Tbsp	**ButterLike Saute Butter**	42.00 g
1	Beaten egg	50.00 g
1/2 cup	Egg substitute	100 g
1 1/2 cup	Skim milk	368.00 g
1 tsp	Vanilla	5.00 g

Directions

In a heavy 8-inch skillet cook **ButterLike** and 1/3 cup **SugarLike** over medium-high heat until **SugarLike** begins to melt, shaking the skillet occasionally to heat evenly. Do not stir. Once the **SugarLike** starts to melt, reduce heat to low and cook about 5 minutes more or until completely melted and golden, stirring as needed with a wooden spoon. Immediately divide the caramelized **SugarLike** among four 6-oz custard cups; tilt custard cups to coat bottoms evenly. Let stand 10 minutes. Meanwhile, combine 1/3 cup **SugarLike**, eggs, milk, and vanilla. Beat until well combined but not foamy. Place the cups in a 2-quart square baking dish on an oven rack. Divide egg mixture among custard cups. If desired, sprinkle dish around custard cups to a depth of 1 inch. Bake in a 325° oven for 30-45 minutes or until a knife inserted near the center comes out clean. Remove cups from water. Cool slightly on a wire rack before serving. (Or, cool completely in custard cups. Cover and chill until serving time.) To unmold flans, loosen edges with a knife, slipping point down sides to let air in. Invert a dessert plate over each flan; turn custard cup and plate over together.

Nutrition Facts				
Serving Size	175 g			
Servings Per Recipe	4			
Amount per serving			High Fat/Sugar Comparison	
Calories	175		250	
Calories from fat	36		60	
		% Daily Value*		% Daily Value*
Total Fat	4 g	**6%**	7 g	**11%**
Saturated Fat	1 g	**5%**	3 g	**15%**
Cholesterol	56 mg	**18%**	170 mg	**57%**
Sodium	119 mg	**5%**	95 mg	**4%**
Total Carbohydrate	41 g	**14%**	39 g	**13%**
Dietary Fiber	8 g	**32%**	0 g	**0%**
Sugars	5 g		37 g	
Other	24 g		0 g	
Protein	9 g		8 g	

*Percent of Daily Values on page a-22

Exchanges and 9 g Carbohydrates Per Serving					
Breads	0.2	Vegetables	0.0	Fruits	0.0
Meats	0.7	Milk	0.3	Fats	0.7

Rich Brownies

The Fat Quotient using **ButterLike** is **5%** instead of **36%**

92% less fat **94% less sugar**

44% less Calories

U.S.	Ingredients	Metric
1 1/3 cup	**ButterLike Baking Butter**	303.00 g
3 3/4 cup	**Granulated SugarLike**	750.00 g
1 3/4 cup	Egg whites	397.00 g
1 1/2 tsp	Vanilla	7.00 g
3 1/2 cup	All-purpose flour	403.00 g
2 cups	Cocoa	476.00 g
1 Tbsp	Baking powder	12.00 g

Directions

Mix softened **ButterLike, SugarLike**, and egg whites until smooth. Add remaining ingredients and mix until combined. Batter will be very thick. Pour into a vegetable sprayed 9x13-inch pan. Bake at 350° for 20-30 minutes. Cool. If desired, dust with **Powdered SugarLike**.

Nutrition Facts				
Serving Size	94 g			
Servings Per Recipe	25			
Amount per serving			High Fat/Sugar Comparison	
Calories	169		300	
Calories from fat	10		110	
		% Daily Value*		% Daily Value*
Total Fat	1 g	**2%**	12 g	**18%**
Saturated Fat	0 g	**0%**	7 g	**35%**
Cholesterol	0 mg	**0%**	90 mg	**30%**
Sodium	135 mg	**6%**	180 mg	**8%**
Total Carbohydrate	51 g	**17%**	45 g	**15%**
Dietary Fiber	8 g	**32%**	0 g	**0%**
Sugars	2 g		31 g	
Other	22 g		0 g	
Protein	4 g		4 g	

*Percent of Daily Values on page a-22

Exchanges and 21 g Carbohydrates Per Serving					
Breads	1.3	Vegetables	0.0	Fruits	0.0
Meats	0.2	Milk	0.1	Fats	0.2

Layered Cream Puff Dessert

The Fat Quotient using **ButterLike** is **11%** instead of **57%**
89% less fat **33% less sugar**
42% less Calories

U.S.	Ingredients	Metric
Crust:		
1/2 cup	**ButterLike Saute Butter**	112.00 g
1 cup	Water	237.00 g
1 cup	All-purpose flour	115.00 g
2 large	Eggs	100.00 g
1/2 cup	Egg whites	114.00 g
Filling:		
2 pkgs	Sugar free instant vanilla pudding mix (3.4-oz)	193.00 g
3 cups	Cold skim milk	735.00 g
1 pkg	Fat free cream cheese, softened (8 oz)	227.00 g
Topping:		
1	Fat free whipped topping (8 oz)	227.00 g

Directions

Crust: In saucepan, bring water and **ButterLike** to boil. Add flour; stir until mixture forms a ball. Remove from heat and cool slightly. Add eggs, one at a time, beating well after each addition. Then add egg whites. Spread on a vegetable sprayed 15x10x1-inch jelly roll pan. Bake at 400° for 30 minutes. Cool but do not prick, leaving surface with its "moon-like" appearance.

Filling: Beat pudding and milk until thick. Add cream cheese; blend well. Spread on crust; refrigerate 20 minutes.

Nutrition Facts				
Serving Size	137 g			
Servings Per Recipe	15			
Amount per serving			High Fat/Sugar Comparison	
Calories		163	280	
Calories from fat		15	160	
	% Daily Value*		% Daily Value*	
Total Fat	2 g	**3%**	18 g	**28%**
Saturated Fat	0.5 g	**3%**	12 g	**60%**
Cholesterol	30 mg	**10%**	95 mg	**32%**
Sodium	430 mg	**18%**	350 mg	**15%**
Total Carbohydrate	27 g	**9%**	24 g	**8%**
Dietary Fiber	0 g	**0%**	0 g	**0%**
Sugars	4 g		6 g	
Other	0 g		0 g	
Protein	7 g		5 g	

*Percent of Daily Values on page a-22

Exchanges and 27 g Carbohydrates Per Serving

Breads	1.2	Vegetables	0.0	Fruits	0.0
Meats	0.2	Milk	0.3	Fats	0.3

Topping: Top with whipped topping. If desired, drizzle **Chocolate Syrup**, page 235, over top and sprinkle with a few nuts.

Note to Diabetics: Substitute whipped topping with 1 cup light whipping cream, 1/4 cup **Granulated SugarLike**, 1 tsp vanilla. Fat will increase to 6.9 grams per serving.

Raisin Pudding

The Fat Quotient using **ButterLike** is **2%** instead of **10%**
86% less fat **78% less sugar**
38% less Calories

U.S.	Ingredients	Metric
1 cup	**Granulated SugarLike**	200.00 g
1 cup	**Brown SugarLike**	200.00 g
2 Tbsp	**ButterLike Saute Butter**	28.00 g
1 cup	All-purpose flour	115.00 g
2 tsp	Baking powder	8.00 g
1/2 cup	Skim milk	123.00 g
1/8 tsp	Salt	.75 g
1 cup	Raisins	145.00 g
2 cups	Boiling water	474.00 g
1/2 tsp	Vanilla extract	2.50 g

Directions

In a small bowl, combine **Granulated SugarLike**, flour, baking powder, milk, and salt. Spread evenly in a vegetable sprayed 9-inch square baking dish. In a saucepan, combine raisins, **Brown SugarLike**, water, and **ButterLike**. Bring to a boil. Stir in vanilla. Pour over flour mixture. Do not stir. Bake at 350° for 30 minutes. If desired, serve warm with fat free whipped topping.

Exchanges and 23 g Carbohydrates Per Serving					
Breads	0.7	Vegetables	0.0	Fruits	0.8
Meats	0.0	Milk	0.1	Fats	0.1

Nutrition Facts				
Serving Size	144 g			
Servings Per Recipe	9			
Amount per serving			High Fat/Sugar Comparison	
Calories		197	320	
Calories from fat		5	30	
	% Daily Value*		% Daily Value*	
Total Fat	0.5 g	**1%**	3.5 g	**5%**
Saturated Fat	0 g	**0%**	2 g	**10%**
Cholesterol	0 mg	**0%**	10 mg	**3%**
Sodium	130 mg	**5%**	170 mg	**7%**
Total Carbohydrate	68 g	**23%**	69 g	**23%**
Dietary Fiber	12 g	**48%**	1 g	**4%**
Sugars	12 g		55 g	
Other	33 g		0 g	
Protein	3 g		2 g	

*Percent of Daily Values on page a-22

Southern Bread Pudding

The Fat Quotient using **ButterLike** is **16%** instead of **40%**
76% less fat **66% less sugar**
40% less Calories

U.S.	Ingredients	Metric
2/3 cup	**Granulated SugarLike**	133.00 g
1/3 cup	**ButterLike Saute Butter**	75.00 g
4 3/4 cup	Skim milk, divided	1163.00 g
1 cup	Egg substitutes	251.00 g
1/4 tsp	Salt	1.50 g
1 tsp	Vanilla extract	5.00 g
11 cups	White bread, cubes	330.00 g
1/2 tsp	Ground cinnamon	1.20 g
2/3 cup	Raisins, optional	97.00 g
Sauce:		
1/3 cup	**Brown SugarLike**	67.00 g
2 Tbsp	**ButterLike Saute Butter**	28.00 g
1/3 cup	**Liquid SugarLike**	113.00 g
1/4 cup	Water	59.00 g
2 Tbsp	Pecans, coarsely chopped	14.00 g
1/2 tsp	Vanilla extract	2.50 g
1/8 tsp	Salt	.75 g

Nutrition Facts				
Serving Size	195 g			
Servings Per Recipe	12			
Amount per serving			High Fat/Sugar Comparison	
Calories		227	380	
Calories from fat		35	150	
	% Daily Value*		% Daily Value*	
Total Fat	4 g	**6%**	17 g	**26%**
Saturated Fat	1 g	**5%**	8 g	**40%**
Cholesterol	5 mg	**2%**	105 mg	**35%**
Sodium	300 mg	**13%**	370 mg	**15%**
Total Carbohydrate	51 g	**17%**	50 g	**17%**
Dietary Fiber	7 g	**28%**	1 g	**4%**
Sugars	11 g		32 g	
Other	17 g		0 g	
Protein	9 g		8 g	

*Percent of Daily Values on page a-22

Exchanges and 27 g Carbohydrates Per Serving					
Breads	1.1	Vegetables	0.0	Fruits	0.4
Meats	0.3	Milk	0.4	Fats	0.6

Directions

In a saucepan, heat 4 cups milk until warm; set aside. In a large mixing bowl, combine remaining milk, egg substitutes, **SugarLike**, salt, and vanilla. Gradually add warmed milk and **ButterLike**, stirring constantly. Add bread cubes; soak 10 minutes. Add cinnamon and raisins. Pour into a 13x9x2-inch vegetable sprayed baking pan. Bake at 400° for 45-60 minutes or until a knife inserted in center comes out clean.

Sauce: Bring water to a boil in a saucepan. Add **Brown SugarLike**; stir to dissolve. Add **Liquid SugarLike**. Bring to a boil; cook 15-20 seconds. Remove from the heat; add remaining ingredients. Cut pudding into squares and serve with sauce.

Bread Pudding

The Fat quotient using **ButterLike** is **14%** instead of **37%**
74% less fat **73% less sugar**
32% less Calories

U.S.	Ingredients	Metric
1/3 cup	**ButterLike Saute Butter**	75.00 g
3/4 cup	**Granulated SugarLike**	150.00 g
1/2 cup	Egg substitutes	126.00 g
2 cups	Skim milk, scalded	490.00 g
1/4 tsp	Salt	1.50 g
1 tsp	Cinnamon	2.30 g
1/2 tsp	Nutmeg	1.00 g
1 tsp	Vanilla extract	5.00 g
4 1/2-5 cups	Soft bread cubes (9 slices)	135.00 g
1/2 cup	Raisins, optional	73.00 g
Sauce:		
5/8 cup	**Granulated SugarLike**	125.00g
1/4 cup	**ButterLike Saute Butter**	56.00 g
2 Tbsp	Cornstarch	16.00 g
1/4 tsp	Salt	1.50 g
1 2/3 cup	Water	395.00 g
3 tsp	Vanilla extract	15.00 g
1/4 tsp	Nutmeg	.55 g

Nutrition Facts				
Serving Size	278 g			
Servings Per Recipe	6			
Amount per serving			High Fat/Sugar Comparison	
Calories		314	460	
Calories from fat		45	180	
		% Daily Value*	% Daily Value*	
Total Fat	5 g	**8%**	19 g	**29%**
Saturated Fat	1.5 g	**8%**	11 g	**55%**
Cholesterol	5 mg	**2%**	120 mg	**40%**
Sodium	390 mg	**16%**	520 mg	**22%**
Total Carbohydrate	81 g	**27%**	65 g	**22%**
Dietary Fiber	12 g	**48%**	1 g	**4%**
Sugars	13 g		48 g	
Other	33 g		0 g	
Protein	9 g		7 g	

*Percent of Daily Values on page a-22

Exchanges and 36 g Carbohydrates Per Serving

Breads	1.4	Vegetables	0.0	Fruits	0.6
Meats	0.3	Milk	0.3	Fats	0.8

Directions

MIx **SugarLike, ButterLike**, and egg substitutes; mix until smooth. Add milk, spices, vanilla, bread cubes, and raisins; stir gently. Pour into a vegetable sprayed 10x6 1/2-inch pan. Bake at 350° for 40-45 minutes or until a knife inserted near edge comes out clean.

Sauce: Combine **SugarLike**, cornstarch, and salt in a saucepan. Stir in water; cook over medium heat for 3 minutes. Remove from heat. Add remaining ingredients. Serve warm with pudding.

Fruit Bread Pudding

The Fat Quotient using **ButterLike** is **10%** instead of **24%**
70% less fat **60% less sugar**
27% less Calories

U.S.	Ingredients	Metric
1/2 cup	**Granulated SugarLike**	100.00 g
1 cup	Egg substitutes	251.00 g
2 1/4 cup	Skim milk	551.00 g
1 Tbsp	Vanilla	15.00 g
1 tsp	Orange peel, finely shredded	2.00 g
1/2 tsp	Ground cardamom or cinnamon	1.00 g
4 cups	Dry french bread or regular bread cubes	120.00 g
1/3 cup	Raisins, cherries or cranberries	48.00 g

Directions

Combine **SugarLike,** egg substitutes, milk, vanilla, orange peel, and cardamom or cinnamon. In a vegetable sprayed 2-quart baking dish, toss together bread cubes and dried fruit; pour egg mixture evenly over bread mixture. Bake in a 350° oven for 40-45 minutes or until a knife inserted near the center comes out clean. Cool slightly.

Streusel-Topped Bread Pudding: Prepare as above, except, for topping, in a small bowl combine 1/4 cup all-purpose flour, 1/4 cup **Brown SugarLike**, and 2 Tbsp softened **ButterLike** until mixture resembles coarse crumbs. Sprinkle over pudding and bake.

Exchanges and 16 g Carbohydrates Per Serving					
Breads	0.5	Vegetables	0.0	Fruits	0.3
Meats	0.5	Milk	0.3	Fats	0.1

Nutrition Facts				
Serving Size	136 g			
Servings Per Recipe	8			
Amount per serving			High Fat/Sugar Comparison	
Calories		139	190	
Calories from fat		15	50	
	% Daily Value*		% Daily Value*	
Total Fat	1.5 g	**2%**	5 g	**8%**
Saturated Fat	0 g	**0%**	2.5 g	**13%**
Cholesterol	0 mg	**0%**	115 mg	**38%**
Sodium	170 mg	**7%**	140 mg	**6%**
Total Carbohydrate	29 g	**10%**	29 g	**10%**
Dietary Fiber	4 g	**16%**	1 g	**4%**
Sugars	8 g		20 g	
Other	9 g		0 g	
Protein	7 g		7 g	

*Percent of Daily Values on page a-22

Bateman's Rice Pudding

The Fat Quotient using **ButterLike** is **9%** instead of **37%**
85% less fat **65% less sugar**
40% less Calories

U.S.	Ingredients	Metric
1/4 cup	**ButterLike Saute Butter**	56.00 g
5/8 cup	**Granulated SugarLike**	125.00 g
2 cups	Rice, cooked	316.00 g
1 1/4 cup	Skim milk	306.00 g
12 oz	Evaporated skim milk	340.00 g
1	Egg yolk	17.00 g
1 Tbsp	Cornstarch	8.00 g
1/2 tsp	Salt	3.00 g
1/2 tsp	Clnnamon	1.20 g
1/2 tsp	Nutmeg	1.00 g
1/2 cup	Raisins	73.00 g

Directions

In a saucepan, mix the **SugarLike**, cornstarch, and salt. Stir in milks and **ButterLike**. Heat until boiling, stirring constantly. Stir in a small amount of the hot mixture into the beaten egg yolk. Stir the yolk mixture back into the saucepan. Add cooked rice, cinnamon, and nutmeg. Stir in the raisins. Cool in the refrigerator.

Nutrition Facts				
Serving Size	311 g			
Servings Per Recipe	4			
Amount per serving			High Fat/Sugar Comparison	
Calories		374	620	
Calories from fat		35	240	
	% Daily Value*		% Daily Value*	
Total Fat	4 g	**6%**	26 g	**40%**
Saturated Fat	1.5 g	**8%**	14 g	**70%**
Cholesterol	60 mg	**20%**	170 mg	**57%**
Sodium	430 mg	**18%**	550 mg	**23%**
Total Carbohydrate	87 g	**29%**	82 g	**27%**
Dietary Fiber	9 g	**36%**	1 g	**4%**
Sugars	16 g		46 g	
Other	23 g		0 g	
Protein	13 g		13 g	

*Percent of Daily Values on page a-22

Exchanges and 55 g Carbohydrates Per Serving					
Breads	1.9	Vegetables	0.0	Fruits	1.0
Meats	0.1	Milk	1.1	Fats	0.7

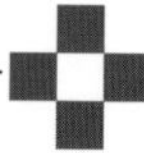

Cranberry Steamed Pudding

The Fat Quotient using ButterLike is 8% instead of 45%
90% less fat **96% less sugar**
50% less Calories

U.S.	Ingredients	Metric
1/2 cup	**Brown SugarLike**	100.00 g
5/8 cup	Hot water	148.00 g
2 tsp	Baking soda	9.20 g
1 1/2 cup	All-purpose flour	173.00 g
2 cups	Fresh or frozen cranberries	220.00 g
1/2 tsp	Salt	3.00 g
Sauce:		
1 cup	**Granulated SugarLike**	200.00 g
1/2 cup	**ButterLike Saute Butter**	110.00 g
1 tsp	Cornstarch	2.70 g
1/8 tsp	Salt	.75 g
1 cup	Evaporated skim milk	255.00 g
1 tsp	Vanilla extract	5.00 g

Directions

Combine all pudding ingredients in order given. Pour into a vegetable sprayed 4-cup pudding mold. Place in a deep kettle on a rack. Fill kettle with boiling water to 1-inch depth; cover and boil gently. Replace water as needed. Steam 1 hour or until pudding tests done. Let stand 5 minutes before unmolding.

Nutrition Facts				
Serving Size	205 g			
Servings Per Recipe	6			
Amount per serving			High Fat/Sugar Comparison	
Calories	310		620	
Calories from fat	30		280	
	% Daily Value*		% Daily Value*	
Total Fat	3 g	**5%**	31 g	**48%**
Saturated Fat	1 g	**5%**	19 g	**95%**
Cholesterol	5 mg	**2%**	100 mg	**33%**
Sodium	710 mg	**30%**	850 mg	**35%**
Total Carbohydrate	87 g	**29%**	80 g	**27%**
Dietary Fiber	14 g	**56%**	2 g	**8%**
Sugars	2 g		50 g	
Other	37 g		0 g	
Protein	8 g		4 g	

*Percent of Daily Values on page a-22

Exchanges and 36 g Carbohydrates Per Serving

Breads	1.9	Vegetables	0.0	Fruits	0.3
Meats	0.0	Milk	0.4	Fats	0.6

Sauce: Combine **SugarLike**, cornstarch, and salt in a saucepan. Add evaporated milk and **ButterLike**. Cook and stir over medium until mixture boils. Boil for 1 minute. Remove from heat; stir in vanilla. Serve warm with pudding.

Blackberry Cobbler

The Fat Quotient using ButterLike is 13% instead of 51%
86% less fat **87% less sugar**
47% less Calories

U.S.	Ingredients	Metric
1/2 cup	**ButterLike Saute Butter**	112.00 g
1/2 cup	**ButterLike Baking Butter**	114.00 g
1 cup	**Granulated SugarLike**	200.00 g
1 cup	Water	237.00 g
1 1/2 cup	All-purpose flour	173.00 g

U.S.	Ingredients	Metric
1 tsp	Baking powder	4.00 g
1/3 cup	Skim milk (room temperature)	82.00 g
2 cups	Fresh or frozen blackberries	288.00 g
1/2 -1 tsp	Ground cinnamon	1.15 g
2 Tbsp	**Granulated SugarLike**	25.00 g

Directions

In a 10-inch vegetable sprayed round or oval baking dish, pour **Saute Butter;** set aside. In a saucepan, heat 1 cup **SugarLike** and water until **SugarLike** dissolves; set aside. Mix flour and baking powder; cut in softened **Baking Butter** until fine crumbs form. Add milk, stirring with a fork until dough leaves sides of bowl. Turn out onto a floured board; knead three or four times. Roll out to an 11x 9-inch rectangle, 1/4-inch thick. Spread berries over dough; sprinkle with cinnamon. Roll up, jelly-roll style. Cut into 1/4-inch thick slices. Lay slices in baking dish. Pour **SugarLike** syrup around slices (syrup will be absorbed). Bake at 350° for 45 minutes. Put cookie sheet under pan to catch the drippings. Sprinkle 2 Tbsp **SugarLike** over top and bake 15 minutes more. Serve warm or cold.

Nutrition Facts				
Serving Size	154 g			
Servings Per Recipe	8			
Amount per serving			High Fat/Sugar Comparison	
Calories	234		440	
Calories from fat	30		230	
	% Daily Value*		% Daily Value*	
Total Fat	3.5 g	**5%**	25 g	**38%**
Saturated Fat	1 g	**5%**	15 g	**75%**
Cholesterol	5 mg	**2%**	65 mg	**22%**
Sodium	115 mg	**5%**	300 mg	**13%**
Total Carbohydrate	61 g	**20%**	50 g	**17%**
Dietary Fiber	9 g	**36%**	2 g	**8%**
Sugars	4 g		31 g	
Other	21 g		0 g	
Protein	4 g		3 g	

*Percent of Daily Values on page a-22

Exchanges and 31 g Carbohydrates Per Serving					
Breads	1.9	Vegetables	0.0	Fruits	0.3
Meats	0.9	Milk	0.9	Fats	0.3

Blackberry Cobbler, Blueberry Peach Cobbler (rectangle glass dish), page 100, and Pumpkin Bars, page 81.

Blueberry Peach Cobbler

The Fat Quotient using **ButterLike** is **6%** instead of **45%**
92% less fat **65% less sugar**
41% less Calories

U.S.	Ingredients	Metric
Filling:		
1/3-1/2 cup	**Granulated SugarLike**	67.00 g
2 cups	Fresh or frozen sliced peaches	340.00 g
4 tsp	Quick-cooking tapioca	13.00 g
2 tsp	Lemon juice	10.00 g
1 cup	Fresh or frozen blueberries	155.00 g
1/4-1/2 tsp	Ground nutmeg	.60 g
Dumplings:		
2 Tbsp	**Granulated SugarLike**	25.00 g
1/4 cup	**ButterLike Baking Butter**	57.00 g
1 cup	All-purpose flour	115.00 g
1 1/2 tsp	Baking powder	6.00 g
1/8 tsp	Salt	.75 g
1 tsp	Grated lemon peel	2.00 g
1/2 cup	Evaporated skim milk	128.00 g

Nutrition Facts				
Serving Size	115 g			
Servings Per Recipe	8			
Amount per serving			High Fat/Sugar Comparison	
Calories	142		240	
Calories from fat	5		100	
	% Daily Value*		% Daily Value*	
Total Fat	1 g	**2%**	12 g	**18%**
Saturated Fat	0 g	**0%**	7 g	**35%**
Cholesterol	0 mg	**0%**	35 mg	**12%**
Sodium	160 mg	**7%**	180 mg	**8%**
Total Carbohydrate	37 g	**12%**	32 g	**11%**
Dietary Fiber	5 g	**20%**	2 g	**8%**
Sugars	6 g		17 g	
Other	8 g		0 g	
Protein	3 g		2 g	

*Percent of Daily Values on page a-22

Exchanges and 24 g Carbohydrates Per Serving

Breads	1.1	Vegetables	0.0	Fruits	0.5
Meats	0.0	Milk	0.2	Fats	0.1

Directions

Filling: In a 1-quart vegetable sprayed baking dish, combine peaches, **SugarLike**, tapioca, and lemon juice. Sprinkle blueberries over top. Sprinkle with nutmeg; set aside.

Dumplings: Combine softened **ButterLike**, **SugarLike**, and evaporated milk. Mix until smooth. Add remaining ingredients. Stir until dough is mixed and moistened. Drop by tablespoon-full over fruit mixture. Bake at 400° for 40-45 minutes or until top is golden brown. Serve warm with ice cream, if desired.

Orange Cream Squares

The Fat Quotient using **ButterLike** is **12%** instead of **33%**
75% less fat **33% less sugar**
32% less Calories

U.S.	Ingredients	Metric
Crust:		
1/4 cup	**Brown SugarLike**	50.00 g
1/4 cup	**ButterLike Saute Butter**	56.00 g
3/4 cup	Low fat graham cracker crumbs	72.00 g
Filling:		
3/4 cup	Skim milk	184.00 g
1 pint	Fat free vanilla ice cream	284.00 g
2 tsp	Grated orange peel	4.00 g
1 pkg	Sugar free instant vanilla pudding mix (3.4 oz)	96.00 g

U.S.	Ingredients	Metric
Glaze:		
1/4 cup	**Granulated SugarLike**	50.00 g
4 tsp	Cornstarch	11.00 g
5/8 cup	Orange juice	158.00 g
2 Tbsp	Lemon juice	31.00 g
1 can	Mandarin oranges (11 oz)	312.00 g

Directions

Crust: Combine ingredients and press into a vegetable sprayed 8-inch square pan; chill.

Filling: Combine milk, softened ice cream, and orange peel in a mixing bowl. Add pudding mix, beating slowly on low speed until well blended. Pour over crust. Chill until set, about 1 hour.

Glaze: Combine **SugarLike**, cornstarch, orange juice, lemon juice, and mandarin orange juice in a saucepan. Bring to a boil. Reduce heat and cook, stirring until mixture thickens, about 2 minutes. Remove from heat and cool. Arrange oranges over filling. Drizzle with glaze. Chill until set.

Note: Diabetics should substitute 1 pint softened sugar free vanilla ice cream for the 1 pint fat free vanilla ice cream. Fat will increase to 4.3 grams; sugar will be reduced to 11 gram per serving.

Nutrition Facts				
Serving Size	145 g			
Servings Per Recipe	9			
Amount per serving			High Fat/Sugar Comparison	
Calories	183		270	
Calories from fat	20		90	
	% Daily Value*		% Daily Value*	
Total Fat	2.5 g	**4%**	10 g	**15%**
Saturated Fat	0.5 g	**3%**	6 g	**30%**
Cholesterol	0 mg	**0%**	30 mg	**10%**
Sodium	410 mg	**17%**	300 mg	**13%**
Total Carbohydrate	43 g	**14%**	42 g	**14%**
Dietary Fiber	3 g	**12%**	0 g	**0%**
Sugars	14 g		21 g	
Other	8 g		0 g	
Protein	5 g		3 g	

*Percent of Daily Values on page a-22

Exchanges and 32 g Carbohydrates Per Serving

Breads	1.8	Vegetables	0.0	Fruits	0.4
Meats	0.0	Milk	0.1	Fats	0.5

Chocolate Souffle

The Fat Quotient using **ButterLike** is **26%** instead of **48%**
68% less fat **89% less sugar**
42% less Calories

U.S.	Ingredients	Metric
1/4 cup	**ButterLike Saute Butter**	56.00 g
3 Tbsp	**ButterLike Baking Butter**	43.00 g
1/2 cup	**Granulated SugarLike**	100.00 g
3 Tbsp	All-purpose flour	22.00 g
3/4 cup	Skim milk	184.00 g
3 Tbsp	Cocoa	45.00 g
2	Egg yolks	33.00 g
3/4 cup	Egg substitutes	188.00 g
1/2 tsp	Vanilla	2.50 g

Directions

Vegetable spray the sides of a 2-quart souffle dish. Sprinkle sides with a little **SugarLike**. Set dish aside. In a small saucepan heat **ButterLike**, flour, and milk. Cook and stir until thickened and bubbly. Add cocoa; stir until combined. Remove from heat. Gradually stir chocolate mixture into beaten egg yolks. Set aside. Beat egg substitutes and vanilla. Gradually add **SugarLike** while beating. Combine mixtures gradually. Transfer to prepared dish. Bake in a 350° oven for 35-40 minutes or until a knife inserted near the center comes out clean. If desired, top with fat free whipped topping. Serve souffle immediately.

Nutrition Facts				
Serving Size	112 g			
Servings Per Recipe	6			
Amount per serving			High Fat/Sugar Comparison	
Calories	152		260	
Calories from fat	40		130	
	% Daily Value*		% Daily Value*	
Total Fat	4.5 g	**7%**	14 g	**22%**
Saturated Fat	1.5 g	**8%**	8 g	**40%**
Cholesterol	75 mg	**25%**	160 mg	**53%**
Sodium	110 mg	**5%**	115 mg	**5%**
Total Carbohydrate	29 g	**10%**	26 g	**9%**
Dietary Fiber	4 g	**16%**	1 g	**4%**
Sugars	2 g		21 g	
Other	12 g		0 g	
Protein	7 g		7 g	

*Percent of Daily Values on page a-22

Exchanges and 13 g Carbohydrates Per Serving

Breads	0.6	Vegetables	0.0	Fruits	0.0
Meats	0.6	Milk	0.1	Fats	0.6

Caramel Pecan Strata

The Fat Quotient using ButterLike is **17%** instead of **51%**
88% less fat **90% less sugar**
64% less Calories

U.S.	**Ingredients**	Metric
6 Tbsp	**ButterLike Baking Butter**	85.00 g
3/4 cup	**Brown SugarLike**	150.00 g
1 1/2 Tbsp	**Liquid SugarLike**	30.00 g
3 Tbsp	Pecans, chopped	20.00 g
8 slices	White bread, crust removed	184.00 g
1 cup	Egg substitutes	244.00 g
1 cup	Skim milk	245.00 g
2/3 tsp	Vanilla	3.30 g
1/4 tsp	Salt	1.50 g

Directions

Make caramel by combining **ButterLike** and **SugarLikes** in a saucepan. Bring to a boil. Pour caramel into a vegetable sprayed 9x9x2-inch pan. Sprinkle with pecans; let cool. Place a layer of bread over caramel; trim as needed. Repeat with second layer; set aside. Whisk milk, eggs, vanilla, and salt together. Pour over bread. Refrigerate, covered, overnight. Bake strata at 350° for 30-40 minutes until puffed. Let strata stand 5-10 minutes before slicing. Serve pieces caramel side up.

Nutrition Facts				
Serving Size	241 g			
Servings Per Recipe	4			
Amount per serving			High Fat/Sugar Comparison	
Calories	324		910	
Calories from fat	50		470	
	% Daily Value*		% Daily Value*	
Total Fat	6 g	**9%**	52 g	**60%**
Saturated Fat	1 g	**5%**	20 g	**100%**
Cholesterol	5 mg	**2%**	285 mg	**95%**
Sodium	610 mg	**25%**	930 mg	**39%**
Total Carbohydrate	80 g	**27%**	93 g	**31%**
Dietary Fiber	15 g	**60%**	2 g	**8%**
Sugars	4 g		41 g	
Other	32 g		0 g	
Protein	13 g		16 g	

*Percent of Daily Values on page a-22

Exchanges and 33 g Carbohydrates Per Serving

Breads	2.1	Vegetables	0.0	Fruits	0.0
Meats	0.9	Milk	0.2	Fats	1.1

Caramel Pecan Strata

Baked Custard

The Fat Quotient using ButterLike is **15%** instead of **30%**
71% less fat **81% less sugar**
41% less Calories

U.S.	Ingredients	Metric
2/3 cup	**Granulated SugarLike**	133.00 g
1/2 cup	Egg whites	114.00 g
2	Whole eggs	100.00 g
1/2 tsp	Salt	3.00 g
1/4 tsp	Nutmeg	.55 g
1/4 tsp	Cinnamon	.58 g
1 Tbsp	Vanilla extract	15.00 g
2 2/3 cup	Skim milk	653.00 g

Directions

In a mixing bowl, combine **SugarLike**, eggs, spices, and vanilla. Blend in milk. Pour in a 1 1/2-quart baking dish. Place baking dish in a cake pan in oven; add 1 inch water to bottom of pan. Bake at 325° for 1 hour or until a knife inserted near middle comes out clean.

Nutrition Facts				
Serving Size	170 g			
Servings Per Recipe	6			
Amount per serving			High Fat/Sugar Comparison	
Calories	124		210	
Calories from fat	15		60	
	% Daily Value*		% Daily Value*	
Total Fat	2 g	**2%**	7 g	**11%**
Saturated Fat	0.5 g	**3%**	3.5 g	**18%**
Cholesterol	75 mg	**25%**	155 mg	**52%**
Sodium	300 mg	**13%**	290 mg	**12%**
Total Carbohydrate	28 g	**9%**	29 g	**10%**
Dietary Fiber	5 g	**20%**	0 g	**0%**
Sugars	5 g		27 g	
Other	16 g		0 g	
Protein	8 g		8 g	

*Percent of Daily Values on page a-22

Exchanges and 7 g Carbohydrates Per Serving

Breads	0.0	Vegetables	0.0	Fruits	0.0
Meats	0.6	Milk	0.4	Fats	0.2

Custard Cooked Rice

The Fat Quotient using ButterLike is **0%** instead of **37%**
100% less fat **63% less sugar**
34% less Calories

U.S.	Ingredients	Metric
1/2 cup +2 Tbsp	**Granulated SugarLike**	125.00 g
2 cups	Skim milk	490.00 g
1 can	Evaporated skim milk (12 oz)	340.00 g
1/2 cup	Raisins	72.50 g
1 Tbsp	Cornstarch	8.00 g
1/4 tsp	Salt	1.50 g
2 cups	Cooked rice	330.00 g
1/2 cup	Egg whites	114.00 g
1/8 tsp	Nutmeg	.30 g
1/8 tsp	Cinnamon	.30 g
1 tsp	Vanilla	4.70 g

Directions

Scald milks with raisins. In a small bowl, combine **SugarLike**, cornstarch, and salt; stir into milk mixture until smooth; add rice. Reheat to a full boil; remove from heat. Add a small amount of rice mixture to egg whites; add egg white mixture into remaining rice mixture. Stir in remaining ingredients.

Nutrition Facts				
Serving Size	186 g			
Servings Per Recipe	8			
Amount per serving			High Fat/Sugar Comparison	
Calories	166		250	
Calories from fat	0		60	
	% Daily Value*		% Daily Value*	
Total Fat	0 g	**0%**	7 g	**11%**
Saturated Fat	0 g	**0%**	3.5 g	**18%**
Cholesterol	5 mg	**2%**	75 mg	**25%**
Sodium	180 mg	**8%**	170 mg	**7%**
Total Carbohydrate	40 g	**13%**	40 g	**13%**
Dietary Fiber	4 g	**16%**	1 g	**4%**
Sugars	9 g		24 g	
Other	11 g		0 g	
Protein	8 g		8 g	

*Percent of Daily Values on page a-22

Exchanges and 35 g Carbohydrates Per Serving

Breads	0.6	Vegetables	0.0	Fruits	0.5
Meats	0.2	Milk	0.6	Fats	0.0

Stirred Custard

The Fat Quotient using **ButterLike** is **35%** instead of **60%**
63% less fat **50% less sugar**
36% less Calories

U.S.	Ingredients	Metric
5 Tbsp	**ButterLike Saute Butter**	70.00 g
1/4 cup	**Granulated SugarLike**	50.00 g
3	Beaten eggs	150.00 g
2 cups	Skim milk	490.00 g
1 tsp	Vanilla	5.00 g

Directions

In a heavy saucepan, combine **SugarLike**, **ButterLike**, eggs, and milk. Cook and stir over medium heat. Continue cooking egg mixture until it coats a metal spoon. Remove from heat. Stir in vanilla. Quickly cool the custard by placing the saucepan into a sink of ice water for 1-2 minutes, stirring constantly. Pour custard mixture into a bowl. Cover the surface with plastic wrap. Chill at least 1 hour. Serve custard over fresh fruit or cake if desired.

Flavored Stirred Custard: Prepare as above, except substitute 2- 3 Tbsp amaretto, orange liqueur, coffee liqueur, rum, brandy, or desired flavor for the vanilla.

Nutrition Facts				
Serving Size	128 g			
Servings Per Recipe	6			
Amount per serving			High Fat/Sugar Comparison	
Calories	116		180	
Calories from fat	15		110	
	% Daily Value*		% Daily Value*	
Total Fat	4.5 g	**7%**	12 g	**18%**
Saturated Fat	1.5 g	**8%**	7 g	**35%**
Cholesterol	110 mg	**37%**	135 mg	**45%**
Sodium	75 mg	**3%**	65 mg	**3%**
Total Carbohydrate	16 g	**5%**	12 g	**4%**
Dietary Fiber	2 g	**8%**	0 g	**0%**
Sugars	4 g		8 g	
Other	6 g		0 g	
Protein	7 g		6 g	

*Percent of Daily Values on page a-22

Exchanges and 8 g Carbohydrates Per Serving					
Breads	0.3	Vegetables	0.0	Fruits	0.3
Meats	0.5	Milk	0.3	Fats	0.6

Stirred Custard

Baked Apples

The Fat Quotient using **ButterLike** is 3% instead of 3%
0% less fat **81% less sugar**
16% less Calories

U.S.	**Ingredients**	Metric
2 Tbsp	**Brown SugarLike**	25.00 g
4 medium	Cooking apples	512.00 g
1/2 cup	Raisins	73.00 g
1/2 tsp	Ground cinnamon	1.20 g
1/4 tsp	Ground nutmeg	.55 g
1/3 cup	Apple juice or water	83.00 g

Directions

Core apples; peel a strip from the top of each. Place apples in a 2-quart casserole dish. Combine the **Brown SugarLike**, raisins, cinnamon, and nutmeg; spoon into the center of the apples. Pour apple juice or water into casserole. Bake apples in a 350° oven for 40-45 minutes or until the apples are tender, basting occasionally. If desired, serve warm with ice cream.

Nutrition Facts				
Serving Size	173 g			
Servings Per Recipe	4			
Amount per serving			High Fat/Sugar Comparison	
Calories	151		180	
Calories from fat	5		5	
	% Daily Value*		% Daily Value*	
Total Fat	0.5 g	**1%**	0.5 g	**1%**
Saturated Fat	0 g	**0%**	0 g	**0%**
Cholesterol	0 mg	**0%**	0 mg	**0%**
Sodium	0 mg	**0%**	5 mg	**0%**
Total Carbohydrate	42 g	**14%**	43 g	**14%**
Dietary Fiber	5 g	**12%**	3 g	**12%**
Sugars	30 g		36 g	
Other	5 g		0 g	
Protein	1 g		1 g	

*Percent of Daily Values on page a-22

Exchanges and 32 g Carbohydrates Per Serving					
Breads	0.0	Vegetables	0.0	Fruits	2.3
Meats	0.0	Milk	0.0	Fats	0.0

Baked Apples

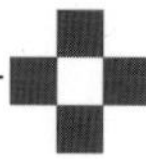

Grandma's Apple Dumplings

The Fat Quotient using ButterLike is 9% instead of 35%
86% less fat **67% less sugar**
45% less Calories

U.S.	Ingredients	Metric
1/2 cup	**Granulated SugarLike**	100.00 g
2 tsp	Maple flavoring	10.00 g
3/4 cup	Water	178.00 g
1	**Mrs. Bateman's Pie Crust**, page 227	307.00 g
1/3 cup	**Granulated SugarLike**	67.00 g
6 small	Baking apples, peeled and cored	768.00 g
3 Tbsp	**ButterLike Saute Butter**	42.00 g

Nutrition Facts				
Serving Size	245 g			
Servings Per Recipe	6			
Amount per serving			High Fat/Sugar Comparison	
Calories	296		530	
Calories from fat	30		190	
	% Daily Value*		% Daily Value*	
Total Fat	3 g	**5%**	21 g	**32%**
Saturated Fat	1 g	**5%**	5 g	**25%**
Cholesterol	5 mg	**2%**	0 mg	**0%**
Sodium	480 mg	**20%**	320 mg	**13%**
Total Carbohydrate	79 g	**26%**	82 g	**27%**
Dietary Fiber	9 g	**12%**	2 g	**8%**
Sugars	17 g		51 g	
Other	23 g		0 g	
Protein	3 g		4 g	

*Percent of Daily Values on page a-22

Exchanges and 47 g Carbohydrates Per Serving

Breads	2.0	Vegetables	0.0	Fruits	1.2
Meats	0.0	Milk	0.0	Fats	0.5

Directions

Maple Syrup: Combine **SugarLike**, maple flavor, and water in small saucepan. Bring to a boil for 2 minutes; cool. This syrup can also be used on pancakes and waffles.

Follow directions for **Mrs. Bateman's Pie Crust** . On a floured surface, roll pastry out to an 18x12-inch rectangle. Cut into six, 6-inch squares. Place an apple on each square. Combine **SugarLike** and **ButterLike**; spoon into apple centers. Moisten edges of pastry; fold up corners to center and pinch to seal. Place on a vegetable sprayed 13x9x2-inch baking pan. Bake at 450° for 15 minutes. Reduce heat to 350° and continue baking until done, about 30 minutes, basting twice with warmed maple syrup. Serve warm.

Apple Kuchen

The Fat Quotient using ButterLike is 3% instead of 14%
86% less fat **97% less sugar**
41% less Calories

U.S.	Ingredients	Metric
1 Tbsp	**ButterLike Baking Butter**	14.00 g
1 cup	**Granulated SugarLike**	200.00 g
6 large	Baking apples, pared and sliced	342.00 g
2 tsp	Cinnamon	4.60 g
1/2 cup	Skim milk	123.00 g
1 cup	All-purpose flour	115.00 g
1 tsp	Baking powder	4.00 g

U.S.	Ingredients	Metric
Sauce:		
1 cup	**Granulated SugarLike**	200.00 g
2 Tbsp	**ButterLike Saute Butter**	28.00 g
2 Tbsp	Cornstarch	16.00 g
1/2 tsp	Salt	3.00 g
2 cups	Cold water	474.00 g
1 tsp	Vanilla extract	5.00 g

Directions

Arrange apples in a 13x9x2-inch baking pan. Combine cinnamon and 1/2 cup **SugarLike**. Reserve 1 Tbsp; sprinkle remaining mixture over apples. In a mixing bowl, combine softened **ButterLike**, milk, remaining **SugarLike**, flour, and baking powder. Drop by tablespoonfuls over apples; sprinkle reserved **SugarLike** on top. Bake at 350° for 35-40 minutes or until golden brown.

Sauce: Combine **SugarLike**, cornstarch, salt, and water in a saucepan. Cook, stirring, over medium heat until thick. Remove from heat; add **ButterLike Saute Butter** and vanilla. Serve sauce and kuchen warm.

Exchanges and 14 g Carbohydrates Per Serving					
Breads	0.7	Vegetables	0.0	Fruits	0.3
Meats	0.0	Milk	0.0	Fats	0.1

Nutrition Facts				
Serving Size	129 g			
Servings Per Recipe	12			
Amount per serving			High Fat/Sugar Comparison	
Calories		136	230	
Calories from fat		5	30	
	% Daily Value*		% Daily Value*	
Total Fat	0.5 g	1%	3.5 g	5%
Saturated Fat	0 g	0%	2 g	10%
Cholesterol	0 mg	0%	10 mg	3%
Sodium	140 mg	6%	170 mg	7%
Total Carbohydrate	47 g	16%	47 g	16%
Dietary Fiber	9 g	36%	1 g	4%
Sugars	1 g		33 g	
Other	24 g		0 g	
Protein	2 g		1 g	

*Percent of Daily Values on page a-22

Cranberry Muffin Dessert

The Fat Quotient using ButterLike is 5% instead of 43%
94% less fat **100% less sugar**
41% less Calories

U.S.	Ingredients	Metric
1/4 cup	**ButterLike Baking Butter**, softened	57.00 g
1/2 cup	**Granulated SugarLike**	100.00 g
1 cup	All-purpose flour	115.00 g
1/2 tsp	Salt	3.00 g
1 1/8 tsp	Baking powder	5.00 g
1/2 cup	Evaporated skim milk	128.00 g
1 1/2 cup	Cranberries, raw, washed	165.00 g
Sauce:		
3 Tbsp	**ButterLike Baking Butter**	43.00 g
1/4 cup	**Granulated SugarLike**	50.00 g
1/4 cup	Evaporated skim milk	64.00 g

Directions

Stir together **SugarLike**, softened **ButterLike**, and 1/4 cup evaporated milk until almost smooth. Blend in remaining ingredients. Fold in cranberries. Put into liners in muffin tin. Bake at 350° for 30 minutes.

Sauce: Mix all ingredients in a heavy saucepan. On a low boil, stir until thick. Drizzle over muffins while warm.

Nutrition Facts				
Serving Size	61 g			
Servings Per Recipe	12			
Amount per serving			High Fat/Sugar Comparison	
Calories		102	180	
Calories from fat		5	80	
	% Daily Value*		% Daily Value*	
Total Fat	0.5 g	1%	8 g	12%
Saturated Fat	0 g	0%	5 g	25%
Cholesterol	0 mg	0%	25 mg	8%
Sodium	190 mg	8%	220 mg	9%
Total Carbohydrate	28 g	9%	23 g	8%
Dietary Fiber	4 g	16%	1 g	4%
Sugars	0 g		12 g	
Other	9 g		0 g	
Protein	2 g		2 g	

*Percent of Daily Values on page a-22

Exchanges and 15 g Carbohydrates Per Serving					
Breads	0.8	Vegetables	0.0	Fruits	0.1
Meats	0.0	Milk	0.2	Fats	0.1

Apple Cobbler

The Fat Quotient using ButterLike is 6% instead of 21%
80% less fat 100% less sugar
30% less Calories

U.S.	Ingredients	Metric
Topping:		
1/3 cup	**ButterLike Baking Butter**	85.00 g
1 1/4 cup	All-purpose flour	144.00 g
1/3 tsp	Salt	2.00 g
1/2 tsp	Baking powder	2.00 g
1/4 cup	Cold water	59.00 g
Filling:		
3 3/4 lb	Canned apple slices, unsweetened	1701.00 g
2 3/8 cup	Water, use as needed	563.00 g
1/4 cup	Cornstarch	32.00 g
1 cup	**Granulated SugarLike**	200.00 g
1 tsp	Cinnamon	2.30 g
1/2 tsp	Nutmeg	1.10 g
1	Egg white	33.00 g

Directions

Pastry Topping: In a large mixing bowl, mix softened **ButterLike**, flour, salt, and baking powder until small crumbs. Add the water and mix just until moistened. Cover and set aside.

Filling: Drain apples, reserving juice. Set apples aside. Add enough water to apple juice to make 2 3/8 cups liquid mixture. Bring remaining liquid mixture to a boil. Add about 1/2 of the **SugarLike**. Gradually add cornstarch mixture to boiling liquid. Cook, stirring constantly, until thickened. Mixture will be very thick. Remove from heat. Blend remaining **SugarLike**, cinnamon, and nutmeg thoroughly into mixture. Add apples to thickened mixture. Stir lightly. Do not break up fruit. Pour apple mixture into a 9x13-inch vegetable sprayed pan. Roll out pastry dough into rectangles about 9x13 inches on a lightly floured surface. Cover apples with pastry. Brush with egg whites. Cut slits in pastry. Bake for 45 minutes in a 425° oven until pastry is brown and filling is bubbly. Cover halfway through baking or when pastry begins to turn gold.

Nutrition Facts				
Serving Size	188 g			
Servings Per Recipe	15			
Amount per serving			High Fat/Sugar Comparison	
Calories	147		210	
Calories from fat	10		50	
	% Daily Value*		% Daily Value*	
Total Fat	1 g	**2%**	5 g	**8%**
Saturated Fat	0 g	**0%**	3 g	**15%**
Cholesterol	0 mg	**0%**	15 mg	**5%**
Sodium	95 mg	**4%**	120 mg	**5%**
Total Carbohydrate	41 g	**14%**	38 g	**1%**
Dietary Fiber	5 g	**20%**	1 g	**4%**
Sugars	0 g		13 g	
Other	10 g		0 g	
Protein	2 g		2 g	

*Percent of Daily Values on page a-22

Exchanges and 26 g Carbohydrates Per Serving

Breads	0.8	Vegetables	0.0	Fruits	1.0
Meats	0.0	Milk	0.0	Fats	0.1

Fruit Crisp

The Fat Quotient using ButterLike is 10% instead of 34%
82% less fat **58% less sugar**
41% less Calories

U.S.	Ingredients	Metric
Filling:		
2-4 Tbsp	**Granulated SugarLike**	25.00 g
5 cups	Sliced, peeled fruit	850.00 g
Topping:		
1/2 cup	**Brown SugarLike**	100.00 g
1/4 cup	**ButterLike Baking Butter**	57.00 g
1/2 cup	Regular rolled oats	117.00 g
1/4 cup	All-purpose flour	29.00 g
1/2 tsp	Baking powder	2.00 g
1/4 tsp	Nutmeg, ginger, or cinnamon	.55 g
1/4 cup	Coconut	19.00 g

Directions

Filling: Thaw fruit, if frozen. Do not drain. Place fruit in a 2-quart square baking dish. Stir in **SugarLike.**

Topping: In a medium bowl, combine **SugarLike**, oats, flour, baking powder, and spice. Cut in softened **ButterLike** until mixture resembles coarse crumbs. Stir in the coconut. Sprinkle over filling.

Bake at 375° for 30-35 minutes or until fruit is tender and topping is golden. If desired, serve warm with ice cream.

Nutrition Facts				
Serving Size	200 g			
Servings Per Recipe	6			
Amount per serving			High Fat/Sugar Comparison	
Calories		172	290	
Calories from fat		20	100	
	% Daily Value*		% Daily Value*	
Total Fat	2 g	**3%**	11 g	**17%**
Saturated Fat	1.5 g	**8%**	5 g	**25%**
Cholesterol	0 mg	**0%**	20 mg	**7%**
Sodium	75 mg	**3%**	90 mg	**4%**
Total Carbohydrate	49 g	**16%**	45 g	**15%**
Dietary Fiber	8 g	**32%**	4 g	**16%**
Sugars	14 g		33 g	
Other	16 g		0 g	
Protein	2 g		3 g	

*Percent of Daily Values on page a-22

Exchanges and 25 g Carbohydrates Per Serving

Breads	0.7	Vegetables	0.0	Fruits	1.0
Meats	0.0	Milk	0.0	Fats	0.4

Fruit Crisp

Trifle

The Fat Quotient using **ButterLike** is **18%** instead of **35%**
67% less fat **75% less sugar**
35% less Calories

U.S.	**Ingredients**	Metric
1 recipe	**Stirred Custard**, page114 or Sugar free instant pudding	762.00 g
1 recipe	**Angel Food Cake**, page 56 or **Hot-Milk Sponge Cake**, page 58	617.00 g
1/2 cup	**Granulated SugarLike**	100.00 g
2 1/2 cup	Peaches, kiwi fruit, or berries	545.00 g
1 Tbsp	Sliced toasted almonds, optional	8.40 g
1 1/2 cup	Fat free whipped topping	96.00 g

Directions

My grandmother, from England, loved this dessert. The trifle was layered in a beautiful glass bowl to show off the striking colors. The pudding can be one of several options: Make the **Stirred Custard**, prepare a package of sugar free vanilla pudding, or simply make a homemade pudding on page 182 of my first cookbook, substituting **SugarLike** and **ButterLike.** The cake can be a leftover white or lemon cake, **Hot-Milk Sponge Cake** or **Angel Food Cake**.

Prepare and cool pudding. Prepare cake and cut into 1-inch cubes (5 cups). Reserve remaining cake for another use. In a serving bowl layer half of cake cubes. Sprinkle **SugarLike** over fruit; stir. Top with half of fruit and half of almonds. Spread with half of the whipped topping. Pour half of the pudding over it. Repeat layers. Cover; chill for 3-24 hours.

Note to Diabetics: Substitute whipped topping with 2 Tbsp **SugarLike**, 1/2 cup light whipping cream, and 1/2 tsp vanilla. Beat until soft peaks form; spread over trifle. Fat will increase to 9 grams per serving, but it will be sugar free.

Nutrition Facts				
Serving Size	266 g			
Servings Per Recipe	8			
Amount per serving			High Fat/Sugar Comparison	
Calories	301		460	
Calories from fat	50		160	
	% Daily Value*		% Daily Value*	
Total Fat	6 g	**9%**	18 g	**28%**
Saturated Fat	2.5 g	**13%**	9 g	**45%**
Cholesterol	80 mg	**27%**	200 mg	**67%**
Sodium	110 mg	**5%**	170 mg	**7%**
Total Carbohydrate	77 g	**26%**	64 g	**21%**
Dietary Fiber	5 g	**20%**	2 g	**8%**
Sugars	11 g		44 g	
Other	47 g		0 g	
Protein	10 g		10 g	

*Percent of Daily Values on page a-22

Exchanges and 25 g Carbohydrates Per Serving

Breads	0.9	Vegetables	0.0	Fruits	0.5
Meats	0.8	Milk	0.2	Fats	0.9

Frozen Mocha Cheesecake

The Fat Quotient using ButterLike is **10%** instead of **55%**
91% less fat **77% less sugar**
46% less Calories

U.S.	Ingredients	Metric
Crust:		
2 Tbsp	**Granulated SugarLike**	25.00 g
1/3 cup	**ButterLike Saute Butter**	75.00 g
1 1/2 cup	Low fat graham cracker crumbs	144.00 g
1 1/2 Tbsp	Cocoa	22.00 g
1/2 tsp	Baking powder	2.00 g
Filling:		
2/3 cup	**Chocolate Syrup**, page 235	227.00 g
1 1/2 cup	**Sweetened Condensed Milk**, page 91	397.00 g
2 Tbsp	**ButterLike Saute Butter**, softened	28.00 g
2 pkg	Fat free cream cheese (8 oz each)	454.00 g
1 Tbsp	Instant coffee granules (optional)	15.00 g
1 tsp	Hot water	5.00 g
2 cups	Fat free whipped topping	144.00 g

Directions

Crust: Combine crust ingredients. Press into the bottom of a vegetable sprayed 9-inch springform pan; set aside.

Filling: Follow directions for **Chocolate Syrup** and **Sweetened Condensed Milk**. Beat softened **ButterLike** and cream cheese in a large mixing bowl until smooth. Gradually add Sweetened Condensed Milk and syrup. Dissolve coffee in water; add to mixing bowl. Fold in whipped topping. Pour into crust; freeze at least 6 hours.

For a low sugar recipe, please substitute 1 cup light whipping cream, whipped with 1/4 cup **SugarLike**. This substitute for the 2 cups fat free whipped topping raises the fat grams to 8 grams, but sugar drops to 5 grams.

Nutrition Facts				
Serving Size	199 g			
Servings Per Recipe	20			
Amount per serving			High Fat/Sugar Comparison	
Calories	199		370	
Calories from fat	80		210	
		% Daily Value*		% Daily Value*
Total Fat	2 g	**3%**	23 g	**35%**
Saturated Fat	1 g	**5%**	14 g	**70%**
Cholesterol	5 mg	**2%**	65 mg	**22%**
Sodium	370 mg	**15%**	290 mg	**12%**
Total Carbohydrate	46 g	**15%**	36 g	**12%**
Dietary Fiber	1 g	**4%**	0g	**0%**
Sugars	6 g		26 g	
Other	22 g		0 g	
Protein	9 g		5 g	

*Percent of Daily Values on page a-22

Exchanges and 23 g Carbohydrates Per Serving

Breads	1.0	Vegetables	0.0	Fruits	0.0
Meats	0.0	Milk	0.7	Fats	1.6

Pumpkin Cheesecake

The Fat Quotient using ButterLike is 7% instead of 64%
95% less fat **61% less sugar**
51% less Calories

U.S.	Ingredients	Metric
Crust:		
1/4 cup	**Granulated SugarLike**	50.00 g
4 Tbsp	**ButterLike Saute Butter**	56.00 g
1 cup	Low fat graham cracker crumbs	96.00 g
1/2 tsp	Baking soda	2.30 g
Filling:		
3/4 cup	**Granulated SugarLike**	150.00 g
1/4 cup	**ButterLike Baking Butter**	57.00 g
2 pkgs	Fat free cream cheese (8 oz each)	454.00 g
1 can	Pumpkin (16 oz)	454.00 g
1 1/4 tsp	Cinnamon	3.00 g
1/2 tsp	Ginger	.90 g
1/2 tsp	Nutmeg	1.10 g
1/4 tsp	Salt	1.50 g
1/2 cup	Egg whites	114.00 g
Topping:		
2 Tbsp	**Granulated SugarLike**	25.00 g
2 cups	Fat free sour cream (16 oz)	512.00 g
1 tsp	Vanilla extract	5.00 g

Directions

Crust: Combine **SugarLike**, **ButterLike**, graham cracker crumbs, and baking soda. Press into bottom of a 9-inch springform pan; chill.

Filling: In a large mixing bowl, mix **SugarLike**, softened **Baking Butter**, softened cream cheese, and egg whites until smooth. Beat in pumpkin, spices, and salt. Pour into crust. Bake at 350° for 50 minutes.

Topping: Combine **SugarLike**, sour cream, and vanilla. Spread over filling; bake 5 minutes more. Cool on rack; chill overnight. Garnish each slice with a pecan half (optional).

Nutrition Facts				
Serving Size	165 g			
Servings Per Recipe	12			
Amount per serving			High Fat/Sugar Comparison	
Calories	188		380	
Calories from fat	15		240	
	% Daily Value*		% Daily Value*	
Total Fat	1.5 g	**2%**	27 g	**42%**
Saturated Fat	0.5 g	**3%**	16 g	**80%**
Cholesterol	0 mg	**0%**	105 mg	**35%**
Sodium	450 mg	**19%**	300 mg	**13%**
Total Carbohydrate	41 g	**14%**	26 g	**9%**
Dietary Fiber	5 g	**20%**	0 g	**0%**
Sugars	7 g		18 g	
Other	14 g		0 g	
Protein	10 g		6 g	

*Percent of Daily Values on page a-22

Exchanges and 22 g Carbohydrates Per Serving

Breads	1.1	Vegetables	0.0	Fruits	0.0
Meats	0.1	Milk	0.7	Fats	0.3

Pumpkin Cheesecake

Cranberry Cheesecake

The Fat Quotient using ButterLike is **11%** instead of **65%**
93% less fat **83% less sugar**
58% less Calories

U.S.	Ingredients	Metric
Crust:		
1/3 cup	**ButterLike Baking Butter**	75.00 g
2 cups	Low fat graham cracker crumbs	193.00 g
Topping:		
2/3 cup	**Granulated SugarLike**	133.00 g
1/3 cup	Water	79.00 g
2 cups	Fresh cranberries	220.00 g
1 tsp	Lemon juice	5.00 g
Filling:		
1 cup	**Granulated SugarLike**	200.00 g
1/2 cup	**ButterLike Baking Butter**	114.00 g
4 pkgs	Fat free cream cheese (8 oz each)	907.00 g
2	Large eggs	100.00 g
3/4 cup	Egg whites	170.00 g
1 Tbsp	Lemon juice	15.00 g

Directions

Crust: Combine crumbs and **Saute Butter**; press into the bottom of a 9-inch vegetable sprayed springform pan. Bake at 300° for 5-8 minutes. Cool.

Topping: Combine water and **SugarLike** in a saucepan. Boil over medium heat for 1 minute. Stir in berries; cover and reduce heat. Cook until most berries have popped, about 3 minutes. Add lemon juice. Press mixture through a sieve or food mill; set aside.

Filling: Mix cream cheese and softened **Baking Butter** in a large mixing bowl until smooth. Gradually beat in **SugarLike**. Add eggs and egg whites, beat well. Add lemon juice. Pour into crust; spoon 4 Tbsp of topping on filling and "marble" with a knife or spatula. Bake at 350° for 45 minutes. Turn oven off; let cake stand in oven 2 hours. Remove from oven; cool. Pour remaining topping on top; refrigerate overnight.

Nutrition Facts				
Serving Size	184 g			
Servings Per Recipe	12			
Amount per serving			High Fat/Sugar Comparison	
Calories	256		610	
Calories from fat	30		400	
	% Daily Value*		% Daily Value*	
Total Fat	3 g	**5%**	44 g	**68%**
Saturated Fat	1 g	**5%**	26 g	**130%**
Cholesterol	40 mg	**13%**	210 mg	**70%**
Sodium	640 mg	**27%**	520 mg	**22%**
Total Carbohydrate	53 g	**18%**	44 g	**15%**
Dietary Fiber	8 g	**32%**	1 g	**4%**
Sugars	5 g		30 g	
Other	20 g		0 g	
Protein	15 g		10 g	

*Percent of Daily Values on page a-22

Exchanges and 25 g Carbohydrates Per Serving

Breads	1.4	Vegetables	0.0	Fruits	0.2
Meats	0.4	Milk	0.5	Fats	0.5

Cranberry Cheesecake

Chocolate Glazed Cheesecake

The Fat quotient using ButterLike is **13%** instead of **63%**
90% less fat **70% less sugar**
38% less Calories

U.S.	Ingredients	Metric
Crust:		
1/4 cup	**Granulated SugarLike**	50.00 g
1/2 cup	**ButterLike Saute Butter**	112.00 g
1 3/4 cup	Crushed low fat graham crackers	186.00 g
2 Tbsp	Cocoa	30.00 g
Filling:		
1/3 cup	**ButterLike Saute Butter**	76.00 g
3/4 cup	**Granulated SugarLike**	150.00 g
19 oz	Fat free cream cheese (divided)	539.00 g
3/4 cup	Egg whites (divided)	170.00 g
1 tsp	Vanilla extract (divided)	341.00 g
6 Tbsp	Cocoa	89.00 g
2 Tbsp	**ButterLike Saute Butter**	28.00 g
1 1/3 cup	Fat free sour cream (divided)	341.00 g
1/3 cup	**Brown SugarLike**	67.00 g
1 Tbsp	All-purpose flour	7.00 g
1/4 tsp	Almond extract	2.00 g
Glaze:		
5 Tbsp	**ButterLike Saute Butter**	70.00 g
1/2 cup	**Powdered SugarLike**	53.00 g
9 Tbsp	Cocoa	48.00 g
1/2 tsp	Vanilla extract	2.50 g
1 Tbsp	Water	15.00 g

Nutrition Facts				
Serving Size	170 g			
Servings Per Recipe	12			
Amount per serving			High Fat/Sugar Comparison	
Calories	279		590	
Calories from fat	35		370	
	% Daily Value*		% Daily Value*	
Total Fat	4 g	**6%**	41 g	**83%**
Saturated Fat	1.5 g	**8%**	23 g	**115%**
Cholesterol	5 mg	**2%**	140 mg	**47%**
Sodium	450 mg	**19%**	390 mg	**16%**
Total Carbohydrate	58 g	**19%**	47 g	**16%**
Dietary Fiber	8 g	**32%**	1 g	**4%**
Sugars	8 g		27 g	
Other	20 g		0 g	
Protein	13 g		8 g	

*Percent of Daily Values on page a-22

Exchanges and 30 g Carbohydrates Per Serving					
Breads	1.8	Vegetables	0.0	Fruits	0.0
Meats	0.2	Milk	0.6	Fats	0.8

Directions

Crust: Combine graham cracker crumbs, **SugarLike**, cocoa, and **ButterLike**; blend well. Press into bottom and 2 inches up the sides of a 9-inch vegetable sprayed springform pan; set aside.

Filling: Beat one 8 oz package of cream cheese and 1/4 cup **Granulated SugarLike** until fluffy. Add 1/4 cup egg whites and 1/4 tsp vanilla; blend well. Combine the 6 Tbsp cocoa and the 2 Tbsp **Saute Butter** and heat in microwave 45 seconds. Stir well. Stir in the chocolate mixture and the 1/3 cup sour cream. Spoon over crust. In another bowl, beat the second 8 oz package of cream cheese, **Brown SugarLike**, and flour until fluffy. Add 1/4 cup egg whites and 1/2 tsp vanilla; blend well. Spoon over chocolate layer. In another bowl, beat remaining 3 oz of cream cheese and remaining **Granulated SugarLike** until fluffy. Blend in last 1/4 cup egg whites. Stir in remaining sour cream and vanilla. Add almond extract. Spoon over cream cheese layer. Bake at 325° for 55 minutes or until center is almost set. Turn off oven and leave cheesecake inside for 30 minutes; open door partway and leave cake in oven another 30 minutes. Remove from oven; cool completely. Refrigerate at least 8 hours.

Glaze: Combine cocoa and **Saute Butter** in top of a double boiler; cook over simmering water until melted. Remove from heat; add remaining ingredients and stir until smooth. Remove cheesecake from pan and spread warm glaze on top just before serving.

Old-Fashioned Ice Cream Roll

The Fat Quotient using ButterLike is 0% instead of 42%
100% less fat 76% less sugar
64% less Calories

U.S.	Ingredients	Metric
3/4 cup	**Granulated SugarLike**	150.00 g
3/4 tsp	Baking powder	3.00 g
1/4 tsp	Salt	1.50 g
1 cup	Egg whites	227.00 g
3/4 cup	All-purpose flour	86.00 g
1 tsp	Vanilla extract	5.00 g
1/2 gal	Fat free vanilla ice cream	1136.00 g
Sauce:		
1 cup	**Brown SugarLike**	200.00 g
1/2 cup	**Granulated SugarLike**	100.00 g
1/2 cup	**Liquid SugarLike**	170.00 g
1/4 tsp	Salt	1.50 g
1 cup	Evaporated skim milk	255.00 g

Nutrition Facts				
Serving Size	292 g			
Servings Per Recipe	8			
Amount per serving			High Fat/Sugar Comparison	
Calories	340		940	
Calories from fat	0		400	
	% Daily Value*		% Daily Value*	
Total Fat	0 g	**0%**	44 g	**68%**
Saturated Fat	0 g	**0%**	26 g	**130%**
Cholesterol	0 mg	**0%**	250 mg	**83%**
Sodium	410 mg	**17%**	350 mg	**15%**
Total Carbohydrate	122 g	**41%**	125 g	**42%**
Dietary Fiber	17 g	**68%**	0 g	**0%**
Sugars	26 g		108 g	
Other	51 g		0 g	
Protein	15 g		11 g	

*Percent of Daily Values on page a-22

Exchanges and 54 g Carbohydrates Per Serving

Breads	3.2	Vegetables	0.0	Fruits	0.0
Meats	0.4	Milk	0.3	Fats	0.0

Directions

In a large mixing bowl, beat baking powder, salt, and egg whites. Add **SugarLike** gradually until the mixture becomes thick. Add flour a little at a time. Stir in vanilla. Spread into a vegetable sprayed wax paper-lined 15x10x1-inch baking pan. Bake at 375° for 10-12 minutes or until light gold. Turn out onto a dish towel sprinkled with **Powdered SugarLike.** Peel off waxed paper and roll up, jelly-roll style; cool. When cool, unroll and spread with ice cream. Roll up again; freeze until firm.

Sauce: Combine **SugarLikes**, evaporated skim milk, and salt in a saucepan. Cook until mixture comes to a full boil. Let boil for 5 minutes. Remove from heat; cool slightly. To serve, slice frozen ice cream roll and pour warm sauce over. Top with pecans if desired.

Variation: Use strawberry ice cream instead of vanilla and eliminate caramel sauce. Garnish with fresh strawberries and whipped topping.

Note to Diabetics: Substitute 1/2 gallon sugar free vanilla ice cream for 1/2 gallon fat free vanilla ice cream. Fat will increase to 8 grams; sugar will decrease to 20 grams per serving.

Strawberry Daiquiri Sorbet

The Fat Quotient using ButterLike is 0% instead of 0%
0% less fat 71% less sugar
62% less Calories

U.S.	Ingredients	Metric
1 cup	**Granulated SugarLike**	200.00 g
1 1/2 cup	Water	356.00 g
8 cups	Strawberries	1192.00 g
1/4 tsp	Rum flavor	1.20 g
2 tsp	Lime peel, finely shredded	4.00 g
1/4 cup	Lime juice	62.00 g
1 Tbsp	Orange flavor	16.00 g
1/4 cup	Orange juice	62.30 g

Directions

In a medium saucepan combine **SugarLike** and water. Cook and stir over high heat until mixture comes to a boil and **SugarLike** dissolves. Remove from heat and cool completely. Place strawberries in a food processor bowl or blender. (For best results, blend half of strawberries at a time). Cover; process or blend until nearly smooth. In a bowl stir together pureed strawberries, rum, lime peel, lime juice, and orange liqueur. Stir in the cooled syrup. Freeze in a 4-quart ice cream freezer according to the manufacturer's directions.

Nutrition Facts				
Serving Size	118 g			
Servings Per Recipe	16			
Amount per serving			High Fat/Sugar Comparison	
Calories		50	80	
Calories from fat		0	0	
	% Daily Value*		% Daily Value*	
Total Fat	0 g	**0%**	0 g	**0%**
Saturated Fat	0 g	**0%**	0 g	**0%**
Cholesterol	0 mg	**0%**	0 mg	**0%**
Sodium	0 mg	**0%**	0 mg	**0%**
Total Carbohydrate	18 g	**6%**	18 g	**6%**
Dietary Fiber	5 g	**20%**	2 g	**8%**
Sugars	5 g		17 g	
Other	9 g		0 g	
Protein	1 g		0 g	

*Percent of Daily Values on page a-22

Exchanges and 4 g Carbohydrates Per Serving

Breads	0.0	Vegetables	0.0	Fruits	0.4
Meats	0.0	Milk	0.0	Fats	0.0

Fresh Berry Sorbet

The Fat Quotient using ButterLike is 0% instead of 0%
0% less fat 74% less sugar
40% less Calories

U.S.	Ingredients	Metric
1/2 cup	**Granulated SugarLike**	100.00 g
4 cups	Hulled strawberries or raspberries	596.00 g
1/2 cup	Water	119.00 g
1 Tbsp	Lemon juice	15.00 g

Nutrition Facts				
Serving Size	119 g			
Servings Per Recipe	7			
Amount per serving			High Fat/Sugar Comparison	
Calories		54	90	
Calories from fat		0	0	
	% Daily Value*		% Daily Value*	
Total Fat	0 g	**0%**	0 g	**0%**
Saturated Fat	0 g	**0%**	0 g	**0%**
Cholesterol	0 mg	**0%**	0 mg	**0%**
Sodium	0 mg	**0%**	0 mg	**0%**
Total Carbohydrate	20 g	**7%**	21g	**7%**
Dietary Fiber	5 g	**20%**	2 g	**8%**
Sugars	5 g		19 g	
Other	10 g		0 g	
Protein	1 g		1 g	

*Percent of Daily Values on page a-22

Directions

In a food processor or blender, whirl berries until smoothly pureed. Pour puree into a strainer; discard seeds. Return puree to food processor and add **SugarLike**, water, and lemon juice. Whirl a few seconds until **SugarLike** is dissolved. Pour into a shallow metal pan and freeze, covered, until solid. Remove ice from freezer and break into chunks with a heavy spoon. In a food processor, whirl ice, about a third at a time, until a smooth slush forms; use on-off bursts at first to break up ice, then whirl continuously. Pour into a bowl and freeze, covered, for at least 1 hour. Before serving, let ice soften at room temperature for about 10 minutes. Makes 3 1/2 cups.

Exchanges and 5 g Carbohydrates Per Serving					
Breads	0.0	Vegetables	0.0	Fruits	0.4
Meats	0.0	Milk	0.0	Fats	0.0

Pineapple Sorbet: Cut 4-lb peeled and cored pineapple into chunks. Puree pineapple; pour into bowl and stir in 1/3 cup **SugarLike**, 1 cup water, and 2 Tbsp lemon juice. Freeze and serve as directed above. Makes 5 cups.

Lemon Sorbet: Cut colored part of lemon peel into 1/2-inch pieces. Blend peel with 1 cup **SugarLike**. Add 1 cup hot water and whirl until **SugarLike** is dissolved. Add 3 cups cold water and 2/3 cup lemon juice. Blend; freeze and serve as directed above. Makes 5 cups.

Chocolate Ice Cream

The Fat Quotient using ButterLike is **3%** instead of **25%**
92% less fat **86% less sugar**
41% less Calories

U.S.	Ingredients	Metric
2 cups	**Granulated SugarLike**	400.00 g
1/4 cup	**ButterLike Baking Butter**	57.00 g
1 quart	Skim milk	980.00 g
1	Egg yolk	17.00 g
1/3 cup	Cocoa	79.00 g
2 Tbsp	All-purpose flour	14.00 g
2 cans	Evaporated skim milk (12 oz each)	680.00 g
2 Tbsp	Vanilla extract	30.00 g

Directions

In a heavy saucepan, combine first six ingredients. Cook until thickened. Add evaporated milk; bring to a boil. Remove from heat and cool. Add vanilla. Pour into the cylinder of an ice cream freezer; add enough skim milk to fill cylinder 3/4 full. Freeze.

Nutrition Facts				
Serving Size	141 g			
Servings Per Recipe	16			
Amount per serving			High Fat/Sugar Comparison	
Calories		129	220	
Calories from fat		5	60	
	% Daily Value*		% Daily Value*	
Total Fat	0.5 g	**1%**	6 g	**9%**
Saturated Fat	0 g	**0%**	3.5 g	**18%**
Cholesterol	15 mg	**5%**	60 mg	**20%**
Sodium	100 mg	**4%**	85 mg	**4%**
Total Carbohydrate	36 g	**12%**	34 g	**11%**
Dietary Fiber	6 g	**24%**	0 g	**0%**
Sugars	4 g		28g	
Other	18 g		0 g	
Protein	6 g		6 g	

*Percent of Daily Values on page a-22

Exchanges and 12 g Carbohydrates Per Serving					
Breads	0.2	Vegetables	0.0	Fruits	0.0
Meats	0.0	Milk	0.6	Fats	0.1

Cherry Ice Cream

The Fat Quotient using **ButterLike** is **0%** instead of **53%**
100% less fat **58% less sugar**
37% less Calories

U.S.	Ingredients	Metric
1/2 cup	**Granulated SugarLike**	100.00 g
1/4 cup	**ButterLike Baking Butter**	57.00 g
1 lb	Fresh or frozen chopped cherries	466.00 g
1 pkg	Sugar free cherry-flavored gelatin	85.00 g
1 cup	Boiling water	237.00 g
1 pkg	Sugar free cook and serve vanilla pudding mix	85.00 g
3 1/2 cup	Skim milk	858.00 g
2 cups	Evaporated skim milk	510.00 g
2 tsp	Vanilla extract	10.00 g

Directions

In a large bowl, combine **SugarLike** and cherries; set aside. Dissolve gelatin in boiling water; set aside. Cook pudding according to package directions, using milk and **ButterLike.** Add to cherries. Stir in evaporated milk, vanilla, and prepared gelatin. Refrigerate, stirring occasionally, until cold. Pour into the cylinder of an ice cream freezer and freeze according to manufacturer's directions.

Nutrition Facts				
Serving Size	150 g			
Servings Per Recipe	16			
Amount per serving			High Fat/Sugar Comparison	
Calories	138		220	
Calories from fat	0		120	
	% Daily Value*		% Daily Value*	
Total Fat	0 g	**0%**	13 g	**20%**
Saturated Fat	0 g	**0%**	8 g	**40%**
Cholesterol	5 mg	**2%**	50 mg	**17%**
Sodium	330 mg	**14%**	200 mg	**8%**
Total Carbohydrate	26 g	**9%**	22 g	**7%**
Dietary Fiber	2 g	**8%**	0 g	**0%**
Sugars	8 g		19 g	
Other	5 g		0 g	
Protein	7 g		5 g	

*Percent of Daily Values on page a-22

Exchanges and 19 g Carbohydrates Per Serving

Breads	0.4	Vegetables	0.0	Fruits	0.5
Meats	0.0	Milk	0.5	Fats	0.0

Strawberry Sherbet

The Fat Quotient using **ButterLike** is **8%** instead of **7%**
25% less fat **41% less sugar**
34% less Calories

U.S.	Ingredients	Metric
1 1/2 cup	**Granulated SugarLike**	300.00 g
4 qts	Fresh strawberries	4192.00 g
2 2/3 cup	Skim milk	653.00 g
2/3 cup	Orange juice	166.00 g
1/8 tsp	Ground cinnamon	.29 g

Nutrition Facts				
Serving Size	166 g			
Servings Per Recipe	32			
Amount per serving			High Fat/Sugar Comparison	
Calories	178		270	
Calories from fat	15		20	
	% Daily Value*		% Daily Value*	
Total Fat	1.5 g	**2%**	2 g	**3%**
Saturated Fat	1 g	**5%**	1.5 g	**8%**
Cholesterol	0 mg	**0%**	5 mg	**2%**
Sodium	10 mg	**0%**	10 mg	**0%**
Total Carbohydrate	44 g	**15%**	60 g	**20%**
Dietary Fiber	6 g	**24%**	2 g	**8%**
Sugars	34 g		58 g	
Other	18 g		0 g	
Protein	2 g		2 g	

*Percent of Daily Values on page a-22

Directions

Combine **SugarLike** and strawberries; let stand until juicy, about 1 1/2 hours. Mash or puree in a blender in several batches. Add milk, orange juice, and cinnamon; blend well. Pour into the cylinder of an ice cream freezer and freeze or pour into ice cube trays without dividers. If preparing in trays, freeze about 3 hours, stirring two or three times.

Exchanges and 33 g Carbohydrates Per Serving					
Breads	0.0	Vegetables	0.0	Fruits	2.2
Meats	0.0	Milk	0.1	Fats	0.3

Butter Pecan Ice Cream

The Fat Quotient using **ButterLike** is **22%** instead of **51%**
79% less fat **85% less sugar**
50% less Calories

U.S.	Ingredients	Metric
1/2 cup	**Brown SugarLike**	100.00 g
1 cup	**Granulated SugarLike**	200.00 g
2/3 cup	**ButterLike Baking Butter**	151.00 g
2 Tbsp	**ButterLike Saute Butter**	28.00 g
1 3/4 cup	Skim milk	429.00 g
1	Egg yolk	17.00 g
1/4 tsp	Salt	1.50 g
2 cups	Skim milk, scalded and cooked	490.00 g
1 1/2 tsp	Vanilla extract	7.00 g
1/4 cup	Pecans, finely chopped	28.00 g

Directions

In a heavy saucepan or top of a double boiler, combine **SugarLikes**, softened **Baking Butter**, 1 3/4 cup skim milk, egg yolk, and salt. Cook over low heat, stirring constantly, until mixture coats a spoon. Cool. Add 2 cups milk and vanilla. Refrigerate for several hours. In a skillet, heat **ButterLike Saute Butter**. Add pecans and saute on medium heat, stirring constantly, being careful not to burn them. Cool. Pour egg mixture into the cylinder of an ice cream freezer; add pecans, stirring to distribute. Freeze. When frozen, pack ice cream in airtight containers and store in freezer.

Exchanges and 9 g Carbohydrates Per Serving					
Breads	0.4	Vegetables	0.0	Fruits	0.0
Meats	0.0	Milk	0.2	Fats	0.4

Nutrition Facts				
Serving Size	91 g			
Servings Per Recipe	16			
Amount per serving			High Fat/Sugar Comparison	
Calories	104		210	
Calories from fat	20		100	
	% Daily Value*		% Daily Value*	
Total Fat	2.5 g	**4%**	12 g	**18%**
Saturated Fat	0.5 g	**3%**	4.5 g	**23%**
Cholesterol	15 mg	**5%**	45 mg	**15%**
Sodium	105 mg	**4%**	90 mg	**4%**
Total Carbohydrate	28 g	**9%**	23 g	**8%**
Dietary Fiber	5 g	**20%**	1 g	**4%**
Sugars	3 g		20 g	
Other	14 g		0 g	
Protein	3 g		3 g	

*Percent of Daily Values on page a-22

Butter Pecan Ice Cream

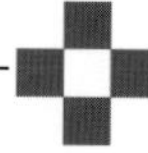

Banana Gelato

The Fat Quotient using ButterLike is **18%** instead of **27%**
56% less fat **60% less sugar**
32% less Calories

U.S.	Ingredients	Metric
1/4 cup	**ButterLike Saute Butter**	56.00 g
3/4 cup	**Granulated SugarLike**	150.00 g
3 cups	Skim milk	735.00 g
3	Strips lemon peel, 2 inches long	10.00 g
1 tsp	Vanilla extract	5.00 g
3	Egg yolks	50.00 g
3 medium	Bananas	342.00 g
3 Tbsp	Lemon juice	46.00 g

Directions

Gelato Base: Combine **SugarLike**, milk, and lemon peel in a saucepan. Cook over medium heat, stirring often, until **SugarLike** dissolves. In medium bowl, beat **ButterLike** and yolks lightly with wire whisk. Gradually whisk in 1 cup hot milk mixture; pour egg mixture into pan, whisking constantly. Cook, stirring, until custard thickens and coats the back of a metal spoon; don't bring to scalding or custard will curdle. Pour custard through a fine wire strainer set over a large bowl. Discard lemon peel. Add vanilla extract. Let gelato base cool; refrigerate, covered, until cold or until next day.

Mash or puree bananas with lemon juice until smooth. In large bowl, stir 1 cup gelato base with banana puree; then gradually stir in remaining gelato base. Pour mixture into container of ice cream maker and freeze. Serve or freeze, covered, for up to 3 weeks. Makes about 1 1/2 quarts.

Variation: Leave bananas and lemon juice out of recipe. Use two whole vanilla beans in gelato base instead of vanilla extract; split beans lengthwise and scrape seeds from pods. Add seeds and pods to milk mixture. Rinse vanilla beans, let dry, and reserve for another use, when discarding lemon peel.

Nutrition Facts

Serving Size 116 g
Servings Per Recipe 12

Amount per serving			High Fat/Sugar Comparison	
Calories	102		150	
Calories from fat	20		45	
	% Daily Value*		% Daily Value*	
Total Fat	2 g	**3%**	4.5 g	**7%**
Saturated Fat	1 g	**5%**	2 g	**10%**
Cholesterol	55 mg	**18%**	115 mg	**38%**
Sodium	35 mg	1%	35 mg	1%
Total Carbohydrate	24 g	**8%**	23 g	**8%**
Dietary Fiber	4 g	**16%**	1 g	**4%**
Sugars	8 g		20 g	
Other	9 g		0 g	
Protein	3 g		4 g	

*Percent of Daily Values on page a-22

Exchanges and 11 g Carbohydrates Per Serving

Breads	0.1	Vegetables	0.0	Fruits	0.5
Meats	0.1	Milk	0.2	Fats	0.3

Chocolate Fudge Pecan Torte

The Fat Quotient using **ButterLike** is **28%** instead of **58%**
78% less fat **61% less sugar**
56% less Calories

U.S.	Ingredients	Metric
Crust:		
1	**Mrs. Bateman's Pie Crust**, page 197	154.00 g
1/8 cup	Pecans, chopped	14.00 g
Filling:		
3/4 cup	**Brown SugarLike**	150.00 g
1 Tbsp	**ButterLike Baking Butter**, softened	14.00 g
3 Tbsp	Unsweetened cocoa	45.00 g
1 Tbsp	Water	15.00 g
1 tsp	Vanilla	5.00 g
1/4 cup	Egg substitute	63.00 g
1/8 cup	Pecans, chopped	14.00 g
1/2 cup	Reduced fat chocolate chips	120.00 g
Topping:		
1/2 cup	Lite whipped topping	32.00 g

Directions

Crust: Follow directions for a **Mrs. Bateman's Pie Crust** . Using a vegetable sprayed 10-inch tart pan with a removable bottom or a vegetable sprayed 9-inch pie pan, press a crust in bottom and up the sides. Before baking, sprinkle 1/8 cup pecans over crust; press firmly into crust. Prick crust. Bake crust 9-11 minutes in a 400° oven.

Filling: In a medium bowl, combine **Brown SugarLike**, cocoa, and water; blend well. Add **ButterLike**, vanilla, and egg substitute; blend until smooth. Pour into baked crust; sprinkle with 1/8 cup pecans and chocolate chips. Bake for 20-30 minutes in a 350° oven or until filling is set. Cool 1 hour or until completely cooled.

Topping: In a small bowl, combine all topping ingredients. Beat until stiff peaks form. Pipe or spoon whipped topping around edge of tart. Store in refrigerator.

Nutrition Facts				
Serving Size	64 g			
Servings Per Recipe	10			
Amount per serving			High Fat/Sugar Comparison	
Calories	160		360	
Calories from fat	45		200	
	% Daily Value*		% Daily Value*	
Total Fat	5 g	**8%**	23 g	**35%**
Saturated Fat	2.5 g	**13%**	9 g	**45%**
Cholesterol	0 mg	**0%**	45 mg	**15%**
Sodium	170 mg	**7%**	160 mg	**7%**
Total Carbohydrate	35 g	**12%**	37 g	**12%**
Dietary Fiber	4 g	**16%**	1 g	**4%**
Sugars	9 g		23 g	
Other	13 g		0 g	
Protein	2 g		3 g	

*Percent of Daily Values on page a-22

Exchanges and 18 g Carbohydrates Per Serving					
Breads	1.2	Vegetables	0.0	Fruits	0.0
Meats	0.1	Milk	0.0	Fats	1.1

Chocolate Fudge Pecan Torte

$1 Million Macadamia Fudge Torte

The Fat Quotient using ButterLike is **15%** instead of **36%**
80% less fat **76% less sugar**
50% less Calories

U.S.	Ingredients	Metric
Filling:		
1/3 cup	**Sweetened Condensed Milk**, page 91	100.00 g
1/2 cup	Reduced fat chocolate chips	120.00 g
Cake:		
3/8 cup	**ButterLike Baking Butter**	85.00 g
1 1/2 cup	**Granulated SugarLike**	300.00 g
1 tsp	Salt	6.00 g
1 tsp	Baking soda	4.60 g
1 tsp	Baking powder	4.00 g
1/3 cup	Cocoa	79.00 g
1 1/2 cup	All-purpose flour	188.00 g
1 1/2 tsp	Cinnamon	3.50 g
1 tsp	Vanilla extract	5.00 g
1 can	Pears (8 oz)	244.00 g
1/2 cup	Egg whites	114.00 g
Topping:		
3 Tbsp	**ButterLike Saute Butter**	42.00 g
1/4 cup	Reduced fat chocolate chips	60.00 g
3 Tbsp	Sliced almonds or nuts	25.00 g
Sauce:		
3/4 cup	**Sweetened Condensed Milk**, page 91	230.00 g
1/2 cup	**Brown SugarLike**	100.00 g
1/2 cup	Skim milk	123.00 g
1/3 cup	**Chocolate Syrup**, page 235	85.00 g

Directions

Filling: Combine filling ingredients in a saucepan. Cook over medium low heat until chocolate is melted, stirring.

Cake: In large mixing bowl combine dry cake ingredients. Reserve 3/4 cup of dry ingredients in second bowl. Place drained pears in blender and blend until smooth. In the first bowl, add the softened **Baking Butter**, pears, egg whites, and vanilla; mix until smooth. Spread batter evenly in vegetable sprayed 10-inch springform pan. Drop filling by teaspoonful over cake batter.

Nutrition Facts				
Serving Size	153 g			
Servings Per Recipe	12			
Amount per serving			High Fat/Sugar Comparison	
Calories	277		550	
Calories from fat	40		200	
	% Daily Value*		% Daily Value*	
Total Fat	4.5 g	**7%**	22 g	**34%**
Saturated Fat	2.5 g	**13%**	10 g	**50%**
Cholesterol	5 mg	**2%**	65 mg	**22%**
Sodium	410 mg	**17%**	480 mg	**20%**
Total Carbohydrate	76 g	**25%**	80 g	**27%**
Dietary Fiber	10 g	**40%**	2 g	**8%**
Sugars	12 g		49 g	
Other	38 g		0 g	
Protein	6 g		8 g	

*Percent of Daily Values on page a-22

Exchanges and 28 g Carbohydrates Per Serving

Breads	1.8	Vegetables	0.0	Fruits	0.1
Meats	0.1	Milk	0.2	Fats	1.1

Topping: Mix **Saute Butter**, nuts, and chocolate chips into the 3/4 cup dry cake ingredients; mix until crumbly. Sprinkle over cake batter. Bake cake for 40-45 minutes in a 350° oven or until top springs back. It is hard to check with a toothpick because the filling never really sets up. Cool 10 minutes. Take off sides of springform pan and cool.

Caramel Sauce: In microwave bowl bring to boil the **Sweetened Condensed Milk**, skim milk, and **Brown SugarLike** for 2 minutes on high or use one of the other caramel sauces in this cookbook.

To serve cake, spread 2 Tbsp of sauce on a serving dish and squirt the **Chocolate Syrup** in a wavy line over sauce. With a butter knife, swirl the Chocolate Syrup into caramel sauce. Serve cake on top decorated sauces. Top with whipped topping if desired.

Glazed Pineapple Pecan Torte

The Fat Quotient using **ButterLike** is **14%** instead of **57%**
91% less fat **90% less sugar**
64% less Calories

U.S.	**Ingredients**	Metric
Crust:		
1	**Mrs. Bateman's Pie Crust**, page 197	154.00 g
Filling:		
3/4 cup	**Granulated SugarLike**	150.00 g
1/2 cup	**ButterLike Baking Butter**, softened	114.00 g
1 pkg	Fat free cream cheese, softened (8 oz)	227.00 g
1 cup	Crushed pineapple	246.00 g
1/2 cup	All-purpose flour	58.00 g
1/8 cup	Pecans, chopped and toasted	14.00 g
Glaze:		
3/4 cup	**Powdered SugarLike**	79.00 g
1/4 cup	Crushed pineapple	62.00 g
1 Tbsp	Pecans, chopped and toasted	7.00 g

Directions

Follow directions for **Mrs. Bateman's Pie Crust**. You may use a vegetable sprayed 10-inch tart pan or a vegetable sprayed 9-inch pie pan. Press crust in bottom and up the sides of the pan. Prick crust. Bake in a 400° oven for 9-11 minutes.

Filling: In a large bowl, combine **SugarLike**, **ButterLike**, and cream cheese; beat until light and fluffy. Add 1 cup pineapple and egg whites; blend well. Lightly spoon flour into measuring cup; level off. Add flour and pecans; blend well. Pour into baked crust; spread evenly. Bake at 325° for 45-55 minutes or until top is light golden brown and center is set. Cool 10 minutes.

Glaze: In a small bowl, combine **Powdered SugarLike** and 1/4 cup pineapple; blend well. Spoon evenly over warm tart; sprinkle with 1 Tbsp pecans. Cool 20 minutes. Refrigerate 1 hour or until completely cooled. Store in refrigerator.

Nutrition Facts				
Serving Size	102 g			
Servings Per Recipe	12			
Amount per serving			High Fat/Sugar Comparison	
Calories	158		440	
Calories from fat	20		250	
	% Daily Value*		% Daily Value*	
Total Fat	2.5 g	**4%**	28 g	**43%**
Saturated Fat	0.5 g	**3%**	14 g	**70%**
Cholesterol	0 mg	**0%**	85 mg	**28%**
Sodium	290 mg	**12%**	340 mg	**14%**
Total Carbohydrate	38 g	**13%**	42 g	**14%**
Dietary Fiber	5 g	**20%**	1 g	**4%**
Sugars	2 g		20 g	
Other	15 g		0 g	
Protein	5 g		4 g	

*Percent of Daily Values on page a-22

Exchanges and 18 g Carbohydrates Per Serving					
Breads	1.0	Vegetables	0.0	Fruits	0.1
Meats	0.2	Milk	0.1	Fats	0.4

Pumpkin Torte

The Fat Quotient using ButterLike is 16% instead of 52%
87% less fat 77% less sugar
43% less Calories

U.S.	Ingredients	Metric
Crust:		
1/3 cup	**Granulated SugarLike**	67.00 g
1/2 cup + 2 Tbsp	**ButterLike Baking Butter**	142.00 g
2 Tbsp	Water	24.00 g
1 1/2 cup	Low fat graham crackers, crushed	144.00 g
Filling:		
2 Tbsp	**ButterLike Baking Butter**, softened	28.40 g
1 1/4 cup	**Granulated SugarLike**, divided	250.00 g
1/2 cup	Egg whites	114.00 g
1 pkg	Fat free cream cheese (8 oz)	227.00 g
1 can	Pumpkin (16 oz)	454.00 g
3	Egg whites	86.00 g
1/2 cup	Skim milk	123.00 g
1/2 tsp	Salt	3.00 g
1 tsp	Cinnamon	2.30 g
1	Envelope unflavored gelatin	7.00 g
1/4 cup	Cold water	59.00 g
1	Lite whipped topping (8 oz)	227.00 g

Directions

Crust: Combine softened **Baking Butter** and other ingredients; press into the bottom of a 13x9x2-inch vegetable sprayed baking pan.

Filling: In a mixing bowl, combine **ButterLike**, 3/4 cup **SugarLike**, egg whites, and cream cheese. Beat until smooth. Spread over crust. Bake at 350° for 20-25 minutes or until top appears set. Cool. Meanwhile, combine pumpkin, egg whites, milk, 1/2 cup **SugarLike**, salt, and cinnamon in a saucepan. Cook, stirring constantly, until mixture thickens; remove from heat. Dissolve gelatin in cold water; add to saucepan. Fold in whipped topping. Spread over cooled torte; chill. Serve with a dollop of whipped topping. Torte keeps well for several days in the refrigerator.

Note to Diabetics: Substitute whipped topping with 1 cup light whipping cream, 1/4 cup **Granulated SugarLike**, and 1 tsp vanilla. Fat will increase to 7.56 grams.

Nutrition Facts				
Serving Size	161 g			
Servings Per Recipe	12			
Amount per serving			High Fat/Sugar Comparison	
Calories	227		400	
Calories from fat	35		210	
	% Daily Value*		% Daily Value*	
Total Fat	4 g	**6%**	23 g	**35%**
Saturated Fat	3 g	**15%**	15 g	**75%**
Cholesterol	0 mg	**0%**	135 mg	**45%**
Sodium	390 mg	**16%**	340 mg	**14%**
Total Carbohydrate	53 g	**18%**	44 g	**15%**
Dietary Fiber	8 g	**32%**	1 g	**4%**
Sugars	7 g		31 g	
Other	20 g		0 g	
Protein	7 g		5 g	

*Percent of Daily Values on page a-22

Exchanges and 25 g Carbohydrates Per Serving

Breads	1.6	Vegetables	0.0	Fruits	0.0
Meats	0.2	Milk	0.2	Fats	0.7

Pumpkin Torte

Main Dishes

Chicken Fajitas, page 167

This main dish section is full of great recipes with a full selection of chicken, beef, pork, and fish dishes.

I am so excited to offer the new **ButterLike Saute Butter** and the **Seasoned Saute Butters**, along with the **ButterLike Saute Butter**, to assist in all types of main dish cooking. The **Saute Butters** have slightly more fat from butter and olive oil than **Baking Butter**, so are more readily spreadable and are a better sauté medium. With only two fat grams per tablespoon, **ButterLike Saute Butters** give any food an intense, real fat taste, yet offer low fat, low calories, and low cholesterol!

Each recipe that uses **ButterLike Saute Butter** as a saute medium has a special symbol ( ) by it. No more sauteing in water or in chicken broth for healthy cooking.

I have assembled many wonderful recipes that use the new **ButterLike Saute Butter** and **ButterLike Seasoned Saute Butters**. I didn't specify which **Saute Butter** to use in most of them. Try our **Butter and Olive Oil**, **Toasted Garlic**, **Toasted Onion**, or **Italian Herb** flavor. The choice is up to you.

Tips on cooking low fat, low calorie, low cholesterol and sugar free main dishes

- Substitute any fat in your recipe one-to-one with **ButterLike Saute Butter** or with the **Flavored Saute Butters**.
- Substitute any sugar into your recipes on a one-to-one replacement with the **SugarLike** products.

- Always use the leanest cuts of meat with the fat trimmed off.
- Substitute boneless skinless chicken breasts for meats that are higher in fat.
- Meats are usually the highest source of fat found in recipes. Slightly cut the serving size of the meats for a healthier diet.

Stir-fried Shrimp and Broccoli, page 157

- Rinse and drain lean ground beef in a colander after browning . (I use this technique often. I brown the meat well, rinse and drain it, and then add the sauteed vegetables and seasoning. I cannot tell a difference in the finished dish and neither can my family.)
- Remove the skin from chicken before serving if it was cooked with the skin on. Recent studies conducted have found that eating chicken without the skin reduce the fat, regardless if it was cooked with the skin or without. I usually use boneless skinless chicken because of ease.
- Here are some techniques to degrease your sauce or gravies.
  - Deglaze your pan using a small amount of cold liquid. (At least 1/4 cup of drippings are necessary for the degreaser cup to work.) Pour drippings into a degreaser cup. Pour off the fat free drippings after the fat has raised to the top. Quit pouring as soon as the fat starts to go into the spout of the cup.
  - Use a plastic baggy to degrease your drippings if you don't have a degreasing cup. Pour drippings into a plastic baggy. Cut or poke a hole in the bottom corner of the baggy. Let the fat free drippings pour into a pan until the fat or grease gets down to the hole. Pinch the hole together and drop the baggy into the garbage. Easy!
  - Pour drippings into a small container and set in the refrigerator until chilled and grease has solidified at the top of the drippings. Spoon off all the solid grease and discard.
  - Add 3 or 4 ice cubes to hot drippings and stir until grease solidifies on the ice. Spoon out with a slotted spoon.
- Use the Substitution Table on page a-16 to substitute other ingredients that are typically high in fat but are not a one-to-one replacement for butter or fat. An example of this is sour cream, cream cheese or cream. I find that I have great success if I use skim milk for the cream, fat free sour cream for the real sour cream, and fat free cream cheese for the cream cheese. The real key to having the end product turn out is to add a small amount of **Baking Butter** or **Saute Butter** to the fat free substitute.
- I went into cheese substitutions in the first cookbook a little more extensively than I will here. If I mix a small amount of a stronger flavored cheese with a low fat or fat free cheese I have greater success in my end recipe. When a recipe calls for sprinkling cheese on top of recipes I always use fat free cheese topping in in place of parmesan cheese.
- Sometimes eggs can be replaced in main dish cooking entirely with egg substitutes. Other dishes such as souffle's need some mix of whole eggs, egg whites or egg substitutes. I recommend you use both egg whites and whole eggs for the most successful recipe.

  Our new **EggLike™** is a natural, dried, whole egg substitute used in baking and cooking. Can be used to substitute any whole egg, 1/4 cup egg whites or egg substitutes in any recipe. See page a-12. **EggLike** is compatible with the recipes in this cookbook. **EggLike** increases volume in cakes and baked products over egg substitutes and egg whites.

Sauteing with ButterLike Saute Butter

- Add **Saute Butter** to a non-stick pan **before** heating to saute vegetables or meats.
- Add enough **Saute Butter** to slightly cover the vegetables and meat. Adjust the size of the pan to fit the amount of the items to be cooked.
- If the **Saute Butter** sticks to the pan, cover it for a few minutes.
- If items need to be browned, some sticking may occur. Sprinkling a small amount of water into the pan and stirring may assist in browning.

Eggs Benedict

The Fat Quotient using **ButterLike** is **42%** instead of **73%**
71% less fat **0% less sugar**
50% less Calories

U.S.	Ingredients	Metric
1/2 recipe	**Hollandaise Sauce**, page 241	97.00 g
4	Eggs	200.00 g
2	English muffins, split	114.00 g
4 slices	Lean bacon	24.00 g

Directions

Fill a vegetable sprayed skillet halfway with water; bring to a boil. Reduce heat to simmering. Break one of the eggs into a measuring cup. Carefully slide egg into simmering water. Repeat with remaining eggs. Simmer eggs, uncovered, for 3 to 5 minutes until whites are set and yolks begin to thicken. Remove poached eggs with slotted spoon and place them in a pan of warm water to keep warm. Place muffin halves, cut sides up, on a baking sheet. Broil 3 to 4 inches from heat for 1 minute or until toasted. Top each half with a slice of bacon; broil 1 minute more or until meat is heated. To serve, top each bacon-topped muffin half with an egg; spoon **Hollandaise Sauce** over eggs. Sprinkle with paprika.

Nutrition Facts				
Serving Size	109 g			
Servings Per Recipe	4			
Amount per serving			High Fat/Sugar Comparison	
Calories		213	430	
Calories from fat		90	310	
	% Daily Value*		% Daily Value*	
Total Fat	10 g	**15%**	35 g	**54%**
Saturated Fat	3 g	**15%**	18 g	**90%**
Cholesterol	295 mg	**98%**	450 mg	**150%**
Sodium	320 mg	**13%**	830 mg	**35%**
Total Carbohydrate	19 g	**6%**	14 g	**5%**
Dietary Fiber	1 g	**4%**	1 g	**4%**
Sugars	1 g		1 g	
Other	0 g		0 g	
Protein	12 g		15 g	

*Percent of Daily Values on page a-22

Exchanges and 18 g Carbohydrates Per Serving					
Breads	1.2	Vegetables	0.0	Fruits	0.0
Meats	1.1	Milk	0.0	Fats	1.5

Basil-Cheese Triangles

The Fat Quotient using ButterLike is 26% instead of 54%
67% less fat **0% less sugar**
30% less Calories

U.S.	Ingredients	Metric
1/4 cup	**ButterLike Saute Butter**	56.00 g
3/4 lb	Fat free monterey jack cheese	340.00 g
1/4 lb	Monterey jack cheese	113.00 g
1/2 cup	Egg substitutes	126.00 g
1 Tbsp	Dried basil leaves	2.40 g
1/4 tsp	White pepper	.60 g
1 pkg	Frozen phyllo sheets, thawed (16 oz)	454.00 g

Directions

Heat oven to 350°. Vegetable spray a cookie sheet. Crumble shredded cheese into a small bowl; mash with fork. Stir in egg substitutes, basil, and white pepper. Cut stack of phyllo sheets lengthwise into thirds. Cover with waxed paper, then with damp towel to prevent them from drying out. For each triangle, use 2 strips of phyllo. Place 1 heaping teaspoon cheese mixture on end of strip; fold phyllo strip end over end, in triangular shape, to opposite end. Place on vegetable sprayed cookie sheet.

Nutrition Facts				
Serving Size	30 g			
Servings Per Recipe	36			
Amount per serving			High Fat/Sugar Comparison	
Calories	70		100	
Calories from fat	20		60	
	% Daily Value*		% Daily Value*	
Total Fat	2 g	**3%**	6 g	**9%**
Saturated Fat	1 g	**5%**	3.5 g	**18%**
Cholesterol	5 mg	**2%**	25 mg	**8%**
Sodium	160 mg	**7%**	150 mg	**6%**
Total Carbohydrate	7 g	**2%**	7 g	**2%**
Dietary Fiber	0 g	**0%**	0 g	**0%**
Sugars	0 g		0 g	
Other	0 g		0 g	
Protein	5 g		4 g	

*Percent of Daily Values on page a-22

Exchanges and 7 g Carbohydrates Per Serving					
Breads	0.5	Vegetables	0.0	Fruits	0.0
Meats	0.4	Milk	0.0	Fats	0.3

Brush **ButterLike** over triangles. Bake at 350° for 20 minutes or until puffed and golden. Serve warm.

Phyllo Triangles

The Fat Quotient using ButterLike is 24% instead of 73%
84% less fat **0% less sugar**
52% less Calories

U.S.	Ingredients	Metric
Filling:		
1/2 cup + 2 Tbsp	**ButterLike Saute Butter**	140.00 g
1/2 lb	Low fat turkey sausage, chopped	227.00 g
1/4 cup	Onion, finely chopped	40.00 g
1/2 cup	Fat free ricotta cheese	124.00 g
1/2 cup	Non fat mozzarella cheese, shredded	60.00 g
1/2 tsp	Dried oregano, crushed	.75 g
12 sheets	Frozen phyllo dough, thawed	228.00 g

Nutrition Facts				
Serving Size	68 g			
Servings Per Recipe	12			
Amount per serving			High Fat/Sugar Comparison	
Calories	130		270	
Calories from fat	35		200	
	% Daily Value*		% Daily Value*	
Total Fat	3.5 g	**5%**	22 g	**34%**
Saturated Fat	1 g	**5%**	6 g	**30%**
Cholesterol	10 mg	**3%**	30 mg	**10%**
Sodium	270 mg	**11%**	380 mg	**16%**
Total Carbohydrate	16 g	**5%**	11 g	**4%**
Dietary Fiber	0 g	**0%**	0 g	**0%**
Sugars	1 g		1 g	
Other	0 g		0 g	
Protein	8 g		8 g	

*Percent of Daily Values on page a-22

Directions

Filling: In a skillet, heat 2 Tbsp **ButterLike**. Cook sausage and onion in **ButterLike** until onion is tender. Combine sausage-onion mixture, cheeses, and oregano; set aside.

Lightly brush a sheet of phyllo with **ButterLike**. Place another sheet of phyllo on top; brush with **ButterLike**. Keep remaining phyllo covered with plastic wrap to prevent it from becoming dry and brittle. Cut the 2 layered sheets crosswise into 6 equal strips, each 14 inches long. Spoon 1 well-rounded teaspoon of filling about an inch from the end of each dough strip. To fold into a triangle, bring a corner over filling so it lines up with other side of strip. Continue folding strip in a triangular shape. Repeat with remaining sheets of phyllo, **ButterLike**, and filling. Place triangles on a baking sheet; brush with **ButterLike**. Bake in a 375° oven for 15 minutes or until golden. If desired, serve with spaghetti sauce.

Exchanges and 16 g Carbohydrates Per Serving

Breads	1.0	Vegetables	0.0	Fruits	0.0
Meats	0.9	Milk	0.0	Fats	0.6

Cheese Souffle

The Fat Quotient using **ButterLike** is **24%** instead of **73%**
84% less fat **25% less sugar**
52% less Calories

U.S.	Ingredients	Metric
1/4 cup	**ButterLike Saute Butter**	56.00 g
1/2 cup	Egg substitute	126.00 g
1/2 cup	Egg whites	114.00 g
1/4 cup	All-purpose flour	29.00 g
1/4 tsp	Dry mustard	.60 g
Dash	Ground red pepper	.23 g
1 cup	Skim milk	245.00 g
1 1/2 cup	Fat free cheddar cheese, shredded	168.00 g
1/4 cup	Sharp cheddar cheese, shredded	28.00 g

Directions

Allow the egg substitute and egg whites to stand at room temperature for 30 minutes.

Cheese Sauce: In a medium saucepan heat **ButterLike**, flour, mustard, and red pepper. Add milk; cook and stir over medium heat until thick and bubbly. Remove from heat. Add cheese, gradually, stirring until melted.

In a medium mixing bowl, slowly add cheese sauce to egg substitutes, stirring constantly. Cool slightly. In a large mixing bowl, beat egg whites on medium speed until stiff peaks form. Gently fold about 1 cup of the stiffly beaten egg whites into cheese sauce. Gradually pour cheese sauce over remaining stiffly beaten egg whites, folding to combine. Pour into vegetable sprayed 1 1/2-quart souffle dish. Bake in a 350° oven 40 minutes or until knife inserted near center comes out clean. Serve immediately.

Nutrition Facts

Serving Size	192 g			
Servings Per Recipe	4			
Amount per serving			High Fat/Sugar Comparison	
Calories	227		470	
Calories from fat	50		340	
	% Daily Value*		% Daily Value*	
Total Fat	6 g	**9%**	38 g	**58%**
Saturated Fat	2.5 g	**13%**	22 g	**110%**
Cholesterol	10 mg	**3%**	315 mg	**105%**
Sodium	480 mg	**20%**	560 mg	**23%**
Total Carbohydrate	16 g	**5%**	10 g	**3%**
Dietary Fiber	0 g	**0%**	0 g	**0%**
Sugars	3 g		4 g	
Other	0 g		0 g	
Protein	26 g		23 g	

*Percent of Daily Values on page a-22

Exchanges and 16 g Carbohydrates Per Serving

Breads	0.7	Vegetables	0.0	Fruits	0.0
Meats	2.7	Milk	0.2	Fats	0.8

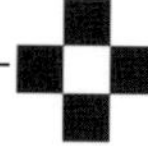

Tomato Souffle

The Fat Quotient using ButterLike is 20% instead of 64%
80% less fat **0% less sugar**
39% less Calories

U.S.	Ingredients	Metric
5 Tbsp	**ButterLike Saute Butter**	70.00 g
3 Tbsp	Non fat parmesan cheese	23.00 g
3 Tbsp	Shallots, chopped	3.00 g
1 1/2 Tbsp	Garlic, minced	43.00 g
2 Tbsp	Fresh tarragon, chopped	57.00 g
1/4 cup	All-purpose flour	29.00 g
1 tsp	Salt	6.00 g
1/2 tsp	Black pepper	1.00 g
2 cups	Ripe tomatoes, peel, seed, chop	442.00 g
2 Tbsp	Tomato paste	33.00 g
1/2 cup	Egg substitutes	126.00 g
5	Egg whites	167.00 g
1/4 tsp	Salt	1.50 g
1/4 tsp	Cream of tartar	.75 g

Nutrition Facts				
Serving Size	167 g			
Servings Per Recipe	6			
Amount per serving			High Fat/Sugar Comparison	
Calories	130		210	
Calories from fat	25		130	
	% Daily Value*		% Daily Value*	
Total Fat	3 g	**5%**	15 g	**23%**
Saturated Fat	1 g	**5%**	8 g	**40%**
Cholesterol	0 mg	**0%**	170 mg	**57%**
Sodium	630 mg	**26%**	700 mg	**29%**
Total Carbohydrate	16 g	**5%**	12 g	**4%**
Dietary Fiber	1 g	**4%**	1 g	**4%**
Sugars	3 g		3 g	
Other	0 g		0 g	
Protein	11 g		8 g	

*Percent of Daily Values on page a-22

Exchanges and 15 g Carbohydrates Per Serving

Breads	0.5	Vegetables	1.3	Fruits	0.0
Meats	1.8	Milk	0.0	Fats	0.4

Directions

Preheat oven to 350°. Vegetable spray a 6 to 8 cup medium to shallow souffle dish. Dust with finely grated parmesan cheese; set aside. Saute shallots in **ButterLike** over medium heat until wilted, about 5 minutes. Add garlic and tarragon, cook a few more minutes. Sprinkle with flour and cook until blended. Add salt, pepper, and tomatoes. Mixture will lump; stir and mash until tomatoes begin to give up their water and a thick paste forms. Stir in tomato paste. Add egg substitutes and cook a few more minutes; set aside. Beat egg whites until foamy. Add salt and cream of tarter. Beat until stiff. Pile whites on top of the tomato mixture and fold in with an over-and-under motion until lightly mixed. Do not overmix; there can be some streaks or white lumps when pouring into prepared souffle dish. Place dish in a larger pan and surround in hot water. Bake at 350° 35-40 minutes, until set. Serve immediately.

Yu-Shiang Chicken or Pork

The Fat Quotient using ButterLike is 19% instead of 66%
89% less fat **75% less sugar**
61% less Calories

U.S.	Ingredients	Metric
Sauce:		
1 Tbsp	**Granulated SugarLike**	12.50 g
1 Tbsp	Vinegar	15.00 g
1 Tbsp	Water	15.00 g
2 Tbsp	Soy sauce	36.00 g
3 Tbsp	Fat free chicken broth	46.00 g
2 tsp	Cornstarch	5.33 g

U.S.	Ingredients	Metric
4 Tbsp	**ButterLike Saute Butter**	56.00 g
1 tsp	Cornstarch	2.70 g
1/4 tsp	Salt	1.50 g
Dash	Pepper	.30 g
1 Tbsp	Water	15.00 g
3/4 lb	Boneless, skinless chicken breasts or pork	340.00 g
2 cloves	Garlic, minced	6.00 g
1 tsp	Fresh ginger	2.00 g
3-4 small	Dried hot red chiles	2.00 g
2/3 cup	Bamboo shoots, sliced	87.00 g
10	Green onions, cut in 2-in. lengths	60.00 g

Directions

Sauce; In a small bowl, combine **SugarLike**, vinegar, water, soy sauce, broth, and cornstarch; set aside.

Cut chicken into matchstick-size pieces. In a bowl, stir together 1 1/2 tsp **ButterLike**, cornstarch, salt, pepper, and water. Add meat and stir to coat; let stand for 15 minutes. Heat a wok or wide frying pan over medium heat. When pan is hot, add 2 Tbsp **ButterLike**. When hot, add garlic, ginger, and chiles; stir once. Add meat and cook, stirring, until lightly browned. Remove from pan. Cut bamboo shoots into matchstick-size pieces. Heat remaining 2 Tbsp **ButterLike** in pan. Add bamboo shoots and onions; cook, stirring, 1 minute. Return meat to pan. Stir sauce; add to pan and cook until sauce boils and thickens, stirring continuously.

Nutrition Facts				
Serving Size	176 g			
Servings Per Recipe	4			
Amount per serving			High Fat/Sugar Comparison	
Calories	164		420	
Calories from fat	30		280	
	% Daily Value*		% Da	
Value*3.				
Total Fat	3.5 g	**5%**	31 g	**48%**
Saturated Fat	1 g	**5%**	9 g	**45%**
Cholesterol	50 mg	**17%**	85 mg	**28%**
Sodium	720 mg	**30%**	760 mg	**32%**
Total Carbohydrate	13 g	**4%**	9 g	**3%**
Dietary Fiber	2 g	**8%**	1 g	**4%**
Sugars	1 g		4 g	
Other	2 g		0 g	
Protein	22 g		25 g	

Exchanges and 11 g Carbohydrates Per Serving

Breads	0.4	Vegetables	0.6	Fruits	0.0
Meats	1.7	Milk	0.0	Fats	0.4

Baked Chicken Paprika

The Fat Quotient using ButterLike is 11% instead of 51%
93% less fat **100% less sugar**
67% less Calories

U.S.	Ingredients	Metric
1/2 tsp	**Granulated SugarLike**	2.00 g
4	Boneless, skinless chicken breast halves	944.00 g
1 tsp	Paprika	2.10 g
3/4 tsp	Salt	4.50 g
1/8 tsp	Pepper	.26 g

Directions

Rinse chicken and pat dry. Place pieces slightly apart on a vegetable sprayed shallow pan. In a small dish, mix **SugarLike**, paprika, salt, and pepper; sprinkle over chicken. Bake 35 minutes in a 400° oven. Turn pieces over and continue to bake until chicken is no longer pink.

Note: Sometimes I drizzle 2 Tbsp **ButterLike Saute Butter** over chicken in pan, before I bake it.

Nutrition Facts				
Serving Size	238 g			
Servings Per Recipe	4			
Amount per serving			High Fat/Sugar Comparison	
Calories	263		780	
Calories from fat	25		410	
	% Daily Value*		% Daily Value*	
Total Fat	3 g	**5%**	45 g	**69%**
Saturated Fat	1 g	**5%**	13 g	**65%**
Cholesterol	135 mg	**45%**	365 mg	**122%**
Sodium	590 mg	**25%**	700 mg	**29%**
Total Carbohydrate	1 g	**0%**	1 g	**0%**
Dietary Fiber	0 g	**0%**	0 g	**0%**
Sugars	0 g		1 g	
Other	1 g		0 g	
Protein	55 g		91 g	

*Percent of Daily Values on page a-22

Exchanges and 0 g Carbohydrates Per Serving

Breads	0.0	Vegetables	0.0	Fruits	0.0
Meats	4.7	Milk	0.0	Fats	0.0

Easy Baked Chicken Kiev

The Fat Quotient using **ButterLike** is **13%** instead of **48%**
80% less fat **0% less sugar**
27% less Calories

U.S.	Ingredients	Metric
1/4 cup	**ButterLike Saute Butter**	56.00 g
5 Tbsp	**ButterLike Saute Butter**	70.00 g
1/2 cup	Fine dry bread crumbs	60.00 g
1/2 cup	Non fat parmesan cheese, grated	60.00 g
1 1/2 tsp	Dry oregano	2.30 g
1/2 tsp	Garlic salt	2.00 g
1/4 tsp	Pepper	.53 g
1 Tbsp	Parsley, chopped	4.00 g
4 oz	Fat free monterey jack cheese	113.00 g
8	Boneless, skinless chicken breast halves	1360.00 g

Nutrition Facts				
Serving Size	216 g			
Servings Per Recipe	8			
Amount per serving			High Fat/Sugar Comparison	
Calories	301		410	
Calories from fat	40		200	
	% Daily Value*		% Daily Value*	
Total Fat	4.5 g	**7%**	22 g	**34%**
Saturated Fat	1.5 g	**8%**	13 g	**65%**
Cholesterol	100 mg	**33%**	150 mg	**50%**
Sodium	580 mg	**24%**	680 mg	**28%**
Total Carbohydrate	11 g	**4%**	6 g	**2%**
Dietary Fiber	1 g	**4%**	0 g	**0%**
Sugars	0 g		0 g	
Other	0 g		0 g	
Protein	50 g		46 g	

*Percent of Daily Values on page a-22

Exchanges and 10 g Carbohydrates Per Serving

Breads	0.7	Vegetables	0.0	Fruits	0.0
Meats	5.7	Milk	0.0	Fats	0.5

Directions

In a shallow bowl, mix crumbs, parmesan cheese, 1 tsp oregano, garlic salt, and pepper; set aside. In a small bowl, mix the 1/4 cup **ButterLike**, parsley, and remaining oregano; set aside. Cut jack cheese into strips about 1/2x1 1/2-inches long; set aside. Cut jack cheese and pat dry. Place each piece between 2 sheets plastic wrap or wax paper; pound with a flat-surfaced mallet until about 1/4-inch thick. Lay each chicken piece flat and spread with an eighth jack cheese strips crosswise at one end. Fold in sides so they overlap; then roll up chicken to enclose end. Fold in sides so they overlap; then roll up chicken to enclose filling. Coat each chicken bundle with **ButterLike**, then with crumb mixture. Arrange bundles, seam side down and slightly apart, in a shallow vegetable sprayed baking pan. Drizzle with remaining **ButterLike**. Refrigerate, covered, for at least 4 hours. Bake, uncovered, about 20 minutes in a 400° oven until meat in center of bundles is no longer pink; cut gently to test.

Chicken and Artichoke Saute

The Fat Quotient using **ButterLike** is **10%** instead of **31%**
72% less fat **0% less sugar**
13% less Calories

U.S.	Ingredients	Metric
2 Tbsp	**ButterLike Saute Butter**	28.00 g
4	Boneless, skinless chicken breast halves	454.00 g
1/4 cup	All-purpose flour	29.00 g
1/4 tsp	Salt	1.50 g
1/4 tsp	Ground sage	.20 g
1/8 tsp	Pepper	.26 g

U.S.	Ingredients	Metric
Sauce:		
1/2 cup	Water	119.00 g
1 can	Artichoke hearts, halved (14 oz)	397.00 g
1 can	Mushrooms, sliced, drained (4 oz)	113.00 g
2 Tbsp	Non fat parmesan cheese, grated	15.00 g
2 Tbsp	Fresh parsley, snipped	7.50 g

Directions

Rinse chicken; pat dry. In a shallow bowl stir together flour, salt, sage, and pepper; reserve 1 Tbsp of the flour mixture. Dip chicken in remaining flour mixture to coat. In a large skillet cook chicken in hot **ButterLike Saute Butter** over medium-high heat about 6 minutes or until chicken is tender and no longer pink. Remove chicken from skillet; cover and keep warm.

Sauce: Stir together reserved flour mixture and water. Add mixture, artichoke hearts, and mushrooms to skillet, scraping up crusty bits from pan. Cook and stir until thick and bubbly. Cook and stir for 2 minutes more. Pour sauce over chicken. Sprinkle with cheese and parsley. Serve immediately.

Exchanges and 14 g Carbohydrates Per Serving

Breads	0.5	Vegetables	1.8	Fruits	0.0
Meats	3.3	Milk	0.0	Fats	0.2

Nutrition Facts				
Serving Size	291 g			
Servings Per Recipe	4			
Amount per serving			High Fat/Sugar Comparison	
Calories		227	260	
Calories from fat		25	80	
	% Daily Value*		% Daily Value*	
Total Fat	2.5 g	**4%**	9 g	**14%**
Saturated Fat	1 g	**5%**	2 g	**10%**
Cholesterol	65 mg	**22%**	70 mg	**23%**
Sodium	520 mg	**22%**	520 mg	**22%**
Total Carbohydrate	15 g	**5%**	13 g	**4%**
Dietary Fiber	1 g	**4%**	1 g	**4%**
Sugars	1 g		1 g	
Other	0 g		0 g	
Protein	33 g		31 g	

*Percent of Daily Values on page a-22

Mexican-Style Chicken Breasts

The Fat Quotient using **ButterLike** is **13%** instead of **37%**
72% less fat **50% more sugar**
23% less Calories

U.S.	Ingredients	Metric
2 Tbsp	**ButterLike Saute Butter**	28.00 g
1	Egg	50.00 g
1 clove	Garlic, minced	3.00 g
1/2 cup	Green chile salsa or taco sauce	124.00 g
1 cup	Fine dry bread crumbs	120.00 g
2 tsp	Chili powder	5.20 g
2 tsp	Ground cumin	9.40 g
1/2 tsp	Ground oregano	.75 g
6	Boneless, skinless chicken breasts	1020.00 g
4-6 cups	Iceberg lettuce, shredded	220.00 g
12-18	Cherry tomatoes	204.00 g
4	Green onions	24.00 g
1/2 cup	Fat free sour cream	128.00 g
1	Lime, cut in wedges	67.00 g

Nutrition Facts				
Serving Size	334 g			
Servings Per Recipe	6			
Amount per serving			High Fat/Sugar Comparison	
Calories		338	440	
Calories from fat		45	170	
	% Daily Value*		% Daily Value*	
Total Fat	5 g	**8%**	18 g	**28%**
Saturated Fat	1 g	**5%**	6 g	**30%**
Cholesterol	135 mg	**45%**	190 mg	**63%**
Sodium	800 mg	**33%**	840 mg	**35%**
Total Carbohydrate	25 g	**8%**	21 g	**7%**
Dietary Fiber	2 g	**8%**	6 g	**24%**
Sugars	3 g		2 g	
Other	0 g		0 g	
Protein	45 g		47 g	

*Percent of Daily Values on page a-22

Exchanges and 23 g Carbohydrates Per Serving

Breads	1.2	Vegetables	0.8	Fruits	0.1
Meats	3.5	Milk	0.2	Fats	0.3

Directions

In a shallow bowl, beat eggs, garlic, and salsa. In another shallow bowl, mix crumbs, chili powder, cumin, and oregano. Rinse chicken and pat dry. Coat each piece of chicken individually with egg mixture, then crumb mixture. Spread **ButterLike** in a vegetable sprayed 10x5-inch baking pan in a 375° oven. Add chicken and turn to coat with **Butterlike.** Bake until meat is no longer pink. Arrange chicken over platter of lettuce. Garnish with cherry tomatoes and a dollop of sour cream; scatter onions over top. Serve with lime wedges.

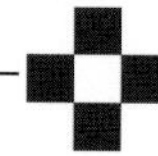

Chicken Breasts with Garden Vegetables

The Fat Quotient using ButterLike is 14% instead of 41%
74% less fat **0% less sugar**
22% less Calories

U.S.	Ingredients	Metric
4 Tbsp	**ButterLike Saute Butter**	56.00 g
1 clove	Garlic	3.00 g
1/4 cup	Onions, chopped	40.00 g
4 oz	Shiitake mushrooms, stems removed, sliced	113.00 g
4	Boneless, skinless chicken breasts	944.00 g
1/2 cup	Green zucchini, thinly sliced	65.00 g
1/2 cup	Yellow squash, thinly sliced	64.00 g
1 large	Sweet red bell pepper, thinly sliced	74.00 g
1/2 tsp	Salt	3.00 g
1/4 tsp	Black pepper	.53 g

Nutrition Facts				
Serving Size	341 g			
Servings Per Recipe	4			
Amount per serving			High Fat/Sugar Comparison	
Calories	320		410	
Calories from fat	45		170	
	% Daily Value*		% Daily Value*	
Total Fat	5 g	**8%**	19 g	**29%**
Saturated Fat	1.5 g	**8%**	9 g	**45%**
Cholesterol	140 mg	**47%**	180 mg	**60%**
Sodium	450 mg	**19%**	550 mg	**23%**
Total Carbohydrate	9 g	**3%**	7 g	**2%**
Dietary Fiber	1 g	**4%**	1 g	**4%**
Sugars	2 g		2 g	
Other	0 g		0 g	
Protein	57 g		55 g	

*Percent of Daily Values on page a-22

Exchanges and 8 g Carbohydrates Per Serving

Breads	0.3	Vegetables	0.9	Fruits	0.0
Meats	4.7	Milk	0.0	Fats	0.4

Directions

Saute the garlic clove, onion, and mushrooms for 3 minutes in 2 Tbsp **ButterLike**. Let cool. Place the chicken breasts on a large piece of aluminum foil and sprinkle with salt and pepper. Top with the mushrooms, then the green zucchini, yellow squash, and red pepper. Lightly salt and pepper vegetables and squirt the remaining **ButterLike** over the vegetable topped chicken. Tightly fold the foil to ensure the juices will not run out. Place on baking sheet and bake at 425° for 20-25 minutes.

Creamy Baked Chicken Breasts

The Fat Quotient using ButterLike is 15% instead of 38%
70% less fat **0% less sugar**
22% less Calories

U.S.	Ingredients	Metric
1/3 cup	**ButterLike Saute Butter**	75.00 g
8	Boneless, skinless chicken breasts, halved	1814.00 g
8 slices	Fat free Swiss cheese	85.00 g
1 can	Low fat cream of chicken soup (10.75 oz)	305.00 g
1/4 cup	Water	59.00 g
2 cups	Seasoned stuffing mix	115.00 g

Nutrition Facts				
Serving Size	307 g			
Servings Per Recipe	8			
Amount per serving			High Fat/Sugar Comparison	
Calories	372		480	
Calories from fat	50		180	
	% Daily Value*		% Daily Value*	
Total Fat	6 g	**9%**	20 g	**31%**
Saturated Fat	1.5 g	**8%**	10 g	**50%**
Cholesterol	135 mg	**457%**	175 mg	**58%**
Sodium	640 mg	**27%**	760 mg	**32%**
Total Carbohydrate	19 g	**6%**	14 g	**5%**
Dietary Fiber	1 g	**4%**	1 g	**4%**
Sugars	1 g		1 g	
Other	0 g		0 g	
Protein	58 g		61 g	

*Percent of Daily Values on page a-22

Directions

Rinse chicken and pat dry. Place pieces apart in shallow baking dish; top each piece with cheese slice. In a small bowl, combine soup and water; spoon evenly over chicken. Coarsely crush stuffing mix and sprinkle over chicken; then drizzle evenly with **ButterLike**. Bake in 350 ° oven 45-55 minutes, until meat is no longer pink.

Note: If you use low fat stuffing mix, fat will be reduced even more.

Exchanges and 18 g Carbohydrates Per Serving					
Breads	0.9	Vegetables	0.0	Fruits	0.0
Meats	4.8	Milk	0.0	Fats	0.4

Lemon and Garlic Grilled Chicken

The Fat Quotient using **ButterLike** is **35%** instead of **51%**
46% less fat **0% less sugar**
21% less Calories

U.S.	Ingredients	Metric
3 Tbsp	**ButterLike Saute Butter**	42.00 g
2	Lemons	216.00 g
1 Tbsp	Fresh rosemary or 1 tsp dried	1.20 g
1/4 tsp	Salt	1.50 g
2 1/2 to 3 lbs	Broiler-fryer chicken	1134.00 g
1/8 tsp	Pepper	.30 g
4 cloves	Garlic, halved	12.00 g
Sauce:		
2 Tbsp	**ButterLike Saute Butter**	28.00 g
3/4 cup	Chicken broth	183.00 g
1 Tbsp	Cornstarch	8.00 g

Nutrition Facts				
Serving Size	271 g			
Servings Per Recipe	6			
Amount per serving			High Fat/Sugar Comparison	
Calories	181		230	
Calories from fat	60		120	
	% Daily Value*		% Daily Value*	
Total Fat	7 g	**11%**	13 g	**20%**
Saturated Fat	2 g	**10%**	6 g	**30%**
Cholesterol	60 mg	**20%**	80 mg	**27%**
Sodium	250 mg	**10%**	340 mg	**14%**
Total Carbohydrate	10 g	**3%**	6 g	**2%**
Dietary Fiber	0 g	**0%**	0 g	**0%**
Sugars	1 g		1 g	
Other	0 g		0 g	
Protein	21 g		21 g	

*Percent of Daily Values on page a-22

Exchanges and 10 g Carbohydrates Per Serving					
Breads	0.3	Vegetables	0.1	Fruits	0.2
Meats	2.3	Milk	0.0	Fats	0.4

Directions

Cut one of the lemons into thin slices. Set aside. Finely shred 1 tsp of lemon peel from the other lemon. Squeeze juice from the lemon. Measure juice. If necessary, add enough water to equal 3 Tbsp total. Set aside 1 Tbsp of the juice. Stir together the lemon peel, the remaining 2 Tbsp lemon juice, **ButterLike**, rosemary, salt, and pepper. Remove the neck and giblets from the chicken. Rinse the chicken on the outside as well as inside the body and neck cavities. Pat dry with paper towels. Place the lemon slices and garlic cloves inside the body cavity. Skewer the neck skin to the back. In a grill with a cover, arrange preheated coals for indirect grilling. Test for medium heat where chicken will cook. Place the chicken, breast side up, on a rack in a roasting pan on the grill rack. Brush the chicken with the lemon-rosemary mixture. Cover and grill for 1-1 1/4 hours or until the chicken is no longer pink and the drumsticks move easily in their sockets, brushing occasionally with the lemon-rosemary mixture.

Sauce: In a small saucepan combine the reserved lemon juice, chicken broth, and cornstarch. Cook and stir until thickened and bubbly. Cook and stir 2 minutes more. Stir in the 2 Tbsp **ButterLike**. Serve with the chicken.

Note: Boneless, skinless chicken breasts are much lower in fat. You can barbeque them with the same sauce using a much shorter cooking time.

Thai Chicken Stir-Fry

The Fat Quotient using **ButterLike** is **20%** instead of **40%**
59% less fat **0% less sugar**
20% less Calories

U.S.	**Ingredients**	Metric
Sauce:		
2 Tbsp	Soy sauce	36.00 g
4 Tbsp	Water	59.00 g
1 tsp	Cornstarch	3.00 g
1/2 tsp	Red pepper, crushed	.90 g
2 Tbsp	**ButterLike Saute Butter**	28.00 g
12 oz	Boneless, skinless, chicken breast	340.00 g
1 tsp	Ground ginger	1.80 g
2 cloves	Garlic, minced	6.00 g
1 cup	Carrots, bias-sliced	212.00 g
1 pkg	Frozen pea pods, thawed (6 oz)	170.00 g
4	Green onions, bias-sliced into 1-inch pieces	24.00 g
1/8 cup	Dry roasted peanuts, chopped	18.00 g

Directions

Sauce: In a small bowl, stir together soy sauce, water, cornstarch, and red pepper. Set aside.

Rinse chicken; pat dry. Cut chicken into 1-inch pieces; set aside. Pour **ButterLike** into wok or large skillet. (Add more as necessary during cooking.) Preheat over medium-high heat. Stir-fry ginger and garlic in hot **ButterLike** for 15 seconds. Add carrots; stir-fry for 2 minutes. Add pea pods and green onions; stir-fry for 2-3 minutes or until crisp-tender. Remove vegetables from wok or skillet. Add chicken to hot wok. Stir-fry for 3-4 minutes or until chicken is no longer pink. Push chicken from center of wok. Stir sauce; add to center of wok. Cook and stir until thickened and bubbly. Return vegetables to wok. Add peanuts. Stir all ingredients together to coat with sauce. Cook and stir 1-2 minutes more or until heated through. If desired, serve at once with rice.

Nutrition Facts				
Serving Size	225 g			
Servings Per Recipe	4			
Amount per serving			High Fat/Sugar Comparison	
Calories	200		250	
Calories from fat	40		100	
	% Daily Value*		% Daily Value*	
Total Fat	4.5 g	**7%**	11 g	**17%**
Saturated Fat	1 g	**5%**	1.5 g	**8%**
Cholesterol	50 mg	**17%**	50 mg	**17%**
Sodium	590 mg	**25%**	600 mg	**25%**
Total Carbohydrate	15 g	**5%**	15 g	**5%**
Dietary Fiber	3 g	**12%**	4 g	**16%**
Sugars	5 g		5 g	
Other	0 g		0 g	
Protein	23 g		25 g	

*Percent of Daily Values on page a-22

Exchanges and 12 g Carbohydrates Per Serving					
Breads	0.3	Vegetables	2.0	Fruits	0.0
Meats	1.8	Milk	0.0	Fats	0.6

Thai Chicken Stir-Fry

Lemon-Basil Chicken

The Fat Quotient using ButterLike is 12% instead of 39%
85% less fat **0% less sugar**
53% less Calories

U.S.	Ingredients	Metric
2 Tbsp	**ButterLike Saute Butter**	28.00 g
2 lbs	Broiler-fryer chicken	907.00 g
1	Lemon	108.00 g
1 clove	Garlic, finely chopped	3.00 g
1 clove	Garlic, thinly sliced	3.00 g
1/4 cup	Fresh basil leaves, chopped	11.00 g

Directions

Heat oven to 375°. Fold wings of chicken across back with tips touching. Grate 2 tsp lemon peel from lemon. Mix lemon peel, **ButterLike**, and chopped garlic; set aside. Cut lemon in half. Rub chicken with juice from half of the lemon. Place sliced garlic, half of the basil, and remaining lemon half in cavity of chicken. Place chicken, breast side up, on rack in shallow roasting pan. Brush **ButterLike** mixture on chicken. Sprinkle evenly with remaining basil, then press basil into chicken. Insert meat thermometer in chicken so tip is in thickest part of inside thigh muscle and does not touch bone.

Nutrition Facts				
Serving Size	177 g			
Servings Per Recipe	6			
Amount per serving			High Fat/Sugar Comparison	
Calories		185	390	
Calories from fat		25	150	
	% Daily Value*		% Daily Value*	
Total Fat	2.5 g	**4%**	17 g	**26%**
Saturated Fat	0.5 g	**3%**	7 g	**35%**
Cholesterol	90 mg	**30%**	1445 mg	**482%**
Sodium	100 mg	**4%**	160 mg	**7%**
Total Carbohydrate	4 g	**1%**	4 g	**1%**
Dietary Fiber	0 g	**0%**	0 g	**0%**
Sugars	0 g		0 g	
Other	0 g		0 g	
Protein	36 g		56 g	

*Percent of Daily Values on page a-22

Lemon-Basil Chicken

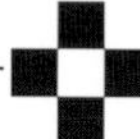

Roast uncovered about 1 1/2 hours, brushing 2 or 3 times with pan drippings, until thermometer reads 180° and juice is no longer pink when center of thigh is cut. Let stand about 15 minutes for easiest carving. Eat the chicken without the skin, in order to keep fat grams low. Skin is very fattening.

Lemon-Basil Chicken with Vegetables: After chicken has roasted 30 minutes, arrange around chicken 6 halves small red potatoes and 1 medium onion, cut into eighths. Brush vegetables with pan drippings and roast uncovered 30 minutes. Add 2 small zucchini, cut crosswise, then lengthwise into eighths; 2 small yellow squash, cut into 1/2-inch slices; and 1 large red bell pepper, cut into 1-inch chunks. Brush vegetables with pan drippings. Roast uncovered about 30 minutes longer or until chicken is done and squash and bell pepper are crisp-tender.

Tarragon Chicken: Omit lemon, garlic, and basil. Mix **ButterLike**, chopped garlic, 1 Tbsp chopped fresh or 1 tsp dried tarragon leaves, 3/4 tsp lemon pepper, and 1/2 tsp onion powder. Brush on chicken before roasting.

Exchanges and 4 g Carbohydrates Per Serving					
Breads	0.1	Vegetables	0.1	Fruits	0.1
Meats	3.0	Milk	0.0	Fats	0.1

Marinated Chicken with Peanut Sauce

The Fat Quotient using **ButterLike** is **26%** instead of **69%**
88% less fat **75% less sugar**
67% less Calories

U.S.	Ingredients	Metric
Marinade:		
1 recipe	**Peanut Sauce**, page 234	254.00 g
1/2 cup	**ButterLike Saute Butter**	112.00 g
2 Tbsp	**Granulated SugarLike**	25.00 g
2 Tbsp	Curry powder	12.00 g
1/2 cup	Soy sauce	144.00 g
4 cloves	Garlic, minced	12.00 g
3 lbs	Boneless, skinless chicken breasts	1360.00 g

Directions

Follow directions for **Peanut Sauce**. Set aside.

Marinade: In a small bowl, stir together **ButterLike**, **SugarLike**, curry powder, soy sauce, and garlic.

Cut chicken into 3/4-inch cubes. Place chicken in a large bowl; pour marinade over chicken. Cover and refrigerate for 4 hours to 2 days; stir occasionally. Thread chicken on metal skewers. Place on grill about 2 inches above a solid bed of medium-hot coals. Cook 8-10 minutes until meat is browned, turning frequently. Serve skewers of chicken with warm Peanut Sauce. Excellent!

Nutrition Facts				
Serving Size	192 g			
Servings Per Recipe	10			
Amount per serving			High Fat/Sugar Comparison	
Calories	273		830	
Calories from fat	70		570	
	% Daily Value*		% Daily Value*	
Total Fat	8 g	**12%**	64 g	**98%**
Saturated Fat	2 g	**10%**	22 g	**110%**
Cholesterol	80 mg	**27%**	190 mg	**63%**
Sodium	980 mg	**41%**	1060 mg	**44%**
Total Carbohydrate	15 g	**5%**	8 g	**3%**
Dietary Fiber	2 g	**8%**	1 g	**4%**
Sugars	1 g		4 g	
Other	2 g		0 g	
Protein	36 g		55 g	

*Percent of Daily Values on page a-22

Exchanges and 11 g Carbohydrates Per Serving					
Breads	0.7	Vegetables	0.1	Fruits	0.0
Meats	2.9	Milk	0.0	Fats	1.2

Chicken Cordon Bleu

The Fat Quotient using **ButterLike** is **14%** instead of **34%**
67% less fat **100% less sugar**
20% less Calories

U.S.	Ingredients	Metric
3 Tbsp	**ButterLike Saute Butter**	42.00 g
4	Fully cooked lean ham, thinly sliced	36.00 g
4	Boneless, skinless chicken breast halves	944.00 g
1/2 cup	Non fat Swiss cheese, shredded	54.00 g
1/3 cup	Fine dry bread crumbs	40.00 g
1 Tbsp	Fresh parsley, snipped	3.80 g
1/8 tsp	Pepper	.26 g
1/4 cup	All-purpose flour	29.00 g

Nutrition Facts				
Serving Size	287 g			
Servings Per Recipe	4			
Amount per serving			High Fat/Sugar Comparison	
Calories	386		480	
Calories from fat	50		160	
	% Daily Value*		% Daily Value*	
Total Fat	6 g	**9%**	18 g	**28%**
Saturated Fat	2 g	**10%**	10 g	**50%**
Cholesterol	150 mg	**50%**	240 mg	**80%**
Sodium	530 mg	**22%**	790 mg	**33%**
Total Carbohydrate	17 g	**6%**	13 g	**4%**
Dietary Fiber	0 g	**0%**	0 g	**0%**
Sugars	0 g		1 g	
Other	0 g		0 g	
Protein	63 g		66 g	

*Percent of Daily Values on page a-22

Exchanges and 17 g Carbohydrates Per Serving

Breads	1.1	Vegetables	0.0	Fruits	0.0
Meats	5.4	Milk	0.0	Fats	0.4

Directions

Cut ham into strips. Place chicken between 2 pieces of plastic wrap. Working from center to the edges, with the flat side of a mallet. pound chicken to 1/8-inch thickness. Remove plastic wrap. Place ham and cheese in center. Fold in sides; overlap ends, forming bundles. Secure with wooden toothpicks. In a shallow dish combine bread crumbs, parsley, and pepper. Roll chicken bundles in flour. Dip into **ButterLike** and then bread crumbs. Bake at 350° for 30 minutes on a vegetable sprayed baking dish until juices run clear.

Chicken Cordon Bleu

Broiled Chicken with Sesame-Ginger Glaze

The fat quotient using ButterLike is 10% instead of 48%
88% less fat **38% less sugar**
47% less Calories

U.S.	Ingredients	Metric
Glaze:		
4 tsp	**Granulated SugarLike**	17.00 g
1/3 cup	Plum sauce or sweet-and-sour	91.00 g
3 Tbsp	Hoisin	54.00 g
2 Tbsp	Soy sauce	36.00 g
4 tsp	Water	20.00 g
1 1/2 tsp	Sesame seed	4.50 g
1/4 tsp	Ground ginger	.45 g
1/4 tsp	Five-spice powder	.70 g
1 clove	Garlic, minced	3.00 g
Dashes	Bottled hot pepper sauce	5.20 g
2-2 1/2 lb	Meaty chicken pieces	907.00 g

Nutrition Facts				
Serving Size	190 g			
Servings Per Recipe	6			
Amount per serving			High Fat/Sugar Comparison	
Calories	208		390	
Calories from fat	20		190	
	% Daily Value*		% Daily Value*	
Total Fat	2.5 g	**4%**	21 g	**32%**
Saturated Fat	0.5 g	**3%**	6 g	**30%**
Cholesterol	90 mg	**30%**	160 mg	**53%**
Sodium	1000 mg	**42%**	1020 mg	**43%**
Total Carbohydrate	10 g	**3%**	10 g	**3%**
Dietary Fiber	1 g	**4%**	0 g	**0%**
Sugars	5 g		8 g	
Other	2 g		0 g	
Protein	36 g		42 g	

*Percent of Daily Values on page a-22

Exchanges and 7 g Carbohydrates Per Serving

Breads	0.4	Vegetables	0.0	Fruits	0.0
Meats	3.0	Milk	0.0	Fats	0.1

Directions

Skin and rinse chicken; pat dry. Place chicken pieces, bone sides up, on the unheated rack of a broiler pan. Broil 4-5 inches from heat about 20 minutes or until lightly browned.

Glaze: In a small saucepan, combine **SugarLike**, plum sauce or sweet-and-sour sauce, hoisin sauce, soy sauce, water, sesame seed, ground ginger, five-spice powder, garlic, and hot pepper sauce. Bring to a boil; reduce heat. Simmer, uncovered, for 2 minutes.

Turn chicken. Broil for 5-15 minutes more or until chicken is tender and no longer pink. Brush with glaze. Broil 2 minutes more.

Chicken Scaloppine

U.S.	Ingredients	Metric
4 Tbsp	**ButterLike Saute Butter**	56.00 g
6	Boneless, skinless chicken breast halves	1020.00 g
1/3 cup	All-purpose flour	38.00 g
2 dashes	Salt	6.00 g
2 dashes	Pepper	2.10 g
1/2 lb	Mushrooms, sliced	227.00 g
1 clove	Garlic, minced	3.00 g
1/4 tsp	Salt	1.50 g
1/4 tsp	Dry marjoram	.15 g
1/4 tsp	Dry thyme	.30 g
1 Tbsp	Lemon juice	15.00 g
1 1/2 tsp	Cornstarch	4.00 g
1/2 cup	Fat free chicken broth	123.00 g
1/2 cup	Non fat parmesan cheese	60.00 g
1	Lemon, cut into wedges	108.00 g

The Fat Quotient using ButterLike is 14% instead of 34%
65% less fat **0% less sugar**
16% less Calories

Directions

Rinse chicken and pat dry. Place individual pieces between 2 sheets of plastic wrap or wax paper; pound with a flat-surfaced mallet until about 1/4-inch thick. Cut chicken into 1-inch wide strips. Dust with flour; sprinkle with salt and pepper. Heat 2 Tbsp **ButterLike** in frying pan over medium heat. Add chicken; cook, turning once, until browned. Cover pan if necessary. Keep warm. Heat remaining **ButterLike** in frying pan over medium heat. Add mushrooms and garlic; cook until soft, stirring often.

Add salt, marjoram, thyme, and lemon juice. Stir cornstarch and broth until smooth; stir into mushroom mixture. Cook, stirring to scrape browned bits free, until sauce boils and thickens. Pour sauce over chicken and sprinkle with cheese. Serve with lemon wedges.

Exchanges and 12 g Carbohydrates Per Serving					
Breads	0.6	Vegetables	0.4	Fruits	0.1
Meats	6.1	Milk	0.0	Fats	0.3

Nutrition Facts				
Serving Size	277 g			
Servings Per Recipe	6			
Amount per serving			High Fat/Sugar Comparison	
Calories	280		340	
Calories from fat	40		120	
	% Daily Value*		% Daily Value*	
Total Fat	4.5 g	**7%**	13 g	**20%**
Saturated Fat	1 g	**5%**	6 g	**30%**
Cholesterol	100 mg	**33%**	120 mg	**40%**
Sodium	730 mg	**30%**	850 mg	**35%**
Total Carbohydrate	12 g	**4%**	9 g	**3%**
Dietary Fiber	0 g	**0%**	0 g	**0%**
Sugars	1 g		1 g	
Other	0 g		0 g	
Protein	48 g		45 g	

*Percent of Daily Values on page a-22

Phyllo Chicken Packets

The Fat Quotient using **ButterLike** is **17%** instead of **64%**
85% less fat **50% more sugar**
45% less Calories

U.S.	Ingredients	Metric
2/3 cup	**ButterLike Saute Butter**	149.00 g
6	Boneless, skinless chicken breasts, halved	1020.00 g
3/4 cup	Green onions, thinly sliced	120.00 g
3/4 cup	Fat free mayonnaise	192.00 g
3 Tbsp	Lemon juice	46.00 g
3/4 tsp	Dried tarragon	.60 g
3 cloves	Garlic, minced	9.00 g
12 sheets	Phyllo dough, thawed (1/3 lb)	151.00 g
	Pepper to taste	2.10 g
	Salt to taste	6.00 g
2 Tbsp	Non fat parmesan cheese	15.00 g

Nutrition Facts				
Serving Size	285 g			
Servings Per Recipe	6			
Amount per serving			High Fat/Sugar Comparison	
Calories	370		670	
Calories from fat	70		430	
	% Daily Value*		% Daily Value*	
Total Fat	7 g	**11%**	48 g	**74%**
Saturated Fat	2 g	**10%**	17 g	**85%**
Cholesterol	100 mg	**33%**	175 mg	**58%**
Sodium	860 mg	**36%**	1020 mg	**43%**
Total Carbohydrate	28 g	**9%**	17 g	**6%**
Dietary Fiber	1 g	**4%**	1 g	**4%**
Sugars	2 g		1 g	
Other	0 g		0 g	
Protein	44 g		43 g	

*Percent of Daily Values on page a-22

Exchanges and 27 g Carbohydrates Per Serving					
Breads	1.7	Vegetables	0.4	Fruits	0.0
Meats	4.1	Milk	0.0	Fats	1.0

Directions

Rinse chicken and pat dry; set aside. In a bowl mix onions, mayonnaise, lemon juice, tarragon, and 2 cloves garlic; set aside. Combine the remaining 1 clove garlic with **Toasted Garlic Saute Butter**. To make each packet, place one phyllo sheet on a flat surface, brush with 2 tsp **Toasted Garlic Saute Butter**. Put a second sheet on top and brush with 2 more tsp **Toasted Garlic Saute Butter**. Sprinkle all sides of one chicken piece with salt and pepper, then spread one side with 1 1/2 Tbsp of the mayonnaise mixture. Place chicken, mayonnaise side down, in center of phyllo about 2 inches from one end. Spread chicken with 1 1/2 more Tbsp mayonnaise mixture. Flip end of phyllo over chicken and roll once; then fold long sides over chicken and roll up completely. Brush packets with remaining **Toasted Garlic ButterLike** and sprinkle with cheese. Arrange phyllo packets, seam side down and slightly apart, in a 10x15-inch rimmed vegetable sprayed baking pan. Bake in a 375° oven 20-25 minutes until golden brown.

Garden Vegetable Stir-Fry

The Fat Quotient using **ButterLike** is **18%** instead of **32%**
57% less fat **29% less sugar**
24% less Calories

U.S.	Ingredients	Metric
Sauce:		
2 tsp	**Granulated SugarLike**	8.33 g
2 Tbsp	Cold water	30.00 g
1 1/2 tsp	Cornstarch	4.00 g
2 Tbsp	Soy sauce	36.00 g
1 Tbsp	Orange juice	16.00 g
Dash	Pepper	.30 g
2 Tbsp	**ButterLike Saute Butter**	28.00 g
1 cup	Green beans, bias-sliced into 1-inch pieces	240.00 g
1 1/2 cup	Cauliflower, 1/2-inch flowerets	150.00 g
1 medium	Onion, cut into thin wedges	80.00 g
1/2 cup	Carrots, thinly bias-sliced	106.00 g
1 small	Zucchini, 1/4-inch slices	130.00 g

Directions

Sauce: Combine water and cornstarch. Stir in soy sauce, orange juice, **SugarLike**, and pepper; Set aside.

Cook beans, covered, in boiling, salted water 2 minutes. Add cauliflower; return to boiling. Reduce heat. Simmer, covered, 1 minute; drain. Pour **ButterLike** into large wok or large skillet. Add more as necessary during cooking. Preheat over medium-high heat. Add onion and carrot; saute 2 minutes. Add beans, cauliflower, and zucchini; saute 3-4 minutes or until vegetables are crisp-tender. Push vegetables from center of wok. Stir sauce. Add sauce to the center of wok. Cook and stir until thickened and bubbly. Stir to coat vegetables with sauce. Cook and stir 1 minute or until heated through.

Nutrition Facts				
Serving Size	207 g			
Servings Per Recipe	4			
Amount per serving			High Fat/Sugar Comparison	
Calories	76		100	
Calories from fat	10		30	
	% Daily Value*		% Daily Value*	
Total Fat	1.5 g	**2%**	3.5 g	**5%**
Saturated Fat	0 g	**0%**	0 g	**0%**
Cholesterol	0 mg	**0%**	0 mg	**0%**
Sodium	710 mg	**30%**	710 mg	**30%**
Total Carbohydrate	16 g	**5%**	13 g	**4%**
Dietary Fiber	4 g	**16%**	3 g	**12%**
Sugars	5 g		7 g	
Other	2 g		0 g	
Protein	3 g		3 g	

*Percent of Daily Values on page a-22

Exchanges and 10 g Carbohydrates Per Serving					
Breads	0.2	Vegetables	1.7	Fruits	0.0
Meats	0.0	Milk	0.0	Fats	0.2

Red Wine-Marinated Steak

The Fat Quotient using **ButterLike** is **28%** instead of **66%**
85% less fat **0% less sugar**
66% less Calories

U.S.	Ingredients	Metric
2 Tbsp	**ButterLike Saute Butter**	28.00 g
1 lb	Boneless beef sirloin steak	454.00 g
1/2 cup	Dry red wine	118.00 g
1/3 cup	Onion, chopped	53.00 g
1/2 tsp	Dried thyme, rosemary, marjoram	.60 g
1/4 tsp	Salt	1.50 g
1/4 tsp	Coarsely ground pepper	.53 g
1 clove	Garlic, minced	3.00 g

Directions

Trim fat from meat. Place meat in a plastic bag set in a shallow dish. For marinade, stir together wine, onion, **ButterLike**, thyme, rosemary, or marjoram, salt, pepper, and garlic. Pour over meat. Close bag. Marinade at room temperature for 30 minutes or in the refrigerator for up to 6 hours, turning bag occasionally. Drain steaks, reserving marinade. Grill steaks on the rack of an uncovered grill directly over medium coals to desired doneness, turning once and brushing once with reserved marinade. (Allow 8-12 minutes for medium rare and 12-15 minutes for medium.) To serve, cut steaks into serving-size pieces.

Indirect grilling: In a grill with a cover arrange preheated coals around a drip pan. Test for medium heat above the pan. Place the steaks on the grill over the drip pan. Cover and grill meat to the desired doneness, brushing once with the reserved marinade.

Exchanges and 11 g Carbohydrates Per Serving					
Breads	0.9	Vegetables	0.2	Fruits	0.0
Meats	0.7	Milk	0.0	Fats	0.6

Nutrition Facts				
Serving Size	165 g			
Servings Per Recipe	4			
Amount per serving			High Fat/Sugar Comparison	
Calories		143	420	
Calories from fat		40	280	
	% Daily Value*		% Daily Value*	
Total Fat	4.5 g	**7%**	31 g	**48%**
Saturated Fat	1.5 g	**8%**	10 g	**50%**
Cholesterol	10 mg	**3%**	110 mg	**37%**
Sodium	330 mg	**14%**	230 mg	**10%**
Total Carbohydrate	14 g	**5%**	2 g	**1%**
Dietary Fiber	3 g	**12%**	0 g	**0%**
Sugars	1 g		1 g	
Other	0 g		0 g	
Protein	8 g		33 g	

*Percent of Daily Values on page a-22

Marinated Barbecued Flank Steak

The Fat Quotient using **ButterLike** is **39%** instead of **64%**
74% less fat **100% less sugar**
57% less Calories

U.S.	Ingredients	Metric
Marinade:		
3 Tbsp	**Granulated SugarLike**	38.00 g
3/4 cup	**ButterLike Saute Butter**	168.00 g
1/4 cup	Soy sauce	72.00 g
2 Tbsp	Vinegar	30.00 g
1 1/2 tsp	Garlic powder	4.20 g
1 1/2 tsp	Ground ginger	2.70 g
1	Green onion, thinly sliced	6.00 g
1 lb	Lean flank steak, trim fat	454.00 g

Directions

Marinade: In a large bowl, stir together **SugarLike**, soy sauce, vinegar, garlic powder, and ginger. Add **ButterLike** and onion.

Place meat in shallow dish and pour marinade over it. Cover and refrigerate, turning meat occasionally, for at least 4 hours. Lift meat from marinade and drain briefly; reserve marinade. Place meat on grill 4-6 inches from medium-hot coals. Cook, turning once and basting occasionally with marinade, until cooked to liking; cut to test. To serve, cut meat across grain into thin slanting slices.

Nutrition Facts				
Serving Size	194 g			
Servings Per Recipe	4			
Amount per serving			High Fat/Sugar Comparison	
Calories		350	810	
Calories from fat		130	530	
	% Daily Value*		% Daily Value*	
Total Fat	15 g	**23%**	58 g	**89%**
Saturated Fat	6 g	**30%**	13 g	**65%**
Cholesterol	55 mg	**18%**	95 mg	**32%**
Sodium	1080 mg	**45%**	1140 mg	**48%**
Total Carbohydrate	25 g	**8%**	16 g	**5%**
Dietary Fiber	2 g	**8%**	0 g	**0%**
Sugars	0 g		13 g	
Other	7 g		0 g	
Protein	34 g		54 g	

*Percent of Daily Values on page a-22

Exchanges and 16 g Carbohydrates Per Serving					
Breads	0.9	Vegetables	0.0	Fruits	0.0
Meats	3.6	Milk	0.0	Fats	1.3

Szechwan Beef Stir-Fry

The Fat Quotient using **ButterLike** is **12%** instead of **42%**
81% less fat **17% less sugar**
32% less Calories

U.S.	**Ingredients**	Metric
Sauce:		
1 tsp	**Granulated SugarLike**	4.00 g
3 Tbsp	Dry sherry or dry white wine	44.00 g
3 Tbsp	Soy sauce	54.00 g
2 Tbsp	Water	30.00 g
2 Tbsp	Hoisin sauce	36.00 g
2 tsp	Cornstarch	5.00 g
2 tsp	Gingerroot, grated	3.60 g
1/2 tsp	Red pepper, crushed	.90 g
1/4 tsp	Black pepper	.50 g
2 cloves	Garlic, minced	6.00 g
3/4 lb	Lean beef sirloin or top round	340.00 g
3 Tbsp	**ButterLike Saute Butter**	42.00 g
1 cup	Carrots, thinly sliced (2 medium)	246.00 g
1 can	Whole baby corn, drained (8 3/4 oz)	248.00 g
1	Red sweet pepper, cut into 1-inch squares	74.00 g
2 cups	Hot cooked rice	372.00 g

Nutrition Facts				
Serving Size	377 g			
Servings Per Recipe	4			
Amount per serving			High Fat/Sugar Comparison	
Calories		347		510
Calories from fat		40		220
	% Daily Value*		% Daily Value*	
Total Fat	4.5 g	**7%**	24 g	**37%**
Saturated Fat	1 g	**5%**	7 g	**35%**
Cholesterol	40 mg	**13%**	75 mg	**25%**
Sodium	1460 mg	**61%**	1460 mg	**61%**
Total Carbohydrate	47 g	**16%**	44 g	**15%**
Dietary Fiber	3 g	**12%**	3 g	**12%**
Sugars	5 g		6 g	
Other	1 g		0 g	
Protein	26 g		29 g	

*Percent of Daily Values on page a-22

Exchanges and 43 g Carbohydrates Per Serving

Breads	2.7	Vegetables	0.8	Fruits	0.0
Meats	2.7	Milk	0.0	Fats	0.5

Szechwan Beef Stir-Fry

Directions

Trim fat from beef. Partially freeze beef. Thinly slice across grain into bite-size strips. Set aside. Cut whole corn in half crosswise; set aside.

Sauce: Stir together **SugarLike**, sherry or wine, soy sauce, water, hoisin sauce, cornstarch, gingerroot, red pepper, black pepper (if desired), and garlic. Set aside.

Pour **ButterLike** into wok or large skillet. (Add more **ButterLike** as necessary during cooking.) Preheat over medium-high heat. Saute carrots in hot **ButterLike** for 2 minutes. Add baby corn and sweet pepper. Saute for 1-2 minutes more or until vegetables are crisp-tender. Remove from wok. Add beef to the hot wok. Add more saute butter if needed. Stir for 2-3 minutes or to desired doneness. Push beef from the center of the wok. Cook and stir till thickened and bubbly. Stir in all cooked meat and vegetables. Cook and stir 1-2 minutes more or until heated through. Serve with rice.

Beef Burgundy Stew

The Fat Quotient using **ButterLike** is **27%** instead of **67%**
84% less fat **0% less sugar**
61% less Calories

U.S.	Ingredients	Metric
Bouquet Garni:		
1	Carrot, quartered	72.00 g
1	Celery top	20.00 g
1	Dry basil leaf	.10 g
2	Parsley sprigs	2.00 g
1 tsp	Dry thyme	1.20 g
1/4 cup	**ButterLike Saute Butter**	56.00 g
16	Small white boiling onions, peeled	85.00 g
6 slices	Diced lean bacon	36.00 g
2 lbs	Boneless lean beef	907.00 g
2 cups	Red wine	472.00 g
2 cloves	Garlic, peeled	6.00 g
2 cups	Small mushrooms, sliced	140.00 g
1 1/2 cups	Water	356.00 g
6 Tbsp	All-purpose flour	43.00 g
1/2 cup	Cold water	119.00 g
	Salt to taste	6.00 g
	Pepper to taste	2.10 g

Nutrition Facts				
Serving Size	290 g			
Servings Per Recipe	8			
Amount per serving			High Fat/Sugar Comparison	
Calories		264		670
Calories from fat		70		450
		% Daily Value*		% Daily Value*
Total Fat	8 g	**12%**	50 g	**77%**
Saturated Fat	3 g	**15%**	21 g	**105%**
Cholesterol	65 mg	**22%**	175 mg	**58%**
Sodium	460 mg	**19%**	580 mg	**24%**
Total Carbohydrate	11 g	**4%**	9 g	**3%**
Dietary Fiber	1 g	**4%**	1 g	**4%**
Sugars	2 g		2 g	
Other	0 g		0 g	
Protein	26 g		45 g	

*Percent of Daily Values on page a-22

Exchanges and 10g Carbohydrates Per Serving					
Breads	0.4	Vegetables	0.7	Fruits	0.0
Meats	2.8	Milk	0.0	Fats	0.9

Directions

Bouquet Garni: Tie carrot, celery, bay leaf, parsley, and thyme in a square of cheesecloth. Set aside.

Trim fat off of beef and cut into 1 to 1 1/2-inch cubes. Heat **ButterLike** in large, heavy pan over medium heat. Add onions and bacon; cook about 10 minutes, stirring often, until onions are lightly browned. Remove onions and bacon; set aside. Add beef to pan, cook a portion at a time; do not crowd. Cook, turning as needed, until well browned.

Return all beef to pan; add red wine, garlic, mushrooms, 1 1/2 cups water, bouquet garni, onions, and bacon. Bring to boil; then reduce heat, cover, and simmer 1 1/2 hours until meat is tender. With a slotted spoon, transfer meat, mushrooms, and onions to a serving dish; keep warm.

Sauce: Pour meat juices through a fine wire strainer set over a medium-size pan; discard residue in strainer. In a small bowl, mix flour and 1/2 cup cold water to make a smooth paste. Stir flour mixture into meat juices; cook over medium heat, stirring constantly, until sauce is thick and smooth. Salt and pepper to taste. Pour sauce over meat and vegetables. Serve over rice, if desired.

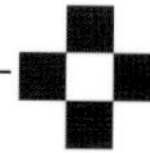

Beef and Bean Tamale Pie

The Fat Quotient using **ButterLike** is **15%** instead of **29%**
54% less fat **40% less sugar**
15% less Calories

U.S.	Ingredients	Metric
10 1/2 oz	Extra lean ground beef	298.00 g
1/2 cup	Onions, chopped	80.00 g
1 Tbsp	Garlic powder	2.80 g
1/3 tsp	Pepper	.70 g
2/3 cup	Canned tomato paste	173.00 g
1 1/8 cup	Tomatoes, with liquid, chopped	270.00 g
1 cup	Water	237.00 g
1 lb	Cooked pinto beans (1/3 lb dry)	454.00 g
2 1/2 tsp	Chili powder	6.50 g
1 1/5 tsp	Ground cumin	2.50 g
1/2 tsp	Paprika	1.00 g
1/2 tsp	Onion powder	1.00 g
Cornmeal	**topping:**	
1 3/4 Tbsp	**Granulated SugarLike**	22.00 g
1 3/4 Tbsp	**ButterLike Baking Butter**	25.00 g
3/4 cup	All-purpose flour	94.00 g
2/3 cup	Cornmeal	92.00 g
1 1/4 tsp	Baking powder	6.00 g
1/4 tsp	Salt	1.50 g
1/3 cup + 1 tsp	Skim milk	98.00 g
1/4 cup	Fat free cheddar cheese	28.00 g
2 Tbsp	Sharp cheddar cheese	31.00 g
2 1/2 Tbsp	Egg substitute	38.00 g

Exchanges and 47 g Carbohydrates Per Serving

Breads	1.0	Vegetables	6.8	Fruits	0.0
Meats	1.5	Milk	0.0	Fats	0.3

Nutrition Facts
Serving Size 196 g
Servings Per Recipe 10

Amount per serving			High Fat/Sugar Comparison	
Calories	340		400	
Calories from fat	50		120	
	% Daily Value*		% Daily Value*	
Total Fat	6 g	**9%**	13 g	**20%**
Saturated Fat	2 g	**10%**	6 g	**30%**
Cholesterol	25 mg	**8%**	60 mg	**20%**
Sodium	400 mg	**17%**	410 mg	**17%**
Total Carbohydrate	52 g	**17%**	51 g	**17%**
Dietary Fiber	3 g	**12%**	2 g	**8%**
Sugars	3 g		5 g	
Other	2 g		0 g	
Protein	22 g		21 g	

*Percent of Daily Values on page a-22

Directions

Brown ground beef. Drain. Rinse with water in a pasta strainer. Add onions, garlic powder, pepper, tomato paste, tomatoes, water, beans, and seasonings. Blend well. Bring to a boil. Reduce heat and simmer for 20-25 minutes. Pour mixture into a vegetable sprayed medium sized casserole dish. Set aside.

Cornmeal topping: Blend softened **ButterLike**, **SugarLike**, flour, cornmeal, baking powder, and salt on low speed for 1 minute. Mix egg substitute and milk. Add to dry ingredients. Blend on medium speed only until dry ingredients are moistened, 2 minutes. Pour batter over meat mixture. Bake at 375° for 30-35 minutes, until lightly browned. Mix cheeses together. Sprinkle cheese over cornbread in each pan. Cut into 10 servings. If desired, serve with taco sauce.

Beef Stroganoff with Noodles

The Fat Quotient using **ButterLike** is **15%** instead of **49%**
83% less fat **60% more sugar**
47% less Calories

U.S.	Ingredients	Metric
4 Tbsp	**ButterLike Saute Butter**	56.00 g
1 lb	Lean round steak, cut 1-inch thick	454.00 g
1/4 cup	Water	59.00 g
1/2 lb	Small white boiling onions, peeled	227.00 g
1/2 lb	Mushrooms, sliced	227.00 g
1 clove	Garlic, minced	3.00 g
3 Tbsp	All-purpose flour	22.00 g
1 can	Condensed consommé (10.5 oz)	298.00 g
1 can	Low fat condensed cream of mushroom soup (10.75 oz)	305.00 g
	Salt to taste	6.00 g
	Pepper to taste	2.10 g
1	Dry bay leaf	.10 g
8 oz	Dry medium-wide noodles	227.00 g
1 cup	Fat free sour cream	256.00 g
2 Tbsp	Parsley, chopped	120.00 g

Directions

Trim fat from steak; cut steak across the grain into 1/4-inch thick slices. Heat 2 Tbsp **ButterLike** in a wide frying pan over medium heat. Add meat, a portion at a time. Cook, turning as needed, until browned. Transfer to a 3-quart baking dish. Stir in water. Heat remaining **ButterLike** in pan. Add onions and cook over medium heat, stirring often, until golden. Add mushrooms and garlic; cook, stirring often until mushrooms are limp. With a slotted spoon, transfer vegetables to baking dish. Stir flour into drippings in pan; cook, stirring, until flour is golden. Remove from heat and gradually stir in consomme and mushroom soup. Salt and pepper to taste. On high heat, bring sauce to a boil, stirring; pour sauce over meat and vegetables. Add bay leaf, cover and bake in a 350° oven 1 1/2 hours, until meat is tender. Stir sour cream into hot meat mixture. Cook noodles according to package directions. Serve mixture warm over noodles. Sprinkle with parsley.

Nutrition Facts				
Serving Size	377 g			
Servings Per Recipe	6			
Amount per serving			High Fat/Sugar Comparison	
Calories	350		660	
Calories from fat	60		330	
	% Daily Value*		% Daily Value*	
Total Fat	6 g	**9%**	36 g	**55%**
Saturated Fat	2 g	**10%**	13 g	**65%**
Cholesterol	65 mg	**22%**	160 mg	**53%**
Sodium	5970 mg	**249%**	6220 mg	**259%**
Total Carbohydrate	38 g	**13%**	28 g	**9%**
Dietary Fiber	2 g	**8%**	2 g	**8%**
Sugars	5 g		2 g	
Other	0 g		0 g	
Protein	33 g		55 g	

*Percent of Daily Values on page a-22

Exchanges and 36 g Carbohydrates Per Serving

Breads	1.4	Vegetables	1.7	Fruits	0.0
Meats	3.6	Milk	0.4	Fats	0.4

Savory Swiss Steak

The Fat Quotient using ButterLike is 19% instead of 39%
63% less fat **27% less sugar**
22% less Calories

U.S.	**Ingredients**	Metric
2 Tbsp	**ButterLike Saute Butter**	28.00 g
1 Tbsp	**Brown SugarLike**	12.50 g
1/2 cup	All-purpose flour	58.00 g
1 Tbsp	Dry mustard	7.20 g
1 lb	Lean round steak, 1-inch thick	680.00 g
1 can	Tomatoes, diced (14.5 oz)	411.00 g
1 cup	Onions, sliced	160.00 g
1/2 cup	Celery, diced	60.00 g
3	Carrots, diced	216.00 g
2 Tbsp	Worcestershire	30.00 g
	Salt to taste	6.00 g
	Pepper to taste	2.10 g

Nutrition Facts				
Serving Size	418 g			
Servings Per Recipe	4			
Amount per serving			High Fat/Sugar Comparison	
Calories	436		560	
Calories from fat	80		220	
	% Daily Value*		% Daily Value*	
Total Fat	9 g	**14%**	24 g	**37%**
Saturated Fat	2.5 g	**13%**	7g	**35%**
Cholesterol	110 mg	**37%**	145 mg	**48%**
Sodium	1010 mg	**42%**	1030 mg	**43%**
Total Carbohydrate	31 g	**10%**	29 g	**10%**
Dietary Fiber	5 g	**20%**	4 g	**16%**
Sugars	8 g		11 g	
Other	2 g		0 g	
Protein	56 g		56 g	

*Percent of Daily Values on page a-22

Exchanges and 24 g Carbohydrates Per Serving

Breads	0.9	Vegetables	2.5	Fruits	0.0
Meats	7.2	Milk	0.0	Fats	0.2

Directions

Trim fat from steak. Mix flour and mustard. Sprinkle flour mixture over steak and pound it in with a cleated meat mallet. Cut steak into serving-size pieces. Heat **ButterLike** in a wide, heavy frying pan over medium heat. Add meat and cook, turning once, until browned. If you are baking meat, transfer it to a shallow baking pan. Add **SugarLike**, tomatoes and their liquid, onions, celery, carrots, and Worcestershire to meat in pan. Salt and pepper to taste. Bring to a boil; then reduce heat, cover and simmer until meat is tender. If baking, cover and bake in a 350° oven about 1 1/2 hours until meat is tender. Serve with noodles.

Shrimp Fajitas

The Fat Quotient using ButterLike is 9% instead of 34%
82% less fat **25% more sugar**
31% less Calories

U.S.	Ingredients	Metric
1 cup	**Great Salsa**, page 8	254.00 g
2 Tbsp	**ButterLike Saute Butter**	28.00 g
1 lb	Medium raw shrimp, shelled, deveined	454.00 g
1 cup	Lightly packed cilantro, chopped	60.00 g
1 clove	Garlic, minced	3.00 g
1/3 cup	Lime juice	82.00 g
6	Fat free flour tortillas	222.00 g
2 large	Green bell peppers, seeded and thinly sliced	340.00 g
1 large	Onion, thinly sliced	160.00 g
1/4 cup	Fat free sour cream	64.00 g

Directions

Prepare **Great Salsa** as directed; set aside.

In a medium bowl, combine shrimp, cilantro, garlic, and lime juice. Let stand at room temperature for 20 minutes. Meanwhile, stack tortillas, wrap in foil, and heat in a 350° oven about 15 minutes until warm and soft. Heat **ButterLike** in a wide non stick frying pan over medium heat. Add bell peppers and onion; cook, stirring occasionally, until vegetables are soft. Lift out vegetables with slotted spoon and keep warm. Add shrimp mixture to pan and cook over high heat, stirring often, just until shrimp are opaque in center; cut to test. You may need to add more **ButterLike**. Stir in vegetables with shrimp. Spoon shrimp mixture into tortillas, top with sour cream, and roll to enclose filling. Add Great Salsa to the individual servings.

Nutrition Facts				
Serving Size	278 g			
Servings Per Recipe	6			
Amount per serving			High Fat/Sugar Comparison	
Calories	200		290	
Calories from fat	20		100	
	% Daily Value*		% Daily Value*	
Total Fat	2 g	**3%**	11 g	**17%**
Saturated Fat	0 g	**0%**	2.5 g	**13%**
Cholesterol	115 mg	**38%**	120 mg	**40%**
Sodium	450 mg	**19%**	430 mg	**18%**
Total Carbohydrate	24 g	**8%**	28 g	**9%**
Dietary Fiber	8 g	**32%**	4 g	**12%**
Sugars	4 g		3 g	
Other	0 g		0 g	
Protein	20 g		20 g	

*Percent of Daily Values on page a-22

Exchanges and 16 g Carbohydrates Per Serving

Breads	1.1	Vegetables	1.1	Fruits	0.1
Meats	1.9	Milk	0.1	Fats	0.1

Salmon in Phyllo

The Fat Quotient using ButterLike is 25% instead of 54%
65% less fat **0% less sugar**
48% less Calories

U.S.	Ingredients	Metric
1/3 cup	**ButterLike Saute Butter**	75.00 g
1 lb	Fresh or frozen skinless salmon	454.00 g
1/4 cup	Fat free sour cream	64.00 g
1 tsp	Dried dillweed	.80 g
Dash	Salt	.75 g
Dash	White pepper	.30 g
8 sheets	Frozen phyllo dough, thawed	152.00 g

Directions

Cut salmon into four 1/2-inch thick fillets. Spread 1 Tbsp of the sour cream over each fillet. Sprinkle with dill, salt, and white pepper; set aside. Unfold phyllo dough; cover with damp towel. Lay a sheet of phyllo dough flat.

Nutrition Facts				
Serving Size	278 g			
Servings Per Recipe	4			
Amount per serving			High Fat/Sugar Comparison	
Calories	325		431	
Calories from fat	81		234	
	% Daily Value*		% Daily Value*	
Total Fat	9 g	**14%**	26g	**40%**
Saturated Fat	2 g	**12%**	13 g	**66%**
Cholesterol	46 mg	**15%**	93 mg	**31%**
Sodium	377 mg	**16%**	537 mg	**22%**
Total Carbohydrate	29 g	**10%**	21 g	**7%**
Dietary Fiber	0 g	**0%**	0 g	**0%**
Sugars	1 g		0 g	
Other	0 g		0 g	
Protein	31 g		30 g	

*Percent of Daily Values on page a-22

Brush phyllo dough with some **ButterLike**. Top with another sheet of phyllo dough.* Brush with more ButterLike. Add 6 more sheets of dough, for a total of 8 sheets, brushing each sheet with **ButterLike**. Cut into four 9x7-inch rectangles. Place a salmon fillet, sour cream side down, in the middle of each dough rectangle. Fold a long side of dough over the salmon; repeat with the other long side, brushing dough with **ButterLike** and pressing lightly. Fold up ends. Repeat with remaining rectangles, **ButterLike**, and salmon to make a total of 4 salmon-phyllo bundles. Arrange bundles, seam sides down, on a baking sheet. Brush the tops with **ButterLike**. Bake in a 375 degree oven for 15 to 18 minutes or till phyllo dough is golden and fish flakes easily with a fork. Serve with Mustard Cream Sauce, page 243.

Anbrea's Favorite Tuna Casserole

The Fat Quotient using ButterLike is 17% instead of 63%
90% less fat **25% less sugar**
69% less Calories

U.S.	Ingredients	Metric
2 Tbsp	**ButterLike Saute Butter**	28.00 g
2 cans	Tuna, packed in water (7 oz)	397.00 g
1 lb	Fat free egg noodles	454.00 g
1 can	Low fat cream of chicken soup (10.75 oz)	298.00 g
1 cup	Non fat mayonnaise	256.00 g
1/4 cup	Onion, chopped	40.00 g
1 cup	Low fat potato chips, crushed	28.00 g
3/4 cup	Non fat cheddar cheese	84.00 g
1/4 cup	Sharp cheddar cheese	62.00 g

Nutrition Facts				
Serving Size	206 g			
Servings Per Recipe	8			
Amount per serving			High Fat/Sugar Comparison	
Calories	244		790	
Calories from fat	40		490	
	% Daily Value*		% Daily Value*	
Total Fat	4.5 g	**7%**	55 g	**85%**
Saturated Fat	2 g	**10%**	15 g	**75%**
Cholesterol	40 mg	**13%**	105 mg	**35%**
Sodium	790 mg	**33%**	3310 mg	**138%**
Total Carbohydrate	28 g	**9%**	44 g	**15%**
Dietary Fiber	0 g	**0%**	1 g	**4%**
Sugars	3 g		4 g	
Other	0 g		0 g	
Protein	21 g		30 g	

*Percent of Daily Values on page a-22

Exchanges and 25 g Carbohydrates Per Serving

Breads	1.4	Vegetables	0.1	Fruits	0.0
Meats	2.4	Milk	0.0	Fats	0.7

Directions

My 15 year old daughter once asked me why I didn't put anything good in my cookbook, like her favorite tuna casserole. I just laughed. I had spent years trying not to make it because Evan, my husband, didn't like tuna casserole especially with crushed potato chips on top. So here's to Anbrea!

Cook and drain the egg noodles according to directions. Saute the chopped onion in the hot **ButterLike** until soft. Mix together in a 4-quart vegetable sprayed or 9x13-inch baking dish the drained tuna, soup, mayonnaise, and onion. Stir in the cooked egg noodles. Spread evenly in pan. Sprinkle on the cheese and crushed potato chips. Bake in 350° oven for 20-25 minutes until hot.

Ginger Shrimp

The Fat Quotient using ButterLike is 12% instead of 38%
77% less fat **83% less sugar**
38% less Calories

U.S.	Ingredients	Metric
5 tsp	**Granulated SugarLike**	21.00 g
4 Tbsp	**ButterLike Saute Butter**	56.00 g
1/4 cup	White vinegar	60.00 g
2 Tbsp	Soy sauce	36.00 g
1 tsp	Cornstarch	2.67 g
2 cloves	Garlic, minced	6.00 g
2 tsp	Fresh ginger, grated	4.00 g
1 lb	Medium raw shrimp, shelled and deveined	454.00 g
2 stalks	Celery, 1/2-inch thick slanting slices	80.00 g
1 can	Bamboo shoots, drained (8 oz)	227.00 g
1/4 cup	Green onions, thinly sliced	40.00 g
1	Green onion, thinly sliced	6.00 g

Directions

In a small bowl, stir together **SugarLike**, vinegar, soy sauce, and cornstarch; set aside. Heat 2 Tbsp **ButterLike** in a wok or frying pan over medium heat. When **ButterLike** is hot, add garlic and ginger; stir once. Add shrimp and cook until opaque in center, stirring continuously. Remove shrimp mixture from pan and set aside. Heat remaining 2 Tbsp **ButterLike** in pan. Add celery, bamboo shoots, and 1/4 cup onions; cook, stirring, for 1 minute. Return shrimp to pan. Stir vinegar mixture and add to pan; cook, stirring, until sauce boils and thickens. Transfer shrimp mixture to a serving dish and sprinkle evenly with sliced onion.

Exchanges and 7 g Carbohydrates Per Serving					
Breads	0.3	Vegetables	0.7	Fruits	0.0
Meats	1.6	Milk	0.0	Fats	0.4

Nutrition Facts				
Serving Size	248 g			
Servings Per Recipe	4			
Amount per serving			High Fat/Sugar Comparison	
Calories	166		260	
Calories from fat	30		130	
	% Daily Value*		% Daily Value*	
Total Fat	3.5 g	**5%**	15 g	**23%**
Saturated Fat	1 g	**5%**	2 g	**10%**
Cholesterol	175 mg	**58%**	175 mg	**58%**
Sodium	740 mg	**31%**	740 mg	**31%**
Total Carbohydrate	15 g	**5%**	11 g	**4%**
Dietary Fiber	4 g	**16%**	2 g	**8%**
Sugars	1 g		6 g	
Other	4 g		0 g	
Protein	21 g		21 g	

*Percent of Daily Values on page a-22

Gingered Plum-Glazed Halibut

The Fat Quotient using **ButterLike** is **12%** instead of **22%**
50% less fat **0% less sugar**
8% less Calories

U.S.	Ingredients	Metric
1 lb	Fresh or frozen halibut, or swordfish	454.00 g
Sauce:		
1/2 cup	Red plum jam	160.00 g
1 Tbsp	Lemon juice	15.00 g
1/8 tsp	Ginger	.25 g
1/8 tsp	Red pepper	.23 g
1/8 tsp	Garlic powder	.35 g
Glaze:		
1 Tbsp	**ButterLike Saute Butter**	14.00 g

Directions

Thaw fish, if frozen. Rinse fish; pat dry with paper towels. Cut in 4 serving size pieces, if necessary. Set aside.

Sauce: In a small bowl combine jam, lemon juice, ginger, red pepper, and garlic powder.

Glaze: In another bowl, combine 3 Tbsp of the sauce with the **ButterLike**. Set remaining sauce aside.

Place the fish on a vegetable sprayed unheated rack of a broiler pan. Lightly brush with half of the glaze. Broil 4-inches from heat for 5 minutes. Using a wide spatula, carefully turn fish over. Lightly brush with remaining glaze. Broil 3-7 minutes more or until fish flakes easily with a fork. Serve fish with the sauce.

Nutrition Facts				
Serving Size	161 g			
Servings Per Recipe	4			
Amount per serving			High Fat/Sugar Comparison	
Calories	230		250	
Calories from fat	30		50	
	% Daily Value*		% Daily Value*	
Total Fat	3 g	**5%**	6 g	**9%**
Saturated Fat	0.5 g	**3%**	2.5 g	**13%**
Cholesterol	35 mg	**12%**	45 mg	**15%**
Sodium	75 mg	**3%**	110 mg	**5%**
Total Carbohydrate	27 g	**9%**	26 g	**9%**
Dietary Fiber	0 g	**0%**	0 g	**0%**
Sugars	24 g		24 g	
Other	0 g		0 g	
Protein	24 g		23 g	

*Percent of Daily Values on page a-22

Exchanges and 27 g Carbohydrates Per Serving					
Breads	0.1	Vegetables	0.0	Fruits	0.0
Meats	3.3	Milk	0.0	Fats	0.1

Flounder and Crab Casserole

The Fat Quotient using **ButterLike** is **14%** instead of **38%**
71% less fat **17% less sugar**
22% less Calories

U.S.	Ingredients	Metric
1/4 cup	**ButterLike Saute Butter**	56.00 g
1 lb	Flounder fillets, 1/2-inch thick	454.00 g
1 1/2 cup	Water	356.00 g
1	Dry bay leaf	.10 g
1/2	Lemon, thinly sliced	54.00 g
1/4 tsp	Salt	1.50 g
1/4 tsp	Pepper	.53 g
1 1/2 cup	Celery, thinly sliced	180.00 g
1 /2 lb	Mushrooms, sliced	227.00 g
1 can	Water chestnuts, drained and sliced (8 oz)	227.00 g
1 small	Green bell pepper, seeded and chopped	170.00 g
5 Tbsp	All-purpose flour	36.00 g
1 1/2 cup	Skim milk	368.00 g
1 tsp	Dry savory	1.40 g
2 tsp	Dijon mustard	10.00 g
1/2 tsp	Liquid hot pepper seasoning	2.60 g
1/4 tsp	Pepper	.53 g
1/2 lb	Crab meat	227.00 g
Dash	Paprika	2.10 g
1/3 cup	Non fat parmesan cheese	40.00 g
1/4 cup	Parsley, chopped	60.00 g

Nutrition Facts				
Serving Size	412 g			
Servings Per Recipe	6			
Amount per serving			High Fat/Sugar Comparison	
Calories	257		330	
Calories from fat	35		130	
		% Daily Value*		% Daily Value*
Total Fat	4 g	**6%**	14 g	**22%**
Saturated Fat	1 g	**5%**	8 g	**40%**
Cholesterol	70 mg	**23%**	100 mg	**33%**
Sodium	680 mg	**28%**	750 mg	**31%**
Total Carbohydrate	20 g	**7%**	18 g	**6%**
Dietary Fiber	4 g	**16%**	4 g	**16%**
Sugars	5 g		6 g	
Other	0 g		0 g	
Protein	35 g		32 g	

*Percent of Daily Values on page a-22

Exchanges and 16 g Carbohydrates Per Serving

Breads	0.5	Vegetables	1.6	Fruits	0.1
Meats	5.3	Milk	0.2	Fats	0.3

Directions

Rinse fish; pat dry, cut into large pieces. In a frying pan, combine water, bay leaf, lemon, salt, and 1/4 tsp pepper. Bring to a boil over high heat; simmer, covered, 5 minutes. Place fish in pan, and simmer, covered, gently until just opaque but still moist in thickest part; cut to test. Lift out fish and drain on paper towels. Break into bite-size pieces; set aside.

Discard poaching liquid from frying pan. Heat **ButterLike** in pan over medium heat. Add celery, mushrooms, water chestnuts, and bell peppers. Cook until mushrooms are soft, stirring often. Add flour; cook, stirring for 1 minute. Remove from heat and stir in milk. Return to heat and cook until sauce boils and thickens, stirring constantly,. Add savory, mustard, hot pepper seasoning, and 1/4 tsp pepper; stir until simmering. Remove from heat. Stir in fish and crab. Spoon mixture into 6 vegetable sprayed 1-1 1/2 cup individual casseroles or in a vegetable sprayed baking dish; sprinkle with paprika. Bake, uncovered, in a 350° oven until hot and bubbly. Sprinkle each serving with cheese and parsley.

Crispy Oven-Fried Fish

The Fat Quotient using **ButterLike** is **11%** instead of **40%**
79% less fat **0% less sugar**
26% less Calories

U.S.	Ingredients	Metric
2 Tbsp	**ButterLike Saute Butter**	28.00 g
1 lb	Cod	454.00 g
1/4 cup	Skim milk	61.00 g
1/4 cup	All-purpose flour	29.00 g
1/3 cup	Fine dry bread crumbs	36.00 g
1/4 cup	Non fat parmesan cheese, grated	30.00 g
1/2 tsp	Dried dillweed	.50 g
1/8 tsp	Pepper	.30 g

Directions

Rinse fish; pat dry with paper towels. Cut into 4 pieces. Place milk in shallow dish. Place flour in another shallow dish. In a third dish, combine bread crumbs, cheese, dillweed, and pepper. Toss with **ButterLike**. Dip pieces of fish in milk, then in flour. Dip again in milk, then in crumb mixture to coat all sides. Place on a vegetable sprayed baking sheet. Bake, uncovered, in a 450° oven for 6-9 minutes or until fish flakes easily with fork.

Exchanges and 14 g Carbohydrates Per Serving					
Breads	1.0	Vegetables	0.0	Fruits	0.0
Meats	4.8	Milk	0.1	Fats	0.3

Nutrition Facts				
Serving Size	160 g			
Servings Per Recipe	4			
Amount per serving			High Fat/Sugar Comparison	
Calories	201		270	
Calories from fat	20		110	
	% Daily Value*		% Daily Value*	
Total Fat	2.5 g	**4%**	12 g	**18%**
Saturated Fat	0.5 g	**3%**	6 g	**30%**
Cholesterol	50 mg	**17%**	125 mg	**42%**
Sodium	240 mg	**10%**	280 mg	**12%**
Total Carbohydrate	15 g	**5%**	14 g	**5%**
Dietary Fiber	1 g	**4%**	1 g	**4%**
Sugars	1 g		1 g	
Other	0 g		0 g	
Protein	27 g		25 g	

*Percent of Daily Values on page a-22

Broiled Basil-Buttered Halibut Steaks

The Fat Quotient using **ButterLike** is **21%** instead of **53%**
71% less fat **0% less sugar**
27% less Calories

U.S.	Ingredients	Metric
3 Tbsp	**ButterLike Saute Butter**	42.00 g
4	Fresh or frozen halibut or sea bass	680.00 g
1 tsp	Dried basil or savory	.80 g
1 Tbsp	Fresh parsley, snipped	3.75 g
2 tsp	Lemon juice	10.00 g

Directions

Thaw fish if frozen. Cut into 1-inch thick steaks. Rinse fish; pat dry with paper towels. Set aside. In a small mixing bowl stir together **ButterLike**, basil, parsley, and lemon juice. Place the fish on the vegetable sprayed unheated rack of a broiler pan. Lightly brush fish with some of the **ButterLike** mixture. Broil 4 inches from the heat for 5 minutes. Using a wide spatula, carefully turn fish over. Lightly brush with more of the **ButterLike** mixture. Broil 3-7 minutes more or until fish flakes easily with a fork.

Nutrition Facts				
Serving Size	184 g			
Servings Per Recipe	4			
Amount per serving			High Fat/Sugar Comparison	
Calories	213		290	
Calories from fat	50		150	
	% Daily Value*		% Daily Value*	
Total Fat	5 g	**8%**	17 g	**26%**
Saturated Fat	1 g	**5%**	8 g	**40%**
Cholesterol	55 mg	**18%**	110 mg	**37%**
Sodium	90 mg	**4%**	220 mg	**9%**
Total Carbohydrate	4 g	**1%**	0 g	**0%**
Dietary Fiber	0 g	**0%**	0 g	**0%**
Sugars	0 g		0 g	
Other	0 g		0 g	
Protein	35 g		34 g	

*Percent of Daily Values on page a-22

Exchanges and 4 g Carbohydrates Per Serving					
Breads	0.2	Vegetables	0.0	Fruits	0.0
Meats	4.9	Milk	0.0	Fats	0.3

Snow Peas with Shrimp

The Fat Quotient using **ButterLike** is **18%** instead of **56%**
80% less fat **25% less sugar**
36% less Calories

U.S.	Ingredients	Metric
1/2 tsp	**Granulated SugarLike**	2.00 g
3 Tbsp	**ButterLike Saute Butter**	42.00 g
1 tsp	Soy sauce	6.00 g
1 1/2 tsp	Cornstarch	4.00 g
1 Tbsp	Cold water	15.00 g
1/2 tsp	Salt	3.00 g
14 large	Raw shrimp, shelled,deveined, halved lengthwise	98.00 g
1/3 cup	Fat free chicken broth	82.00 g
1/2 cup	Water chestnuts, thinly sliced	88.00 g
1 1/2 cup	Chinese pea pods, remove ends and strings	129.00 g
1/2 large	Onion, halved crosswise, cut into thin wedges	160.00 g
2 small	Stalks celery, 1/4-inch slanting slices	80.00 g

Nutrition Facts				
Serving Size	177 g			
Servings Per Recipe	4			
Amount per serving			High Fat/Sugar Comparison	
Calories	102		160	
Calories from fat	20		90	
	% Daily Value*		% Daily Value*	
Total Fat	2 g	**3%**	10 g	**15%**
Saturated Fat	0.5 g	**3%**	6 g	**30%**
Cholesterol	40 mg	**13%**	60 mg	**20%**
Sodium	450 mg	**19%**	600 mg	**25%**
Total Carbohydrate	14 g	**5%**	11 g	**4%**
Dietary Fiber	3 g	**12%**	3 g	**12%**
Sugars	3 g		4 g	
Other	1 g		0 g	
Protein	6 g		6 g	

*Percent of Daily Values on page a-22

Exchanges and 10 g Carbohydrates Per Serving

Breads	0.3	Vegetables	1.5	Fruits	0.0
Meats	0.4	Milk	0.0	Fats	0.3

Directions

In a small bowl, stir together **SugarLike**, soy sauce, cornstarch, and water; set aside. Heat **ButterLike** in a wok or a wide frying pan over medium heat. When hot, add salt and shrimp. Cook, stirring, until shrimp are opaque in center; cut to test. Add broth, water chestnuts, pea pod, onion, and celery. Cover and cook, stirring once, for 1 1/2 minutes. Stir soy sauce mixture and add to pan; cook, stirring until sauce thickens. Serve over rice.

Grilled Halibut

The Fat Quotient using **ButterLike** is **19%** instead of **33%**
50% less fat **66% less sugar**
13% less Calories

U.S.	Ingredients	Metric
2 Tbsp	**ButterLike Saute Butter**	28.00 g
1 Tbsp	**Granulated SugarLike**	12.50 g
2 lb	Halibut steaks, 3/4 to 1-inch thick	907.00 g
3 Tbsp	Soy sauce	54.00 g
2 Tbsp	Lemon juice	31.00 g
1 Tbsp	Worcestershire sauce	15.00 g
3/4 tsp	Ground ginger	1.40 g
1 clove	Garlic	3.00 g
1/8 tsp	Pepper	.30 g
1	Lemon, cut into wedges	108.00 g

Directions

Rinse fish and pat dry. In a shallow dish, combine **ButterLike**, **SugarLike**, soy sauce, lemon juice, worcestershire, ginger, garlic, and pepper. Add fish and turn to coat. Refrigerate, covered for 1-2 hours, turning occasionally. Place fish on a vegetable sprayed grill 4-6 inches above bed of coals. Cover barbecue; adjust vents as needed to maintain even heat. Cook, turning once, while fish is just opaque but still moist in thickest part; cut to test. Serve with lemon wedges.

Exchanges and 4 g Carbohydrates Per Serving					
Breads	0.1	Vegetables	0.0	Fruits	0.1
Meats	4.3	Milk	0.1	Fats	0.1

Nutrition Facts				
Serving Size	193 g			
Servings Per Recipe	6			
Amount per serving			High Fat/Sugar Comparison	
Calories		192	220	
Calories from fat		40	70	
	% Daily Value*		% Daily Value*	
Total Fat	4 g	**6%**	8 g	**12%**
Saturated Fat	0.5 g	**3%**	3 g	**15%**
Cholesterol	50 mg	**17%**	60 mg	**20%**
Sodium	620 mg	**26%**	660 mg	**28%**
Total Carbohydrate	7 g	**2%**	6 g	**2%**
Dietary Fiber	1 g	**4%**	0 g	**0%**
Sugars	1 g		3 g	
Other	2 g		0 g	
Protein	32 g		32 g	

*Percent of Daily Values on page a-22

Ultimate Baked Halibut

The Fat Quotient using ButterLike is **20%** instead of **76%**
86% less fat **80% more sugar**
47% less Calories

U.S.	Ingredients	Metric
1/2 cup	**ButterLike Saute Butter**	112.00 g
1 cup	Fat free sour cream	256.00 g
2 Tbsp	Lemon juice	31.00 g
4	Halibut steaks	348.00 g
1 large	Onion, sliced	160.00 g
1/2 cup	Fat free cheddar cheese	60.00 g

Directions

Combine **ButterLike**, sour cream, and lemon juice in a small non stick pan. Stir over medium high heat until bubbling. Cover and set aside. Lay 1/2 of the sliced onion rings loosely in the bottom of a vegetable sprayed 8x12-inch casserole dish. Spoon 1/2 of sauce over onions. Place halibut over onions. Make sure steaks do not overlap. Lay remaining onions over halibut steaks. Sprinkle with grated cheese. Bake uncovered for 45 minutes in a 350° oven.

Nutrition Facts				
Serving Size	242 g			
Servings Per Recipe	4			
Amount per serving			High Fat/Sugar Comparison	
Calories		270	510	
Calories from fat		60	390	
	% Daily Value*		% Daily Value*	
Total Fat	6 g	**9%**	43 g	**66%**
Saturated Fat	1.5 g	**8%**	26 g	**130%**
Cholesterol	30 mg	**10%**	135 mg	**45%**
Sodium	230 mg	**10%**	410 mg	**17%**
Total Carbohydrate	24 g	**8%**	7 g	**2%**
Dietary Fiber	1 g	**4%**	1 g	**4%**
Sugars	5 g		1 g	
Other	0 g		0 g	
Protein	26 g		24 g	

*Percent of Daily Values on page a-22

Exchanges and 23 g Carbohydrates Per Serving					
Breads	0.6	Vegetables	0.5	Fruits	0.0
Meats	3.0	Milk	0.8	Fats	0.8

Scampi

The Fat Quotient using ButterLike is 23% instead of 66%
82% less fat **0% less sugar**
48% less Calories

U.S.	Ingredients	Metric
1/4 cup	**ButterLike Saute Butter**	56.00 g
1 Tbsp	Green onion thinly sliced	10.00 g
4-5 cloves	Garlic, minced	12.00 g
2 tsp	Lemon juice	10.00 g
1/4 tsp	Salt	1.50 g
3/4 lb	Medium raw shrimp, shelled and deveined	340.00 g
1/4 tsp	Lemon peel, grated	.50 g
2 Tbsp	Parsley, minced	7.50 g
Dash	Liquid hot pepper seasoning	.65 g
1	Lemon, cut into wedges	108.00 g

Directions

Heat **ButterLike** in a wide frying pan over medium heat. Stir in onion, garlic, lemon juice, and salt; cook, until bubbly, stirring often. Add shrimp and cook, stirring occasionally, until opaque in center; cut to test. Stir in lemon peel, parsley, and hot pepper seasoning. Serve with lemon wedges.

Nutrition Facts				
Serving Size	273 g			
Servings Per Recipe	2			
Amount per serving			High Fat/Sugar Comparison	
Calories	233		450	
Calories from fat	50		300	
	% Daily Value*		% Daily Value*	
Total Fat	6 g	**9%**	33 g	**51%**
Saturated Fat	2 g	**10%**	16 g	**80%**
Cholesterol	265 mg	**88%**	330 mg	**110%**
Sodium	610 mg	**25%**	860 mg	**36%**
Total Carbohydrate	17 g	**6%**	9 g	**3%**
Dietary Fiber	0 g	**0%**	0 g	**0%**
Sugars	2 g		2 g	
Other	0 g		0 g	
Protein	31 g		29 g	

*Percent of Daily Values on page a-22

Exchanges and 17 g Carbohydrates Per Serving

Breads	0.6	Vegetables	0.5	Fruits	0.4
Meats	2.4	Milk	0.0	Fats	0.8

Stir-Fried Shrimp and Broccoli

The Fat Quotient using ButterLike is 8% instead of 6%
38% less fat **43% less sugar**
52% less Calories

U.S.	Ingredients	Metric
1 1/2 tsp	**Granulated SugarLike**	6.25 g
3 Tbsp	**ButterLike Saute Butter**	42.00 g
1 lb	Shrimp or 12 oz scallops	340.00 g
3 Tbsp	Red wine vinegar	48.00 g
3 Tbsp	Soy sauce	54.00 g
3 Tbsp	Water	44.00 g
1 Tbsp	Cornstarch	8.00 g
2 cloves	Garlic, minced	6.00 g
2 cups	Broccoli flowerets	368.00 g
1 cup	Carrots, thinly bias-sliced	156.00 g
1 small	Onion, halved lengthwise and sliced	6.00 g
1 cup	Fresh mushrooms, sliced	70.00 g
2 cups	Hot cooked rice	316.00 g

Nutrition Facts				
Serving Size	366 g			
Servings Per Recipe	4			
Amount per serving			High Fat/Sugar Comparison	
Calories	274		570	
Calories from fat	25		40	
	% Daily Value*		% Daily Value*	
Total Fat	2.5 g	**4%**	4 g	**6%**
Saturated Fat	0.5 g	**3%**	2 g	**10%**
Cholesterol	30 mg	**10%**	35 mg	**12%**
Sodium	960 mg	**40%**	990 mg	**41%**
Total Carbohydrate	42 g	**14%**	113 g	**38%**
Dietary Fiber	5 g	**20%**	5 g	**20%**
Sugars	4 g		7 g	
Other	1 g		1 g	
Protein	21 g		21 g	

*Percent of Daily Values on page a-22

Directions

Thaw shrimp or scallops, if frozen. If using fresh shrimp, peel, and devein. Rinse shrimp or scallops; pat dry with paper towels. Cut any large scallops in half. Set aside. In a small mixing bowl combine vinegar, soy sauce, water, cornstarch, and **SugarLike**; set aside. Heat **ButterLike** in wok or large skillet over medium-high heat. Stir-fry the garlic in the hot **ButterLike** for 15 seconds. Add the mushrooms; stir-fry for 1-2 minutes more or until vegetables are crisp-tender. Remove vegetables from wok with slotted spoon. Stir vinegar mixture. Add to wok and bring to a boil. Add shrimp or scallops and cook about 3 minutes or until shrimp turn pink or scallops are opaque. Stir in vegetables; heat through. Serve with pasta or rice.

Exchanges and 36 g Carbohydrates Per Serving					
Breads	1.8	Vegetables	2.0	Fruits	0.0
Meats	2.0	Milk	0.0	Fats	0.4

Stir-Fried Shrimp and Broccoli

Caribbean Pork Chops

The Fat Quotient using **ButterLike** is **32%** instead of **51%**
54% less fat **66% less sugar**
26% less Calories

U.S.	**Ingredients**	Metric
1 Tbsp	**Brown SugarLike**	12.50 g
1 Tbsp	**ButterLike Saute Butter**	14.00 g
3/4 cup	Water	178.00 g
1/3 cup	Lemon juice	81.00 g
1/3 cup	Onion, chopped	53.00 g
1 Tbsp	Green onion, chopped	3.60 g
3/4 tsp	Salt	4.50 g
3/4 tsp	Ground allspice	1.40 g
3/4 tsp	Ground cinnamon	2.00 g
3/4 tsp	Pepper	1.60 g
1/2 tsp	Ground thyme	.70 g
1/4 tsp	Ground red pepper (cayenne)	.45 g
6	Lean pork chops, about 5/8-inch thick	444.00 g

Directions

Place all ingredients except pork in blender. Cover and blend until well blended. Reserve 1/2 cup of the marinade; cover and refrigerate for basting. Trim excess fat from pork. Place pork in shallow glass or plastic dish. Pour remaining marinade over pork. Cover and refrigerate at least 12 hours, but no longer than 24 hours. Heat coals or gas grill. Remove pork from marinade; discard marinade.

Nutrition Facts				
Serving Size	133 g			
Servings Per Recipe	6			
Amount per serving			High Fat/Sugar Comparison	
Calories	170		230	
Calories from fat	60		120	
	% Daily Value*		% Daily Value*	
Total Fat	6 g	**9%**	13 g	**20%**
Saturated Fat	2.5 g	**13%**	4 g	**20%**
Cholesterol	60 mg	**20%**	65 mg	**22%**
Sodium	340 mg	**14%**	350 mg	**15%**
Total Carbohydrate	6 g	**2%**	5 g	**2%**
Dietary Fiber	1 g	**4%**	1 g	**4%**
Sugars	1 g		3 g	
Other	2 g		0 g	
Protein	23 g		24 g	

*Percent of Daily Values on page a-22

Exchanges and 3 g Carbohydrates Per Serving

Breads	0.1	Vegetables	0.1	Fruits	0.1
Meats	2.9	Milk	0.0	Fats	0.5

Cover and grill pork 4-5 inches from medium heat for 8-11 minutes, turning frequently and brushing with reserved marinade, until medium done (160°) and slightly pink when cut near bone. Discard any remaining basting marinade.

Spicy Pork Tenderloins

The Fat Quotient using **ButterLike** is **25%** instead of **55%**
76% less fat **100% less sugar**
48% less Calories

U.S.	**Ingredients**	Metric
1/4 cup	**Granulated SugarLike**	50.00 g
2	Pork tenderloins (1 1/2 lbs), trim fat	680.00 g
1/4 cup	Prepared mustard	60.00 g
1/4 tsp	Salt	1.50 g
1/4 tsp	Chili powder	.65 g

Directions

Fold and tie narrow ends of tenderloin under for even thickness. In a large bowl, stir together **SugarLike**, mustard, salt, and chili powder. Add meat and turn to coat. Cover and refrigerate, turning meat occasionally, for at least 4 hours. Set meat on grill above drip pan. Cover barbecue and adjust vents as needed to maintain an even heat. Cook until the meat thermometer inserted in thickest part of meat registers 150°-155°. To serve, cut meat across the grain into thin slanting slices; discard string.

Exchanges and 0 g Carbohydrates Per Serving					
Breads	0.0	Vegetables	0.0	Fruits	0.0
Meats	4.8	Milk	0.0	Fats	0.0

Nutrition Facts				
Serving Size	132 g			
Servings Per Recipe	6			
Amount per serving			High Fat/Sugar Comparison	
Calories		215	410	
Calories from fat		50	230	
	% Daily Value*		% Daily Value*	
Total Fat	6 g	**9%**	25 g	**38%**
Saturated Fat	2 g	**10%**	9 g	**45%**
Cholesterol	80 mg	**27%**	100 mg	**33%**
Sodium	300 mg	**13%**	280 mg	**12%**
Total Carbohydrate	8 g	**3%**	9 g	**3%**
Dietary Fiber	2 g	**8%**	0 g	**0%**
Sugars	0 g		8 g	
Other	6 g		0 g	
Protein	33 g		36 g	

*Percent of Daily Values on page a-22

Gingered Black Peppered Pork Tenderloins

The Fat Quotient using **ButterLike** is **25%** instead of **58%**
82% less fat **33% less sugar**
58% less Calories

U.S.	Ingredients	Metric
2 tsp	**Granulated SugarLike**	8.33 g
2	Lean pork tenderloins (3/4 lb ea)	544.00 g
1/3 cup	Apple juice	83.00 g
1 Tbsp	Gingerroot, finely chopped	6.00 g
2 Tbsp	Low sodium soy sauce	36.00 g
1 clove	Garlic, finely chopped	3.00 g
2 tsp	Coarse pepper	4.20 g

Directions

Fold thin ends of pork under so pork is an even thickness; secure with toothpicks. Mix remaining ingredients, except pepper in shallow glass or plastic dish. Add pork, turning to coat with marinade. Cover and refrigerate, turning occasionally, at least 8 hours but no longer than 12 hours. Prepare grill, arranging coals around edge of firebox. Place aluminum foil drip pan under grilling area. Remove pork from marinade; reserve marinade. Roll pork in coarsely ground pepper. Cover and grill 4-5 inches from medium heat
25-30 minutes, brushing occasionally with marinade and turning once, until medium done (160°). Discard any remaining marinade. Remove toothpicks. Cut pork across grain into thin slices.

Nutrition Facts				
Serving Size	114 g			
Servings Per Recipe	6			
Amount per serving			High Fat/Sugar Comparison	
Calories		165	390	
Calories from fat		40	230	
	% Daily Value*		% Daily Value*	
Total Fat	4.5 g	**7%**	25 g	**38%**
Saturated Fat	1.5 g	**8%**	9 g	**45%**
Cholesterol	70 mg	**23%**	100 mg	**33%**
Sodium	250 mg	**10%**	410 mg	**17%**
Total Carbohydrate	4 g	**1%**	4 g	**1%**
Dietary Fiber	1 g	**4%**	0 g	**0%**
Sugars	2 g		3 g	
Other	1 g		0 g	
Protein	26 g		36 g	

*Percent of Daily Values on page a-22

Exchanges and 2 g Carbohydrates Per Serving					
Breads	0.0	Vegetables	0.0	Fruits	0.1
Meats	3.8	Milk	0.0	Fats	0.0

Pork Medallions with Dijon Mushroom Sauce

The Fat Quotient using ButterLike is 29% instead of 75%
86% less fat **50% less sugar**
63% less Calories

U.S.	Ingredients	Metric
4 Tbsp	**ButterLike Saute Butter**	56.00 g
1	Shallot, finely chopped (2 Tbsp)	1.80 g
1 jar	Sliced mushrooms, drained (4.5 oz)	128.00 g
1/2 lb	Lean pork tenderloin, 8 slices	227.00 g
1/8 tsp	Salt	.75 g
1/8 tsp	Pepper	.30 g
1 Tbsp	Apple juice	16.00 g
1 Tbsp	Dijon mustard	15.00 g
1/2 cup	Evaporated skim milk	128.00 g
4 to 6	Fresh thyme sprigs or basil leaves	2.00 g

Directions

Heat 1 Tbsp of the **ButterLike** in a medium skillet over medium heat. Add shallot and mushrooms; cook and stir 1 minute or until tender. Remove from skillet. Add remaining **ButterLike** to skillet. Add pork; cook 8-10 minutes or until browned and no longer pink; turning slices halfway through cooking. Cover, if necessary. Sprinkle with salt and pepper. Remove from skillet; Cover to keep warm. Gradually add apple juice to skillet; stir in mustard and milk. Bring to a boil. Boil 1-2 minutes or until slightly thickened, stirring constantly.

Nutrition Facts				
Serving Size	287 g			
Servings Per Recipe	2			
Amount per serving			High Fat/Sugar Comparison	
Calories	342		920	
Calories from fat	100		690	
	% Daily Value*		% Daily Value*	
Total Fat	11 g	**17%**	77 g	**118%**
Saturated Fat	3.5 g	**18%**	40 g	**200%**
Cholesterol	95 mg	**32%**	275 mg	**92%**
Sodium	330 mg	**14%**	560 mg	**23%**
Total Carbohydrate	21 g	**7%**	7 g	**2%**
Dietary Fiber	1 g	**4%**	1 g	**4%**
Sugars	2 g		4 g	
Other	0 g		0 g	
Protein	40 g		51 g	

*Percent of Daily Values on page a-22

Exchanges and 20 g Carbohydrates Per Serving

Breads	0.6	Vegetables	0.7	Fruits	0.1
Meats	4.8	Milk	0.6	Fats	0.8

Add mushroom mixture; cook 1 minute or until thoroughly heated. To serve, arrange 4 pork slices on each plate; spoon sauce over pork. Garnish with thyme. If desired, serve with hot cooked white and wild rice.

Barbecued Pork Sandwiches

The Fat Quotient using ButterLike is 30% instead of 52%
78% less fat **40% less sugar**
62% less Calories

U.S.	Ingredients	Metric
Seasoning mixture:		
1/2 tsp	Salt	3.00 g
1/2 tsp	Black pepper	1.00 g
1/4 tsp	Celery seed	.40 g
1/8 tsp	Onion powder	.26 g
1/8 tsp	Garlic powder	.35 g
1/8 tsp	Ground cloves	.26 g
Dash	Ground red pepper	.23 g
3 lb	Boneless pork shoulder roast	1360.00 g

U.S.	Ingredients	Metric
Sauce:		
2 Tbsp	**Brown SugarLike**	25.00 g
1 can	Tomato sauce (8 oz)	227.00 g
1 cup	Catsup	240.00 g
1 cup	Onion, chopped	160.00 g
1/2 cup	Green sweet pepper, chopped	68.00 g
1/4 cup	Vinegar	60.00 g
2 Tbsp	Worcestershire sauce	30.00 g
1 Tbsp	Prepared mustard	15.00 g
2 tsp	Chili powder	5.20 g
1 clove	Garlic, minced	3.00 g
12	French-style rolls, split and toasted	456.00 g

Directions

Seasoning mixture: In a small mixing bowl combine salt, black pepper, celery seed, onion powder, garlic powder, cloves, and red pepper. Trim fat from meat. Rub mixture evenly onto meat.

In a grill with a cover, arrange preheated coals for indirect grilling. Test for medium heat where meat will cook. Place the meat on a rack in a roasting pan on the grill rack. Add 1/2-inch water to pan. Cover and grill about 4 hours or until meat is extremely tender, adding more water to pan, if necessary. Remove pork roast from grill. Let pork roast stand, 30 minutes, covered loosely with foil.

Sauce: In a medium saucepan combine tomato sauce, catsup, onion, sweet pepper, vinegar, brown **SugarLike**, worcestershire sauce, mustard, chili powder, and garlic. Bring to boiling. Reduce heat and simmer, covered, for 15 minutes. Shred pork with 2 forks. Stir shredded pork into sauce. Heat through. Spoon pork onto toasted rolls.

Nutrition Facts				
Serving Size	221 g			
Servings Per Recipe	12			
Amount per serving			High Fat/Sugar Comparison	
Calories	272		710	
Calories from fat	80		370	
	% Daily Value*		% Daily Value*	
Total Fat	9 g	**14%**	41 g	**63%**
Saturated Fat	3 g	**15%**	15 g	**75%**
Cholesterol	50 mg	**17%**	140 mg	**47%**
Sodium	770 mg	**32%**	860 mg	**36%**
Total Carbohydrate	30 g	**10%**	31 g	**10%**
Dietary Fiber	2 g	**8%**	1 g	**4%**
Sugars	3 g		5 g	
Other	2 g		0 g	
Protein	18 g		53 g	

*Percent of Daily Values on page a-22

Exchanges and 26 g Carbohydrates Per Serving					
Breads	1.7	Vegetables	0.5	Fruits	0.0
Meats	1.9	Milk	0.0	Fats	0.6

Oven-Fried Pork Chops

The Fat Quotient using **ButterLike** is **31%** instead of **52%**
58% less fat **0% less sugar**
29% less Calories

U.S.	**Ingredients**	Metric
2 Tbsp	**ButterLike Saute Butter**	2800 g
4	Lean pork loin chops	296.00 g
1/4 cup	Egg whites, beaten	57.00 g
2 Tbsp	Skim milk	31.00 g
1/4 tsp	Pepper	.53 g
1 cup	Herb-seasoned stuffing mix	57.00 g

Directions

Trim fat from meat. Pour **ButterLike** into vegetable sprayed 13x9x2-inch baking pan. Combine egg whites, milk, and pepper. Dip chops into egg mixture. Coat with stuffing mix. Place in pan. Bake in a 425° oven for 10 minutes. Turn chops. Bake about 10 minutes more or until no pink remains and juices run clear.

Nutrition Facts				
Serving Size	117 g			
Servings Per Recipe	4			
Amount per serving			High Fat/Sugar Comparison	
Calories	235		330	
Calories from fat	70		170	
	% Daily Value*		% Daily Value*	
Total Fat	8 g	**12%**	19 g	**29%**
Saturated Fat	2.5 g	**13%**	8 g	**40%**
Cholesterol	60 mg	**20%**	135 mg	**45%**
Sodium	270 mg	**11%**	350 mg	**15%**
Total Carbohydrate	14 g	**5%**	12 g	**4%**
Dietary Fiber	1 g	**4%**	1 g	**4%**
Sugars	1 g		1 g	
Other	0 g		0 g	
Protein	26 g		28 g	

*Percent of Daily Values on page a-22

Exchanges and 13 g Carbohydrates Per Serving					
Breads	0.9	Vegetables	0.0	Fruits	0.0
Meats	3.1	Milk	0.0	Fats	0.8

Marinated Chicken Pizza

The Fat Quotient using ButterLike is 21% instead of 40%
64% less fat **0% less sugar**
15% less Calories

U.S.	Ingredients	Metric
1 recipe	**Pizza Crust**, page 28	610.00 g
Marinade:		
3 Tbsp	**ButterLike Saute Butter**	42.00 g
1/3 cup	Balsamic vinegar	91.00 g
1/8 tsp	Salt	3.00 g
1/8 tsp	Garlic pepper	3.20 g
6 each	Boneless, skinless chicken breasts	533.00 g
2 Tbsp	**ButterLike Saute Butter**	28.00 g
4-6 large	Fresh tomatoes, thinly sliced	615.00 g
1 large	Red pepper, chopped	74.00 g
1 cup	Artichoke hearts, canned	168.00 g
5/8 cup	Grated azaago cheese or parmesan	50.00 g
1/2 cup	Non fat parmesan cheese	60.00 g
1 1/2 cup	Grated fontina cheese	85.00 g

Nutrition Facts				
Serving Size	148 g			
Servings Per Recipe	16			
Amount per serving			High Fat/Sugar Comparison	
Calories	197		230	
Calories from fat	40		90	
	% Daily Value*		% Daily Value*	
Total Fat	4.5 g	**7%**	10 g	**15%**
Saturated Fat	2 g	**10%**	5 g	**25%**
Cholesterol	30 mg	**10%**	40 mg	**13%**
Sodium	430 mg	**18%**	460 mg	**19%**
Total Carbohydrate	23 g	**8%**	21 g	**7%**
Dietary Fiber	2 g	**8%**	2 g	**8%**
Sugars	3 g		3 g	
Other	0 g		0 g	
Protein	16 g		14 g	

*Percent of Daily Values on page a-22

Exchanges and 21 g Carbohydrates Per Serving

Breads	1.2	Vegetables	0.6	Fruits	0.0
Meats	2.0	Milk	0.0	Fats	0.4

Directions

Marinade: Mix together marinade ingredients. Marinade the chicken at least four hours.

Prepare **Pizza Crust** according to the directions. A pre-made crust is very convenient to use, just make sure you check the fat content.

Wash and cube chicken. Heat frying pan and add 2 Tbsp **ButterLike.** Add the chicken as soon as **ButterLike** gets hot. Saute until chicken is barely done; Cover. Divide the tomato slices and cover pizza crust. Spread out the cooked chicken, sliced artichoke hearts, and red pepper over prepared crust. Mix together the cheese. You don't have to use azaago cheese if you don't have any, but it is worth the extra effort. The flavor is wonderful. Set aside 1/2 cup of cheese. Divide the remaining cheese and sprinkle over the pizza. Follow the directions for baking the finished pizza in the Pizza Crust recipe. Sprinkle the remaining cheese over the pizza right when you take it out of the oven. Makes 2 large pizzas.

Basil Prosciutto Pizza

The Fat Quotient using **ButterLike** is **18%** instead of **33%**

50% less fat **0% less sugar**

9% less Calories

U.S.	Ingredients	Metric
1 recipe	**Pizza Crust**, page 28	610.00 g
2 Tbsp	**ButterLike Saute Butter or Toasted Garlic Saute Butter**	28.00 g
1/4 tsp	Red pepper flakes	.50 g
3 Tbsp	Fresh basil, chopped	8.00 g
4-6 large	Fresh tomatoes, thinly sliced	615.00 g
2	Large potatoes, thinly sliced	404.00 g
1/2 cup	Lean ham or prosciutto, thinly sliced	70.00 g
1/2 cup	Azaago cheese or parmesan	40.00 g
1/2 cup	Non fat parmesan cheese	60.00 g
1 1/2 cup	Grated fontina cheese	85.00 g
Sprinkle	Garlic pepper	.80 g

Directions

Prepare **Pizza Crust** according to the directions. A pre-made crust is very convenient to use, just make sure you check the fat content.

Brush on **ButterLike Saute Butter or Toasted Garlic Saute Butter** over prepared crust. Sprinkle with red pepper flakes (this is optional if you don't like your pizza spicy hot). Divide evenly the chopped basil over the crust. Cover the crust with the thinly sliced tomatoes. Cover the tomatoes with very thinly sliced raw potatoes. Sprinkle the garlic pepper over the pizza. Combine the cheese and reserve 1/2 cup. Sprinkle the major portion of the cheese over the pizza. Follow directions for baking the finished pizza in the Pizza Crust recipe. During the last 3 minutes of baking, add the very thinly sliced small pieces of prosciutto so it doesn't get over cooked. Sprinkle the remaining cheese over the freshly baked pizza immediately and serve. Delicious! Makes 2 large pizzas.

Nutrition Facts				
Serving Size	120 g			
Servings Per Recipe	16			
Amount per serving			High Fat/Sugar Comparison	
Calories	172		190	
Calories from fat	30		70	
	% Daily Value*		% Daily Value*	
Total Fat	3.5 g	**5%**	7 g	**11%**
Saturated Fat	2 g	**10%**	4 g	**20%**
Cholesterol	10 mg	**3%**	20 mg	**7%**
Sodium	280 mg	**12%**	290 mg	**12%**
Total Carbohydrate	26 g	**9%**	25 g	**8%**
Dietary Fiber	2 g	**8%**	2 g	**8%**
Sugars	2 g		2 g	
Other	0 g		0 g	
Protein	9 g		8 g	

*Percent of Daily Values on page a-22

Exchanges and 24 g Carbohydrates Per Serving					
Breads	1.5	Vegetables	0.3	Fruits	0.0
Meats	1.5	Milk	0.0	Fats	0.3

Garlic Basil Tomato Pie

The Fat Quotient using **ButterLike** is **25%** instead of **48%**
61% less fat **50% less sugar**
27% less Calories

U.S.	**Ingredients**	Metric
2-4 tsp	**ButterLike Saute Butter**	9.00 g
8 oz	Pizza dough	227.00 g
1/2 cup	Fresh basil, chopped	21.00 g
1-3 tsp	Garlic, minced	2.80 g
6 oz	Provolone cheese, thinly sliced	170.00 g
8	Italian plum tomatoes, thinly sliced	227.00 g
1/4 cup	Non fat parmesan cheese or romano cheese, grated	30.00 g

Directions

Heat oven to 375°. Vegetable spray 10-inch pie pan or tart pan. Separate dough into 4 rectangles. Place rectangles in vegetable sprayed pan. Press evenly over bottom and up sides; firmly press edges and perforations to seal. Prick dough with fork. Bake at 375° for 15-17 minutes or until golden brown. Meanwhile, in small saucepan, combine **ButterLike**, basil and garlic. Cook over low heat just until heated, stirring occasionally. Cover to keep warm. Arrange half of the provolone cheese slices over partially baked crust; top with half of the tomatoes. Sprinkle with 2 Tbsp of the parmesan cheese. Repeat layers with remaining provolone cheese, tomatoes, and parmesan cheese. Spoon basil mixture over pie; sprinkle with pepper.

Exchanges and 11 g Carbohydrates Per Serving					
Breads	0.7	Vegetables	0.2	Fruits	0.0
Meats	1.5	Milk	0.0	Fats	0.2

Nutrition Facts				
Serving Size	69 g			
Servings Per Recipe	10			
Amount per serving			High Fat/Sugar Comparison	
Calories	124		170	
Calories from fat	30		80	
	% Daily Value*		% Daily Value*	
Total Fat	3.5 g	**5%**	9 g	**14%**
Saturated Fat	2 g	**10%**	4.5 g	**23%**
Cholesterol	10 mg	**3%**	20 mg	**7%**
Sodium	300 mg	**13%**	370 mg	**15%**
Total Carbohydrate	13 g	**4%**	11 g	**4%**
Dietary Fiber	2 g	**8%**	0 g	**0%**
Sugars	1 g		2 g	
Other	0 g		0 g	
Protein	10 g		10 g	

*Percent of Daily Values on page a-22

Garlic Basil Tomato Pie

Mushroom Enchiladas

The Fat Quotient using ButterLike is 17% instead of 55%
82% less fat **11% less sugar**
42% less Calories

U.S.	Ingredients	Metric
Sauce:		
2 Tbsp	**ButterLike Saute Butter**	28.00 g
2 tsp	**Granulated SugarLike**	8.00 g
1 large	Onion, chopped	160.00 g
2 cloves	Garlic	6.00 g
1 can	Tomato sauce (15 oz)	425.00 g
3/4 cup	Water	178.00 g
1 Tbsp	Chili powder	7.80 g
2 tsp	Dry oregano	3.00 g
1 tsp	Salt	6.00 g
1 tsp	Ground cumin	4.70 g
1 tsp	Ground coriander	1.60 g
	Liquid hot pepper seasoning to taste	5.20 g
Filling:		
1/4 cup	**ButterLike Saute Butter**	56.00 g
1 1/2 lb	Mushrooms	680.00 g
7 oz can	Green chiles, diced	199.00 g
1 cup	Green onion, sliced	160.00 g
1 cup	Plain non fat yogurt	227.00 g
1 pkg	Fat free cream cheese, cut (3 oz)	85.00 g
2 Tbsp	All-purpose flour	14.40 g
	Salt to taste	6.00 g
	Pepper to taste	2.10 g
10	Corn tortillas	250.00 g
1 1/2 cup	Fat free jack cheese, shredded	170.00 g

Directions

Sauce: Heat **ButterLike** in a frying pan over medium heat. Add onion; cook about 7 minutes until golden, stirring often. Add **SugarLike**, garlic, tomato sauce, water, chili powder, oregano, salt, cumin, and coriander. Season to taste with hot sauce. Bring to a boil; then reduce heat, cover, and simmer 10 minutes. Keep warm.

Filling: Heat **ButterLike** in a frying pan over medium heat. Add mushrooms and cook, stirring often, until mushrooms are soft. Reduce heat to low and add chiles, onion, yogurt, cream cheese, and flour; cook, stirring constantly, until mixture has thickened. Remove from heat; season to taste with salt and pepper.

Work with one tortilla at a time. Using tongs, dip each tortilla into enchilada sauce for a few seconds to soften; place on a vegetable sprayed 9x13-inch pan and spoon 1/3 to 1/2 cup of the filling down the center of tortilla. Roll tortilla around filling to enclose, then turn seam side down. Arrange filled tortillas side by side, completely covering pan bottom. If sauce becomes to thick, thin with water. Pour remaining sauce evenly over enchiladas. Bake, covered, in a 375° oven for 20 minutes. Uncover baking pan and sprinkle jack cheese evenly over enchilada. Continue to bake, uncovered, until cheese is melted. Serve warm.

Nutrition Facts				
Serving Size	537 g			
Servings Per Recipe	5			
Amount per serving			High Fat/Sugar Comparison	
Calories	370		640	
Calories from fat	60		350	
	% Daily Value*		% Daily Value*	
Total Fat	7 g	**11%**	39 g	**60%**
Saturated Fat	1 g	**5%**	22 g	**110%**
Cholesterol	0 mg	**0%**	95 mg	**32%**
Sodium	2110 mg	**88%**	2160 mg	**90%**
Total Carbohydrate	58 g	**19%**	51 g	**17%**
Dietary Fiber	8 g	**32%**	7 g	**28%**
Sugars	8 g		9 g	
Other	1 g		0 g	
Protein	26 g		21 g	

*Percent of Daily Values on page a-22

Exchanges and 49 g Carbohydrates Per Serving					
Breads	2.1	Vegetables	3.8	Fruits	0.0
Meats	0.8	Milk	0.5	Fats	0.7

Chicken Fajitas

The Fat Quotient using **ButterLike** is **9%** instead of **40%**
81% less fat **0% less sugar**
23% less Calories

U.S.	Ingredients	Metric
4	Boneless, skinless chicken breasts	944.00 g
Marinade:		
2 Tbsp	**ButterLike Saute Butter**	28.00 g
2 Tbsp	White wine vinegar	30.00 g
2 Tbsp	Fat free chicken stock	30.00 g
1 Tbsp	Onion, minced	6.00 g
1 Tbsp	Cilantro, chopped	3.00 g
1/2 tsp	Cumin	2.40 g
1/2 tsp	Chili pepper	1.20 g
1 medium	Yellow bell pepper, cut into strips	186.00 g
1 medium	Red bell pepper, cut into strips	186.00 g
1/2	White onion, cut into strips	57.00 g
1/4 cup	White wine	59.00 g
1/2 cup	Fat free chicken stock	120.00 g
6	Fat free flour or corn tortillas,	222.00 g

Nutrition Facts				
Serving Size	312 g			
Servings Per Recipe	6			
Amount per serving			High Fat/Sugar Comparison	
Calories	280		360	
Calories from fat	25		140	
	% Daily Value*		% Daily Value*	
Total Fat	3 g	**5%**	16 g	**25%**
Saturated Fat	1 g	**5%**	4.5 g	**23%**
Cholesterol	90 mg	**30%**	110 mg	**37%**
Sodium	300 mg	**13%**	470 mg	**20%**
Total Carbohydrate	20 g	**7%**	16 g	**5%**
Dietary Fiber	6 g	**24%**	6 g	**24%**
Sugars	0 g		0 g	
Other	0 g		0 g	
Protein	40 g		38 g	

*Percent of Daily Values on page a-22

Exchanges and 14 g Carbohydrates Per Serving

Breads	1.0	Vegetables	1.0	Fruits	0.0
Meats	3.2	Milk	0.0	Fats	0.3

Directions

Marinade: Combine **ButterLike**, white wine vinegar, chicken stock, minced onion, cilantro, and seasonings; set aside.

Cut chicken breasts into 1/2-inch strips. Soak in marinade for 1-10 hours. Saute chicken in marinade plus 1/4 cup chicken stock. Cut red and yellow peppers and 1/2 of an onion into thin strips. Saute vegetables until tender with white wine and 1/4 cup chicken stock; add more stock as necessary to prevent scorching.

Serve with 1 warm flour or corn tortilla.

Chicken Fajitas

Fajitas

The Fat Quotient using ButterLike is 14% instead of 39%
82% less fat **56% more sugar**
48% less Calories

U.S.	Ingredients	Metric
1/2 recipe	**Great Salsa**, page 8 (2 cups)	509.00 g
1/3 cup	**ButterLike Saute Butter**	75.00 g
1 1/2 lbs	Lean flank steak	680.00 g
1/2 cup	Lime juice	123.00 g
4 cloves	Garlic, minced	12.00 g
1 1/2 tsp	Ground cumin	7.00 g
1 tsp	Dry oregano	1.50 g
1/2 tsp	Pepper	1.00 g
4-5 small	Onions, unpeeled, halved lengthwise	488.00 g
3 cans	Fat free refried beans (1 lb each)	1360.00 g
2 cups	Fat free sour cream	512.00 g
1/2 cup	Cilantro sprigs	30.00 g
20	Fat free flour tortillas	740.00 g

Nutrition Facts				
Serving Size	454 g			
Servings Per Recipe	10			
Amount per serving			High Fat/Sugar Comparison	
Calories		491	870	
Calories from fat		60	340	
	% Daily Value*		% Daily Value*	
Total Fat	7 g	**11%**	38 g	**58%**
Saturated Fat	2.5 g	**13%**	14 g	**70%**
Cholesterol	30 mg	**10%**	950 mg	**32%**
Sodium	1280 mg	**53%**	1360 mg	**57%**
Total Carbohydrate	66 g	**22%**	73 g	**24%**
Dietary Fiber	20 g	**80%**	11 g	**44%**
Sugars	9 g		4 g	
Other	0 g		0 g	
Protein	34 g		59 g	

*Percent of Daily Values on page a-22

Exchanges and 46 g Carbohydrates Per Serving					
Breads	3.7	Vegetables	1.1	Fruits	0.1
Meats	2.7	Milk	0.5	Fats	0.2

Directions

Follow directions for **Great Salsa**.

Cut steaks crosswise into 12-inch lengths, then arrange in a 9x13-inch dish. In a small bowl, whisk together **ButterLike**, lime juice, garlic, cumin, oregano, and pepper. Pour over meat; turn meat to coat. Place onion halves, cut side down, in marinade alongside meat. Refrigerate, covered, for at least 4 hours, turning meat occasionally. Place onion halves on a vegetable sprayed grill 4-6 inches above hot coals. Cook 7 minutes; turn over. Lift meat from marinade and drain briefly; reserve marinade. Set meat on grill. Generously brush marinade over meat and onion halves. Cook onion halves 5-9 more minutes until soft and browned. Cook meat, turning once, until done to your liking. Place meat and onions on a carving board. Cut meat across grain into thin slanting slices. Heat tortillas on grill as needed until softened. Divide Great Salsa, meat, onions, sour cream, and cilantro sprigs equally among 20 tortillas. Top with beans. Fold to enclose filling; eat out of hand.

Beef Fajitas

The Fat Quotient using ButterLike is 12% instead of 31%
73% less fat **33% more sugar**
33% less Calories

U.S.	Ingredients	Metric
1 lb	Lean beef round steak	454.00 g
Marinade:		
1 Tbsp	**ButterLike Saute Butter**	1400 g
1/2 cup	Fat free Italian salad dressing	124.00 g
1/2 cup	Salsa	32.00 g
2 Tbsp	Lime or lemon juice	31.00 g
1 tsp	Worcestershire sauce	5.00 g
12	Fat free flour tortillas (7-inch)	444.00 g
1 medium	Onion, sliced in thin rings	160.00 g
1 medium	Sweet pepper, cut in thin strips	74.00 g
2/3 cup	Tomato, chopped	161.00 g

Directions

Trim fat from meat. Partially freeze. Thinly slice across grain into bite-size strips. Place in a plastic bag set in a deep bowl.

Marinade: Combine salad dressing, salsa, lime juice, and worcestershire sauce. Pour over meat. Close the bag. Marinate in refrigerator for 6-24 hours, turning occasionally.

Wrap tortillas in foil. Heat in a 350° oven for 10 minutes. Meanwhile, pour **ButterLike** into a large skillet (add more **ButterLike** as necessary during cooking). Preheat over medium-high heat. Cook onion in **ButterLike** for 1 1/2 minutes stirring occasionally. Add sweet pepper strips; cook and stir 1 1/2 minutes more or until crisp-tender. Remove from skillet. Add half of the undrained beef strips to hot skillet. Cook and stir for 2-3 minutes or to desired doneness. Remove beef. Drain well. Repeat with remaining beef. Return all beef and vegetables to skillet. Add tomato, cook, stirring occasionally. Fill warmed tortillas with beef mixture. If desired, add sour cream, guacamole, or avocado dip, cheese, or additional salsa. Roll up fajitas.

Nutrition Facts				
Serving Size	250 g			
Servings Per Recipe	6			
Amount per serving			High Fat/Sugar Comparison	
Calories	290		430	
Calories from fat	40		140	
	% Daily Value*		% Daily Value*	
Total Fat	4 g	**6%**	15 g	**23%**
Saturated Fat	1.5 g	**8%**	5 g	**25%**
Cholesterol	65 mg	**22%**	70 mg	**23%**
Sodium	830 mg	**35%**	640 mg	**27%**
Total Carbohydrate	33 g	**11%**	44 g	**15%**
Dietary Fiber	13 g	**52%**	3 g	**12%**
Sugars	3 g		2 g	
Other	0 g		0 g	
Protein	30 g		31 g	

*Percent of Daily Values on page a-22

Exchanges and 20 g Carbohydrates Per Serving					
Breads	1.9	Vegetables	0.7	Fruits	0.0
Meats	3.5	Milk	0.0	Fats	0.1

Enchilada Sauce

The fat quotient using **ButterLike** is **13%** instead of **50%**
80% less fat **0% less sugar**
24% less Calories

U.S.	Ingredients	Metric
2 Tbsp	**ButterLike Saute Butter**	28.00 g
3 cups	Tomato juice	732.00 g
3 Tbsp	All-purpose flour	23.00 g
3 Tbsp	Chili powder	23.00 g
1 tsp	Oregano	1.50 g
3 cloves	Garlic, minced	9.00 g
1/2 tsp	Salt	3.00 g

Directions

Combine all ingredients with a wire whisk in a 2-quart saucepan. Bring to a full boil and reduce heat; cook 5 minutes.

Enchilada: Use sauce by dipping corn tortilla in sauce then putting in a filling. Pour additional sauce over filled enchilada. Sprinkle with cheese and heat in oven until cheese melts. Sprinkle with chopped green onions. Fillings can include cooked cubed chicken, cheese, **Spicy Meat**, page 170, cooked shrimp, shredded pork, shredded beef, or browned, rinsed lean ground beef that has been seasoned.

Nutrition Facts				
Serving Size	68 g			
Servings Per Recipe	12			
Amount per serving			High Fat/Sugar Comparison	
Calories	34		45	
Calories from fat	5		20	
	% Daily Value*		% Daily Value*	
Total Fat	0.5 g	**1%**	2.5 g	**4%**
Saturated Fat	0 g	**0%**	1.5 g	**8%**
Cholesterol	0 mg	**0%**	5 mg	**2%**
Sodium	330 mg	**14%**	350 mg	**15%**
Total Carbohydrate	6 g	**2%**	5 g	**2%**
Dietary Fiber	1 g	**4%**	1 g	**4%**
Sugars	2 g		2 g	
Other	0 g		0 g	
Protein	1 g		1 g	

*Percent of Daily Values on page a-22

Exchanges and 5 g Carbohydrates Per Serving					
Breads	0.1	Vegetables	0.5	Fruits	0.0
Meats	0.0	Milk	0.0	Fats	0.1

Spicy Meat Filling

The Fat Quotient using ButterLike is 16% instead of 69%
88% less fat **0% less sugar**
51% less Calories

U.S.	Ingredients	Metric
2 Tbsp	**ButterLike Saute Butter**	28.00 g
1 large	Onion, finely chopped	160.00 g
2 cloves	Garlic, minced	6.00 g
4 cups	Boneless, skinless chicken breasts	560.00 g
1 can	Red chile sauce (10 oz)	284.00 g
1/2 tsp	Ground cinnamon	1.20 g
1/2 tsp	Ground cumin	2.40 g
2-4 Tbsp	Diced green chiles	30.00 g
	Salt to taste	6.00 g

Directions

Heat **ButterLike** in a frying pan over medium heat. Add onion and garlic. Cook, stirring often, until onion is soft. Stir in chicken, chile sauce, cinnamon, cumin, and chiles. Salt to taste. Bring to a boil; then reduce heat and simmer 5 minutes, uncovered. If desired, enclose filling in warmed flour or corn tortillas.

Variation: Beef or pork may be used in place of chicken.

Nutrition Facts				
Serving Size	108 g			
Servings Per Recipe	10			
Amount per serving			High Fat/Sugar Comparison	
Calories	84		170	
Calories from fat	10		120	
	% Daily Value*		% Daily Value*	
Total Fat	1.5 g	**2%**	13 g	**20%**
Saturated Fat	0 g	**0%**	4.5 g	**23%**
Cholesterol	35mg	**12%**	35 mg	**12%**
Sodium	290 mg	**12%**	280 mg	**12%**
Total Carbohydrate	4 g	**1%**	3 g	**1%**
Dietary Fiber	1 g	**4%**	1 g	**4%**
Sugars	0 g		0 g	
Other	0 g		0 g	
Protein	14 g		10 g	

*Percent of Daily Values on page a-22

Exchanges and 3 g Carbohydrates Per Serving					
Breads	0.1	Vegetables	0.3	Fruits	0.0
Meats	1.1	Milk	0.0	Fats	0.1

Pasta

Tuscan Rigatoni and White Beans, page 185

I am pleased to share with you this section of classic pasta dishes made low fat, low calorie and low cholesterol. There is such a significant difference in the amount of fat found in these pasta dishes versus the high fat versions! I'm sure you will be absolutely amazed at what dishes you can now eat and not feel guilty. The real butter and olive oil in **ButterLike Saute Butter** and the **Seasoned Saute Butter's** make your Pasta Dishes rich and delicious.

Tips for successful pasta dishes using the Bateman Products

- Please read "Tips on cooking low fat, low calorie, low cholesterol and sugar free main dishes", page 127; and "Sauteing with **ButterLike Saute Butter**", page 128.
- Cook your pasta just until Al Dente.
- Avoiding overcooked pasta is easy. When pasta is Al Dente, take it out of the hot water and drain. Keep a kettle of water boiling until your sauce is ready. Drop your cooked pasta into the boiling water to heat it back up. Add the hot noodles to your hot pasta sauce and serve immediately.
- If cheese is called for in your sauce recipe, add it last. Do not bring your sauce to a boil after adding your cheese. Heat slowly until cheese is melted and serve. Boiling your sauce will make the cheese tough.
- Grating great cheese over your steaming hot pasta is a way to use less cheese yet add more flavor. Add it as a flavoring, not as a meat group.

Pesto for Pasta, page 175

Homemade Pasta

The Fat Quotient using ButterLike is 3% instead of 20%
89% less fat **0% less sugar**
10% less Calories

U.S.	**Ingredients**	Metric
1 Tbsp	**ButterLike Saute Butter**	14.00 g
2 1/3 cup	Regular flour or semolina	268.00 g
1 tsp	Dried basil or marjoram, crushed	.80 g
1/2 tsp	Salt	3.00 g
1/2 cup	Egg whites	114.00 g
1/3 cup	Water	79.00 g

Directions

In bowl, mix 2 cups of flour, basil or marjoram, optional, and salt. Make a well in center of mixture. In another bowl combine egg whites, water, and **ButterLike**; mix into dry mixture. Sprinkle kneading surface with remaining flour. Knead dough 8 to 10 minutes until dough is smooth and elastic. Cover dough; let rest 10 minutes. Divide dough into 4 equal portions. On floured surface, roll each portion into a 12-inch square, 1/16-inch thick. Let stand, uncovered, 20 minutes. (If using a pasta machine, pass each portion through until dough is 1/16-inch thick.) Cut and shape as desired. Let pasta dry completely by hanging it from a pasta-drying rack, clothes hanger, or spread on wire cooling rack. To store, place in airtight container and refrigerate up to 3 days or dry pasta for at least 1 hour and seal in a freezer bag or freezer container and freeze up to 8 months. Cook homemade pasta until tender but firm. Drain well. Makes 1 pound fresh pasta.

Whole wheat pasta: Substitute whole wheat flour for all-purpose flour; omit herbs. I use a pasta machine that rolls out the pasta dough, because it is quick and easy to roll thin layers of pasta dough and it cuts just as fast.

Food processor directions: Place steel blade in food processor bowl. Process flour, herbs, salt, and egg whites until mixture forms fine crumbs. Continue processing, while **ButterLike** and water are poured through feed tube. Dough should form a ball. Transfer dough to floured surface. Cover; let dough rest 10 minutes. Continue as directed.

Nutrition Facts				
Serving Size	80 g			
Servings Per Recipe	6			
Amount per serving			High Fat/Sugar Comparison	
Calories	180		200	
Calories from fat	5		40	
	% Daily Value*		% Daily Value*	
Total Fat	0.5 g	**1%**	4.5 g	**7%**
Saturated Fat	0 g	**0%**	1 g	**5%**
Cholesterol	0 mg	**0%**	70 mg	**23%**
Sodium	230 mg	**10%**	210 mg	**9%**
Total Carbohydrate	35 g	**12%**	34 g	**11%**
Dietary Fiber	1 g	**4%**	1 g	**4%**
Sugars	1 g		1 g	
Other	0 g		0 g	
Protein	7 g		7 g	

*Percent of Daily Values on page a-22

Exchanges and 34 g Carbohydrates Per Serving					
Breads	2.3	Vegetables	0.0	Fruits	0.0
Meats	0.3	Milk	0.0	Fats	0.1

Homemade Pasta with Fresh Tomato Sauce, page 244

Marinara Sauce

The Fat Quotient using ButterLike is 15% instead of 40%
75% less fat **0% less sugar**
33% less Calories

U.S.	Ingredients	Metric
1/4 cup	**ButterLike Saute Butter**	56.00 g
1/2 to 1 Tbsp	**Granulated SugarLike**	12.50 g
3 large	Onions, coarsely chopped	480.00 g
3 cloves	Garlic, minced	9.00 g
6 lbs	Ripe tomatoes, peeled and chopped	2721.00 g
1 cup	Fresh basil leaves, chopped	42.00 g
	Salt to taste	6.00 g
	Pepper to taste	2.10 g

Directions

Heat **ButterLike** in a frying pan over medium heat. Add onions and garlic; cook, stirring often, 20 minutes until onions are golden brown. Add tomatoes and basil. Cook over medium heat 45-60 minutes, uncovered, stirring occasionally, until sauce is reduced to about 2 quarts. Add **SugarLike**. Season to taste with salt and pepper. Store, covered, in refrigerator for up to 1 week. Reheat to boiling before serving. Makes 2 quarts.

Nutrition Facts				
Serving Size	104 g			
Servings Per Recipe	32			
Amount per serving			High Fat/Sugar Comparison	
Calories		30	45	
Calories from fat		5	20	
	% Daily Value*		% Daily Value*	
Total Fat	0.5 g	**1%**	2 g	**3%**
Saturated Fat	0 g	**0%**	0 g	**0%**
Cholesterol	0 mg	**0%**	0 mg	**0%**
Sodium	80 mg	**3%**	80 mg	**3%**
Total Carbohydrate	6 g	**2%**	6 g	**2%**
Dietary Fiber	1 g	**4%**	1 g	**4%**
Sugars	3 g		3 g	
Other	0 g		0 g	
Protein	1 g		1 g	

*Percent of Daily Values on page a-22

Exchanges and 5 g Carbohydrates Per Serving

Breads	0.0	Vegetables	1.0	Fruits	0.0
Meats	0.0	Milk	0.0	Fats	0.1

Pesto for Pasta

The Fat Quotient using ButterLike is 13% instead of 38%
74% less fat **0% less sugar**
22% less Calories

U.S.	Ingredients	Metric
Pesto:		
1/4 cup	**ButterLike Saute Butter**	56.00 g
1 cup	Fresh packed basil leaves	42.00 g
1/2 cup	Fresh Parsley	30.00 g
1/2 cup	Non fat parmesan cheese, grated	60.00 g
2 Tbsp	Pine nuts, walnuts, or almonds	20.00 g
1 clove	Garlic, raw, quartered	3.00 g
1/4 tsp	Salt	1.50 g
12 oz.	Spaghetti or fettuccine, dried.	340.00 g

Nutrition Facts				
Serving Size	138 g			
Servings Per Recipe	4			
Amount per serving			High Fat/Sugar Comparison	
Calories		430	550	
Calories from fat		60	210	
	% Daily Value*		% Daily Value*	
Total Fat	6 g	**9%**	23 g	**35%**
Saturated Fat	1.5 g	**8%**	4.5 g	**23%**
Cholesterol	0 mg	**0%**	10 mg	**3%**
Sodium	350 mg	**15%**	340 mg	**14%**
Total Carbohydrate	70 g	**23%**	67 g	**22%**
Dietary Fiber	3 g	**12%**	3 g	**12%**
Sugars	3 g		3 g	
Other	0 g		0 g	
Protein	22 g		18 g	

*Percent of Daily Values on page a-22

Directions

Pesto: Blend together basil, parsley, cheese, nuts, garlic, and salt, scraping sides often. Slowly add **ButterLike Saute Butter**. Blend to the consistency of soft butter. Cook fettuccine or spaghetti 8-10 minutes or until tender but still firm. Drain well. Toss together with pesto.

Note: If you leave the nuts out of this recipe you would have 3.6 grams of fat per serving.

Exchanges and 67 g Carbohydrates Per Serving					
Breads	4.5	Vegetables	0.2	Fruits	0.0
Meats	4.0	Milk	0.0	Fats	1.0

Pesto for Pasta

Alfredo Sauce

The Fat Quotient using ButterLike is **23%** instead of **86%**
86% less fat **0% less sugar**
45% less Calories

U.S.	Ingredients	Metric
1/2 cup	**ButterLike Saute Butter**	112.00 g
2/3 cup	Skim milk	163.00 g
1/4 tsp	Pepper	.50 g
1/8 tsp	Nutmeg	.30 g
1 cup	Non fat parmesan cheese, grated	120.00 g

Directions

Place **ButterLike** and milk in a 10-inch heavy skillet over medium-low heat. Cook, stirring constantly, until blended and mixture bubbles for 2 minutes. Stir in pepper and nutmeg. Remove from heat. Gradually stir in parmesan cheese until thoroughly blended and fairly smooth. Return skillet briefly to heat if necessary to completely blend cheese. Don't let sauce bubble or cheese will become lumpy and tough. Remove from heat. Pour over pasta and serve.

Nutrition Facts				
Serving Size	66 g			
Servings Per Recipe	6			
Amount per serving			High Fat/Sugar Comparison	
Calories		120	220	
Calories from fat		25	190	
	% Daily Value*		% Daily Value*	
Total Fat	3 g	**5%**	21 g	**32%**
Saturated Fat	1 g	**5%**	13 g	**65%**
Cholesterol	5 mg	**2%**	60 mg	**20%**
Sodium	270 mg	**11%**	620 mg	**26%**
Total Carbohydrate	7 g	**2%**	2 g	**1%**
Dietary Fiber	0 g	**0%**	0 g	**0%**
Sugars	1 g		1 g	
Other	0 g		0 g	
Protein	14 g		7 g	

*Percent of Daily Values on page a-22

Exchanges and 7 g Carbohydrates Per Serving					
Breads	0.4	Vegetables	0.0	Fruits	0.0
Meats	5.3	Milk	0.1	Fats	0.6

Red Clam Sauce

The fat quotient using ButterLike is **25%** instead of **53%**
65% less fat **0% less sugar**
25% less Calories

U.S.	Ingredients	Metric
1/4 cup	**ButterLike Saute Butter**	56.00 g
1 pint	Fresh small clams, reserve liquid	400.00 g
3 cloves	Garlic, finely chopped	9.00 g
1 can	Whole italian tomatoes, chopped	794.00 g
1 Tbsp	Fresh parsley, chopped	3.80 g
1 tsp	Salt	6.00 g
1 small	Red chili, seeded, finely chopped	14.00 g

Directions

Chop clams; reserve. Heat **ButterLike** in 3-quart saucepan over medium-high heat. Cook garlic in **ButterLike**, stirring frequently. Stir in tomatoes and chili. Cook 3 minutes, stirring frequently. Stir in clam liquid. Bring to boil; reduce heat to low. Simmer uncovered 10 minutes. Stir in clams, parsley and salt. Cover and simmer about 15 minutes, stirring occasionally, until clams are tender.

Nutrition Facts				
Serving Size	214 g			
Servings Per Recipe	6			
Amount per serving			High Fat/Sugar Comparison	
Calories		128	170	
Calories from fat		30	90	
	% Daily Value*		% Daily Value*	
Total Fat	3.5 g	**5%**	10 g	**15%**
Saturated Fat	1 g	**5%**	6 g	**30%**
Cholesterol	55 mg	**18%**	75 mg	**25%**
Sodium	1020 mg	**43%**	1100 mg	**46%**
Total Carbohydrate	11 g	**4%**	8 g	**3%**
Dietary Fiber	2 g	**8%**	1 g	**4%**
Sugars	4 g		4 g	
Other	0 g		0 g	
Protein	13g		12 g	

*Percent of Daily Values on page a-22

Exchanges and 9 g Carbohydrates Per Serving					
Breads	0.2	Vegetables	1.4	Fruits	0.0
Meats	1.2	Milk	0.0	Fats	0.3

Broccoli-Shrimp Fettuccine

The Fat Quotient using ButterLike is **14%** instead of **48%**
78% less fat **0% less sugar**
25% less Calories

U.S.	Ingredients	Metric
1 Tbsp	**ButterLike Saute Butter**	14.00 g
10 oz	**Alfredo sauce**, pg 176	284.00 g
1 pkg	Frozen ready-to-cook shrimp (12 oz)	340.00 g
4 cups	Fresh broccoli flowerets	352.00 g
1 pkg	Uncooked fettuccine (9 oz)	255.00 g
1 large	Shallot, minced	6.00 g
1 can	Diced tomatoes, undrained (14.5 oz)	411.00 g
1 Tbsp	Tomato paste	17.00 g
1/2 tsp	Fennel seed, crushed	1.00 g
1/2 cup	Non fat parmesan cheese (2 oz)	60.00 g

Nutrition Facts				
Serving Size	290 g			
Servings Per Recipe	6			
Amount per serving			High Fat/Sugar Comparison	
Calories		324	430	
Calories from fat		45	210	
	% Daily Value*		% Daily Value*	
Total Fat	5 g	**8%**	23 g	**35%**
Saturated Fat	1 g	**5%**	12 g	**60%**
Cholesterol	95 mg	**32%**	145 mg	**48%**
Sodium	450 mg	**19%**	730 mg	**30%**
Total Carbohydrate	33 g	**11%**	29 g	**10%**
Dietary Fiber	2 g	**8%**	2 g	**8%**
Sugars	3 g		3 g	
Other	0 g		0 g	
Protein	34 g		26 g	

*Percent of Daily Values on page a-22

Directions

Follow directions for **Alfredo Sauce,** page 176.

In large saucepan, bring 6 cups water to a boil. Add shrimp and broccoli; cook 2-3 minutes or until shrimp turns pink. Drain. In medium bowl, combine shrimp, broccoli and Alfredo Sauce. Cook fettuccine to desired doneness as directed on package. Meanwhile, in a medium saucepan, heat **ButterLike** until hot. Add shallot; cook 1 minute. Stir in tomatoes, tomato paste and fennel seed; simmer 10 minutes. Drain fettuccine; arrange 1/3 of fettuccine in vegetable sprayed 12 x 8-inch baking pan. Cover with half of tomato mixture. Top with 1/3 of fettuccine and shrimp-broccoli mixture. Top with remaining fettuccine and remaining tomato mixture. Sprinkle with cheese. Bake at 375° for 35-40 minutes or until mixture is thoroughly heated and cheese is melted. Let stand 10 minutes before serving.

Exchanges and 31 g Carbohydrates Per Serving					
Breads	1.7	Vegetables	0.8	Fruits	0.0
Meats	7.9	Milk	0.1	Fats	0.8

Chicken Tetrazzini

The Fat Quotient using ButterLike is **14%** instead of **55%**
83% less fat **50% less sugar**
36% less Calories

U.S.	Ingredients	Metric
1/3 cup + 2 Tbsp	**ButterLike Saute Butter**	103.00 g
5 Tbsp	All-purpose flour	36.00 g
2 1/2 cup	Fat free chicken broth	613.00 g
1 1/4 cup	Skim milk	306.00 g
1/2 cup	Water	119.00 g
3/4 cup	Non fat parmesan cheese, grated	90.00 g
3/4 lb	Mushrooms, sliced	340.00 g
8 oz	Dry pasta strands, cooked and drained	304.00 g
3 cups	Skinless chicken breast, thinly sliced	420.00 g
	Salt to taste	6.00 g

Nutrition Facts				
Serving Size	292 g			
Servings Per Recipe	8			
Amount per serving			High Fat/Sugar Comparison	
Calories	316		490	
Calories from fat	45		270	
	% Daily Value*		% Daily Value*	
Total Fat	5 g	**8%**	30 g	**46%**
Saturated Fat	1 g	**5%**	14 g	**70%**
Cholesterol	70 mg	**23%**	130 mg	**43%**
Sodium	520 mg	**22%**	850 mg	**35%**
Total Carbohydrate	37 g	**12%**	34 g	**11%**
Dietary Fiber	1 g	**4%**	1 g	**4%**
Sugars	4 g		2 g	
Other	0 g		0 g	
Protein	29 g		22 g	

*Percent of Daily Values on page a-22

Exchanges and 36 g Carbohydrates Per Serving					
Breads	2.3	Vegetables	0.4	Fruits	0.0
Meats	4.1	Milk	0.1	Fats	0.4

Directions

Heat 4 Tbsp **ButterLike** in a pan over medium heat. Add flour, stirring. Remove from heat and gradually stir in broth, milk, and water. Return to heat; cook 3 minutes, stirring continuously. Stir in 1/2 cup cheese. Measure out 1 cup of sauce; set aside. Stir remaining cheese into remaining sauce. Remove from heat. Heat remaining **ButterLike** in a wide frying pan over medium heat. Add mushrooms and cook, stirring often, until lightly browned. Set aside a few mushroom slices; add remaining mushrooms, pasta, and chicken to sauce in pan. Season mixture to taste with salt and pour into large, shallow vegetable sprayed baking pan. Spoon reserved 1 cup sauce evenly over chicken mixture; then scatter reserved mushroom slices over top. Bake in a 375° oven about 15 minutes, until bubbly and heated through. Then broil 4 to 5 inches below heat just until top is lightly browned.

Chicken Vegetable Tetrazzini

The Fat Quotient using **ButterLike** is **13%** instead of **28%**
61% less fat **0% less sugar**
12% less Calories

U.S.	**Ingredients**	Metric
4 Tbsp	**ButterLike Saute Butter**	56.00 g
1 pkg	Refrigerated linguine (9 oz)	255.00 g
6	Boneless, skinless chicken breasts	1416.00 g
2 cloves	Garlic, minced	6.00 g
1 1/2 cup	Frozen broccoli cuts, thawed	203.00 g
1 jar	Carrots, drained, sliced (15 oz)	425.00 g
1 jar	Mushrooms, drained, sliced (4.5 oz)	128.00 g
2/3 cup	Skim milk	163.00 g
1 can	Low fat cream of chicken soup (10.75 oz)	305.00 g
1/3 cup	Non fat parmesan cheese, grated	40.00 g

Nutrition Facts				
Serving Size	499 g			
Servings Per Recipe	6			
Amount per serving			High Fat/Sugar Comparison	
Calories	501		570	
Calories from fat	60		160	
	% Daily Value*		% Daily Value*	
Total Fat	7 g	**11%**	18 g	**28%**
Saturated Fat	1.5 g	**8%**	6 g	**30%**
Cholesterol	140 mg	**47%**	160 mg	**53%**
Sodium	690 mg	**29%**	930 mg	**39%**
Total Carbohydrate	40 g	**13%**	36 g	**12%**
Dietary Fiber	3 g	**12%**	3 g	**12%**
Sugars	5 g		5 g	
Other	0 g		0 g	
Protein	67 g		65 g	

*Percent of Daily Values on page a-22

Exchanges and 37 g Carbohydrates Per Serving

Breads	1.6	Vegetables	1.4	Fruits	0.0
Meats	6.5	Milk	0.1	Fats	0.5

Directions

Cut chicken into 1-inch chunks. Cook linguine to desired doneness as directed on package. Drain. Meanwhile, heat 2 Tbsp **ButterLike** in large skillet or Dutch oven over medium heat until hot. Add chicken; cook and stir 4-5 minutes or until no longer pink. Remove chicken from skillet; cover to keep warm. In same skillet, heat 2 Tbsp **ButterLike** over medium heat. Add garlic, broccoli, carrots and mushrooms; cook 4-5 minutes or until vegetables are tender, stirring occasionally. Stir in milk, soup, cheese, and chicken; cook 1-2 minutes or until thoroughly heated. Stir in linguine; cook 2 minutes or until thoroughly heated, stirring occasionally. Add salt and pepper to taste; sprinkle with parsley.

Sausage Rigatoni

The Fat Quotient using **ButterLike** is **21%** instead of **65%**
83% less fat **17% less sugar**
49% less Calories

U.S.	**Ingredients**	Metric
1 tsp	**Granulated SugarLike**	4.00 g
1 Tbsp	**ButterLike Saute Butter**	14.00 g
8 oz	Uncooked rigatoni	227.00 g
1 lb	Low fat turkey sausage, 1/4-inch slices	454.00 g
1 can	Crushed tomatoes, undrained (28 oz)	794.00 g
1 1/2 oz	Sun-dried tomatoes	43.00 g
3/4 cup	Water	178.00g
2 tsp	Dried basil	1.60 g
1/2 tsp	Dried thyme leaves	.60 g
2 cloves	Garlic, minced	6.00 g

Directions

Cook rigatoni to desired doneness as directed on package. Meanwhile, in large saucepan, brown sausage in **ButterLike** over medium-high heat. Stir in **SugarLike**, crushed tomatoes, sun-dried tomatoes, water, basil, thyme and garlic. Bring to a boil. Reduce heat; simmer 10-15 minutes. Drain rigatoni. Serve sausage mixture over rigatoni.

Exchanges and 27 g Carbohydrates Per Serving					
Breads	1.0	Vegetables	0.5	Fruits	0.0
Meats	3.0	Milk	0.0	Fats	0.2

Nutrition Facts				
Serving Size	430 g			
Servings Per Recipe	4			
Amount per serving			High Fat/Sugar Comparison	
Calories	253		500	
Calories from fat	50		330	
	% Daily Value*		% Daily Value*	
Total Fat	6 g	**9%**	36 g	**55%**
Saturated Fat	2 g	**10%**	12 g	**60%**
Cholesterol	70 mg	**23%**	115 mg	**38%**
Sodium	800 mg	**33%**	1540 mg	**64%**
Total Carbohydrate	29 g	**10%**	19 g	**6%**
Dietary Fiber	1 g	**4%**	1 g	**4%**
Sugars	5 g		6 g	
Other	1 g		0 g	
Protein	22 g		26 g	

*Percent of Daily Values on page a-22

Scallop and Red Pepper Pasta

The Fat Quotient using ButterLike is **12%** instead of **39%**
76% less fat **0% less sugar**
26% less Calories

U.S.	Ingredients	Metric
1/2 cup	**ButterLike Saute Butter**	112.00 g
1	Lemon	108.00 g
12 oz	Dry spaghetti	340.00 g
1 lb	Scallops	454.00 g
3 large	Red bell peppers, seeded	510.00 g
2 cloves	Garlic, minced	6.00 g
1/4-1/2 tsp	Red pepper flakes, crushed	25.00 g
3/4 cup	Fat free chicken broth	184.00 g
1/4 cup	Lemon juice	61.00 g
3/4 cup	Parsley, finely chopped	45.00 g
	Salt to taste	6.00 g
	Pepper to taste	2.10 g

Nutrition Facts				
Serving Size	309 g			
Servings Per Recipe	6			
Amount per serving			High Fat/Sugar Comparison	
Calories	365		490	
Calories from fat	45		190	
	% Daily Value*		% Daily Value*	
Total Fat	5 g	**8%**	21 g	**32%**
Saturated Fat	1 g	**5%**	2.5 g	**13%**
Cholesterol	30 mg	**10%**	25 mg	**8%**
Sodium	530 mg	**22%**	620 mg	**26%**
Total Carbohydrate	59 g	**20%**	53 g	**18%**
Dietary Fiber	3 g	**12%**	3 g	**12%**
Sugars	5 g		5 g	
Other	0 g		0 g	
Protein	23 g		22 g	

*Percent of Daily Values on page a-22

Exchanges and 56 g Carbohydrates Per Serving					
Breads	3.2	Vegetables	0.7	Fruits	0.2
Meats	1.8	Milk	0.0	Fats	0.6

Directions

Finely shred colored part of lemon peel; set aside. In a large pan, cook pasta in salted boiling water until tender to bite. Drain, rinse with cold water, and drain again; set aside. Rinse scallops and pat dry. If using sea scallops, cut into 1/4-inch thick slices. Set aside. Heat **ButterLike** in a wide frying pan over medium heat. Add bell peppers cut into thin slices, garlic, and red pepper flakes; cook, stirring, for 1 minute. Add broth and lemon juice to pan; bring to boil. Add scallops; cook, covered until opaque in center. Remove from heat. Lift scallops and peppers from pan with slotted spoon and set aside. Add pasta to pan juices; lift and mix with 2 forks until pasta is hot. Pour pasta and sauce into a serving dish. Top with scallops and peppers; then sprinkle with parsley and lemon peel. Season to taste with salt and pepper. Before serving, mix lightly with a serving fork and spoon.

Prosciutto Pasta Shells

The Fat Quotient using ButterLike is 12% instead of 45%
82% less fat **46% less sugar**
31% less Calories

U.S.	Ingredients	Metric
2 Tbsp	**ButterLike Saute Butter**	28.00 g
12	Jumbo pasta shells	170.00 g
2 cloves	Garlic, minced	6.00 g
3/4 cup	Cooked prosciutto or fat free ham	113.00 g
1 cup	Non fat ricotta cheese	248.00 g
1/3 cup	Non fat parmesan cheese, grated	40.00 g
1 Tbsp	Fresh basil, chopped	2.70 g
1	Egg	50.00 g
14 oz	Low fat spaghetti sauce	397.00 g

Directions

Chop prosciutto or ham. Cook pasta to desired doneness as directed on package. Meanwhile, heat **ButterLike** in medium skillet over medium heat until hot. Add garlic and prosciutto; cook 2 to 3 minutes or until garlic is light golden brown. In medium bowl, combine half of ham mixture with ricotta cheese, parmesan cheese, basil and egg whites; mix well. Stir spaghetti sauce into ham mixture remaining in skillet. Drain pasta shells; rinse with cold water to cool. Drain well. Spoon ricotta mixture into shells; place in vegetable sprayed 8-inch baking dish. Spoon spaghetti sauce mixture over shells; cover with foil. Bake at 375° for 35-40 minutes or until mixture is thoroughly heated.

Nutrition Facts				
Serving Size	264 g			
Servings Per Recipe	4			
Amount per serving			High Fat/Sugar Comparison	
Calories		386	560	
Calories from fat		50	250	
	% Daily Value*		% Daily Value*	
Total Fat	5 g	**8%**	28 g	**43%**
Saturated Fat	1.5 g	**8%**	10 g	**50%**
Cholesterol	65 mg	**22%**	110 mg	**37%**
Sodium	770 mg	**32%**	850 mg	**35%**
Total Carbohydrate	52 g	**17%**	52 g	**17%**
Dietary Fiber	2 g	**8%**	3 g	**12%**
Sugars	7 g		13 g	
Other	0 g		0 g	
Protein	30 g		25 g	

*Percent of Daily Values on page a-22

Exchanges and 50 g Carbohydrates Per Serving					
Breads	3.4	Vegetables	0.1	Fruits	0.0
Meats	4.9	Milk	0.0	Fats	0.7

Penne Provencal

The Fat Quotient using ButterLike is 8% instead of 23%
70% less fat **33% less sugar**
13% less Calories

U.S.	Ingredients	Metric
2 tsp	**Granulated SugarLike**	8.33 g
2 Tbsp	**ButterLike Saute Butter**	28.00 g
8 oz	Uncooked Penne, tube pasta (2 cups)	227.00 g
3 cups	Eggplant, peeled, diced,	246.00 g
2 cans	Diced tomatoes, undrained (14.5oz each)	822.00 g
1 can	Navy beans, drained, rinsed (15 oz)	425.00 g
3 cloves	Garlic, minced	9.00 g
1 medium	Onion, chopped	160.00 g
2 Tbsp	Fresh Italian parsley, chopped	7.50 g

Nutrition Facts				
Serving Size	322 g			
Servings Per Recipe	6			
Amount per serving			High Fat/Sugar Comparison	
Calories		174	200	
Calories from fat		15	50	
	% Daily Value*		% Daily Value*	
Total Fat	1.5 g	**2%**	5 g	**8%**
Saturated Fat	0g	**0%**	1 g	**5%**
Cholesterol	15 mg	**5%**	10mg	**3%**
Sodium	360 mg	**15%**	360 mg	**15%**
Total Carbohydrate	33 g	**11%**	29 g	**10%**
Dietary Fiber	6 g	**24%**	5 g	**20%**
Sugars	2 g		3g	
Other	1 g		0 g	
Protein	8 g		8 g	

*Percent of Daily Values on page a-22

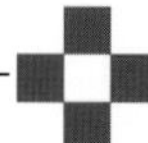

Directions

Saute garlic and onion in **ButterLike** until tender. Cook penne to desired doneness as directed on package. Meanwhile, in dutch oven or large saucepan, combine **SugarLike**, eggplants, tomatoes, beans, onion, and garlic; mix well. Bring to boil over medium-heat. Reduce heat; simmer 10-15 minutes or until eggplant is tender. If desired, add salt and pepper to taste. Drain penne. Add to eggplant mixture; toss gently to mix. Sprinkle with parsley.

Exchanges and 26 g Carbohydrates Per Serving					
Breads	1.6	Vegetables	1.1	Fruits	0.0
Meats	0.3	Milk	0.0	Fats	0.2

Linguine with Red Clam Sauce

The Fat Quotient using ButterLike is **14%** instead of **28%**
58% less fat **0% less sugar**
14% less Calories

U.S.	Ingredients	Metric
1 recipe	**Red Clam Sauce**, page 177	1284.00 g
6 cups	Cooked linguine or penne pasta	422.00 g

Directions

Follow **Red Clam Sauce**. Cook linguine in a large pot of water. Boil uncovered 2-4 minutes, stirring occasionally, until firm but tender. Begin testing for doneness when linguine rises to surface of water. Drain linguine. Toss linguine and sauce. Sprinkle with parsley.

Nutrition Facts				
Serving Size	284 g			
Servings Per Recipe	6			
Amount per serving			High Fat/Sugar Comparison	
Calories	327		380	
Calories from fat	50		110	
	% Daily Value*		% Daily Value*	
Total Fat	5 g	**8%**	12 g	**18%**
Saturated Fat	1 g	**5%**	6 g	**30%**
Cholesterol	55 mg	**18%**	75 mg	**25%**
Sodium	1030 mg	**43%**	1110 mg	**46%**
Total Carbohydrate	51 g	**17%**	48 g	**16%**
Dietary Fiber	3 g	**12%**	3 g	**12%**
Sugars	5 g		5 g	
Other	0 g		0 g	
Protein	20 g		19 g	

*Percent of Daily Values on page a-22

Exchanges and 48 g Carbohydrates Per Serving					
Breads	2.6	Vegetables	1.4	Fruits	0.0
Meats	1.2	Milk	0.0	Fats	0.7

Linguine with Roasted Vegetables

The Fat Quotient using ButterLike is 14% instead of 43%
77% less fat **0% less sugar**
29% less Calories

U.S.	Ingredients	Metric
3 Tbsp	**ButterLike Saute Butter**	42.00 g
4	Tomatoes, peeled and coarsely chopped	492.00 g
1	Eggplant, unpeeled, cubed	82.00 g
1	Red bell pepper, cut into 1-inch pieces	170.00 g
1	Zucchini, sliced	301.00 g
4 cloves	Garlic, minced	12.00 g
1 tsp	Dried basil leaves	.80 g
1/2 tsp	Salt	3.00 g
1/8 tsp	Pepper	.30 g
6 oz	Uncooked linguine	170.00 g
2 oz	Non fat parmesan cheese, shredded	57.00 g

Nutrition Facts				
Serving Size	222 g			
Servings Per Recipe	6			
Amount per serving			High Fat/Sugar Comparison	
Calories	163		230	
Calories from fat	20		100	
	% Daily Value*		% Daily Value*	
Total Fat	2.5 g	**4%**	11 g	**17%**
Saturated Fat	0 g	**0%**	3g	**15%**
Cholesterol	0 mg	**0%**	5 mg	**2%**
Sodium	330 mg	**14%**	390 mg	**16%**
Total Carbohydrate	26 g	**9%**	24 g	**8%**
Dietary Fiber	3 g	**12%**	3 g	**12%**
Sugars	5g		5 g	
Other	0 g		0 g	
Protein	11 g		8 g	

*Percent of Daily Values on page a-22

Exchanges and 23 g Carbohydrates Per Serving

Breads	1.1	Vegetables	1.4	Fruits	0.0
Meats	2.5	Milk	0.0	Fats	0.4

Directions

In a large bowl, combine tomatoes, eggplant, bell pepper, zucchini and garlic. Toss with 2 Tbsp of the **ButterLike**, basil, salt and pepper. Place vegetables on vegetable sprayed 15x10x1-inch baking pan. Bake at 450° for 12-15 minutes or until vegetables are tender and lightly browned. Meanwhile, cook linguine to desired doneness as directed on package. Drain linguine; return to saucepan or place in serving bowl. Add remaining **ButterLike** and roasted vegetables; toss gently to mix. Sprinkle with parmesan cheese.

Chicken Chili Pasta

The Fat Quotient using ButterLike is 10% instead of 15%
36% less fat **0% less sugar**
2% less Calories

U.S.	Ingredients	Metric
2 Tbsp	**ButterLike Saute Butter**	28.00 g
8 oz	Uncooked rotini (3 cups)	227.00 g
3	Boneless, skinless chicken breast halves	708.00 g
1 large	Onion, chopped	160.00 g
1 can	Spicy chili beans, undrained (15 oz)	425.00 g
1 can	Diced tomatoes, undrained (14.5 oz)	411.00 g
1 tsp	Chili powder	2.60 g
1/2 tsp	Cumin	2.40 g
2 tsp	Dried cilantro	1.60 g

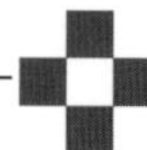

Directions

Cut chicken into bite-size strips. Cook rotini to desired doneness as directed on package. Meanwhile, in large skillet, heat **ButterLike** over medium heat until hot. Add chicken and onion; cook and stir 5-7 minutes or until chicken is lightly browned. Stir in chili beans, tomatoes, chili powder and cumin. Bring to a boil. Reduce heat; simmer 10-15 minutes or until onion is tender and chicken is no longer pink. Drain rotini. Serve chili over rotini; sprinkle with cilantro.

Exchanges and 29 g Carbohydrates Per Serving					
Breads	1.5	Vegetables	1.8	Fruits	0.0
Meats	4.0	Milk	0.0	Fats	0.4

Nutrition Facts				
Serving Size	491 g			
Servings Per Recipe	4			
Amount per serving			High Fat/Sugar Comparison	
Calories	402		410	
Calories from fat	40		60	
	% Daily Value*		% Daily Value*	
Total Fat	4.5 g	**7%**	7 g	**11%**
Saturated Fat	1 g	**5%**	1.5 g	**8%**
Cholesterol	120 mg	**40%**	120 mg	**40%**
Sodium	280 mg	**12%**	280 mg	**12%**
Total Carbohydrate	38 g	**13%**	36 g	**12%**
Dietary Fiber	9 g	**36%**	9 g	**36%**
Sugars	8 g		8 g	
Other	0 g		0 g	
Protein	52 g		51 g	

*Percent of Daily Values on page a-22

Garden Vegetable Fettuccine

The Fat Quotient using ButterLike is **11%** instead of **35%**
75% less fat **0% less sugar**
19% less Calories

U.S.	**Ingredients**	Metric
2 Tbsp	**ButterLike Saute Butter**	28.00 g
8 oz	Dry or fresh fettuccine	227.00 g
6 slices	Lean bacon, 1/2-inch pieces	36.00 g
6 cloves	Garlic, minced	18.00 g
1 large	Onion, chopped	160.00 g
1 large	Zucchini, cut into 1/2-inch cubes	680.00g
1 small	Red or green bell pepper, seeded	170.00 g
3 large	Tomatoes, cut into 1/2-inch cubes	369.00 g
1/2 cup	Parsley, chopped	30.00 g
1/2 cup	Fresh basil, chopped or 2 Tbsp dried basil	21.00 g
	Salt to taste	3.00 g
	Pepper to taste	1.00 g
1/2 cup	Non fat parmesan cheese, grated	60.00 g

Nutrition Facts				
Serving Size	451 g			
Servings Per Recipe	4			
Amount per serving			High Fat/Sugar Comparison	
Calories	372		460	
Calories from fat	40		160	
	% Daily Value*		% Daily Value*	
Total Fat	4.5 g	**7%**	18 g	**28%**
Saturated Fat	1 g	**5%**	5 g	**25%**
Cholesterol	60 mg	**20%**	70 mg	**23%**
Sodium	650 mg	**27%**	660 mg	**28%**
Total Carbohydrate	59 g	**20%**	57 g	**19%**
Dietary Fiber	6 g	24%	6 g	**24%**
Sugars	10 g		10 g	
Other	0 g		0 g	
Protein	24 g		19 g	

*Percent of Daily Values on page a-22

Exchanges and 53 g Carbohydrates Per Serving					
Breads	2.8	Vegetables	2.8	Fruits	0.0
Meats	4.0	Milk	0.0	Fats	0.5

Directions

In a large pan, cook pasta in 2 1/2 quarts of boiling salted water until barely tender. Drain and place in serving bowl. Cook bacon in frying pan over medium heat, stirring often, until crisp. Remove bacon from pan, drain, and set aside. Discard all but 1/2 Tbsp of the drippings. Add **ButterLike**, garlic and onion to drippings in pan and cook stirring often, until onion is soft. Increase heat to medium-high and add zucchini and bell pepper; cook, stirring, until zucchini is tender-crisp. Add tomatoes, parsley, and basil. Cook, stirring, until heated through. Season to taste with salt and pepper. Pour vegetable sauce over pasta and sprinkle with bacon; toss gently. Sprinkle with parmesan cheese.

Spinach Pesto Manicotti

The Fat Quotient using ButterLike is **25%** instead of **56%**
78% less fat **81% less sugar**
50% less Calories

U.S.	Ingredients	Metric
1/2 cup	**Pesto for Pasta**, page 175	113.00 g
8 oz	Uncooked manicotti	227.00 g
1/2 lb	Extra lean ground beef	227.00 g
9 oz	Frozen spinach, thawed, drained	255.00 g
4 oz	Non fat mozzarella cheese	113.00 g
1	Egg	50.00 g
1 jar	Low fat spaghetti sauce (20 oz)	567.00 g

Directions

Follow directions for **Pesto for Pasta** on page 175. Cook manicotti to desired doneness as directed on package. Meanwhile, in a large bowl combine ground beef, spinach, cheese, pesto, and egg. If desired, add salt and pepper; mix well. For easier stuffing, place beef mixture in resealable plastic freezer bag. Seal bag; cut off 1 corner. Drain manicotti; rinse with cold water. Drain well. Fill each manicotti by squeezing beef mixture into manicotti; place in vegetable sprayed 13 x 9-inch baking dish. Pour spaghetti sauce over manicotti; cover with foil. Bake at 400° for 30-40 minutes or until filling is no longer pink in center.

Nutrition Facts				
Serving Size	259 g			
Servings Per Recipe	6			
Amount per serving			High Fat/Sugar Comparison	
Calories	327		660	
Calories from fat	80		370	
	% Daily Value*		% Daily Value*	
Total Fat	9 g	**14%**	41 g	**63%**
Saturated Fat	3 g	**15%**	13 g	**65%**
Cholesterol	85 mg	**28%**	140 mg	**47%**
Sodium	480 mg	**20%**	850 mg	**35%**
Total Carbohydrate	30 g	**10%**	39 g	**13%**
Dietary Fiber	3 g	**12%**	6 g	**24%**
Sugars	3 g		16 g	
Other	0 g		0 g	
Protein	31 g		32 g	

*Percent of Daily Values on page a-22

Exchanges and 27 g Carbohydrates Per Serving					
Breads	1.6	Vegetables	0.5	Fruits	0.0
Meats	4.8	Milk	0.0	Fats	0.8

Tuscan Rigatoni and White Beans

The Fat Quotient using ButterLike is **10%** instead of **37%**
80% less fat **50% more sugar**
28% less Calories

U.S.	Ingredients	Metric
2 Tbsp	**ButterLike Saute Butter**	28.00 g
2 cups	Uncooked Rigatoni Pasta (6 oz.)	181.00 g
1 large	Onion, chopped	160.00 g
10 oz	Low fat smoked turkey sausage, sliced	284.00 g
15-16 oz	Cannellini beans, rinsed	425.00 g
1/3 cup	Sun dried tomatoes, chopped	813.00 g
1/3 cup	Chicken broth	81.00 g
1 Tbsp	Fresh or 1 tsp dried rosemary	1.20 g
1/3 cup	Non fat parmesan cheese, shredded	40.00 g

Nutrition Facts				
Serving Size	336 g			
Servings Per Recipe	6			
Amount per serving			High Fat/Sugar Comparison	
Calories	441		610	
Calories from fat	45		220	
	% Daily Value*		% Daily Value*	
Total Fat	5 g	**8%**	25 g	**38%**
Saturated Fat	1.5 g	**8%**	10 g	**50%**
Cholesterol	40 mg	**13%**	70 mg	**23%**
Sodium	640 mg	**27%**	1080 mg	**45%**
Total Carbohydrate	69 g	**23%**	66 g	**22%**
Dietary Fiber	10 g	**40%**	10 g	**40%**
Sugars	4g		2 g	
Other	0 g		0 g	
Protein	31 g		32 g	

*Percent of Daily Values on page a-22

Directions

Cook and drain pasta as directed on package. While pasta is cooking, saute onion and sausage with **ButterLike** in a 12-inch skillet over medium-high heat 2-3 minutes, stirring occasionally, until onion is tender. Gently stir in pasta and remaining ingredients except cheese. Cook 3-5 minutes or

Exchanges and 59 g Carbohydrates Per Serving					
Breads	4.1	Vegetables	0.5	Fruits	0.0
Meats	5.3	Milk	0.0	Fats	0.5

until hot. Sprinkle each serving with cheese.

**Increase in sugar is from the fat free items

Tuscan Rigatoni

Angel Hair Spaghetti with Meat Sauce

The Fat Quotient using ButterLike is **26%** instead of **40%**
43% less fat **0% less sugar**
14% less Calories

U.S.	Ingredients	Metric
2 Tbsp	**ButterLike Saute Butter**	28.00 g
1/2 cup	Onion, chopped	80.00 g
1/2 cup	Green pepper, chopped	113.00 g
2 cloves	Garlic	6.00 g
1 lb	Lean ground beef	454.00 g
3 1/2 cups	Tomatoes, crushed (28.5 oz)	721.00 g
2 cups	Water	474.00 g
2/3 cup	Tomato paste	176.00 g
1 Tbsp	Fresh parsley	.90 g
2 tsp	Dried oregano leaves	3.00 g
1/2 tsp	Salt	3.00 g
1/4 tsp	Black pepper	.53 g
16 oz	Angel hair pasta	454.00 g

Directions

Saute vegetables in **ButterLike**; set aside. Brown and rinse ground beef. Cook angel hair pasta according to package directions. Combine sauteed vegetables, cooked meat, tomatoes, water, tomato paste, parsley, oregano, salt and pepper and simmer 20 minutes to an hour. Serve on hot angel hair pasta. Sprinkle with parmesan cheese, if desired.

Exchanges and 23 g Carbohydrates Per Serving					
Breads	1.1	Vegetables	1.7	Fruits	0.0
Meats	2.3	Milk	0.0	Fats	0.3

Nutrition Facts				
Serving Size	314 g			
Servings Per Recipe	8			
Amount per serving			High Fat/Sugar Comparison	
Calories	267		310	
Calories from fat	70		130	
	% Daily Value*		% Daily Value*	
Total Fat	8 g	**12%**	14 g	**22%**
Saturated Fat	3 g	**15%**	4.5 g	**23%**
Cholesterol	40 mg	**13%**	45 mg	**15%**
Sodium	460 mg	**19%**	460 mg	**19%**
Total Carbohydrate	26 g	**9%**	25 g	**8%**
Dietary Fiber	3 g	**12%**	3 g	**12%**
Sugars	4 g		4 g	
Other	0 g		0 g	
Protein	21 g		20 g	

*Percent of Daily Values on page a-22

Filled Pasta with Vegetables

The Fat Quotient using ButterLike is **23%** instead of **57%**
84% less fat **23% more sugar**
60% less Calories

U.S.	**Ingredients**	Metric
1/4 cup	**ButterLike Saute Butter**	56.00 g
8 oz	Fresh or frozen low-fat filled pasta	227.00 g
1 medium	Zucchini, cut into 1/4-inch cubes	454.00 g
1 small	Bell pepper, seeded and finely diced	170.00 g
1 clove	Garlic, minced	3.00 g
1/2 tsp	Dry thyme	.60 g
1 1/2 tsp	Almonds, slivered	4.00 g
	Salt to taste	3.00 g
	Pepper to taste	1.00 g
1/4 cup	Non fat parmesan cheese, grated	30.00 g

Nutrition Facts				
Serving Size	474 g			
Servings Per Recipe	2			
Amount per serving			High Fat/Sugar Comparison	
Calories	314		780	
Calories from fat	70		440	
	% Daily Value*		% Daily Value*	
Total Fat	8 g	**12%**	49 g	**75%**
Saturated Fat	2.5 g	**13%**	11 g	**55%**
Cholesterol	15 mg	**5%**	85 mg	**28%**
Sodium	1010 mg	**42%**	1230 mg	**51%**
Total Carbohydrate	42 g	**14%**	60 g	**20%**
Dietary Fiber	6 g	**24%**	8 g	**32%**
Sugars	13 g		10 g	
Other	0 g		0 g	
Protein	20 g		26 g	

*Percent of Daily Values on page a-22

Directions

In a pan, cook pasta according to package directions; drain well. Meanwhile, heat **ButterLike** in a frying pan over medium heat. Add zucchini, bell pepper, garlic, and thyme; cook, stirring often, for 3 minutes. Add nuts; continue to cook, stirring, until zucchini and nuts begin to brown. Add hot pasta; mix gently. Season to taste with salt and pepper. Sprinkle with cheese.

Exchanges and 36 g Carbohydrates Per Serving					
Breads	1.3	Vegetables	2.5	Fruits	0.0
Meats	4.2	Milk	0.0	Fats	1.1

Fettuccine with Vegetables and Ham

The Fat Quotient using ButterLike is 13% instead of 35%
69% less fat 25% more sugar**
17% less Calories

U.S.	Ingredients	Metric
2 Tbsp	**ButterLike Saute Butter**	28.00 g
6 oz	Dried fettuccine, broken	170.00 g
1 medium	Fennel bulb, trimmed and cut	131.00 g
1/2 lb	Fresh asparagus, 1-inch slices	227.00 g
1 1/2 cup	Tomatoes, peeled, seeded, chopped	363.00 g
2 oz	Fat free ham (1/3 cup)	57.00 g
1/4 cup	Non fat parmesan cheese	30.00 g

Directions

Cook fettuccine in a large pot for 6 to 8 minutes or until tender but still firm. Drain well. Return fettuccine to warm saucepan. Cook fennel in a medium skillet in hot **ButterLike** for 3 minutes. Add asparagus; cook about 4 minutes more or until nearly tender. Add more **ButterLike** if needed. Add tomatoes and thin strips of ham; cook about 2 minutes or until heated through. Add vegetable mixture to fettuccine; toss gently to mix. Sprinkle with parmesan cheese. Season to taste with salt and pepper.

Nutrition Facts				
Serving Size	335 g			
Servings Per Recipe	3			
Amount per serving			High Fat/Sugar Comparison	
Calories	340		410	
Calories from fat	45		140	
	% Daily Value*		% Daily Value*	
Total Fat	5 g	**8%**	16 g	**25%**
Saturated Fat	1 g	**5%**	3.5 g	**18%**
Cholesterol	55 mg	**18%**	70 mg	**23%**
Sodium	650 mg	**27%**	660 mg	**28%**
Total Carbohydrate	52 g	**17%**	49 g	**16%**
Dietary Fiber	4 g	**16%**	4 g	**16%**
Sugars	4 g		3 g	
Other	0 g		0 g	
Protein	22 g		18 g	

*Percent of Daily Values on page a-22

Exchanges and 48 g Carbohydrates Per Serving					
Breads	2.9	Vegetables	1.7	Fruits	0.0
Meats	3.1	Milk	0.0	Fats	0.3

**Increase in sugar is from the fat free items

Fettuccine with Four Cheeses

The Fat Quotient using ButterLike is 20% instead of 69%
85% less fat 33% more sugar**
47% less Calories

U.S.	Ingredients	Metric
1/4 cup	**ButterLike Saute Butter**	56.00 g
1/2 cup	Onion, minced	80.00 g
1 Tbsp	Garlic, minced	8.40 g
1 cup	Fat free ricotta cheese	248.00 g
2 oz	Goat cheese, may substitute another cheese	57.00 g
1/2 tsp	Salt	3.00 g
1/8 tsp	Cayenne pepper	.23 g
1 1/2 oz	Non fat parmesan cheese	43.00 g
1 lb	Fettuccine	454.00 g
1/2 cup	**ButterLike Saute Butter**, heated	112.00 g
1/2 lb	Fat free mozzarella cheese, cubed	227.00 g
2 Tbsp	Fresh chives, chopped	6.00 g

Nutrition Facts				
Serving Size	216 g			
Servings Per Recipe	6			
Amount per serving			High Fat/Sugar Comparison	
Calories	319		600	
Calories from fat	70		420	
	% Daily Value*		% Daily Value*	
Total Fat	7 g	**11%**	46 g	**71%**
Saturated Fat	2 g	**10%**	17 g	**85%**
Cholesterol	40 mg	**13%**	120 mg	**40%**
Sodium	670 mg	**28%**	650 mg	**27%**
Total Carbohydrate	33 g	**11%**	24 g	**8%**
Dietary Fiber	1 g	**4%**	1 g	**4%**
Sugars	3 g		2 g	
Other	0 g		0 g	
Protein	30 g		21 g	

*Percent of Daily Values on page a-22

Directions

Cook fettuccine to desired doneness as directed on package. Saute the onion and garlic in **ButterLike** until just wilted, 4-5 minutes. Stir in ricotta and goat cheese. Allow to heat and melt over low heat, stirring. Mix in salt, cayenne pepper, and parmesan cheese. Toss pasta and **ButterLike** together, then add ricotta mixture and toss again. Add the mozzarella and chives and toss quickly. Serve pasta before mozzarella has a chance to completely melt. Serve on individual warmed plates, with additional Parmesan on the side if desired.

Variation: Add chopped lean ham and peas for a meal in one.

**Increase in sugar is from the fat free items

Exchanges and 32 g Carbohydrates Per Serving					
Breads	1.9	Vegetables	0.2	Fruits	0.0
Meats	4.2	Milk	0.0	Fats	1.3

Ricotta-Vegetable Lasagna

The Fat Quotient using ButterLike is **13%** instead of **38%**
78% less fat **20% more sugar****
18% less Calories

U.S.	Ingredients	Metric
1 Tbsp	**ButterLike Saute Butter**	14.00 g
9	Uncooked lasagna noodles	766.00 g
1 lb	Frozen broccoli, carrots, and water chestnuts vegetable mix	454.00 g
1 pkg	Frozen spinach, thawed, drained, chopped (9 oz)	255.00 g
1 carton	Low fat ricotta cheese (15 oz)	425.00 g
2 tsp	Dried basil leaves	1.60 g
1 clove	Garlic, minced	3.00 g
1/2 cup	Egg whites	114.00 g
3/4 cup	Non fat parmesan cheese, shredded	90.00 g
2 cans	Italian-style tomatoes, chopped (28 oz each)	793.00 g

Directions

Cook lasagna noodles to desired doneness as directed on package, adding frozen vegetables during last 5 minutes of cooking time. Meanwhile in medium bowl, combine spinach, ricotta cheese, basil, garlic, and egg whites; mix well. If desired, add salt and pepper to taste. Drain lasagna noodles and vegetables; rinse with cold water to cool. To assemble, place 3 lasagna noodles over bottom of a 13x9-inch vegetable sprayed dish. Spoon and spread 1/3 of ricotta mixture over noodles; top with 1/3 of vegetables, 1/3 of parmesan cheese and 1/3 of tomatoes. Repeat layers two more times. Drizzle top with **ButterLike**. Bake at 375° for 30-40 minutes or until heated thoroughly and bubbly. Let stand 10 minutes before serving.

**Increase in sugar is from the fat free items

Nutrition Facts				
Serving Size	245 g			
Servings Per Recipe	12			
Amount per serving			High Fat/Sugar Comparison	
Calories	184		225	
Calories from fat	20		80	
	% Daily Value*		% Daily Value*	
Total Fat	2 g	**4%**	9 g	**14%**
Saturated Fat	1 g	**5%**	4.5 g	**23%**
Cholesterol	27 mg	**8%**	80 mg	**27%**
Sodium	345 mg	**10%**	200 mg	**8%**
Total Carbohydrate	23 g	**7%**	23 g	**7%**
Dietary Fiber	3 g	**12%**	3 g	**12%**
Sugars	5 g		4 g	
Other	0 g		0 g	
Protein	16 g		12 g	

*Percent of Daily Values on page a-22

Exchanges and 20 g Carbohydrates Per Serving					
Breads	1.1	Vegetables	0.8	Fruits	0.0
Meats	2.9	Milk	0.0	Fats	0.2

Pasta with Fresh Tomato and Basil Sauce

The Fat Quotient using **ButterLike** is **10%** instead of **26%**
66% less fat **0% less sugar**
19% less Calories

U.S.	Ingredients	Metric
2 Tbsp	**ButterLike Saute Butter**	28.00 g
1/4 cup	Onion, finely chopped	40.00 g
2 cloves	Garlic, minced	6.00 g
3 lbs or 4 cups	Tomatoes	1360.00 g
2 tsp	Dried basil, crushed	1.60 g
6 oz.	Spaghetti, dried	170.00 g
1/4 tsp	Salt	
1/4 tsp	Pepper	

Directions

Sauce: Cook onion and garlic in hot **Saute Butter** until tender (but not brown). Stir in tomatoes, salt, and pepper. Bring to a boil, reduce heat, simmer uncovered 35-40 minutes. Add basil, cook 5 minutes more.

While sauce is simmering cook spaghetti. Drain and serve.

Nutrition Facts				
Serving Size	268 g			
Servings Per Recipe	6			
Amount per serving			High Fat/Sugar Comparison	
Calories	170		210	
Calories from fat	15		50	
	% Daily Value*		% Daily Value*	
Total Fat	2 g	**3%**	6 g	**9%**
Saturated Fat	0 g	**0%**	1 g	**5%**
Cholesterol	0 mg	**0%**	0 mg	**0%**
Sodium	25 mg	**1%**	25 mg	**1%**
Total Carbohydrate	34 g	**11%**	33 g	**11%**
Dietary Fiber	3 g	**12%**	3 g	**12%**
Sugars	7 g		7 g	
Other	g		0 g	
Protein	4 g		6 g	

*Percent of Daily Values on page a-22

Exchanges and 31 g Carbohydrates Per Serving

Breads	1.5	Vegetables	1.8	Fruits	0.0
Meats	0.0	Milk	0.0	Fats	0.1

Noodles Romanoff

The Fat Quotient using **ButterLike** is **4%** instead of **55%**
94% less fat **80% more sugar****
25% less Calories

U.S.	Ingredients	Metric
2 Tbsp	**ButterLike Saute Butter**	28.00 g
4 cups	Uncooked wide noodles (8 oz)	227.00 g
2 cups	Fat free sour cream	512.00 g
1/4 cup	Non fat parmesan cheese, grated	30.00 g
1 Tbsp	Fresh chives, chopped	3.00 g
1/2 tsp	Salt	3.00 g
1/8 tsp	Pepper	.30 g
1 clove	Garlic, crushed	3.00 g
1/4 cup	Non fat parmesan cheese, grated	30.00 g

Directions

Cook noodles as directed on package. While noodles are cooking, mix sour cream, 1/4 cup cheese, chives, salt, pepper and garlic. Drain noodles. Stir **ButterLike** into noodles. Stir in sour cream mixture. Place on warm platter. Sprinkle with 1/4 cup cheese.

**Increase in sugar comes from the fat free items.

Nutrition Facts				
Serving Size	105 g			
Servings Per Recipe	8			
Amount per serving			High Fat/Sugar Comparison	
Calories	209		280	
Calories from fat	10		150	
	% Daily Value*		% Daily Value*	
Total Fat	1 g	**2%**	17 g	**26%**
Saturated Fat	0 g	**0%**	10 g	**50%**
Cholesterol	0 mg	**0%**	40 mg	**13%**
Sodium	290 mg	**12%**	300 mg	**13%**
Total Carbohydrate	35 g	**12%**	24 g	**8%**
Dietary Fiber	1 g	**4%**	1 g	**4%**
Sugars	5 g		1 g	
Other	0 g		0 g	
Protein	12 g		8 g	

*Percent of Daily Values on page a-22

Exchanges and 34 g Carbohydrates Per Serving

Breads	1.9	Vegetables	0.0	Fruits	0.0
Meats	2.0	Milk	0.6	Fats	0.2

Pasta with Carbonara Sauce

The Fat Quotient using ButterLike is 14% instead of 48%
79% less fat   0% less sugar
23% less Calories

U.S.	Ingredients	Metric
1/4 cup	**ButterLike Saute Butter**	56.00 g
1/4 lb	Low fat sausage	113.00 g
1/4 lb	Low fat cooked ham, finely chopped	113.00 g
8 oz	Dry spaghetti	227.00 g
1/2 cup	Parsley, minced	30.00 g
1/4 cup	Egg substitutes	63.00 g
1 whole	Egg, beaten	50.00 g
Dash	Pepper	.30 g
1/2 cup	Non fat parmesan cheese, grated	60.00

Directions

Crumble sausage into frying pan. Add 2 Tbsp **ButterLike**; cook over medium-low heat, stirring occasionally, until sausage is lightly browned. Remove from heat; keep hot. In a large pan, cook pasta in about 2 1/2 quarts of boiling salted water until barely tender. Drain and transfer to serving bowl. Add remaining **ButterLike** and parsley to hot pasta; toss lightly. Add eggs and hot sausage mixture; toss until pasta is evenly coated. Sprinkle with pepper and cheese; toss gently. Offer additional cheese to add to taste.

Nutrition Facts				
Serving Size	178 g			
Servings Per Recipe	4			
Amount per serving			High Fat/Sugar Comparison	
Calories		399	520	
Calories from fat		50	250	
	% Daily Value*		% Daily Value*	
Total Fat	6 g	**9%**	28 g	**43%**
Saturated Fat	2 g	**10%**	14 g	**70%**
Cholesterol	80 mg	**27%**	235 mg	**78%**
Sodium	660 mg	**28%**	960 mg	**40%**
Total Carbohydrate	50 g	**17%**	44 g	**15%**
Dietary Fiber	2 g	**8%**	2 g	**8%**
Sugars	1 g		1 g	
Other	0 g		0 g	
Protein	27 g		24 g	

*Percent of Daily Values on page a-22

Exchanges and 48 g Carbohydrates Per Serving

Breads	3.1	Vegetables	0.1	Fruits	0.0
Meats	5.7	Milk	0.0	Fats	0.5

Pasta with Broccoli and Ricotta

The Fat Quotient using ButterLike is 5% instead of 34%
88% less fat   50% more sugar**
23% less Calories

U.S.	Ingredients	Metric
2 Tbsp	**ButterLike Saute Butter**	28.00 g
5	Green onions, thinly sliced	30.00 g
1 lb	Broccoli flowerets, cut into bite-size pieces	454.00 g
1/4 cup	Water	59.00 g
	Salt to taste	3.00 g
	Pepper to taste	2.00 g
12 oz	Dry pasta	340.00 g
1 1/2 cup	Fat free ricotta cheese	372.00 g
1/4 cup	Non fat parmesan cheese, grated	30.00

Nutrition Facts				
Serving Size	330 g			
Servings Per Recipe	4			
Amount per serving			High Fat/Sugar Comparison	
Calories		433	560	
Calories from fat		25	190	
	% Daily Value*		% Daily Value*	
Total Fat	2.5 g	**4%**	21 g	**32%**
Saturated Fat	1g	**5%**	10 g	**50%**
Cholesterol	10 mg	**3%**	50 mg	**17%**
Sodium	1110 mg	**46%**	710 mg	**30%**
Total Carbohydrate	70 g	**23%**	67 g	**22%**
Dietary Fiber	2 g	**8%**	2 g	**8%**
Sugars	4 g		2 g	
Other	0 g		0g	
Protein	32 g		26 g	

*Percent of Daily Values on page a-22

Directions

Heat **ButterLike** in a frying pan over medium heat. Add onions; cook, stirring often. Add broccoli; cook, until bright green. Add 1/4 cup water and bring to a boil; reduce heat, cover, and simmer until broccoli is tender-crisp. Remove from heat; add salt and pepper to taste and keep warm. In a large pan, cook pasta in 3 quarts of boiling salted water until barely tender. Drain, reserving 1/4 cup of the cooking water. Transfer to a serving bowl. Add broccoli mixture and ricotta cheese to pasta; toss gently until combined. If needed, add reserved pasta water to moisten. Sprinkle with parmesan cheese.

Exchanges and 68 g Carbohydrates Per Serving

Breads	4.4	Vegetables	0.9	Fruits	0.0
Meats	3.8	Milk	0.0	Fats	0.5

**Increase in sugar is from the fat free items.

Lazy-Day Overnight Lasagna

The Fat Quotient using **ButterLike** is **19%** instead of **56%**
87% less fat **62% less sugar**
61% less Calories

U.S.	Ingredients	Metric
1 Tbsp	**ButterLike Saute Butter**	1400 g
1 lb	Lean ground beef, rinsed	454.00 g
1 jar	Low fat spaghetti sauce (28 oz)	794.00 g
1 can	Tomatoes, chopped (14.5 oz)	411.00 g
15 oz	Non fat ricotta cheese	425.00 g
2 Tbsp	Fresh chives, chopped	.40 g
1/2 tsp	Dried oregano leaves	.75 g
1/4 cup	Egg whites	57.00 g
8 oz	Uncooked lasagna noodles	1280.00 g
2 Tbsp	Non fat parmesan cheese, grated	15.00 g
16 oz	Non fat mozzarella cheese, sliced	454.00 g

Directions

Brown beef in large skillet over medium-high heat; rinse and drain well. Add spaghetti sauce and tomatoes; blend well. In medium bowl, combine **ButterLike**, ricotta cheese, chives, oregano and egg whites; mix well. To assemble, place a layer of uncooked lasagna noodles in a vegetable sprayed 13 x 9-inch baking dish or lasagna pan, spread 1 1/2 cups of the meat mixture and mozzarella cheese. Repeat with another layer of noodles, 1 1/2 cups meat sauce and remaining noodles, ricotta cheese mixture and mozzarella cheese. Top with remaining meat sauce. Sprinkle with parmesan cheese. Cover; refrigerate 12 hours or overnight. Uncover baking dish; bake at 350° for 50-60 minutes or until bubbly. Cover; let stand 15 minutes before serving.

Nutrition Facts				
Serving Size	325 g			
Servings Per Recipe	12			
Amount per serving			High Fat/Sugar Comparison	
Calories	382		990	
Calories from fat	70		560	
		% Daily Value*		% Daily Value*
Total Fat	8 g	**12%**	62 g	**95%**
Saturated Fat	2.5 g	**13%**	35 g	**175%**
Cholesterol	70 mg	**23%**	275 mg	**92%**
Sodium	500 mg	**21%**	740 mg	**31%**
Total Carbohydrate	40 g	**13%**	49 g	**16%**
Dietary Fiber	2 g	**8%**	3 g	**12%**
Sugars	5 g		13 g	
Other	0 g		0 g	
Protein	36 g		59 g	

*Percent of Daily Values on page a-22

Exchanges and 38 g Carbohydrates Per Serving

Breads	2.4	Vegetables	0.0	Fruits	0.0
Meats	4.0	Milk	0.0	Fats	0.6

Lasagna

The Fat Quotient using **ButterLike** is **17%** instead of **57%**
79% less fat **25% less sugar**
32% less Calories

U.S.	Ingredients	Metric
Sauce:		
2 Tbsp	**ButterLike Saute Butter**	28.00 g
12 oz	Extra lean ground beef	340.00 g
1 cup	Onion, chopped (1 large)	160.00 g
2 cloves	Garlic, minced	6.00 g
1 can	Tomatoes, cut-up (7.5 oz)	213.00 g
1 can	Tomato sauce (8 oz)	227.00 g
1 can	Tomato paste (6 oz)	170.00 g
2 tsp	Dried basil, crushed	1.60 g
1 tsp	Dried oregano, crushed	1.50 g
1/4 tsp	Pepper	.50 g
6	Dry lasagna noodles	170.00 g
Filing:		
1/4 cup	Egg whites	57.00 g
2 cups	Non fat ricotta or cottage cheese	452.00 g
1/3 cup	Non fat parmesan cheese	40.00 g
3 Tbsp	Fresh snipped parsley, optional	2.70 g
6 oz	Non fat mozzarella cheese, shredded	170.00 g

Nutrition Facts				
Serving Size	255 g			
Servings Per Recipe	8			
Amount per serving			High Fat/Sugar Comparison	
Calories	312		460	
Calories from fat	50		260	
	% Daily Value*		% Daily Value*	
Total Fat	6 g	**9%**	29 g	**45%**
Saturated Fat	2 g	**10%**	13 g	**65%**
Cholesterol	30 mg	**10%**	105 mg	**35%**
Sodium	660 mg	**28%**	730 mg	**30%**
Total Carbohydrate	29 g	**10%**	27 g	**9%**
Dietary Fiber	2 g	**8%**	2 g	**8%**
Sugars	3 g		4 g	
Other	0 g		0 g	
Protein	33 g		23 g	

*Percent of Daily Values on page a-22

Exchanges and 27 g Carbohydrates Per Serving

Breads	1.2	Vegetables	1.5	Fruits	0.0
Meats	4.8	Milk	0.0	Fats	0.3

Directions

Sauce: In skillet, heat **ButterLike** until hot. Add onion and garlic cloves; saute until heated through. In a medium saucepan cook meat until brown. Rinse and drain meat. Stir in onions, garlic, undrained tomatoes, tomato sauce, tomato paste, basil, oregano, and pepper. Bring to a boil, reduce heat. Cover; simmer 15 minutes, stirring occasionally. Meanwhile, cook noodles for 10-12 minutes or until tender but still firm. Drain noodles; rinse with cold water. Drain well.

Filling: Combine egg whites, ricotta cheese or drained cottage cheese, parmesan cheese, and, if desired, parsley. Layer half of the cooked noodles in a 20-quart rectangular baking dish. Spread with half of the filling. Top with half of the meat sauce and half of the mozzarella cheese. Repeat layers. If desired, sprinkle additional parmesan cheese on top. Bake in a 375° oven for 30-35 minutes or until heated through. Let stand 10 minutes before serving.

Pasta with Marinara Sauce

The Fat Quotient using **ButterLike** is **13%** instead of **38%**
75% less fat **14% less sugar**
27% less Calories

U.S.	Ingredients	Metric
2 Tbsp	**ButterLike Saute Butter**	28.00 g
1/2 tsp	**Granulated SugarLike**	2.00 g
1 cup	Onion, chopped (1 large)	160.00 g
1/2 cup	Green sweet pepper, chopped	68.00 g
1/4 cup	Carrot, coarsely chopped	36.50 g
1/4 cup	Celery, sliced	53.00 g
2 cloves	Garlic, minced	6.00 g
2 cups	Tomatoes, peeled, chopped	480.00 g
1/3 cup	Tomato paste (3 oz)	87.00 g
2 tsp	Fresh basil or 3/4 tsp dried	1.80 g
2 tsp	Fresh oregano or 1/2 tsp dried	1.50 g
1 tsp	Fresh thyme or 1/4 tsp dried	.30 g
1/4 cup	Water	59.00 g
1/2 tsp	Salt	3.00 g
1/8 tsp	Pepper	.26 g
4 oz	Dried spaghetti or linguine	113.00 g

Directions

In a large skillet cook onion, sweet pepper, carrot, celery, and garlic in **ButterLike** until tender. Stir in **SugarLike**, tomatoes, tomato paste, basil, oregano, thyme, water, salt, and pepper. Bring to a boil; reduce heat. Cover and simmer 30 minutes. If necessary, uncover and simmer 10-15 minutes more or to desired consistency; stir occasionally. Meanwhile, cook spaghetti 10-12 minutes or until tender but still firm. Drain well. Serve with sauce.

Exchanges and 23 g Carbohydrates Per Serving					
Breads	0.7	Vegetables	3.0	Fruits	0.0
Meats	0.0	Milk	0.0	Fats	0.3

Nutrition Facts				
Serving Size	275 g			
Servings Per Recipe	4			
Amount per serving			High Fat/Sugar Comparison	
Calories	139		190	
Calories from fat	20		70	
	% Daily Value*		% Daily Value*	
Total Fat	2 g	3%	8 g	12%
Saturated Fat	0.5 g	3%	1 g	5%
Cholesterol	0 mg	0%	0 mg	0%
Sodium	350 mg	15%	350 mg	15%
Total Carbohydrate	28 g	9%	26 g	9%
Dietary Fiber	4 g	16%	4 g	16%
Sugars	6 g		7 g	
Other	1 g		0 g	
Protein	5 g		4 g	

*Percent of Daily Values on page a-22

Orange Shrimp with Fettuccine

The Fat Quotient using ButterLike is **10%** instead of **15%**

33% less fat **0% less sugar**

2% less Calories

U.S.	Ingredients	Metric
3 Tbsp	**ButterLike Saute Butter**	42.00 g
1/2 tsp	Sesame oil	1.00 g
12 oz	Fresh or frozen shrimp, peeled	340.00 g
6 oz	Dried fettuccine or linguine	170.00 g
1	Red or green sweet pepper, 3/4-inch squares	74.00 g
1/2 tsp	Orange peel, finely shredded	1.00 g
2/3 cup	Orange juice	166.00 g
1 Tbsp	Cornstarch	8.00 g
1 tsp	Instant Chicken bouillon granules	4.00 g
1/4 tsp	Salt	1.50 g
1/8 tsp	Ground red pepper	.23 g
6 oz pkg	Frozen pea pods, thawed	170.00 g
2	Oranges, peeled and sectioned	262.00 g

Nutrition Facts				
Serving Size	310 g			
Servings Per Recipe	4			
Amount per serving			High Fat/Sugar Comparison	
Calories	353		360	
Calories from fat	35		60	
	% Daily Value*		% Daily Value*	
Total Fat	4g	6%	6 g	9%
Saturated Fat	1g	5%	1 g	5%
Cholesterol	150 mg	50%	145 mg	48%
Sodium	820 mg	34%	810 mg	34%
Total Carbohydrate	53 g	18%	50 g	17%
Dietary Fiber	3 g	12%	3 g	12%
Sugars	12 g		12 g	
Other	0 g		0 g	
Protein	27 g		26 g	

*Percent of Daily Values on page a-22

Exchanges and 50 g Carbohydrates Per Serving					
Breads	2.3	Vegetables	1.0	Fruits	0.7
Meats	2.8	Milk	0.0	Fats	0.5

Directions

Cook fettuccine for 8-10 minutes or until tender but still firm. Drain well; keep warm. Meanwhile, in a large skillet cook sweet pepper in 1/2 Tbsp hot **ButterLike** and sesame oil for 1-2 minutes or until crisp-tender. Remove sweet pepper. Add shrimp to skillet; cook and stir about 2 minutes or until shrimp turns pink. Remove shrimp. Combine 1 tsp **ButterLike**, orange peel, orange juice, cornstarch, bouillon granules, salt, and ground red pepper; add to skillet. Cook and stir until thickened and bubbly. Return shrimp and sweet pepper to skillet; stir to coat. Gently stir in pea pods and orange sections; heat through. Serve shrimp mixture over fettuccine.

Pie

Sour Cream Raisin Pie, page 204

Have you dreamed of a delicious pie that was really low in fat? A piece of a two crusted fruit pie made with **Mrs. Bateman's' Products** has less fat than a piece of bread and butter. We have reduced the fat so low in our pies that the pie crust is tender, but not as flaky as most high fat pies. Try using a partial fat replacement rather than a one-to-one replacement if you want your pie flaky, but not so low in fat. **SugarLike** has made it possible to make sugar free fruit fillings that can be baked and not lose their sweetness.

Tips for successful pie making using the Bateman Products

- I recommend that you use the recipe given in this cookbook for **Mrs. Bateman's Baking Butter Pie Crust**, and carefully follow the directions. If you use your own recipe for pie crusts, you need to add leavening (1/4 tsp of baking soda or baking powder per cup of flour) and enough liquid so that your dough will roll out easily. **Mrs. Bateman's Pie Crust** recipe directions offers excellent tips for baking low fat pie crusts using any recipe.
- The bottom crust may begin to absorb fruit juice and become soggy if allowed to sit for a few days after baking.
- Pies may be made up in advance, wrapped, and frozen. When ready, take them from the freezer, defrost, and bake at 350° for 50-60 minutes. Unbaked crusts may be rolled out, placed in pie tins, wrapped in tin foil and then in plastic, and frozen.

Meringue Orange Pie, page 203

Mrs. Bateman's Pie Crust

The Fat Quotient using **ButterLike** is **8%** instead of **74%**
95% less fat **100% less sugar**
51% less Calories

U.S.	Ingredients	Metric
7/8 cup	**ButterLike Baking Butter**	199.00 g
1 Tbsp	**Granulated SugarLike**	13.00 g
1 1/4 cup	Cake flour	136.00 g
1/4 tsp	Baking powder	1.00 g
1/4 tsp	Baking soda	1.00 g
1 tsp	Salt	6.00 g
1 tsp	Vinegar	15.00 g
1	Egg white	28.00 g

Directions

Place dry ingredients in mixing bowl and stir with a fork. If the **ButterLike** is cold, soften for 10-30 seconds in the microwave. Cut pre-measured **Baking Butter** into the flour mixture with a pastry cutter or two butter knives until you have small crumbs. If using a mixer or food processor, watch as you mix in the **ButterLike**; stop when crumbs are quite small. Use ice cold water and vinegar and **gradually** pour in as the mixer is mixing. At certain altitudes and humidity levels, the dough may not require the full amount of water. You want the flour pretty much picked up off the bottom of the mixer. There will be a little left. The dough pulls together on the paddle of your mixer. The dough should be pliable. Add a small amount of water if the dough is too dry. If your dough seems too soft to roll out, add a small amount of flour. It should not fall apart when you roll out and lift into a pan. Let dough rest for a few minutes before rolling

Generously flour the table and place 1/3 of the dough in the center. Cover the top with flour and start to roll out. Lift the round piece as you roll and keep putting flour underneath to prevent sticking. When the circle is slightly bigger than the vegetable sprayed pie pan, stop. Let the dough rest for a few minutes. Fold the dough in half and lift it into pie pan and open it up. Fit it down into the pan and then trim off the overhang. For a single crust, crimp the edges. If using a top crust, then fill the pie crust with filling, wet the edges and place a rolled out pie crust on the top of the filling. Crimp the edges, make vent designs if desired, and brush with egg white to help it brown. If the filling is sweet, I sprinkle the top crust with granulated sugar.

Nutrition Facts				
Serving Size	19 g			
Servings Per Recipe	20			
Amount per serving			High Fat/Sugar Comparison	
Calories	54		110	
Calories from fat	5		80	
	% Daily Value*		% Daily Value*	
Total Fat	0.5 g	**1%**	9 g	**14%**
Saturated Fat	0 g	**0%**	5g	**25%**
Cholesterol	0 mg	**0%**	25 mg	**8%**
Sodium	180 mg	**8%**	230 mg	**10%**
Total Carbohydrate	11 g	**4%**	6 g	**2%**
Dietary Fiber	0 g	**0%**	0 g	**0%**
Sugars	0 g		1 g	
Other	1 g		0 g	
Protein	1 g		1 g	

*Percent of Daily Values on page a-22

Exchanges and 10 g Carbohydrates Per Serving					
Breads	0.7	Vegetables	0.0	Fruits	0.0
Meats	0.0	Milk	0.0	Fats	0.1

Bake single crusts at 350° for 20-25 minutes. Avoid overcooking. Remove from oven even if not as brown as traditional crusts. Follow cooking times in recipe directions for double crusts. Cover the edges of the pie crust with tin foil to prevent over crisping. Brush crust with egg whites to achieve a golden brown. Makes 2 1/2 crusts.

Mrs. Bateman's Graham Cracker Crust

The Fat Quotient using **ButterLike** is **19%** instead of **56%**
80% less fat **33% less sugar**
42% less Calories

U.S.	Ingredients	Metric
1/3 cup	**ButterLike Saute Butter**	75.00 g
3 Tbsp	**Granulated SugarLike**	38.00 g
1 1/4 cup	Low fat graham cracker crumbs	120.00 g
1/8 tsp	Baking soda	.60 g

Directions

In a mixing bowl combine all ingredients and mix until moistened. Press crumb mixture evenly on the bottom and sides of a vegetable sprayed 9-inch pie pan. Bake at 350° for 15 minutes. Cool. Fill with any kind of filling desired. Makes 1 crust.

Nutrition Facts				
Serving Size	29 g			
Servings Per Recipe	8			
Amount per serving			High Fat/Sugar Comparison	
Calories	93		160	
Calories from fat	20		90	
	% Daily Value*		% Daily Value*	
Total Fat	2 g	**3%**	10 g	**15%**
Saturated Fat	0.5 g	**3%**	5 g	**25%**
Cholesterol	0 mg	**0%**	20 mg	**7%**
Sodium	120 mg	**5%**	230 mg	**10%**
Total Carbohydrate	20 g	**7%**	16 g	**5%**
Dietary Fiber	2 g	**8%**	0 g	**0%**
Sugars	4 g		6 g	
Other	3 g		0 g	
Protein	2 g		2 g	

*Percent of Daily Values on page a-22

Exchanges and 15 g Carbohydrates Per Serving					
Breads	1.0	Vegetables	0.0	Fruits	0.0
Meats	0.0	Milk	0.0	Fats	0.4

Orange Blossom Strawberry Pie

The Fat Quotient using **ButterLike** is **7%** instead of **30%**
88% less fat **72% less sugar**
43% less Calories

U.S.	Ingredients	Metric
1	**Mrs. Bateman's Pie Crust**, page 197	154.00 g
3/4 cup	**SugarLike Granulated Sugar**	150.00 g
3 Tbsp	Cornstarch	24.00 g
1 tsp	Orange peel, grated	2.00 g
6-7 cup	Strawberries, hulled	894.00 g
6 Tbsp	Water	89.00 g
2 Tbsp	Frozen orange juice concentrate, thawed	31.00 g

Directions

Follow directions for one **Mrs. Bateman's Pie Crust**, baked.

In a 1-1 1/2 quart pan, combine **SugarLike**, cornstarch, and orange peel. In a blender or food processor, whirl 2 cups of the least perfect strawberries with water until smoothly pureed. Blend puree into **SugarLike** mixture. Bring to a boil, stirring often. Remove from heat; stir in orange juice. Arrange remaining strawberries, tips up, in baked pastry. Spoon hot glaze over berries, covering completely. Refrigerate until glaze is cool and set. If made ahead, refrigerate, covered, until next day. Serve with fat free whipped topping or lite whipping cream, whipped with **SugarLike** and vanilla.

Nutrition Facts				
Serving Size	168 g			
Servings Per Recipe	8			
Amount per serving			High Fat/Sugar Comparison	
Calories		137	240	
Calories from fat		10	70	
	% Daily Value*		% Daily Value*	
Total Fat	1 g	**2%**	8 g	**12%**
Saturated Fat	0 g	**0%**	2 g	**10%**
Cholesterol	0 mg	**0%**	0 mg	**0%**
Sodium	180 mg	**8%**	125 mg	**5%**
Total Carbohydrate	41 g	**14%**	40 g	**13%**
Dietary Fiber	7 g	**28%**	3 g	**12%**
Sugars	7 g		25 g	
Other	14 g		0 g	
Protein	2 g		2 g	

*Percent of Daily Values on page a-22

Exchanges and 19 g Carbohydrates Per Serving					
Breads	0.9	Vegetables	0.0	Fruits	0.6
Meats	0.0	Milk	0.0	Fats	0.1

Baked Lemon Pie

The Fat Quotient using **ButterLike** is 13% instead of 34%
79% less fat **92% less sugar**
46% less Calories

U.S.	Ingredients	Metric
1	**Mrs. Bateman's Pie Crust**, page 197	154.00 g
1 1/2 cup	**Granulated SugarLike**	300.00 g
2 Tbsp	**ButterLike Saute Butter**	28.00 g
1/3 cup	All-purpose flour	38.00 g
1/4 tsp	Salt	1.50 g
1/2 tsp	Lemon peel, grated	1.00 g
5 Tbsp	Lemon juice	76.00 g
3	Eggs, separated	150.00 g
1 1/2 cup	Skim milk	368.00 g

Nutrition Facts				
Serving Size	140 g			
Servings Per Recipe	8			
Amount per serving			High Fat/Sugar Comparison	
Calories		201	370	
Calories from fat		30	130	
	% Daily Value*		% Daily Value*	
Total Fat	3 g	**5%**	14 g	**22%**
Saturated Fat	1 g	**5%**	5 g	**25%**
Cholesterol	85 mg	**28%**	95 mg	**32%**
Sodium	300 mg	**13%**	270 mg	**11%**
Total Carbohydrate	56 g	**19%**	55 g	**18%**
Dietary Fiber	9 g	**36%**	0 g	**0%**
Sugars	3 g		39 g	
Other	28 g		0 g	
Protein	6 g		6 g	

*Percent of Daily Values on page a-22

Exchanges and 19 g Carbohydrates Per Serving					
Breads	1.0	Vegetables	0.0	Fruits	0.0
Meats	0.3	Milk	0.2	Fats	0.4

Directions

Follow directions for one **Mrs. Bateman's Pie Crust**, unbaked.

In small bowl, beat egg yolks with milk until well blended. Stir **SugarLike**, **ButterLike**, flour, salt, lemon peel, and lemon juice into mixture. In another medium bowl, beat egg whites until soft peaks form. Gently fold whites into lemon mixture. Pour filling into pastry shell. Bake on lowest rack at 375° until top is lightly browned and center jiggles only slightly when shaken. If crust begins to brown excessively, drape with foil. Serve cool. If made ahead, refrigerate, covered, up to 5 hours.

To Die For Pecan Pie

The Fat Quotient using ButterLike is 21% instead of 42%
73% less fat **97% less sugar**
50% less Calories

U.S.	Ingredients	Metric
1	**Mrs. Bateman's Pie Crust**, page 197	307.00 g
1/2 cup	**ButterLike Baking Butter**	114.00 g
1 cup	**Granulated SugarLike**	200.00 g
2 cups	**Liquid SugarLike**	680.00 g
3/4 cup	Egg whites	170.00 g
3	Large eggs	150.00 g
1 tsp	Salt	6.00 g
1 tsp	Vanilla	5.00 g
3/4 cup	Pecan halves	81.00 g

Directions

Follow directions for one **Mrs. Bateman's Pie Crust**, unbaked.

Mix softened **ButterLike**, **SugarLike**, and egg whites until smooth. Add the rest of the ingredients, except the pecans. Mix until combined. Pour filling into crust. Top with pecans. Bake at 350° for 60-70 minutes. Edges stay softer if covered with tin foil.

Nutrition Facts				
Serving Size	107 g			
Servings Per Recipe	16			
Amount per serving			High Fat/Sugar Comparison	
Calories	208		410	
Calories from fat	50		170	
	% Daily Value*		% Daily Value*	
Total Fat	5 g	**8%**	19 g	**29%**
Saturated Fat	1 g	**5%**	7 g	**35%**
Cholesterol	40 mg	**13%**	95 mg	**32%**
Sodium	380 mg	**16%**	400 mg	**17%**
Total Carbohydrate	57 g	**19%**	55 g	**18%**
Dietary Fiber	10 g	**40%**	0 g	**0%**
Sugars	1 g		33 g	
Other	30 g		0 g	
Protein	4 g		4 g	

*Percent of Daily Values on page a-22

Exchanges and 17 g Carbohydrates Per Serving					
Breads	1.0	Vegetables	0.0	Fruits	0.0
Meats	0.3	Milk	0.0	Fats	0.9

All-American Strawberry Pie

The Fat Quotient using **ButterLike** is **10%** instead of **53%**
91% less fat **71% less sugar**
49% less Calories

U.S.	Ingredients	Metric
1	**Mrs. Bateman's Pie Crust**, page 197	154.00 g
3/4 cup	**Granulated SugarLike**	150.00 g
2 Tbsp	**ButterLike Baking Butter**	28.00 g
2 Tbsp	**ButterLike Saute Butter**	28.00 g
1/4 cup	**Powdered SugarLike**	26.00 g
1/2 cup	All-purpose flour	58.00 g
1/4 tsp	Salt	1.50 g
3 cups	Skim milk	735.00 g
1	Egg yolk	17.00 g
1 1/2 tsp	Vanilla extract	7.40 g
1 cup	Evaporated skim milk, partially frozen	255.00 g
1 tsp	Vanilla extract	5.00 g
1 pint	Fresh strawberries, halved	298.00 g
1 cup	Fresh or frozen blueberries	145.00 g

Directions

Follow directions for one **Mrs. Bateman's Pie Crust**, baked.

Freeze evaporated milk about 1 hour before whipping. In a 3-quart saucepan, combine **Granulated SugarLike**, flour, and salt. Add milk, stirring until smooth. Cook and stir over medium heat until thickened. Stir a small amount of milk mixture into egg yolk, then return all to saucepan. Cook, stirring, for 3 minutes. Remove from heat; stir in softened **ButterLikes** and vanilla. Cool 20 minutes. Pour into baked pie crust. Chill several hours until firm. Whip evaporated milk and **Powdered SugarLike**; spread half over pie filling. Arrange berries on top. Dollop or pipe remaining cream around edge of pie.

Nutrition Facts				
Serving Size	238 g			
Servings Per Recipe	8			
Amount per serving			High Fat/Sugar Comparison	
Calories	233		460	
Calories from fat	25		240	
	% Daily Value*		% Daily Value*	
Total Fat	2.5 g	**4%**	27 g	**42%**
Saturated Fat	1 g	**5%**	13 g	**65%**
Cholesterol	30 mg	**10%**	140 mg	**47%**
Sodium	350 mg	**15%**	290 mg	**12%**
Total Carbohydrate	55 g	**18%**	47 g	**16%**
Dietary Fiber	7 g	**28%**	2 g	**8%**
Sugars	8 g		28 g	
Other	17 g		0 g	
Protein	8 g		7 g	

*Percent of Daily Values on page a-22

Exchanges and 31 g Carbohydrates Per Serving

Breads	1.3	Vegetables	0.0	Fruits	0.3
Meats	0.1	Milk	0.6	Fats	0.4

Caribbean Truffle Pie

The Fat Quotient using ButterLike is 15% instead of 54%
87% less fat **68% less sugar**
52% less Calories

U.S.	Ingredients	Metric
Crust:		
1	**Mrs. Bateman's Pie Crust**, page 197	154.00 g
2 Tbsp	Coconut flakes	15.00 g
Streusel:		
4 tsp	**ButterLike Saute Butter**	19.00 g
1/4 cup	**Granulated SugarLike**	50.00 g
1/4 cup	All-purpose flour	31.00 g
1/8 cup	Coconut flakes	15.00 g
Filling:		
1/2 cup	**Granulated SugarLike**	100.00 g
1 pkg	Lemon pudding and pie dry mix (2.8 oz)	85.00 g
3 Tbsp	Lime juice	46.00 g
1/2 cup	Egg beaters	122.00 g
2 cup	Water	474.00 g
1 tsp	Lime peel, grated	2.00 g
2 oz	White chocolate, broken up	56.00 g
1 pkg	Fat free cream cheese, softened (8 oz)	227.00 g
6 Tbsp	Fat free sour cream	96.00 g
Topping and Garnish:		
1	Fat Free whipped topping (8 oz)	227.00 g
1	Lime, sliced	57.00 g

Nutrition Facts				
Serving Size	222 g			
Servings Per Recipe	8			
Amount per serving			High Fat/Sugar Comparison	
Calories	273		570	
Calories from fat	40		310	
	% Daily Value*		% Daily Value*	
Total Fat	4.5 g	**7%**	34 g	**52%**
Saturated Fat	3 g	**15%**	20 g	**100%**
Cholesterol	5 mg	**2%**	120 mg	**40%**
Sodium	500 mg	**21%**	310 mg	**13%**
Total Carbohydrate	57 g	**19%**	56 g	**19%**
Dietary Fiber	5 g	**20%**	1 g	**4%**
Sugars	11 g		34 g	
Other	14 g		0 g	
Protein	9 g		8 g	

*Percent of Daily Values on page a-22

Exchanges and 38 g Carbohydrates Per Serving					
Breads	1.8	Vegetables	0.0	Fruits	0.3
Meats	0.3	Milk	0.4	Fats	0.8

Directions

Crust: Follow directions for one **Mrs. Bateman's Pie Crust**, unbaked. Brush with egg whites. Sprinkle with coconut. Bake 25 minutes at 350°.

Streusel: In a small bowl, combine flour and **SugarLike**. Stir in **ButterLike** until mixture resembles coarse crumbs. Stir in coconut. Spread mixture in a vegetable sprayed pan. Bake at 425° for 4-8 minutes or until golden brown, stirring every minute; set aside.

Filling: In a saucepan combine **SugarLike**, pudding mix, lime juice, and egg beaters; mix well. Stir in water. Cook and stir over medium heat until mixture comes to a full boil. Remove from heat; stir in lime peel. In a small bowl, combine white chocolate pieces and 1/2 cup of the hot pudding mixture; stir until pieces are melted.

In a small bowl, beat cream cheese until light and fluffy. Add white chocolate mixture; beat until smooth. Spoon and spread over baked crust. Stir sour cream into remaining pie filling mixture; blend well. Spoon and spread over cream cheese layer. Refrigerate 2 hours or until well chilled.

Topping/Garnish: Pipe whipped topping around edge of pie. Garnish with lime slices. Sprinkle streusel in center of pie. Store in refrigerator.

Meringue Orange Pie

The Fat Quotient using **ButterLike** is **9%** instead of **29%**
83% less fat **81% less sugar**
44% less Calories

U.S.	Ingredients	Metric
1	**Mrs. Bateman's Pie Crust**, page 197	154.00 g
Filling:		
1 1/2 cup	**Granulated SugarLike**	300.00 g
3 Tbsp	**ButterLike Baking Butter**	43.00 g
1/4 cup + 2 Tbsp	Cornstarch	48.00 g
1/4 tsp	Salt	1.50 g
3 cups	Orange juice	747.00 g
1/4 cup	Egg whites, well beaten	57.00 g
2	Egg yolks	33.00 g
1/4 cup + 2 Tbsp	Lemon juice	92.00 g
1 1/2 tsp	Grated orange peel	3.00 g
Meringue:		
1/2 cup	**Granulated SugarLike**	100.00 g
1/2 cup	Egg whites	114. 00 g
1/4 tsp	Cream of tartar	.75 g

Nutrition Facts				
Serving Size	214 g			
Servings Per Recipe	8			
Amount per serving			High Fat/Sugar Comparison	
Calories	258		460	
Calories from fat	20		130	
	% Daily Value*		% Daily Value*	
Total Fat	2.5 g	**4%**	15 g	**23%**
Saturated Fat	1 g	**5%**	6 g	**30%**
Cholesterol	55 mg	**18%**	120 mg	**40%**
Sodium	320 mg	**13%**	270 mg	**11%**
Total Carbohydrate	79 g	**26%**	**76 g**	**25%**
Dietary Fiber	12 g	**48%**	0 g	**0%**
Sugars	11 g		59 g	
Other	37 g		0 g	
Protein	5 g		5 g	

*Percent of Daily Values on page a-22

Exchanges and 30 g Carbohydrates Per Serving					
Breads	1.3	Vegetables	0.0	Fruits	0.7
Meats	0.4	Milk	0.0	Fats	0.3

Directions

Follow directions for one **Mrs. Bateman's Pie Crust**, baked.

Filling: In a 2-3 quart saucepan, combine **SugarLike**, cornstarch and salt. Using a wire whisk, gradually blend in orange juice until smooth. Add eggs and blend thoroughly. Add lemon juice and **ButterLike**. Cook on medium heat as mixture thickens. Boil slowly for 1 minute. Remove from heat; stir in peel. Pour hot filling into baked pie crust. Let stand, allowing a thin film to form on top.

Meringue: Beat egg whites in a small mixing bowl until foamy. Add cream of tartar; beat on high until soft peaks form. Reduce speed to medium; add **SugarLike** gradually, about 1 Tbsp at a time. Beat on high until stiff and glossy. Spoon meringue around edge of filling. Using a spatula, push meringue gently against inner edge of crust, sealing well. Swirl meringue into center of pie. Bake at 350° for 12-15 minutes or until meringue is golden brown. Cool on wire rack for 2 hours before serving. To cut, use a sharp knife dipped in hot water.

Sour Cream Raisin Pie

The Fat Quotient using ButterLike is 6% instead of 36%
89% less fat **58% less sugar**
36% less Calories

U.S.	**Ingredients**	Metric
Filling:		
1	**Mrs. Bateman's Pie Crust**, page 197	154.00 g
2/3 cup	**Granulated SugarLike**	133.00 g
1 cup	Raisins	145.00 g
3 Tbsp	Cornstarch	24.00 g
1/8 tsp	Salt	.75 g
1/8 tsp	Ground cloves	.26 g
1/2 tsp	Ground cinnamon	1.00 g
1 cup	Fat free sour cream	256.00 g
1	Egg yolk	17.00 g
1/4 cup	Egg whites	57.00 g
1/2 cup	Skim milk	123.00 g
Meringue:		
5 Tbsp	**Granulated SugarLike**	63.00 g
3	Egg whites	85.00 g

Directions

Follow directions for one **Mrs. Bateman's Pie Crust**, baked.

Filling: In a small saucepan, place raisins and enough water to cover; bring to a boil. Turn off heat; set aside. In a heavy saucepan, combine **SugarLike**, cornstarch, salt, cloves, and cinnamon. Stir in sour cream. Beat in eggs. Add milk; cook over medium heat, stirring constantly, until pudding comes to a boil and is very thick. Remove from heat. Drain raisins, reserving 1/2 cup liquid. Stir liquid into filling. Add raisins. Pour into baked pie crust.

Meringue: In a small mixing bowl, beat egg whites with salt until foamy. Gradually add **SugarLike**, about 1 tablespoon at a time; beat until stiff and glossy. Spread over pie, making sure meringue covers all of the filling. Bake at 350° for 10-15 minutes or until light golden brown. Serve warm or cold. Store leftovers in the refrigerator.

Nutrition Facts				
Serving Size	132 g			
Servings Per Recipe	8			
Amount per serving			High Fat/Sugar Comparison	
Calories	225		350	
Calories from fat	15		120	
	% Daily Value*		% Daily Value*	
Total Fat	1.5 g	**2%**	14 g	**22%**
Saturated Fat	0.5 g	**3%**	6 g	**30%**
Cholesterol	30 mg	**10%**	95 mg	**32%**
Sodium	350 mg	**15%**	260 mg	**11%**
Total Carbohydrate	59 g	**20%**	52 g	**17%**
Dietary Fiber	7 g	**28%**	1 g	**4%**
Sugars	15 g		36 g	
Other	19 g		0 g	
Protein	6 g		5 g	

*Percent of Daily Values on page a-22

Exchanges and 33 g Carbohydrates Per Serving

Breads	1.1	Vegetables	0.0	Fruits	1.0
Meats	0.3	Milk	0.4	Fats	0.2

Double Crusted Pecan Pie Danish

The Fat Quotient using **ButterLike** is **20%** instead of **52%**
82% less fat **68% less sugar**
53% less calories

U.S.	Ingredients	Metric
2	**Mrs. Bateman's Pie Crust**, page 197	308.00 g
Filling:		
1/2 cup	**Powdered SugarLike**	60.00 g
2 Tbsp	**ButterLike Saute Butter**	28.00 g
1/3 cup	Apricot or other flavor jam	107.00 g
1 pkg	Fat free cream cheese, softened (3 oz)	85.00 g
1/4 cup	Pecans, finely chopped	.25 g
Topping:		
1/2 cup	**Granulated SugarLike**	100.00 g
1 Tbsp	**ButterLike Saute Butter**	14.00 g
1-3 tsp	**Powdered SugarLike**	7.50 g
1/3 cup	**Liquid SugarLike**	113.00 g
1 Tbsp	All-purpose flour	7.20 g
2 Tbsp	Fat free sour cream	32.00 g
1/2 tsp	Vanilla	2.50 g
1/4 cup	Egg whites	57.00 g
1/8 cup	Pecans, chopped	14.00 g

Directions

Follow directions for two **Mrs. Bateman's Pie Crust**, using a vegetable sprayed 10-inch tart pan with removable bottom. Place bottom crust in pan; press bottom and sides until dough stays attached. Trim edges if necessary.

Filling: Place cookie sheet in oven to preheat. In a small bowl, combine all filling ingredients except pecans; blend well. Stir in pecans. Spread mixture over bottom of prepared crust. Top with second crust; press edges together to seal. Place pie on heated cookie sheet. Bake at 400° for 15-20 minutes or until golden brown.

Topping: Combine **Granulated SugarLike**, **Liquid SugarLike**, **ButterLike Saute Butter**, flour, sour cream, vanilla, and egg whites; blend until smooth. Stir in pecans. Pour topping over partially baked pie. Bake at 375° an additional 18-28 minutes or until golden brown. Cool 10 minutes. Lightly sprinkle **Powdered SugarLike** over pie. Cool 2 hours or until completely cooled. Store in refrigerator.

Nutrition Facts				
Serving Size	80 g			
Servings Per Recipe	12			
Amount per serving			High Fat/Sugar Comparison	
Calories	180		380	
Calories from fat	35		200	
	% Daily Value*		% Daily Value*	
Total Fat	4 g	**6%**	22 g	**34%**
Saturated Fat	1 g	**5%**	7 g	**35%**
Cholesterol	5 mg	**2%**	35 mg	**12%**
Sodium	300 mg	**13%**	240 mg	**10%**
Total Carbohydrate	44 g	**15%**	45 g	**15%**
Dietary Fiber	5 g	**20%**	1 g	**4%**
Sugars	6 g		19 g	
Other	16 g		5 g	
Protein	3 g		2 g	

*Percent of Daily Values on page a-22

Exchanges and 23 g Carbohydrates Per Serving

Breads	1.1	Vegetables	0.0	Fruits	0.0
Meats	0.1	Milk	0.1	Fats	0.7

Yogurt Lemon Pie

The Fat Quotient using **ButterLike** is **10%** instead of **58%**
88% less fat **31% less sugar**
30% less Calories

U.S.	**Ingredients**	Metric
1	**Mrs. Bateman's Graham Cracker Crust**, page 198	233.00 g
3 Tbsp	**ButterLike Baking Butter**, softened	43.00 g
1/3 cup	Skim milk	82.00 g
1 pkg	Fat free cream cheese (8 oz)	227.00 g
1 pkg	Sugar free instant lemon pudding mix (3.4 oz)	100.00 g
2 cups	Non fat plain yogurt	454.00 g

Directions

Follow directions for **Mrs. Bateman's Graham Cracker Crust,** baked.

In a mixing bowl, beat softened **ButterLike**, milk, and softened cream cheese until smooth. Stir in yogurt until smooth. Add pudding mix and blend until mixture begins to thicken. Spoon into baked and cooled pie crust. Serve immediately or refrigerate until serving time. If desired, garnish with whipped topping and lemon peel strips.

Nutrition Facts				
Serving Size	142 g			
Servings Per Recipe	8			
Amount per serving			High Fat/Sugar Comparison	
Calories	217		310	
Calories from fat	25		180	
	% Daily Value*		% Daily Value*	
Total Fat	2.5 g	**4%**	20 g	**31%**
Saturated Fat	1 g	**5%**	10 g	**50%**
Cholesterol	0 mg	**0%**	40 mg	**13%**
Sodium	530 mg	**22%**	410 mg	**17%**
Total Carbohydrate	41 g	**14%**	27 g	**9%**
Dietary Fiber	0 g	**0%**	0 g	**0%**
Sugars	9 g		13 g	
Other	5 g		0 g	
Protein	9 g		6 g	

*Percent of Daily Values on page a-22

Exchanges and 36 g Carbohydrates Per Serving

Breads	2.0	Vegetables	0.0	Fruits	0.0
Meats	0.0	Milk	0.7	Fats	0.5

Salads

Fiesta Chicken Salad, page 220

It is new and exciting to think we could actually make our own low fat salad dressings to accompany our salads. I have assembled here a cross section of several commonly used salad dressings. All of the salads were a breeze to put together and you will find them very tasty! This Section really shows how versatile the **ButterLike** and **SugarLike** products are.

Tips on successful salads and salad dressings using the Bateman Products

- Please read "Sauteing with **ButterLike Saute Butter**", page 128.
- A blender or a good whip are the best tools for making good salad dressings. The ingredients must be well blended for the best flavor.
- Chilling most dressings before serving also makes them taste better.
- Do not put your salad dressings on your salads to early. Pour on your dressing and serve.
- **ButterLike Saute Butter** and **Seasoned Saute Butters** are recommended for salad dressings. Add SugarLike gradually and blend well between additions.

Tomato and Avocado Salad with Mogul Dressing, page 226

Green Onion Dressing

The Fat Quotient using ButterLike is **47%** instead of **90%**
86% less fat **0% less sugar**
73% less Calories

U.S.	Ingredients	Metric
3 Tbsp	**ButterLike Saute Butter**	42.00 g
1/4 cup	White vinegar	60.00 g
2 Tbsp	Lemon juice	30.50 g
1/2 tsp	Garlic salt	1.80 g
1/8 tsp	Seasoned pepper	.35 g
1/2 cup	Green onions, thinly sliced	80.00 g

Directions

In a small bowl, whisk together the dressing ingredients. Serve as a coating or topping for a salad.

Nutrition Facts				
Serving Size	27 g			
Servings Per Recipe	8			
Amount per serving			High Fat/Sugar Comparison	
Calories		19	70	
Calories from fat		5	60	
	% Daily Value*		% Daily Value*	
Total Fat	1 g	**2%**	7 g	**11%**
Saturated Fat	0 g	**0%**	1 g	**5%**
Cholesterol	0 mg	**0%**	0 mg	**0%**
Sodium	60 mg	**3%**	60 mg	**3%**
Total Carbohydrate	3 g	**1%**	1 g	**0%**
Dietary Fiber	0 g	**0%**	0 g	**0%**
Sugars	0 g		0 g	
Other	0 g		0 g	
Protein	0 g		0 g	

*Percent of Daily Values on page a-22

Exchanges and 3 g Carbohydrates Per Serving

Breads	0.1	Vegetables	0.1	Fruits	0.0
Meats	0.0	Milk	0.0	Fats	0.2

Buttermilk Dressing

The Fat Quotient using ButterLike is **16%** instead of **96%**
97% less fat **0% less sugar**
82% less Calories

U.S.	Ingredients	Metric
2 Tbsp	**ButterLike Saute Butter**	28.00 g
1/3 cup	Non fat buttermilk	82.00 g
1/4 cup	Green onions, sliced	40.00 g
1/4 cup	Parsley, coarsely chopped	15.00 g
1/4 cup	Watercress, coarsely chopped	8.50 g
1/2 tsp	Dry tarragon	.80 g
2 tsp	Lemon juice	10.00 g
1/2 tsp	Anchovy paste	3.50 g
1/2 cup	Fat free mayonnaise	128.00 g
	Salt to taste	3.00 g
	Pepper to taste	1.00 g

Directions

In a blender or food processor, combine **ButterLike**, buttermilk, onions, parsley, watercress, tarragon, lemon juice, and anchovy paste; whirl until herbs are finely chopped. Add mayonnaise; whirl until blended. Season to taste with salt and pepper. Store, covered, in refrigerator for up to a week. Makes 1 cup.

Nutrition Facts				
Serving Size	40 g			
Servings Per Recipe	8			
Amount per serving			High Fat/Sugar Comparison	
Calories		28	160	
Calories from fat		5	150	
	% Daily Value*		% Daily Value*	
Total Fat	0.5 g	**1%**	17 g	**26%**
Saturated Fat	0 g	**0%**	1.5 g	**8%**
Cholesterol	0 mg	**0%**	10 mg	**3%**
Sodium	260 mg	**11%**	310 mg	**13%**
Total Carbohydrate	4 g	**1%**	2 g	**1%**
Dietary Fiber	0 g	**0%**	0 g	**0%**
Sugars	1 g		1 g	
Other	0 g		0 g	
Protein	1 g		1 g	

*Percent of Daily Values on page a-22

Exchanges and 4 g Carbohydrates Per Serving

Breads	0.2	Vegetables	0.1	Fruits	0.0
Meats	0.0	Milk	0.0	Fats	0.1

Cooked Salad Dressing

The Fat Quotient using ButterLike is 30% instead of 54%
66% less fat 66% less sugar
40% less Calories

U.S.	Ingredients	Metric
2 Tbsp	**Granulated SugarLike**	25.00 g
2 Tbsp	**ButterLike Saute Butter**	28.00 g
1/4 cup	Flour	29.00 g
1 tsp	Dry mustard, ground	5.00 g
1/2 tsp	Salt	3.00 g
1 1/2 cup	Skim milk	368.00 g
1/3 cup	White vinegar	80.00 g
2	Egg yolks, slightly beaten	33.00 g

Directions

Blend **SugarLike**, flour, mustard and salt in a 2-quart saucepan. Gradually stir in milk; bring to boil over medium heat, stirring constantly for 1 minute. Gradually blend half the hot mixture into the egg yolks; return this mixture back to saucepan. Boil, stirring, 1 minute then remove from heat. Stir in **ButterLike** and vinegar. Refrigerate covered, for 2 hours or until chilled. Store, covered, in refrigerator. Makes 2 cups.

Nutrition Facts				
Serving Size	36 g			
Servings Per Recipe	16			
Amount per serving			High Fat/Sugar Comparison	
Calories		30		50
Calories from fat		10		30
	% Daily Value*		% Daily Value*	
Total Fat	1 g	2%	3 g	5%
Saturated Fat	0 g	0%	1 g	5%
Cholesterol	30 mg	10%	30 mg	10%
Sodium	90 mg	4%	90 mg	4%
Total Carbohydrate	5 g	2%	4 g	1%
Dietary Fiber	0 g	0%	0 g	0%
Sugars	1 g		3 g	
Other	1 g		0 g	
Protein	1 g		1 g	

*Percent of Daily Values on page a-22

Exchanges and 4 g Carbohydrates Per Serving					
Breads	0.1	Vegetables	0.0	Fruits	0.0
Meats	0.1	Milk	0.1	Fats	0.1

Creamy French Dressing

The Fat Quotient using ButterLike is 47% instead of 96%
83% less fat 100% less sugar
66% less Calories

U.S.	Ingredients	Metric
2 Tbsp	**Granulated SugarLike**	25.00 g
3/4 cup	**ButterLike Saute Butter**	168.00 g
3 Tbsp	Vinegar	45.00 g
2 tsp	Paprika	4.20 g
1 tsp	Worcestershire sauce	5.00 g
1/4 tsp	Salt	1.50 g
1/4 tsp	Dry mustard	.60 g
1/8 tsp	Garlic powder	.40 g
Dash	Ground red pepper	.20 g

Nutrition Facts				
Serving Size	23 g			
Servings Per Recipe	11			
Amount per serving			High Fat/Sugar Comparison	
Calories		48		140
Calories from fat		20		130
	% Daily Value*		% Daily Value*	
Total Fat	2.5 g	4%	15 g	23%
Saturated Fat	1 g	5%	2 g	10%
Cholesterol	0 mg	0%	0 mg	0%
Sodium	60 mg	3%	60 mg	3%
Total Carbohydrate	8 g	3%	3 g	1%
Dietary Fiber	1 g	4%	0 g	0%
Sugars	0 g		2 g	
Other	2 g		0 g	
Protein	1 g		0 g	

*Percent of Daily Values on page a-22

Directions

In a small mixing bowl, blender container, or food processor bowl, combine vinegar, **SugarLike**, paprika, worcestershire sauce (if desired), salt, dry mustard, garlic powder, and red pepper. With mixer, blender, or food processor, slowly add **ButterLike** in a thin, steady stream. (This should take 2-3 minutes.) Continue mixing, blending, or processing until mixture is thick. Serve immediately or cover and store in the refrigerator for up to 2 weeks. Stir before serving.

Exchanges and 5 g Carbohydrates Per Serving					
Breads	0.3	Vegetables	0.0	Fruits	0.0
Meats	0.0	Milk	0.0	Fats	0.5

Orange-Basil Vinaigrette

The Fat Quotient using ButterLike is **17%** instead of **63%**
86% less fat **0% less sugar**
46% less Calories

U.S.	Ingredients	Metric
2 Tbsp	**ButterLike Saute Butter**	28.00 g
1 cup	Orange juice	249.00 g
2 tsp	Cornstarch	5.33 g
1/3 cup	White vinegar	80.00 g
2 tsp	Dijon mustard	10.00 g
2 tsp	Dry basil	1.60 g

Directions

In a small saucepan, stir orange juice and cornstarch until cornstarch dissolves. Bring to a boil over medium heat; boil, stirring for 30 seconds. Pour into a small bowl and refrigerate until cold. Then whisk in **ButterLike**, vinegar, mustard, and basil until blended. Store, covered, in refrigerator. Makes 1 cup.

Nutrition Facts				
Serving Size	47 g			
Servings Per Recipe	8			
Amount per serving			High Fat/Sugar Comparison	
Calories	27		50	
Calories from fat	5		30	
	% Daily Value*		% Daily Value*	
Total Fat	0.5 g	**1%**	3.5 g	**5%**
Saturated Fat	0 g	**0%**	0 g	**0%**
Cholesterol	0 mg	**0%**	0 mg	**0%**
Sodium	10 mg	**0%**	10 mg	**0%**
Total Carbohydrate	5 g	**2%**	4 g	**1%**
Dietary Fiber	0 g	**0%**	0 g	**0%**
Sugars	3 g		3 g	
Other	0 g		0 g	
Protein	0 g		0 g	

*Percent of Daily Values on page a-22

Exchanges and 5 g Carbohydrates Per Serving					
Breads	0.1	Vegetables	0.0	Fruits	0.2
Meats	0.0	Milk	0.0	Fats	0.1

Tart-Hot Dressing

The Fat Quotient using ButterLike is 0% instead of 0%
0% less fat 100% less sugar
33% less Calories

U.S.	Ingredients	Metric
1 tsp	**Granulated SugarLike**	4.00 g
2 Tbsp	Lime juice	31.00 g
2 Tbsp	Soy sauce	36.00 g
1 Tbsp	Fresh ginger, minced	10.00 g
1/2 tsp	Red pepper flakes	.90 g

Directions

In a small bowl, whisk together all ingredients. Serve over salad.

Exchanges and 2 g Carbohydrates Per Serving					
Breads	0.0	Vegetables	0.0	Fruits	0.0
Meats	0.0	Milk	0.0	Fats	0.0

Nutrition Facts				
Serving Size	20 g			
Servings Per Recipe	4			
Amount per serving			High Fat/Sugar Comparison	
Calories	10		15	
Calories from fat	0		0	
	% Daily Value*		% Daily Value*	
Total Fat	0 g	0%	0 g	0%
Saturated Fat	0 g	0%	0 g	0%
Cholesterol	0 mg	0%	0 mg	0%
Sodium	500 mg	21%	500 mg	21%
Total Carbohydrate	3 g	1%	3 g	1%
Dietary Fiber	0 g	0%	0 g	0%
Sugars	0 g		1 g	
Other	1 g		0 g	
Protein	1 g		1 g	

*Percent of Daily Values on page a-22

Spicy French Dressing

The Fat Quotient using ButterLike is 0% instead of 27%
100% less fat 98% less sugar
46% less Calories

U.S.	Ingredients	Metric
1/3 cup	**Catsup**, page 245	174.00 g
1/2 cup	**Granulated SugarLike**	100.00 g
2 Tbsp	**ButterLike Saute Butter**	28.00 g
1/2 cup	Cider vinegar	120.00 g
1 Tbsp	All-purpose flour	7.20 g
1 tsp	Salt	6.00 g
1 tsp	Worcestershire sauce	5.00 g
1 medium	Onion, finely chopped	120.00 g
1 clove	Garlic, minced	3.00 g
1/2 tsp	Paprika	1.00 g
1 tsp	Celery seeds	2.00 g

Directions

Follow directions for **Catsup**. Set aside.

Combine **SugarLike**, vinegar, and flour in a small pan. Cook over medium heat for 5 minutes until bubbly, stirring continuously. Blend vinegar mixture, salt, worcestershire, onion, garlic, and paprika in a blender or food processor until smooth. On lowest speed, gradually add **ButterLike**. Transfer dressing to a bowl and stir in Catsup and celery seeds. Store covered in the refrigerator for up to 2 weeks. Makes 2 cups.

Nutrition Facts				
Serving Size	35 g			
Servings Per Recipe	16			
Amount per serving			High Fat/Sugar Comparison	
Calories	27		50	
Calories from fat	0		15	
	% Daily Value*		% Daily Value*	
Total Fat	0 g	0%	1.5 g	2%
Saturated Fat	0 g	0%	0 g	0%
Cholesterol	0 mg	0%	0 mg	0%
Sodium	190 mg	8%	190 mg	8%
Total Carbohydrate	9 g	3%	9 g	3%
Dietary Fiber	2 g	8%	0 g	0%
Sugars	1 g		7 g	
Other	5 g		0 g	
Protein	0 g		0 g	

*Percent of Daily Values on page a-22

Exchanges and 2 g Carbohydrates Per Serving					
Breads	0.1	Vegetables	0.2	Fruits	0.0
Meats	0.0	Milk	0.0	Fats	0.1

Thousand Island Dressing

The Fat Quotient using ButterLike is 31% instead of 90%
93% less fat **0% less sugar**
81% less Calories

U.S.	Ingredients	Metric
1/4 cup	**Spicy Chili Sauce**, page 241	67.00 g
2 Tbsp	**ButterLike Saute Butter**	28.00 g
1 cup	Fat free mayonnaise	256.00 g
2 tsp	Onion, minced	6.70 g
1 Tbsp	Green bell pepper, minced	14.00 g
1 Tbsp	Pimento	14.00 g
2 Tbsp	Sweet pickle relish	30.00 g
1	Hard-cooked egg, finely chopped	50.00 g
	Salt to taste	3.00 g
	Pepper to taste	1.00 g

Directions

Follow directions for **Spicy Chili Sauce**.

In a small bowl, stir together 1/4 cup Spicy Chili Sauce, **ButterLike**, mayonnaise, onion, bell pepper, pimento, pickle relish, and egg. Store covered in refrigerator. Makes 1 3/4 cups.

Nutrition Facts				
Serving Size	34 g			
Servings Per Recipe	14			
Amount per serving			High Fat/Sugar Comparison	
Calories	29		150	
Calories from fat	5		140	
	% Daily Value*		% Daily Value*	
Total Fat	1 g	**2%**	15 g	**23%**
Saturated Fat	0 g	**0%**	2.5 g	**13%**
Cholesterol	15 mg	**5%**	25 mg	**8%**
Sodium	240 mg	**10%**	230 mg	**10%**
Total Carbohydrate	5 g	**2%**	2 g	**1%**
Dietary Fiber	0 g	**0%**	0 g	**0%**
Sugars	1 g		1 g	
Other	0 g		0 g	
Protein	1 g		1 g	

*Percent of Daily Values on page a-22

Exchanges and 5 g Carbohydrates Per Serving

Breads	0.2	Vegetables	0.1	Fruits	0.0
Meats	0.1	Milk	0.1	Fats	0.1

Prosciutto Dressing

The Fat Quotient using ButterLike is 35% instead of 81%
83% less fat **0% less sugar**
61% less Calories

U.S.	Ingredients	Metric
5 Tbsp	**ButterLike Saute Butter**, divided	70.00 g
1/4 lb	Fat free ham or prosciutto	113.00 g
2 cloves	Garlic, minced or pressed	6.00 g
3 Tbsp	Lemon juice	46.00 g
2 tsp	Dijon mustard	10.00 g

Directions

Thinly slice prosciutto or ham into fine slivers. Place in a wide frying pan and add 2 Tbsp **ButterLike** and garlic. Cook over medium heat 8-10 minutes, stirring often, until prosciutto and garlic are golden. Remove from heat and stir in 3 Tbsp **ButterLike**, lemon juice, and dijon mustard. If made ahead, pour into small jar, cover, and let stand until next day. Stir before using.

Nutrition Facts				
Serving Size	31 g			
Servings Per Recipe	8			
Amount per serving			High Fat/Sugar Comparison	
Calories	39		100	
Calories from fat	15		80	
	% Daily Value*		% Daily Value*	
Total Fat	1.5 g	**2%**	9 g	**14%**
Saturated Fat	0 g	**0%**	1.5 g	**8%**
Cholesterol	0 mg	**0%**	10 mg	**3%**
Sodium	180 mg	**8%**	180 mg	**8%**
Total Carbohydrate	4 g	**1%**	1 g	**0%**
Dietary Fiber	0 g	**0%**	0 g	**0%**
Sugars	1 g		1 g	
Other	0 g		0 g	
Protein	3 g		3 g	

*Percent of Daily Values on page a-22

Exchanges and 4 g Carbohydrates Per Serving

Breads	0.2	Vegetables	0.1	Fruits	0.0
Meats	0.3	Milk	0.0	Fats	0.3

Blue Cheese Dressing

The Fat Quotient using **ButterLike** is **37%** instead of **81%**
89% less fat **0% less sugar**
72% less Calories

U.S.	Ingredients	Metric
2 Tbsp	**ButterLike Saute Butter**	28.00 g
3/4 cup	Non fat buttermilk	184.00 g
2 Tbsp	Parsley, chopped	7.50 g
2 Tbsp	Non fat plain yogurt	28.00 g
2 Tbsp	White vinegar	30.00 g
2 Tbsp	Blue-veined cheese	14.00 g
1 Tbsp	Shallot, minced	.90 g
	White pepper to taste	2.40 g

Directions

In a blender or food processor, combine **ButterLike**, buttermilk, parsley, yogurt, cheese, and shallot; whirl until smooth. Season to taste with white pepper. Store covered in a refrigerator. Makes 1 cup.

Nutrition Facts				
Serving Size	37 g			
Servings Per Recipe	8			
Amount per serving			High Fat/Sugar Comparison	
Calories	28		100	
Calories from fat	10		80	
	% Daily Value*		% Daily Value*	
Total Fat	1 g	**2%**	9 g	**14%**
Saturated Fat	0.5 g	**3%**	1 g	**5%**
Cholesterol	5 mg	**2%**	5 mg	**2%**
Sodium	50 mg	**2%**	230 mg	**10%**
Total Carbohydrate	3 g	**1%**	2 g	**1%**
Dietary Fiber	0 g	**0%**	0 g	**0%**
Sugars	1 g		1 g	
Other	0 g		0 g	
Protein	2 g		1 g	

*Percent of Daily Values on page a-22

Exchanges and 3 g Carbohydrates Per Serving

Breads	0.0	Vegetables	0.0	Fruits	0.0
Meats	0.0	Milk	0.0	Fats	0.0

Olive-Pecan Chicken Slaw

The Fat Quotient using **ButterLike** is **33%** instead of **72%**
86% less fat **0% less sugar**
69% less Calories

U.S.	Ingredients	Metric
Dressing:		
1/2 tsp	**Granulated SugarLike**	2.00 g
1/2 cup	Fat free mayonnaise	128.00 g
2 Tbsp	Lemon juice	31.00 g
1 tsp	Dijon mustard	5.00 g
1/4 tsp	Pepper	.53 g
Salad:		
2 tsp	**ButterLike Saute Butter**	9.33 g
1/8 cup	Pecans	14.00 g
2 cups	Cabbage, shredded	140.00 g
1 1/2 cup	Cooked chicken breast, cubed	140.00 g
1 medium	Red apple, cored and diced	138.00 g
1 jar	Pimentos, drained and diced (2 oz)	57.00 g
1 1/2 oz	Ripe olives, sliced	43.00 g
1/4 cup	Celery, thinly sliced	30.00 g

Nutrition Facts				
Serving Size	123 g			
Servings Per Recipe	6			
Amount per serving			High Fat/Sugar Comparison	
Calories	110		350	
Calories from fat	35		250	
	% Daily Value*		% Daily Value*	
Total Fat	4 g	**6%**	28 g	**43%**
Saturated Fat	0.5 g	**3%**	5 g	**25%**
Cholesterol	20 mg	**7%**	60 mg	**20%**
Sodium	250 mg	**10%**	270 mg	**11%**
Total Carbohydrate	10 g	**3%**	8 g	**3%**
Dietary Fiber	1 g	**4%**	2 g	**8%**
Sugars	5 g		5 g	
Other	0 g		0 g	
Protein	8 g		16 g	

*Percent of Daily Values on page a-22

Directions

Dressing: In a serving bowl, stir all dressing ingredients together. Set aside.

Salad: Heat **ButterLike** in a wide frying pan over medium heat. Add pecans and cook several minutes, stirring often, until a darker brown. Drain on paper towels. Combine cabbage, chicken, apple, pimentos, olives, celery, and dressing; toss to coat evenly. Sprinkle pecans over salad; season to taste with salt.

Exchanges and 9 g Carbohydrates Per Serving					
Breads	0.2	Vegetables	0.5	Fruits	0.3
Meats	1.1	Milk	0.0	Fats	0.5

Lemon-Mint Pea and Pastina Salad

The Fat Quotient using ButterLike is **20%** instead of **63%**
82% less fat **0% less sugar**
44% less Calories

U.S.	Ingredients	Metric
1/2 cup	**ButterLike Saute Butter**	112.00 g
1 cup	Tiny pasta shapes	38.00 g
1 lb	Frozen tiny peas, thawed	454.00 g
1 cup	Celery, chopped	120.00 g
1/2 cup	Green onions, sliced	80.00 g
1/2 cup	Fresh mint, chopped	85.00 g
1/4 cup	Lemon juice	61.00 g
2 tsp	Lemon peel, grated	4.00 g

Directions

Cook pasta, then rinse with cold water and drain. Combine pasta, peas, celery, onions, and chopped mint. In a small bowl whisk **ButterLike**, lemon juice, and lemon peel. Add to pea mixture; mix well. Salt and pepper to taste. Store, covered, in refrigerator.

Nutrition Facts				
Serving Size	119 g			
Servings Per Recipe	8			
Amount per serving			High Fat/Sugar Comparison	
Calories	113		200	
Calories from fat	25		130	
	% Daily Value*		% Daily Value*	
Total Fat	2.5 g	**4%**	14 g	**22%**
Saturated Fat	1 g	**5%**	2 g	**10%**
Cholesterol	5 mg	**2%**	5 mg	**2%**
Sodium	65 mg	**3%**	65 mg	**3%**
Total Carbohydrate	18 g	**6%**	14 g	**5%**
Dietary Fiber	4 g	**16%**	4 g	**16%**
Sugars	4 g		4 g	
Other	0 g		0 g	
Protein	5 g		4 g	

*Percent of Daily Values on page a-22

Exchanges and 14 g Carbohydrates Per Serving					
Breads	1.1	Vegetables	0.2	Fruits	0.0
Meats	0.0	Milk	0.0	Fats	0.4

Dilled Pea Salad

The Fat Quotient using ButterLike is **14%** instead of **39%**
79% less fat **0% less sugar**
39% less Calories

U.S.	Ingredients	Metric
3 Tbsp	**ButterLike Saute Butter**	42.00 g
2 pkgs	Frozen peas (10 oz each)	567.00 g
2 Tbsp	Lemon juice	31.00 g
3/4 tsp	Dry dill weed	.75 g
1/4 tsp	Dried basil	.20 g
1 clove	Garlic, peeled	3.00 g
1 cup	Celery, thinly sliced	120.00 g
6	Butter lettuce leaves, rinsed, crisped	45.00 g

Directions

Cook peas according to package directions; drain, reserving 1/3 cup of the cooking water. In a large bowl, combine **ButterLike**, peas, reserved cooking water, lemon juice, dill weed, basil, and garlic. Season to taste with salt and pepper. Cover and refrigerate for 1 hour. Discard garlic. Add celery and toss lightly. Place a lettuce leaf on 6 salad plates; top equally with pea mixture.

Nutrition Facts				
Serving Size	135 g			
Servings Per Recipe	6			
Amount per serving			High Fat/Sugar Comparison	
Calories	98		160	
Calories from fat	10		60	
	% Daily Value*		% Daily Value*	
Total Fat	1.5 g	**2%**	7 g	**11%**
Saturated Fat	0 g	**0%**	1.5 g	**8%**
Cholesterol	0 mg	**0%**	105 mg	**35%**
Sodium	100 mg	**4%**	135 mg	**6%**
Total Carbohydrate	17 g	**6%**	15 g	**5%**
Dietary Fiber	6 g	**24%**	6 g	**24%**
Sugars	6 g		6 g	
Other	0 g		0 g	
Protein	6 g		8 g	

*Percent of Daily Values on page a-22

Exchanges and 11 g Carbohydrates Per Serving

Breads	1.0	Vegetables	0.2	Fruits	0.0
Meats	0.0	Milk	0.0	Fats	0.2

Dilled Pea Salad

Layered Chicken Salad

The Fat Quotient using **ButterLike** is **10%** instead of **76%**
96% less fat **0% less sugar**
71% less Calories

U.S.	Ingredients	Metric
1 Tbsp	**Granulated SugarLike**	12.50 g
6 cup	Iceberg lettuce, shredded	330.00 g
1 2/3 cup	Bean sprouts	113.00 g
1 can	Water chestnuts, drained, sliced (8 oz)	227.00 g
1/2 cup	Green onion, thinly sliced	80.00 g
1 medium	Cucumber, thinly sliced	65.00 g
4 cups	Boneless, skinless chicken breasts, cooked	560.00 g
2 pkgs	Frozen chinese pea pods (6 oz each)	340.00 g
2 cups	Fat free mayonnaise	512.00 g
2 tsp	Curry powder	4.00 g
1/2 tsp	Ground ginger	.90 g
1/8 cup	Spanish peanuts, optional	14.00 g
12-18	Cherry tomatoes, cut into halves	306.00 g

Directions

Cut cooked chicken into 2-3 inch long strips. Spread lettuce evenly in a wide glass serving bowl. Top with bean sprouts, water chestnuts, onions, cucumber, and chicken; arrange ingredients in layers. Pat pea pods dry and arrange evenly over chicken. In a small bowl, stir together **SugarLike**, mayonnaise, curry powder, and ginger. Spread mayonnaise mixture over pea pods. Cover and refrigerate for several hours or until next day. Garnish salad with peanuts (optional) and cherry tomato halves.

Nutrition Facts				
Serving Size	214 g			
Servings Per Recipe	12			
Amount per serving			High Fat/Sugar Comparison	
Calories	129		450	
Calories from fat	15		340	
	% Daily Value*		% Daily Value*	
Total Fat	1.5 g	**2%**	38 g	**58%**
Saturated Fat	0 g	**0%**	4.5 g	**23%**
Cholesterol	25 mg	**8%**	65 mg	**22%**
Sodium	400 mg	**17%**	340 mg	**14%**
Total Carbohydrate	14 g	**5%**	11 g	**4%**
Dietary Fiber	3 g	**12%**	3 g	**12%**
Sugars	4 g		4 g	
Other	1 g		0 g	
Protein	13 g		16 g	

*Percent of Daily Values on page a-22

Exchanges and 10 g Carbohydrates Per Serving

Breads	0.3	Vegetables	1.3	Fruits	0.0
Meats	1.0	Milk	0.0	Fats	0.1

Hot Bacon Spinach Salad

The Fat Quotient using ButterLike is 23% instead of 60%
83% less fat 71% less sugar
54% less Calories

U.S.	Ingredients	Metric
1/2 cup	**Brown SugarLike**	100.00 g
3 Tbsp	**ButterLike Saute Butter**	42.00 g
1/2 lb	Lean bacon	227.00 g
1/2 cup	Balsamic vinegar	113.00 g
1 large	Red onion, thinly sliced	85.00 g
4 cups	Fresh spinach leaves, torn	224.00 g
2 large	Eggs, hard boiled, sliced	100.00 g
1/4 tsp	Garlic pepper	.80 g

Directions

Wash and tear spinach and put in a large salad bowl. Toss in the red onion slices and arrange the hard boiled eggs on top. Cook bacon in frying pan until crisp. Drain on paper towels. Remove and discard most of drippings being careful to leave the small brown bacon pieces in pan. Stir in the **ButterLike** while trying to get the small pieces of bacon off the bottom of the pan. Heat, adding the balsamic vinegar and the **Brown SugarLike**. Stir in the garlic pepper. Sprinkle the crumbled bacon on top of the salad and pour the hot dressing over the salad. Serve immediately.

Nutrition Facts				
Serving Size	112 g			
Servings Per Recipe	8			
Amount per serving			High Fat/Sugar Comparison	
Calories	138		300	
Calories from fat	30		180	
	% Daily Value*		% Daily Value*	
Total Fat	3.5 g	5%	20 g	31%
Saturated Fat	1 g	5%	8 g	40%
Cholesterol	65 mg	22%	90 mg	30%
Sodium	460 mg	19%	560 mg	23%
Total Carbohydrate	22 g	7%	20 g	7%
Dietary Fiber	4 g	16%	1 g	4%
Sugars	5 g		17 g	
Other	9 g		0 g	
Protein	11 g		11 g	

*Percent of Daily Values on page a-22

Exchanges and 9 g Carbohydrates Per Serving					
Breads	0.1	Vegetables	0.4	Fruits	0.0
Meats	0.2	Milk	0.0	Fats	1.2

Chinese Chicken Salad

The Fat Quotient using ButterLike is 22% instead of 64%
86% less fat 75% less sugar
61% less Calories

Exchanges and 16 g Carbohydrates Per Serving					
Breads	1.0	Vegetables	0.3	Fruits	0.0
Meats	3.4	Milk	0.0	Fats	1.1

U.S.	Ingredients	Metric
Dressing:		
2 tsp	**ButterLike Saute Butter**	9.33 g
1 tsp	**Granulated SugarLike**	4.00 g
3/4 tsp	Dry mustard	1.80 g
1 tsp	Lemon peel, grated	2.00 g
1 Tbsp	Soy sauce	18.00 g
1 Tbsp	Lemon juice	15.00 g
Salad:		
1/2 cup	**ButterLike Saute Butter**	112.00 g
1 1/2 lb	Boneless, skinless chicken breasts	680.00 g
1/4 cup	All-purpose flour	29.00 g

U.S.	Ingredients	Metric
1/8 tsp	Ground cloves	.26 g
1/8 tsp	Anise seeds	.26 g
1/8 tsp	Ground cinnamon	.29 g
1/8 tsp	Ground ginger	.23 g
1/2 tsp	Salt	3.00 g
1/8 tsp	Pepper	.26 g
1 Tbsp	Sesame seeds	9.00 g
4 cups	Iceberg lettuce, finely shredded	220.00 g
3	Green onions, thinly sliced	18.00 g
1 large	Bunch cilantro, rinsed, stemmed	4.00 g

Directions

Dressing: In a small bowl, whisk together all dressing ingredients. Set aside.

Salad: Rinse chicken; pat dry. Trim all fat off and cube chicken in bite-size pieces. In a shallow dish, mix flour, spices, salt, and pepper. Coat chicken in flour mixture and shake off excess. Saute chicken in **ButterLike**. Cook, turning after 5 or 6 minutes, until meat is no longer pink. Drain on paper towels; let cool briefly. Toast sesame seeds in a frying pan over medium heat, stirring often, until golden. Let cool. Arrange lettuce in a large serving bowl; top with chicken, onions, and cilantro. Sprinkle with sesame seeds. Stir dressing, then drizzle over salad and toss. Serve immediately. Excellent with 1 cup chowmein noodles tossed in salad.

Nutrition Facts				
Serving Size	282 g			
Servings Per Recipe	4			
Amount per serving			High Fat/Sugar Comparison	
Calories	326		830	
Calories from fat	70		540	
	% Daily Value*		% Daily Value*	
Total Fat	8 g	**12%**	59 g	**91%**
Saturated Fat	2.5 g	**13%**	10 g	**50%**
Cholesterol	105 mg	**35%**	105 mg	**35%**
Sodium	670 mg	**28%**	810 mg	**34%**
Total Carbohydrate	19 g	**6%**	23 g	**8%**
Dietary Fiber	2 g	**8%**	7 g	**28%**
Sugars	1 g		4 g	
Other	1 g		0 g	
Protein	43 g		51 g	

*Percent of Daily Values on page a-22

French Salad

The Fat Quotient using ButterLike is **20%** instead of **58%**
82% less fat **0% less sugar**
47% less Calories

U.S.	Ingredients	Metric
Dressing:		
3/4 cup	**ButterLike Saute Butter**	168.00 g
1/4 cup	Red wine vinegar	64.00 g
2 Tbsp	Chives, snipped	6.00 g
2 Tbsp	Parsley, finely chopped	7.50 g
Salad:		
4 large	Thin-skinned potatoes, scrubbed	808.00 g
1 1/2 lb	Green beans, ends and strings removed	680.00 g
2 large	Tomatoes, cut into wedges	246.00 g
1/4 cup	Ripe olives, pitted	35.00 g
6	Lettuce leaves, rinsed and crisped	120.00 g
1 can	Water-packed tuna (6.125 oz)	174.00 g

Directions

Dressing: In a small bowl, whisk **ButterLike**, vinegar, chives, and parsley. Salt and pepper to taste; cover and set aside.

Salad: Cook potatoes in boiling water 25 minutes until tender when pierced. Drain, immerse in ice water until cool; drain again. Peel and slice potatoes; place in bowl and pour just enough dressing over slices to coat them. Mix gently, cover, and refrigerate for at least 2 hours. Cut beans into 1 1/2 inch pieces and cook in boiling water until tender-crisp. Drain, immerse in ice water until cool; drain again. Arrange potatoes, beans, and tomatoes in separate mounds on platter. Garnish with olives. Just before serving, arrange lettuce leaves around edge of platter. Drain tuna, leaving in can. Invert can on top of salad. Carefully lift off. Pour remaining dressing over all ingredients.

Nutrition Facts				
Serving Size	433 g			
Servings Per Recipe	5			
Amount per serving			High Fat/Sugar Comparison	
Calories	323		610	
Calories from fat	60		360	
	% Daily Value*		% Daily Value*	
Total Fat	7 g	**11%**	39 g	**60%**
Saturated Fat	2 g	**10%**	6 g	**30%**
Cholesterol	10 mg	**3%**	140 mg	**47%**
Sodium	490 mg	**20%**	930 mg	**39%**
Total Carbohydrate	59 g	**20%**	50 g	**17%**
Dietary Fiber	7 g	**28%**	7 g	**28%**
Sugars	7 g		7 g	
Other	0 g		0 g	
Protein	9 g		14 g	

*Percent of Daily Values on page a-22

Exchanges and 53 g Carbohydrates Per Serving					
Breads	3.0	Vegetables	1.4	Fruits	0.0
Meats	0.1	Milk	0.0	Fats	1.3

Deviled Eggs with Homemade Salad Dressing

The Fat quotient using **ButterLike** is **45%** instead of **70%**
57% less fat **100% less sugar**
33% less Calories

U.S.	Ingredients	Metric
Dressing:		
1/2 cup	**ButterLike Baking Butter**	114.00 g
2 1/2 Tbsp	**Granulated SugarLike**	31.00 g
2	Egg yolks	33.00 g
3 tsp	Vinegar	15.00 g
1/3 tsp	Mustard	2.00 g
Dash	Salt	1.00 g
12	Hard boiled eggs	600.00 g
2 Tbsp	Pickle relish	30.00 g
1/4 tsp	Paprika	1.00 g

Nutrition Facts				
Serving Size	34 g			
Servings Per Recipe	24			
Amount per serving			High Fat/Sugar Comparison	
Calories	60		90	
Calories from fat	30		60	
	% Daily Value*		% Daily Value*	
Total Fat	3 g	**5%**	7 g	**11%**
Saturated Fat	1 g	**5%**	3.5 g	**18%**
Cholesterol	125 mg	**42%**	135 mg	**45%**
Sodium	75 mg	**3%**	100 mg	**4%**
Total Carbohydrate	5 g	**2%**	2 g	**1%**
Dietary Fiber	0 g	**0%**	0 g	**0%**
Sugars	0 g		1 g	
Other	1 g		0 g	
Protein	3 g		3 g	

*Percent of Daily Values on page a-22

Exchanges and 4 g Carbohydrates Per Serving

Breads	0.2	Vegetables	0.0	Fruits	0.0
Meats	0.5	Milk	0.0	Fats	0.4

Directions

Dressing: Place room temperature egg yolks into a blender. Turn on and add the **ButterLike** by tablespoonfuls until all added. Turn off and scrape sides. Turn back on and add vinegar and remaining ingredients until well mixed. Season to taste.

Slice hard boiled eggs in half and scoop out the yolks and place in a bowl. Using a fork, mash the yolks until the lumps are gone. Lightly salt the mashed yolks and mix the salad dressing into them. I like to add pickle relish at this point. It is optional. Either spoon the deviled eggs into the egg white half or fill a pastry bag with the deviled egg mixture and pipe into the egg white half. There should be enough to mound. Sprinkle with paprika. Chill until ready to serve.

Fiesta Chicken Salad

The Fat Quotient using **ButterLike** is **19%** instead of **38%**
57% less fat **0% less sugar**
15% less Calories

U.S.	Ingredients	Metric
1/4 cup	**ButterLike Saute Butter**	56.00 g
6	Boneless, skinless chicken breast halves	1416.00 g
1/2 cup	Egg whites or egg substitutes	114.00 g
1 1/4 cup	Medium chunky salsa	310.00 g
1 1/3 cup	Plain bread crumbs	144.00 g
1 tsp	Salt	6.00 g
1 tsp	Cumin	5.00 g
1 tsp	Chile powder	2.60 g
1/2 tsp	Ground oregano	.75 g
4	Green onions, sliced	24.00 g
1 pkg	Mixed salad greens (1 lb)	454.00 g
3	Medium tomatoes, chopped	369.00 g
1 bottle	Red wine vinegar/dressing (8 oz)	227.00 g
1	Avocado, peeled, sliced	237.00 g
1 cup	Fat free sour cream	256.00 g

Directions

Heat oven to 400°. Place **ButterLike** in a 15x10x1-inch vegetable sprayed baking pan. Tilt pan to coat with **ButterLike**. Halve chicken breasts lengthwise; then cut crosswise into 1/2-inch slices. In a large bowl, beat egg whites; stir in chicken and 1/4 cup of the salsa. In a shallow bowl, combine bread crumbs, salt, cumin, chili powder, and oregano; mix well. Add chicken pieces to bread crumb mixture, a few at a time; turn to coat. Place coated chicken in **ButterLike**-coated pan. Bake at 400° for 15-20 minutes or until chicken is no longer pink. Reserve 1 Tbsp of the green onions for garnish. In a large bowl, combine remaining onions, salad greens, and tomatoes; toss gently. Pour half of the dressing over salad; toss to coat. Arrange evenly on 8 individual plates. Spoon chicken into center of each salad. Top each with 1 Tbsp sour cream and about 1/2 tsp reserved green onions. Garnish each plate with avocado slices. Serve with remaining half of salad dressing, 1/2 cup sour cream, and 1 cup salsa.

Nutrition Facts				
Serving Size	453 g			
Servings Per Recipe	8			
Amount per serving			High Fat/Sugar Comparison	
Calories	427		500	
Calories from fat	80		190	
	% Daily Value*		% Daily Value*	
Total Fat	9 g	**14%**	21 g	**32%**
Saturated Fat	1 g	**5%**	9 g	**45%**
Cholesterol	105 mg	**35%**	185 mg	**62%**
Sodium	1290 mg	**54%**	1330 mg	**55%**
Total Carbohydrate	37 g	**12%**	30 g	**10%**
Dietary Fiber	5 g	**20%**	5 g	**20%**
Sugars	15 g		15 g	
Other	0 g		0 g	
Protein	49 g		48 g	

*Percent of Daily Values on page a-22

Exchanges and 32 g Carbohydrates Per Serving					
Breads	1.6	Vegetables	1.1	Fruits	0.0
Meats	3.7	Milk	0.3	Fats	1.2

Fiesta Chicken Salad

Potato Salad

The Fat Quotient using ButterLike is 9% instead of 49%
88% less fat 0% less sugar
39% less Calories

U.S.	Ingredients	Metric
1/2 cup	**ButterLike Saute Butter**	112.00 g
3 1/2 lb	Medium, red, thin-skinned potatoes	1587.00 g
3 cloves	Garlic, minced or pressed	9.00 g
1/4 cup	Sweet pickle relish	60.00 g
1/2 cup	Fat free mayonnaise	128.00 g
1 can	Sliced ripe olives, drained (2.25 oz)	64.00 g
1/2 cup	Celery, thinly sliced	60.00 g
1/2 cup	Green onions, thinly sliced	80.00 g
1 jar	Sliced pimentos, drained (2 oz)	28.00 g

Directions

Wash and cook potatoes in boiling water 20 minutes until tender throughout when pierced. Drain and let cool briefly; cut into 1/2-inch cubes and place in a large bowl. Add **ButterLike** and garlic; mix lightly until potatoes are well coated. Let stand until cool. Add pickle relish, mayonnaise, olives, celery, and onions to potatoes. Mix lightly until combined. Season to taste with salt or pepper. Cover and refrigerate for at least 3 hours or until the next day. Just before serving, garnish salad with pimentos and parsley.

Nutrition Facts				
Serving Size	213 g			
Servings Per Recipe	10			
Amount per serving			High Fat/Sugar Comparison	
Calories	232		380	
Calories from fat	25		190	
	% Daily Value*		% Daily Value*	
Total Fat	2.5 g	**4%**	21 g	**32%**
Saturated Fat	0.5 g	**3%**	2.5 g	**13%**
Cholesterol	0 mg	**0%**	5 mg	**2%**
Sodium	220 mg	**9%**	190 mg	**8%**
Total Carbohydrate	49 g	**16%**	44 g	**15%**
Dietary Fiber	4 g	**16%**	4 g	**16%**
Sugars	3 g		3 g	
Other	0 g		0 g	
Protein	5 g		4 g	

*Percent of Daily Values on page a-22

Exchanges and 45 g Carbohydrates Per Serving

Breads	2.6	Vegetables	0.4	Fruits	0.0
Meats	0.0	Milk	0.0	Fats	0.5

Potato Salad

Danish Potato Salad

The Fat Quotient using **ButterLike** is **32%** instead of **73%**
79% less fat **0% less sugar**
52% less Calories

U.S.	Ingredients	Metric
2 Tbsp	**ButterLike Saute Butter**	28.00 g
1 tsp	Granulated SugarLike	4.00 g
1 clove	Garlic, peeled and halved	3.00 g
1/4 cup	Tarragon vinegar	64.00 g
1 tsp	Salt	
1/2 tsp	Dry dill weed or 1 1/2 tsp fresh dill	.50 g
1 lb	New potatoes, peeled	454.00 g
3	Eggs, hard-boiled	150.00 g
2	Green onions, sliced	12.00 g
3 large	Radishes, sliced	13.50 g
1/3 cup	Fat free mayonnaise	85.00 g

Nutrition Facts			High Fat/Sugar Comparison	
Serving Size	137 g			
Servings Per Recipe	6			
Amount per serving				
Calories	100		210	
Calories from fat	30		150	
	% Daily Value*		% Daily Value*	
Total Fat	3.5 g	**5%**	17 g	**26%**
Saturated Fat	1 g	**5%**	2.5 g	**13%**
Cholesterol	105 mg	**35%**	115 mg	**38%**
Sodium	670 mg	**28%**	640 mg	**27%**
Total Carbohydrate	13 g	**4%**	10 g	**3%**
Dietary Fiber	1 g	**4%**	1 g	**4%**
Sugars	1 g		1 g	
Other	1 g		0 g	
Protein	4 g		4 g	

*Percent of Daily Values on page a-22

Exchanges and 11 g Carbohydrates Per Serving

Breads	0.7	Vegetables	0.1	Fruits	0.0
Meats	0.5	Milk	0.0	Fats	0.4

Directions

In a large bowl combine **ButterLike** and garlic. Let stand for 10 minutes; discard garlic or use **Toasted Garlic Saute Butter**. Stir in **SugarLike**, vinegar, salt, and dill weed; set aside. Cook potatoes in boiling water 20 minutes until tender throughout when pierced. Drain and let cool briefly; cut into 1/2-inch cubes. Add to dressing and toss to coat. Cover and refrigerate for at least 1 hour or until next day. Just before serving, chop 2 of the eggs. Add chopped eggs, onions, radishes, and mayonnaise to potatoes; mix gently. Cut remaining egg into wedges; garnish salad with egg wedges and sprinkle with parsley.

Danish Potato Salad

Black Bean, Corn, and Pepper Salad

The Fat Quotient using **ButterLike** is **8%** instead of **17%**
57% less fat **0% less sugar**
12% less Calories

U.S.	**Ingredients**	Metric
2 Tbsp	**ButterLike Saute Butter**	28.00 g
2 cans	Black or white beans (15 oz each)	202.00 g
1 1/2 cup	Fresh corn kernels	203.00 g
1 large	Red bell pepper, seeded and diced	170.00 g
2 small	Fresh jalapeno chilies, seeded and minced	38.00 g
1/2 cup	Cilantro, chopped, firmly packed	30.00 g
1/4 cup	Lime juice	62.00 g
10	Lettuce leaves, rinsed and crisped	200.00 g

Directions

Drain and rinse beans. In a large bowl, mix **ButterLike**, beans, corn, bell pepper, chilies, cilantro, and lime juice. Season to taste with salt and pepper. Cover and refrigerate for at least 1 hour or until next day. Transfer bean mixture to a salad bowl lined with lettuce leaves. Serve warm or at room temperature.

Nutrition Facts				
Serving Size	155 g			
Servings Per Recipe	6			
Amount per serving			High Fat/Sugar Comparison	
Calories	168		190	
Calories from fat	15		30	
	% Daily Value*		% Daily Value*	
Total Fat	1.5 g	**2%**	3.5 g	**5%**
Saturated Fat	0 g	**0%**	0.5 g	**3%**
Cholesterol	0 mg	**0%**	0 mg	**0%**
Sodium	110 mg	**5%**	110 mg	**5%**
Total Carbohydrate	31 g	**10%**	30 g	**10%**
Dietary Fiber	7 g	**28%**	7 g	**28%**
Sugars	3 g		3 g	
Other	0 g		0 g	
Protein	10 g		10 g	

*Percent of Daily Values on page a-22

Exchanges and 24 g Carbohydrates Per Serving					
Breads	1.9	Vegetables	0.2	Fruits	0.0
Meats	0.6	Milk	0.0	Fats	0.2

Spinach Salad and Almond Dressing

The Fat Quotient using **ButterLike** is **48%** instead of **81%**
78% less fat **0% less sugar**
62% less Calories

U.S.	**Ingredients**	Metric
Dressing:		
7 Tbsp	**ButterLike Saute Butter**	98.00 g
1/4 cup	Slivered almonds or pine nuts	34.00 g
2 1/2 Tbsp	Wine vinegar	40.00 g
1/8 tsp	Ground nutmeg	.30 g
1/2 tsp	Lemon peel, grated	1.00 g
1/2 tsp	Dried tarragon	.40 g
Salad:		
1 1/2 lb	Spinach, rinsed, stems removed	680.00 g

Nutrition Facts				
Serving Size	107 g			
Servings Per Recipe	8			
Amount per serving			High Fat/Sugar Comparison	
Calories	75		200	
Calories from fat	40		160	
	% Daily Value*		% Daily Value*	
Total Fat	4 g	**6%**	18 g	**28%**
Saturated Fat	1 g	**5%**	8 g	**40%**
Cholesterol	0 mg	**0%**	30 mg	**38%**
Sodium	10 mg	**0%**	115 mg	**10%**
Total Carbohydrate	7 g	**2%**	4 g	**1%**
Dietary Fiber	1 g	**4%**	1 g	**4%**
Sugars	1 g		1 g	
Other	0 g		0 g	
Protein	3 g		5 g	

*Percent of Daily Values on page a-22

Directions

Dressing: Spread almonds in a shallow baking pan and toast about 5-8 minutes in a 350° oven, stirring occasionally, until lightly browned. Let cool. In a bowl, combine **ButterLike**, almonds, wine vinegar, nutmeg, lemon peel, and tarragon. Cover and let stand at room temperature for at least 30 minutes or until next day.

Salad: Select large leaves from spinach and use to line 8 salad plates. Cut remaining leaves into thin slivers; mount on plates. Stir dressing to blend, then drizzle over salads. Salt to taste.

Exchanges and 6 g Carbohydrates Per Serving					
Breads	0.3	Vegetables	0.6	Fruits	0.0
Meats	0.0	Milk	0.0	Fats	0.8

Southwestern Grilled Chicken Salad

The Fat Quotient using **ButterLike** is **13%** instead of **44%**
79% less fat **0% less sugar**
32% less Calories

U.S.	Ingredients	Metric
	Orange Sauce, page 234	185.00 g
4	Boneless, skinless chicken breasts, halved	472.00 g
1/4 tsp	Salt	1.50 g
1/4 tsp	Pepper	.53 g
1/4 cup	Fat free caesar dressing	59.00 g
2 Tbsp	Chopped fresh cilantro	4.80 g
2 Tbsp	Canned chopped green chilies	30.00 g
8 cups	Bite-size pieces romaine	448.00 g
1 large	Red bell pepper, sliced	186.00 g

Directions

Follow directions for **Orange Sauce**.

Heat coals or gas grill. Brush chicken with **Orange Sauce**. Cover and grill chicken 5-6 inches from medium heat 15-20 minutes, turning once, until meat of chicken is no longer pink when centers of thickest pieces are cut. Sprinkle with salt and pepper. Cover and refrigerate chicken at least 1 hour until chilled. Cut each chicken breast half into slices. Mix dressing, cilantro, and chilies. Place 2 cups romaine on each of 4 serving plates. Top with bell pepper slices and 1 half chicken breast sliced. Serve with dressing mixture.

Nutrition Facts				
Serving Size	347 g			
Servings Per Recipe	4			
Amount per serving			High Fat/Sugar Comparison	
Calories		238	350	
Calories from fat		30	150	
	% Daily Value*		% Daily Value*	
Total Fat	3.5 g	**5%**	17 g	**26%**
Saturated Fat	1 g	**5%**	5 g	**25%**
Cholesterol	70 mg	**23%**	90 mg	**30%**
Sodium	630 mg	**26%**	550 mg	**23%**
Total Carbohydrate	20 g	**7%**	18 g	**6%**
Dietary Fiber	3 g	**12%**	3 g	**12%**
Sugars	3 g		3 g	
Other	0 g		0 g	
Protein	31 g		31 g	

*Percent of Daily Values on page a-22

Exchanges and 17 g Carbohydrates Per Serving					
Breads	0.2	Vegetables	1.1	Fruits	0.6
Meats	2.3	Milk	0.0	Fats	0.3

Tomato & Avocado Salad w/ Mogul Dressing

The Fat Quotient using ButterLike is **55%** instead of **85%**
72% less fat **0% less sugar**
57% less Calories

U.S.	Ingredients	Metric
Dressing:		
1/2 cup	**ButterLike Saute Butter**	112.00 g
2 Tbsp	Tarragon vinegar	32.00 g
1 tsp	Dry basil	.80 g
1/8 tsp	Ground cloves	.26 g
1/8 tsp	Anise seeds	.26 g
1/8 tsp	Ground cinnamon	.29 g
1/8 tsp	Ground ginger	.23 g
1/2 tsp	Lemon juice	2.50 g
1 clove	Garlic, minced or pressed	3.00 g
1/8 tsp	Dry mustard	.30 g
1/8 tsp	Pepper	.26 g
Salad:		
2 large	Tomatoes	246.00 g
2	Cucumbers	602.00 g
1/2	Avocado	119.00 g

Nutrition Facts				
Serving Size	140 g			
Servings Per Recipe	8			
Amount per serving			High Fat/Sugar Comparison	
Calories		73	170	
Calories from fat		40	150	
	% Daily Value*		% Daily Value*	
Total Fat	4.5 g	**7%**	16 g	**25%**
Saturated Fat	0.5 g	**3%**	1.5 g	**8%**
Cholesterol	0 mg	**0%**	0 mg	**0%**
Sodium	5 mg	**0%**	10 mg	**0%**
Total Carbohydrate	8 g	**3%**	4 g	**1%**
Dietary Fiber	3 g	**12%**	7 g	**28%**
Sugars	3 g		3 g	
Other	0 g		0 g	
Protein	2 g		2 g	

*Percent of Daily Values on page a-22

Exchanges and 5 g Carbohydrates Per Serving

Breads	0.3	Vegetables	0.7	Fruits	0.0
Meats	0.0	Milk	0.0	Fats	0.8

Directions

Dressing: In a small bowl, whisk all dressing ingredients together. Salt to taste. Pour into a serving container, cover, and refrigerate for at least 2 hours.

Salad: Peel and thinly slice tomatoes and cucumbers; pit, peel, and slice avocado. Arrange tomatoes and avocado slices on a platter. Stir dressing to blend, then drizzle half of it over vegetables. Garnish with lettuce and cucumbers, if desired. Offer remaining dressing to add to individual servings.

Tomato and Avocado Salad with Mogul Dressing

Roasted Eggplant, Pepper, and Onion Salad

The Fat Quotient using ButterLike is 15% instead of 60%
88% less fat **0% less sugar**
48% less Calories

U.S.	**Ingredients**	Metric
2 Tbsp	**ButterLike Saute Butter**	28.00 g
1 1/2 small	Eggplants, halved lengthwise	82.00 g
1	Red bell pepper, halved lengthwise	170.00 g
1/2 large	Green bell pepper, seeded	85.00 g
1 medium	Onion with peel, cut in half	120.00 g
2 Tbsp	White wine vinegar	30.00 g
1 Tbsp	Balsamic vinegar	17.00 g
1 Tbsp	Capers	15.00 g
2 tsp	Garlic, finely chopped	5.60 g
1 Tbsp	Fresh parsley, chopped	3.80 g

Directions

Set oven control to broil. Place eggplant, bell peppers and onion, cut sides down, on rack in broiler pan. Broil with tops 4-6 inches from heat about 10 minutes or until skins are blistered. Turn vegetables; broil 5-8 minutes longer or just until eggplant is tender and light brown. Place vegetables in large paper bag or on plastic wrap; seal tightly. Let stand at room temperature 20 minutes. Peel eggplants; cut each half lengthwise in half, then cut crosswise into 1-inch slices. Peel bell peppers; cut crosswise in half, then cut into 1-inch strips. Peel and chop onion. Beat remaining ingredients except parsley with wire whisk in large bowl. Add vegetables; toss gently until evenly coated. Sprinkle with parsley. Cover and refrigerate at least 2 hours until chilled.

Nutrition Facts				
Serving Size	79 g			
Servings Per Recipe	7			
Amount per serving			High Fat/Sugar Comparison	
Calories	31		60	
Calories from fat	5		35	
	% Daily Value*		% Daily Value*	
Total Fat	0.5 g	**1%**	4 g	**6%**
Saturated Fat	0 g	**0%**	0.5 g	**3%**
Cholesterol	0 mg	**0%**	0 mg	**0%**
Sodium	80 mg	**3%**	80 mg	**3%**
Total Carbohydrate	6 g	**2%**	5 g	**2%**
Dietary Fiber	1 g	**4%**	1 g	**4%**
Sugars	2 g		2 g	
Other	0 g		0 g	
Protein	1 g		1 g	

*Percent of Daily Values on page a-22

Exchanges and 5 g Carbohydrates Per Serving

Breads	0.1	Vegetables	0.6	Fruits	0.0
Meats	0.0	Milk	0.0	Fats	0.1

Roasted Potato and Carrot Salad

The Fat Quotient using **ButterLike** is **4%** instead of **16%**
75% less fat **15% less sugar**
15% less calories

U.S.	Ingredients	Metric
2 Tbsp	**ButterLike Saute Butter**	28 00 g
2 lb	Thin-skinned potatoes, scrubbed	907.00 g
8 large	Carrots, peeled, 1-inch chunks	907.00 g
Dressing:		
1 Tbsp	**Granulated SugarLike**	12.50 g
2 tsp	Orange peel, grated	4.00 g
1/2 cup	Orange juice	125.00 g
2 Tbsp	White vinegar	30.00 g
2 Tbsp	Fresh basil, chopped	5.30 g
2 tsp	Dijon mustard	10.00 g
1 tsp	Ground cumin	5.00 g
2 cloves	Garlic, minced or pressed	6.00 g
1	Fresh jalapeno chile, seeded, minced	19.00 g

Directions

Cut potatoes into 1-inch chunks. Combine potatoes with 1 Tbsp **ButterLike** in a vegetable sprayed 10 x15-inch rimmed baking pan. Combine carrots and remaining 1 Tbsp **ButterLike** in another vegetable sprayed 10x15-inch rimmed baking pan. Bake potatoes and carrots 35-40 minutes in a 475° oven, turning occasionally, until richly browned. Let roasted vegetables cool until warm.

Dressing: In a small bowl whisk together all dressing ingredients. Combine dressing with potatoes and carrots in a shallow serving bowl. Toss gently. Garnish with basil sprigs. Season to taste with salt and pepper.

Nutrition Facts				
Serving Size	257 g			
Servings Per Recipe	8			
Amount per serving			High Fat/Sugar Comparison	
Calories	196		230	
Calories from fat	10		35	
	% Daily Value*		% Daily Value*	
Total Fat	1 g	**2%**	4 g	**6%**
Saturated Fat	0 g	**0%**	0.5 g	**3%**
Cholesterol	0 mg	**0%**	0 mg	**0%**
Sodium	95 mg	**4%**	90 mg	**4%**
Total Carbohydrate	45 g	**15%**	45 g	**15%**
Dietary Fiber	7 g	**28%**	6 g	**24%**
Sugars	11 g		13 g	
Other	1 g		0 g	
Protein	4 g		4 g	

*Percent of Daily Values on page a-22

Exchanges and 37 g Carbohydrates Per Serving					
Breads	1.7	Vegetables	2.4	Fruits	0.1
Meats	0.0	Milk	0.0	Fats	0.1

Sauces

Peanut Sauce, page 234; Lemon Sauce, page 238; and Cherry Sauce, page 232

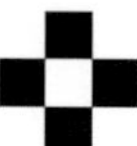

Your cream and normally rich sauces can now all be made low fat, sugar free, and absolutely delicious. **SugarLike** makes sweet sauces incredibly decadent and impossible to believe that they are sugar free and low fat too! I had a woman call me once and asked if I had ever made a hollandaise sauce using the **Baking Butter**. I told her I had never tried, but I asked her to call me back and tell me how it worked. She called me back a few minutes later, very excited to report her success in making a recipe that she had been unable to eat previously because of health reasons. Please follow the following tips for easy sauce making.

Tips on successful sauces using the Bateman Products

- Please read "Tips on cooking low fat, low calorie, low cholesterol and sugar free main dishes", page 127; and "Tips on successful sauces using the Bateman Products", page 128.
- Follow the recipe directions if you are using one of the **Saute Butters**. You may substitute **Baking Butter** for a sauce that calls for **Saute Butter**, but should whisk the **ButterLike** into the other ingredients rather than melt the **ButterLike** first. This is because there is so little real fat in the **ButterLike**.
- Make sure you cook sauces long enough to blend the flavors together.
- Cook sauces that have flour or cornstarch in them for five minutes after they start to boil. That way the starch is properly cooked and loses the flour taste.
- When sauces are made with **SugarLike**, it helps to gradually add the **SugarLike** and mix in completely before adding more. This helps avoid lumps.
- Sauces can be canned without losing their sweetness.

Basic Cream Sauce

The fat quotient using ButterLike is 10% instead of 71%
93% less fat **5% less sugar**
48% less Calories

U.S.	Ingredients	Metric
3 Tbsp	**ButterLike Baking** or **Saute Butter**	42.00 g
1 cup	Skim milk	246.00 g
3 Tbsp	All-purpose flour	21.00 g
1/2 tsp	Salt	3.00 g

Directions

Whisk flour, salt, and milk together in a saucepan. Add **ButterLike** to milk mixture. Stir and cook over medium heat until bubbly and hot. Use in any way you would normally use a cream sauce. Makes approximately 1 cup plus.

Exchanges and 26 g Carbohydrates Per Serving					
Breads	1.3	Vegetables	0.0	Fruits	0.0
Meats	0.0	Milk	0.5	Fats	0.3

Nutrition Facts				
Serving Size	157 g			
Servings Per Recipe	26			
Amount per serving			High Fat/Sugar Comparison	
Calories		140	270	
Calories from fat		15	190	
	% Daily Value*		% Daily Value*	
Total Fat	1.5 g	**2%**	22 g	**34%**
Saturated Fat	1 g	**5%**	13 g	**65%**
Cholesterol	5 mg	**2%**	65 mg	**22%**
Sodium	730 mg	**30%**	820 mg	**34%**
Total Carbohydrate	27 g	**9%**	15 g	**5%**
Dietary Fiber	0 g	**0%**	0 g	**0%**
Sugars	5 g		6 g	
Other	1 g		0 g	
Protein	6 g		5 g	

*Percent of Daily Values on page a-22

Raspberry Sauce

The fat quotient using ButterLike is 0% instead of 0%
0% less fat **62% less sugar**
33% less Calories

U.S.	Ingredients	Metric
1/3 cup	**Granulated SugarLike**	67.00 g
3 cup	Fresh or frozen raspberries	369.00 g
1 tsp	Cornstarch	2.70 g

Directions

Thaw the berries, if frozen. Do not drain. Place half of the berries in a blender or food processor bowl. Cover and blend or process until berries are smooth. Press berries through a fine-mesh sieve; discard seeds. Repeat with remaining berries. (You should have about 1/2 cup sieved puree from each 1 1/2 cups berries.) In a medium saucepan stir together **SugarLike** and cornstarch. Add sieved berries. Cook and stir over medium heat until thickened and bubbly. Cook and stir for 2 minutes more. Remove from heat. Cool to room temperature before serving.

Strawberry Sauce: Prepare as above, except substitute strawberries for raspberries and do not sieve.

Nutrition Facts				
Serving Size	55 g			
Servings Per Recipe	8			
Amount per serving			High Fat/Sugar Comparison	
Calories		40	60	
Calories from fat		0	0	
	% Daily Value*		% Daily Value*	
Total Fat	0 g	**0%**	0 g	**0%**
Saturated Fat	0 g	**0%**	0 g	**0%**
Cholesterol	0 mg	**0%**	0 mg	**0%**
Sodium	0 mg	**0%**	0 mg	**0%**
Total Carbohydrate	14 g	**5%**	14 g	**5%**
Dietary Fiber	5 g	**20%**	3 g	**12%**
Sugars	5 g		13 g	
Other	6 g		0 g	
Protein	0 g		0 g	

*Percent of Daily Values on page a-22

Exchanges and 3 g Carbohydrates Per Serving					
Breads	0.0	Vegetables	0.0	Fruits	0.3
Meats	0.0	Milk	0.0	Fats	0.0

Cranberry Sauce

The fat quotient using **ButterLike** is **0%** instead of **0%**
0% less fat **100% less sugar**
48% less Calories

U.S.	Ingredients	Metric
1 cup	**Granulated SugarLike**	200.00 g
1 cup	Water	237.00 g
2 cups	Cranberries	220.00 g

Directions

In medium saucepan, combine **SugarLike** and water. Bring to a boil, stirring to dissolve **SugarLike**. Boil rapidly for 5 minutes. Add cranberries. Return to a boil; reduce heat. Boil gently, uncovered, over medium-high heat for 3-4 minutes or until skins pop, stirring occasionally. Remove from heat. Serve warm or chilled with poultry or pork. Makes 2 cups.

Molded Cranberry Sauce: Prepare as above, except gently boil cranberry mixture for 13-16 minutes or until a drop gels on a cold plate. Pour into 1 1/2 cup mold and chill until firm.

Nutrition Facts				
Serving Size	41 g			
Servings Per Recipe	16			
Amount per serving			High Fat/Sugar Comparison	
Calories		31	60	
Calories from fat		0	0	
	% Daily Value*		% Daily Value*	
Total Fat	0 g	**0%**	0 g	**0%**
Saturated Fat	0 g	**0%**	0 g	**0%**
Cholesterol	0 mg	**0%**	0 mg	**0%**
Sodium	0 mg	**0%**	0 mg	**0%**
Total Carbohydrate	14 g	**5%**	14 g	**5%**
Dietary Fiber	4 g	**16%**	1 g	**4%**
Sugars	0 g		12 g	
Other	9 g		0 g	
Protein	0 g		0 g	

*Percent of Daily Values on page a-22

Exchanges and 1 g Carbohydrates Per Serving

Breads	0.0	Vegetables	0.0	Fruits	0.1
Meats	0.0	Milk	0.0	Fats	0.0

Cherry Sauce

The Fat Quotient using **ButterLike** is **0%** instead of **0%**
0% less fat **75% less sugar**
35% less Calories

U.S.	Ingredients	Metric
1/2 cup	**Granulated SugarLike**	100.00 g
2 Tbsp	All-purpose flour	14.00 g
1/2 cup	Water	119.00 g
2 cups	Fresh, tart cherries, pitted	310.00 g
1 Tbsp	Orange juice	16.00 g

Directions

In a medium saucepan stir together **SugarLike** and flour; stir in water. Add cherries. Cook and stir over medium heat until thickened and bubbly. Cook and stir for 2 minutes more. Remove saucepan from heat. Stir in the juice. Serve warm. Or, cool to room temperature to serve.

Nutrition Facts				
Serving Size	35 g			
Servings Per Recipe	16			
Amount per serving			High Fat/Sugar Comparison	
Calories		26	40	
Calories from fat		0	0	
	% Daily Value*		% Daily Value*	
Total Fat	0 g	**0%**	0 g	**0%**
Saturated Fat	0 g	**0%**	0 g	**0%**
Cholesterol	0 mg	**0%**	0 mg	**0%**
Sodium	0 mg	**0%**	0 mg	**0%**
Total Carbohydrate	9 g	**3%**	10 g	**3%**
Dietary Fiber	2 g	**8%**	0 g	**0%**
Sugars	2 g		8 g	
Other	5 g		0 g	
Protein	0 g		0 g	

*Percent of Daily Values on page a-22

Exchanges and 2 g Carbohydrates Per Serving

Breads	0.0	Vegetables	0.0	Fruits	0.2
Meats	0.0	Milk	0.0	Fats	0.0

Caramel Sauce

The fat quotient using ButterLike is 0% instead of 23%
100% less fat **100% less sugar**
50% less Calories

U.S.	Ingredients	Metric
1/2 cup	**Brown SugarLike**	100.00 g
2 Tbsp	**Liquid SugarLike**	42.50 g
1 Tbsp	**ButterLike Saute Butter**	14.00 g
1 Tbsp	Cornstarch	16.00 g
1/4 cup	Water	59.00 g
1/3 cup	Evaporated skim milk	85.00 g
1/2 tsp	Vanilla	2.50 g

Directions

In a heavy saucepan combine **Brown SugarLike** and cornstarch. Stir in water. Stir in **Liquid SugarLike** and evaporated milk. Cook and stir until bubbly, mixture may curdle. Cook and stir for 2 minutes more. Remove saucepan from heat; stir in **ButterLike** and vanilla. Serve warm or cool over ice cream, baked fruits, or cake. Cover and chill any leftovers.

Nutrition Facts				
Serving Size	39 g			
Servings Per Recipe	8			
Amount per serving			High Fat/Sugar Comparison	
Calories	50		100	
Calories from fat	0		25	
	% Daily Value*		% Daily Value*	
Total Fat	0 g	**0%**	2.5 g	**4%**
Saturated Fat	0 g	**0%**	1.5 g	**8%**
Cholesterol	0 mg	**0%**	10 mg	**3%**
Sodium	15 mg	**1%**	30 mg	**1%**
Total Carbohydrate	19 g	**6%**	18 g	**6%**
Dietary Fiber	4 g	**0%**	0 g	**0%**
Sugars	0 g		15 g	
Other	12 g		0 g	
Protein	1 g		0 g	

*Percent of Daily Values on page a-22

Exchanges and 3 g Carbohydrates Per Serving

Breads	0.1	Vegetables	0.0	Fruits	0.0
Meats	0.0	Milk	0.1	Fats	0.1

Caramel Sauce and Old-Fashioned Ice Cream Roll, page 115

Peanut Sauce

The Fat Quotient using **ButterLike** is **51%** instead of **78%**
63% less fat **0% less sugar**
44% less Calories

U.S.	Ingredients	Metric
1/3 cup	**ButterLike Saute Butter**	75.00 g
1/3 cup	Low fat peanut butter, crunchy	96.00 g
1/4 cup	Boiling water	59.00 g
1 Tbsp	Grated gingerroot or 1 tsp ground	5.40 g
1 Tbsp	Lemon juice	15.00 g
1 tsp	Red pepper flakes	2.00 g
1 tsp	Dried red pepper, crushed	2.00 g

Directions

Mix all ingredients until smooth. Baste on barbequed poultry, fish, or meat. Excellent sauteed on meat and served with pasta. It turns your pasta and chicken into Thai chicken.

Nutrition Facts				
Serving Size	42 g			
Servings Per Recipe	6			
Amount per serving			High Fat/Sugar Comparison	
Calories	124		220	
Calories from fat	70		170	
	% Daily Value*		% Daily Value*	
Total Fat	7 g	**11%**	19 g	**29%**
Saturated Fat	1.5 g	**8%**	7 g	**35%**
Cholesterol	0 mg	**0%**	20 mg	**7%**
Sodium	115 mg	**5%**	170 mg	**7%**
Total Carbohydrate	12 g	**4%**	6 g	**2%**
Dietary Fiber	1 g	**4%**	2 g	**8%**
Sugars	2 g		2 g	
Other	0 g		0 g	
Protein	4 g		6 g	

*Percent of Daily Values on page a-22

Exchanges and 11 g Carbohydrates Per Serving

Breads	0.7	Vegetables	0.0	Fruits	0.0
Meats	0.3	Milk	0.0	Fats	1.4

Orange Sauce

The Fat Quotient using **ButterLike** is **20%** instead of **60%**
81% less fat **0% less sugar**
44% less Calories

U.S.	Ingredients	Metric
1/4 cup	**ButterLike Saute Butter**	56.00 g
1/4 cup	Lemon juice	61.00 g
2 Tbsp	Lemon peel, grated	12.00 g
1/2 tsp	Salt	3.00 g
1	Clove garlic, crushed	3.00 g
1/2 cup	Orange juice concentrate	142.00 g

Directions

Place all ingredients in a blender and blend until smooth. This sauce is great on poultry or fish. It will cover 1 1/2 lbs of chicken.

Nutrition Facts				
Serving Size	46 g			
Servings Per Recipe	6			
Amount per serving			High Fat/Sugar Comparison	
Calories	67		120	
Calories from fat	15		70	
	% Daily Value*		% Daily Value*	
Total Fat	1.5 g	**2%**	8 g	**12%**
Saturated Fat	0 g	**0%**	5 g	**25%**
Cholesterol	0 mg	**0%**	20 mg	**7%**
Sodium	200 mg	**8%**	280 mg	**12%**
Total Carbohydrate	13 g	**4%**	10 g	**3%**
Dietary Fiber	0 g	**0%**	0 g	**0%**
Sugars	0 g		0 g	
Other	0 g		0 g	
Protein	1 g		1 g	

*Percent of Daily Values on page a-22

Exchanges and 13 g Carbohydrates Per Serving

Breads	0.2	Vegetables	0.0	Fruits	0.6
Meats	0.0	Milk	0.0	Fats	0.3

Chocolate Syrup

The fat quotient using **ButterLike** is **5%** instead of **40%**	
95% less fat	**93% less sugar**
55% less Calories	

U.S.	Ingredients	Metric
1/2 cup	**ButterLike Baking Butter**	114.00 g
1 1/2 cup	**Granulated SugarLike**	300.00 g
1/4 cup	Cocoa	60.00 g
1/2 cup	Skim milk	123.00 g
1 tsp	Vanilla extract	5.00 g

Directions

Combine all ingredients in a large microwavable bowl, large enough to prevent boiling over. Cook on high for 30 seconds; stir. Repeat cooking and stirring until **ButterLike** and **SugarLike** are dissolved. Pour into a container and let cool. Cover and store in refrigerator.

Nutrition Facts				
Serving Size	60 g			
Servings Per Recipe	10			
Amount per serving			High Fat/Sugar Comparison	
Calories		98	220	
Calories from fat		5	90	
	% Daily Value*		% Daily Value*	
Total Fat	0.5 g	**1%**	10 g	**15%**
Saturated Fat	0 g	**0%**	6 g	**30%**
Cholesterol	0 mg	**0%**	30 mg	**10%**
Sodium	60 mg	**3%**	110 mg	**5%**
Total Carbohydrate	37 g	**12%**	32 g	**11%**
Dietary Fiber	7 g	**28%**	0 g	**0%**
Sugars	2 g		30 g	
Other	22 g		0 g	
Protein	1 g		1 g	

*Percent of Daily Values on page a-22

Exchanges and 8 g Carbohydrates Per Serving					
Breads	0.4	Vegetables	0.0	Fruits	0.0
Meats	0.0	Milk	0.1	Fats	0.1

Easy Caramel Sauce

The fat quotient using **ButterLike** is **24%** instead of **65%**	
85% less fat	**100% less sugar**
58% less Calories	

U.S.	Ingredients	Metric
1 cup	**ButterLike Saute Butter**	224.00 g
1 cup	**Granulated SugarLike**	200.00 g
1 cup	Evaporated skim milk	256.00 g

Directions

Combine all ingredients in a heavy saucepan. Bring to a slow rolling boil and boil for 2 hour until, darkened in color and reduced in size. Cool and store. Pour over ice cream. Or, use in any recipe calling for caramel. It will be easier to spoon out if placed in a microwave for 30 seconds before serving.

Nutrition Facts				
Serving Size	43 g			
Servings Per Recipe	16			
Amount per serving			High Fat/Sugar Comparison	
Calories		75	180	
Calories from fat		20	120	
	% Daily Value*		% Daily Value*	
Total Fat	2 g	**3%**	13 g	**20%**
Saturated Fat	0.5 g	**3%**	8 g	**40%**
Cholesterol	5 mg	**2%**	35 mg	**12%**
Sodium	20 mg	**1%**	1400 mg	**6%**
Total Carbohydrate	19 g	**6%**	14 g	**5%**
Dietary Fiber	3 g	**12%**	0 g	**0%**
Sugars	0 g		12 g	
Other	9 g		0 g	
Protein	2 g		1 g	

*Percent of Daily Values on page a-22

Exchanges and 7 g Carbohydrates Per Serving					
Breads	0.3	Vegetables	0.0	Fruits	0.0
Meats	0.0	Milk	0.2	Fats	0.4

Coconut Sauce

The Fat Quotient using **ButterLike** is **38%** instead of **81%**
85% less fat **100% less sugar**
68% less Calories

U.S.	**Ingredients**	Metric
1/4 cup + 3 Tbsp	**ButterLike Saute Butter**	99.00 g
1 cup	Shallots or red onion, minced	14.40 g
4 cloves	Garlic, minced	12.00 g
3 Tbsp	Fresh ginger, finely minced	18.00 g
1 tsp	Ground turmeric	2.20 g
1/2-1 tsp	Red pepper flakes, crushed	50.00 g
1/2 tsp	Ground coriander	.80 g
2 cup	Fat free chicken broth	490.00 g
3/4 cup	Skim milk	184.00 g
1 1/2 tsp	Coconut flavoring	7.40 g
1/4 cup	Lemon juice	61.00 g

Directions

In a wide frying pan, combine 3 Tbsp **ButterLike**, shallots, garlic, ginger, turmeric, red pepper, and coriander. Cook over medium heat, stirring often, until shallots are very soft. Add **ButterLike**, chicken broth, skim milk, and coconut flavoring. Cook, stirring, until hot. Stir in lemon juice. Serve hot or cold with vegetables.

Nutrition Facts				
Serving Size	94 g			
Servings Per Recipe	10			
Amount per serving			High Fat/Sugar Comparison	
Calories	60		190	
Calories from fat	20		150	
	% Daily Value*		% Daily Value*	
Total Fat	2.5 g	**4%**	17 g	**26%**
Saturated Fat	0.5 g	**3%**	9 g	**45%**
Cholesterol	0 mg	**0%**	0 mg	**0%**
Sodium	25 mg	**1%**	240 mg	**10%**
Total Carbohydrate	9 g	**3%**	6 g	**2%**
Dietary Fiber	0 g	**0%**	0 g	**0%**
Sugars	2 g		0 g	
Other	0 g		0 g	
Protein	2 g		4 g	

*Percent of Daily Values on page a-22

Exchanges and 9 g Carbohydrates Per Serving					
Breads	0.2	Vegetables	0.1	Fruits	0.0
Meats	0.1	Milk	0.1	Fats	0.3

Rich Hot Fudge Sauce

The fat quotient using **ButterLike** is **22%** instead of **45%**
72% less fat **53% less sugar**
42% less Calories

U.S.	Ingredients	Metric
1/4 cup	**ButterLike Saute Butter**	56.00 g
2/3 cup	**Granulated SugarLike**	133.00 g
3/4 cup	Reduced fat chocolate pieces	180.00 g
1 can	Evaporated skim milk (5 oz)	142.00 g

Directions

In a heavy saucepan, melt chocolate. Add **ButterLike** and **SugarLike**; gradually stir in evaporated milk. Bring mixture to a boil; reduce heat. Boil gently over low heat for 8 minutes, stirring frequently. Remove pan from heat. Cool slightly. Serve warm over ice cream. Cover and chill leftovers.

Peanut Butter-Fudge Sauce: Prepare as above except, after cooking for 8 minutes, stir in 1/4 cup reduced fat peanut butter. Makes 1 1/2 cups.

Nutrition Facts				
Serving Size	43 g			
Servings Per Recipe	12			
Amount per serving			High Fat/Sugar Comparison	
Calories	104		180	
Calories from fat	25		80	
	% Daily Value*		% Daily Value*	
Total Fat	2.5 g	**4%**	9 g	**14%**
Saturated Fat	2.5 g	**13%**	6 g	**30%**
Cholesterol	0 mg	**0%**	15 mg	**5%**
Sodium	15 mg	**1%**	70 mg	**3%**
Total Carbohydrate	24 g	**8%**	22 g	**7%**
Dietary Fiber	3 g	**12%**	0 g	**0%**
Sugars	9 g		19 g	
Other	8 g		0 g	
Protein	2 g		2 g	

*Percent of Daily Values on page a-22

Exchanges and 13 g Carbohydrates Per Serving					
Breads	0.8	Vegetables	0.0	Fruits	0.0
Meats	0.0	Milk	0.1	Fats	0.8

Hot Fudge Sauce

The Fat Quotient using **ButterLike** is **4%** instead of **42%**
95% less fat **93% less sugar**
55% less Calories

U.S.	Ingredients	Metric
1/2 cup	**ButterLike Baking Butter**	114.00 g
1 1/2 cup	**Granulated SugarLike**	300.00 g
1/4 cup	Cocoa	60.00 g
1/2 cup	Skim milk	123.00 g
1 tsp	Vanilla	5.00 g

Directions

Combine all ingredients, except vanilla. Cook and stir until **ButterLike** is dissolved. Cook until sauce holds together in a soft ball. Stir in 1 tsp vanilla. Add cherry extract for a cherry fudge sauce.

Exchanges and 8 g Carbohydrates Per Serving					
Breads	0.4	Vegetables	0.0	Fruits	0.0
Meats	0.0	Milk	0.1	Fats	0.1

Nutrition Facts				
Serving Size	60 g			
Servings Per Recipe	10			
Amount per serving			High Fat/Sugar Comparison	
Calories	100		220	
Calories from fat	5		90	
	% Daily Value*		% Daily Value*	
Total Fat	0.5 g	**1%**	10 g	**15%**
Saturated Fat	0 g	**0%**	6 g	**30%**
Cholesterol	0 mg	**0%**	30 mg	**10%**
Sodium	60mg	**3%**	110 mg	**5%**
Total Carbohydrate	37 g	**12%**	32 g	**11%**
Dietary Fiber	7 g	**28%**	0 g	**0%**
Sugars	2 g		30 g	
Other	22 g		0 g	
Protein	1 g		1 g	

*Percent of Daily Values on page a-22

Lemon Sauce

The fat quotient using **ButterLike** is **0%** instead of **23%**
100% less fat **100% less sugar**
47% less Calories

U.S.	Ingredients	Metric
1/4 cup	**Granulated SugarLike**	50.00 g
2 tsp	**ButterLike Saute Butter**	9.33 g
1/2 cup	Water	119.00 g
1 Tbsp	Cornstarch	8.00 g
1/4 tsp	Lemon peel, finely shredded	.50 g
1 Tbsp	Lemon juice	15.00 g

Directions

In a small saucepan combine **SugarLike**, water, cornstarch, lemon peel, and lemon juice. Cook and stir until thickened and bubbly. Cook and stir 2 minutes more. Remove from heat; stir in **ButterLike**. Serve warm.

Lemon Sauce

Nutrition Facts				
Serving Size	40 g			
Servings Per Recipe	5			
Amount per serving			High Fat/Sugar Comparison	
Calories	32		60	
Calories from fat	0		15	
	% Daily Value*		% Daily Value*	
Total Fat	0 g	**0%**	1.5 g	**2%**
Saturated Fat	0 g	**0%**	1 g	**5%**
Cholesterol	0 mg	**0%**	5 mg	**2%**
Sodium	0 mg	**0%**	20 mg	**1%**
Total Carbohydrate	12 g	**4%**	12 g	**4%**
Dietary Fiber	2 g	**8%**	0 g	**0%**
Sugars	0 g		10 g	
Other	7 g		0 g	
Protein	0 g		0 g	

*Percent of Daily Values on page a-22

Exchanges and 3 g Carbohydrates Per Serving					
Breads	0.1	Vegetables	0.0	Fruits	0.0
Meats	0.0	Milk	0.0	Fats	0.1

Whipped Cream

The fat quotient using ButterLike is 80% instead of 64%
20% less fat **100% less sugar**
36% less Calories

U.S.	Ingredients	Metric
1/4 cup	**Granulated SugarLike**	50.00 g
1 tsp	Vanilla	5.00 g
7/8 cup	Lite whipping cream	209.00 g

Directions

In a chilled bowl, beat whipping cream with chilled beaters of an electric mixer on medium speed until peaks form. Add **SugarLike** and vanilla. Serve on top of pies, cakes, hot drinks or cream puffs.

Flavored Whipped Cream: Prepare as above, except add one of the following along with the vanilla: 2 Tbsp unsweetened cocoa powder plus 1 Tbsp additional **SugarLike**; 2 Tbsp amaretto or coffee, hazelnut, orange, or praline liqueur; 1 tsp instant coffee crystals; 1/2 tsp almond extract; 1/2 tsp finely shredded lemon, orange, or lime peel; or 1/4 tsp ground cinnamon, nutmeg, or ginger.

Nutrition Facts				
Serving Size	17 g			
Servings Per Recipe	16			
Amount per serving			High Fat/Sugar Comparison	
Calories	45		70	
Calories from fat	35		45	
	% Daily Value*		% Daily Value*	
Total Fat	4 g	**6%**	5 g	**8%**
Saturated Fat	2.5 g	**13%**	3.5 g	**18%**
Cholesterol	15 mg	**5%**	20 mg	**7%**
Sodium	0 mg	**0%**	5 mg	**0%**
Total Carbohydrate	4 g	**1%**	4 g	**1%**
Dietary Fiber	1 g	**4%**	0 g	**0%**
Sugars	0 g		3 g	
Other	2 g		0 g	
Protein	0 g		0 g	

*Percent of Daily Values on page a-22

Exchanges and 1 g Carbohydrates Per Serving

Breads	0.0	Vegetables	0.0	Fruits	0.0
Meats	0.0	Milk	0.0	Fats	0.8

Vanilla Sauce

The Fat quotient using ButterLike is 0% instead of 64%
100% less fat **100% less sugar**
38% less Calories

U.S.	Ingredients	Metric
3 Tbsp	**Granulated SugarLike**	38.00 g
1	Egg	50.00 g
1/3 cup	Skim milk	82.00 g
1/2 cup	Evaporated skim milk	128.00 g
1 tsp	Vanilla extract	5.00 g

Directions

Place evaporated skim milk in freezer, just until the milk starts to freeze. In a small saucepan combine **SugarLike**, egg, and milk. Cook and stir until mixture is thickened and bubbly. Remove from heat. Cool mixture; chill at least 1 hour. Just before serving, beat the evaporated milk and vanilla until soft peaks form; fold into egg mixture. Cover and chill any leftovers.

Nutrition Facts				
Serving Size	25 g			
Servings Per Recipe	12			
Amount per serving			High Fat/Sugar Comparison	
Calories	24		70	
Calories from fat	0		45	
	% Daily Value*		% Daily Value*	
Total Fat	0 g	**0%**	5 g	**8%**
Saturated Fat	0 g	**0%**	3 g	**15%**
Cholesterol	20 mg	**7%**	50 mg	**17%**
Sodium	20 mg	**1%**	10 mg	**0%**
Total Carbohydrate	5 g	**2%**	4 g	**1%**
Dietary Fiber	1 g	**4%**	0 g	**0%**
Sugars	0 g		3 g	
Other	2 g		0 g	
Protein	2 g		1 g	

*Percent of Daily Values on page a-22

Exchanges and 3 g Carbohydrates Per Serving

Breads	0.0	Vegetables	0.0	Fruits	0.0
Meats	0.1	Milk	0.1	Fats	0.0

Teriyaki Sauce

The Fat Quotient using **ButterLike** is **31%** instead of **90%**
86% less fat **100% less sugar**
60% less Calories

U.S.	Ingredients	Metric
2 Tbsp	**Catsup**, page 245	65.00 g
1/4 cup	**ButterLike Saute Butter**	56.00 g
1/4 cup	Soy sauce	72.00 g
1 Tbsp	White vinegar	15.00 g
1/4 tsp	Pepper	.53 g
2 cloves	Garlic, minced	6.00 g

Directions

Follow directions for **Catsup**.

Combine 2 tablespoons Catsup, **ButterLike**, soy sauce, vinegar, pepper, and garlic. Serve with pork, chicken, shrimp, fish, or vegetables.

Nutrition Facts				
Serving Size	43 g			
Servings Per Recipe	5			
Amount per serving			High Fat/Sugar Comparison	
Calories	44		110	
Calories from fat	15		100	
	% Daily Value*		% Daily Value*	
Total Fat	1.5 g	**2%**	11 g	**17%**
Saturated Fat	0.5 g	**3%**	1.5 g	**8%**
Cholesterol	0 mg	**0%**	0 mg	**0%**
Sodium	870 mg	**36%**	880 mg	**37%**
Total Carbohydrate	6 g	**2%**	3 g	**1%**
Dietary Fiber	0 g	**0%**	0 g	**0%**
Sugars	0 g		1 g	
Other	1 g		0 g	
Protein	2 g		1 g	

*Percent of Daily Values on page a-22

Exchanges and 5 g Carbohydrates Per Serving

Breads	0.2	Vegetables	0.2	Fruits	0.0
Meats	0.0	Milk	0.0	Fats	0.3

Raspberry Glaze

The fat quotient using **ButterLike** is **15%** instead of **45%**
88% less fat **89% less sugar**
63% less Calories

U.S.	Ingredients	Metric
2 Tbsp	**ButterLike Saute Butter**	28.00 g
1/2 cup	**Granulated SugarLike**	100.00 g
1 cup	Raspberries, fresh or frozen	144.00 g
1/4 cup	Red wine vinegar	64.00 g
2 Tbsp	Fresh cilantro	24.00 g
1/2 tsp	Pepper	1.00 g

Directions

Place all ingredients in a blender. Blend until smooth. This sauce is excellent brushed on barbequed chicken, steak, and fish. The glaze may also be added to sauteed chicken, steak or fish.

Nutrition Facts				
Serving Size	60 g			
Servings Per Recipe	6			
Amount per serving			High Fat/Sugar Comparison	
Calories	60		160	
Calories from fat	5		80	
	% Daily Value*		% Daily Value*	
Total Fat	1 g	**2%**	8 g	**12%**
Saturated Fat	0 g	**0%**	5 g	**25%**
Cholesterol	0 mg	**0%**	20 mg	**7%**
Sodium	0 mg	**0%**	85 mg	**4%**
Total Carbohydrate	21 g	**7%**	20 g	**7%**
Dietary Fiber	5 g	**20%**	1 g	**4%**
Sugars	2 g		18 g	
Other	12 g		0 g	
Protein	1 g		0 g	

*Percent of Daily Values on page a-22

Exchanges and 4 g Carbohydrates Per Serving

Breads	0.1	Vegetables	0.0	Fruits	0.2
Meats	0.0	Milk	0.0	Fats	0.1

Spicy Chili Sauce

The fat quotient using ButterLike is 0% instead of 50%
100% less fat **50% less sugar**
58% less Calories

U.S.	Ingredients	Metric
2 Tbsp	**ButterLike Saute Butter**	28.00 g
2 Tbsp	**Brown SugarLike**	25.00 g
1 cup	Whole tomatoes	206.00 g
1/2 cup	Onion, chopped	80.00 g
3 Tbsp	Lemon juice	46.00 g
2 tsp	Tarragon vinegar	11.00 g
1 clove	Garlic, minced	3.00 g
1/2 tsp	Liquid hot pepper seasoning	2.50 g
1/4 tsp	Dry mustard	.60 g
1/4 tsp	Salt	1.50 g

Directions

Pulse tomatoes in blender or food processor 3 or 4 times. In small pan, stir together all ingredients. Bring mixture to a boil over high heat. Reduce heat and simmer, uncovered 5 minutes. Makes 1 1/4 cups.

Nutrition Facts				
Serving Size	34 g			
Servings Per Recipe	12			
Amount per serving			High Fat/Sugar Comparison	
Calories	19		45	
Calories from fat	0		20	
	% Daily Value*		% Daily Value*	
Total Fat	0 g	**0%**	2.5 g	**4%**
Saturated Fat	0 g	**0%**	0 g	**0%**
Cholesterol	0 mg	**0%**	0 mg	**0%**
Sodium	85 mg	**4%**	250 mg	**10%**
Total Carbohydrate	4 g	**1%**	5 g	**2%**
Dietary Fiber	1 g	**4%**	1 g	**4%**
Sugars	1 g		2 g	
Other	2 g		0 g	
Protein	0 g		1 g	

*Percent of Daily Values on page a-22

Exchanges and 1 g Carbohydrates Per Serving

Breads	0.1	Vegetables	0.2	Fruits	0.0
Meats	0.0	Milk	0.0	Fats	0.1

Hollandaise Sauce

The fat quotient using ButterLike is 60% instead of 100%
74% less fat **0% less sugar**
52% less Calories

U.S.	Ingredients	Metric
1/2 cup	**ButterLike Saute Butter**	112.00 g
3	Egg yolks, beaten	50.00 g
1 Tbsp	Water	15.00 g
1 Tbsp	Lemon juice	15.00 g
Dash	Salt	.75 g
Dash	White pepper	.30 g

Directions

In the top of a double boiler combine egg yolks, water, lemon juice, salt, and pepper. Add 1/3 of **ButterLike**. Place over boiling water (upper pan should not touch water). Cook, stirring rapidly with a whisk, while sauce begins to thicken. Add the remaining **ButterLike**, 1/3 at a time, stirring constantly. Continue to cook and stir until sauce thickens (about 2 minutes more). Immediately remove from heat. If sauce is too thick or curdles,whisk in 1-2 tablespoons hot water. Serve with cooked vegetables, poultry, fish, or eggs.

Nutrition Facts				
Serving Size	32 g			
Servings Per Recipe	6			
Amount per serving			High Fat/Sugar Comparison	
Calories	81		170	
Calories from fat	50		170	
	% Daily Value*		% Daily Value*	
Total Fat	5 g	**8%**	19 g	**29%**
Saturated Fat	1.5 g	**8%**	11 g	**55%**
Cholesterol	110 mg	**37%**	150 mg	**50%**
Sodium	55 mg	**2%**	210 mg	**9%**
Total Carbohydrate	6 g	**2%**	0 g	**0%**
Dietary Fiber	0 g	**0%**	0 g	**0%**
Sugars	0 g		0 g	
Other	0 g		0 g	
Protein	2 g		2 g	

*Percent of Daily Values on page a-22

Exchanges and 6 g Carbohydrates Per Serving

Breads	0.4	Vegetables	0.0	Fruits	0.0
Meats	0.2	Milk	0.0	Fats	0.9

Bearnaise Sauce

The fat quotient using **ButterLike** is **56%** instead of **95%**
74% less fat **0% less sugar**
56% less Calories

U.S.	Ingredients	Metric
1/2 cup	**ButterLike Saute Butter**	112.00 g
3 Tbsp	White wine vinegar	45.00 g
1 tsp	Green onion, finely chopped	3.33 g
1/4 tsp	Dried tarragon, crushed	.20 g
Dash	Dried chervil, crushed	.08 g
1/8 tsp	White pepper	.30 g
3	Egg yolks, beaten	50.00 g
1 Tbsp	Water	15.00 g

Directions

In a small saucepan, combine vinegar, green onion, tarragon, chervil, and pepper. Bring to a boil; boil, uncovered, on high 2 minutes or until reduced by half. In top of a double boiler, combine vinegar mixture, egg yolks, and water. Add 1/3 cup **ButterLike**. Place over boiling water; upper pan should not touch water. Cook, stirring rapidly with whisk, until sauce begins to thicken. Add the remaining **ButterLike**, 1/3 at a time, stirring constantly. Continue to cook and stir 1-2 more minutes until sauce thickens. Immediately remove saucepan from heat. If sauce is too thick or curdles, immediately whisk in 1-2 tablespoons hot water. Serve with beef, pork, and poultry.

Nutrition Facts				
Serving Size	38 g			
Servings Per Recipe	6			
Amount per serving			High Fat/Sugar Comparison	
Calories	80		180	
Calories from fat	50		170	
	% Daily Value*		% Daily Value*	
Total Fat	5 g	**8%**	19 g	**29%**
Saturated Fat	1.5 g	**8%**	11 g	**55%**
Cholesterol	110 mg	**37%**	185 mg	**62%**
Sodium	0 mg	**0%**	160 mg	**7%**
Total Carbohydrate	6 g	**2%**	0 g	**0%**
Dietary Fiber	0 g	**0%**	0 g	**0%**
Sugars	0 g		0 g	
Other	0 g		0 g	
Protein	2 g		2 g	

*Percent of Daily Values on page a-22

Exchanges and 6 g Carbohydrates Per Serving

Breads	0.4	Vegetables	0.0	Fruits	0.0
Meats	0.2	Milk	0.0	Fats	0.9

Bordelaise Sauce

The Fat Quotient using **ButterLike** is **23%** instead of **80%**
78% less fat **0% less sugar**
22% less Calories

U.S.	Ingredients	Metric
3 Tbsp	**ButterLike Saute Butter**	42.00 g
1 1/2 cup	Water	356.00 g
3/4 cup	Dry red wine	177.00 g
2 Tbsp	Shallot or onion, finely chopped	1.80 g
1 tsp	Instant beef bouillon granules	4.00 g
1/2 tsp	Dried thyme	.60 g
1	Bay leaf	.10 g
2 Tbsp	All-purpose flour	14.40 g
1 Tbsp	Snipped fresh parsley	3.80 g

Nutrition Facts				
Serving Size	75 g			
Servings Per Recipe	8			
Amount per serving			High Fat/Sugar Comparison	
Calories	39		50	
Calories from fat	5		40	
	% Daily Value*		% Daily Value*	
Total Fat	1 g	**2%**	4.5 g	**7%**
Saturated Fat	0 g	**0%**	3 g	**15%**
Cholesterol	0 mg	**0%**	10 mg	**3%**
Sodium	95 mg	**4%**	140 mg	**6%**
Total Carbohydrate	4 g	**1%**	2 g	**1%**
Dietary Fiber	0 g	**0%**	0 g	**0%**
Sugars	0 g		0 g	
Other	0 g		0 g	
Protein	1 g		0 g	

*Percent of Daily Values on page a-22

Directions

In a medium saucepan, combine water, red wine, shallot or onion, bouillon granules, thyme, and bay leaf. Bring to a boil, reduce heat. Simmer, uncovered, for 15-20 minutes (you should have about 1 1/3 cups). Remove bay leaf. Stir together **ButterLike** and flour. Add 1/2 cup of wine mixture to paste. Stir until flour is well blended. Add to remaining wine mixture. Cook and stir until thickened and bubbly. Cook and stir for 1 minute more. Stir in parsley. Serve with broiled or grilled meats.

Exchanges and 4 g Carbohydrates Per Serving					
Breads	0.2	Vegetables	0.0	Fruits	0.0
Meats	0.0	Milk	0.0	Fats	0.3

Mustard Cream Sauce

The fat quotient using **ButterLike** is **23%** instead of **63%**
71% less fat **100% more sugar**
24% less Calories

U.S.	Ingredients	Metric
3 Tbsp	**ButterLike Saute Butter**	42.00 g
1/3 cup	Dry white wine	79.00 g
3 Tbsp	Shallots, finely chopped	3.00 g
7/8 cup	Skim milk	214.00 g
4 tsp	All-purpose flour	9.60 g
1/8 tsp	White pepper	.30 g
1 Tbsp	Dijon-style mustard	15.00 g

Directions

Combine wine and shallots. Bring to a boil; reduce heat. Simmer, uncovered, for 8-10 minutes or until the liquid is reduced to about 3 Tbsp, stirring occasionally. Stir **ButterLike** and milk into flour. Stir into wine mixture with white pepper. Cook and stir over medium heat until thickened and bubbly. Stir in mustard. Cook and stir for 1 minute more. May be served over chicken, meat, or vegetables.

Note: Substitute 1/3 cup chicken broth for wine if desired.

Nutrition Facts				
Serving Size	91 g			
Servings Per Recipe	4			
Amount per serving			High Fat/Sugar Comparison	
Calories	76		100	
Calories from fat	20		70	
	% Daily Value*		% Daily Value*	
Total Fat	2 g	**3%**	7 g	**11%**
Saturated Fat	0.5 g	**3%**	4.5 g	**23%**
Cholesterol	5 mg	**2%**	20 mg	**7%**
Sodium	50 mg	**2%**	50 mg	**2%**
Total Carbohydrate	9 g	**3%**	6 g	**2%**
Dietary Fiber	0 g	**0%**	0 g	**0%**
Sugars	3 g		0 g	
Other	0 g		0 g	
Protein	3 g		2 g	

*Percent of Daily Values on page a-22

Exchanges and 9 g Carbohydrates Per Serving					
Breads	0.3	Vegetables	0.0	Fruits	0.0
Meats	0.0	Milk	0.2	Fats	0.5

Barbecue Sauce

The Fat Quotient using **ButterLike** is **0%** instead of **0%**
0% less fat **71% less sugar**
25% less Calories

U.S.	Ingredients	Metric
2 Tbsp	**Granulated SugarLike**	25.00 g
1 cup	**Catsup**, page 245	1043.00 g
1/2 cup	Water	119.00 g
1/4 cup	Finely chopped onion	40.00 g
1/4 cup	Vinegar	60.00 g
1 Tbsp	Worcestershire sauce	15.00 g
1/4 tsp	Celery seed	.40 g
1/4 tsp	Salt	1.50 g
	Several dashes hot pepper sauce	5.20 g

Directions

Follow directions for **Catsup**. In a saucepan combine **SugarLike**, catsup, water, onion, vinegar, worcestershire sauce, celery seed, salt, and hot pepper sauce. Bring to a boil; reduce heat. Simmer, uncovered, for 10-15 minutes or to desired consistency. Brush on beef, pork, or poultry during last 10-20 minutes of grilling or roasting. If desired, pass any remaining sauce. Makes 1 3/4 cups sauce.

Hot Barbecue Sauce: Prepare as above, except add 1 tsp chili powder and 1/2 tsp ground red pepper with the Catsup.

Nutrition Facts				
Serving Size	93 g			
Servings Per Recipe	14			
Amount per serving			High Fat/Sugar Comparison	
Calories		30	40	
Calories from fat		0	0	
	% Daily Value*		% Daily Value*	
Total Fat	0 g	**0%**	0 g	**0%**
Saturated Fat	0 g	**0%**	0 g	**0%**
Cholesterol	0 mg	**0%**	0 mg	**0%**
Sodium	330 mg	**14%**	330 mg	**14%**
Total Carbohydrate	9 g	**3%**	9 g	**3%**
Dietary Fiber	1 g	**4%**	1 g	**4%**
Sugars	2 g		7 g	
Other	5 g		0 g	
Protein	1 g		1 g	

*Percent of Daily Values on page a-22

Exchanges and 3 g Carbohydrates Per Serving

Breads	0.0	Vegetables	0.6	Fruits	0.0
Meats	0.0	Milk	0.0	Fats	0.0

Tangy Mustard Barbecue Sauce: Prepare as above, except omit celery seed. Add 2 tablespoons prepared mustard and 1/4 teaspoon garlic powder with the Catsup.

Fresh Tomato Sauce

The fat quotient using **ButterLike** is **0%** instead of **60%**
100% less fat **0% less sugar**
49% less Calories

U.S.	Ingredients	Metric
1-2 Tbsp	**ButterLike Saute Butter**	14.00 g
1 small	Onion, chopped	80.00 g
2 cloves	Garlic, minced or crushed	6.00 g
2 cup	Canned tomatoes, chopped	412.00 g
2 Tbsp	Fresh basil, chopped	5.30 g
1 tsp	Dried oregano	1.50 g

Directions

Heat the **ButterLike** in a skillet over medium heat; add onion and saute 5 more minutes. Add garlic and cook 2 minutes. Add remaining ingredients. Salt and pepper to taste. Cook 5 minutes. Then reduce heat to low and simmer, uncovered, for 10-15 minutes. Serves as a side dish or over tortellini, ravioli, or rice. Makes 2 cups.

Exchanges and 3 g Carbohydrates Per Serving					
Breads	0.0	Vegetables	0.3	Fruits	0.0
Meats	0.0	Milk	0.0	Fats	0.0

Nutrition Facts				
Serving Size	65 g			
Servings Per Recipe	8			
Amount per serving			High Fat/Sugar Comparison	
Calories		23	45	
Calories from fat		0	30	
	% Daily Value*		% Daily Value*	
Total Fat	0 g	**0%**	3.5 g	**5%**
Saturated Fat	0 g	**0%**	0 g	**0%**
Cholesterol	0 mg	**0%**	0 mg	**0%**
Sodium	110 mg	**5%**	110 mg	**5%**
Total Carbohydrate	4 g	**1%**	3 g	**1%**
Dietary Fiber	1 g	**4%**	1 g	**4%**
Sugars	2 g		2 g	
Other	0 g		0 g	
Protein	1 g		1 g	

*Percent of Daily Values on page a-22

Catsup

The fat quotient using **ButterLike** is **0%** instead of **0%**
0% less fat **60% less sugar**
16% less Calories

U.S.	Ingredients	Metric
1 cup	**Granulated SugarLike**	200.00 g
8 lb	Tomatoes	3628.00 g
1/2 cup	Onion, chopped	80.00 g
1/4 tsp	Ground red pepper	.50 g
1 cup	White vinegar	240.00 g
1 1/2 inch	Stick cinnamon, broken	2.30 g
1 1/2 tsp	Whole cloves	2.40 g
1 tsp	Celery seed	1.60 g
1 Tbsp	Salt	18.00 g

Directions

Core and quarter tomatoes; drain. In an 8- or 10-quart kettle combine tomatoes, onion, and red pepper. Bring to a boil; cook 30 minutes, stirring often. Press through food mill or sieve. Discard seeds and skins. Return to kettle; add **SugarLike**. Bring to a boil; reduce heat. Simmer 3-4 hours or until reduced by half, stirring occasionally. In a saucepan bring vinegar cinnamon, cloves, and celery seed to a boil. Remove from heat. Strain vinegar mixture into tomato mixture; discard spices. Add salt. Simmer for 60 minutes or to desired consistency, stirring often.

Boiling-Water Canning: Ladle hot Catsup into hot, clean half-pint jars, leaving a 1/8-inch headspace. Wipe jar rims and adjust lids. Process in a boiling-water canner for 15 minutes.

Freezing: Place kettle in ice water; stir to cool. Ladle into freezer containers, leaving a 1/2-inch headspace. Seal, label, and freeze up to 10 months.

Nutrition Facts				
Serving Size	65 g			
Servings Per Recipe	64			
Amount per serving			High Fat/Sugar Comparison	
Calories		21	25	
Calories from fat		0	0	
	% Daily Value*		% Daily Value*	
Total Fat	0 g	**0%**	0 g	**0%**
Saturated Fat	0 g	**0%**	0 g	**0%**
Cholesterol	0 mg	**0%**	0 mg	**0%**
Sodium	230 mg	**10%**	230 mg	**10%**
Total Carbohydrate	5 g	**2%**	5 g	**2%**
Dietary Fiber	1 g	**4%**	1 g	**4%**
Sugars	2 g		5 g	
Other	2 g		0 g	
Protein	1 g		1 g	

*Percent of Daily Values on page a-22

Exchanges and 2 g Carbohydrates Per Serving					
Breads	0.0	Vegetables	0.5	Fruits	0.0
Meats	0.0	Milk	0.0	Fats	0.0

Cocktail Sauce

The Fat Quotient using **ButterLike** is **0%** instead of **0%**
0% less fat **57% less sugar**
12% less Calories

U.S.	Ingredients	Metric
3/4 cup	**Catsup**, page 245	782.00 g
2 Tbsp	Lemon/lime juice	31.00 g
2 Tbsp	Green onions, thinly sliced	20.00 g
1 Tbsp	Prepared horseradish	15.00 g
2 tsp	Worcestershire sauce, optional	10.00 g
1 tsp	Bottled hot pepper sauce, optional	5.20 g

Directions

Follow directions for **Catsup**. In a mixing bowl, combine Catsup, lemon juice, green onion, horseradish, worcestershire sauce, and hot pepper sauce. Cover and store in a refrigerator for up to 2 weeks. Serve with fish or seafood.

Nutrition Facts				
Serving Size	108 g			
Servings Per Recipe	8			
Amount per serving			High Fat/Sugar Comparison	
Calories		35	40	
Calories from fat		0	0	
	% Daily Value*		% Daily Value*	
Total Fat	0 g	**0%**	0 g	**0%**
Saturated Fat	0 g	**0%**	0 g	**0%**
Cholesterol	0 mg	**0%**	0 mg	**0%**
Sodium	390 mg	**16%**	390 mg	**16%**
Total Carbohydrate	9 g	**3%**	9 g	**3%**
Dietary Fiber	1 g	**4%**	1 g	**4%**
Sugars	3 g		7 g	
Other	5 g		0 g	
Protein	1 g		1 g	

*Percent of Daily Values on page a-22

Exchanges and 3 g Carbohydrates Per Serving

Breads	0.0	Vegetables	0.7	Fruits	0.0
Meats	0.0	Milk	0.0	Fats	0.0

Tartar Sauce

The Fat Quotient using **ButterLike** is **0%** instead of **96%**
100% less fat **100% less sugar**
84% less Calories

U.S.	Ingredients	Metric
2 Tbsp	**ButterLike Saute Butter**	28.00 g
1 cup	Fat free mayonnaise	256.00 g
1/4 cup	Sweet or dill pickles, finely chopped	39.00 g
1 Tbsp	Onion, finely chopped	10.00 g
1 Tbsp	Fresh parsley, snipped	4.00 g
1 Tbsp	Diced pimiento	12.00 g
1 tsp	Lemon juice	5.00 g

Directions

In a bowl, combine the **ButterLike,** mayonnaise, pickles, onion, parsley, pimiento, and lemon juice. Cover; chill for at least 2 hours before serving. Store in refrigerator for up to 2 weeks. Serve with fish or seafood. Makes 1 1/4 cups sauce.

Nutrition Facts				
Serving Size	35 g			
Servings Per Recipe	10			
Amount per serving			High Fat/Sugar Comparison	
Calories		25	160	
Calories from fat		0	160	
	% Daily Value*		% Daily Value*	
Total Fat	0 g	**0%**	17 g	**26%**
Saturated Fat	0 g	**0%**	3 g	**15%**
Cholesterol	0 mg	**0%**	15 mg	**5%**
Sodium	220 mg	**9%**	170 mg	**7%**
Total Carbohydrate	4 g	**1%**	0 g	**0%**
Dietary Fiber	0 g	**0%**	0 g	**0%**
Sugars	1 g		0 g	
Other	0 g		0 g	
Protein	0 g		0 g	

*Percent of Daily Values on page a-22

Exchanges and 4 g Carbohydrates Per Serving

Breads	0.2	Vegetables	0.0	Fruits	0.0
Meats	0.0	Milk	0.0	Fats	0.1

Pearl Onion Chutney

The Fat Quotient using ButterLike is 0% instead of 10%
100% less fat **33% less sugar**
27% less Calories

U.S.	Ingredients	Metric
2 Tbsp	**ButterLike Baking Butter**	28.00 g
1/4 cup	**Brown SugarLike**	50.00 g
10 small	Pearl onions	122.00 g
1 medium	Yellow onion, chopped	120.00 g
2 cloves	Garlic, minced	6.00 g
1 lb	Whole tomatoes, peeled, chopped	454.00 g
1/2 cup	Golden raisins	83.00 g
3/4 cup	Cider vinegar	180.00 g
1 tsp	Ground ginger	1.80 g
1/4 tsp	Ground cloves	.50 g
1/2 tsp	Ground nutmeg	1.00 g

Directions

Cut an X on the bottom of the pearl onions and blanch 60 seconds in boiling water. Carefully remove skin leaving the onions whole and base intact. Heat the **ButterLike** in a 3-quart heavy stainless steel saucepan and saute the chopped onion over medium heat for 3 minutes. Add the garlic and saute for 2 minutes. Add the rest of the ingredients and simmer on low, uncovered, until the sauce has thickened and the onions are tender, about 40 minutes. Salt and pepper to taste. Cool and spoon into a serving bowl. Makes 2 1/2 cups.

Nutrition Facts				
Serving Size	52 g			
Servings Per Recipe	20			
Amount per serving			High Fat/Sugar Comparison	
Calories	33		45	
Calories from fat	0		0	
	% Daily Value*		% Daily Value*	
Total Fat	0 g	**0%**	0.5 g	**1%**
Saturated Fat	0 g	**0%**	0 g	**0%**
Cholesterol	0 mg	**0%**	0 mg	**0%**
Sodium	75 mg	**3%**	70 mg	**3%**
Total Carbohydrate	9 g	**3%**	9 g	**3%**
Dietary Fiber	1 g	**4%**	1 g	**4%**
Sugars	4 g		6 g	
Other	2 g		0 g	
Protein	1 g		0 g	

*Percent of Daily Values on page a-22

Exchanges and 6 g Carbohydrates Per Serving					
Breads	0.0	Vegetables	0.4	Fruits	0.2
Meats	0.0	Milk	0.0	Fats	0.0

Garlic Dipping Butter

The fat quotient using ButterLike is 51% instead of 100%
82% less fat **0% less sugar**
35% less Calories

U.S.	Ingredients	Metric
1/2 cup	**ButterLike Saute Butter**	112.00 g
3 cloves	Garlic, minced	9.00 g

Directions

Saute garlic in a small amount of **ButterLike**. Add to the rest of the **ButterLike** and heat. Serve hot with vegetables, meats, or fish.

Exchanges and 6 g Carbohydrates Per Serving					
Breads	0.4	Vegetables	0.1	Fruits	0.0
Meats	0.0	Milk	0.0	Fats	0.6

Nutrition Facts				
Serving Size	20 g			
Servings Per Recipe	6			
Amount per serving			High Fat/Sugar Comparison	
Calories	53		150	
Calories from fat	25		150	
	% Daily Value*		% Daily Value*	
Total Fat	3 g	**5%**	17 g	**26%**
Saturated Fat	1 g	**5%**	10 g	**50%**
Cholesterol	5 mg	**2%**	45 mg	**15%**
Sodium	0 mg	**0%**	170 mg	**7%**
Total Carbohydrate	6 g	**2%**	1 g	**0%**
Dietary Fiber	0 g	**0%**	0 g	**0%**
Sugars	0 g		0 g	
Other	0 g		0 g	
Protein	1 g		0 g	

*Percent of Daily Values on page a-22

Lemon-Soy Marinade

The Fat Quotient using **ButterLike** is **20%** instead of **60%**
75% less fat **0% less sugar**
27% less Calories

U.S.	**Ingredients**	Metric
2 Tbsp	**ButterLike Saute Butter**	28.00 g
1/3 cup	Soy sauce	96.00 g
1/2 cup	Lemon juice	122.00 g
4	Garlic cloves, raw	12.00 g
2 Tbsp	Fresh ginger, minced	12.00 g

Directions

In a bowl, stir together **ButterLike**, soy sauce, lemon juice, garlic, and ginger. Makes about 1 cup.

Nutrition Facts				
Serving Size	34 g			
Servings Per Recipe	8			
Amount per serving			High Fat/Sugar Comparison	
Calories	22		30	
Calories from fat	5		15	
	% Daily Value*		% Daily Value*	
Total Fat	0.5 g	**1%**	2 g	**3%**
Saturated Fat	0 g	**0%**	0 g	**0%**
Cholesterol	0 mg	**0%**	0 mg	**0%**
Sodium	690 mg	**29%**	690 mg	**29%**
Total Carbohydrate	4 g	**1%**	3 g	**1%**
Dietary Fiber	0 g	**0%**	0 g	**0%**
Sugars	0 g		0 g	
Other	0 g		0 g	
Protein	1 g		1 g	

*Percent of Daily Values on page a-22

Exchanges and 4 g Carbohydrates Per Serving

Breads	0.1	Vegetables	0.1	Fruits	0.1
Meats	0.0	Milk	0.0	Fats	0.1

Side Dishes

Brown and Wild Rice Pilaf, page 267; Marinade Barbeque Flank Steak, page 145; and Pickled Beets, page 67

I am quite pleased with the selection of side dish recipes put together in this Cookbook. There are many sauté recipes (indicated with a saute symbol), and recipes for buttery tasting vegetables, that are not normally found in a low fat cookbook. Now there is no reason to give up eating your favorite foods because they were too high in calories or fat. Simply prepare them using the Bateman products and they will be rich, flavorful, and healthy too.

Tips on successful side dish cooking using the Bateman Products

- Please read "Tips on cooking low fat, low calorie, low cholesterol and sugar free main dishes". page 127.

Sauteing with ButterLike Saute Butter

- Add **Saute Butter** to a non-stick pan **before** heating to saute vegetables or meats.
- Add enough **Saute Butter** to slightly cover the vegetables and meat. Adjust the size of the pan to fit the amount of the items to be cooked.
- If the **Saute Butter** sticks to the pan, cover it for a few minutes.
- If items need to be browned, some sticking may occur. Sprinkling a small amount of water into the pan and stirring may assist in browning.

Old-Fashioned Baked Beans

The Fat Quotient using ButterLike is 5% instead of 28%
90% less fat **80% less sugar**
42% less Calories

U.S.	Ingredients	Metric
3/4 cup	**Brown SugarLike**	150.00 g
1 lb	Dry navy or great northern beans	454.00 g
1/4 lb	Lean bacon, cut up	113.00 g
1 cup	Onion, chopped	160.00 g
1/3 cup	Water	79.00 g
1 tsp	Dry mustard	2.40 g
1/2 tsp	Salt	3.00 g

Directions

Rinse beans. In a large pot combine beans and 8 cups water. Bring to a boil; reduce heat. Simmer for 2 minutes. Remove from heat. Cover and let stand for 1 hour. (Or place beans in a pot of water. Cover and let soak in a cool place overnight.) Drain and rinse beans. Return beans to pot. Stir in 8 cups fresh water. Bring to a boil; reduce heat. Cover and simmer for 1-1 1/2 hours or until tender, stirring occasionally. Drain beans, reserving liquid. In a 2 1/2-quart casserole dish combine the beans, bacon, and onion. Stir in 1 cup of the reserved bean liquid, **SugarLike**, water, dry mustard, salt, and pepper. Bake, covered, in a 300° oven for about 2 1/2 hours or to desired consistency, stirring occasionally. If necessary, add additional reserved bean liquid.

Nutrition Facts

Serving Size	80 g			
Servings Per Recipe	12			
Amount per serving			High Fat/Sugar Comparison	
Calories	92		160	
Calories from fat	5		45	
	% Daily Value*		% Daily Value*	
Total Fat	0.5 g	**1%**	5 g	**8%**
Saturated Fat	0 g	**0%**	1.5 g	**8%**
Cholesterol	5 mg	**2%**	10 mg	**3%**
Sodium	320 mg	**13%**	350 mg	**15%**
Total Carbohydrate	22 g	**7%**	22 g	**7%**
Dietary Fiber	3 g	**12%**	0 g	**0%**
Sugars	1 g		5 g	
Other	9 g		0 g	
Protein	6 g		6 g	

*Percent of Daily Values on page a-22

Exchanges and 10 g Carbohydrates Per Serving

Breads	0.5	Vegetables	0.2	Fruits	0.0
Meats	0.2	Milk	0.0	Fats	0.3

Easy Baked Beans

The Fat Quotient using ButterLike is 4% instead of 19%
85% less fat **63% less sugar**
30% less Calories

U.S.	Ingredients	Metric
1 cup	**Brown SugarLike**	200.00 g
1/2 lb	Lean bacon, sliced	227.00 g
4 large	Onions, thinly sliced (2 lb)	907.00 g
1 1/2 tsp	Dry mustard	3.60 g
1/2 cup	Cider vinegar	120.00 g
2 cans	Butter beans (15 oz each)	851.00 g
1 can	Green lima beans (15 oz)	425.00 g
1 can	Red kidney beans (15 oz)	425.00 g
1 can	White or navy beans (28 oz)	794.00 g

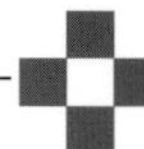

Directions

In a frying pan, cook bacon over medium heat until crisp. Lift out, drain, crumble, and set aside. Discard drippings, but do not wipe pan clean. Add onions to drippings and stir to coat. Stir in **SugarLike**, mustard, and vinegar. Cook over medium heat about 1 minute, stirring occasionally. Drain and rinse butter beans, lima beans, and kidney beans. In a 3-3 1/2-quart baking pan, combine butter beans, lima beans, kidney beans, and white or navy beans. Add onion-vinegar mixture and all but 2 Tbsp of the bacon; stir gently until blended. Bake, covered, 1 1/4-1 1/2 hours in a 350° oven until bubbly and heated through. Sprinkle with reserved bacon before serving.

Exchanges and 42 g Carbohydrates Per Serving					
Breads	3.2	Vegetables	0.9	Fruits	0.0
Meats	1.1	Milk	0.0	Fats	0.7

Nutrition Facts				
Serving Size	329 g			
Servings Per Recipe	12			
Amount per serving			High Fat/Sugar Comparison	
Calories	338		480	
Calories from fat	15		90	
	% Daily Value*		% Daily Value*	
Total Fat	1.5 g	**2%**	10 g	**15%**
Saturated Fat	0 g	**0%**	3.5 g	**18%**
Cholesterol	10 mg	**3%**	15 mg	**5%**
Sodium	910 mg	**38%**	950 mg	**40%**
Total Carbohydrate	72 g	**24%**	72 g	**24%**
Dietary Fiber	17 g	**68%**	13 g	**52%**
Sugars	10 g		27 g	
Other	13 g		0 g	
Protein	23 g		24 g	

*Percent of Daily Values on Page a-22

Buttered Green Beans and Onions

The Fat Quotient using ButterLike is **13%** instead of **45%**
78% less fat **0% less sugar**
23% less Calories

U.S.	Ingredients	Metric
3 Tbsp	**ButterLike Saute Butter**	42.00 g
2 lb	Frozen cut green beans	907.00 g
1 clove	Garlic	3.00 g
1/4 cup	Minced parsley	15.00 g
1/2 tsp	Salt	3.00 g
Dash	Pepper	.26 g
Dash	Ground nutmeg	.28 g
1 lb	Small white onions, drained	454.00 g

Directions

Cook beans according to package directions until tender-crisp. Drain; immerse in ice water until cool and drain again. Heat **ButterLike** in a wide frying pan over medium heat. Add garlic, parsley, salt, pepper, and nutmeg. Cook, stirring often, for 3 minutes. Add beans and onions. Cook, stirring occasionally, until heated through.

Nutrition Facts				
Serving Size	178 g			
Servings Per Recipe	8			
Amount per serving			High Fat/Sugar Comparison	
Calories	69		90	
Calories from fat	5		40	
	% Daily Value*		% Daily Value*	
Total Fat	1 g	**2%**	4.5 g	**7%**
Saturated Fat	0 g	**0%**	3 g	**15%**
Cholesterol	0 mg	**0%**	10 mg	**3%**
Sodium	470 mg	**20%**	510 mg	**21%**
Total Carbohydrate	12 g	**4%**	11 g	**4%**
Dietary Fiber	3 g	**12%**	3 g	**12%**
Sugars	5 g		5 g	
Other	0 g		0 g	
Protein	1 g		1 g	

*Percent of Daily Values on page a-22

Exchanges and 9 g Carbohydrates Per Serving					
Breads	0.1	Vegetables	2.2	Fruits	0.0
Meats	0.0	Milk	0.0	Fats	0.2

Sugared Green Beans with Cranberries

The Fat Quotient using **ButterLike** is **5%** instead of **4%**
0% less fat **75% less sugar**
30% less Calories

U.S.	Ingredients	Metric
2 Tbsp	**Granulated SugarLike**	25.00 g
1 1/2 lb	Green beans	680.00 g
1 tsp	Orange peel, grated	2.00 g
1/2 cup	Dried cranberries	55.00 g

Directions

Heat beans and orange peel in 1 inch water; bring to boil in 2-quart saucepan. Boil uncovered 5 minutes; reduce heat. Cover and simmer 10-15 minutes or until beans are crisp-tender; drain. Toss beans, cranberries and **SugarLike**.

Nutrition Facts				
Serving Size	191 g			
Servings Per Recipe	4			
Amount per serving			High Fat/Sugar Comparison	
Calories	78		110	
Calories from fat	45		240	
	% Daily Value*		% Daily Value*	
Total Fat	0.5 g	**1%**	0.5 g	**1%**
Saturated Fat	0 g	**0%**	0 g	**0%**
Cholesterol	0 mg	**0%**	0 mg	**0%**
Sodium	5 mg	**0%**	5 mg	**0%**
Total Carbohydrate	21 g	**7%**	24 g	**8%**
Dietary Fiber	8 g	**32%**	6 g	**24%**
Sugars	3 g		12 g	
Other	5 g		0 g	
Protein	3 g		3 g	

*Percent of Daily Values on page a-22

Exchanges and 8 g Carbohydrates Per Serving

Breads	0.0	Vegetables	2.4	Fruits	0.1
Meats	0.0	Milk	0.0	Fats	0.0

Three Green Vegetable Casserole

The Fat Quotient using **ButterLike** is **13%** instead of **65%**
89% less fat **0% less sugar**
51% less Calories

U.S.	Ingredients	Metric
2 Tbsp	**ButterLike Saute Butter**	28.00 g
1 pkg	Frozen baby lima beans (10 oz)	284.00 g
1 pkg	Frozen cut green beans (9 oz)	255.00 g
1/4 cup	Onion, finely chopped	40.00 g
1 Tbsp	All-purpose flour	7.20 g
1/2 cup	Fat free sour cream	128.00 g
1/2 cup	Fat free mayonnaise	128.00 g
1/2 tsp	Dried basil	.40 g
1 pkg	Frozen peas, thawed (10 oz)	284.00 g
Dash	Salt	3.00 g
Dash	Pepper	1.00 g
1/2 cup	Fat free cheddar cheese	56.00 g
1/4 cup	Sharp cheddar cheese	68.00 g

Nutrition Facts				
Serving Size	128 g			
Servings Per Recipe	10			
Amount per serving			High Fat/Sugar Comparison	
Calories	123		250	
Calories from fat	15		160	
	% Daily Value*		% Daily Value*	
Total Fat	2 g	**3%**	18 g	**28%**
Saturated Fat	1 g	**5%**	6 g	**30%**
Cholesterol	5 mg	**2%**	35 mg	**12%**
Sodium	440 mg	**18%**	570 mg	**24%**
Total Carbohydrate	18 g	**6%**	15 g	**5%**
Dietary Fiber	4 g	**16%**	4 g	**16%**
Sugars	4 g		4 g	
Other	0 g		0 g	
Protein	7 g		7 g	

*Percent of Daily Values on page a-22

Directions

Cook lima beans and green beans separately in boiling water until tender-crisp. Do not over cook. Rinse and drain with cold water. Heat **ButterLike** in a frying pan over medium heat. Add onion and cook, stirring often, until soft. Stir in flour and cook, stirring, for 1 minute. Remove from heat. Add sour cream, mayonnaise and basil; stir until blended. Stir in lima beans, green beans, and peas. Season to taste with salt and pepper. Spoon into a 2-quart baking dish and sprinkle with cheese. Bake, uncovered, in a 325° oven 20-30 until heated through.

Exchanges and 14 g Carbohydrates Per Serving					
Breads	0.9	Vegetables	0.4	Fruits	0.0
Meats	0.4	Milk	0.2	Fats	0.3

Green Bean Casserole

The Fat Quotient using ButterLike is **16%** instead of **71%**
89% less fat **0% less sugar**
52% less Calories

U.S.	Ingredients	Metric
3 Tbsp	**ButterLike Saute Butter**	42.00 g
1 pkg	Frozen cut green beans (9 oz)	255.00 g
1medium	Onion, chopped	120.00 g
1 clove	Garlic, minced	3.00 g
1/2	Green bell pepper, seeded and chopped	85.00 g
2 jars	Pimentos, sliced or chopped (2oz)	14.00 g
2 tsp	Prepared mustard	10.00 g
1 can	Tomato sauce (8 oz)	28.00 g

Directions

Cook beans according to package directions, until tender-crisp. Drain, immerse in ice water to cool; drain again. Heat **ButterLike** in a frying pan over medium heat. Add onions, garlic, bell pepper, and pimentos; cook, stirring often, until onions are soft. Stir in beans, mustard, tomato sauce, and cheese. Spoon into a shallow 1-quart baking dish.

Bake in a 350° oven for 25 minutes, until cheese is melted.

Nutrition Facts				
Serving Size	167 g			
Servings Per Recipe	4			
Amount per serving			High Fat/Sugar Comparison	
Calories	114		240	
Calories from fat	15		170	
	% Daily Value*		% Daily Value*	
Total Fat	2 g	**3%**	19 g	**29%**
Saturated Fat	0.5 g	**3%**	12 g	**60%**
Cholesterol	0 mg	**0%**	55 mg	**18%**
Sodium	360 mg	**15%**	430 mg	**18%**
Total Carbohydrate	13 g	**4%**	8 g	**3%**
Dietary Fiber	3 g	**12%**	3 g	**12%**
Sugars	3 g		3 g	
Other	0 g		0 g	
Protein	11 g		8 g	

*Percent of Daily Values on page a-22

Exchanges and 10 g Carbohydrates Per Serving					
Breads	0.2	Vegetables	1.5	Fruits	0.0
Meats	1.0	Milk	0.0	Fats	0.3

Green Beans Amandine

The Fat Quotient using **ButterLike** is **40%** instead of **63%**
64% less fat **0% less sugar**
44% less Calories

U.S.	Ingredients	Metric
1 Tbsp	**ButterLike Saute Butter**	14.00 g
1/2 lb	Green beans	227.00 g
1 Tbsp	Slivered almonds	8.40 g
1 tsp	Lemon juice	5.00 g

Directions

Cut beans into 1-inch pieces. Cook beans, covered, in a small amount of boiling water 20-25 minutes until tender-crisp, or according to package directions. Drain; keep warm. Meanwhile, cook and stir almonds in **ButterLike** over medium heat until golden. Remove from heat; stir in lemon juice. Stir almond mixture into beans. Serve.

Nutrition Facts				
Serving Size	85 g			
Servings Per Recipe	3			
Amount per serving			High Fat/Sugar Comparison	
Calories	56		100	
Calories from fat	20		70	
	% Daily Value*		% Daily Value*	
Total Fat	2.5 g	**4%**	7 g	**11%**
Saturated Fat	0 g	**0%**	3 g	**15%**
Cholesterol	0 mg	**0%**	10 mg	**3%**
Sodium	0 mg	**0%**	45 mg	**2%**
Total Carbohydrate	8 g	**3%**	7 g	**2%**
Dietary Fiber	3 g	**12%**	3 g	**12%**
Sugars	2 g		2 g	
Other	0 g		0 g	
Protein	2 g		3 g	

*Percent of Daily Values on page a-22

Exchanges and 5 g Carbohydrates Per Serving

Breads	0.1	Vegetables	1.1	Fruits	0.0
Meats	0.0	Milk	0.0	Fats	0.4

Tiny Carrots with Dill Butter

The Fat Quotient using **ButterLike** is **31%** instead of **70%**
78% less fat **0% less sugar**
52% less Calories

U.S.	Ingredients	Metric
2 Tbsp	**ButterLike Saute Butter**	28.00 g
1 pkg	Tiny, whole carrots (16 oz)	454.00 g
1/2 tsp	Dried dillweed	1.50 g
1 Tbsp	Lemon juice	15.00 g
1/4 tsp	Salt	1.50 g
1/8 tsp	Pepper	.30 g

Directions

In a medium saucepan cook carrots, covered, in a small amount of boiling water about 10 minutes or until tender-crisp; drain. Stir **ButterLike**, dillweed, lemon juice, salt, and pepper into carrots; toss lightly to coat.

Nutrition Facts				
Serving Size	125 g			
Servings Per Recipe	4			
Amount per serving			High Fat/Sugar Comparison	
Calories	43		90	
Calories from fat	15		60	
	% Daily Value*		% Daily Value*	
Total Fat	1.5 g	**2%**	7 g	**11%**
Saturated Fat	0 g	**0%**	4 g	**20%**
Cholesterol	0 mg	**0%**	15 mg	**5%**
Sodium	380 mg	**16%**	440 mg	**18%**
Total Carbohydrate	8 g	**3%**	6 g	**2%**
Dietary Fiber	2 g	**8%**	2 g	**8%**
Sugars	4 g		4 g	
Other	0 g		0 g	
Protein	1 g		1 g	

*Percent of Daily Values on page a-22

Exchanges and 6 g Carbohydrates Per Serving

Breads	0.2	Vegetables	0.9	Fruits	0.0
Meats	0.0	Milk	0.0	Fats	0.2

Mustard-Glazed Carrots

The Fat Quotient using **ButterLike** is **17%** instead of **42%**
71% less fat **29% less sugar**
30% less Calories

U.S.	**Ingredients**	Metric
3 Tbsp	**ButterLike Saute Butter**	42.00 g
2 Tbsp	**Brown SugarLike**	25.00 g
2 lbs	Carrots, cut into 1/4-inch slanting slices	907.00 g
1/2 cup	Water	119.00 g
3 Tbsp	Dijon mustard	45.00 g
1 Tbsp	Chopped parsley	3.75 g

Directions

Place carrots in a 3-quart pan. Add water and bring to a boil over high heat; reduce heat, cover, and let simmer 10 minutes until carrots are tender-crisp. Drain. Stir in **ButterLike**, **SugarLike**, and mustard. Cook over medium heat, stirring until carrots are evenly glazed. Sprinkle with parsley.

Nutrition Facts				
Serving Size	190 g			
Servings Per Recipe	6			
Amount per serving			High Fat/Sugar Comparison	
Calories	105		150	
Calories from fat	20		60	
	% Daily Value*		% Daily Value*	
Total Fat	2 g	**3%**	7 g	**11%**
Saturated Fat	0 g	**0%**	4 g	**20%**
Cholesterol	0 mg	**0%**	15 mg	**5%**
Sodium	120 mg	**5%**	180 mg	**8%**
Total Carbohydrate	22 g	**7%**	20 g	**7%**
Dietary Fiber	1 g	**4%**	0 g	**0%**
Sugars	10 g		14 g	
Other	3 g		0 g	
Protein	2 g		2 g	

*Percent of Daily Values on page a-22

Exchanges and 18 g Carbohydrates Per Serving					
Breads	0.2	Vegetables	2.7	Fruits	0.0
Meats	0.0	Milk	0.0	Fats	0.2

Walter's Lentils

The Fat Quotient using **ButterLike** is **4%** instead of **20%**
80% less fat **0% less sugar**
13% less Calories

U.S.	**Ingredients**	Metric
1/4 cup	**ButterLike Saute Butter**	56.00 g
1 pkg	Lentils, washed, cleaned (1 lb)	454.00 g
1 large	Onion, chopped	85.00 g
3 cloves	Garlic, minced	28.00 g
1 can	Tomato paste (6 oz)	170.00 g
2 cups	Carrots, sliced	312.00 g
1/4 tsp	Pepper	.53 g
1 tsp	Salt	6.00 g
1-2 Tbsp	Red wine vinegar	17.00 g

Directions

In a pan, cook lentils in water for 30 minutes; drain. Add more water to cover half of lentils; set aside. Saute the onion and garlic in the **ButterLike** until tender. Add carrots, onion mixture, tomato paste, salt, and garlic pepper to the lentils and cook until water is reduced and vegetables and lentils are tender. Season with the red wine vinegar. Adjust seasoning.

Nutrition Facts				
Serving Size	113 g			
Servings Per Recipe	10			
Amount per serving			High Fat/Sugar Comparison	
Calories	199		230	
Calories from fat	10		45	
	% Daily Value*		% Daily Value*	
Total Fat	1 g	**2%**	5 g	**8%**
Saturated Fat	0 g	**0%**	3 g	**15%**
Cholesterol	0 mg	**0%**	15 mg	**5%**
Sodium	420 mg	**18%**	470 mg	**20%**
Total Carbohydrate	38 g	**13%**	36 g	**12%**
Dietary Fiber	4 g	**16%**	4 g	**16%**
Sugars	5 g		5 g	
Other	0 g		0 g	
Protein	10 g		10 g	

*Percent of Daily Values on page a-22

Exchanges and 34 g Carbohydrates Per Serving					
Breads	1.9	Vegetables	1.6	Fruits	0.0
Meats	0.5	Milk	0.0	Fats	0.2

Pennsylvania Red Cabbage

The Fat Quotient using ButterLike is **10%** instead of **24%**
80% less fat **78% less sugar**
53% less Calories

U.S.	Ingredients	Metric
2 Tbsp	**Brown SugarLike**	25.00 g
1 Tbsp	**ButterLike Saute Butter**	14.00 g
2 Tbsp	Vinegar	30.00 g
2 Tbsp	Water	30.00 g
1/4 tsp	Caraway seed	.53 g
2 cups	Red or green cabbage, shredded	140.00 g
3/4 cup	Apple, coarsely chopped	128.00 g
Dash	Salt	
Dash	Pepper	

Directions

In a large skillet combine the **Brown SugarLike**, vinegar, water, **ButterLike**, caraway seed, 1/4 tsp salt, and dash of pepper. Cook for 2-3 minutes or until hot, stirring occasionally. Stir in the cabbage and apple. Cook, covered, over medium-low heat about 5 minutes or until cabbage is tender-crisp, stirring occasionally.

Nutrition Facts				
Serving Size	123 g			
Servings Per Recipe	3			
Amount per serving			High Fat/Sugar Comparison	
Calories	90		190	
Calories from fat	10		45	
	% Daily Value*		% Daily Value*	
Total Fat	1 g	**2%**	5 g	**8%**
Saturated Fat	0 g	**0%**	0.5 g	**3%**
Cholesterol	0 mg	**0%**	0 mg	**0%**
Sodium	10 mg	**0%**	15 mg	**1%**
Total Carbohydrate	19 g	**6%**	35 g	**12%**
Dietary Fiber	4 g	**16%**	5 g	**20%**
Sugars	6 g		27 g	
Other	6 g		0 g	
Protein	1 g		1 g	

*Percent of Daily Values on page a-22

Exchanges and 9 g Carbohydrates Per Serving

Breads	0.1	Vegetables	0.5	Fruits	0.4
Meats	0.0	Milk	0.0	Fats	0.1

Pennsylvania Red Cabbage

Corn Casserole

The Fat Quotient using **ButterLike** is **11%** instead of **48%**
85% less fat **50% less sugar**
37% less Calories

U.S.	Ingredients	Metric
1 Tbsp	**ButterLike Saute Butter**	14.00 g
1 can	Cream-style corn (17 oz)	482.00 g
1 cup	Evaporated skim milk	255.00 g
1/2 cup	Fat free salted cracker crumbs	56.00 g
2	Eggs, beaten	100.00 g
1 medium	Onion, minced	120.00 g
1/4 tsp	Salt	1.50 g
1/8 tsp	Pepper	.26 g
1 1/2 cup	Fat free sharp cheddar cheese	170.00 g

Directions

In a large bowl, combine corn, milk, crumbs, eggs, onion, salt, and pepper; stir until blended. Spoon half of corn mixture into a vegetable sprayed 8-inch square baking pan; sprinkle with half of cheese. Evenly spoon the remaining corn mixture over cheese; then top with remaining cheese. Bake in a 350° oven about 35 minutes until mixture is set and cheese is golden.

Nutrition Facts				
Serving Size	200 g			
Servings Per Recipe	6			
Amount per serving			High Fat/Sugar Comparison	
Calories	200		320	
Calories from fat	20		160	
	% Daily Value*		% Daily Value*	
Total Fat	2.5 g	**4%**	17 g	**26%**
Saturated Fat	0.5 g	**3%**	9 g	**45%**
Cholesterol	75 mg	**25%**	150 mg	**50%**
Sodium	740 mg	**31%**	650 mg	**27%**
Total Carbohydrate	34 g	**11%**	26 g	**9%**
Dietary Fiber	2 g	**8%**	2 g	**8%**
Sugars	1 g		2 g	
Other	0 g		0 g	
Protein	14 g		15 g	

*Percent of Daily Values on page a-22

Exchanges and 32 g Carbohydrates Per Serving

Breads	1.8	Vegetables	0.3	Fruits	0.0
Meats	1.0	Milk	0.4	Fats	0.3

Sauteed Mushrooms

The Fat Quotient using **ButterLike** is **56%** instead of **80%**
69% less fat **0% less sugar**
70% less Calories

U.S.	Ingredients	Metric
3 Tbsp	**ButterLike Saute Butter**	42.00 g
1 lb	Mushrooms	454.00 g

Directions

Rinse and drain mushrooms. Use whole or sliced mushrooms. Heat **ButterLike** in a medium skillet over medium heat. When hot, add mushrooms; saute, stirring occasionally, until heated through. Season to taste with salt and pepper.

Exchanges and 4 g Carbohydrates Per Serving

Breads	0.2	Vegetables	0.8	Fruits	0.0
Meats	0.0	Milk	0.0	Fats	0.2

Nutrition Facts				
Serving Size	83 g			
Servings Per Recipe	6			
Amount per serving			High Fat/Sugar Comparison	
Calories	40		90	
Calories from fat	20		80	
	% Daily Value*		% Daily Value*	
Total Fat	2.5 g	**4%**	8 g	**12%**
Saturated Fat	0 g	**0%**	1 g	**5%**
Cholesterol	0 mg	**0%**	0 mg	**0%**
Sodium	0 mg	**0%**	0 mg	**0%**
Total Carbohydrate	4 g	**1%**	2 g	**1%**
Dietary Fiber	0 g	**0%**	0 g	**0%**
Sugars	1 g		1 g	
Other	0 g		0 g	
Protein	3 g		2 g	

*Percent of Daily Values on page a-22

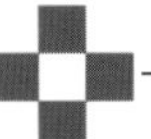

Caramelized Onions

The Fat Quotient using ButterLike is 16% instead of 49%
83% less fat **67% less sugar**
47% less Calories

U.S.	Ingredients	Metric
2 Tbsp	**ButterLike Saute Butter**	28.00 g
4 tsp	**Brown SugarLike**	17.00 g
2 large	White or red onion, 3/4-inch cubes	320.00 g

Directions

In a medium skillet cook onions, covered, in hot **ButterLike** over medium-low heat for 13-15 minutes or until onions are tender. Uncover; add **SugarLike**. Cook and stir over medium-high heat for 4-5 minutes or until onions are golden. Serve hot over burgers, prime rib, or beef steaks. Add more **ButterLike** if needed. To caramelize vegetables, I find that if I let them begin to stick to the pan, they brown better. When brown, sprinkle the pan with water and stir; the caramelized bits stir right up in the vegetables. Delicious!

Nutrition Facts				
Serving Size	91 g			
Servings Per Recipe	4			
Amount per serving			High Fat/Sugar Comparison	
Calories		58	110	
Calories from fat		10	60	
	% Daily Value*		% Daily Value*	
Total Fat	1 g	**2%**	6 g	**9%**
Saturated Fat	0 g	**0%**	4 g	**20%**
Cholesterol	0 mg	**0%**	15 mg	**5%**
Sodium	0 mg	**0%**	65 mg	**3%**
Total Carbohydrate	13 g	**4%**	11 g	**4%**
Dietary Fiber	2 g	**8%**	1 g	**4%**
Sugars	2 g		6 g	
Other	3 g		0 g	
Protein	1 g		1 g	

*Percent of Daily Values on page a-22

Exchanges and 8 g Carbohydrates Per Serving					
Breads	0.2	Vegetables	1.0	Fruits	0.0
Meats	0.0	Milk	0.0	Fats	0.2

Seasoned Baked Onions

The Fat Quotient using ButterLike is 15% instead of 68%
83% less fat **25% less sugar**
26% less Calories

U.S.	Ingredients	Metric
2 Tbsp	**ButterLike Saute Butter**	28.00 g
20 small	Boiling onions, peeled	366.00 g
1	Chicken bouillon cube	4.00 g
3/4 cup	Water	178.00 g
1/2 tsp	Ground sage	.35 g
1/4 tsp	Pepper	.50 g
1 1/2 tsp	Cornstarch	4.00 g
1 Tbsp	Cold water	15.00 g
1/4 cup	Low fat croutons, slightly crushed	7.50 g
2 Tbsp	Non fat parmesan cheese, grated	15.00 g
1 Tbsp	Parsley, chopped	4.00 g

Nutrition Facts				
Serving Size	124 g			
Servings Per Recipe	5			
Amount per serving			High Fat/Sugar Comparison	
Calories		59	80	
Calories from fat		10	50	
	% Daily Value*		% Daily Value*	
Total Fat	1 g	**2%**	6 g	**9%**
Saturated Fat	0 g	**0%**	3.5 g	**18%**
Cholesterol	0 mg	**0%**	15 mg	**5%**
Sodium	510 mg	**21%**	560 mg	**23%**
Total Carbohydrate	9 g	**3%**	7 g	**2%**
Dietary Fiber	1 g	**4%**	1 g	**4%**
Sugars	3 g		4 g	
Other	0 g		0 g	
Protein	2 g		1 g	

*Percent of Daily Values on page a-22

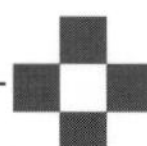

Directions

Arrange onions in a single layer in an 8- or 9-inch vegetable sprayed baking dish. In small pan, crush bouillon cube; add **ButterLike** and water. Heat over medium heat, stirring often, until bouillon cube is dissolved. Stir in sage and pepper. Pour over onions. Cover and bake in a 350° oven about 1 hour until onions are tender. Transfer onions to serving dish with a slotted spoon; keep warm. Blend cornstarch and cold water; set aside. Pour cooking juices into a small pan. Stir in cornstarch mixture and cook, stirring, until sauce boils and thickens. Pour over onions. In a bowl, combine croutons, cheese, and parsley; sprinkle evenly over onions.

Exchanges and 8 g Carbohydrates Per Serving					
Breads	0.3	Vegetables	1.0	Fruits	0.0
Meats	0.8	Milk	0.0	Fats	0.2

Onion Tarts

The Fat Quotient using ButterLike is **18%** instead of **60%**

81% less fat **0% less sugar**

40% less Calories

U.S.	Ingredients	Metric
1	**Mrs. Bateman's Pie Crust**, page 227	154.00 g
3 Tbsp	**ButterLike Saute Butter**	42.00 g
2 large	Onions, thinly chopped	320.00 g
3/4 cup	Egg substitutes	188.00 g
1/4 cup	Skim milk	61.00 g
	Pepper	1.00 g
	Salt	3.00 g
2 Tbsp	Chives, chopped	2.40 g
1/2 tsp	Ground mace	.80 g
1 tsp	Dried mustard	2.40 g

Directions

Follow directions for **Mrs. Bateman's Pie Crust**, page 197, unbaked.

Roll pastry into 1/8-inch thick rectangles. Using a 3-inch round pastry cutter, cut out 12 circles and fit into vegetable sprayed tartlet tins. Pat pastry up the sides and around the rims of molds and press down with fork tines. Chill in refrigerator. Heat **ButterLike** in a skillet over medium heat and saute onions for 5 minutes. Remove onions from the skillet and allow to cool. In a small bowl, beat together eggs and milk. Stir in the pepper, chives, mace, and mustard. Spoon onion into tart shells and pour egg mixture over top. Bake 350° on the top rack of the oven for 15-20 minutes, until a knife inserted in the center comes out clean.

Nutrition Facts				
Serving Size	65 g			
Servings Per Recipe	12			
Amount per serving			High Fat/Sugar Comparison	
Calories		72	120	
Calories from fat		15	70	
	% Daily Value*		% Daily Value*	
Total Fat	1.5 g	**2%**	8 g	**12%**
Saturated Fat	0 g	**0%**	2 g	**10%**
Cholesterol	0 mg	**0%**	55 mg	**18%**
Sodium	250 mg	**10%**	95 mg	**4%**
Total Carbohydrate	11 g	**4%**	10 g	**3%**
Dietary Fiber	1 g	**4%**	1 g	**4%**
Sugars	1 g		1 g	
Other	1 g		0 g	
Protein	3 g		3 g	

*Percent of Daily Values on page a-22

Exchanges and 9 g Carbohydrates Per Serving					
Breads	0.5	Vegetables	0.3	Fruits	0.0
Meats	0.3	Milk	0.0	Fats	0.2

Sauteed Onions

The Fat Quotient using ButterLike is 20% instead of 70%
86% less fat **50% more sugar**
52% less Calories

U.S.	Ingredients	Metric
3 Tbsp	**ButterLike Saute Butter**	42.00 g
2 large	Onions, thinly sliced	400.00 g

Directions

Heat **ButterLike** in a medium skillet over medium heat. Add onions; saute, stirring occasionally, until heated through. Salt and pepper to taste.

Exchanges and 7 g Carbohydrates Per Serving

Breads	0.2	Vegetables	0.8	Fruits	0.0
Meats	0.0	Milk	0.0	Fats	0.2

Nutrition Facts				
Serving Size	74 g			
Servings Per Recipe	6			
Amount per serving			High Fat/Sugar Comparison	
Calories	44		90	
Calories from fat	10		60	
	% Daily Value*		% Daily Value*	
Total Fat	1 g	**2%**	7 g	**11%**
Saturated Fat	0 g	**0%**	1 g	**5%**
Cholesterol	0 mg	**0%**	0 mg	**0%**
Sodium	0 mg	**0%**	0 mg	**0%**
Total Carbohydrate	8 g	**3%**	6 g	**2%**
Dietary Fiber	1 g	**4%**	1 g	**4%**
Sugars	2 g		1 g	
Other	0 g		0 g	
Protein	1 g		1 g	

*Percent of Daily Values on page a-22

Onion Pie

The Fat Quotient using ButterLike is 16% instead of 39%
64% less fat **20% less sugar**
14% less Calories

U.S.	Ingredients	Metric
5 Tbsp	**ButterLike Saute Butter**	70.00 g
4 large	Onions	907.00 g
	Salt	6.00 g
4 slices	White bread	92.00 g
1/2 cup	Grated non fat parmesan cheese	60.00 g
1/2 cup	Egg substitute	126.00 g
1/4 tsp	Pepper	.53 g
1 cup	Skim milk	245.00 g
2-4 Tbsp	Green onions, sliced thin	20.00 g

Directions

Halve large onions lengthwise, then thinly slice crosswise. Heat 3 Tbsp **ButterLike** in a frying pan over medium heat. Add onions and cook about 30 minutes, stirring often, until lightly browned. Salt to taste. While onions are cooking, toast bread and spread with remaining **ButterLike**. Tear or cut toast into 1/2-inch squares and scatter over bottom of a vegetable sprayed 8-inch square or 8x12-inch oval baking dish. Evenly spoon onions over toast and sprinkle with cheese. In a small bowl, beat egg substitute, pepper, and milk; pour over onions.

Nutrition Facts				
Serving Size	191 g			
Servings Per Recipe	8			
Amount per serving			High Fat/Sugar Comparison	
Calories	138		160	
Calories from fat	20		70	
	% Daily Value*		% Daily Value*	
Total Fat	2.5 g	**4%**	7 g	**11%**
Saturated Fat	0.5 g	**3%**	4 g	**20%**
Cholesterol	0 mg	**0%**	70 mg	**23%**
Sodium	490 mg	**20%**	500 mg	**21%**
Total Carbohydrate	19 g	**6%**	17 g	**6%**
Dietary Fiber	3 g	**12%**	3 g	**12%**
Sugars	4 g		5 g	
Other	0 g		0 g	
Protein	10 g		7 g	

*Percent of Daily Values on page a-22

Exchanges and 16 g Carbohydrates Per Serving

Breads	0.5	Vegetables	1.4	Fruits	0.0
Meats	2.2	Milk	0.1	Fats	0.3

Cover and refrigerate for at least 10 hours or until next day. Bake, uncovered, in a 350° oven until center of pie jiggles only slightly when dish is gently shaken. Sprinkle with green onions.

Artichokes au Gratin

The Fat Quotient using **ButterLike** is **17%** instead of **59%**
83% less fat **0% less sugar**
42% less Calories

U.S.	Ingredients	Metric
1 Tbsp	**ButterLike Saute Butter**	14.00 g
1 pkg	Frozen artichoke hearts (9 oz)	255.00 g
1 Tbsp	Grated non fat parmesan cheese	7.50 g
1 Tbsp	Fine dry bread crumbs	7.00 g
1/4 tsp	Paprika	.53 g
Sauce:		
2 Tbsp	**ButterLike Saute Butter**	28.00 g
1 cup	Fresh mushrooms, sliced	70.00 g
1 Tbsp	All-purpose flour	7.00 g
1 tsp	Dijon-style mustard	5.00 g
1/8 tsp	Salt	.75 g
1/8 tsp	Dried marjoram or thyme, crushed	.08 g
2/3 cup	Skim milk	163.00 g
	Pepper	.26 g

Directions

Cook artichoke hearts according to package directions; drain. Combine cheese, bread crumbs, and paprika; stir in **ButterLike**. Set aside artichokes and crumb mixture.

Sauce: In a medium saucepan cook mushrooms in **ButterLike** over medium-high heat 3 minutes or until almost tender. Stir in flour, mustard, salt, marjoram, and pepper. Add milk all at once. Cook and stir 1 minute more. Stir in the artichoke hearts. Transfer mixture to a 1-quart casserole dish. Sprinkle crumb mixture over the artichoke hearts. Bake, uncovered, in a 350° oven about 20 minutes or until bubbly.

Nutrition Facts				
Serving Size	186 g			
Servings Per Recipe	3			
Amount per serving			High Fat/Sugar Comparison	
Calories	133		230	
Calories from fat	25		140	
	% Daily Value*		% Daily Value*	
Total Fat	2.5 g	**4%**	15 g	**23%**
Saturated Fat	1 g	**5%**	9 g	**45%**
Cholesterol	5 mg	**2%**	40 mg	**13%**
Sodium	270 mg	**11%**	390 mg	**16%**
Total Carbohydrate	21 g	**7%**	17 g	**6%**
Dietary Fiber	5 g	**20%**	5 g	**20%**
Sugars	4 g		4 g	
Other	0 g		0 g	
Protein	8 g		7 g	

*Percent of Daily Values on page a-22

Exchanges and 16 g Carbohydrates Per Serving					
Breads	0.5	Vegetables	2.0	Fruits	0.0
Meats	0.7	Milk	0.2	Fats	0.4

Baked Potatoes

The Fat Quotient using **ButterLike** is **5%** instead of **21%**
79% less fat **0% less sugar**
18% less Calories

U.S.	Ingredients	Metric
2 Tbsp	**ButterLike Saute Butter**	28.00 g
4	Potatoes	808.00 g

Directions

Wash, dry, and pierce potatoes with a fork. Brush potatoes with **ButterLike**. Bake potatoes in a 375° oven for 45-60 minutes or microwave on high power for 8 minutes per potato, turning every few minutes. Test by inserting a small knife or fork in the center. Split baked potatoes open and fluff with a fork. Serve with desired toppings.

Nutrition Facts				
Serving Size	209 g			
Servings Per Recipe	4			
Amount per serving			High Fat/Sugar Comparison	
Calories		239	290	
Calories from fat		10	70	
	% Daily Value*		% Daily Value*	
Total Fat	1.5 g	**2%**	7 g	**11%**
Saturated Fat	0 g	**0%**	1 g	**5%**
Cholesterol	0 mg	**0%**	0 mg	**0%**
Sodium	15 mg	**1%**	15 mg	**1%**
Total Carbohydrate	53 g	**18%**	51 g	**17%**
Dietary Fiber	5 g	**20%**	5 g	**20%**
Sugars	3 g		3 g	
Other	0 g		0 g	
Protein	5 g		5 g	

*Percent of Daily Values on page a-22

Exchanges and 48 g Carbohydrates Per Serving

Breads	3.0	Vegetables	0.0	Fruits	0.0
Meats	0.0	Milk	0.0	Fats	0.2

Best Ever Garlicky Potatoes

The Fat Quotient using **ButterLike** is **7%** instead of **26%**
79% less fat **0% less sugar**
17% less Calories

U.S.	Ingredients	Metric
2 Tbsp	**ButterLike Saute Butter**	26.00 g
3 large	Red thin-skinned potatoes, scrubbed & cut into eighths	606.00 g
1 medium	Onion, cut into eighths	120.00 g
3 cloves	Garlic, peeled & halved	9.00 g
Dash	Salt	3.00 g
Dash	Pepper	1.00 g

Directions

Scrub potatoes and cut into eighths. Place **ButterLike** in 9x13-inch vegetable sprayed baking pan. Add potatoes, onion, and garlic to pan and stir to coat. Bake about 30 minutes at 400°, stirring occasionally, until potatoes are golden brown and tender when pierced. Season vegetables to taste with salt and pepper.

Nutrition Facts				
Serving Size	192 g			
Servings Per Recipe	4			
Amount per serving			High Fat/Sugar Comparison	
Calories		199	240	
Calories from fat		10	60	
	% Daily Value*		% Daily Value*	
Total Fat	1.5 g	**2%**	7 g	**11%**
Saturated Fat	0 g	**0%**	2.5 g	**13%**
Cholesterol	0 mg	**0%**	10 mg	**3%**
Sodium	300 mg	**13%**	340 mg	**14%**
Total Carbohydrate	44 g	**15%**	42 g	**14%**
Dietary Fiber	4 g	**16%**	4 g	**16%**
Sugars	3 g		3 g	
Other	0 g		0 g	
Protein	4 g		4 g	

*Percent of Daily Values on page a-22

Exchanges and 40 g Carbohydrates Per Serving

Breads	2.3	Vegetables	0.5	Fruits	0.0
Meats	0.0	Milk	0.0	Fats	0.2

Easy Roasted Potatoes

The Fat Quotient using **ButterLike** is **12%** instead of **36%**
75% less fat **0% less sugar**
27% less Calories

U.S.	Ingredients	Metric
1/4 cup	**ButterLike Saute Butter**	56.00 g
6	Whole potatoes, washed and cubed	606.00 g
1 large	Onion, chopped	160.00 g
1/4 tsp	Salt	1.50 g
1/8 tsp	Pepper	.30 g

Directions

Place cubed potatoes and onions in a 9x13-inch vegetable sprayed baking pan. Mix **ButterLike** into the vegetables until covered. Sprinkle with salt and pepper. Cover with tinfoil and bake at 350° for 30 minutes or until potatoes are tender. This is excellent made with the **Toasted Onion Saute Butter** or **Toasted Garlic Saute Butter.**

Nutrition Facts				
Serving Size	69 g			
Servings Per Recipe	12			
Amount per serving			High Fat/Sugar Comparison	
Calories		73	100	
Calories from fat		5	35	
	% Daily Value*		% Daily Value*	
Total Fat	1 g	**2%**	4 g	**6%**
Saturated Fat	0 g	**0%**	2.5 g	**13%**
Cholesterol	0 mg	**0%**	10 mg	**3%**
Sodium	55 mg	**2%**	95 mg	**4%**
Total Carbohydrate	15 g	**5%**	14 g	**5%**
Dietary Fiber	1 g	**4%**	1 g	**4%**
Sugars	1 g		1 g	
Other	0 g		0 g	
Protein	2 g		1 g	

*Percent of Daily Values on page a-22

Exchanges and 14 g Carbohydrates Per Serving					
Breads	0.8	Vegetables	0.2	Fruits	0.0
Meats	0.0	Milk	0.0	Fats	0.1

Roasted Red and Yellow Potatoes

The Fat Quotient using **ButterLike** is **5%** instead of **19%**
80% less fat **0% less sugar**
17% less Calories

U.S.	Ingredients	Metric
3 Tbsp	**ButterLike Saute Butter**	42.00 g
3 small	Sweet potatoes or yams, scrubbed	342.00 g
2 lb	Medium red potatoes	907.00 g
3 medium	Onions, quartered	360.00 g
Dash	Salt	3.00 g
Dash	Pepper	1.00 g

Directions

Halve sweet potatoes lengthwise; cut crosswise into 1-inch pieces. Scrub and quarter red potatoes. In a shallow baking pan, combine **ButterLike**, sweet potatoes, red potatoes, and onions; toss gently to coat vegetables with **ButterLike**. Bake in a 425° oven 55 minutes until vegetables are browned and tender throughout when pierced. Season to taste with salt and pepper.

Nutrition Facts				
Serving Size	207 g			
Servings Per Recipe	8			
Amount per serving			High Fat/Sugar Comparison	
Calories		199	240	
Calories from fat		10	50	
	% Daily Value*		% Daily Value*	
Total Fat	1 g	**2%**	5 g	**8%**
Saturated Fat	0 g	**0%**	0.5 g	**3%**
Cholesterol	0 mg	**0%**	0 mg	**0%**
Sodium	160 mg	**7%**	160 mg	**7%**
Total Carbohydrate	45 g	**15%**	43 g	**14%**
Dietary Fiber	5 g	**20%**	5 g	**20%**
Sugars	8 g		8 g	
Other	0 g		0 g	
Protein	4 g		4 g	

*Percent of Daily Values on page a-22

Exchanges and 40 g Carbohydrates Per Serving					
Breads	2.4	Vegetables	0.6	Fruits	0.0
Meats	0..0	Milk	0.0	Fats	0.2

Broccoli with Almonds and Rice

The Fat Quotient using ButterLike is **19%** instead of **48%**
78% less fat **13% less sugar**
44% less Calories

U.S.	**Ingredients**	Metric
2 Tbsp	**ButterLike Saute Butter**	28.00 g
1/8 cup	Slivered almonds	17.00 g
1/2 cup	Long-grain white rice	48.00 g
1/4 cup	Golden raisins	41.00 g
1 1/2 tsp	Chili powder	3.90 g
2 cups	Fat free chicken broth	490.00 g
1 1/4 lbs	Broccoli	567.00 g

Directions

Toast almonds in a frying pan over medium heat, stirring, until lightly browned. Remove from pan; set aside. Add **ButterLike**, rice, raisins, and chili powder to pan. Cook about 5 minutes, stirring, until rice is opaque. Add broth and stir until blended. Bring to a boil over high heat; then simmer, covered, until rice is barely tender. Trim and discard ends of broccoli stalks. Cut flowerets; peel stalks and cut crosswise into thin slices; set aside. After rice has cooked for 15 minutes, arrange flowerets and stalks on top of rice. Cover and continue cooking broccoli until tender-crisp.

Nutrition Facts				
Serving Size	299 g			
Servings Per Recipe	4			
Amount per serving			High Fat/Sugar Comparison	
Calories	169		300	
Calories from fat	35		140	
	% Daily Value*		% Daily Value*	
Total Fat	3.5 g	**5%**	16 g	**25%**
Saturated Fat	0.5 g	**3%**	2.5 g	**13%**
Cholesterol	0 mg	**0%**	5 mg	**2%**
Sodium	60 mg	**3%**	800 mg	**33%**
Total Carbohydrate	26 g	**9%**	27 g	**9%**
Dietary Fiber	3 g	**12%**	3 g	**12%**
Sugars	7 g		8 g	
Other	0 g		0 g	
Protein	9 g		12 g	

*Percent of Daily Values on page a-22

Exchanges and 23 g Carbohydrates Per Serving					
Breads	0.8	Vegetables	1.0	Fruits	0.5
Meats	0.2	Milk	0.0	Fats	0.7

Gently stir broccoli into rice mixture; spoon onto platter. Sprinkle with toasted almonds.

Baked Lemon Rice Pilaf

The Fat Quotient using ButterLike is **0%** instead of **32%**
100% less fat **100% less sugar**
26% less Calories

U.S.	**Ingredients**	Metric
2 Tbsp	**ButterLike Saute Butter**	14.00 g
2 cup	Fat free chicken broth	490.00 g
1 cup	Long-grain white rice	95.00 g
2 tsp	Lemon peel, grated	4.00 g
2 Tbsp	Lemon juice	31.00 g
1/4 cup	Green onion, sliced	40.00 g

Nutrition Facts				
Serving Size	112 g			
Servings Per Recipe	6			
Amount per serving			High Fat/Sugar Comparison	
Calories	74		100	
Calories from fat	0		30	
	% Daily Value*		% Daily Value*	
Total Fat	0 g	**0%**	3.5 g	**5%**
Saturated Fat	0 g	**0%**	1.5 g	**8%**
Cholesterol	0 mg	**0%**	5 mg	**2%**
Sodium	20 mg	**1%**	540 mg	**23%**
Total Carbohydrate	15 g	**5%**	16 g	**5%**
Dietary Fiber	0 g	**0%**	0 g	**0%**
Sugars	0 g		1 g	
Other	0 g		0 g	
Protein	2 g		3 g	

*Percent of Daily Values on page a-22

Directions

In a 1 1/2- to 2-quart baking dish, mix **ButterLike**, broth, rice, lemon peel, lemon juice, and onions. Bake, covered, in a 350° oven 45-55 minutes until rice is tender to bite.

Exchanges and 15 g Carbohydrates Per Serving					
Breads	0.9	Vegetables	0.1	Fruits	0.0
Meats	0.1	Milk	0.0	Fats	0.1

Brown Rice Vegetable Casserole

The Fat Quotient using ButterLike is **11%** instead of **38%**
80% less fat **0% less sugar**
33% less Calories

U.S.	Ingredients	Metric
1 Tbsp	**ButterLike Saute Butter**	14.00 g
2 1/2 cup	Water	593.00 g
2	Chicken bouillon cubes	8.00 g
1 cup	Long-grain brown rice	168.00 g
1 lb	Broccoli	454.00 g
1 small	Head cauliflower	635.00 g
2 medium	Crookneck squash or zucchini	907.00 g
1/4 cup	Celery, sliced	30.00 g
1/4 lb	Mushrooms, sliced	113.00 g
1/4 cup	Carrot, shredded	28.00 g
1/4 cup	Green onions, sliced	40.00 g
1/2 tsp	Soy sauce	3.00 g
1 can	Mild green chile salsa (7 oz)	199.00 g
20	Cherry tomatoes	340.00 g
3 slices	Fat free jack cheese	85.00 g
3 slices	Fat free cheddar cheese	85.00 g
1 Tbsp	Salted roasted sunflower seeds	8.00 g

Nutrition Facts				
Serving Size	618 g			
Servings Per Recipe	6			
Amount per serving			High Fat/Sugar Comparison	
Calories		242	360	
Calories from fat		30	140	
	% Daily Value*		% Daily Value*	
Total Fat	3 g	**5%**	15 g	**23%**
Saturated Fat	0 g	**0%**	7 g	**35%**
Cholesterol	0 mg	**0%**	35 mg	**12%**
Sodium	850 mg	**35%**	850 mg	**35%**
Total Carbohydrate	39 g	**13%**	38 g	**13%**
Dietary Fiber	9 g	**36%**	9 g	**36%**
Sugars	10 g		10 g	
Other	0 g		0 g	
Protein	19 g		18 g	

*Percent of Daily Values on page a-22

Exchanges and 30 g Carbohydrates Per Serving					
Breads	1.3	Vegetables	3.1	Fruits	0.0
Meats	0.9	Milk	0.0	Fats	0.2

Directions

Combine water and bouillon cubes in a 2-quart pan. Bring to boil over high heat. Add **ButterLike** and rice; reduce heat, simmer, covered, until rice is tender. Remove from heat and uncover. Cut broccoli flowerets into bite-size pieces, leaving about 2 inches of stem. Break cauliflower into bite-size flowerets. Cut squash into 1/2-inch thick slices. Cover and steam until all vegetables are tender-crisp. Add mushrooms, cover, and steam for 2 more minutes; remove from heat. Add carrot, onions, and soy sauce to rice; stir gently until combined. Spread rice mixture evenly in a vegetable sprayed 2-quart baking dish. Spoon salsa over rice. Top with steamed vegetables and cherry tomatoes. Cut each slice of cheese in half; then cover casserole with alternate slices of jack and cheddar cheese, overlapping edges slightly. Bake, uncovered, in a 350° oven 15-20 minutes until heated through. Sprinkle with sunflower seeds.

Brown and Wild Rice Pilaf

The Fat Quotient using ButterLike is **12%** instead of **22%**
50% less fat **0% less sugar**
11% less Calories

U.S.	**Ingredients**	Metric
1 Tbsp	**ButterLike Saute Butter**	14.00 g
1 cup	Fresh mushrooms, sliced	70.00 g
1/4 cup	Green onion, sliced	6.00 g
1 can	Chicken broth (14.5 oz)	411.00 g
1/2 cup	Brown rice, uncooked	95.00 g
1/3 cup	Wild rice, uncooked, rinsed	51.00 g
1/4 cup	Carrot, shredded	28.00 g
1/2 tsp	Dried basil, crushed	.40 g
1/8 tsp	Pepper	.26 g
1/2 cup	Frozen peas	80.00 g

Directions

In a medium saucepan cook mushrooms and green onion in **ButterLike** until tender. Carefully add chicken broth; bring to boil. Stir in rices, carrot, basil, and pepper. Return to boiling; reduce heat. Simmer, covered, about 40 minutes or until the rices are tender and most of the broth is absorbed. Stir in frozen peas. Simmer for 3-5 minutes more or until heated through, stirring occasionally.

Nutrition Facts				
Serving Size	189 g			
Servings Per Recipe	4			
Amount per serving			High Fat/Sugar Comparison	
Calories	179		200	
Calories from fat	20		45	
	% Daily Value*		% Daily Value*	
Total Fat	2.5 g	**4%**	5 g	**8%**
Saturated Fat	0.5 g	**3%**	2.5 g	**13%**
Cholesterol	0 mg	**0%**	10 mg	**3%**
Sodium	40 mg	**2%**	70 mg	**3%**
Total Carbohydrate	33 g	**11%**	32 g	**11%**
Dietary Fiber	2 g	**8%**	2 g	**8%**
Sugars	2 g		2 g	
Other	0 g		0 g	
Protein	6 g		6 g	

*Percent of Daily Values on page a-22

Exchanges and 3 g Carbohydrates Per Serving

Breads	2.1	Vegetables	0.3	Fruits	0.0
Meats	0.2	Milk	0.0	Fats	0.3

Walter's Greek Vegetable Rice

The Fat Quotient using **ButterLike** is **9%** instead of **35%**
79% less fat **0% less sugar**
22% less Calories

U.S.	Ingredients	Metric
1/4 cup	**ButterLike Saute Butter**	56.00 g
2 cups	Long-grain rice, uncooked	632.00 g
2	Chicken bouillon cubes	8.00 g
1/2 tsp	Salt	3.00 g
1/4 tsp	Garlic pepper	.80 g
1 Tbsp	Red wine vinegar	17.00 g
3 small	Summer squash, sliced	450.00 g
2 cups	Fresh spinach, torn	112.00 g
4 cups	Water	948.00 g

Directions

This is an easy delicious dish that is great to use up fresh produce out of the garden. In a 4-quart saucepan add the water, rice, garlic pepper, and salt. Cover and cook 10 minutes and add the vegetables, **ButterLike**, and the red wine vinegar. Continue cooking until the liquid is absorbed and the rice is tender. Adjust seasoning.

Nutrition Facts				
Serving Size	278 g			
Servings Per Recipe	8			
Amount per serving			High Fat/Sugar Comparison	
Calories	141		180	
Calories from fat	15		70	
	% Daily Value*		% Daily Value*	
Total Fat	1.5 g	**2%**	7 g	**11%**
Saturated Fat	0 g	**0%**	1 g	**5%**
Cholesterol	0 mg	**0%**	0 mg	**0%**
Sodium	450 mg	**19%**	450 mg	**19%**
Total Carbohydrate	28 g	**9%**	26 g	**9%**
Dietary Fiber	1 g	**4%**	1 g	**4%**
Sugars	2 g		2 g	
Other	0 g		0 g	
Protein	3 g		3 g	

*Percent of Daily Values on page a-22

Exchanges and 27 g Carbohydrates Per Serving

Breads	1.9	Vegetables	0.1	Fruits	0.0
Meats	0.0	Milk	0.0	Fats	0.3

Risotto Milanese

The Fat Quotient using **ButterLike** is **19%** instead of **68%**
83% less fat **0% less sugar**
37% less Calories

U.S.	Ingredients	Metric
1/2 cup + 2 Tbsp	**ButterLike Saute Butter**	140.00 g
1 cup	Onions, chopped	170.00 g
10 oz	Arborio rice	284.00 g
16	Saffron threads	28.00 g
3/4 cup	White wine	177.00 g
2 qt	Chicken stock	907.00 g
Dash	Salt	.75 g
Dash	Black pepper	.26 g
1/3 cup	Non fat parmesan cheese	40.00 g

Directions

Cook onions in 1/2 cup **ButterLike** until transparent. Add rice and cook 2 minutes. Add saffron and wine. Reduce by 1/2 over medium heat, about 15 minutes. Stirring constantly, add 1/2 cup stock at a time until absorbed. Cook 15-18 minutes until al dente. Remove from heat and vigorously stir in 2 Tbsp **ButterLike** and parmesan cheese. Serve hot.

Nutrition Facts				
Serving Size	437 g			
Servings Per Recipe	4			
Amount per serving			High Fat/Sugar Comparison	
Calories	288		460	
Calories from fat	50		320	
	% Daily Value*		% Daily Value*	
Total Fat	6 g	**9%**	35 g	**54%**
Saturated Fat	2 g	**10%**	9 g	**45%**
Cholesterol	5 mg	**2%**	20 mg	**7%**
Sodium	2210 mg	**92%**	2260 mg	**94%**
Total Carbohydrate	38 g	**13%**	28 g	**9%**
Dietary Fiber	1 g	**4%**	1 g	**4%**
Sugars	2 g		2 g	
Other	0 g		0 g	
Protein	12 g		7 g	

*Percent of Daily Values on page a-22

Exchanges and 37 g Carbohydrates Per Serving

Breads	2.1	Vegetables	0.5	Fruits	0.0
Meats	2.7	Milk	0.0	Fats	1.5

Creamed Spinach

The Fat Quotient using ButterLike is 21% instead of 64%
83% less fat **0% less sugar**
50% less Calories

U.S.	Ingredients	Metric
5 Tbsp	**ButterLike Saute Butter**	70.00 g
1 large	Onion, minced	160.00 g
2 Tbsp	All-purpose flour	14.00 g
1 cup	Fat free chicken broth	245.00 g
6 Tbsp	Skim milk	92.00 g
1/4 tsp	Ground nutmeg	.55 g
2 pkgs	Frozen chopped spinach (10 oz each)	567.00 g
Dash	Salt	6.00 g
Dash	Pepper to taste	2.10 g

Directions

Heat **ButterLike** in a wide frying pan over medium heat. Add onion; cook, stirring often, until lightly browned. Stir in flour and cook, stirring, for 1 minute. Remove from heat and gradually stir in broth, milk, and nutmeg. Return to heat and bring to a boil; stirring for 1 minute. Add spinach, thawed and squeezed dry; stir until blended. Remove from heat; season to taste with salt and pepper.

Nutrition Facts				
Serving Size	193 g			
Servings Per Recipe	6			
Amount per serving			High Fat/Sugar Comparison	
Calories	85		170	
Calories from fat	20		110	
	% Daily Value*		% Daily Value*	
Total Fat	2 g	**3%**	12 g	**18%**
Saturated Fat	0.5 g	**3%**	8 g	**40%**
Cholesterol	0 mg	**0%**	35 mg	**12%**
Sodium	490 mg	**20%**	710 mg	**30%**
Total Carbohydrate	14 g	**5%**	10 g	**3%**
Dietary Fiber	3 g	**12%**	3 g	**12%**
Sugars	1 g		1 g	
Other	0 g		0 g	
Protein	5 g		5 g	

*Percent of Daily Values on page a-22

Exchanges and 11 g Carbohydrates Per Serving					
Breads	0.4	Vegetables	1.4	Fruits	0.0
Meats	0.1	Milk	0.1	Fats	0.4

Sauteed Spinach and Cucumber

The Fat Quotient using ButterLike is 28% instead of 70%
81% less fat **0% less sugar**
51% less Calories

U.S.	Ingredients	Metric
5 Tbsp	**ButterLike Saute Butter**	70.00 g
2 large	Bunches spinach (2 lbs)	907.00 g
1	Cucumber	301.00 g
1 Tbsp	Balsamic vinegar	17.00 g
Dash	Salt	3.00 g
Dash	Pepper	1.00 g

Nutrition Facts				
Serving Size	325 g			
Servings Per Recipe	4			
Amount per serving			High Fat/Sugar Comparison	
Calories	112		230	
Calories from fat	30		160	
	% Daily Value*		% Daily Value*	
Total Fat	3.5 g	**5%**	18 g	**28%**
Saturated Fat	1 g	**5%**	2.5 g	**13%**
Cholesterol	5 mg	**2%**	0 mg	**0%**
Sodium	530 mg	**22%**	530 mg	**22%**
Total Carbohydrate	17 g	**6%**	11 g	**4%**
Dietary Fiber	7 g	**28%**	7 g	**28%**
Sugars	4 g		4 g	
Other	0 g		0 g	
Protein	8 g		7 g	

*Percent of Daily Values on page a-22

Directions

Remove tough stems and discard blemished leaves from spinach. Wash in cold water. Peel cucumber and halve lengthwise; use a teaspoon to remove and discard seeds. Cut cucumber halves into crosswise 1/8-inch thick slices; set aside. Place damp spinach in heavy skillet. Cook, covered, over medium heat, stirring occasionally, 5-10 minutes or until wilted. Drain spinach in colander. Heat **ButterLike** in same skillet over medium heat. Add spinach and cucumber slices; saute 3-4 minutes, or until heated through. Sprinkle with vinegar; season with salt and pepper.

Exchanges and 10 g Carbohydrates Per Serving					
Breads	0.4	Vegetables	2.0	Fruits	0.0
Meats	0.0	Milk	0.0	Fats	0.5

Spinach Cauliflower Toss

The Fat Quotient using ButterLike is **56%** instead of **79%**
74% less fat **0% less sugar**
64% less Calories

U.S.	Ingredients	Metric
1/3 cup	**ButterLike Saute Butter**	75.00 g
1/8 cup	Slivered Almonds or pine nuts	17.00 g
1/2 lb	Spinach, rinsed, stems removed	227.00 g
1/2	Head cauliflower	476.00 g
1/2 large	Avocado	119.00 g
1 Tbsp	Lemon juice	15.00 g
3 Tbsp	White wine vinegar	45.00 g
1 clove	Garlic, minced or pressed	3.00 g
1/2 tsp	Salt	3.00 g
1/2 tsp	Dry mustard	1.20 g
1/2 tsp	Dry basil	0.40 g
1/4 tsp	Pepper	0.50 g
1/4 tsp	Nutmeg	0.50 g

Directions

Spread almonds in a shallow baking pan and toast about 5-8 minutes in a 350° oven, stirring occasionally, until lightly browned. Let cool. Tear spinach leaves into bite-size pieces. Cut cauliflower flowerets into 1/4-inch thick slices. Place spinach and cauliflower in a serving bowl. Pit, peel, and slice avocado; sprinkle with lemon juice to coat. Add avocado to vegetables. In a small bowl, whisk together **ButterLike**, garlic, vinegar, salt, mustard, basil, pepper, and nutmeg. You may use **Toasted Garlic ButterLike** in place of the garlic and **ButterLike**. Pour dressing over vegetables. Add almonds and mix gently to coat.

Nutrition Facts				
Serving Size	164 g			
Servings Per Recipe	6			
Amount per serving			High Fat/Sugar Comparison	
Calories	96		260	
Calories from fat	60		210	
	% Daily Value*		% Daily Value*	
Total Fat	6 g	**9%**	23 g	**35%**
Saturated Fat	1 g	**5%**	8 g	**40%**
Cholesterol	0 mg	**0%**	30 mg	**10%**
Sodium	220 mg	**9%**	340 mg	**14%**
Total Carbohydrate	8 g	**3%**	5 g	**2%**
Dietary Fiber	5 g	**20%**	7 g	**28%**
Sugars	2 g		2 g	
Other	0 g		0 g	
Protein	4 g		7 g	

*Percent of Daily Values on page a-22

Exchanges and 3 g Carbohydrates Per Serving					
Breads	0.3	Vegetables	0.7	Fruits	0.0
Meats	0.0	Milk	0.0	Fats	1.2

Apricot Glazed Squash

The Fat Quotient using ButterLike is 20% instead of 49%
79% less fat **0% less sugar**
51% less Calories

U.S.	Ingredients	Metric
3 Tbsp	**Strawberry Jam**, page 61 use peach or apricots	62.00 g
1/4 cup	**ButterLike Saute Butter**	56.00 g
1 1/2 lbs	Banana squash, peeled and seeded	680.00 g
2 Tbsp	Water	30.00 g
1 Tbsp	Frozen orange juice concentrate, thawed	18.00 g
1/8 tsp	Ground cloves	.26 g
1/4 tsp	Salt	1.50 g
Dash	Pepper	.26 g

Nutrition Facts				
Serving Size	212 g			
Servings Per Recipe	4			
Amount per serving			High Fat/Sugar Comparison	
Calories	113		220	
Calories from fat	20		110	
	% Daily Value*		% Daily Value*	
Total Fat	2.5 g	**4%**	12 g	**18%**
Saturated Fat	0.5 g	**3%**	8 g	**40%**
Cholesterol	0 mg	**0%**	35 mg	**12%**
Sodium	780 mg	**33%**	910 mg	**38%**
Total Carbohydrate	26 g	**9%**	24 g	**8%**
Dietary Fiber	0 g	**0%**	0 g	**0%**
Sugars	1 g		1 g	
Other	8 g		0 g	
Protein	3 g		2 g	

*Percent of Daily Values on page a-22

Exchanges and 18 g Carbohydrates Per Serving

Breads	0.3	Vegetables	2.3	Fruits	0.1
Meats	0.0	Milk	0.0	Fats	0.5

Directions

Follow directions for **Strawberry Jam**, except substitute peaches or apricots for strawberries.

Cut banana squash into 1/4-inch cubes. Heat **ButterLike** in a frying pan over medium heat. Add squash and 2 Tbsp water; stir to coat. Cover and cook over high heat, stirring occasionally, just until squash is tender and liquid is absorbed; add more water if needed to prevent sticking. Reduce heat to low and stir in orange juice concentrate, jam, cloves, salt, and pepper. Cook, stirring gently, until squash is evenly glazed.

Grilled Thai Marinated Summer Squash

The Fat Quotient using ButterLike is 9% instead of 53%
86% less fat **0% less sugar**
17% less Calories

U.S.	Ingredients	Metric
1 Tbsp	**ButterLike Saute Butter**	14.00 g
1 medium	Zucchini	454.00 g
1 medium	Yellow summer squash	454.00 g
1/4 cup	Fat free chicken broth	61.00 g
1 Tbsp	Lime juice	15.00 g
1/8 tsp	Dried mint leaves	.10 g
1/8 tsp	Dried basil leaves	.10 g
1/2 tsp	Ginger root, finely chopped	3.00 g
1/2 tsp	Jalapeno, finely chopped	1.40 g
1 tsp	Low sodium soy sauce	5.60 g

Directions

Place zucchini and squash in square baking dish, 8x8x2-inches. Mix remaining ingredients; pour over vegetables. Cover and let stand at least 1 hour, but no longer than 2 hours. Heat coals or gas grill. Remove vegetables from marinade; reserve marinade. Cover and grill vegetables 4 inches from medium heat for 10-15 minutes. Turn 2 or 3 times with marinade, until golden brown and tender. Cut each crosswise into 4 pieces. Toss with any remaining marinade.

Exchanges and 5 g Carbohydrates Per Serving					
Breads	0.1	Vegetables	1.7	Fruits	0.0
Meats	0.0	Milk	0.0	Fats	0.1

Nutrition Facts				
Serving Size	138 g			
Servings Per Recipe	4			
Amount per serving			High Fat/Sugar Comparison	
Calories		50	60	
Calories from fat		5	35	
	% Daily Value*		% Daily Value*	
Total Fat	0.5 g	**1%**	3.5 g	**5%**
Saturated Fat	0 g	**0%**	0.5 g	**3%**
Cholesterol	0 mg	**0%**	0 mg	**0%**
Sodium	55 mg	**2%**	115 mg	**5%**
Total Carbohydrate	6 g	**2%**	5 g	**2%**
Dietary Fiber	1 g	**4%**	1 g	**4%**
Sugars	1 g		1 g	
Other	0 g		0 g	
Protein	1 g		1 g	

*Percent of Daily Values on page a-22

Broiled Zucchini Slices

The Fat Quotient using **ButterLike** is **36%** instead of **90%**
83% less fat **0% less sugar**
49% less Calories

U.S.	Ingredients	Metric
2 Tbsp	**ButterLike Saute Butter**	28.00 g
2 cloves	Garlic, minced	6.00 g
1/2 tsp	Dried rosemary	.60 g
1/2 tsp	Cracked black pepper	1.00 g
1/8 tsp	Salt	.75 g
2 medium	Zucchini or squash, sliced 1/4-inch thick	390.00 g

Directions

In a saucepan over medium heat cook garlic in **ButterLike** for 30 seconds. Stir in rosemary, pepper, and salt. Drizzle mixture over zucchini; toss to coat. Arrange zucchini in a single layer in a 15x10-inch baking pan. Broil about 5 inches from heat 5-6 minutes or until tender, turning once.

Nutrition Facts				
Serving Size	106 g			
Servings Per Recipe	4			
Amount per serving			High Fat/Sugar Comparison	
Calories		36	71	
Calories from fat		10	60	
	% Daily Value*		% Daily Value*	
Total Fat	1 g	**2%**	6 g	**9%**
Saturated Fat	0 g	**0%**	4 g	**20%**
Cholesterol	0 mg	**0%**	15 mg	**5%**
Sodium	75 mg	**3%**	140 mg	**6%**
Total Carbohydrate	6 g	**2%**	4 g	**1%**
Dietary Fiber	1 g	**4%**	1 g	**4%**
Sugars	2 g		2 g	
Other	0 g		0 g	
Protein	1 g		1 g	

*Percent of Daily Values on page a-22

Exchanges and 5 g Carbohydrates Per Serving					
Breads	0.2	Vegetables	0.3	Fruits	0.0
Meats	0.0	Milk	0.0	Fats	0.2

Baked Squash with Maple Butter

The Fat Quotient using **ButterLike** is **18%** instead of **36%**
63% less fat **75% less sugar**
27% less Calories

U.S.	Ingredients	Metric
1/2 cup	**ButterLike Saute Butter**	112.00 g
6 Tbsp	**Liquid SugarLike**	128.00 g
1 tsp	Maple extract	5.00 g
1/2 tsp	Ground cinnamon	1.20 g
1/4 tsp	Ground ginger	.50 g
1/4 tsp	Ground allspice	.50 g
3 large	Acorn squash	680.00 g
	Salt to taste	18.00 g

Directions

In a small bowl, combine **ButterLike**, **SugarLike**, maple flavoring, cinnamon, ginger, and allspice. Halve squash lengthwise; remove seeds. Place halves, cut sides down, in a large baking pan. Pour 1 inch of boiling water into pan. Bake, covered, in a 350° oven about 45 minutes, until squash is tender. Remove squash and discard water. Return squash to pan, placing halves cut side up. Sprinkle lightly with salt. Place a sixth of the **ButterLike** mixture in cavity of each squash half. Cover and bake in a 400° oven until heated through. To serve, arrange in a serving dish; at the table, scoop squash from skins onto individual plates.

Nutrition Facts				
Serving Size	77 g			
Servings Per Recipe	12			
Amount per serving			High Fat/Sugar Comparison	
Calories	73		100	
Calories from fat	15		35	
	% Daily Value*		% Daily Value*	
Total Fat	1.5 g	**2%**	4 g	**6%**
Saturated Fat	0 g	**0%**	2.5 g	**13%**
Cholesterol	0 mg	**0%**	10 mg	**3%**
Sodium	100 mg	**4%**	140 mg	**6%**
Total Carbohydrate	18 g	**6%**	15 g	**5%**
Dietary Fiber	2 g	**8%**	0 g	**0%**
Sugars	2 g		8 g	
Other	5 g		0 g	
Protein	1 g		1 g	

*Percent of Daily Values on page a-22

Exchanges and 11 g Carbohydrates Per Serving					
Breads	0.8	Vegetables	0.0	Fruits	0.0
Meats	0.0	Milk	0.0	Fats	0.3

Butter Pecan-Topped Sweet Potatoes

The Fat Quotient using **ButterLike** is **17%** instead of **46%**
80% less fat **48% less sugar**
46% less Calories

U.S.	Ingredients	Metric
3/4 cup	**Brown SugarLike**	150.00 g
1/2 cup	**ButterLike Saute Butter**	112.00 g
3 lb	Sweet potatoes or yams, scrubbed	1360.00 g
1	Egg	50.00 g
1 tsp	Salt	6.00 g
1 tsp	Ground cinnamon	2.30 g
1/2 cup	Orange juice	125.00 g
1/8 cup	Pecan halves	14.00 g

Nutrition Facts				
Serving Size	227 g			
Servings Per Recipe	8			
Amount per serving			High Fat/Sugar Comparison	
Calories	242		450	
Calories from fat	40		210	
	% Daily Value*		% Daily Value*	
Total Fat	4.5 g	**7%**	23 g	**35%**
Saturated Fat	1 g	**5%**	9 g	**45%**
Cholesterol	30 mg	**10%**	85 mg	**28%**
Sodium	320 mg	**13%**	460 mg	**19%**
Total Carbohydrate	57 g	**19%**	56 g	**19%**
Dietary Fiber	5 g	**20%**	1 g	**4%**
Sugars	21 g		40 g	
Other	14 g		0 g	
Protein	4 g		5 g	

*Percent of Daily Values on page a-22

Directions

Cook sweet potatoes in boiling water until tender throughout when pierced. Drain and let cool briefly; then peel and place in a large bowl. Using an electric mixer or potato masher, beat potatoes until almost smooth. Add egg, 1/4 cup **SugarLike**, 1/4 cup **ButterLike**, salt, cinnamon, and orange juice. Continue to beat until moist and fluffy, adding more orange juice if needed. Spread mixture in a shallow 1 1/2- to 2-quart baking dish. Top with pecans, sprinkle with remaining 1/2 cup **SugarLike**, and drizzle with remaining 1/4 cup **ButterLike**. Bake, uncovered, in a 375° oven about 20 minutes until heated through.

Exchanges and 38 g Carbohydrates Per Serving					
Breads	2.0	Vegetables	0.0	Fruits	0.1
Meats	0.1	Milk	0.0	Fats	0.7

Yam and Cashew Casserole

The Fat Quotient using ButterLike is **6%** instead of **29%**
81% less fat **67% less sugar**
28% less Calories

U.S.	Ingredients	Metric
1/4 cup	**Granulated SugarLike**	50.00 g
3 Tbsp	**ButterLike Saute Butter**	42.00 g
2 1/2 lb	Yams or sweet potatoes, scrubbed	1134.00 g
1 tsp	Ground cinnamon	2.30 g
1/4 tsp	Salt	1.50 g
1/4 cup	Egg whites	57.00 g
1/4 cup	Pineapple juice, unsweetened	63.00 g
1/4 cup	Apple juice, unsweetened	62.00 g
1/8 cup	Salted cashews, coarsely chopped	17.00 g

Nutrition Facts				
Serving Size	238 g			
Servings Per Recipe	6			
Amount per serving			High Fat/Sugar Comparison	
Calories	286		400	
Calories from fat	25		110	
	% Daily Value*		% Daily Value*	
Total Fat	2.5 g	**4%**	13 g	**20%**
Saturated Fat	0.5 g	**3%**	5 g	**25%**
Cholesterol	0 mg	**0%**	50 mg	**17%**
Sodium	130 mg	**5%**	190 mg	**8%**
Total Carbohydrate	66 g	**22%**	67 g	**22%**
Dietary Fiber	2 g	**8%**	1 g	**4%**
Sugars	4 g		12 g	
Other	6 g		0 g	
Protein	5 g		6 g	

*Percent of Daily Values on page a-22

Directions

Cook yams in boiling water until tender throughout. Drain and let cool briefly; then peel and place in a large bowl. Using an electric mixer or a potato masher, beat yams until almost smooth. Add **SugarLike**, cinnamon, salt, egg whites, and pineapple juice, and apple juice. Continue to beat until mixture is moist and fluffy, adding more fruit juice if needed. Beat in 2 Tbsp **ButterLike**. Season to taste with more salt or **SugarLike**, if desired. Spread yam mixture in a small frying pan over medium heat. Add cashews and cook, stirring often, until lightly toasted. Sprinkle over yam mixture. Bake, uncovered, in a 375° oven until heated through.

Exchanges and 58 g Carbohydrates Per Serving					
Breads	2.9	Vegetables	0.0	Fruits	0.2
Meats	0.1	Milk	0.0	Fats	0.5

Ratatouille

The Fat Quotient using ButterLike is 20% instead of 56%
80% less fat 0% less sugar
43% less Calories

U.S.	Ingredients	Metric
1/2 cup	**ButterLike Saute Butter**	112.00 g
2 large	Onions, sliced	320.00 g
2 cloves	Garlic, minced	6.00 g
1	Eggplant, unpeeled, cut in 1/2 (1lb)	82.00 g
6 medium	Zucchini, thickly sliced	2721.00 g
2	Green or red bell peppers, seeded, cut	340.00 g
1 tsp	Dry basil	.80 g
1/2 cup	Parsley, minced	30.00 g
4 large	Tomatoes, cut into chunks	907.00 g
	Salt to taste	6.00 g

Nutrition Facts				
Serving Size	566 g			
Servings Per Recipe	8			
Amount per serving			High Fat/Sugar Comparison	
Calories	136		240	
Calories from fat	30		130	
	% Daily Value*		% Daily Value*	
Total Fat	3 g	**5%**	15 g	**23%**
Saturated Fat	1 g	**5%**	2 g	**10%**
Cholesterol	0 mg	**0%**	0 mg	**0%**
Sodium	320 mg	**13%**	320 mg	**13%**
Total Carbohydrate	25 g	**8%**	21 g	**7%**
Dietary Fiber	7 g	**28%**	7 g	**28%**
Sugars	13 g		13 g	
Other	0 g		0 g	
Protein	7 g		6 g	

*Percent of Daily Values on page a-22

Exchanges and 18 g Carbohydrates Per Serving					
Breads	0.3	Vegetables	3.7	Fruits	0.0
Meats	0.0	Milk	0.0	Fats	0.4

Directions

Heat 1/4 cup of the **ButterLike** in a frying pan over medium heat. Add onions and garlic and cook, stirring often, until onions are soft but not browned. Stir in eggplant, zucchini, bell peppers, basil, and minced parsley; add more **ButterLike** as needed to prevent sticking. Reduce heat, cover, and simmer, stirring occasionally, for about 30 minutes. Stir in tomatoes. Cover and continue to simmer, stirring occasionally, for about 15 more minutes. If ratatouille appears soupy, simmer, uncovered, until almost all liquid has evaporated. Season to taste with salt. May be served cold or hot.

Frittata Puff

The Fat Quotient using ButterLike is 24% instead of 68%
82% less fat 0% less sugar
47% less Calories

U.S.	Ingredients	Metric
1/4 cup	**ButterLike Saute Butter**	56.00 g
3	Eggs	150.00 g
1/2 cup	Egg substitute	123.00 g
1 cup	Fat free cottage cheese	226.00 g
1/4 cup	All-purpose flour	29.00 g
1/2 tsp	Baking powder	2.00 g
1/2 tsp	Salt	3.00 g
2 cups	Non fat shredded jack cheese (8 oz)	227.00 g
1 can	Diced green chilies (4 oz)	113.00 g

Directions

In a large bowl beat eggs until thick and lemon-colored. Stir in **ButterLike**, cottage cheese, flour, baking powder, and salt. Then add cheese and chilies; stir just until combined. If serving as a main dish, pour egg mixture into a vegetable sprayed 8-inch baking pan. Bake 35 minutes in a 350° oven or until the edges are browned and the center is firm. If serving as an appetizer, spoon egg mixture into tiny 1-inch vegetable sprayed muffin pans, using 1 1/2 Tbsp egg mixture per pan. Bake 15 minutes in a 350° oven until firm.

Exchanges and 7 g Carbohydrates Per Serving					
Breads	0.4	Vegetables	0.1	Fruits	0.0
Meats	1.7	Milk	0.0	Fats	0.4

Nutrition Facts				
Serving Size	116 g			
Servings Per Recipe	8			
Amount per serving			High Fat/Sugar Comparison	
Calories		133	250	
Calories from fat		30	180	
	% Daily Value*		% Daily Value*	
Total Fat	3.5 g	**5%**	19 g	**29%**
Saturated Fat	1 g	**5%**	10 g	**50%**
Cholesterol	80 mg	**27%**	180 mg	**60%**
Sodium	580 mg	**24%**	610 mg	**25%**
Total Carbohydrate	8 g	**3%**	4 g	**1%**
Dietary Fiber	1 g	**4%**	0 g	**0%**
Sugars	0 g		0 g	
Other	0 g		0 g	
Protein	16 g		14 g	

*Percent of Daily Values on page a-22

Fried Green Tomatoes

The Fat Quotient using ButterLike is **18%** instead of **56%**
78% less fat **0% less sugar**
31% less Calories

U.S.	Ingredients	Metric
4 Tbsp	**ButterLike Saute Butter**	56.00 g
1 large	Egg	50.00 g
2 Tbsp	Skim milk	31.00 g
	Salt to taste	.75 g
	Pepper to taste	.30 g
6 medium	Green tomatoes	738.00 g
1/2 cup	All-purpose flour	58.00 g
1/2 cup	Seasoned fat free cracker crumbs	56.00 g

Directions

Beat the egg, milk, salt, and pepper together in a mixing bowl. Dip tomato slices in flour, then into egg mixture, and finally into cracker crumbs. Heat 2 Tbsp of the **ButterLike** in a skillet over medium heat. Add crumbed tomato slices to hot **ButterLike** without overcrowding. Saute the slices 3 minutes each side until crispy golden brown; cover if necessary. Remove to a plate and serve immediately or keep warm in low oven. Repeat with remaining **ButterLike** and tomato slices.

Nutrition Facts				
Serving Size	247 g			
Servings Per Recipe	4			
Amount per serving			High Fat/Sugar Comparison	
Calories		200	290	
Calories from fat		35	170	
	% Daily Value*		% Daily Value*	
Total Fat	4 g	**6%**	18 g	**28%**
Saturated Fat	1 g	**5%**	3 g	**15%**
Cholesterol	55 mg	**18%**	55 mg	**18%**
Sodium	110 mg	**5%**	210 mg	**9%**
Total Carbohydrate	36 g	**12%**	17 g	**9%**
Dietary Fiber	3 g	**12%**	3 g	**12%**
Sugars	6 g		6 g	
Other	0 g		0 g	
Protein	7 g		6 g	

*Percent of Daily Values on page a-22

Exchanges and 33 g Carbohydrates Per serving					
Breads	1.8	Vegetables	1.4	Fruits	0.0
Meats	0.2	Milk	0.0	Fats	0.6

Tomato Souffle

The Fat Quotient using ButterLike is 20% instead of 64%
80% less fat **0% less sugar**
39% less Calories

U.S.	Ingredients	Metric
5 Tbsp	**ButterLike Saute Butter**	70.00 g
3 Tbsp	Non fat parmesan cheese	23.00 g
3 Tbsp	Shallots, chopped	3.00 g
1 1/2 Tbsp	Garlic, minced	43.00 g
2 Tbsp	Fresh tarragon, chopped	57.00 g
1/4 cup	All-purpose flour	29.00 g
1 tsp	Salt	6.00 g
1/2 tsp	Black pepper	1.00 g
2 cups	Ripe tomatoes, peel, seed, chop	442.00 g
2 Tbsp	Tomato paste	33.00 g
1/2 cup	Egg substitutes	126.00 g
5	Egg whites	167.00 g
1/4 tsp	Salt	1.50 g
1/4 tsp	Cream of tartar	.75 g

Nutrition Facts				
Serving Size	167 g			
Servings Per Recipe	6			
Amount per serving			High Fat/Sugar Comparison	
Calories	130		210	
Calories from fat	25		130	
	% Daily Value*		% Daily Value*	
Total Fat	3 g	**5%**	15 g	**23%**
Saturated Fat	1 g	**5%**	8 g	**40%**
Cholesterol	0 mg	**0%**	170 mg	**57%**
Sodium	630 mg	**26%**	700 mg	**29%**
Total Carbohydrate	16 g	**5%**	12 g	**4%**
Dietary Fiber	1 g	**4%**	1 g	**4%**
Sugars	3 g		3 g	
Other	0 g		0 g	
Protein	11 g		8 g	

*Percent of Daily Values on page a-22

Exchanges and 15 g Carbohydrates Per Serving

Breads	0.5	Vegetables	1.3	Fruits	0.0
Meats	1.8	Milk	0.0	Fats	0.4

Directions

Preheat oven to 350°. Vegetable spray a 6-8 cup medium to shallow souffle dish. Dust with finely grated parmesan cheese; set aside. Saute shallots in **ButterLike** over medium heat until wilted, about 5 minutes. Add garlic and tarragon, cook a few more minutes. Sprinkle with flour and cook until well blended. Add salt, pepper, and tomatoes. Mixture will lump; stir and mash until tomatoes begin to give up their water and a thick paste forms. Stir in tomato paste. Add egg substitutes and cook a few more minutes; set aside. Beat egg whites until foamy. Add salt and cream of tarter. Beat until stiff. Pile whites on top of the tomato mixture and fold in with an over-and-under motion until lightly mixed. Do not over mix; there can be some streaks or white lumps when pouring into prepared souffle dish. Place dish in a larger pan and surround in hot water. Bake 35-40 minutes, until set. Serve immediately.

Spinach-Stuffed Tomatoes

The Fat Quotient using ButterLike is 20% instead of 38%
60% less fat **0% less sugar**
23% less Calories

U.S.	Ingredients	Metric
2 Tbsp	**ButterLike Saute Butter**	28.00 g
8 medium	Tomatoes	984.00 g
1 medium	Onion, finely chopped (3/4 cup)	83.00 g
2 cloves	Garlic, crushed or minced	6.00 g
2 lb	Fresh spinach, steamed and chopped	907.00 g
1 cup	Dried bread crumbs	45.00 g
1	Egg, beaten	50.00 g
1 tsp	Dried thyme leaves	1.20 g
1 tsp	Dried oregano leaves	1.50 g

Directions

Halve tomatoes horizontally and remove seeds and juice. Place tomato halves in a lightly vegetable sprayed baking dish. Heat **ButterLike** in a skillet over medium heat and saute onion 3 minutes. Add garlic and saute 2 minutes longer. Remove from heat and stir in spinach, bread crumbs, egg, thyme, and oregano. Salt and pepper to taste. Spoon the mixture into the hollowed tomato halves and bake in a 350° oven for 35-40 minutes, until hot and golden.

Exchanges and 10 g Carbohydrates Per Serving					
Breads	0.3	Vegetables	1.9	Fruits	0.0
Meats	0.1	Milk	0.0	Fats	0.2

Nutrition Facts				
Serving Size	263 g			
Servings Per Recipe	8			
Amount per serving			High Fat/Sugar Comparison	
Calories		92	120	
Calories from fat		20	45	
	% Daily Value*		% Daily Value*	
Total Fat	2 g	3%	5 g	8%
Saturated Fat	0.5 g	3%	1 g	5%
Cholesterol	25 mg	8%	25 mg	8%
Sodium	170 mg	7%	170 mg	7%
Total Carbohydrate	15 g	5%	14 g	5%
Dietary Fiber	5 g	20%	5 g	20%
Sugars	5 g		5 g	
Other	0 g		0 g	
Protein	6 g		6 g	

*Percent of Daily Values on page a-22

Stir-Fried Ginger-Mustard Turnips

The Fat Quotient using ButterLike is **14%** instead of **70%**
80% less fat **0% less sugar**
29% less Calories

U.S.	Ingredients	Metric
3 Tbsp	**ButterLike Baking Butter**	43.00 g
1 lb	Turnips, peeled and sliced, 1/4-inch	454.00 g
2 cloves	Garlic, minced	6.00 g
1 tsp	Ground ginger	1.80 g
2 Tbsp	Prepared mustard, spicy or sweet	30.00 g

Directions

Heat the **ButterLike** in a large skillet. Add turnip pieces and saute 5 minutes. If turnips tend to stick, cover and continue cooking. Add garlic and ginger; saute 3 more minutes. Remove from heat and coat with mustard. Spoon into dish and serve immediately.

Nutrition Facts				
Serving Size	134 g			
Servings Per Recipe	4			
Amount per serving			High Fat/Sugar Comparison	
Calories		64	90	
Calories from fat		10	60	
	% Daily Value*		% Daily Value*	
Total Fat	1 g	2%	5 g	11%
Saturated Fat	0 g	0%	1 g	5%
Cholesterol	0 mg	0%	0 mg	0%
Sodium	150 mg	6%	105 mg	4%
Total Carbohydrate	15 g	5%	14 g	5%
Dietary Fiber	1 g	4%	1 g	4%
Sugars	4 g		4 g	
Other	0 g		0 g	
Protein	1 g		1 g	

*Percent of Daily Values on page a-22

Exchanges and 14 g Carbohydrates Per Serving					
Breads	0.4	Vegetables	1.3	Fruits	0.0
Meats	0.0	Milk	0.0	Fats	0.1

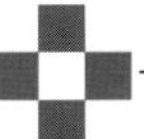

Cajun Oven-Fried Vegetables

The Fat Quotient using ButterLike is 8% instead of 38%
86% less fat **0% less sugar**
30% less Calories

U.S.	Ingredients	Metric
2 Tbsp	**ButterLike Saute Butter**	28.00 g
1/2 cup	Egg whites	114.00 g
1 cup	Unseasoned dry bread crumbs	108.00 g
1/2 tsp	Cajun seasoning	2.00 g
1 can	Whole mushrooms (8 oz)	227.00 g
1 medium	Zucchini, diagonal 1/2-inch slices	195.00 g
1 medium	Bell pepper, 1/2-inch strips	170.00 g

Directions

Heat oven to 375°. Vegetable spray cookie sheet. Beat **ButterLike** and egg whites in a small bowl. Mix bread crumbs and cajun seasoning in a small bowl. Dip mushrooms, zucchini, and bell peppers into egg mixture, then coat with bread crumb mixture. Arrange vegetables in single layer, so pieces are not touching each other, on cookie sheet. Bake 20-25 minutes, turning after 10 minutes, until coating is golden brown. Serve hot.

Nutrition Facts				
Serving Size	71 g			
Servings Per Recipe	12			
Amount per serving			High Fat/Sugar Comparison	
Calories		56	80	
Calories from fat		9	30	
	% Daily Value*		% Daily Value*	
Total Fat	.5 g	**1%**	3.5 g	**0%**
Saturated Fat	0 g	**0%**	1.5 g	**0%**
Cholesterol	0 mg	**0%**	40 mg	**3%**
Sodium	115 mg	**2%**	130 mg	**1%**
Total Carbohydrate	9 g	**3%**	8 g	**3%**
Dietary Fiber	1 g	**4%**	1 g	**4%**
Sugars	0 g		0 g	
Other	0 g		0 g	
Protein	1 g		1 g	

*Percent of Daily Values on page a-22

Exchanges and 8 g Carbohydrates Per Serving					
Breads	0.2	Vegetables	0.1	Fruits	0.0
Meats	0.0	Milk	0.0	Fats	0.1

Grilled Vegetables

The Fat Quotient using ButterLike is 31% instead of 81%
83% less fat **0% less sugar**
56% less Calories

U.S.	Ingredients	Metric
1/3 cup	**ButterLike Saute Butter**	75.00 g
2 lbs	Vegetables, choices follow	907.00 g
2 Tbsp	Minced fresh thyme	6.00 g
2 Tbsp	Fresh oregano	6.00 g
2 Tbsp	Fresh rosemary	6.00 g
2 Tbsp	Fresh tarragon	6.00 g
	Salt to taste	6.00 g
	Pepper to taste	2.10 g

Nutrition Facts				
Serving Size	127 g			
Servings Per Recipe	8			
Amount per serving			High Fat/Sugar Comparison	
Calories		44	100	
Calories from fat		15	80	
	% Daily Value*		% Daily Value*	
Total Fat	1.5 g	**2%**	9 g	**14%**
Saturated Fat	0 g	**0%**	1 g	**5%**
Cholesterol	0 mg	**0%**	0 mg	**0%**
Sodium	290 mg	**12%**	290 mg	**12%**
Total Carbohydrate	7 g	**2%**	4 g	**1%**
Dietary Fiber	2 g	**8%**	2 g	**8%**
Sugars	3 g		3 g	
Other	0 g		0 g	
Protein	2 g		1 g	

*Percent of Daily Values on page a-22

Directions

To blanch vegetables, cook 2 lb of chosen vegetables in boiling water until tender. Remove with tongs. Cool in ice water. To grill vegetables, combine **ButterLike** and herbs or use **Seasoned ButterLike** instead; brush over vegetables. Grill on a vegetable sprayed grill 4-6 inches above coals. Cook, turning often and brushing with mixture to keep moist, until vegetables are hot, tender, and covered with brown streaks. Salt and pepper to taste.

Bell Peppers: Cut in quarters; remove seeds. Grill 8-10 minutes.

Eggplant: Cut lengthwise into 1 1/2-inch wide wedges. Blanch 2-3 minutes; grill until very soft 12-15 minutes.

Mushrooms: Grill 10 minutes. Thread small and button mushrooms on skewers. Grill large mushrooms whole.

Onions: Halve small onions; quarter large onions. Thread skewers through layers, arranging pieces to lie flat. Grill 15-20 minutes. (Green Onions: Trim root ends and top 2 inches of green tops. Grill 8-10 minutes.)

Potatoes: Scrub well; cut lengthwise into 1-inch wedges. Blanch 4-5 minutes; grill 8-10 minutes.

Summer Squash: If thicker than 1 inch, halve lengthwise. Blanch 2-3 minutes. Grill 8-10 minutes.

Tomatoes: Cut into halves. Grill 8-12 minutes.

Exchanges and 5 g Carbohydrates Per Serving					
Breads	0.2	Vegetables	0.7	Fruits	0.0
Meats	0.0	Milk	0.0	Fats	0.3

Chinese Celery Cabbage Stir-Fry

The Fat Quotient using **ButterLike** is **12%** instead of **41%**
80% less fat **0% less sugar**
33% less Calories

U.S.	Ingredients	Metric
2 Tbsp	**ButterLike Saute Butter**	28.00 g
2 lb	Cabbage, 2-inch pieces	907.00 g
3/4 cup	Water	178.00 g
1/4 cup	Rice vinegar	68.00 g
2 Tbsp	Soy sauce	36.00 g
1 1/2 Tbsp	Cornstarch	12.00 g
1 Tbsp	Fresh ginger, grated	5.40 g
1 3-inch	Hot chile, without stem, thinly sliced	35.00 g

Directions

Heat the **ButterLike** in a wok over medium heat. Add the cabbage and cook 3 minutes, stirring frequently. Remove cabbage mixture from wok and into dish. Combine the water, rice vinegar, soy sauce, cornstarch, and grated ginger. Pour into the wok and stir constantly until it thickens, in about 1 minute. Return cabbage to the wok, add the sliced hot chilies, and stir-fry for 1 minute. Serve immediately.

Nutrition Facts				
Serving Size	212 g			
Servings Per Recipe	6			
Amount per serving			High Fat/Sugar Comparison	
Calories		74	110	
Calories from fat		10	45	
	% Daily Value*		% Daily Value*	
Total Fat	1 g	**2%**	5 g	**8%**
Saturated Fat	0 g	**0%**	0 g	**0%**
Cholesterol	0 mg	**0%**	0 mg	**0%**
Sodium	480 mg	**20%**	480 mg	**20%**
Total Carbohydrate	15 g	**5%**	14 g	**5%**
Dietary Fiber	3 g	**12%**	3 g	**12%**
Sugars	8 g		8 g	
Other	0 g		0 g	
Protein	3 g		2 g	

*Percent of Daily Values on page a-22

Exchanges and 12 g Carbohydrates Per Serving					
Breads	0.4	Vegetables	1.6	Fruits	0.0
Meats	0.0	Milk	0.0	Fats	0.1

Soups

Minestrone Genovese, page 284

Bateman Saute Butters work beautifully in soups. In this section there are many soups that start by sauteing vegetables. These will be marked by the special Saute Symbol ( ). These soups end up rich and buttery tasting and I am very pleased to offer this new addition to the Cookbook.

Tips on successful soups using the Bateman Products

Sauteing with ButterLike Saute Butter

- Add **Saute Butter** to a non stick pan **before** heating to saute vegetables or meats.
- Add enough **Saute Butter** to slightly cover the vegetables and meat. Adjust the size of the pan to fit the amount of the items to be cooked.
- If the **Saute Butter** sticks to the pan, cover it for a few minutes.
- If items need to be browned, some sticking may occur. Sprinkling a small amount of water into the pan and stirring may assist in browning.

Tortellini Soup with Hot Pepper Cream

The Fat Quotient using ButterLike is **22%** instead of **58%**
74% less fat **0% less sugar**
31% less Calories

U.S.	Ingredients	Metric
Tortellini Soup:		
2 Tbsp	**ButterLike Saute Butter**	28.00 g
1 small	Yellow onion, halved and peeled	80.00 g
2 medium	Carrots, peeled	170.00 g
1 can	Peeled Italian plum tomatoes (14 oz)	397.00 g
1 cup	Tomato puree	252.00 g
3 cups	Water	711.00 g
1 lb	Low fat cheese tortellini	454.00 g
1/2 cup	Evaporated skim milk	128.00 g
Creamy Hot Pepper Sauce:		
Dash	Salt	.75 g
Dash	Pepper	.26 g
1/2 cup	**ButterLike Saute Butter**	112.00 g
2-3 cloves	Garlic, peeled and crushed	6.00 g
4 oz	Roasted red peppers, drained	113.00 g
1 Tbsp	Lemon juice	15.00 g
2	Egg yolks	33.00 g
1/2 tsp	Cayenne pepper	.90 g
1/2 tsp	Crushed red pepper flakes	.90 g
To taste	Salt	3.00 g
1 tsp	Parsley, chopped	1.25 g

Nutrition Facts				
Serving Size	418 g			
Servings Per Recipe	6			
Amount per serving			High Fat/Sugar Comparison	
Calories	247		360	
Calories from fat	60		210	
	% Daily Value*		% Daily Value*	
Total Fat	6 g	**9%**	23 g	**35%**
Saturated Fat	2.5 g	**13%**	11 g	**55%**
Cholesterol	85 mg	**28%**	180 mg	**60%**
Sodium	610 mg	**25%**	640 mg	**27%**
Total Carbohydrate	38 g	**13%**	25 g	**8%**
Dietary Fiber	4 g	**16%**	4 g	**16%**
Sugars	9 g		9 g	
Other	0 g		0 g	
Protein	11 g		13 g	

*Percent of Daily Values on page a-22

Exchanges and 34 g Carbohydrates Per Serving

Breads	1.0	Vegetables	2.9	Fruits	0.0
Meats	0.3	Milk	0.2	Fats	0.8

Directions

Tortellini Soup: Coarsely chop onions and carrots. Heat **ButterLike** in heavy saucepan over medium heat. Add onions and carrots; saute 3 minutes or until slightly softened. Stir in tomatoes with juice, breaking up with wooden spoon. Stir in puree and water; bring to boil over high heat. Add tortellini; cover and simmer 10-12 minutes until tortellini is tender, over low heat. Add evaporated milk to saucepan and stir to blend. Season soup very lightly with salt and pepper. Keep warm over low heat until ready to serve.

Creamy Hot Pepper Sauce: Blend garlic, roasted peppers, lemon juice, egg yolks, cayenne, and red pepper flakes. While blending, add **ButterLike** in a thin, steady stream, stopping often to scrape sides with spatula. Add salt to taste. Spoon over Tortellini Soup, divided into 6 bowls. Top each bowl with parsley.

Hamburger Soup

The Fat Quotient using ButterLike is 29% instead of 51%
68% less fat 0% less sugar
44% less Calories

U.S.	Ingredients	Metric
2 Tbsp	**ButterLike Saute Butter**	28.00 g
1 lb	Extra lean ground beef	454.00 g
Dash	Pepper	.75 g
1/2 tsp	Oregano	.75 g
1/2 tsp	Basil	.4 g
1/8 tsp	Seasoned salt	.60 g
1 pkg	Onion soup mix (1.5 oz)	39.00 g
6 cups	Water	1422.00 g
1 can	Tomato sauce (8 oz)	227.00 g
1 Tbsp	Soy sauce	18.00 g
1 cup	Celery, sliced	120.00 g
1/4 cup	Celery leaves, coarsely chopped	30.00 g
1 cup	Carrots, diced	110.00 g
1/3 cup	Dried split peas	66.00 g
1 cup	Dry elbow macaroni	105.00 g

Nutrition Facts				
Serving Size	327 g			
Servings Per Recipe	8			
Amount per serving			High Fat/Sugar Comparison	
Calories	248		440	
Calories from fat	70		220	
	% Daily Value*		% Daily Value*	
Total Fat	8 g	**12%**	25 g	**38%**
Saturated Fat	3 g	**15%**	9 g	**45%**
Cholesterol	45 mg	**15%**	70 mg	**23%**
Sodium	830 mg	**35%**	850 mg	**35%**
Total Carbohydrate	23 g	**8%**	22 g	**7%**
Dietary Fiber	4 g	**16%**	4 g	**16%**
Sugars	2 g		2 g	
Other	0 g		0 g	
Protein	21 g		32 g	

*Percent of Daily Values on page a-22

Exchanges and 19 g Carbohydrates Per Serving

Breads	1.2	Vegetables	0.8	Fruits	0.0
Meats	2.5	Milk	0.0	Fats	0.4

Directions

Heat **ButterLike** in a deep 4-5 quart pan over medium heat. Crumble in beef and cook, stirring often, until browned. Rinse meat. Return to pan and add pepper, oregano, basil, seasoned salt, and onion soup mix. Stir in the water, tomato sauce, and soy sauce. Bring to a boil; then reduce heat, cover, and simmer for about 15 minutes. Add celery, celery leaves, carrots, and peas; cover and simmer for 30 more minutes. Add macaroni, cover, and simmer until tender to bite (10-15 minutes); add more water, if needed. Season to taste with salt.

Green Pea and Ham Soup

The Fat Quotient using ButterLike is 20% instead of 42%
63% less fat 0% less sugar
23% less Calories

U.S.	Ingredients	Metric
4 Tbsp	**ButterLike Saute Butter**	56.00 g
1/4 lb	Extra lean ham steak, 1/2-inch thick	113.00 g
1/3 cup	Celery, finely chopped	40.00 g
1/2 cup	Carrots, finely chopped	55.00 g
1 cup	Onions, finely chopped	160.00 g
1/2 lb	Fresh button mushrooms, sliced	227.00 g
1 clove	Garlic, minced	3.00 g
4 cups	Chicken stock, heated	907.00 g
1 tsp	Salt	6.00 g
1/2 tsp	Paprika	1.00 g
1/4 tsp	Black pepper, finely ground	.50 g
1/2 cup	Boston head lettuce, shredded	82.00 g
2 cups	Green peas, shelled	340.00 g

Nutrition Facts				
Serving Size	332 g			
Servings Per Recipe	6			
Amount per serving			High Fat/Sugar Comparison	
Calories	131		170	
Calories from fat	25		80	
	% Daily Value*		% Daily Value*	
Total Fat	3 g	**5%**	8 g	**12%**
Saturated Fat	1 g	**5%**	3.5 g	**18%**
Cholesterol	6 mg	**2%**	20 mg	**7%**
Sodium	2070 mg	**86%**	2170 mg	**90%**
Total Carbohydrate	17 g	**6%**	14 g	**5%**
Dietary Fiber	4 g	**16%**	4 g	**16%**
Sugars	4 g		4 g	
Other	0 g		0 g	
Protein	10 g		10 g	

*Percent of Daily Values on page a-22

Directions

Heat **ButterLike** in a deep saucepan and add finely diced ham. Saute over medium heat until ham begins to crisp. Remove, drain, and reserve. Add celery, carrots, and onions; saute until vegetables wilt and begin to turn golden, about 3 minutes. Add mushrooms and continue cooking for 2 minutes more, tossing all the while. Stir in garlic, then add chicken stock, salt, paprika, and pepper. Add lettuce and peas to the soup. Bring to a boil and then reduce heat to a simmer. Cook for 10 minutes and turn off heat. Stir in reserved ham and allow to sit for 15 minutes before serving.

Exchanges and 13 g Carbohydrates Per Serving					
Breads	0.7	Vegetables	1.0	Fruits	0.0
Meats	0.6	Milk	0.0	Fats	0.3

Minestrone Genovese

The fat quotient using ButterLike is **4%** instead of **25%**

87% less fat | **0% less sugar**

76% less Calories

U.S.	Ingredients	Metric
	Pesto Sauce, page 175	179.00 g
2	Leeks, raw	248.00 g
3 quarts	Fat free chicken broth	2940.00 g
2 large	Carrots, cut into 1/2-inch chunks	144.00 g
2 large	Stalks celery, thinly sliced	120.00 g
30 oz	White kidney beans, drained, rinsed	851.00 g
2 cups	Dry elbow macaroni	210.00 g
1 lb	Squash or yellow zucchini, 1/2-inch chunks	454.00 g
1 large	Red bell pepper, seeded, 1/2-inch pieces	170.00 g
1 pkg	Frozen tiny peas, thawed (1 lb)	454.00 g

Nutrition Facts				
Serving Size	481 g			
Servings Per Recipe	12			
Amount per serving			High Fat/Sugar Comparison	
Calories	415		540	
Calories from fat	20		140	
	% Daily Value*		% Daily Value*	
Total Fat	2 g	**3%**	15 g	**23%**
Saturated Fat	0.5 g	**3%**	3 g	**15%**
Cholesterol	0 mg	**0%**	5 mg	**2%**
Sodium	350 mg	**15%**	1060 mg	**44%**
Total Carbohydrate	72 g	**24%**	72 g	**24%**
Dietary Fiber	15 g	**60%**	15 g	**60%**
Sugars	5 g		5 g	
Other	0 g		0 g	
Protein	28 g		30 g	

*Percent of Daily Values on page a-22

Exchanges and 57 g Carbohydrates Per Serving					
Breads	4.2	Vegetables	1.4	Fruits	0.0
Meats	3.2	Milk	0.0	Fats	0.2

Directions

Prepare **Pesto Sauce** as directed.

Cut off and discard root ends of leeks. Trim tops, leaving about 3 inches of green leaves. Discard coarse outer leaves. Split leeks in half lengthwise and rinse well; then thinly slice crosswise. In a 8- to 10-quart pan, combine leeks, broth, carrots, and celery. Bring to a boil over high heat; then reduce heat, cover, and simmer 10 minutes until macaroni is just tender to bite. Add beans, macaroni, squash, and the bell pepper. Bring to a boil; then reduce heat, cover and simmer about 10 minutes. Add peas; bring again to a boil over high heat. Stir 1/2 cup of the Pesto Sauce into soup. If made ahead, let cool; then cover and refrigerate until next day. Serve cold or at room temperature, or reheat to serve hot. To serve, ladle soup into bowls. Offer remaining Pesto Sauce, salt, and pepper to add taste.

Mushroom Velvet Soup

The Fat Quotient using **ButterLike** is **13%** instead of **73%**
91% less fat **75% less sugar**
52% less Calories

U.S.	Ingredients	Metric
1/4 cup	**ButterLike Saute Butter**	56.00 g
1/2 lb	Mushrooms, sliced	227.00 g
1 medium	Onion, coarsely chopped	120.00 g
2/3 cup	Parsley, finely chopped	40.00 g
1 Tbsp	All-purpose flour	7.00 g
1 can	Fat free beef broth (14.5 oz)	411.00 g
1 cup	Fat free sour cream	256.00 g

Directions

Heat **ButterLike** in a wide frying pan over medium heat. Add mushrooms, onion, and parsley. Cook, stirring, until mushrooms are soft. Stir in flour and cook, stirring, for 1 minute; then stir in broth. Bring to a boil over high heat, stirring constantly. In a blender or food processor, whirl half the soup with 1/2 cup of the sour cream until smooth. Repeat to puree remaining soup with remaining 1/2 cup sour cream. To serve, return soup to pan and heat thoroughly; do not boil. Ladle into bowls or mugs.

Nutrition Facts				
Serving Size	186 g			
Servings Per Recipe	6			
Amount per serving			High Fat/Sugar Comparison	
Calories		101	210	
Calories from fat		15	150	
	% Daily Value*		% Daily Value*	
Total Fat	1.5 g	**2%**	17 g	**26%**
Saturated Fat	.5 g	**3%**	10 g	**50%**
Cholesterol	0 mg	**0%**	40 mg	**13%**
Sodium	85 mg	**4%**	340 mg	**14%**
Total Carbohydrate	16 g	**5%**	10 g	**3%**
Dietary Fiber	1 g	**4%**	1 g	**4%**
Sugars	4 g		1 g	
Other	0 g		0 g	
Protein	6 g		3 g	

*Percent of Daily Values on page a-22

Exchanges and 15 g Carbohydrates Per Serving					
Breads	0.5	Vegetables	0.7	Fruits	0.0
Meats	0.1	Milk	0.4	Fats	0.3

Curried Carrot-Peanut Soup

The Fat Quotient using **ButterLike** is **27%** instead of **37%**
50% less fat **14% less sugar**
32% less Calories

U.S.	Ingredients	Metric
2 Tbsp	**ButterLike Saute Butter**	28.00 g
1 lb	Carrots, chopped	454.00 g
6 cups	Fat free chicken broth	1470.00 g
1/2 cup	Onion, finely chopped	80.00 g
1/8 cup	Reduced fat peanut butter	36.00 g
1 clove	Garlic, minced or pressed	3.00 g
2 Tbsp	Curry powder	12.00 g
1/4 cup	Rice	41.00 g
2 cups	Small broccoli flowerets (6 oz)	176.00 g

Nutrition Facts				
Serving Size	383 g			
Servings Per Recipe	6			
Amount per serving			High Fat/Sugar Comparison	
Calories		116	170	
Calories from fat		30	70	
	% Daily Value*		% Daily Value*	
Total Fat	3.5 g	**5%**	7 g	**11%**
Saturated Fat	.5 g	**3%**	1.5 g	**8%**
Cholesterol	0 mg	**0%**	0 mg	**0%**
Sodium	87 mg	**4%**	140 mg	**7%**
Total Carbohydrate	16 g	**5%**	16 g	**5%**
Dietary Fiber	2 g	**8%**	2 g	**8%**
Sugars	6 g		7 g	
Other	0 g		0 g	
Protein	6 g		10 g	

*Percent of Daily Values on page a-22

Directions

In a 4- to 5-quart saucepan, combine carrots and 3 cups broth. Boil over high heat; then reduce heat to medium, cover, and boil gently 25-30 minutes until carrots are very tender to bite. Drain carrots; reserve broth. Puree carrots in a blender or food processor. Return puree to pan with reserved cooking broth and stir until blended. Stir in **ButterLike**, remaining 3 cups broth, onion, peanut butter, garlic, curry powder, and rice. Bring to a boil over high heat; reduce heat, cover, and simmer, stirring occasionally, 30-40 minutes until rice is tender to bite. Add broccoli; cook 5 minutes until tender when pierced. To serve, ladle into bowls.

Exchanges and 14 g Carbohydrates Per Serving					
Breads	0.3	Vegetables	1.8	Fruits	0.0
Meats	0.5	Milk	0.0	Fats	0.5

Creamed Green Vegetable Soup

The Fat Quotient using ButterLike is **9%** instead of **23%**
71% less fat **8% less sugar**
22% less Calories

U.S.	Ingredients	Metric
2 Tbsp	**ButterLike Saute Butter**	28.00 g
1/2 tsp	**Granulated SugarLike**	2.00 g
1 medium	Onion, chopped	120.00 g
1/4 cup	Celery leaves, chopped	2.0.00 g
6 cups	Broccoli or halved brussel sprouts	1212.00 g
2 cups	Vegetable stock	454.00 g
1 1/2 cup	Skim milk	368.00 g
1/4 tsp	Ground mace	.43 g
1/4 tsp	Fresh dill, chopped	.56 g
1/4 cup	Chives, chopped	5.00 g

Directions

Heat the **ButterLike** in a 4-quart saucepan and saute the onion and celery leaves for 5 minutes over medium heat. Add the broccoli or brussel sprouts to the pan with stock and milk. Cover and bring to a boil over high heat. Reduce the heat and simmer for 15 minutes. Place one third of the soup at a time in a food processor, blender, or food mill. Puree the mixture. Return the soup to the pot and stir in the **SugarLike**, mace, dill, salt, and pepper. Add enough milk to thin mixture to a moderately thick, souplike texture. Heat through for 5 minutes. Ladle into soup bowls and garnish with chopped chives.

Nutrition Facts

Serving Size	552 g			
Servings Per Recipe	4			
Amount per serving			High Fat/Sugar Comparison	
Calories		211	270	
Calories from fat		20	70	
	% Daily Value*		% Daily Value*	
Total Fat	2 g	**3%**	7 g	**11%**
Saturated Fat	.5 g	**3%**	2.5 g	**13%**
Cholesterol	5 mg	**2%**	10 mg	**3%**
Sodium	1120 mg	**47%**	1120 mg	**47%**
Total Carbohydrate	39 g	**13%**	36 g	**12%**
Dietary Fiber	13 g	**52%**	13 g	**52%**
Sugars	11 g		12 g	
Other	1 g		0 g	
Protein	15 g		15 g	

*Percent of Daily Values on page a-22

Exchanges and 26 g Carbohydrates Per Serving					
Breads	0.2	Vegetables	5.7	Fruits	0.0
Meats	0.0	Milk	0.3	Fats	0.2

Garden Fresh Vegetable Soup

The Fat Quotient using **ButterLike** is **14%** instead of **25%**
66% less fat **0% less sugar**
40% less Calories

U.S.	Ingredients	Metric
3 Tbsp	**ButterLike Saute Butter**	42.00 g
1 large	Onion, chopped	160.00 g
2 cloves	Garlic, minced or pressed	6.00 g
6 cups	Prepared vegetables	660.00 g
2 quarts	Fat free beef broth	1920.00 g
1 can	Red kidney beans, drained (15 oz)	425.00 g
1/2 tsp	Dry basil	.70 g
1/2 tsp	Dry oregano	.75 g
1/2 tsp	Dry rosemary	.60 g
1 can	Tomato sauce (8 oz)	227.00 g
2 large	Tomatoes, seeded and chopped	246.00 g
2/3 cup	Dry elbow macaroni or spaghetti	70.00 g
2 cups	Shredded cabbage, spinach, or chard	140.00 g

Directions

Heat **ButterLike** in pan. Add onion, garlic, and prepared vegetables. Cook over medium heat until onion is soft. Add broth, kidney beans, basil, oregano, and rosemary. Bring to a simmer; cover and simmer 30 minutes. Add tomato sauce, tomatoes, and macaroni to pan. Return to a simmer; cover and simmer 10-15 minutes until macaroni is tender to bite. Stir cabbage, spinach, or chard into soup. Cover and simmer 5 minutes, just until wilted. Season to taste with salt and pepper. To serve, ladle soup into bowls. If desired, sprinkle with grated fat free cheese.

Nutrition Facts				
Serving Size	487 g			
Servings Per Recipe	8			
Amount per serving			High Fat/Sugar Comparison	
Calories	198		330	
Calories from fat	25		80	
		% Daily Value*		% Daily Value*
Total Fat	3 g	**5%**	9 g	**14%**
Saturated Fat	.5 g	**3%**	3 g	**15%**
Cholesterol	0 mg	**0%**	25 mg	**8%**
Sodium	520 mg	**22%**	1180 mg	**49%**
Total Carbohydrate	34 g	**11%**	45 g	**15%**
Dietary Fiber	8 g	**32%**	8 g	**32%**
Sugars	9 g		9 g	
Other	0 g		0 g	
Protein	11 g		16 g	

*Percent of Daily Values on page a-22

Exchanges and 26 g Carbohydrates Per Serving

Breads	1.1	Vegetables	3.0	Fruits	0.0
Meats	0.7	Milk	0.0	Fats	0.4

Curried Cauliflower Soup

The Fat Quotient using **ButterLike** is **12%** instead of **45%**
79% less fat **0% less sugar**
23% less Calories

U.S.	Ingredients	Metric
3 Tbsp	**ButterLike Saute Butter**	42.00 g
2 lb	Cauliflower, separated into flowerets	907.00 g
1 large	Sweet onion, finely chopped	200.00 g
1 large	Red bell pepper, finely chopped	170.00g
2 large	Celery ribs, finely chopped	120.00g
4 cloves	Garlic, finely minced	12.00 g
2 Tbsp	All-purpose flour	14.00g
3 Tbsp	Mild curry powder	18.00g

U.S.	Ingredients	Metric
2 tsp	Ground coriander	3.20 g
2 tsp	Turmeric powder	4.40 g
1 tsp	Ground cumin	4.70 g
2 cups	Skim milk	490.00 g
1 1/2 cup	Vegetable stock	340.00 g
1 cup	Fat free sour cream	256.00 g
1/4 cup	Fresh parsley, chopped	15.00 g

Directions

Steam the cauliflower flowerets in 1/2 cup water in a covered dish in the microwave 12-15 minutes, until tender (or on top of the stove in a covered pan in 1 inch of water). Heat the **ButterLike** in a 4-quart saucepan over medium heat, add the chopped onion, bell pepper, celery, and garlic. Saute for 10 minutes stirring occasionally. Combine the flour, curry powder, coriander, turmeric, and cumin. Stir into the onion mixture and cook 5 minutes. Pour in the vegetable stock and milk. Cook for 8-10 minutes, stirring frequently, until the liquid thickens. Stir the cauliflower flowerets into the pan and continue cooking for 5 minutes, until heated through. Remove from heat. Stir a little of the hot soup into the sour cream and spoon this mixture back into the simmering liquid in the pan. Stir to combine. Serve immediately garnished with chopped parsley.

Nutrition Facts				
Serving Size	433 g			
Servings Per Recipe	6			
Amount per serving			High Fat/Sugar Comparison	
Calories	184		240	
Calories from fat	20		110	
	% Daily Value*		% Daily Value*	
Total Fat	2.5 g	**4%**	12 g	**18%**
Saturated Fat	.5 g	**3%**	3.5 g	**18%**
Cholesterol	0 mg	**0%**	15 mg	**5%**
Sodium	620 mg	**26%**	600 mg	**25%**
Total Carbohydrate	32 g	**11%**	24 g	**8%**
Dietary Fiber	7 g	**28%**	7 g	**28%**
Sugars	11 g		11 g	
Other	0 g		0 g	
Protein	11 g		9 g	

*Percent of Daily Values on page a-22

Exchanges and 25 g Carbohydrates Per Serving

Breads	0.5	Vegetables	1.9	Fruits	0.0
Meats	0.0	Milk	0.7	Fats	0.2

Spinach Tortellini Soup

The Fat Quotient using ButterLike is **11%** instead of **51%**
88% less fat **0% less sugar**
45% less Calories

U.S.	**Ingredients**	Metric
2 Tbsp	**ButterLike Saute Butter**	28.00 g
1 1/2 cup	Onions, chopped	240.00 g
4 cloves	Garlic, minced	12.00 g
8 oz	Fresh mushrooms, sliced	227.00 g
4 cans	Fat free chicken broth (14.5 oz each)	1644.00 g
9 oz	Low fat cheese-filled tortellini	255.00 g
3 cups	Chopped fresh spinach	168.00 g
1/3 cup	Non fat parmesan cheese, shredded	40.00 g

Directions

Heat **ButterLike** in a large saucepan over medium heat until hot. Add onions; cook and stir 2-3 minutes or until tender. Add garlic and mushrooms; cook and stir 2 minutes. Add broth; bring to a boil. Add tortellini; return to a boil. Boil 5-7 minutes or until tortellini are of desired doneness. Stir in spinach; cook 1-2 minutes or until wilted. Top each serving with cheese.

Nutrition Facts				
Serving Size	436 g			
Servings Per Recipe	6			
Amount per serving			High Fat/Sugar Comparison	
Calories	126		230	
Calories from fat	15		120	
	% Daily Value*		% Daily Value*	
Total Fat	1.5 g	**2%**	13 g	**20%**
Saturated Fat	.5 g	**3%**	5 g	**25%**
Cholesterol	5 mg	**2%**	30 mg	**10%**
Sodium	260 mg	**11%**	1100 mg	**46%**
Total Carbohydrate	17 g	**6%**	14 g	**5%**
Dietary Fiber	2 g	**8%**	3 g	**12%**
Sugars	3 g		3 g	
Other	0 g		0 g	
Protein	11 g		14 g	

*Percent of Daily Values on page a-22

Exchanges and 15 g Carbohydrates Per Serving

Breads	0.4	Vegetables	1.5	Fruits	0.0
Meats	2.2	Milk	0.0	Fats	0.1

Chicken and Angel Hair Soup

The Fat Quotient using ButterLike is 12% instead of 27%
56% less fat **0% less sugar**
2% less Calories

U.S.	Ingredients	Metric
2 tbsp	**ButterLike Saute Butter**	28.00 g
4	Boneless, skinless chicken breasts, halved	680.00 g
1/4 cup	Shallots, finely chopped	4.00 g
1 clove	Garlic, minced or pressed	3.00 g
1/4 tsp	Dry thyme	.30 g
1/8 tsp	White pepper	.30 g
1 can	Fat free chicken broth (14.5 oz)	411.00 g
1 1/2 cup	Water	356.00 g
1/2 cup	Dry white wine	118.00 g
1 medium	Carrot, thinly sliced	72.00 g
2 oz	Dry capellini (angel hair pasta)	57.00 g
2 cups	Shredded Swiss chard	72.00 g
1 medium	Tomato, seeded, chopped	123.00 g

Nutrition Facts				
Serving Size	481 g			
Servings Per Recipe	4			
Amount per serving			High Fat/Sugar Comparison	
Calories	296		300	
Calories from fat	35		80	
	% Daily Value*		% Daily Value*	
Total Fat	4 g	**6%**	9 g	**14%**
Saturated Fat	1 g	**5%**	4.5 g	**23%**
Cholesterol	115 mg	**38%**	130 mg	**43%**
Sodium	190 mg	**8%**	290 mg	**12%**
Total Carbohydrate	15 g	**5%**	13 g	**4%**
Dietary Fiber	2 g	**8%**	2 g	**8%**
Sugars	3 g		3 g	
Other	0 g		0 g	
Protein	42 g		42 g	

*Percent of Daily Values on page a-22

Exchanges and 13 g Carbohydrates Per Serving

Breads	0.7	Vegetables	0.8	Fruits	0.0
Meats	3.5	Milk	0.0	Fats	0.6

Directions

Rinse chicken, pat dry, and cut into bite-size pieces. Set aside. Heat **ButterLike** in a deep 3- to 4-quart pan over medium heat. Add shallots and cook about 3 minutes, stirring often, until soft. Stir in garlic, thyme, white pepper, and chicken. Cook about 3 minutes, stirring often, until chicken is no longer pink; cover if necessary. Add broth, water, wine, and carrots. Bring to a boil over high heat, cover, and boil gently about 5 minutes until carrots are tender. Add capellini. Bring to a boil over high heat; boil 4-5 minutes, stirring often, until pasta is barely tender. Add chard and tomato; cover, remove from heat, and let stand just until tomato is heated through. Season soup to taste with salt.

Black Bean and Macaroni Soup

The Fat Quotient using ButterLike is 8% instead of 26%
75% less fat **17% less sugar**
54% less Calories

U.S.	Ingredients	Metric
1/4 cup	**ButterLike Saute Butter**	56.00 g
1 tsp	**Granulated SugarLike**	4.00 g
1 cup	Dried black beans	176.00 g
8 cups	Chicken stock	1817.00 g
2 small	Bay leaves	.20 g
1 large	Onion, coarsely chopped	160.00 g
1 clove	Garlic, finely chopped	3.00 g
1 cup	Tomatoes, drained, chopped	2442.00 g
1 Tbsp	Red wine vinegar	16.00 g
1/4 tsp	Black pepper	.50 g
1 1/2 cup	Elbow macaroni	158.00 g
2 large	Red bell peppers, roasted, peeled	340.00 g

Directions

Wash beans; cover with an inch of water and bring to a rapid boil. Boil 2 minutes and turn off heat. Allow to sit, covered, for 1 hour. Drain beans and cover with 3 cups of chicken stock. Bring to a boil and turn heat down to a simmer. Add bay leaves. Simmer until beans start to get tender, about 1 hour and 30 minutes. Meanwhile, heat **ButterLike** and saute the onion until wilted and starting to brown, about 5 minutes. Stir in the garlic and continue to cook for another minute or so. Scrape the onion-garlic mixture into the beans and add the tomatoes. Continue cooking, adding more stock if necessary, until beans are done. This can take up to another hour. Add **SugarLike**, red wine vinegar, pepper, and remaining stock. Boil macaroni in very well salted water for 6 minutes. Drain and add to the bean mixture along with the diced red pepper. Simmer just long enough to completely cook the macaroni. Allow to sit for about 5 minutes before serving. Salt or season to taste. Sprinkle with chopped flat-leaf parsley and green onion, if desired.

Nutrition Facts				
Serving Size	862 g			
Servings Per Recipe	6			
Amount per serving			High Fat/Sugar Comparison	
Calories	283		620	
Calories from fat	45		240	
	% Daily Value*		% Daily Value*	
Total Fat	2.5 g	**4%**	10 g	**15%**
Saturated Fat	.5 g	**3%**	1.5 g	**8%**
Cholesterol	0 mg	**0%**	0 mg	**0%**
Sodium	2770 mg	**115%**	2770 mg	**115%**
Total Carbohydrate	51 g	**17%**	48 g	**16%**
Dietary Fiber	9 g	**36%**	9 g	**36%**
Sugars	5 g		6 g	
Other	1 g		0 g	
Protein	15 g		14 g	

*Percent of Daily Values on page a-22

Exchanges and 41 g Carbohydrates Per Serving					
Breads	2.7	Vegetables	1.3	Fruits	0.0
Meats	0.5	Milk	0.0	Fats	0.3

Black Bean and Pepper Chili

The Fat Quotient using **ButterLike** is **6%** instead of **29%**

82% less fat **29% more sugar**

18% less Calories

U.S.	**Ingredients**	Metric
2 Tbsp	**ButterLike Saute Butter**	28.00 g
9 cloves	Garlic, finely chopped	27.00 g
1	Fresh poblano pepper, finely chopped	19.00 g
1/2 tsp	Dried cayenne pepper	.90 g
1 large	Sweet pepper, chopped (1 cup)	74.00 g
2 large	Onions, chopped (2 cups)	320.00 g
2 large	Carrots, chopped	144.00 g
1 rib	Celery, chopped (3/4 cup)	90.00 g
2 lb	Ripe tomatoes, pureed (3 cups)	907.00 g
6 cups	Cooked black beans	1032.00 g
1 Tbsp	Ground coriander	5.00 g
1 Tbsp	Ground cumin	14.00 g
1 Tbsp	Dried oregano	4.50 g
1 cup	Fat free sour cream	256.00 g
6	Jalapeno peppers, thinly sliced	78.00 g

Directions

Heat the **ButterLike** in a large saucepan or heavy pot. Add the garlic, peppers, onions, carrots, and celery. Stir and saute over medium heat for 10 minutes. Stir in the pureed tomatoes, cooked beans and seasonings. Lower the heat and simmer the chili for 20 minutes. Serve the chili on rice and garnish with sour cream and sliced jalapenos.

Nutrition Facts				
Serving Size	375 g			
Servings Per Recipe	8			
Amount per serving			High Fat/Sugar Comparison	
Calories	280		340	
Calories from fat	20		100	
	% Daily Value*		% Daily Value*	
Total Fat	2 g	**3%**	11 g	**17%**
Saturated Fat	0 g	**0%**	4.5 g	**23%**
Cholesterol	0 mg	**0%**	15 mg	**5%**
Sodium	400 mg	**17%**	400 mg	**17%**
Total Carbohydrate	51 g	**17%**	46 g	**15%**
Dietary Fiber	15 g	**60%**	15 g	**60%**
Sugars	9 g		7 g	
Other	0 g		0 g	
Protein	16 g		15 g	

*Percent of Daily Values on page a-22

Exchanges and 36 g Carbohydrates Per Serving					
Breads	2.3	Vegetables	2.3	Fruits	0.0
Meats	0.8	Milk	0.3	Fats	0.1

Spring Garden Soup

The Fat Quotient using ButterLike is 15% instead of 49%
83% less fat 0% less sugar
46% less Calories

U.S.	Ingredients	Metric
1/4 cup	**ButterLike Saute Butter**	56.00 g
2 cups	Carrots, diced	292.00 g
1 can	Fat free chicken broth (49.5 oz)	1403.00 g
2 cups	Asparagus, thinly sliced (3/4 lb)	268.00 g
1/2 cup	Green onions, thinly sliced	80.00 g
10 oz	Frozen peas, or 2 cups shelled	284.00 g
1/4 cup	Parsley, minced	15.00 g

Directions

Heat **ButterLike** in a deep 5-quart saucepan over medium-low heat. Add carrots and cook, stirring often, until tender-crisp to bite (5-7 minutes). Add broth and bring to a boil over high heat. Add asparagus and onions. Reduce heat to medium-low, cover, and simmer until asparagus is tender to bite (about 5 minutes). Stir in peas and parsley. Season to taste with salt and pepper. To serve, ladle soup into bowls or mugs.

Nutrition Facts				
Serving Size	240 g			
Servings Per Recipe	10			
Amount per serving			High Fat/Sugar Comparison	
Calories	59		110	
Calories from fat	10		50	
	% Daily Value*		% Daily Value*	
Total Fat	1 g	**2%**	6 g	**9%**
Saturated Fat	0 g	**0%**	3.5 g	**18%**
Cholesterol	0 mg	**0%**	15 mg	**5%**
Sodium	130 mg	**5%**	590 mg	**25%**
Total Carbohydrate	9 g	**3%**	8 g	**3%**
Dietary Fiber	3 g	**12%**	3 g	**12%**
Sugars	3 g		3 g	
Other	0 g		0 g	
Protein	4 g		5 g	

*Percent of Daily Values on page a-22

Exchanges and 6 g Carbohydrates Per Serving

Breads	0.4	Vegetables	0.7	Fruits	0.0
Meats	0.2	Milk	0.0	Fats	0.2

Steak and Mushroom Soup

The Fat Quotient using ButterLike is 17% instead of 71%
89% less fat 33% less sugar
54% less Calories

U.S.	Ingredients	Metric
Marinade		
2/3 cup	**ButterLike Baking Butter**	151.00 g
1 Tbsp	**Brown SugarLike**	12.50 g
2 Tbsp	Lemon juice	31.00 g
2 Tbsp	Soy sauce	36.00 g
1 tsp	Dijon mustard	5.00 g
1 clove	Garlic, finely minced	3.00 g
1/3 cup	**ButterLike Saute Butter**	75.00 g
1 1/2 lb	Lean steak, cut into 1-in cubes	680.00 g
3 medium	Onions	480.00 g
2 small	Carrots, scraped, finely chopped	144.00 g
2 small	Celery ribs, finely chopped	150.00 g
1 lb	Fresh button mushrooms, thick sliced	454.00 g
2 Tbsp	Flour	14.00 g
5-6 cups	Low fat beef stock	1134.00 g
1 1/2 tsp	Salt	9.00 g
1/4 tsp	Black pepper	.53 g
1 large	Bay leaf	.10 g
1 1/4 lbs	Fresh spinach	567.00 g

Nutrition Facts				
Serving Size	493 g			
Servings Per Recipe	8			
Amount per serving			High Fat/Sugar Comparison	
Calories	264		580	
Calories from fat	45		410	
	% Daily Value*		% Daily Value*	
Total Fat	5 g	**8%**	46 g	**71%**
Saturated Fat	1.5 g	**8%**	10 g	**50%**
Cholesterol	40 mg	**13%**	55 mg	**18%**
Sodium	2110 mg	**88%**	2030 mg	**85%**
Total Carbohydrate	30 g	**10%**	17 g	**6%**
Dietary Fiber	4 g	**16%**	3 g	**12%**
Sugars	4 g		6 g	
Other	2 g		0 g	
Protein	26 g		26 g	

*Percent of Daily Values on page a-22

Exchanges and 24 g Carbohydrates Per Serving

Breads	1.0	Vegetables	2.3	Fruits	0.0
Meats	2.7	Milk	00	Fats	0.5

Directions

Marinade: Whisk ingredients together. Add cubed steak; submerge steak completely. Set aside for 1 hour.

Coarsely chop half of the onions; thinly slice the other half. Heat 1/2 of the **ButterLike** in a large stockpot. Add the chopped onion, carrot, and celery. Cook over medium heat until nicely golden, but not burned, about 5 minutes. Add mushrooms and continue cooking until they are just wilted, several more minutes. Remove and set aside. Wipe out any lingering bits of vegetable and add the remaining **ButterLike**. Pat the steak cubes dry and flour them, shaking off excess. Brown in **ButterLike** over medium heat. Don't let the flour burn. Remove and set aside. Return cooked vegetables, mushrooms, and sliced onions to the pot. Add 5 cups beef stock. Bring to a simmer and add salt, pepper, and a bay leaf. Simmer 15 minutes, skimming if necessary. Add steak and simmer for 10 more minutes before adding spinach. You may add more stock here if the soup is too thick. Simmer just long enough for spinach to become tender. Do not overcook. Season, if desired.

Corn Chowder

The Fat Quotient using ButterLike is **8%** instead of **31%**
81% less fat **75% more sugar**
30% less Calories

U.S.	Ingredients	Metric
2 Tbsp	**ButterLike Saute Butter**	28.00 g
3 slices	Lean bacon	18.00 g
1 large	Onion, chopped	160.00 g
1 large	Russet potato, peeled and diced	202.00 g
1 cup	Water	237.00 g
2 cans	Cream style corn (17 oz each)	964.00 g
1/3 cup	Canned diced green chilies	80.00 g
2 oz	Sliced pimentos, drained	57.00 g
2 cups	Skim milk	490.00 g

Directions

Cook bacon in a 4-quart pan over medium heat until crisp. Lift out, drain, crumble, and set aside. Discard drippings. Pour 2 Tbsp **ButterLike** into a pan and add onion; cook, stirring often, until onion is soft (about 5 minutes). Stir in potato and water. Bring to a boil over high heat; then reduce heat, cover, and simmer until potato is tender when pierced (about 15 minutes). Stir in corn, chilies, pimentos, and milk. Season to taste with garlic salt and pepper. Heat until steaming; do not boil. To serve, ladle soup into bowls and garnish with bacon.

Nutrition Facts				
Serving Size	279 g			
Servings Per Recipe	8			
Amount per serving			High Fat/Sugar Comparison	
Calories	160		230	
Calories from fat	10		80	
	% Daily Value*		% Daily Value*	
Total Fat	1.5 g	**2%**	8 g	**12%**
Saturated Fat	0 g	**0%**	5 g	**25%**
Cholesterol	5 mg	**2%**	25 mg	**8%**
Sodium	460 mg	**19%**	470 mg	**20%**
Total Carbohydrate	35 g	**12%**	33 g	**11%**
Dietary Fiber	3 g	**12%**	3 g	**12%**
Sugars	4 g		1 g	
Other	0 g		0 g	
Protein	6 g		6 g	

*Percent of Daily Values on page a-22

Exchanges and 32 g Carbohydrates Per Serving

Breads	1.9	Vegetables	0.4	Fruits	0.0
Meats	0.0	Milk	0.2	Fats	0.3

Broccoli Soup

The Fat Quotient using ButterLike is **21%** instead of **60%**
81% less fat **0% less sugar**
47% less Calories

U.S.	Ingredients	Metric
5 Tbsp	**ButterLike Saute Butter**	70.00 g
2 cups	Water	474.00 g
1 1/2 lb	Broccoli, finely chopped	680.00 g
3/4 cup	Celery, chopped	90.00 g
2 Tbsp	Flour	14.00 g
2 1/2 cup	Water	593.00 g
1 Tbsp	Instant chicken bouillon	12.00 g
3/4 tsp	Salt	4.50 g
1/8 tsp	Pepper	.30 g
Dash	Ground nutmeg	.30 g
1/3 cup	Skim milk	82.00 g

Directions

Bring 2 cups water to a boil. Add broccoli and celery. Cover and boil until tender, about 10 minutes. Do not drain. Heat 2 Tbsp **ButterLike** in a saucepan; add flour. Cook, stirring constantly, until mixture is smooth and bubbly. Remove from heat. Stir in 2 1/2 cups water. Heat to boiling; stirring constantly. Boil and stir 1 minute. Stir into broccoli mixture. Add bouillon, salt, pepper, and nutmeg. Return to a boil. Remove from heat. Whip 3 Tbsp **ButterLike** and milk; add to mixture. If desired, top with shredded cheese.

Nutrition Facts				
Serving Size	253 g			
Servings Per Recipe	8			
Amount per serving			High Fat/Sugar Comparison	
Calories		63	120	
Calories from fat		15	80	
	% Daily Value*		% Daily Value*	
Total Fat	1.5 g	**2%**	8 g	**12%**
Saturated Fat	0 g	**0%**	5 g	**25%**
Cholesterol	0 mg	**0%**	25 mg	**8%**
Sodium	650 mg	**27%**	680 mg	**28%**
Total Carbohydrate	10 g	**3%**	7 g	**2%**
Dietary Fiber	3 g	**12%**	3 g	**12%**
Sugars	2 g		2 g	
Other	0 g		0 g	
Protein	4 g		3 g	

*Percent of Daily Values on page a-22

Exchanges and 7 g Carbohydrates Per Serving

Breads	0.3	Vegetables	1.0	Fruits	0.0
Meats	0.0	Milk	0.0	Fats	0.3

Index

Index